THE
FLAVOR
BIBLE

THE FLAVOR BIBLE

THE ESSENTIAL GUIDE TO CULINARY CREATIVITY, BASED ON THE WISDOM OF AMERICA'S MOST IMAGINATIVE CHEFS

KAREN PAGE AND **ANDREW DORNENBURG**

PHOTOGRAPHS BY BARRY SALZMAN

LITTLE, BROWN AND COMPANY   NEW YORK • BOSTON • LONDON

Little, Brown and Company
Hachette Book Group
237 Park Avenue
New York, NY 10017
www.hachettebookgroup.com

First Edition: September 2008
Sixth Printing, 2011

Little, Brown and Company is a division of Hachette Book Group, Inc.
The Little, Brown name and logo are trademarks of Hachette Book Group, Inc.

The publisher is not responsible for websites (or their content) that are not owned
by the publisher.

Library of Congress Cataloging-in-Publication Data

Page, Karen.
  The flavor bible : the essential guide to culinary creativity,
based on the wisdom of America's most imaginative chefs /
Karen Page and Andrew Dornenburg. — 1st ed.
      p. cm.
  Includes index.
  ISBN-13: 978-0-316-11840-8
  ISBN-10: 0-316-11840-0
  1. Cookery.   2. Gastronomy.   I. Dornenburg, Andrew.   II. Title.
  TX651.P34 2008
  641.5 — dc22   2007033064

Book and jacket design by Wilcox Design

Printed in Singapore

*At times our own light goes out and is rekindled by a spark
from another person. Each of us has cause to think with deep gratitude
of those who have lighted the flame within us.*

— ALBERT SCHWEITZER

To Daniel Boulud, Patrick O'Connell, and Jean-Georges Vongerichten —
the leading lights of culinary creativity of their generation —
whose sparks always rekindle our flame

Gastronomy is the rational study of all related to man as he is eating. Its purpose is to keep humankind alive with the best possible food.

— JEAN-ANTHELME BRILLAT-SAVARIN (1755–1826)

In what art or science could improvements be made that would more powerfully contribute to increase the comforts and enjoyments of mankind?

— SIR BENJAMIN THOMPSON, COUNT RUMFORD

(IN A 1794 ESSAY ON THE ART OF COOKERY)

CONTENTS

PREFACE

"When we no longer have good cooking in the world, we will have no literature, nor high and sharp intelligence, nor friendly gatherings, nor social harmony."
— MARIE-ANTOINE CARÊME, CHEF (1784–1833)

"Good cooking is an art, as well as a form of intense pleasure. . . . A recipe is only a theme, which an intelligent cook can play each time with a variation."
— MADAME JEHANE BENOÎT, CHEF (1904–1987)

"You have to love either what you are going to eat, or the person you are cooking for. Then you have to give yourself up to cooking. Cuisine is an act of love."
— ALAIN CHAPEL, CHEF (1937–1990)

The first quotation suggests why we do what we do, while the others suggest how. We published our first book in 1995, and it is exciting as we approach the publication of *The Flavor Bible* in 2008 to witness the realm of good cooking as it reaches a new "tipping point."

No longer content simply to replicate others' recipes, today's cooks — professionals and amateurs alike — increasingly seek to create their own dishes. In doing so, they celebrate the creative *process* of cooking as much as the finished *product*.

Cooking at its most basic level is a creative act, one of transforming food through the application of heat and the incorporation of other ingredients. But there are different orders of creativity, and merely following a recipe is a creative act of the most basic order, like painting by numbers.

When accomplished cooks grow restless, they start to analyze instructions before following them to see if they can improve upon the results, thus raising the act of cooking to a creative act of a higher order. As their experience grows, cooks are able to bring greater intuition and even inspiration to their cooking.

Traditional cookbooks are aimed at first-order cooks. Every cook owes a debt of gratitude to those who have brought progress to cuisine throughout history — those who famously codified classic cuisines through the painstaking chronicling of recipes, from Auguste Escoffier in France to others around the globe. Appreciation is also due to those who have elevated and expanded the range of available ingredients and techniques, the essential building blocks of cooking.

Over the years, cookbooks have come to dictate precise measurement of ingredients along with instructions for their preparation and assembly, which has done much to improve the general accessibility of recipes. However, they also have come to provide a false sense of security for which the unsuspecting cook pays a price. When a recipe is rigidly scripted and blindly followed, it negates the cook's own creative instincts and good judgment — not to mention much of the pleasure of truly "being" in the moment.

————

"Great cooks rarely bother to consult cookbooks."
— CHARLES SIMIC, U.S. POET LAUREATE

Those with the urge to innovate had long been on their own in the kitchen until many adopted our 1996 book, *Culinary Artistry*, as their muse. That book sought to break the mold of contemporary prescriptive cookbooks and to restore the creative instinct to chefs. Drawing on classic flavor combinations and preparations, it put the wisdom of history at cooks' fingertips for the first time — and with the same ease with which writers consulted a thesaurus.

As time passed, it became clear that chefs were thinking of flavors and their combination in new ways, beyond the classics chronicled in *Culinary Artistry*. Meanwhile, the gap between professionals and amateur cooks narrowed, as the latter installed Viking ranges at home to prepare a burgeoning array of new ingredients, with their TVs transformed into virtual twenty-four-hour cooking schools, given the advent of culinary programming.

————

"Food without wine is a corpse; wine without food is a ghost.
United and well matched, they are as body and soul: living partners."
— ANDRÉ SIMON, CHEF (1877–1970)

Since the year 2000 we have been studying the new ways in which flavors are being combined. It has been a privilege to interview many of the country's most imaginative chefs and other food and drink experts (turning to an entirely different lineup from those we spoke to for *Culinary Artistry*). Some are well-established industry pioneers, while others have risen on the scene in recent years. All have wowed us with their savory cuisines and/or desserts, and often in spots less traveled, from Dallas to New Orleans to Hoboken. We've also combed the most recent culinary literature published in 2000 or later.

The first result was our 2006 book, *What to Drink with What You Eat*, which celebrated the harmonious combination of food and drink and, indeed, their inseparability, as suggested by the André Simon quotation.

The second result is *The Flavor Bible*, which, like *Culinary Artistry*, is not intended to be prescriptive; rather, it is an empowerment tool. *The Flavor Bible* is a comprehensive, easy-to-use single-volume reference of more than six hundred alphabetical entries listing modern-day compatible flavors, chronicling new flavor synergies in the new millennium.

Our books *Culinary Artistry* (classic flavor combinations before 1996), *The Flavor Bible* (modern flavor combinations since 2000), and *What to Drink with What You Eat* (classic and modern food and drink combinations) are essential to use in concert, as each covers different aspects of food and drink flavor harmony.

Flavor Combinations

CULINARY ARTISTRY			THE FLAVOR BIBLE	
Classics	1996	2000	2006	2008

Food and Drink Combinations

	WHAT TO DRINK WITH WHAT YOU EAT			
Classics	1996	2000	2006	2008

We believe cooking will continue to evolve, and not only as a means of "doing" (i.e., putting dinner on the table, or "problem-solving" by "following a recipe"). Over time, we believe more people — including, perhaps, yourself — will have discovered it as a way of "being" in the world. We have learned enough over the past decade or two to question why cooking is done one way versus another. This thoughtful sensory engagement leads to a store of experiences that allow us to bring more intuition to the cooking process, synthesizing what we've done before into innovative approaches to creating a dish. Ultimately, cooking offers the opportunity to be immersed in one's senses and in the moment like no other activity, uniting the inner and outer selves. At these times, cooking transcends drudgery and becomes a means of meditation and even healing.

It is little surprise to us, then, that when U.S. Poet Laureate Charles Simic was asked by the *New York Times Magazine*'s Deborah Solomon earlier this year, "What advice would you give to people who are looking to be happy?" his response was "For starters, learn how to cook."

We hope this book makes you happy — literally.

— KAREN PAGE AND ANDREW DORNENBURG
New York City
April 2008

Chapter

FLAVOR = TASTE + MOUTHFEEL + AROMA + "THE X FACTOR": LEARNING TO RECOGNIZE THE LANGUAGE OF FOOD

Magical dishes, magical words: A great cook is, when all is said and done, a great poet. . . . For was it not a visit from the Muses that inspired the person who first had the idea of marrying rice and chicken, grape and thrush, potatoes and entrecôte, Parmesan and pasta, eggplant and tomato, Chambertin and cockerel, liqueur brandy and woodcock, onion and tripe?
— MARCEL E. GRANCHER, *CINQUANTE ANS À TABLE* (1953)

FLAVOR = TASTE + MOUTHFEEL + AROMA + "THE X FACTOR"

Taste = What is perceived by the taste buds
Mouthfeel = What is perceived by the rest of the mouth
Aroma = What is perceived by the nose
"The X Factor" = What is perceived by the other senses — plus the heart, mind, and spirit

---

Our taste buds can perceive only four basic tastes: sweet, salty, sour, and bitter. The essence of great cooking is to bring these four tastes into balanced harmony to create deliciousness. It's that simple — and that difficult. After all, flavor is a function not only of taste, but also of smell, touch, sight, and sound. Because we're human beings, other nonphysical factors come into play, including our emotions, thoughts, and spirits.

Learning to recognize as well as manipulate both the obvious and subtle components of flavor will make you a much better cook. This book will be your companion in the kitchen whenever you wish to create deliciousness.

Learning to cook like a great chef is within the realm of possibility. However, it is something that is rarely taught; it must be "caught."

Everyone who cooks — or even merely seasons their food at the table before eating — can benefit from mastering the basic principles of making food taste great. This complex subject is simplified by one thing: while the universe may contain a vast number of ingredients and a virtually infinite number of ingredient combinations, the palate can register only the four basic tastes.

Great food balances these tastes beautifully. A great cook knows how to taste, to discern what is needed, and to make adjustments. Once you learn how to season and how to balance tastes, a whole new world opens up to you in cooking. Of course, several factors conspire against your ever doing so — not the least of which is a culture that sees the publication of thousands of new cookbooks annually featuring recipes that promise to dazzle you and your guests if you follow them to the letter. And yet you're often left wondering why the results aren't as delicious as promised. That's because great cooking is never as simple as merely following a recipe. The best cooking requires a discerning palate to know when a dish needs a little something or other — and what to add or do to elevate its flavor.

WHAT IS PERCEIVED BY THE MOUTH

Taste Buds

Sweetness. Saltiness. Sourness. Bitterness. Every delicious bite you've ever tasted has been a result of these four tastes coming together on your taste buds. We taste them as individual notes, and in concert. Each taste affects the other. For example, bitterness suppresses sweetness. In addition, different tastes affect us in different ways. Saltiness stimulates the appetite, while sweetness satiates it. Take the time to explore the four basic tastes.

Sweetness

It takes the greatest quantity of a substance that is sweet (versus salty, sour, or bitter) to register on our taste buds. However, we can appreciate the balance and "roundness" that even otherwise imperceptible sweetness adds to savory dishes. Sweetness can work with bitterness, sourness — even saltiness. Sweetness can also bring out the flavors of other ingredients, from fruits to mint.

Saltiness

When we banished more than thirty of America's leading chefs to their own desert islands with only ten ingredients to cook with for the rest of their lives (*Culinary Artistry*, 1996), the number-one ingredient they chose was salt. Salt is nature's flavor enhancer. It is the single most important taste for making savory food delicious. (Sweetness, by the way, plays the same role in desserts.)

Sourness

Sourness is second only to salt in savory food and sugar in sweet food in its importance as a flavor enhancer. Sour notes — whether a squeeze of lemon or a drizzle of vinegar — add sparkle and brightness to a dish. Balancing a dish's acidity with its other tastes is critical to the dish's ultimate success.

Bitterness

Humans are most sensitive to bitterness, and our survival wiring allows us to recognize it in even relatively tiny amounts. Bitterness balances sweetness, and can also play a vital role in cutting richness in a dish. While bitterness is more important to certain people than to others, some chefs see it as an indispensable "cleansing" taste — one that makes you want to take the next bite, and the next.

Umami (Savoriness)

In addition to the four basic tastes, there is growing evidence of a fifth taste, *umami*, which we first wrote about in 1996 in *Culinary Artistry*. It is often described as the savory or meaty "mouth-filling" taste that is noticeable in such ingredients as anchovies, blue cheese, mushrooms, and green tea, and in such flavorings as monosodium glutamate (MSG), which is the primary component of branded seasonings such as Ac´cent.

Mouthfeel

In addition to its sense of taste, the mouth has a sense of "touch" and can register other sensations, such as temperature and texture, that all play a role in flavor. These aspects of food, generally characterized as mouthfeel, help to bring food into alignment with our bodies, and bring some of a dish's greatest interest and pleasure. The crunchiness and crispiness of a dish contribute sound as well as textural appeal.

Temperature

I always pay attention to temperature. I look at what I feel like eating now. If it is cold and rainy outside, I make sure that soup is on the menu. If it is hot outside, I make sure there are lots of salads on the menu.
— **ANDREW CARMELLINI,** A VOCE (NEW YORK CITY)

Temperature is one of the foremost among the other sensations that can be perceived by the mouth. The temperature of our food even affects our perception of its taste; for example, coldness suppresses sweetness. Boston pastry chef Rick Katz, with whom Andrew cooked at Lydia Shire's restaurant Biba, first taught him the lesson of pulling out the ice cream a few minutes before serving so that the slight rise in temperature could maximize its flavor.

A food's temperature can affect both the perception and enjoyment of a dish. A chilled carrot soup on a hot summer day — and hot roasted carrots on a cold winter day — could be said to be "healing" through their ability to bring our bodies into greater alignment with our environment.

Texture

I would never serve pike on a base of chowder, because balance and texture are so important when it comes to creating a dish. Is there a rich component, a lean component, a crunchy component, and a cleansing component? Are all the taste sensors activated so that you want to go back for a second bite? Cod works better over a richer preparation like chowder. I would also make sure to choose the right technique for the cod: I would not poach it, because if it is poached it would be silky on silky. If it is seared, it is crunchy on silky — which is more appealing because of the contrast.
— **SHARON HAGE,** YORK STREET (DALLAS)

A food's texture is central to its ability to captivate and to please. We value pureed and/or creamy foods (such as soups and mashed potatoes) as "comfort" foods, and crunchiness and crispiness (such as nachos and caramel corn) as "fun" foods. We enjoy texture as it activates our other senses, including touch, sight, and sound.

While babies by necessity eat pureed foods, most adults enjoy a variety of textures, particularly crispiness and crunchiness, which break up the smoothness of texture — or even the simple monotony — of dishes.

Piquancy

Our mouths can also sense what we often incorrectly refer to as "hotness," meaning piquancy's "sharpness" and/or "spiciness" — whether boldly as in chile peppers, or more subtly as in a sprinkle of cayenne pepper. Some people find the experience of these *picante* (as the Spanish refer to it, or *piccante* as the Italians do) tastes more pleasurable than others.

Astringency

Our mouths "pucker" to register astringency. This is a drying sensation caused by the tannins in red wine or strong tea, and occasionally in foods such as walnuts, cranberries, and unripe persimmons.

WHAT IS PERCEIVED BY THE NOSE

Aroma

Aroma is thought to be responsible for as much as 80 percent or more of flavor. This helps to explain the popularity of aromatic ingredients, from fresh herbs and spices to grated lemon zest. Incorporating aromatic ingredients can enhance the aroma of your dish and, in turn, its flavor.

Some qualities are perceived through both the sense of taste and smell, such as:

Pungency

Pungency refers to the taste and aroma of such ingredients as horseradish and mustard that are as irritating — albeit often pleasantly — to the nose as they are to the palate.

Chemesthesis

Chemesthesis refers to other sensations that tickle (e.g., the tingle of carbonated beverages) or play tricks on (e.g., the false perception of "heat" from chile peppers, or "cold" from peppermint) our gustatory senses.

WHAT IS PERCEIVED BY THE HEART, MIND, AND SPIRIT

"The X Factor"

When we are present to what we are eating, food has the power to affect our entire selves. We experience food not only through our five physical senses — including our sense of sight, which we ad-

---

Heightening Flavor with Dominique and Cindy Duby of Wild Sweets

We believe that food preparation is 60 percent ingredients and 40 percent technique.
— **DOMINIQUE AND CINDY DUBY,** WILD SWEETS (VANCOUVER)

Flavor is the combination of the taste you experience on your tongue and the aroma you experience through your nose. We believe that as much as 90 percent of what we perceive as taste is actually aroma. When you eat a pineapple, the flavor really comes through the nose. So, if your pineapple is not ripe, it won't have much aroma. It may taste sweet, but it won't taste like pineapple.

There are two ways to bring flavor to a dish, through aroma or through chemical reaction. We always say that cooking is no different from doing a lab experiment: The minute you add heat to a raw product, you are changing the status of that product. When you use the Maillard reaction — which is what happens when you sear a piece of meat — you are getting a reaction of caramelization from the carbohydrates and amino acids. This chemical reaction creates flavor.

To add aroma to a dish, think of a piece of fish cooked in broth with herbs or lemon. The problem is that the flavor escapes into the air. If you walk into a room and it smells great, that means there is not much flavor left in the dish. The aroma has escaped. So, if you want to add aroma to a dish, the best way is through *sous-vide* cooking [which cooks encased food at long, slow temperatures]. This method traps the aroma into what you are cooking without letting it escape.

The problem is that *sous vide* is not available for home cooks. What a home cook can do is "sealed cooking," where you take a heavy-duty freezer ziplock bag, put in what you want to cook with the liquid, then cook it over a steady heat on your stove. Another method that works is putting the bag in a pot with a single-cup water heater that goes to about 140 degrees Fahrenheit and, from time to time, stirring the water. [Note: Care must be taken with this low-temperature method of cooking to avoid food poisoning.]

This is a way to put — and keep — a lot of flavor in whatever you are cooking.

dress first below — but also emotionally, mentally, and even spiritually.

The Visual

The visual presentation of a dish can greatly enhance the pleasure we derive from it. Just a few decades ago, it was still possible to taste a dish with the eyes, but only those who'd spent time in world-class kitchens knew the tricks of such artistic plate presentation. Since the advent of *Art Culinaire* and the Web, it's become easier to reproduce a great dish's elaborate form than its exquisite flavor.

How a dish looks can also affect our perception of its flavor in more direct ways; for example, the deeper the color of a berry sorbet, the more berry flavor is perceived. The stronger the connection between a particular food and a particular color, the stronger the flavor impact — such as berries with red, lemon with yellow, and lime with green.

The Emotional

I say all the time that [my mother's Spanish potato and egg tortilla] is my favorite because it conveys a point: that sentimental value comes above all else.
— **FERRAN ADRIA,** EL BULLI (SPAIN)

Compatible Flavors

An essential aspect of great cooking is harnessing compatible flavors — which involves knowing which herbs, spices, and other flavorings best accentuate particular ingredients.

A process of trial and error over centuries resulted in classic cuisines and dishes, some of which feature timeless combinations of beloved flavor pairings — for example, basil with tomatoes, rosemary with lamb, and tarragon with lobster.

However, today it's possible to use scientific techniques to analyze similar molecular structures to come up with new, compatible pairing possibilities, as odd as some might sound — such as jasmine with pork liver, parsley with banana, or white chocolate with caviar.

We taste with our hearts as much as with our tongues. What else could explain adult preferences for one's mother's dishes over those prepared by a great chef? This also helps to explain the lasting appeal of traditional dishes and cuisines of countries around the globe, which stem from our love for their cultures, their people, and the deeply rooted culinary traditions that have sustained them over centuries.

The Mental

If we ate only for sustenance, we could probably survive on nutritive pills and water. But we also eat for pleasure. Because we typically eat three times a day, 365 days a year, we enjoy novelty, such as a twist on the traditional construct of a dish. Increasingly, since the 1980s and the advent of "tall" food, chefs have played with the presentation of their ingredients. Since the 1990s, the advent of avant-garde cuisine and so-called molecular gastronomy has seen chefs experiment more and more with both the chemical composition and presentation of dishes as well.

The Spiritual

The preparation, cooking, and eating of food is a sacrament. Treating it as such has the potential to elevate the quality of our daily lives like nothing else. Several of the world's leading chefs have worked to perfect each aspect of the dining encounter — from the food and drink to the ambiance to the service — to raise the overall experience to a new level imbued not only with pleasure, comfort, and interest, but also with meaning.

Choosing a Cooking Technique with Michael Anthony of Gramercy Tavern in New York City

When we look at an ingredient, we ask, "How can we maximize the inherent flavor or quality of what this is?" As in any other progressive modern kitchen, there is a fascination with examining all the new techniques we can get our hands on. We have used *sous vide* [i.e., cooking vacuum-packed ingredients at low temperatures for long periods of time], but we are far from letting any technique drive a dish.

Alice Waters described something cooked via *sous vide* as "dead" food. I can understand her opinion because she is all about inflecting that "fresh-cut crunch" feeling into her food. *Sous vide* is all about a long, slow cooking process — and those products calling for that [such as tougher cuts of meat] will be awesome.

Why we choose any specialized piece of equipment for a dish always gets back to good old-fashioned cooking principles: What is the best way of capturing flavors?

That is how choosing a technique fits into my cooking.

I'm excited to eat in restaurants that are pushing the boundaries of presentation and technique. Yet my personal take on food that is too technically driven is that technique comes first and taste comes second. I feel the meals that hit home are ones where the flavor is there and you are eating a meal in a distinct time and place. I love it when people look back on a meal, and the time of year is what made it special. The ingredients they tasted seemed naturally a part of that moment because that is what is available then.

Sometimes straightforward flavors are the ones people can latch on to, even though the ingredients can be very sophisticated behind the scenes. If, ultimately, the flavor combination is one that is simple and straightforward, with an impressive balance of acidity and bitterness, and you remember it, then you win as a diner. Sometimes the meals that hit home are not the ones that were the most complicated.

FLAVOR FROM THE INSIDE OUT

America's foremost chefs reached the pinnacle of their profession through their painstaking attention to every aspect of their cuisine and the restaurant experience. Chefs bring their own unique approaches to their cuisines, which are arguably rooted in either the physical, emotional, mental, or spiritual — although they can span two, three, or even all of them.

Chefs whose focus celebrates the **physical** realm include **Alice Waters** of Chez Panisse in Berkeley, California, with her pathbreaking focus on the quality of ingredients sourced and served, and **Dan Barber** of Blue Hill at Stone Barns in Pocantico Hills, New York, whose on-premises greenhouse, gardens, and pastures grow and raise much of what the restaurant serves.

Celebrating the **emotional** realm are those chefs whose cuisines are closely tied to a specific culture, its people, and their traditions. It includes chefs such as **Rick Bayless**, whose Frontera Grill and Topolobampo in Chicago elevate Mexican cuisine, and **Vikram Vij** and **Meeru Dhalwala**, whose Vij's and Rangoli restaurants in Vancouver honor and celebrate the cooking of India and tap Indian women exclusively to staff their kitchens.

Easily identifiable as part of the **mental** realm are chefs whose efforts are reconceptualizing how food can be manipulated and presented, such as Chicago's **Grant Achatz** of Alinea (with signature dishes such as bacon on a clothesline) and **Homaro Cantu** of Moto (whose dishes include incorporating edible paper printed with soy-based inks, and a doughnut soup that looks like eggnog and tastes just like a doughnut).

Through the elevation not only of their cuisines but of the creation and orchestration of ambiance and service as well, chefs such as **Daniel Boulud** of New York's Restaurant Daniel and **Patrick O'Connell** of The Inn at Little Washington in Virginia transcend the prior three categories to bring the dining experience to another level in the **spiritual** realm.

In the pages that follow, we'll share chefs' reflections on working in the first three realms. (As for their thoughts on the fourth, we invite you to visit or revisit our book *Culinary Artistry*.)

The Physical Realm

My motto has always been: Find the best ingredients possible, and listen to what they tell you about how they want to be prepared. Mess with them as little as you can. Keep their integrity, but at the same time, focus their flavor, which is where creativity comes in.
— **VITALY PALEY,** PALEY'S PLACE (PORTLAND, OREGON)

The best chefs work with the best ingredients available to them. The *very* best chefs don't settle for this, and seek out even better ingredients through working with foragers, developing relationships with farmers and other purveyors, and even growing their own produce and raising their own animals.

Monica Pope of T'afia in Houston

My cooking changed radically when we started hosting a farmers' market [located at T'afia]. I remember when I was cooking in California, and chefs would be waiting for an ingredient to come into season. When it arrived, their philosophy would be "Let's just slice it and not screw it up." I thought, "That is just not the way restaurants work." It's hard to believe that now I am saying the same thing that they used to say.

Since the advent of the farmers' market, when I get a product, it is phenomenal — because it was picked at the right time and has never even been refrigerated before it comes to my door. Sometimes I feel guilty because people will love something, and ask what I did to it. Often the answer is "Very little."

Our zucchini salad is a perfect example of celebrating what comes to our door. We get baby zucchini and we shave them raw. Then we add a flavored pecan oil, raw local pecan halves, shaved pecorino cheese, Mexican marigold, and a pinch of salt.

We also think a lot about the best way to present these ingredients. The salad has to be interesting the whole way through, and I want the customer to have the experience of interacting with it themselves. I want them to have the experience of lifting a shaved piece of cheese after their bite of crunchy yellow or light-green squash. They will see that the salad is dressed with oil, but then have to search and realize that it is pecan oil. Then they will take the next bite and get the herb that has a minty note to it. To achieve this, I will taste a dish night after night to make sure it is "eating" the way I want it to eat.

Michael Anthony of Gramercy Tavern in New York City

You want to have an infatuation with the ingredients you cook with. You want to tap all the hopes and dreams that went into producing that ingredient. You need to think, "Is this ingredient not only up to par, but is it brilliant?" When it is cooked, you want whoever bites into what you made to think that the flavor is bright, interesting, and delicious.

I take a simple approach to my food, but simple food does not mean unmanipulated food. Sometimes simple food is simply boring.

When I cook, I am looking to pull myself back from a dish rather than add to a dish. I would rather a dish feel too simple than too fussy. So, sticking to my core principles, I never want to overload a dish with too many ingredients. But cooking is not always one-two-three. Sometimes you need some extra ingredients as long as they work dynamically.

Dan Barber of Blue Hill at Stone Barns in Pocantico Hills, New York

Our pork dish starts not at the table with the cut of pork on the plate, but in the field with what kind of pork we choose to raise for our restaurant. I make a lot of decisions to get the most "pigness" out of our pork dish. We raise Berkshire pigs, which have a great flavor. They are an older breed that has a flavor profile that

newer breeds don't have. The pig has a great intramuscular profile that allows it to develop a better flavor.

We feed our pigs organic grains and that makes a huge difference. We feed them a wide variety of grains and they forage as well. We are also careful of how much corn the pigs eat. I proved unequivocally this summer the difference feed makes. We had a problem getting organic grain for about eight weeks and had to use conventional grain that has more corn in it because it is cheap to use in the feed. I tasted our pork that was raised exactly the same way side by side with the only change being the feed, and the flavor was as different as night and day. The flavor of the two was so different that a child could tell them apart.

We also make sure our pigs are slaughtered in a less stressful way. This makes for a calmer pig, and you can see a difference in the meat and taste the difference [in the texture] on the plate.

At Blue Hill when you order the pork at our restaurant, you don't know what cut you will be getting. We serve leg, shoulder, rack, loin, and belly; it is a mix on the plate. This makes for a more interesting experience, because you get a variety of flavors and textures. We keep the dish pretty straightforward. We will serve it with Brussels sprout leaves and chickpeas.

We don't want to do anything to hide the flavor. We make a pork stock, infuse it with more roasted scraps and bones to make a pork second [also known as a *remoulage*], then do one more pass with more pork and very little wine. This is water that has been infused with pork three times.

Depending on the season, I will make an infusion with herbs like a tea and add a little to the sauce if I want to add more flavor. The reason I do an infusion is to make sure the flavor is so light that you don't even know it is there.

The Emotional Realm

I have no professional cooking training. My starting point was, What do I know? I know Indian spices and flavors.

— **MEERU DHALWALA,** VIJ'S (VANCOUVER)

There are many emotional connections to draw from when creating dishes — from the bounty of a particular country and its historic evolution into a national cuisine, to the classic dishes of that culture, and of the families and even individual cooks within it — as each might bring a unique twist to the standards.

Maricel Presilla of Cucharamama and Zafra in Hoboken, New Jersey

I'm Cuban — but whether you are Cuban, Venezuelan, Chilean [or another nationality], there is an enormous pride in the flavors of your region and of your childhood. It is like mother's milk, your first compass. It doesn't matter how much you travel or how much you expand your palate: You always come back to this notion of basic flavors and ingredients, time and again.

For me, being a Cuban from eastern Cuba is my anchor. I am from Santiago, which has a very defined cuisine. It is more influenced by the neighboring islands such as Jamaica and Haiti, which both have European influences as well. The cooks from those islands brought flavors with them like allspice, which is not used in the rest of Cuba. My family uses allspice lavishly in our adobo and in other dishes. I use it a lot as well — and it is one of my favorite spices. Our cooking has more complexity than the food of Havana because of these influences.

We have the most interesting cuisine in the world — and I am not kidding. I have traveled throughout South America, cooking with chefs as well as elderly women, not to mention studying the history of our cuisine from pre-Columbian cooking through the influence of Spanish medieval cooking.

What is fascinating is that there is a lot of structure to our cooking and clearly defined rules to our seasoning.

I have learned how all these flavors work in their nationalities and regions, making Latin America my "backyard" of flavor. I am like a painter, and every painter has his or her own palette. I use this analogy because my father was a painter, and there are colors that he would never use that would not be on his palette.

When I want to be creative, I am comfortable reaching across topographical boundaries. However, I do so with an understanding of all the basic elements of flavor in South American cuisine because I have studied them, eaten them, and lived them!

Vikram Vij of Vij's and Rangoli in Vancouver

The three secrets to my cooking? Number one, my wife, Meeru. Number two, treating the spices with integrity. And number three, using local produce as much as possible.

My own mother is from the northern part of India, so my style and flavors are a combination of different whole and ground spices. I love fenugreek and cinnamon and other aromatics. But one of my [signature dishes] is actually called Mother-in-Law's Pork Curry, because it is based on a recipe my mother-in-law gave me for stewed meat.

I wanted to make something new and was talking to Meeru, who told me her mother used to make a curry with lamb, cream, masala, and some other spices and that they loved it. I decided to try it with pork instead of lamb. It was vindaloo style with vinegar, and green onions added right at the end so that they stayed really fresh. There were too many spices in it to list on the menu so it just made sense to name the dish after her instead.

When I opened my first restaurant, I didn't have a liquor license and did not want to serve [soda] pop or anything with artificial ingredients or preservatives. I remembered growing up in India and having lemon water with a hint of salt and pepper as a homemade lemonade. [At Vij's,] we made some lemonade and added a little ginger, a pinch of salt, and sparkling water to give the refreshing effervescence of [soda] pop. We started out serving it with pepper as well, but customers couldn't get used to seeing black pepper in a drink.

It is wonderful at the beginning of the meal to refresh your palate.

Meeru Dhalwala Vij of Vij's and Rangoli in Vancouver

While working in India for eleven months, I visited Gujarat. Having been raised in the United States, to me "Indian food" was what my mom cooked. I had no idea there were other kinds!

If you watch a Bollywood movie, you see that the Punjabis and the Gujaratis make a lot of fun of each other. The Gujaratis find us Punjabis very volatile and show-offy. They will say, "Just like your cuisine, you are all fiery and hot!" We Punjabis, on the other hand, think the Gujaratis are quiet and dull. Of course, for me, that has all changed — I love all Indians.

In Gujarat, at the end of cooking a curry, they would add a teaspoon of sugar and a half a lime. The first time I tasted this, it was awful — but then I found out that the cook of the house was a crappy cook! When I had it done correctly, it was delicious, and had a nice, mellow aftertaste. So, I incorporated lime into my cooking after eating Gujarati food in India.

My kitchen is staffed by Punjabi women, who had a hard time using lime because it was not part of their cooking in Punjab. When they tasted it, they thought, "Yuck! What's the point?" Since my Punjabi cooks don't like lime, this led me to start using kaffir lime. I had more control over the recipes' flavor because I could just say, "Add 15 leaves to the recipe." And I learned that turmeric and lime leaf are wonderful together, by the way.

The Mental Realm

My menu may read as unusual, but everything is really just a slight flip on a traditional flavor profile. If I pull out one acid, I replace it with another. If I make a tagine *traditionally, it will have preserved lemon. Then I'll ask, "Would it work with lime or orange juice?" It is still the same flavor profile in that it will still have a cutting acid — just maybe not the one that would be used traditionally.*

— BRAD FARMERIE, PUBLIC (NEW YORK CITY)

In modern architecture and design, form is said to follow function. In the cutting-edge world of avant-garde cuisine, which turns classic dishes inside out for the sake of argument or even simple amusement, form follows flavor.

Homaro Cantu of Moto in Chicago

Moto is not meant to be an everyday experience. Neither is Charlie Trotter's [also in Chicago] or Daniel [in New York City]. Someone could say that these chefs are just cooking for themselves, and that is true to a certain extent. I am doing this style of [avant-garde] cooking because I am bored with other dishes. If I was all about the customer and just wanted to make people happy, I would cook paella, pizza, and burgers all day. Everyone would have smiles on their faces!

There is a little bit of selfishness, but there is also playfulness. We have to make sure guests are happy, and that our dishes are both inventive and seasonal. What is happening [in the world] right now is that we are expanding our repertoire of what good food is.

At Moto, when we start out with a concept, flavor is the most important thing but also the last thing we think about. Something might taste great, but who cares? What are *we* going to do with it? As it pertains to us, we look at a concept. Then it evolves into something where we tweak the flavor a little bit to make it taste more like it "should." For example, once we wanted to make a cookie with a really concentrated flavor. So, we threw cookies into the dehydrator, and turned them into powder. This created a new building block for flavor. [Instead of the flour you would normally use in your dough,] you weigh the powdered cookies out as your starch in your normal cookie recipe. But this starch is now a carrier of flavor for the end product — so the resulting cookie now tastes more like it "should" than it would have just using regular flour.

A lot of our food is rooted in classic combinations — and it has to be. Why? The process by which we go about creating is so foreign that we have to make something that you are familiar with eating. In a tapas restaurant, you have had generations of trial and error to create a dish through local ingredients and techniques that have evolved into something that tastes good. For example, olives marinated with garlic and parsley has been around for a hundred years. Now, there is nothing wrong with that. But, for us, the idea of marinating olives with garlic and parsley is not fun. So, we are going to make a dish where the olives are actually the parsley and the garlic is the olives and so on. But it tastes like something you'd want.

What's in a Pancake? Yes, we do serve real food. We got some BLiS syrup [handcrafted aged maple syrup] in the kitchen which is used by other top chefs around the country. This stuff is liquid gold! This syrup is aged in small bourbon barrels in Canada and is $20 for a small [375 ml] bottle. The maker even hand-stamps each bottle with wax and writes the label by hand. When we got it in, we knew we had to do something with it.

We decided to make a pancake dish. We started with the question "How can we make this dish taste more like pancakes than pancakes?" So, we pureed cooked pancakes, then adjusted the liquid with milk. The cool thing about making a pancake puree out of cooked pancakes is that you can alter the concentration levels. You can't alter the concentration levels when you are making straight pancakes.

We wanted to trick the customer into thinking that they were going to eat a hot pancake topped with this syrup. Believability is so important in the process, so we even execute the dish in front of them [in the dining room]. We bring out a metal plate that looks hot [but is frozen and steaming from being immersed in nitrogen]. The pancake batter is then shot from a syringe. The batter freezes when it hits the metal. When we serve it, we top it with the BLiS syrup. Ninety-nine percent of the people who were served this dish swore they were getting a hot flapjack, and it was only when they tasted it that they learned it was cold.

Contrarian by Nature People want to say that wine is natural and has been around a thousand years. But is it natural or unnatural? We don't know. You have people in a foreign country stepping all over these grapes, putting foot fungus in there, and then creating a fermented thing that is controlled. I don't think that wine is all that natural! Every time you turn on the blender and puree something, you are crossing the line of natural versus unnatural. Nature did not intend for an electric motor to spin a blade and turn a solid into a liquid.

If you think an unripe green tomato tastes better than a ripe heirloom red tomato picked off the vine in August, then by all means eat the green tomato. That is flavor preference. What if I feed you an unripe green tomato but alter its taste so it tastes *better* than a vine-ripened red tomato? When we pick it off the vine earlier, it has a different quality — it is sharper. So, we will pair something that maybe should not go with it, like Parmesan cheese pureed with butter. This will make it a little richer and compensate for the overtannic, overacidic qualities of the tomato. [If you enjoy it,] then you have succumbed to not following the seasons.

In the same manner, we'll serve a dish of unripe things that taste ripe because they are together! What do I prefer? Of course I prefer the vine-ripened tomato at the end of August. We would make the other dish just to ask the question.

Creating New Flavors I disagree with the notion that there are no new flavors. Maybe there are no new products, even though we don't know everything that exists in the sea. To create a new flavor, all you have to do is dissect an ingredient. For example, if I take an avocado and put it into a centrifuge, we would separate the fat and the water. The water will carry the avocado taste. If I take that water and create a snow with it or make it into a pill, it will have a much different taste than avocado, because avocado is thought of as something that is rich. But there would be no richness here; it is a completely different product. We just made up a new flavor.

So now if I want to mimic an avocado, I would have to serve something rich with it. I could serve something dairy with it, like brown butter. I now have something that would go with a classical turbot dish with brown butter and capers, whereas fresh avocado would not have paired up with that dish very well.

Katsuya Fukushima of minibar in Washington, DC

I like to work with classic, preexisting flavor combinations that people can recognize. They may not recognize anything from the textures I use, but they will find recognition in the flavors.

To make our "Philly Cheesesteak," we start with the bread. We put pita dough through a pasta machine so that it gets really thin, but puffs way up when you cook it. For the cheese element, we use a Vermont and Wisconsin cheddar cheese mousse that we pipe into the pita. For the beef, we serve seared Kobe beef. For the onions, we spread on caramelized onion puree. We then top that with truffles. So you have bread, cheese, beef, and onion, just like a Philly cheesesteak. We add the truffles just to push it over the top.

CHEFS' STRATEGIES FOR BALANCING FLAVORS

On every forkful — regardless of what's on the fork — there has to be salt, acid, and heat. . . . However, unless you are serving a pepper-crusted dish, or a lemon or vinegar dish, your seasoning should never be detected. Instead, your beans should taste like beans, and your rabbit should taste like rabbit. Diners don't need to know how much salt, acid, and heat are in the dish — and none should be obvious. You'll also have minor supporting players in a dish, such as the aromatic or picante levels that might come from your mirepoix or sofrito [a well-cooked sauce of tomatoes, garlic, onions, and herbs] or whatever else went in there. But when a diner tastes your dishes, all you want them to be thinking about is those beans, or that rabbit.
— **SHARON HAGE,** YORK STREET (DALLAS)

Over the past fifteen years, we have interviewed many chefs in an effort to understand how some of America's best chefs approach creating great food. What we learned is that there are as many approaches as chefs themselves. While some strategies overlap, others are unique and display strong self-knowledge as to what makes their individual cuisines so original and compelling.

Traci Des Jardins of Jardinière in San Francisco

The most important aspect of any dish is balance — between acid, fat, salt, and sweetness. It is the key to making food taste good.

The same is true in pastry. I am constantly working with my pastry chef when I taste desserts with her. I will taste something and say it is too sweet — that it is missing the acid balance, and needs some fat and a little salt. Using salt in pastry brings out the flavor, just as it does in savory food. When it comes to dessert, people think more in a "monochromatic" sweet fashion. But sweets need balance, too.

My favorite flavor is the harmony of these elements working together, whether it is sweet or savory.

Marcel Desaulniers of The Trellis in Williamsburg, Virginia

My cooking philosophy has always been simple: Don't complicate things, and let the food speak for itself. I want the food to leave a clean taste in your mouth, and that goes for savory food as well as desserts.

We don't use a lot of spices because they can have an intensity of flavor that can overwhelm other flavors. People can't restrain themselves with certain ingredients — and, often, it's garlic. At The Trellis, we use garlic in only one recipe: a dressing that has been on the menu for twenty-six years. Herbs can be overused as well, too. Rosemary and basil, which I love, are constantly overused, which results in a bitter flavor.

I tell cooks, "When in doubt, don't use it." The food you are starting with already has its own intrinsic flavor, whether it is a scallop or a filet of beef. Whatever you do to embellish the flavor should be a very minor part of the relationship, rather than sharing the stage fifty-fifty.

I thought of myself as a saucier from my days in New York, yet when I opened this restaurant in Williamsburg, it was not the way I wanted to present the food. Rather than sauces, I wanted to use vegetables and fruits as the accompaniments. They provide moisture as a natural component and they work on the plate, but not as a fifty-fifty partner.

An example of where fruit works great as a component is on our pork dish: We serve pork loin medallions, grilled sausage, sweet potatoes, tender cooked string beans, and bourbon-glazed peaches. So this is a dish with no sauce, except the juice from the peaches.

Carrie Nahabedian of Naha in Chicago

You should always season something right from the start, and not just at the end. If you just add salt and pepper at the end, you are not doing a soup justice. You want those flavors to blossom.

Take our butternut squash soup as an example. We start our soup with hefty pieces of slab bacon, so we are already starting off with a lot of flavor. From there, we add the mirepoix and make sure it gets nice and caramelized. Then we start adding our salt, fresh-cracked pepper, and thyme sprig.

Next, we add roasted squash. The reason we roast it before it goes in the soup is because you can taste what state the squash is in. It may need a little help because it needed to age a couple more weeks in the cellar before we got it, so we may add a garnet yam. Now, we taste the soup and decide what kind of sweetness to add. That could be honey, molasses, or maple sugar — not just [white] sugar.

Next, we puree the soup and pass it [through a fine-mesh strainer] to achieve its smooth texture.

To the soup base, we add the garnishes. We already have bacon, but some smoked duck will be good, too. We add spaghetti squash and fried parsnips for additional texture and, in the case of the parsnips, sweetness as well. For a last note, we add a drizzle of maple syrup or barrel-aged sherry. These things just seal the soup so that the flavors all escalate. It is important to not rush things so that your flavors come together.

Andrew Carmellini of A Voce in New York City

Any kind of sauce boils down to acid, salt, sweetness, and two kinds of spice: savory spice, meaning cumin- or coriander-type spices, and heat spice, meaning chiles or pepper flakes. You can be making a vinaigrette or a Thai curry or a bouillabaisse, but its seasoning involves the same principles on the palate. As long as you can manipulate those things, you can get your palate excited.

If something is heavy or fatty on the tongue, add some vinegar or lemon or another type of acid. If you were making a Thai-style coconut curry that is too fatty and rich from the coconut milk, you would add some grated lime zest, lime juice, and a splash of fish sauce to cut the richness.

When you are adjusting the seasoning of a dish, you need to think about its origin. That is why traveling is so important. For example, you wouldn't use rice wine vinegar in a French bouillabaisse, but you might use a little bit of chili flakes. You must understand the historical context of a dish, which is why you wouldn't thicken an Indian curry with strawberries.

Sharon Hage of York Street in Dallas

When I am building a dish, I use a tray we call "the four seasons," which is *fleur de sel* [salt]; red pepper flakes, the ultimate marriage of heat and fruit; dry mustard, which I use all the time; and sumac, which is an acidic component.

When I make a dish, it starts with the dry ingredients first, and the salt is the first dry ingredient. Then I add the heat layer, such as a jalapeño or horseradish. Then I add acid: lemon juice, vinegar, *verjus*, or all three. Then, at the last second, I add the fat component — the oil or butter — to the sauce, which brings it all together.

Brad Farmerie of Public in New York City

When I come up with a new dish, I am looking at two things: The first is building up the richness, and the second is cutting that richness with acidity, spice, or herbaceousness.

I start by thinking, What is the rich component? How can I build richness? If it is a protein, we may cure the meat or fry the fish. If it is a vegetarian dish, I may start with eggplant, which is meaty, so I will build it up with miso or tahini, which will make it even richer and meatier. This is really important in a vegetarian dish, because I hate those flimsy veg plates of grilled vegetables and a lot of salad!

Texture is another way of building richness. If you add miso or tahini, that adds richness and texture. An emulsification also gives a sense of richness in your mind and across your palate. One way to add rich texture in a "fakey-jakey" way is to add palm sugar. It is [a less] sweet sugar, and we will shave it into a dish halfway through the cooking and temper it with tamarind. We use it so subtly that you don't even know it is there.

Now that I have my richness, the question becomes, "How can we cut that richness so it is light on the palate and in the belly?" We use a tremendous amount of acid, but it is always in check with what is on the plate. Choosing the right acid or herb will leave a light feeling on the palate and cut a rich dish.

With any fried food, you need a big zap of acidity to get through it. With fried fish, we will use preserved lemon, yogurt, or yuzu with a white soy dipping sauce.

Cured meat is almost the epitome of richness. Cured meats have a salinity to them, and quite often there is sugar to balance the salt as well. You need some punchy flavors to cut the meat, or it will just be heavy on the palate. Traditionally, you would use capers or caper berries. Mustard fruits [known in Italy as *mostarda,* these are fruits preserved in mustard-flavored sweet syrup] are another traditional approach. I like them because you have the added element of spice. We make our own mustard fruits and bastardize them a little by using kumquats, baby apricots, and gooseberries, which are not traditional in Italy. These fruits simply have beautiful flavor and color. The other thing we do is use whole mustard seeds. Mustard fruits are typically [made through] a refined process in that they become like a clear jam. We leave ours a little rougher and fold in a little dry mustard in the end to make the colors of the citrus fruits really pop.

Another way we cut richness is by using sweet-and-sour poached vegetables and fruit. We'll poach fennel or pearl onions in a sweet-sour liquid with licorice and star anise. The family of apples, pears, and quince also holds up very well, as do sour poached plums.

I like aromatic spices [for their ability to cut richness]. If I'm working on a dish inspired by India, my inspirations are the flavors of clove, cardamom, and coriander seed. They are aromatic spices that really cut the fat of a dish, so the dish is not big, fat, and flabby on the palate. Fresh turmeric gives you fruitiness and upfront flavor with a touch of acid that perks up a dish. If you add fresh turmeric to your curry, you will make a world of difference by adding this one small thing.

If I'm working on a dish inspired by Southeast Asia, I like galangal, lemongrass, and ginger. They all have natural acidity and zingy spice that will perk up anything. Even if you are not adding acid to coconut milk but just adding aromatics, it won't taste heavy.

Emily Luchetti, pastry chef at Farallon in San Francisco

I want my flavors to be clean, crisp, accentuated, and distinguished. From there, I look at what I feel like making. If I have peaches, do I want to make a trifle or a napoleon or something else? What is the star of the plate? Is it one thing and everything else is going to be showing it off? Or are there two main flavors that are both going to have equal billing? I make a peach-blueberry trifle that has a mascarpone cream and is pretty intense. It is one of my favorite summer things to make. The peaches and blueberries are both the stars. If you make a pumpkin-cranberry upside-down cake, the pumpkin is the star and the cranberry is an accent.

You have to look at the ingredient and ask, "How am I going to bring out the best of its flavors? Do I cook it, or leave it alone? Does this piece of fruit need to be intensified because it wants to be the star, or is it not good enough on its own?" When you are working with fresh or dried fruit, the most important thing is the balance of sugar, salt, and lemon. If I am mixing fresh fruit for a shortcake or crisp, I always add some lemon juice and salt, because — just like in savory cooking — it helps bring out the flavor. We are talking a half teaspoon to a teaspoon of lemon and a large pinch of kosher salt.

Whenever you are cooking fruit with sugar to serve with something, taste the fruit first. If it is the peak of summer, that fruit may not need sugar. If you added some anyway, it would dull the flavors and make it taste too sweet. So, taste your fruit — and trust your palate! People trust their palates for savory food all the time. They'll taste a tomato sauce and know it needs some salt. You need to trust your palate for sugar as well. You know when something is too sugary or salty.

When you are working with fresh fruit, the fruit has to be the guide. If you eat a piece of fresh fruit by itself, it is a dessert. So you want the dessert, in the end, to taste better than the fruit itself. To do that, you need to add things that go naturally. Blueberries and peaches go well together. Vanilla goes with practically any fruit. Almonds go with most fruits because they are light nuts that have a lot of flavor but not a lot of fat. Just starting with things that naturally go together, you will have a greater rate of success.

People will read that I think three flavors work in a dessert — then they'll say, "Well, you used *four*. . . ." That is not the point — the point is knowing when to stop! Too many chefs start adding things that in the end all taste muddled, because nothing can stand out on its own. When you are more restrictive, each thing tastes good on its own — and the dessert becomes more than the sum of its parts. It is hard to know when to stop. Many chefs seem to think, "Oh, I'll just add this dot of mango. . . ." Well, the taste of that one acidic dot can set the whole dessert off.

———————————

Flavor is a "language" that anyone who loves the pleasures of the palate will find to be well worth mastering. Once you master the language of flavor, you can use it to communicate — and become a better cook.

2

Chapter

GREAT COOKING = MAXIMIZING FLAVOR + PLEASURE BY TAPPING BODY + HEART + MIND + SPIRIT: COMMUNICATING VIA THE LANGUAGE OF FOOD

Happy and successful cooking doesn't rely only on know-how. It comes from the heart, makes great demands on the palate, and needs enthusiasm and a deep love of food to bring it to life.

— GEORGES BLANC, MICHELIN THREE-STAR CHEF IN VONNAS, FRANCE

The defining trait of a great cook is more than a great palate, and more than great technique; it is sound judgment. It is not only knowing what to do with ingredients, but also when, where, why, and how to serve them. Cooking involves the thoughtful combination and manipulation of ingredients. Good cooking results in those ingredients tasting even better. Great cooking not only celebrates the ingredients, but also celebrates the moment.

Recipes evolved as a way to teach less experienced cooks how to prepare particular dishes, by providing specific proportions of compatible ingredients along with step-by-step instructions. However, anyone who believes that every recipe followed verbatim will always produce consistent results is kidding themselves, given the diversity within individual ingredients, whether the sweetness of fruit or the thickness of a fish fillet. Slavish followers of recipes, who treat them as gospel instead of guidelines, make the mistake of putting more faith in someone else's instructions than they do in themselves. Many people would do better in the kitchen if they *didn't* blindly follow recipes. In fact, following recipes may be holding *you* back from achieving your potential as a cook.

Take the time to learn and master some of the general principles of how to make food taste great — such as what to pair with various ingredients, and how to prepare them — which is the subject of this book. After all, more than a dozen years after the advent of the Food Network turned every TV set in this country into a virtual 24/7 cooking school, supplementing the burgeoning food programming on many of the other major channels, Americans are better-trained cooks than at any previous point in history. Most of us can now whip up a dish with our general knowledge of how to boil pasta, sauté an onion, or grill a steak. Today, long, detailed recipes are rarely needed for most cooking (with the exception of baking, whose chemistry requires precise measurements).

Training wheels can be useful when first learning to ride a bike, as can "painting by numbers" when first learning to paint. Likewise, following a recipe can be useful when first learning to cook — for understanding the order of completing certain steps, and internalizing their intrinsic logic. But great cooking should be more akin to meditation: you — and all of your senses — are in the moment, and fully awake and aware. You can taste the ingredients, and know what you need to do to make them taste their best. You know, as chef Judy Rodgers famously told us for our book *Becoming a Chef*, to "look out the window and see what the weather is and decide what the soup wants to be." Be fully grounded in the moment that is part of that second, that minute, that hour, that day, that month, that season, that year of your life — all at once.

To elevate your cooking to a whole new level, develop a better appreciation for the essence of ingredients, which provides insight into when and how to best use them. Celebrating the essence of ingredients allows you to work with them more intuitively and effectively. This book will help you decide what ingredients to reach for in the kitchen, and why, and what to do with them when you do.

HOW TO MAKE FOOD TASTE GREAT

A great cook is able to make food taste great by doing two basic things:

1. Understanding the essence of the **moment,** which comprises everything from the meal's driving force to the occasion, to the weather, to the available time, budget, and/or other resources (for example, ingredients, equipment, etc.).

2. Understanding the essence of the **ingredients,** which comprises their season, regionality, weight and volume, function, flavor, and/or flavor affinities.

The deeper your understanding of both, the greater your ability to bring them together into a dish that is the perfect expression of the ingredients and the moment.

Understanding the Essence of the Moment

Why do you need or want to cook in the first place? In a day and age when more of the meals we consume are prepared *outside* the home than *at* home, cooking has become relatively infrequent. So, what's driving *you*?

Always keep in mind your starting point in the kitchen, the reference point serving as the inspiration for your cooking — which can be virtually anything. Following its essence logically or intuitively will lead you to each subsequent step toward creating something delicious. Your starting point is your initial desire. It may be an ingredient, or a dish, or a country: you're excited to prepare the first heirloom tomatoes of summer; you're craving your grandmother's cheesecake; or you want a dish that will take you to Italy to relive the flavors you enjoyed on your last vacation.

Other factors provide the parameters of how you'll act on that desire. They might be time ("I want to spend the day cooking for pleasure" versus "I have only fifteen minutes to get something on the table"), budget ($5/person versus "money is no object, so bring on the truffles"), occasion (dinner on a Tuesday night, or someone's birthday), availability of ingredients (your neighbors just gave you fresh vegetables from their garden), season (the arrival of the first asparagus of spring, or the last corn of Indian summer), weather (wanting a chilled lunch to help you cool off on a hot summer day), or something else.

Your starting point, whatever it is, has an essence: Your desire to host a barbecue to celebrate the beautiful summer weather will bring up associations that will in turn bring up other associations, until you have a long list of associations, for example:

- Desire to enjoy the 80-degree sunny summer day (starting point: season, weather)
   → Have a summer barbecue (craving)
   → Invite friends over to enjoy it, too
- Prefer to cool down (function)
   → Serve cold drinks
   → Serve at least some chilled dishes
- Serve corn bought at the market this morning (available resources)
   → Serve corn salsa on grilled chicken or fish
   → Serve corn on the cob
- Have best friends over for dinner (guests)
   → Everyone eats chicken
   → One of them is from New England and can bring lobster
- Avoid turning the oven on (temperature)
   → Cook outside → fire up the grill
   → Cook on the stovetop only → boil water

So, starting with your driving factor and its essence, you can follow these associations to their logical conclusion and come up with the perfect meal. For one person, it might be serving grilled chicken with a corn salsa in the backyard. For another, it might be hosting a lobster and corn boil in an air-conditioned dining room. It's all about taking everything into consideration at once, and using sound judgment to determine how to proceed.

Occasion

Even if it wasn't the driving force behind why you're cooking in the first place, you'll still want to consider the importance and significance of the meal. A quick dinner on a time-pressed weeknight will be different from a dinner made on the weekend when there is more time to enjoy the sensual process of cooking. Keep the occasion in mind when planning your meal, with the knowledge that any meal can be elevated to a special occasion — or simplified in a crunch. The elements of breakfast take on a different level of importance when they are used for a special brunch. A quick fried egg and a toasted English muffin on a Tuesday can morph into poached eggs with Canadian bacon with hollandaise sauce on an English muffin for a weekend brunch, or vice versa.

But a true special occasion — a birthday, anniversary, or holiday — definitely calls for something equally special to celebrate it. If lack of time is a factor, a birthday isn't the time to undertake making and decorating a cake from scratch. However, it might inspire you to pick up a half gallon of the birthday boy or girl's favorite ice cream, toast some pecans, and whip up some homemade chocolate sauce — which would take only minutes, as opposed to hours.

Weather

While seasonality will drive your choice of ingredients, the weather will drive your decision as to how to prepare and serve them. On the coldest days, you'll want to warm your home as well as your body with slow-braised dishes, soups, and stews, and on warmer days, you'll want to keep your home (and yourself) cooler by doing more grilling or on the hottest days serving quick-cooked or even chilled dishes — no matter what season those days may fall in.

Some cooks believe you can serve anything at any time of the year. Our eyebrows have raised upon seeing heavy braised dishes on restaurant menus in August. However, chefs have defended them by arguing that once someone is seated in an air-conditioned dining room, they forget what it's like outside! Those chefs may be giving customers what they want while they are at the table . . . but what happens when those same customers leave the restaurant after finishing their braised short ribs and walk out into the heat and humidity? They might feel as out of sorts as they would wearing long wool overcoats on such a night! A lighter meal on a hot night won't sap your energy in the same way. Even in the middle of summer, there will be unseasonably cool days that might suggest a warm dish that would offend the sensibilities on the season's hottest, most sweltering day. Even during the dead of winter, the sun can break through and create an unseasonably warm day on which hot, slow-cooked braised dishes would not be appealing.

Considering the weather means taking into consideration the natural rhythms of nature. One of the easiest clues available to inform your cooking is to look out the window, and ask yourself what you feel like eating. If you look out the window on a sunny summer morning, are you more tempted by hot oatmeal — or by granola and yogurt? That afternoon, as the temperature rises, does your mouth water thinking of hot tomato soup — or chilled gazpacho? That night, does the temperature fall enough to make you want to turn on the oven to roast a chicken — or would you rather grill it on your stovetop?

On our first visit to a certain New York City restaurant on one of the hottest nights of summer, we were surprised to be sent an *amuse-bouche* from the kitchen that was a tall glass of hot yellow pepper soup. While the soup itself might have been made from seasonal ingredients and tasty in a vacuum, unfortunately what we remember even more vividly was how unappealing we found it, especially as our first taste after a sweltering taxi ride to the restaurant. If the same soup had been served to us cold, we expect it would have been more successful as the welcoming gesture it was intended to be.

Understanding the Essence of the Ingredients

Once you're clear about "the problem" of what to cook, the right ingredients, well prepared, provide the ideal "solution." To prepare any ingredients well, it's vital to understand and respect their essence.

What do we mean when we talk about an ingredient's "essence"? Every ingredient has associations with it, and the sum total of those associations comprises its essence. An ingredient's essence is more than its flavor. Take two sample ingredients, both salty:

- What comes to mind when you think of soy sauce? Common associations besides its saltiness might include Asia (region), rice (as a common flavoring for), and/or scallions (compatible ingredient).
- What comes to mind when you think of Parmesan cheese? Aside from saltiness (flavor), its common associations might include Italy (region), pasta or pizza (which it is a common flavoring for), and/or basil and tomatoes (compatible ingredients).

While certain other ingredients — such as chicken, garlic, and onions, which are all used around the world — may be neutral in their universality, many ingredients are rooted in distinct associations.

Some of the primary aspects of any ingredient's essence include its **seasonality**, its **taste**, its **volume**, its **function**, its **regionality**, its **weight**, and its **flavor affinities**. While the importance of each factor varies, depending on the dish, the goal when cooking is to ensure that all of these factors are respected in the ingredient's use.

Seasonality

It is almost a cliché to talk about seasonality if you are a New American chef. You are cooking that way naturally. I had a customer complain that his favorite pea ravioli was not on the menu. I explained that peas were not very good at the time, so that we were featuring corn ravioli. I don't focus on making an ingredient that is not at its peak taste better; I simply take it off the menu. Chefs still pay more attention to seasonality than customers do. We still have diners who want berries in the middle of February!

— **ANDREW CARMELLINI,** A VOCE (NEW YORK CITY)

Cooking with ingredients at their seasonal peak is such a central tenet of good cooking that it bears constant repeating. In stores across the country, you can find almost any ingredient at almost any time of year. However, an ingredient's mere availability offers no assurances of its quality.

Each season suggests a different palette of ingredients, and different ways of preparing and serving them. Classic holiday dishes represent time-tested ways of celebrating the season: Picture a grilled hamburger followed by a red, white, and blue strawberry shortcake accented with blueberries and whipped cream served on the Fourth of July, or roasted turkey with stuffing, cranberry sauce, and pumpkin pie on Thanksgiving. (If you're not convinced of the perfection of each dish's expression of the season and occasion, just imagine eating each menu on the *other* holiday!) Each season also suggests its own beverages; for example, summer calls more often for lighter-bodied white and rosé wines, just as winter calls for fuller-bodied reds.

Taste

Every ingredient has its *stereotypical* taste (bananas are sweet), plus its *actual* taste, which may be a function of its age or ripeness. For example, a banana may increase noticeably in sweetness as it ripens and its color changes from green to yellow to brown. That is why it's crucial to taste your ingredients when cooking.

If you don't — and, as a result, don't end up making other adjustments (for example, slightly decreasing the amount of sugar used when using very ripe bananas) — you'll find your dishes to be out of balance. Even seemingly similar ingredients (such as regular versus aged balsamic vinegar, or Italian versus Thai basil) can vary dramatically.

Weight

It was through our study of wine that we developed an appreciation for the critical role of understanding a wine's body, or weight — and, in turn, the relative weights of various foods. In fact, weight has eclipsed color as the key factor in pairing wine with food.

Weight and season often go hand in hand, as we crave lightness in summer and heavier dishes when temperatures fall. In summer, that craving for lightness could be satisfied with a salad of fresh greens topped with shrimp or chicken and tossed in a vinaigrette. Our winter cravings for more substance and warmth might lead us to a hearty stew made with red meat and root vegetables in their own thick sauce.

There is a spectrum of wine and ingredients that suggests itself for warmer versus cooler seasons or days, as well as for lighter versus heavier appetites:

	Light	*Medium*	*Heavy*
White Wines	Riesling	Sauvignon Blanc	Chardonnay
Red Wines	Pinot Noir	Merlot	Cabernet Sauvignon
Vegetables	Bibb lettuce	Carrots	Celery root
Grains	Couscous	Rice	Bulgur wheat
Fruits	Watermelon	Apples	Bananas
Seafood	Shrimp, sole	Salmon, tuna	
White Meat		Chicken, pork, veal	
Red Meat			Beef, lamb, venison
Sauces	Citrus/lemon Vinaigrette	Butter/cream Olive oil	Demi-glace Meat stock

Volume

One important aspect of an ingredient's flavor essence is its "volume." Think of a stereo dial with "1" indicating a "quiet" seasoning of chopped parsley, and "10" suggesting a "loud" mound of freshly chopped habanero chile peppers. You'll use them very differently to create very different effects, while striving to achieve the same all-important balance in the final dish.

So, is the ingredient you're working with quiet, moderate, or loud? You need to be aware of an ingredient's volume whenever combining it with other ingredients. If a dish is overspiced to the point where you can't taste its essence, it's wrong. Consider:

Proteins
Light and/or quiet: fish, shellfish, tofu
Medium and/or moderate: white meat (chicken, pork, veal)
Heavy and/or loud: red meat (beef, lamb, venison)

Cooking Techniques
Light and/or quiet: poaching, steaming
Medium and/or moderate: frying, sautéing
Heavy and/or loud: braising, stewing

Herbs
Light and/or quiet: chervil, parsley
Medium and/or moderate: dill, lemon thyme
Heavy and/or loud: rosemary, tarragon

Function

Different tastes serve different functions. Saltiness stimulates thirst (think of all those free salty peanuts in bars!), while sourness quenches it (think lemonade). Saltiness heightens the appetite, making this flavor especially effective in appetizers. Bitterness also stimulates the appetite, and can promote the other tastes with which it is paired while adding a note of lightness to a dish. Sourness is refreshing, and adds a fresh note to any dish to which it is added. Sweetness is famously satiating, making it ideal (not to mention customary) to end a meal with a sweet dessert, or at least a sweet note (such as a cheese course with honey or sweet figs).

Certain foods, such as the spices cinnamon and nutmeg, are thought of as "warming" foods, so their addition to dishes is thought to add a warming quality that might be especially welcomed on a cold day. There are also "cooling" foods (such as cucumber and mint) that can be used just as judiciously.

Keeping an ingredient's function in mind will help you use it most wisely, and avoid unfortunate mismatches of flavor and function. We still remember an otherwise delicious beet salad we were once served as an appetizer in New Orleans that was so sweet it killed our appetite for the rest of our meal.

Region

Determining the region that will serve as the reference point for whatever you're cooking is one of the easiest ways to create successful flavor marriages in the kitchen. Thinking regionally is as important to good pairing as thinking seasonally is to good cooking. Many people are familiar with the maxim "If it grows together, it goes together," and this is still the best place to start as a guide. Knowing what country you want to draw on will narrow your list of ingredient choices, often for the better! For example, as chicken is the world traveler of ingredients, if you're making a chicken dish, you'll especially need to decide on a region of inspiration. Are you going to root your dish in Mexico by topping it with salsa, or take it to France by finishing it with a mustard cream sauce? The accompaniments you choose will reinforce the dish's sense of place. Would rice and beans, or boiled new potatoes, be most appealing served alongside it?

Flavor Affinities

A perfect ingredient served plainly can be an extraordinary thing, whether a perfectly ripe and sweet piece of fruit, or a silky slice of raw fish as sashimi. But in the real world, perfect ingredients are all too rare — and there are few ingredients whose flavors can't be helped along by a pinch of this or a splash of that. A sprinkle of sugar will bring out the flavor of strawberries. A squeeze of lime will bring out a melon's sweetness. A drizzle of vinegar will provide a tasty counterpoint for salty French fries.

Understanding what herbs, spices, and other seasonings will best bring out the flavor of whatever it is you're cooking is some of the most important knowledge any cook can master. The pages that follow emphasize modern-day flavor affinities that have been proved in some of the best-respected kitchens in this country in this millennium.

———————

Studying the language and syntax of ingredients in these pages will allow you access to the collective wisdom — and impeccably sound judgment — of some of America's most imaginative chefs.

Chapter

3

FLAVOR MATCHMAKING: THE CHARTS

Good cooking does not depend on whether the dish is large or small, expensive or economical. If one has the art, then a piece of celery or salted cabbage can be made into a marvelous delicacy; whereas if one has not the art, all the greatest delicacies and rarities of land, sea or sky are of no avail.

— YUAN MEI, EIGHTEENTH-CENTURY CHINESE POET

When you're creating in the kitchen, the starting point for a dish or a menu can be literally anything. It can begin with the seasonal availability of a particular ingredient — vegetable, fruit, meat, or seafood — or even a cooking style, such as grilling in the summer or braising in the winter. It can begin with a craving for the flavors of a particular country or region: the garlic and herbs of Provence, or the garlic and ginger of Asia. Or it can begin with simple curiosity, the urge to experiment with a new ingredient or technique.

Recognizing this, we've provided a similarly broad range of starting points in the A-to-Z (achiote seeds to zucchini blossoms) lists that follow: the seasons (with listings for autumn, spring, summer, and winter); an extensive variety of vegetables, fruits, meat, seafood, and other ingredients; dozens of world cuisines; and a broad array of flavorings and seasonings (from avocado oil to fennel pollen to Kaffir lime), including dozens of different salts, peppers, herbs, spices, oils, and vinegars.

Below each, we've distilled and summarized key aspects of an ingredient's essence: its season, taste, weight, volume, and primary function. You'll also find its most recommended cooking techniques and some useful tips to keep in mind when working with it. After all, some ingredients lend themselves to being prepared in a particular manner: While chicken is versatile enough to be cooked in a number of ways, delicate fish beg to be served lightly cooked or even raw, while tougher cuts of meat beg to be braised or stewed.

When perusing the listings of compatible flavors, readers of our book *What to Drink with What You Eat* will recognize our ranking system to let you know which pairings are truly stellar. Those ingredients that appear in **BOLD CAPS** with an asterisk (*) are ethereal, time-honored classics: these "marriages made in heaven" comprise the top 1 or 2 percent of pairings. Next we have very highly recommended pairings in **BOLD CAPS**. **Bold**, noncapitalized listings are frequently recommended pairings; and plain text pairings are recommended pairings. But remember: Even when just a single top expert recommends a flavor combination, it's very high praise indeed.

In some cases, we've also noted flavor pairings to **AVOID** or steer clear of, to prevent overpowering or clashing with your star ingredient.

For many listings, we've also indicated "flavor trios" and other "flavor cliques" to get you started on compound flavor combinations. In other cases, you'll find some of America's most creative chefs' signature dishes, so you can gain inspiration from some of the most celebrated restaurant kitchens across the country.

Throughout these pages, you'll also find several insightful sidebars on cooking with herbs, mushrooms, pastas, steaks, and more. They'll serve to help you learn not only the "whats" of combining flavors, but also the "whys" and "hows."

Keep an eye out for the distinctions being made among ingredients. After all, not even all salts are created equal. As you hone your selections, you'll hone the quality of the flavors you're able to create.

Since the turn of the new millennium, we have traveled throughout the United States and Canada, spending thousands of hours interviewing dozens of the most creative chefs and other experts on their most recommended flavor pairings. We've scoured these experts' memories — along with their post-1999 restaurant menus, Web sites, cookbooks, and other highly recommended books — for pairing insights. Then we synthesized their advice into the comprehensive, easy-to-use listings that follow. These listings represent a treasure trove of pairing ideas for you to put to work in your own kitchen.

Armed with the extensive information that follows, you'll learn how to better show off virtually any ingredient, or to recreate the flavors of any world cuisine, you can think of. From here on out, you'll have the expert advice of some of America's most imaginative culinarians at your disposal when you want to inspire your own creativity. Whether you're exploring a new-to-you ingredient or looking for additional ideas for working with an ingredient you've cooked a thousand times, you'll find insightful tips and a plethora of pairings here.

MATCHING FLAVORS

KEY: Flavors mentioned in regular type are pairings suggested by one or more experts.

Those in **bold** were recommended by a number of experts.

Those in **BOLD CAPS** were very highly recommended by an even greater number of experts.

Those in *BOLD CAPS** with an asterisk (*) are "Holy Grail" pairings that are the most highly recommended by the greatest number of experts.

SEASON: The ingredient's seasonal peak(s)

TASTE: The ingredient's primary taste(s), e.g., bitter, salty, sour, sweet

FUNCTION: The ingredient's intrinsic property, e.g., cooling vs. warming

WEIGHT: The ingredient's relative density, e.g., from light to heavy

VOLUME: The ingredient's relative flavor "loudness," e.g., from quiet to loud

TECHNIQUES: The most commonly used techniques to prepare the ingredient

TIPS: Suggestions for using the ingredient

FLAVOR AFFINITIES: Compatible flavor groups

AVOID: Incompatible flavors

ACHIOTE SEEDS
beef
chicken
chiles
citrus (e.g., sour orange)
fish
game birds (e.g., duck, quail)
garlic
Mexican cuisine, esp. Yucatán
oil
pork
shellfish, e.g., lobster, shrimp
shrimp

Flavor Affinities
achiote + pork + sour orange

ACIDITY (See Sourness)

AFGHAN CUISINE
almonds
barley
breads
cardamom
chile pepper
cinnamon
cloves
coriander
cucumber
cumin
dill
fennel
fruits, esp. dried
ginger
grapes
kebabs
lamb
mint
mushrooms
nuts, e.g., almonds
pasta
rice, basmati
sesame
tomatoes and tomato sauce
turmeric
yogurt

Flavor Affinities
almonds + cardamom + sugar
cucumber + mint + yogurt

AFRICAN CUISINE
(See also Ethiopian and
Moroccan Cuisines)
bananas
bell peppers
braised dishes

chicken
chile peppers, esp. West African
coconuts
corn
fish, esp. coastal
fruits, esp. tropical
garlic
goat
greens, esp. steamed or stewed
mangoes
melons
okra
onions
papayas
peanuts
peas, esp. black-eyed
plantains
soups
stews, esp. meat or vegetable
sweet potatoes
tomatoes
watermelon
yams, esp. West African

AFRICAN CUISINE (NORTH) (See also Moroccan Cuisine)
bell peppers
braised dishes
chicken
chickpeas
couscous
cucumbers
cumin
eggplant
fish
garlic
lamb
mint
parsley
rice
stewed dishes
tomatoes
wheat

Flavor Affinities
cumin + garlic + mint, esp.
   Northeast Africa

AFRICAN CUISINE (SOUTH)
beans
carrots
chile peppers
cinnamon
cloves
fenugreek
garlic
ginger
lamb
onions
peas
pumpkin
stews
tomatoes
turmeric

Flavor Affinities
lamb + chile peppers + garlic +
   onions

AFRICAN CUISINE (WEST)
bananas
bell peppers
braised dishes
chicken
chile peppers
corn
goat
mangoes
okra
papayas
peanuts
plantains
rice
soups
stewed dishes
sweet potatoes
tomatoes
wheat
yams

Flavor Affinities
chile peppers + peanuts +
   tomatoes

ALLSPICE
Season: autumn–winter
Taste: sweet
Weight: medium
Volume: loud
Tips: Add early in cooking.

apples
baked goods
beans
BEEF, esp. braised, corned, grilled, ground, raw, roasted, or stewed
beets
breads, esp. breakfast
cabbage
cakes
Caribbean cuisine
carrots
chicken (e.g., Jamaican style)
chickpeas
chile peppers
cinnamon
cloves
cookies
coriander
currants, esp. black
curries and curry powder
Eastern Mediterranean cuisine
eggplant
English cuisine
fish, esp. grilled
fruits, fruit compotes, and jams
game and game birds (e.g., quail)
garlic
ginger
goat
grains
ham
herring, pickled
Indian cuisine
JAMAICAN CUISINE (e.g., jerk dishes)
ketchup
lamb
mace
MEATS, red, esp. braised, grilled, or roasted

In Jamaica, **allspice** is their pepper. It's fruitier than black peppercorns. I think it's especially nice with braised and roasted meats.

— **BRADFORD THOMPSON**, MARY ELAINE'S AT THE PHOENICIAN (SCOTTSDALE, ARIZONA)

Mexican cuisine
Middle Eastern cuisine
mushrooms
mustard
North American cuisine
nutmeg
nuts
onions
pepper, black
pies
pineapple
pork
PUMPKIN
rabbit
rice
rosemary
salsas and sauces
sauerkraut
sausages
soups
spiced cakes
spinach
squash, winter
stews
stocks and broths, chicken
sweet potatoes
thyme
tomatoes
turnips
vegetables, esp. root
West Indies cuisine

Flavor Affinities
allspice + beef + onions
allspice + garlic + pork

ALMOND OIL
(See Oil, Almond)

ALMONDS
Taste: sweet
Botanical relatives: peaches

Function: warming
Weight: medium
Volume: quiet

amaretto
anise, esp. green
apples
apricots
beans
blackberries
brandy
BUTTER, UNSALTED
butterscotch
caramel
cardamom
cayenne
cheese: goat, manchego, ricotta
cherries, esp. sour
chicken
CHOCOLATE: DARK, MILK
chocolate, white
cinnamon
coconut
coffee
cornmeal
corn syrup
crab
cranberries
CREAM
cream cheese
crème fraîche
crust: pastry, pie
currants
figs
fish
French pastries
fruits, most
garlic
grapes
Greek cuisine
greens, salad
hazelnuts

HONEY
ice cream
Indian cuisine
Italian sauces
lamb
lavender
lemon: juice, zest
liqueurs, fruit (including orange)
mascarpone
Mediterranean cuisine
Mexican beverages and mole sauces
milk, sweetened condensed
molasses
Moroccan cuisine
nectarines
oats
olive oil
olives
orange: juice, zest
paprika
passion fruit
peaches
pears
pecans
pepper, ground
pine nuts
plums
praline
prunes
quince
raisins, esp. white
raspberries
rhubarb
rice
rosemary
rum
salt: kosher, sea
shellfish
sherry
Spanish cuisine, esp. sauces
strawberries
sugar: brown, white
tea
Turkish cuisine
VANILLA
walnuts

Almonds are fairly versatile in that their flavor is not very specific. When they are manufactured, then they have a distinct flavor: think of Frangelico, almond oil, or marzipan in dessert. In these cases, the almond has a very distinct flavor.
— MARCEL DESAULNIERS, THE TRELLIS (WILLIAMSBURG, VIRGINIA)

If you have some beautiful **almonds**, there are so many things you can do. You can grind them and make a frangipane and put it in puff pastry. You can put them into biscotti, a cake, or almond ice cream.
— EMILY LUCHETTI, FARALLON (SAN FRANCISCO)

Flavor Affinities
almonds + chocolate + coconut
almonds + coffee + orange
almonds + green anise + figs
almonds + honey + orange zest + raisins

AMARETTO (sweet almond liqueur)
almonds
apricots
butter
cherries
chocolate
coffee
cream
hazelnuts
Italian cuisine
peaches
pork
sugar

ANCHOVIES
Taste: salty
Weight: light
Volume: loud

almonds
basil
beans, green
bell peppers, esp. roasted
capers
carrots
cauliflower
celery
cheese: manchego, mozzarella, Parmesan
chives

eggs, hard-boiled
fennel
GARLIC
lemon, juice
lobster
mayonnaise
Mediterranean cuisine
mustard (e.g., Dijon)
nectarines
OLIVE OIL
olives (e.g., black, green, niçoise)
onions
orange, zest
parsley, flat-leaf
pasta
pepper: black, white

No country in the world has **anchovies** like Spain. They are sophisticated, and the ones from the north of Spain are best because they are bigger. Spanish anchovies are not salty, either. Once you eat one, your life changes forever! I pay a lot for my anchovies — up to seventy-five cents per fillet — and will have to charge $9 for a plate. My customers will say that is too much to pay, and I agree — but if you don't pay, you don't taste. Lately, I have been combining anchovies with nectarines, which I love. I will make a vinaigrette with Pedro Ximénez [i.e., PX sherry], sherry vinegar, and olive oil and it is the perfect dressing — and unique.
— JOSÉ ANDRÉS, CAFÉ ATLÁNTICO (WASHINGTON, DC)

peppers, piquillo
pizza
potatoes
puttanesca sauce (key ingredient)
red pepper flakes
romaine lettuce
rosemary
salads, esp. Caesar (key
   ingredient)
salmon
salt: kosher, sea
shallots
sherry, PX
tapenade (key ingredient)
thyme
tomatoes
tuna
**vinegar: champagne, red wine,
   sherry**

Flavor Affinities
anchovies + lemon + olive oil +
   rosemary

ANGELICA
Taste: bitter, sweet
Volume: loud
Tips: Add late in cooking; use in
baking.
Use to balance high-acid fruit, to
reduce the need for sweeteners.

almonds
anise
apricots
candy
cream and ice cream
custards
desserts
fish
fruits
ginger: fresh, candied
hazelnuts
juniper berries
lavender
lemon balm
liqueurs
mushrooms

Angelica pairs well with fresh or candied ginger. And angelica with
rhubarb really intensifies the flavor of the rhubarb.
— **JERRY TRAUNFELD,** THE HERBFARM (WOODINVILLE, WASHINGTON)

nutmeg
oranges
pepper, black
plums
*RHUBARB
salads
shellfish
strawberries

Flavor Affinities
angelica + cream + rhubarb

ANISE (See also Anise,
Star, and Fennel)
Function: warming
Weight: light–medium
Volume: moderate–loud
Tips: Add early in cooking.

allspice
almonds
apples
baked goods, esp. cakes, cookies
beets
breads, esp. rye
cabbage
cakes
cardamom
carrots
cauliflower
cheese, esp. goat and ricotta
chestnuts
Chinese cuisine
cinnamon
cloves
coffee
cookies
crab
cream

cumin
dates
desserts
duck
fennel seeds
figs
FISH
fruit
garlic
ginger
hazelnuts
lemon
lentils
mayonnaise
Mediterranean cuisine
melon
Middle Eastern cuisine
mole sauce
Moroccan cuisine
mussels
nutmeg
nuts
orange
parsnips
peaches
pears
pepper
pickles
pineapple
plums
pork
Portuguese cuisine
Provençal cuisine (French)
prunes
pumpkin
quince
raisins
rhubarb
salumi

Anise seeds and fennel are used for braising our pork belly. Fennel and
pork is a natural, just like in Italian sausage.
— **CARRIE NAHABEDIAN,** NAHA (CHICAGO)

sauerkraut
Scandinavian cuisine
shellfish
soups, esp. fish
star anise
STEWS, ESP. FISH
strawberries
sugar
sweet potatoes
tea
vanilla
vegetables, root
Vietnamese cuisine
walnuts

ANISE HYSSOP

Season: late spring–summer
Taste: sweet
Weight: light–medium
Volume: quiet–moderate

apricots
basil
beans, green
beets
berries, esp. blueberries
beverages
carrots
cherries
chervil
chicken
cream and ice cream
currants
custards
desserts
fennel bulb
fish
FRUITS, ESP. SUMMER
honey
lavender
lemon
lychees
marjoram
melons
mint
nectarines
oranges
parsley

parsnips
peaches
pears
plums
pork
raspberries
rice
salads: fruit, green
shellfish (e.g., shrimp)
shrimp
spinach
squash, winter
stone fruits (e.g., peaches)
sweet potatoes
tarragon
teas
tomatoes
vegetables, root
watermelon
zucchini

ANISE, STAR

Taste: sweet, bitter
Weight: medium
Volume: moderate–loud
Tips: Add at the beginning of the cooking process. Use in stir-fries.

allspice
baked goods (e.g., breads, pastries)
beef
beverages
cardamom
chestnuts

chicken
chile peppers
chili powder
CHINESE CUISINE
chocolate, esp. milk
cinnamon
citrus zest
cloves
coriander
cumin
curry powder (ingredient)
duck
eggs
fennel seeds
figs
fish
FIVE-SPICE POWDER
fruits, esp. tropical
garlic
ginger
Indian cuisine
kumquats
leeks
lemongrass
lime, zest
liqueurs
mace
Malaysian cuisine
mangoes
maple syrup
meats, esp. fatty
nutmeg
orange, zest
oxtails
pears, esp. poached

As a kid, I hated black jelly beans. But I have grown to like all the various forms of anise, and **star anise** is one of my favorites. My favorite application is when it is infused with milk chocolate. It then has an almost malty-caramely quality to it. It adds that little something that people can't quite identify. I also love pears with anise, which works well with roasted or poached pears.
— **MICHAEL LAISKONIS,** LE BERNARDIN (NEW YORK CITY)

I love using **star anise** in dishes from meats to desserts. I love how it can be kind of meaty in a stew, or kind of sweet, adding bright, warm notes to a pumpkin dessert.
— **TONY LIU,** AUGUST (NEW YORK CITY)

pepper: black, Szechuan
pineapple
plums, esp. poached
pork
poultry
pumpkin
raspberries
root vegetables
salmon
sauces
scallions
scallops
shellfish
shrimp
soups
soy sauce
stews
stocks: beef, chicken
sweet potatoes
tamarind
teas
tuna
turmeric
vanilla
vegetables, esp. root
Vietnamese cuisine (e.g., *pho*)
wine, rice

Flavor Affinities

star anise + cream + maple
star anise + milk + milk chocolate
    + orange zest + sugar
star anise + pork + soy sauce +
    sugar

APPETIZERS

Tips: Saltiness stimulates
appetite.
    Serve small portions so as not
to satiate the appetite too early in
a meal.
    Accompany appetizers with
light-bodied wines.

Dishes

Insalata A Voce: Green Apple, Marcona Almonds, Watercress, Pecorino
— Andrew Carmellini, A Voce (New York City)

**Apple and Eggplant Croûte with Apple Butter, Cranberry Compote, and
Lemon-Poached Apples**
— Dominique and Cindy Duby, Wild Sweets (Vancouver)

Apple Softcake with Dark Chocolate and Cinnamon Soup
— Dominique and Cindy Duby, Wild Sweets (Vancouver)

Sautéed Apples, Olive Oil Sponge, Maple–Brown Butter Ice Cream
— Johnny Iuzzini, pastry chef, Jean Georges (New York City)

Poached Granny Smith Apples, Wildflower Honey, and Belgian Endive Leaves
— Thomas Keller, The French Laundry (Yountville, California)

Apple-Lychee Sorbet
— Michael Laiskonis, pastry chef, Le Bernardin (New York City)

Caramelized Apple Sundae with Butter Pecan Ice Cream
— Emily Luchetti, Farallon (San Francisco)

Warm Granny Smith Apple Tart with Buttermilk Ice Cream
— Patrick O'Connell, The Inn at Little Washington (Washington, Virginia)

APPLES

Season: autumn
Taste: sweet, astringent
Function: cooling
Weight: medium
Volume: quiet–moderate

Techniques: bake, caramelize,
deep-fry (e.g., as fritters), grill,
poach, raw, sauté, stew

allspice
almonds

The combination of **apple** and celery works. A tart green apple sorbet is not going to knock your socks off, because you are programmed to know it. When you add the flavor of celery, you get something new. I also love the flavors of apple and fennel together, especially in sorbet.

— **MICHAEL LAISKONIS**, LE BERNARDIN (NEW YORK CITY)

I make an **apple** confit of thinly sliced apples with cinnamon caramel powder layered between the apples and baked slowly. When the dish is served, next to the apples is a small pile of dates poached in syrup with vanilla. The other flavors on the plate are lemon confit, quince, raw apple with apple cider gelée, and *ras el hanout* (a Moroccan spice blend).

For this dish you need a contrast for the sweetness, so the role of the lemon confit is to cleanse and refresh. If the confit was not there, you would have a bite of the sweet date and be done. The date and lemon is like a salad. The line drawing this together is the quince and dates that come from the Middle East and that was the line to *ras el hanout*.

— **MICHAEL LAISKONIS**, LE BERNARDIN (NEW YORK CITY)

If you cook **apples** on top of the stove, some varieties will have a lot of juice while others will have none at all. Fuji, Gala, and Golden Delicious apples tend to be juicy, while Granny Smith apples are often drier. With different types of apples, you often don't know exactly what they will do. So if I'm going to serve apples with gingerbread, I will sauté them in a little sugar and see what happens. If they are letting out a bunch of juice, I won't add much sugar. If they are dry, I'll add some apple juice or Calvados.

— **EMILY LUCHETTI**, FARALLON (SAN FRANCISCO)

When I make an **apple** pie, I won't use any fewer than three different kinds of apples for their different textures and sweetnesses, which ensures that every single bite is interesting. I'll use Galas or Golden Delicious apples for their sweetness in the middle of the pie, and soft Jonathans or McIntoshes on top for their ability to melt into the others, and Braeburns or Granny Smiths on the bottom for their ability to stay firm. . . . I can't imagine an apple pie without cinnamon, a splash of lemon juice, and a pinch of salt.

— **SHARON HAGE**, YORK STREET (DALLAS)

Apples and caramel are a wonderful combination and depending on what nut you add it will take the combination in very different directions. If you add pecans, it would make the combination a heavier winter dessert, versus adding almonds, which would keep it lighter. Both work; you just need to decide how heavy you want the dish.

— **EMILY LUCHETTI**, FARALLON (SAN FRANCISCO)

apple cider or juice
applejack
apricots: dried, jam, puree
Armagnac
bacon
bay leaf
beef
blackberries
bourbon
brandy, esp. apple
brioche
BUTTER, UNSALTED
butterscotch
cabbage, red
CALVADOS
CARAMEL
cardamom
celery
celery root
cheese: Camembert, cheddar, goat, Gruyère
cherries: dried, fresh
chestnuts
chicken
chives
cider
***CINNAMON**
cloves
cognac
Cointreau
coriander
cranberries
CREAM AND ICE CREAM
crème anglaise (sauce)
crème fraîche
crust: pastry, pie
cumin
currants, esp. black, and currant jelly
curry powder
custards
dates
duck
eggplant
fennel
French cuisine, esp. from Normandy
frisée
ginger

Apple and shiso work well together. I especially like them together in a sorbet. I will use a Granny Smith apple that has a nice tartness combined with a little sugar, lemon, and then the shiso. The shiso has a cumin and cinnamon flavor that is a natural with apple.

— **JERRY TRAUNFELD**, THE HERBFARM (WOODINVILLE, WASHINGTON)

If you stay in the boundaries of what people think a dessert should be it gets very hard to do something new. We explain that they already eat carrot cake. We think parsnip will work instead of carrot and that kabocha squash will work instead of pumpkin in a pie.

When people see eggplant in a dessert they automatically think it will not work. You have to hide the unusual element and play up what people know already. The boundaries are limitless when you think of all the crossovers between sweet and savory. Duck à l'orange is a fruit and meat combined, so why not use bacon in a dessert? A pancake with maple syrup and bacon on the plate is really sweet and savory. So people already eat these combinations unconsciously.

For our apple-eggplant dessert, we start with a *choux* dough piecrust. Then we layer an almond cream-like custard. Then we alternate **apple** and eggplant slices side by side. We use baby eggplant because it has a spongy texture and sucks up moisture from the cream that can otherwise make the crust soggy and absorb the juice and flavor from the apples that would normally just evaporate. So when you eat the eggplant and apples, the eggplant tastes like apples.

— **DOMINIQUE AND CINDY DUBY**, WILD SWEETS (VANCOUVER)

I have always been very fond of chef Frédy Girardet [who earned three Michelin stars at his restaurant in Switzerland before retiring in 1996]. When I was young, I cooked almost every recipe from his book and visited his restaurant. One of his most interesting desserts was an **apple** dessert made of apples in the shape of little balls. The dessert broke away from cooking apples whole in the traditional way, which alone inspired me. He cooked them over a very high heat for two minutes and put them into a red wine reduction that had cinnamon, orange peel, and sugar. This was put onto a sheet tray that needed to be shaken for an hour so the apples would not dry out. The apples would absorb these flavors like a sponge and would then be served with vanilla ice cream.

In that spirit, we transformed this dessert. We transformed the wine by "espherication" so that it creates a bubble of liquid that explodes in your mouth. We cut apples with a melon baller, then vacuum-packed the apples with the wine but cooked it in such a way that the apples stayed hard and absorbed the wine flavor.

— **JOSÉ ANDRÉS**, CAFÉ ATLÁNTICO (WASHINGTON, DC)

We serve a dish of smoked oysters with **apples.** We smoke the oysters over applewood, and so it seemed logical to add apple to the dish. We serve it with a puree of apple with juniper that just plays beautifully off the oyster.

— **KATSUYA FUKUSHIMA**, MINIBAR (WASHINGTON, DC)

goose
hazelnuts
honey, esp. chestnut, wildflower
horseradish
ice cream
Kirsch
lavender
LEMON: JUICE, ZEST
lemon thyme
lychees
Madeira
maple syrup
mayonnaise
meringue
molasses
mustard
nutmeg
nuts
oatmeal and oats
oil: canola, hazelnut, walnut
olive oil
onions, esp. green, red
orange: juice, zest
parsley
peanuts and peanut butter
pears
pecans
pepper, black
pies
pineapple
pine nuts
pistachios
plums
pomegranates
pork
poultry
prunes
puff pastry
pumpkin
quince
raisins, esp. seedless, white
rhubarb
rice and rice pudding
rosemary
RUM: DARK, LIGHT
salads: fruit, green
salt, kosher
sauerkraut
sherry

soups
sour cream
star anise
SUGAR: BROWN, WHITE
sweet potatoes
tarragon
tarts
thyme
vanilla
verjus
vermouth
vinegar: apple cider, raspberry
WALNUTS
wine: red, dry white
yogurt

Flavor Affinities
apples + almonds + caramel
apples + almonds + Armagnac + crème fraîche + raisins
apples + apricots + pine nuts + rosemary
apples + brown sugar + cream + walnuts
apples + Calvados + cranberries + maple syrup
apples + caramel + cinnamon
apples + caramel + cinnamon + dates + lemon confit + quince + *ras el hanout* + vanilla
apples + caramel + peanuts
apples + caramel + pecans
apples + caramel + pistachios + vanilla
apples + celery + walnuts
apples + cinnamon + cranberries
apples + cinnamon + dark chocolate + yams
apples + cream + ginger
apples + ginger + hazelnuts
apples + ginger + lemon + quince + sugar
apples + honey + lemon thyme
apples + raisins + rum
apples + red cabbage + cinnamon

APRICOTS — IN GENERAL

Season: summer
Taste: sweet
Weight: medium
Volume: moderate
Techniques: bake, grill, poach, raw, stew

allspice
ALMONDS
amaretto
anise
apples
apricot brandy
bananas
blackberries
blueberries

brandy
butter, unsalted
caramel
cardamom
cayenne
cheese (e.g., Brie, Reblochon, ricotta)
cheesecake
cherries
chicken
chocolate, white
cinnamon
coconut
coffee and espresso
cognac
coriander
cranberries
CREAM AND ICE CREAM
crème anglaise
custards (e.g., crème brûlée)
duck
foie gras
game
garlic
ginger
hazelnuts
honey
ice cream, esp. vanilla
Kirsch
lamb
LEMON: juice, zest
lemon verbena
liqueurs: apricot, nut
maple syrup
mascarpone
Mediterranean cuisine
meringue
Middle Eastern stews
mint (garnish)
Moroccan cuisine
nectarines
nutmeg
nuts
oats and oatmeal
onions, esp. yellow
orange: juice, zest
orange liqueur
peaches

pepper, black
pineapple
pine nuts
pistachios
plums
pork
poultry
praline
prunes
raisins
raspberries
rice pudding
rosemary
rum
saffron
salads, esp. fruit, green
Sauternes
sour cream
strawberries
SUGAR: brown, white
tea: apple, apricot, Earl Grey
*****VANILLA**
vinegar, red wine
walnuts
wine: sweet, white
yogurt

Flavor Affinities

apricots + almonds + cream +
   sugar
apricots + almonds + meringue +
   Moscato d'Asti
apricots + apples + pine nuts +
   rosemary
apricots + cranberries + white
   chocolate
apricots + oranges + sugar +
   vanilla + walnuts

Apricots are much better cooked than raw. It is rare that you find a fruit that reaches its full potential as cooked rather than raw, but an apricot is one. A so-so apricot poached will turn into heaven. They are great with either chamomile or lavender.
— **GINA DEPALMA**, BABBO (NEW YORK CITY)

Apricot is a fruit you need to cook to help unleash its flavors. A bite of raw apricot is kind of bland and doesn't excite very much. If you throw that same apricot into the oven and heat it up a bit, it turns into a whole different fruit. Apricot with vanilla is a match made in heaven.
— **EMILY LUCHETTI**, FARALLON (SAN FRANCISCO)

APRICOTS, DRIED
Techniques: poach, stew

allspice
cherries, dried
cinnamon
currants
custard
French toast
ginger
hazelnuts
honey
ice cream
lemon: juice, zest
Madeira
Moroccan cuisine
orange: juice, zest
pancakes/crepes
pistachios
pork
prunes
pumpkin seeds
raisins
rice pudding
sugar
tamarind paste
vanilla
wine, sweet white (e.g., Muscat)

Flavor Affinities

dried apricots + dried cherries +
   ginger + orange + pistachios

ARGENTINIAN CUISINE
(See also Latin American Cuisine)
beef
corn
peaches
pumpkin
sweet potatoes

AROMA
When looking to make a big
   impact with aroma, turn to:
chocolate
cinnamon
herbs
pineapple
sous-vide cooking
spices
star anise
truffles
vanilla

We believe as much as 90 percent of flavor is due to **aroma** as oppposed to taste.
— **DOMINIQUE AND CINDY DUBY**,
WILD SWEETS (VANCOUVER)

ARTICHOKES
Season: spring–early autumn
Weight: medium
Volume: moderate–loud
Techniques: bake, boil, braise, broil, deep-fry, grill, raw, roast, sauté, steam, stew

aioli
anchovies
arugula
bacon
basil
bay leaf
beans, fava
beets
bell peppers, esp. roasted
bread crumbs
butter
capers
carrots

Dishes

Fettuccine with House-Made Pancetta, Artichokes, Lemon, and Hot Chiles
— Mario Batali, Babbo (New York City)

Spring Artichoke Fritto with Yogurt, Mint, and Lemon Aioli
— Andrew Carmellini, A Voce (New York City)

My mom made **artichokes** that we dipped in mayonnaise, so I tweaked that idea for the stuffed artichoke we serve here. *Panko* bread crumbs are mixed with chopped mint, salted, and stuffed into the artichoke cavity. The homemade mayonnaise I serve is made with eggs and just a little olive oil but mostly melted butter, which makes it richer and more flavorful — which is based on how it is made for the Chinese dish of shrimp and walnuts. The mayonnaise is then seasoned with anchovies, red pepper flakes, and onion confit.

— TONY LIU, AUGUST (NEW YORK CITY)

cashews
celery
cheese: **Emmental, goat, Gruyère, Parmesan**
chervil
chicken
chives
coriander
cream
crème fraîche
eggs: yolk, hard-boiled
French cuisine
GARLIC
grapefruit
ham (e.g., Serrano)
hazelnuts
hollandaise sauce
Italian cuisine
leeks
LEMON: confit, juice, zest
lobster
mayonnaise
Mediterranean cuisine
MINT
Moroccan cuisine
mushrooms
mustard, Dijon
nuts: cashews, hazelnuts, walnuts
oil: hazelnut, peanut
OLIVE OIL

olives: black, niçoise
ONIONS, ESP. SWEET AND YELLOW
orange
pancetta
PARSLEY, FLAT-LEAF
PEPPER: BLACK, WHITE
pesto
piquillo peppers
potatoes
prosciutto
radicchio

red pepper flakes
rice
risotto
rosemary
saffron
sage
salads
SALT, KOSHER
savory
shallots
shellfish (e.g., crab)
sherry, dry
shrimp
soy sauce
Spanish cuisine
spinach
stock, chicken
sugar (pinch)
tapenade
tarragon, fresh
THYME, FRESH
TOMATOES
truffles, black
tuna
vinaigrette
vinegar: balsamic, rice, sherry, white wine
walnuts
WINE, DRY WHITE
yogurt

Flavor Affinities

artichokes + butter + garlic + lemon + parsley
artichokes + cream + Parmesan cheese + thyme
artichokes + garlic + lemon
artichokes + garlic + lemon + mint
artichokes + garlic + lemon + olive oil
artichokes + garlic + lemon + olive oil + thyme
artichokes + garlic + mint
artichokes + garlic + Parmesan cheese + thyme
artichokes + garlic + sage
artichokes + lemon + mint + yogurt
artichokes + lemon + onions
artichokes + mushrooms + onions + sausage
artichokes + olive oil + Parmesan cheese + white truffles

ARTICHOKES, JERUSALEM

Season: autumn–spring
Weight: medium
Volume: moderate
Techniques: bake, blanche, cream, fry, roast, sauté

anise
bacon
bay leaf
butter
celery
cheese, goat
chervil
chives
coriander
cream
cumin
dill
fennel leaves
fennel seeds
garlic
ginger
hazelnuts
leeks
lemon, juice
mace
meats, esp. roasted
morels
nutmeg
oil: nut, sunflower seed
olive oil
onions
parsley, flat-leaf
pepper, black
potatoes
rosemary
sage
salmon
salt, sea

shallots
stock, chicken
tarragon
thyme
vinegar
wine, dry white

Flavor Affinities
Jerusalem artichoke + goat cheese
   + hazelnuts
Jerusalem artichoke + lemon +
   morels

Dishes

Jerusalem Artichoke Soup, Sweet Garlic Flan, "Sockeye" Salmon Tartare, Poached Quail Egg, and Crisp Sunchokes
— Carrie Nahabedian, Naha (Chicago)

Dishes

Arugula Risotto with Roquefort and Pignoli Nuts
— Gabriel Kreuther, The Modern (New York City)

Arugula Salad with Cucumber, Mt. Vikos Feta, Mint, Coriander Vinaigrette, and Niçoise Olives
— Judy Rodgers, Zuni Café (San Francisco)

Sautéed Arugula with Paneer Cheese and Roasted Cashews
— Vikram Vij and Meeru Dhalwala, Vij's (Vancouver)

ARUGULA (See also Lettuces
— Bitter Greens and Chicories)

Season: spring–summer
Taste: bitter
Weight: light–medium
Volume: moderate–loud
Techniques: braise, raw (salads), sauté, soups, wilt

almonds
basil
beans, white
bell peppers, esp. red
cheese: Cabrales, feta, **goat**,
   mozzarella, **Parmesan**
chicken
cilantro

clams
corn
cucumbers
dill
eggs, esp. hard-boiled
endive
fennel
fish (e.g., salmon, tuna)
garlic
grapes
Italian cuisine
lemon juice
lettuces
lovage
Mediterranean cuisine
mesclun salad greens (key
   ingredient)
mint
mushrooms
mussels
nuts
olive oil
olives, black
oranges, esp. blood
pancetta
parsley
pasta
pears
pesto
pine nuts
potatoes
prosciutto
radicchio
radishes
risotto
salads and salad greens

salt, esp. sea
shallots
shellfish (e.g., shrimp)
tomatoes
tuna
vinaigrettes
vinegar: balsamic, champagne, red wine, sherry, white wine
watercress

Flavor Affinities

arugula + balsamic vinegar + lemon + olive oil + Parmesan cheese

arugula + Cabrales cheese + endive + grapes

arugula + cucumber + feta cheese + mint

arugula + endive + radicchio

arugula + fennel + pears

arugula + pears + prosciutto

ASIAN CUISINE

(See Chinese, Japanese, Vietnamese, etc. Cuisines)

ASPARAGUS

Season: spring
Weight: light–medium
Volume: moderate
Techniques: blanch, boil, deep-fry, grill, pan roast, simmer, steam, stir-fry

almonds
anchovies
artichokes
basil
bay leaf
beets
bread crumbs
butter, brown
BUTTER, UNSALTED
capers
caraway seeds
carrots
cayenne
CHEESE: chèvre, Fontina, goat,
Muenster, PARMESAN, PECORINO, ricotta, Romano
chervil
chives
crab
cream, heavy
crème fraîche
dill
EGGS AND EGG DISHES (e.g., coddled, hard-boiled omelets)
fava beans
French cuisine
garlic
ginger
ham
hollandaise sauce
Italian cuisine
leeks
LEMON: JUICE, ZEST
lemon thyme

lime, juice
lobster
Marsala wine
mascarpone
mayonnaise
mushrooms, esp. cremini, **morels**, shiitakes
mustard, Dijon
oil: hazelnut, peanut, sesame, truffle
OLIVE OIL
onions, esp. spring, yellow
orange
oysters
pancetta
parsley, flat-leaf
pasta
peas
PEPPER: BLACK, WHITE
peppers, piquillo

Dishes

Ricotta Gnocchi with Asparagus, Morels, and Pine Nuts
— Dan Barber, Blue Hill at Stone Barns (Pocantico Hills, New York)

Asparagus and Ricotta "Mezzalune" with Spring Onion Butter
— Mario Batali, Babbo (New York City)

Salad of Sacramento Delta Green Asparagus, Spring Garlic, Marinated Sweet Peppers, with Young Arugula and Yellow Pepper Gastrique
— Thomas Keller, The French Laundry (Yountville, California)

Warm Salad of Sacramento Delta Green Asparagus, Melted Cipollini Onion Rings, Soft-Boiled Hen Egg, and Country Bread Croutons
— Thomas Keller, The French Laundry (Yountville, California)

Green Asparagus Soup with Gyromitre Mushrooms and Soft-Poached Farm Egg
— Gabriel Kreuther, The Modern (New York City)

Warm Salad of Grilled Asparagus and Prawns with a Sherry Vinaigrette
— Patrick O'Connell, The Inn at Little Washington (Washington, Virginia)

Vegetarian Sushi: Asparagus and Roasted Bell Pepper Roll
— Kaz Okochi, Kaz Sushi Bistro (Washington, DC)

Asparagus and Morel Mushroom Salad: Pancetta, Fiddlehead Ferns, Vermont Shepherd Cheese, and a Mushroom Reduction
— Alfred Portale, Gotham Bar and Grill (New York City)

Terrine of Green and White Asparagus, Roasted Beet Root Salad, Asparagus Juices
— Rick Tramonto, Tru (Chicago)

pistachios
potatoes
prosciutto
ramps
rice and risotto
saffron
sage
salmon
SALT: KOSHER, SEA
sauce: béchamel, brown butter,
    Mornay
savory
scallions
sesame seeds
shallots
shrimp
soups
sour cream
soy sauce
spinach
stocks: chicken, vegetable
tarragon
thyme, fresh
tomatoes
turnips
vermouth
vinaigrette: mustard, sherry
vinegar: champagne, **red wine,**
    sherry, **white wine**
wine, dry white (e.g., Muscat)
yogurt

Flavor Affinities

asparagus + capers + ham + shrimp
asparagus + cayenne + lime
asparagus + chervil + chives + garlic + morel mushrooms + shallots
asparagus + crab + morel mushrooms + ramps
asparagus + garlic + ginger + sesame
asparagus + garlic + leeks + onions + potatoes
asparagus + goat cheese + mascarpone + thyme
asparagus + ham + morel mushrooms + Parmesan cheese
asparagus + lemon + olive oil + black pepper
asparagus + morel mushrooms + ramps
asparagus + Parmesan cheese + eggs
asparagus + Parmesan cheese + pancetta + vinaigrette
asparagus + prosciutto + goat cheese + chervil

ASPARAGUS, WHITE

Season: spring
Weight: light
Volume: quiet–moderate
Techniques: blanch, boil, sauté, steam
Tips: Covered to deprive it of sunlight while growing, white asparagus is lighter in flavor and texture than green asparagus.

butter
cheese, Parmesan
chicken
crab
eggs: whole, yolks
ham
hazelnuts
lemon
mushrooms (e.g., cepes, morels, porcini)
mustard
oil, truffle
olive oil
parsley
pepper, black
salt, sea
sauces: hollandaise, mayonnaise, romesco
shallots

Daniel Humm of New York's Eleven Madison Park on Making Asparagus Soup

Making and seasoning soup is one of the best ways to learn about flavor. Let's make asparagus soup:

- You need a lot of asparagus flavor.
- You need acidity.
- You need sweetness that will come from the asparagus.
- You need the right amount of salt.
- You need just the right amount of spice, so that it doesn't actually taste spicy. We use a lot of cayenne, but you would never know it is there; it is just an accent.
- You need fresh lime juice to finish.

Soup is a play of balance when you have a lot of flavor. You can add a lot of salt and it won't taste salty. You can add a lot of acid and it won't taste acidic. But you still have a bold-flavored soup. It's like winemaking; at some point, there is a balance of all the flavors.

The first thing you need to do is get all the asparagus flavor into the soup at the start. We save our asparagus liquid from all the asparagus we cook to use for asparagus stock.

Making the soup: We sweat the asparagus [that is, cook it over low heat in a little fat, generally in a covered pot or pan] very slowly. When we add wine, we do it multiple times, adding a little at a time and reducing it, then repeating the process. What this does is concentrate the flavor at each step. It makes a big difference [before adding the asparagus liquid].

Finishing the soup: A soup may taste seasoned, but it still needs to be "woken up." You taste the asparagus, but maybe it doesn't blow you away at first. To do that, you need acid and cayenne. We season the soup with lime because it is a stronger acid and yet has less flavor than lemon. If I use lemon to get as much acid as I need for the soup, I will need to use so much that the soup will taste lemony instead.

shrimp
stock, chicken
sugar (pinch)
tarragon
vinaigrette
vinegar: champagne, white
wine, Riesling

Flavor Affinities
white asparagus + hazelnuts + Parmesan cheese + truffle oil
white asparagus + lemon + cepes mushrooms + parsley
white asparagus + mustard + olive oil + vinegar

ASTRINGENCY
Taste: astringent
Function: cooling

apples (astringent-sweet)
artichokes
asparagus
bananas, unripe (astringent-sweet)
basil
beans
berries
broccoli
buckwheat
cashews
cauliflower
coffee
cranberries
figs (astringent-sweet)
fruits: dried, raw, unripe
grapes (astringent-sour-sweet)
hazelnuts
herbs
honey
legumes
lentils
lettuce
mace
marjoram
okra
parsley
peaches (astringent-sweet)
pears (astringent-sweet)
persimmons
plums (astringent-sweet)
pomegranates (astringent-sour-sweet)
quinoa
rhubarb
rye
saffron
sprouts
tea
turmeric
turnips
vegetables, raw
walnuts

AUSTRALIAN CUISINE
barbecued foods
beef
cheese
fish
fruits, fresh
lamb
nuts, macadamia
seafood
shellfish, esp. shrimp
vegetables, fresh
wines
yabbies

NOTE: *Akin to the "New American" cuisine that incorporates ingredients and techniques from around the world, "Mod Oz" (modern Australian) cuisine combines its British heritage with influences from other parts of Europe as well as Asia.*

AUSTRIAN CUISINE
beer
cinnamon
coffee
cream
desserts
dumplings
goulash
marjoram
meat, esp. beef or pork
paprika
parsley
pastries
potatoes
schnitzel
soups, esp. with dumplings or noodles
stews
strudel
wine

AUTUMN
Weather: typically cool
Techniques: braise, glaze, roast

almonds (peak: October)
apples (peak: September–November)
artichokes (peak: September–October)
basil (peak: September)
beans (peak: September)
bell peppers (peak: September)
broccoli
broccoli rabe (peak: July–December)
Brussels sprouts (peak: November–February)
cakes, esp. served warm
cantaloupe (peak: June–September)
caramel
cardoons (peak: October)
cauliflower
celery root (peak: October–November)
chard (peak: June–December)

The earthy flavors of **autumn** come together in our chanterelle mushroom and lentil soup with sautéed foie gras.

— **HIRO SONE AND LISSA DOUMANI,** TERRA (ST. HELENA, CALIFORNIA)

In the **autumn,** I use walnut vinegar, which is red wine vinegar with macerated walnuts in it. It is great on a dish of sweetbreads and hazelnuts.

— **ANDREW CARMELLINI,** A VOCE (NEW YORK CITY)

When I think of **autumn,** I think of apples, pears, quince — which is so underrated — figs, and pumpkins.

I work with apples and pears, which you can start using in September, especially with the early apples like Gravenstein in the Bay Area. I try not to use pumpkin until close to Halloween, because no matter what you do with it, it will still taste like pumpkin. It's not like berries or apples that you can do a thousand things with. As a pastry chef, if I serve pumpkin too soon, people will get sick of it — and if I take it off the menu, there is nothing to replace it with. So I try to wait so I don't peak too early.

Figs are great for fall. The problem with figs is that there are not that many fig lovers out there. There are a lot more peach, chocolate, and apple lovers than there are fig lovers. When I make a fig dessert, I'll pair it with a raspberry or late summer fruit so it's more likely to meet with customer acceptance.

In the fall, I'll make more cakes. Fall also turns into caramel season, and fall fruits work so well with caramel. I keep a lighter hand with caramel in the fall because it is being combined with fruit versus chocolate.

— **EMILY LUCHETTI,** FARALLON (SAN FRANCISCO)

chestnuts (peak: October–November)
chile peppers
coconut (peak: October–November)
corn (peak: September)
cranberries (peak: September–December)
cucumbers (peak: September)
dates
duck
eggplant (peak: August–November)
fennel
figs (peak: September–October)
foie gras
garlic (peak: September)

gooseberries (peak: June–September)
grains
grapes (peak: September)
heavier dishes
huckleberries (peak: August–September)
kale (peak: November–January)
kohlrabi (peak: September–November)
lentils
lovage (peak: September–October)
lychee nuts (peak: September–November)
mushrooms: chanterelles (peak: April–October), porcini (peak: September–October)

nectarines (peak: July–September)
nuts
okra (peak: July–September)
oranges, blood (peak: November–February)
oysters (peak: September–April)
partridge (peak: November–December)
passion fruit (peak: November–February)
pears (peak: July–October)
peas (peak: June–September)
persimmons (peak: October–January)
pheasant (peak: October–December)
pistachios (peak: September)
plums (peak: July–October)
polenta
pomegranates (peak: October–December)
pumpkins (peak: September–December)
quinces (peak: October–December)
salsify (peak: November–January)
scallops
seeds, sunflower
spices, warming (e.g., black peppercorns, cayenne, cinnamon, chili powder, clove, cumin, mustard, etc.)
squash, winter (peak: October–December)
stuffing
sweetbreads
sweet potatoes (peak: November–January)
tomatoes (peak: September)
turkey
vinegar, red wine
walnuts
watermelon (peak: July–September)
yams (peak: November)
zucchini (peak: June–October)

Dishes

Avocado and Grapefruit with Poppy Seed Dressing
— Ann Cashion, Cashion's Eat Place (Washington, DC)

Creamy Avocado Pudding with Pink Grapefruit Reduction and Candied Zest
— Dominique and Cindy Duby, Wild Sweets (Vancouver)

AVOCADO OIL (See Oil, Avocado)

AVOCADOS

Season: spring–summer
Botanical relatives: allspice, bay leaf
Weight: medium–heavy
Volume: quiet
Techniques: raw
Tips: Use to add richness to a dish.

arugula
bacon
basil and Thai basil
beans, black
bell peppers, esp. red
butter, unsalted
Central American cuisine
chayote
chervil
chicken
chile peppers: chipotle, jalapeño, serrano
chives
cilantro
corn and masa
crab
cream, heavy
crème fraîche
cucumbers
cumin
dashi
endive, esp. Belgian
fennel
fish
frisée
fruits, esp. tropical
garlic
grapefruit
guacamole (key ingredient)
jicama
lemon: juice, zest
LIME, JUICE
lobster
mangoes
mayonnaise
Mexican cuisine
oil, canola
olive oil
ONIONS, ESP. RED, spring, white
orange
parsley, flat-leaf
pepper: black, white
radishes
rocket
sake
salads, esp. green, seafood
salsa
SALT: KOSHER, SEA
sandwiches
scallions
shellfish (e.g., shrimp)
shrimp
smoked fish (e.g., trout)
soups
sour cream
Southwestern cuisine
soy sauce
spinach
stocks: chicken, vegetable
Tabasco sauce
tarragon
tequila
tomatillos
tomatoes
vinaigrette
VINEGAR: balsamic, cider, tarragon, white wine
walnuts, oil
yogurt

Flavor Affinities

avocado + bacon + scallions + tomatoes
avocado + basil + red onions + tomatoes + balsamic vinegar
avocado + chiles + cilantro + lime + black pepper + salt + scallions
avocado + cilantro + lime juice
avocado + crab + grapefruit + tomato
avocado + crème fraîche + grapefruit
avocado + endive + frisée + lemon juice + sea salt
avocado + jalapeño chiles + cilantro + cumin + garlic + lime + onion
avocado + lemon + smoked trout

Avocados are so rich that we always season them with a lot of *fleur de sel* and lemon juice, and toss them with frisée and endive. Avocados need something bitter for balance.
— **SHARON HAGE,** YORK STREET (DALLAS)

BACON

Taste: salty
Weight: medium
Volume: moderate
Techniques: broil, roast, sauté

aioli
avocados
beans (e.g., black, fava, green)
breakfast
butter, unsalted

celery
chervil
chicken
eggs
French cuisine
frisée
greens (e.g., arugula)
Italian cuisine
lentils
lettuce
maple syrup
mayonnaise
mushrooms, esp. chanterelles
olive oil
onions
parsnips
peas
pepper, black
potatoes
risotto
salads
salmon
salt
scallops
shallots
spinach
squash, winter
stews
stock, chicken
tomatoes
vinegar

Flavor Affinities

bacon + arugula + egg + pork belly
bacon + chanterelle mushrooms + chicken + potatoes
bacon + chanterelle mushrooms + salmon + shallots
bacon + hard-boiled eggs + spinach + balsamic vinegar
bacon + lettuce + tomatoes
bacon + onions + vinegar
bacon + shallots + vinegar
bacon + spinach + winter squash

Bacon can be salt, fat, and/or smoke, depending on the bacon you choose. You can also play with its texture, depending on whether you are using pork belly or crispy bacon. It is wonderful with vegetables. The fat is delicious, so if you are braising onions in bacon fat, reduce that down, and add a little onion *jus* and vinegar, you have a great sauce. Bacon just brings another layer of flavor to the vegetables. My dish of Berkshire pork chop with scarlet turnips, roasted rhubarb, and smoked bacon with cherry-almond salsa seca represents the relationship between fat, salt, sugar, and acid; they are all there. The bacon brings complexity to the pork; the cherry brings acid balance; and the almond brings a different kind of fat with crunch. The almonds in the dish are marcona, and every tenth one is extremely bitter, which adds another layer of complexity.
— **TRACI DES JARDINS,** JARDINIÈRE (SAN FRANCISCO)

Dishes

Braised Bacon with Spring Vegetables and White Horseradish Broth
— Dan Barber, Blue Hill at Stone Barns (Pocantico Hills, New York)

Smoked Bacon and Egg Ice Cream with Pain Perdu, Tea Jelly
— Heston Blumenthal, The Fat Duck (England)

Berkshire Pork Chop with Scarlet Turnips, Roasted Rhubarb, and Smoked Bacon with Cherry-Almond Salsa Seca
— Traci Des Jardins, Jardinière (San Francisco)

BALANCE

Tips: Seek balance in every dish you make:
- tastes (e.g., sourness vs. saltiness; sweetness vs. bitterness)
- richness (e.g., fat) vs. relief (e.g., acidity, bitterness)
- temperatures (e.g., hot vs. cold)
- textures (e.g., creamy vs. crunchy)

Balance taste by adding its opposite or its complement.

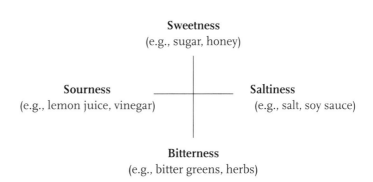

Sweetness
(e.g., sugar, honey)

Sourness
(e.g., lemon juice, vinegar)

Saltiness
(e.g., salt, soy sauce)

Bitterness
(e.g., bitter greens, herbs)

BALSAMIC VINEGAR
(See Vinegar, Balsamic)

BANANAS

Season: winter
Taste: sweet, astringent
Function: cooling
Weight: medium
Volume: quiet
Techniques: bake, broil, caramelize, deep-fry, grill, poach, raw, sauté
Tips: Sugar enhances the flavor of bananas.

allspice
almonds
apricots
Armagnac
baked goods (e.g., muffins, quick
    breads)
banana liqueur
blackberries
blueberries
brandy
breakfast
butter, unsalted
buttermilk
butterscotch
cakes
Calvados
CARAMEL
cardamom
cashews
cherries
chile peppers: habanero, jalapeño,
    serrano
CHOCOLATE: dark, white
cinnamon
cloves
**COCONUT AND COCONUT
    MILK**
coffee
cognac
CREAM AND ICE CREAM
cream cheese
crème anglaise

crème fraîche
curries
custard
dates
desserts
figs, dried
ginger
guava
hazelnuts
honey
Kirsch
LEMON, JUICE
lemongrass

lime, juice
macadamia
mangoes: green, ripe
maple syrup
meringue
nutmeg
oats and oatmeal
oil, vegetable
orange
pancakes
papaya
parsley
passion fruit

Dishes

Chocolate-Banana Flan, Exotic Fruit Jelly, Spiced Fritters, Faux Foie Gras Emulsion, and Cumin Gel
— Dominique and Cindy Duby, Wild Sweets (Vancouver)

Sticky Toffee Pudding with Bananas, Medjool Dates, Oatmeal Ice Cream, Root Beer Reduction
— Gale Gand, pastry chef, Tru (Chicago)

Banana-Coconut Split with Vanilla Ice Cream, Candied Coconut, Dulce de Leche, Fudge Sauce
— Emily Luchetti, pastry chef, Farallon (San Francisco)

Caramelized Banana Tart with Coconut Ice Cream
— Patrick O'Connell, The Inn at Little Washington (Washington, Virginia)

Banana Tempura with Black Raspberry Ice Cream
— Kaz Okochi, Kaz Sushi Bistro (Washington, DC)

Macadamia Nut Tart with Banana-Rum Ice Cream
— Hiro Sone and Lissa Doumani, Terra (St. Helena, California)

Banana-Toffee Tart
— Sandy D'Amato, Sanford (Milwaukee)

Banana Tempura with Mango Ice Cream
— Sushi-Ko (Washington, DC)

Banana Crème Brûlée, Citrus-Pistachio Biscuit, Beurre Noisette Ice Cream, Peanut Caramel
— Michael Laiskonis, pastry chef, Le Bernardin (New York City)

Caramelized Banana, Smoked Chocolate Ice Cream, Stout
— Sam Mason, wd-50 (New York City)

Dover Sole with "Mostly Traditional Flavors" and Sliced Banana
— Grant Achatz, Alinea (Chicago)

A **banana** in a dessert is an instant sell. Everyone loves caramelized bananas!

— **GINA DEPALMA,** BABBO (NEW YORK CITY)

I hate overripe **bananas.** We'll actually freeze whole, unpeeled bananas, which will continue to ripen in the freezer and turn black. When we want bananas to use as a puree, we'll pull them out and let them thaw before pureeing, and then add them to a cake or mousse. The flavor is much better this way.

— **DOMINIQUE DUBY,** WILD SWEETS (VANCOUVER)

I serve a **banana** crème brûlée that is not made in ramekins (the usual individual serving cups) but cut out of a sheet pan and caramelized. I serve this set up in a grid with two squares of crème brûlée, one topped with a little citrus, the other with caramelized bananas — alternated with citrus biscuit, one topped with a brown butter ice cream, and the other with caramelized banana. So I have these three flavors — banana, citrus, and brown butter — tied together with a salted peanut–caramel sauce.

— **MICHAEL LAISKONIS,** LE BERNARDIN (NEW YORK CITY)

A **banana**'s ripeness will determine what you do with it. I like my bananas yellow and firm. If you are going to make a bananas Foster and your bananas are very yellow, you can cook them longer and they won't fall apart or turn to mush. If you start with a banana that is pretty brown, the second you add heat, it falls apart. A brown banana gives me shivers!

— **EMILY LUCHETTI,** FARALLON (SAN FRANCISCO)

peanuts and peanut butter
pecans
pepper, black
pineapple
pistachios
pomegranate
puddings
raisins
raspberries: red, black
rice
RUM
salads, fruit
sesame seeds
smoothies and shakes
sour cream
strawberries
SUGAR: BROWN, WHITE
sweet potatoes

Tabasco sauce
vanilla
vinegar, white
walnuts
yogurt

Flavor Affinities
banana + blackberries + cream
banana + brown butter + caramel + citrus + peanuts
banana + caramel + chocolate
banana + caramel + crème fraîche + lemongrass
banana + coconut + cream
banana + cream + honey + macadamia nuts + vanilla
banana + cream + mango
banana + dates + oatmeal
banana + honey + sesame seeds
banana + macadamia nuts + rum
banana + oats + pecans

BARLEY
Taste: sweet, astringent
Function: cooling
Techniques: simmer

beef
butter
garlic
lemon thyme
mirepoix (carrots, celery, onions)
mushrooms: cultivated, wild (e.g., shiitakes)
olive oil
onions
oregano
parsley, flat-leaf
pepper, white
sage
salt, kosher
savory
scallions
soups
stocks: chicken, vegetable
thyme
tomatoes
vinegar, sherry

(See also Basil, Thai, and Lemon Basil)

Season: summer
Taste: sweet
Weight: light, soft-leaved
Volume: mild–moderate
Tips: Add just before serving. Use to add a note of freshness to a dish.

apricots
Asian cuisine
beans: green, white
bell peppers, esp. red, roasted
berries
blueberries
breads
broccoli
Cambodian cuisine
capers
carrots
CHEESE: feta, goat, MOZZARELLA, PARMESAN, PECORINO, RICOTTA
chicken
chile peppers
chives
chocolate, white
cilantro
cinnamon
coconut milk
corn
crab
cream and ice cream
cucumber
custards
duck
eggplant
EGGS AND EGG DISHES (e.g., omelets)
fennel
fish, esp. grilled or poached
French cuisine
***GARLIC**
ginger, fresh
honey
ITALIAN CUISINE
lamb

lemon, juice
lemon verbena
lime, juice
liver
marjoram
meats
Mediterranean cuisine
mint
mussels
mustard: powder, seeds
nectarines
OLIVE OIL
olives
onions
orange
oregano
Parmesan cheese
parsley, flat-leaf
PASTA DISHES AND SAUCES

peaches
peas
pepper: black, white
PESTO (key ingredient)
pineapple
pine nuts
pizza
pork
potatoes
poultry
rabbit
raspberries
rice
rosemary
salads and salad dressings
salmon
salt: kosher, sea
sauces
scallops

I use **basil** a lot. I will add it at the very end of cooking a dish, and it will totally change where the dish is going. Added at the last second, it gives a minty freshness that was not there before. Basil says "fresh" and "alive" to me. And although you can get it year-round, I associate it with summer.

I think particularly of fish and shellfish with basil. I cook a lobster with a sauce of sweet Muscat or Sauternes, curry, and lime. This is a dish that has been played with. The shells have been chopped up, added to mirepoix, and turned into sauce. Then there's wine. So when the basil hits, you have this whole new thing going on. It opens up the dish and makes it light. It goes against the "worked-on" aspect of the dish.

In Thai cooking, you will find coconut milk–based curry that will have whole leaves of basil in it. Basil becomes something of a vegetable served this way.

— **DAVID WALTUCK**, CHANTERELLE (NEW YORK CITY)

I love **basil** in syrups. It works with strawberries and any citrus fruit. The trio I use the most for summer fruits like berries is basil, lemon, and vanilla. I have even macerated cherry tomatoes in this combination and made them into a fruit crisp.

— **MICHAEL LAISKONIS**, LE BERNARDIN (NEW YORK CITY)

I love **basil**. It is more familiar than cilantro, and more people like it. I use it in ceviche instead of cilantro because it is not as pungent. I combine hamachi tuna with tomato, watermelon, yuzu, and sesame seeds with fresh basil and basil oil.

— **KATSUYA FUKUSHIMA**, MINIBAR (WASHINGTON, DC)

sea bass
shellfish
shrimp
soups, esp. Asian, bean, chowder, vegetable
soy sauce
spinach
squash, summer
summer vegetables
Thai cuisine (e.g., green curries)
thyme
*****TOMATOES and tomato sauces**
tuna
vanilla
veal
vegetables, esp. summer
Vietnamese cuisine
vinaigrettes
vinegar: balsamic, sherry
watermelon
ZUCCHINI

AVOID
tarragon

Flavor Affinities
basil + coconut + curry
basil + garlic + olive oil + salt
basil + garlic + olive oil + Parmesan cheese + pine nuts
basil + hamachi tuna + tomatoes + watermelon
basil + lemon + vanilla
basil + mozzarella cheese + tomatoes
basil + olive oil + Parmesan cheese

BASIL, LEMON (See Lemon Basil)

BASIL, THAI
Taste: anise- or licorice-like

Asian cuisines
beef
coconut milk
curries

I use this in lots of vegetarian dishes because it gives them some oomph. It also works well with meat dishes, from beef to carpaccio to venison. I make a **Thai basil** pesto but make a few adjustments to the recipe or else it can look bruised and take on a funky color. We will add a little pumpkin seed oil to keep it a deep, rich green.
— **BRAD FARMERIE**, PUBLIC (NEW YORK CITY)

ginger
lemongrass
noodles and noodle dishes
oils, esp. pumpkin seed
salads
seafood
soups, esp. Asian
Thai cuisine
vegetarian dishes
venison

Flavor Affinities
Thai basil + beef + pumpkin seed oil
Thai basil + coconut milk + ginger

BASS (See also Bass, Sea, and Bass, Striped)
Weight: light
Volume: quiet
Techniques: bake, broil, deep-fry, poach, roast, sauté, steam

artichoke
bay leaf
carrots
cayenne
celery
chervil
fennel
garlic
lemon
olive oil

onions
orange: juice, zest
parsley, flat-leaf
pepper: black, white
saffron
salmon
salt, sea
shallots
sole
star anise
stock, fish
tarragon
tomatoes and tomato paste
vanilla
wine, white

BASS, BLACK
Weight: medium
Volume: quiet

asparagus
basil
beets
butter
cabbage, savoy
carrots
celery
chestnuts
chile peppers, jalapeño
chives
chutney
cilantro
coriander
duck, Peking

Black bass is a fish that can go with the most exotic flavors. We serve black bass with Peking duck, green papaya salad, and a very light, thin chutney sauce. I love Peking duck and find the flavor very soft and not "duck-y" or aggressive.
— **ERIC RIPERT**, LE BERNARDIN (NEW YORK CITY)

In my **black sea bass** in a tamarind-ginger sauce with minted baby onions dish, the tamarind is acidic, and ginger is a nice flavor bridge. I put mint in the onions to cut their sweetness.

— GABRIEL KREUTHER, THE MODERN (NEW YORK CITY)

Dishes

Paupiette of Black Sea Bass in a Crisp Potato Shell, with Tender Leeks and Syrah Sauce
— Daniel Boulud, Daniel (New York City)

Sesame-Crusted Chilean Sea Bass with Baby Shrimp, Clams, and Artichokes
— Patrick O'Connell, The Inn at Little Washington (Washington, Virginia)

Black Bass with Porcini Mushrooms, Braised Parsnips, and Chestnuts
— David Pasternak, Esca (New York City)

Grilled Pacific Sea Bass for Two with Marinated Blood Orange and Lime
— David Pasternak, Esca (New York City)

Crisp Black Sea Bass with Olive-Caper Emulsion
— Alfred Portale, Gotham Bar and Grill (New York City)

Spice-Crusted Black Sea Bass in Sweet and Sour Jus
— Jean-Georges Vongerichten, Jean Georges (New York City)

endive
fennel
garlic
ginger
ham
honey
leeks
lemon
lemon, preserved
lime
marjoram
mint
mushrooms, porcini
mustard
olive oil
onions
orange, juice
oregano
papaya
parsley, flat-leaf
parsnips
peas
pepper, white
raisins
saffron

salt, sea
scallions
scallops
shallots
shrimp
squash: hubbard, yellow
stock, chicken
tarragon
thyme
tomatoes
tuna
turnips
vinegar: champagne, red wine
wine: red, white
zucchini

Flavor Affinities

black bass + chutney + papaya
black bass + new potatoes + shrimp

BASS, SEA

Season: winter–spring
Weight: medium
Volume: quiet

Techniques: bake, broil, ceviche, deep-fry, grill, pan roast, poach, roast, sauté, steam

almonds
anchovies
artichokes
bacon
basil
bay leaf
beans, esp. green or white
beets
bell peppers: red, green
bread crumbs
BUTTER: clarified, salted, unsalted
capers
cardamom
carrots
cayenne
celery
chervil
chives
cilantro
citrus
coriander
corn
cream
crème fraîche
fennel
garlic, fresh
ginger, fresh
hazelnuts
honey
leeks
lemon: juice, zest
lemon, preserved
lentils
lime, juice
marjoram
mayonnaise
mint
mirepoix (carrots, celery, onions)
mirin
MUSHROOMS, esp. button, porcini, or shiitake
mustard, Dijon
new potatoes

oil: canola, peanut, sesame
olive oil
olives, black
onions: pearl, yellow
oregano
parsley, flat-leaf
PEPPER: black, white
potatoes, esp. as a crust, mashed
radishes
rhubarb
saffron
sake
salmon roe
SALT, KOSHER
sauces: beurre blanc, brown
   butter
scallops
sesame seeds
shallots
shiso
shrimp
soy sauce
spearmint
spinach, esp. baby
star anise
stocks: chicken, fish, vegetable
sugar
tamarind
tarragon
thyme, fresh
TOMATOES: cherry, grape, juice,
   roasted
vanilla
vermouth
VINEGAR: champagne, red wine,
   rice, **sherry**, white wine
wine, dry white
yuzu juice
zucchini

Flavor Affinities

sea bass + artichokes + basil +
   chives + green beans + lemon +
   new potatoes
sea bass + bacon + corn + fava
   beans
sea bass + mushrooms + sesame
   seeds + shrimp

Striped bass is a hearty fish and is one of my favorites. I love roasting it with the skin on to a crisp, and finishing it with butter, garlic, and thyme. It's a fish that pairs well with meat, whether bacon, sweetbreads, or braised pork.

— **BRADFORD THOMPSON,** MARY ELAINE'S AT THE PHOENICIAN (SCOTTSDALE, ARIZONA)

Dishes

Wild Carolina Coast Striped Bass "Riviera" with a Salad of Shaved Fennel, Arugula, and Babaganoush, Cured Tomatoes, Spanish Olives, and Yellow Pepper Broth
— Carrie Nahabedian, Naha (Chicago)

Roasted Local Wild Striped Bass with Hubbard Squash, Caramelized Apple, and Wild Mushrooms
— David Pasternak, Esca (New York City)

Poached Atlantic Striped Bass, Pasilla Chili, Cocoa, Duck Consommé
— Rick Tramonto, Tru (Chicago)

BASS, STRIPED

Weight: medium
Volume: quiet
Techniques: bake, braise, broil, deep-fry, grill, pan roast, poach, raw, roast, sauté, sear, steam

artichokes
bacon
bay leaf
beets
bell peppers: red, yellow
bok choy
butter: clarified, unsalted
buttermilk
calamari
carrots
cauliflower
cayenne
celery
chanterelles
chervil
chile peppers: dried, fresh
   (e.g., jalapeño)
chives
cilantro
clams
corn
cream
cucumber
curries and curry powder
dill
fava beans
fennel
fish sauce
garlic
ginger
hollandaise sauce
horseradish
leeks
lemon: juice, zest
lemon verbena
lime, juice
mint
monkfish
mushrooms, shiitake
mustard, Dijon
OIL: canola, peanut, sesame,
   vegetable
olive oil
olives, picholine
onions: pearl, red
orange
paprika, sweet
parsley, flat-leaf
PEPPER: BLACK, GREEN, WHITE
potatoes

prosciutto
rosemary
sage
SALT: KOSHER, SEA
sauerkraut
scallions
sesame seeds
shallots
sour cream
soy sauce
squid
squid ink
stocks: fish, shellfish
Tabasco sauce
thyme, fresh
tomatoes
truffles, black
VINEGAR: champagne, red wine,
   sherry, white wine
walnuts
wine: port, dry white, Riesling
zucchini

Flavor Affinities

striped bass + bacon + sauerkraut
striped bass + bok choy + fish sauce
striped bass + clam broth + marjoram + spinach
striped bass + curry + sour cream
striped bass + fennel + olives + tomatoes
striped bass + garlic + lemon + thyme
striped bass + leeks + lemon juice + Dijon mustard
striped bass + leeks + shiitake mushrooms

I am a little too fond of **bay leaf.** I use it a lot. I probably have a fondness for it because I associate it with so many childhood flavors, like pot roast. It has a hearty quality to it and I associate it with stocks and big flavors. I will use fresh or dried bay leaf. Fresh bay leaf has fresher flavor and is surprisingly more intense than dried bay leaf, but it's still not as dramatic a difference as you can find with other herbs when it comes to fresh versus dried.

— **DAVID WALTUCK,** CHANTERELLE (NEW YORK CITY)

Inexperienced cooks will throw a handful of **bay leaves** into 40 gallons of veal stock. What happens next is they go to make a sauce and can't figure out what to do about the medicinal taste. It's the bay leaf! I'll explain they only need two or three at the most.

— **CARRIE NAHABEDIAN,** NAHA (CHICAGO)

BAY LEAF

Taste: sweet, bitter
Weight: light, tough-leaved
Volume: quiet–loud, depending on quantity used
Techniques: can stand up to cooking (e.g., simmer, stew)

allspice
apples
beans: dried, white
beef
braised dishes
caramel
cauliflower
celery leaf
cheese dishes
chestnuts
chicken
corn
cream and ice cream
custards
dates
desserts
duck
figs
fish
French cuisine
game
game birds
garlic
grains
juniper berries
lamb
lemon, juice
lentils
marinades
marjoram
meats
Mediterranean cuisine
mole sauce
Moroccan cuisine
onions
parsley
pâté
pears
pepper, black
polenta
pork
pot roast
potatoes
poultry
prunes
pumpkin
quail
**rice (e.g., rice pudding) and
   risotto**
rosemary
sage
salmon
sauces
sausage

savory
shellfish, shrimp
SOUPS
spinach
squash: summer, winter
STEWS
STOCKS AND BROTHS
strawberries
swordfish
thyme
tomatoes and tomato sauces
tuna
turkey
Turkish cuisine
vanilla
veal
venison
vinegar

BEANS — IN GENERAL

(See also specific beans below)
carrots
celery
garlic
lemon
marjoram
mint
onions
PARSLEY
rosemary
sage
salt
***SAVORY**
thyme
vinegar

BEANS, BLACK

Weight: medium–heavy
Volume: moderate
Techniques: simmer

allspice
apples
avocado
bacon
bay leaf
beer
bell peppers: green, red
butter

Dishes

Black Bean Soup Flavored with Grilled Wild Ramps, Avocado Leaf, and Cilantro, Studded with Sweet Roasted Chayote and Corn, Topped with Green Chile Salsa and Crispy Tortilla Strips
— Rick Bayless, Frontera Grill (Chicago)

Black Bean Tamales Filled with Homemade Goat Cheese in "Guisado" of Wild and Woodland Mushrooms, Organic Roasted Tomatoes, Green Chile, and Mint; Watercress Salad
— Rick Bayless, Frontera Grill (Chicago)

Black Beans Fried with Garlic, Onion, and Epazote, Topped with Mexican Fresh Cheese
— Rick Bayless, Frontera Grill (Chicago)

Carribbean cuisine
carrots
cayenne
celery
celery root
Central American cuisine
cheese: cheddar, dry feta, farmer's, Parmesan, queso fresco, smoked
CHILE PEPPERS: ancho, cachuca, chipotle, jalapeño
chili powder, ancho
chives
CILANTRO
cream
crème fraîche
CUMIN
duck
egg, esp. hard-boiled
epazote
fennel seeds
GARLIC
ginger
ham and ham hocks
lemon
lime, juice
maple syrup
Mexican cuisine, esp. in the South
OIL: canola, **olive**, peanut, safflower, vegetable
olive oil
ONIONS: red, white, yellow
orange: fruit, juice, zest
oregano, dried

PARSLEY, FLAT-LEAF
pepper: black, white
red pepper flakes
rice
rosemary
salsa
SALT, ESP. KOSHER
salt pork
sausage
SAVORY
scallions
shallots
sherry
shrimp
soups
SOUR CREAM
South American cuisine
Southwestern cuisine
spinach
STOCKS: BEEF, CHICKEN, VEGETABLE
sugar: brown, white
Tabasco sauce
thyme
tomatoes and tomato paste
vinegar: cider, red wine, sherry, white wine
wine: Madeira, sherry
yogurt

Flavor Affinities

black beans + cumin + green bell peppers + oregano
black beans + lemon + sherry

BEANS, BROAD (See Beans, Fava)

BEANS, BUTTER (See Beans, Lima)

BEANS, CANNELLINI
(See also Beans, White)
Weight: medium
Volume: quiet–moderate
Techniques: braise, puree, simmer

bacon
carrots
celery
clams
garlic
Italian cuisine
lamb
lemon
olive oil

onions, esp. Spanish
paprika, sweet
PARSLEY, FLAT-LEAF
pepper, black
saffron
salads
salt, kosher
sausages (e.g., chorizo)
SAVORY
soups
stock, chicken
tarragon
thyme
tomatoes, esp. plum

BEANS, FAVA (aka Broad Beans or Horse Beans)
Season: spring–summer
Taste: bitter
Weight: light–medium
Volume: moderate
Techniques: boil, puree, simmer

Asian cuisine
bacon
basil
butter, unsalted
CHEESE: dry feta, manchego, Parmesan, pecorino, ricotta, sheep's milk
chile peppers
chives, fresh
cilantro
corn
cream
cumin
curry
dill
duck
falafel (key ingredient)
fennel
fish (e.g., salmon)
garlic
gnocchi
greens, bitter
ham
herbs
Italian cuisine
lamb
leeks
lemon, juice
lentils
lobster
Mediterranean cuisine
Mexican cuisine
Middle Eastern cuisine
mint (e.g., Italian cuisine)
Moroccan cuisine
OIL, walnut
OLIVE OIL
onions, esp. spring
orange, zest
oregano
PARSLEY, FLAT-LEAF
pasta
peas
pepper, black
poultry (e.g., turkey)
prosciutto
rabbit
radishes

Dishes
Cannellini Bean Soup with Smoked Trout Croquette and Pumpkin Seed Oil
— Gabriel Kreuther, The Modern (New York City)

Fava beans have a great flavor. Cooks in the past would blanch them, and the flavor would be left in the water. Today, what I like to do with favas and other vegetables is to put them in a pan with a little water, olive oil, or butter, and to cover them while they cook. That way, all the flavor stays in the vegetables. If I could cook for my customers the way I like to cook and eat at home, I would sweat some spring onions in a pan with butter or oil, covered, to keep in the flavor. Then I'd add the shucked fava beans and let them cook with a little water. At the last second, I'd toss in some chopped parsley or basil, and there's your sauce. This would be great under some fish. If you added some thyme and maybe a little lamb *jus*, it would also work with lamb.

— TRACI DES JARDINS, JARDINIÈRE (SAN FRANCISCO)

Fava beans have a very delicate flavor, I like them raw and tender by themselves — or combined with sheep's milk cheese and olive oil. However, I wouldn't use an olive oil that's too peppery or spicy, because it would overwhelm them.

— TONY LIU, AUGUST (NEW YORK CITY)

rice and risotto
rosemary
sage, fresh
salads
salt: kosher, sea
SAVORY (e.g., as in French
   cuisine)
shellfish (e.g., lobster)
shallots
soups
spinach
steak
stir-fries
stock, chicken
thyme
tomatoes
vinaigrette
vinegar, cider
walnuts
yogurt

Flavor Affinities
fava beans + basil + spring onions
fava beans + garlic + olive oil + rosemary
fava beans + lamb + thyme
fava beans + olive oil + pecorino cheese + prosciutto
fava beans + olive oil + thyme
fava beans + sheep's milk cheese + olive oil

BEANS, FLAGEOLET
Weight: light–medium
Volume: quiet
Techniques: simmer

apples
arugula
basil
bay leaf
butter
carrots
cassoulet
celery
cheese, esp. manchego or
   pecorino
chicken
cream
fines herbes
fish (e.g., cod)
French cuisine, esp. Provençal

garlic
*LAMB
lemon, juice
lime
marjoram
olive oil
onions, esp. red, sweet, yellow
orange
PARSLEY
pasta
pepper, black
pork, esp. roasted
poultry
salads
salt
SAVORY
shallots
soups
stocks: chicken, vegetable
tarragon
thyme
tomatoes and tomato sauces
vinegar, red wine
wine, dry white

Flavor Affinities
flageolet beans + garlic + thyme

BEANS, GARBANZO
(See Chickpeas)

BEANS, GREEN
Season: summer–autumn
Weight: light–medium
Volume: moderate
Techniques: boil, grill, sauté, steam, stir-fry

almonds
anchovies
bacon
BASIL

Dishes
Pasta with Basil Pesto, Green Beans, and Potatoes
— Lidia Bastianich, Felidia (New York City)

bay leaf
beans, shell
bell pepper, red
bread crumbs
butter, unsalted
capers
carrots
cayenne
CHEESE: Asiago, blue, feta, goat,
  PARMESAN
chervil
chickpeas
chile peppers
chives
cilantro
coconut
corn
cream
crème fraîche
cumin
curry leaves
dill
eggs, esp. hard-boiled
fennel
French cuisine
garlic
ginger, fresh
ham (e.g., Serrano)
lemon, juice
lemon balm
lime, juice
lovage
marjoram
Mediterranean cuisine
mint
mushrooms
mustard, Dijon
mustard seeds, black
nuts
OIL: peanut, sesame
OLIVE OIL
olives: black, niçoise
ONIONS, esp. green, pearl, or red
oregano
pancetta
paprika: smoked, sweet
PARSLEY
peanuts

pepper: black, white
Pernod
pork
potatoes
prosciutto
red pepper flakes
rosemary
sage
salt, kosher
SAVORY, SUMMER
shallots
shrimp
soy sauce
stock, chicken
sugar
tamari
tarragon
thyme
TOMATOES
vinaigrettes
VINEGAR: red wine, rice wine,
  sherry, tarragon, white wine
walnuts
yogurt

Flavor Affinities
green beans + anchovies + garlic +
  Parmesan cheese + walnuts
green beans + mustard + prosciutto
  + vinaigrette + walnuts

BEANS, KIDNEY

Taste: sweet-astringent
Function: cooling
Weight: medium
Volume: moderate
Techniques: boil, simmer

bacon
bay leaf
bell pepper, esp. red
cardamom
carrots
cayenne
chile peppers: dried red, fresh
  green
chili
chorizo

cinnamon
cloves
coriander
cumin
curry leaves
garam masala
garlic
ginger
Indian cuisine
Italian cuisine, esp. Tuscan
olive oil
onions, esp. red, sweet, white
PARSLEY
pepper, black
pork
potatoes
saffron
salt
sauerkraut
SAVORY
thyme
tomatoes
turmeric
wine, red

BEANS, LIMA

Season: summer
Taste: bitter
Weight: medium
Volume: moderate
Techniques: simmer, steam

bacon
bay leaf
butter
Central American cuisine
chile peppers
cilantro
cream
cumin
curries
dill
fish
garlic
greens, bitter
ham and ham hocks
herbs
leeks

lemon, juice
mint
New England cuisine (e.g., succotash)
olive oil
onions
oregano
PARSLEY, FLAT-LEAF
pepper, ground
poultry, esp. chicken
rosemary
sage
salt, kosher
savory
shallots
shellfish (e.g., shrimp)
sorrel
soul food cuisine
Southern cuisine (American)
spinach
steak
succotash (key ingredient)
thyme
tomatoes and tomato sauce
tuna
vinegar

BEANS, NAVY

Weight: medium
Volume: moderate
Techniques: simmer

bacon
baked beans
basil
bay leaf
cayenne
cheese: Parmesan, ricotta
chili powder
garlic
ketchup
molasses
mustard: Dijon, yellow
olive oil
ONIONS, ESP. YELLOW
PARSLEY
pasta
pepper

salads
salt, kosher
SAVORY
soups
sugar, brown
thyme
tomatoes
vinegar, red wine

BEANS, PINTO

Season: winter
Weight: medium
Volume: moderate
Techniques: refry, simmer

bacon
cheese: feta, queso fresco
chile peppers: chipotle, jalapeño, poblano, serrano
chili
cilantro
cumin
epazote
garlic
Mexican cuisine, esp. northern
mint
oil: safflower, vegetable
onions, white
oregano, dried
paprika
PARSLEY
pork
refried beans (key ingredient)
SALT
SAVORY
scallions
sour cream
Southwestern cuisine
tequila
tomatoes

Dishes

A Latin Cassoulet of White Beans, Sausages, Smoked Bacon, and Kale Braised Slowly in the Wood-Burning Oven, with Spicy Sauce and Rice
— Maricel Presilla, Cucharamama (Hoboken, New Jersey)

Soup: White Bean Puree with Rosemary Oil
— Judy Rodgers, Zuni Café (San Francisco)

Flavor Affinities
pinto beans + bacon + poblano chiles + tomatoes

BEANS, RED

Weight: medium
Volume: moderate
Techniques: simmer

bell peppers, esp. green
chile peppers
chili (key ingredient)
chorizo
garlic
Mexican cuisine
olive oil
onions
PARSLEY
pork
sausage
SAVORY
Southwestern cuisine
stews

BEANS, WHITE

(e.g., Cannellini, Navy)
Season: winter
Weight: medium
Volume: moderate

ale or beer, dark
ancho chili powder
apricots, dried
arugula
bacon
basil
bay leaf
bouquet garni
bourbon
broccoli rabe

butter, unsalted
carrots
celery
cheese: manchego, **Parmesan**, Pecorino Romano
chile peppers, dried
chives
cloves
cream
fennel
GARLIC
ginger, ground
Italian cuisine
ham
lamb
lemon, juice
maple syrup
mirepoix (carrots, celery, onions)
molasses
mushrooms, wild
mustard, dry
OIL, peanut
OLIVE OIL
ONIONS (e.g., cipollini, red, sweet)
PARSLEY, FLAT-LEAF
pasta
PEPPER: black, white
pork
prosciutto
red pepper flakes
rosemary
rum, dark
sage
SALT: KOSHER, SEA
SAVORY
shallots
soups
squash, winter
stocks: chicken, vegetable
sugar, brown
tarragon
thyme
tomatoes and tomato paste
truffles
vinegar: balsamic, cider, red wine
wine, dry white

Flavor Affinities

white beans + olive oil + pecorino cheese
white beans + olive oil + rosemary + balsamic vinegar
white beans + broccoli rabe + wild mushrooms

BEEF — IN GENERAL

Taste: sweet
Function: heating
Weight: medium–heavy
Volume: moderate
Techniques: See also individual cuts of beef.
Tips: Clove adds richness to beef.

allspice
bacon
basil
bay leaf
beans, green
béarnaise sauce
beer
bouquet garni
brandy
butter, unsalted
capers
carrots
cayenne
celery
cheese, blue (e.g., Cabrales)
chiles, esp. dried and pasilla
chives
chocolate and cocoa powder
cilantro
cinnamon
cloves
coffee and espresso
cognac
coriander
corn
cornichons
cream
cumin
curry
fat: chicken, goose
foie gras
GARLIC
ginger
herbs
horseradish
hyssop
leeks
marrow, beef
mint
miso, red
mushrooms, esp. porcini or shiitake
mustard, Dijon

Dishes

"Brasato al Barolo" Braised Beef with Porcini Mushrooms
— Mario Batali, Babbo (New York City)

Mochomos: Crispy, Crunchy Shredded Montana Natural Beef with Crispy White Onion Strings, Guacamole, Spicy Chile Salsa, and Warm Tortillas for Making Soft Tacos
— Rick Bayless, Topolobampo (Chicago)

Balsamic-Caramel Beef Cubes with Sticky Rice and Toasted Coconut
— Monica Pope, T'afia (Houston)

Chateaubriand, Wild Mushrooms, Porcini-Flavored Diced Yukon Gold Potatoes, Syrah Sauce
— Michel Richard, Citronelle (Washington, DC)

Ground Beef with Cream and Fenugreek on Yucca
— Vikram Vij and Meeru Dhalwala, Vij's (Vancouver)

I love blue cheese with **beef.** We make a dish with blue cheese sauce that has chicken stock, Dijon mustard, truffle juice, and fresh truffle. This is a sauce that has many layers of flavor. The mustard is barely there but adds much more flavor to the sauce than vinegar or lemon would. The sauce is served on a [beef] filet that has been poached in spiced red wine. The poaching liquid is made with Cabernet Sauvignon that has been reduced for 25 minutes to concentrate its flavor, juniper berries, pepper, star anise, fennel seeds, and cloves. The cooked tannin in the wine really brings up the meaty flavor of the beef.

— **GABRIEL KREUTHER,** THE MODERN (NEW YORK CITY)

All cuts of **beef** have a different flavor profile: There is the big beefy flavor of the strip steak, the luxurious tenderness of filet mignon, and the juicy, fatty mouthfeel of a great rib eye. Skirt steak is a juicy cut that is great served as an open-faced sandwich. Hanger steak has an offal quality to it and is different from all the others. Braised short ribs pick up all of the flavors of what they are cooked with, developing layers of deep, dark beef flavor after being cooked on the bone for hours.

— **MICHAEL LOMONACO,** PORTER HOUSE NEW YORK (NEW YORK CITY)

We make a wood-grilled 18-ounce "prime" rib eye of **beef** with a gratin of macaroni and goat cheese, glazed shallots, oxtail red wine sauce, and *fleur de sel.* This dish is meat on meat on meat! We have the steak, oxtail sauce, and shallots braised in veal stock. This dish has so much flavor. You have the richness and fattiness of the rib eye, and we grill it over a wood fire that takes it to a whole other place. Top it with a drizzle of olive oil, the *fleur de sel,* cracked pepper, and then add rich oxtail sauce to it. People go crazy for it.

— **CARRIE NAHABEDIAN,** NAHA (CHICAGO)

oil: canola, sesame
olive oil
ONIONS: green, red, Spanish, yellow
orange
oregano
parsley, flat-leaf
PEPPER: BLACK, white
potatoes
red pepper flakes
rosemary
saffron
salt: *fleur de sel,* **kosher**
shallots
soy sauce
spinach (accompaniment)
stocks: beef, chicken, veal

sugar (pinch)
tarragon
thyme
tomatoes and tomato paste
truffles
turnips
vinaigrette

vinegar: cider, red wine, rice wine, sherry, tarragon
wine: red (e.g., Cabernet Sauvignon, Merlot), Madeira
zucchini

Flavor Affinities
beef + beer + onions
beef + garlic + ginger
beef + garlic + tomatoes
beef + mushrooms + potatoes
beef + mushrooms + red wine
beef + porcini mushrooms + red wine

BEEF — BRISKET
Techniques: barbecue, braise, corn, roast, simmer, smoke

barbecue rub
barbecue sauce
bay leaf
beer
cabbage, with corned beef brisket
chili powder
cinnamon
cumin
fennel seeds
garlic
horseradish
maple syrup
mirepoix
mustard
olive oil
onions
pasilla peppers
pepper, black

You can braise **brisket** for hours, and it still tastes like brisket, making it ideal to prepare for large parties. Nothing is better than what the Texans do with brisket, and that is barbecue. I also noticed that Texans get the fattiest brisket I have ever seen, so the fat just melts away and the meat is self-basting. My favorite barbecued brisket is from Mueller's outside of Austin. He cooks it about twenty hours and then wraps it in brown butcher paper to let it rest — which I think is the key to his barbecue.

— **MICHAEL LOMONACO,** PORTER HOUSE NEW YORK (NEW YORK CITY)

potatoes
rosemary
salt
soups
star anise
stews
stock, beef
sugar, brown
thyme
tomatoes and tomato paste
vinegar: sherry, wine
wine, red

BEEF — CHEEKS
Techniques: braise

apples
bay leaf
butter, unsalted
carrots
celery
celery root
chives
cinnamon
cloves
garlic
horseradish
leeks
mustard
oil, peanut
onions
pasta (e.g., gnocchi, ravioli)
pepper, black
potatoes, esp. mashed and/or
    new
risotto
rosemary
salt, kosher
stock, chicken
tarragon
thyme, fresh
tomatoes
vegetables, root
vinegar, balsamic
wine, red (e.g., Burgundy)

Dishes

Kobe Beef, Sautéed Foie Gras, Shaved Black Truffle, Madeira Sauce on an Onion Bun
— Hubert Keller, Burger Bar (Las Vegas)

Kobe Beef Carpaccio, Shaved Parmesan, Arugula, and Horseradish Sauce
— Frank Stitt, Highlands Bar and Grill (Birmingham, Alabama)

BEEF — KOBE
arugula
cheese, Parmesan
chives
garlic
ginger
horseradish
Japanese cuisine
Madeira
mushrooms
oil, sesame
olive oil
onions
pepper, black
salt, sea
sesame seeds
soy sauce
truffles, black
yuzu juice

BEEF — LOIN (aka shell, sirloin, tenderloin)
Techniques: pan roast, roast

butter, unsalted
five-spice powder
ginger
oil, peanut
paprika
pepper: black, white
rosemary, fresh
salt: kosher, sea
sauces
soy sauce
thyme, fresh
wasabi

Dishes

Cream of Sweet Onion, Braised Beef Oxtail, Aged Parmesan Tuile
— Jean Joho, Everest (Chicago)

BEEF — OXTAILS
Techniques: braise, stew

allspice
anise
basil
bay leaf
beans, esp. white
beer
bell peppers
cheese: Asiago, pecorino
garlic
ginger
gnocchi
leeks
Madeira
mushrooms
mustard
olive oil
ONIONS
orange
parsley, flat-leaf
parsnips
pasta (e.g., ravioli, tortellini)
pepper, black
potatoes, esp. mashed
risotto
salt
scallops
shallots
soups
stews
stocks: beef, chicken
thyme
tomatoes and tomato sauce
WINE, RED
wine, white

Flavor Affinities

oxtails + parsnips + red wine

oxtails + red wine + thyme + tomatoes

BEEF — RIBS

Techniques: barbecue, braise, (dry) roast

barbecue sauce
spice rub

BEEF — ROAST

Techniques: roast

brandy
chocolate
coffee
garlic
horseradish
mushrooms, wild
rosemary
sauces: béarnaise, red wine (esp. Madeira or port)
soy sauce
thyme
wine, red

BEEF — ROUND

Techniques: grill, sauté, stir-fry

bell peppers: red, green
chili powder
cilantro
cumin
garlic
lime, juice
olive oil
onions, red
parsley
radishes
Tabasco sauce

BEEF — SHANK

Techniques: braise

garlic
ginger

lemon
onions, green
paprika
pepper, black
sesame oil
soy sauce
sugar

BEEF — SHORT LOIN

This is the T-bone steak. When it is cut double cut [that is, twice as thick], that is when it is a porterhouse. The story goes that it was first served in Lower Manhattan in 1815 at a porter house. The owner ran out of his usual cut of meat, and when a customer asked for something to go with his porter [beer], the owner cut him this huge piece of meat. It became known as a "porterhouse" steak. The porterhouse steak is part filet mignon and part strip steak. It is the perfect grilling steak. You get the tenderness of the filet, and the big beefy chewiness of the strip steak.

— **MICHAEL LOMONACO,** PORTER HOUSE NEW YORK (NEW YORK CITY)

BEEF — SHORT RIBS

Techniques: barbecue, braise, stew

bacon
basil
bay leaf
beer or ale
butter, unsalted
carrots
celery: stalk, leaves
celery root
chervil
chile peppers, esp. hot cherry
chives
cilantro
cinnamon

coriander
garam masala (Indian cuisine)
GARLIC
ginger
gremolata
grits
horseradish
leeks
lemon: juice, zest
lime
mirepoix
mushrooms: porcini, wild
mustard: Dijon, Meaux
molasses
OIL: canola, corn, grapeseed, hazelnut, peanut, sesame, vegetable, walnut
olive oil
ONIONS, esp. green, pearl, white, or yellow
orange: juice, zest
oregano
parsley, flat-leaf
parsnips
peas

Vikram Vij of Vancouver's Vij's on Beef Short Ribs in Cinnamon

For braising, I prefer to use cinnamon bark. Cinnamon stick is pretty, but it is steamed and rolled and a little too manipulated. In this dish, cinnamon bark is big and intense and not needed for presentation. At the end of the braise, you pull it out and throw it away. This dish is cooked for four hours and the cinnamon flavor does not cook out. In the end, the cinnamon imparts a delicate, sweet, aromatic flavor. It adds contrast to the chile flavor from the curry. If this dish ever has too much cinnamon flavor, you can counterbalance it with rice or yogurt that has a little salt and pepper in it.

— **VIKRAM VIJ,** VIJ'S (VANCOUVER)

PEPPER: black, Szechuan, white

potatoes, esp. mashed

prosciutto

rosemary

sage

salt, kosher

savory

shallots

sherry, dry

soy sauce

star anise

STOCK: BEEF, CHICKEN, VEAL

sugar: brown, white (pinch)

tamarind

tarragon

THYME, FRESH

tomatoes, tomato paste, and
    tomato sauce

turnips (accompaniment)

vinegar: balsamic, sherry

WINE, DRY RED (e.g., Barolo,
    Cabernet Sauvignon, Merlot,
    Zinfandel)

wine, white, esp. fruity

Worcestershire sauce

Dishes

Short Ribs with Braised Boston Lettuce, Peppered Shallot Confit
— Daniel Boulud, Daniel (New York City)

Braised Short Ribs with Parsnip Puree, Porcini Mushrooms, and Barolo
— Scott Bryan, Veritas (New York City)

Slow-Roasted Short Ribs with Stone-Ground Grits
— Cesare Casella, Maremma (New York City)

Garlic Braised Short Ribs with Parsnip Puree, Baby Round Carrots in Carrot Butter, Haricots Verts, and Cabernet Sauce
— Bob Kinkead, Colvin Run (Vienna, Virginia)

Braised Short Ribs of Beef with Soft Grits and Meaux Mustard Sauce
— Gray Kunz, Café Gray (New York City)

Braised Short Ribs of Beef, Wild Boar Bacon, and Cauliflower Puree with Roasted Winter Root Vegetables and Cipollini Onions, Smoked "Manuka" Sea Salt, and Herb Salad
— Carrie Nahabedian, Naha (Chicago)

Short Ribs Braised and Then Caramelized on the Grill with Ginger and Soy
— Kaz Okochi, Kaz Sushi Bistro (Washington, DC)

Braised Short Ribs in Red Wine Sauce, Brown Loaf Sugar and Mustard Crust, Stir-Fried Quinoa and Swiss Chard
— Maricel Presilla, Cucharamama (Hoboken, New Jersey)

Beef Short Ribs in Cinnamon and Red Wine Curry
— Vikram Vij and Meeru Dhalwala, Vij's (Vancouver)

Short ribs are a luxurious cut of meat, because they are braised for three to three and a half hours. We don't braise our ribs in red wine, but in Yuengling Porter, which has ethereal chocolate notes in the aroma. In the sauce with the beer is mirepoix, a sachet of herbs, lots of peppercorns, and chiles. I went to a charity event where they served short ribs for six hundred guests, and one reason it worked is because it is a cut that allows for a great margin of error. You cook it until it is well done and falling-off-the-bone tender. Falling-off-the-bone tender is one of the appeals of a braised dish. It is sensual. Get yourself a glass of good spicy Syrah with that short rib dish and think great thoughts!
— **MICHAEL LOMONACO,** PORTER HOUSE NEW YORK (NEW YORK CITY)

Flavor Affinities

short ribs + bay leaf + beer + mushrooms + mustard

short ribs + beer + garlic + horseradish + onions + potatoes + tomatoes

short ribs + carrots + mushrooms + parsnips

short ribs + celery root + horseradish

short ribs + cinnamon + tomatoes + red wine

short ribs + horseradish + lemon + parsley

short ribs + onions + potatoes + red wine

short ribs + potatoes + root vegetables

BEEF — STEAK: IN GENERAL

Techniques: broil, grill, sauté

aligot (French garlic-cheesy pureed potatoes)

allspice

arugula

basil

bay leaf

béarnaise sauce

brandy

butter, unsalted

capers

cayenne

celery root

chard

cheese, Parmesan

chile peppers

chives

cilantro

cloves

cognac

coriander

cream

cumin

five-spice powder

fish sauce, Thai

GARLIC

ginger, fresh

herbs, esp. *herbes de Provence*

honey

horseradish

juniper berries

lemon: juice, zest

lemongrass

lime, juice

marrow

mushrooms (e.g., chanterelles, cremini, shiitake)

mustard, Dijon

oil: canola, grapeseed, sesame, vegetable

olive oil

onions: red, white

parsley, flat-leaf

PEPPER: black, green, pink, Szechuan, white

port

potatoes, French fries

red pepper flakes

rice

rosemary

salt, kosher

scallions

shallots

sherry, dry

soy sauce

stocks: beef, veal

sugar (pinch)

tamarind

tarragon

thyme

vinegar: balsamic, champagne, Chinese black, cider, red wine, rice wine, sherry, white wine

watercress

WINE, DRY RED (e.g., Beaujolais, Chianti)

Flavor Affinities

steak + arugula + Parmesan cheese + balsamic vinegar

steak + bacon + potatoes + red wine

steak + Chianti + lemon + salt

steak + cremini mushrooms + watercress

steak + horseradish + mustard + potatoes

steak + shallots + red wine

BEEF — STEAK: CHUCK

Techniques: braise, grill, stew

This cut is really beefy, flavorful, and fatty, but tough. **Chuck steak** can be grilled, but it also works well for braising. A chuck also makes a good cut for stew because it has nice fat. When I was growing up, a "steak Episole" was chuck steak that had good fat, was seared well, and then cooked slowly with tomatoes, onions, and fresh oregano. You may not see chuck steak a lot on menus, but you see it a lot in burgers. In fact, this is my favorite meat for a burger. I like my mix to be 75 to 80 percent lean and 20 to 25 percent fat.

— **MICHAEL LOMONACO,** PORTER HOUSE NEW YORK (NEW YORK CITY)

I like to keep it simple and serve **steak** au poivre with a peppercorn crust and deglazed with bourbon or even good ole American rye, which has more flavor. I also like steak with a margarita sauce, which is a good, zingy sauce made with tequila, orange, and lemon zest, and finished with roasted chile peppers.

— **MICHAEL LOMONACO,** PORTER HOUSE NEW YORK (NEW YORK CITY)

BEEF — STEAK: FILET MIGNON (aka Beef Tenderloin)

Techniques: broil, grill, sauté

bacon
butter, unsalted
cognac
cream
foie gras
garlic
leeks
mushrooms, esp. morels, porcini
oil, peanut
olive oil
onions
pepper: black, green
port
potatoes
rosemary
salt
shallots
sherry
stocks: beef, mushroom, veal
thyme
vinegar, balsamic
wine: dry red, Madeira

BEEF — STEAK: FLANK

Techniques: broil, grill, sauté, stir-fry

chile peppers, esp. chipotle or jalapeño
cilantro
cumin
garlic
hoisin sauce
honey
lime, juice
molasses
mustard, brown
oil: peanut, sesame
olive oil
oregano
salsa, esp. tomato
salt
soy sauce

Dishes

Seared Rib Eye, Caramelized Yukon Gold Potatoes, and Chanterelles
— Daniel Boulud, Daniel (New York City)

Strip Loin Poached in Butter and Roasted with Sea Salt, Short Ribs Stuffed in Cremini Mushrooms with Potato Boulangère, Spinach Puree, and Foie Gras Hollandaise
— Jeffrey Buben, Vidalia (Washington, DC)

Dry-Aged New York Steak with Slow-Cooked Broccoli, Garlic, and Lemon, Fingerling Potatoes, Niçoise Olive Jus
— Traci Des Jardins, Jardinière (San Francisco)

Skirt Steak Marinated in Seville Oranges and Lime Juice
— Maricel Presilla, Zafra (Hoboken, New Jersey)

Strawberry Mountain New York Strip, Grilled Lettuce, Olive Oil–Poached Tomato, and Lemon Cream
— Cory Schreiber, Wildwood (Portland, Oregon)

Cast Iron–Seared Porcini-Crusted New York Sirloin Steak, Roasted Garlic Mash Potatoes, Black Trumpet Ragout, Braised Kale, Rum au Poivre
— Allen Susser, Chef Allen's (Aventura, Florida)

Filet mignon gets no respect from many chefs because it doesn't have much beef flavor, but it is still the most popular cut in restaurants. I like to sear it and pan roast it with a little olive oil or an olive oil and butter combination. It is not a well-used muscle on the inside of the short loin, so filet is always tender. On the other side of the bone from the more worked side of the strip steak is the tail end of the filet. Béarnaise sauce [i.e., vinegar, shallots, egg yolks, butter, etc.] is a classic accompaniment to filet mignon.
— **MICHAEL LOMONACO,** PORTER HOUSE NEW YORK (NEW YORK CITY)

Dishes

Grilled Filet Mignon, Crisp Potatoes, Spinach, and Roasted Garlic Custard
— Alfred Portale, Gotham Bar and Grill (New York City)

Tournedos of Beef Tenderloin Worthy of a Splurge: Twin Filets of Beef Tenderloin Set on Brioche Toast, Slathered with Foie Gras Butter, and Served with Truffle Sauce, Port-Braised Cipollini Onions, Fingerling Potatoes, Spring Mushrooms, and Leek Puree
— Janos Wilder, Janos (Tucson)

sugar
thyme
vinegar, balsamic

Dishes

Flank Steak with Marinated Mushrooms, Artichokes, Tomatoes, Summer Squash, Whipple Farm Greens, Yellow Taxi Tomato Vinaigrette, and Basil-Garlic Aioli
— Jeffrey Buben, Vidalia (Washington, DC)

Green Peppercorn Marinated Flank Steak with Balsamic Roasted Onions, Tomatoes, and Thai Barbecue Sauce
— Charlie Trotter, Trotter's to Go (Chicago)

Miso-marinated grilled **steak** will help to release the flavors of everything else you pair with it. Use red miso alone, or in combination with garlic, ginger, mirin [sweet rice wine], sesame oil, soy sauce, and/or sugar.
— HIRO SONE, TERRA (ST. HELENA, CALIFORNIA)

BEEF — STEAK: HANGER
Techniques: broil, grill, sauté

bell peppers
brandy
celery root
ginger
mushrooms
mustard
onions
parsnips
pepper, black
salsa verde
scallions
soy sauce
thyme
wine, red

Dishes

Hanger Steak Pizzaiola with Local Peppers, Salsa Verde, Natural Juices
— Andrew Carmellini, A Voce (New York City)

BEEF — STEAK: RIB EYE
Techniques: broil, grill, sauté, stir-fry

garlic
mushrooms, porcini (dried)
olive oil
oregano
pepper, black
red pepper flakes
rosemary
vinegar: balsamic, red wine

BEEF — STEAK: SKIRT
Techniques: broil, grill, sauté

allspice
anchovies
butter
capers
chile peppers, ancho
cinnamon
cumin
endive, Belgian
garlic
lime: juice, zest
mustard
oil, canola
olive oil
onions, red
oregano
paprika
parsley, flat-leaf
red pepper flakes
rosemary
salt: kosher, sea
scallions
soy sauce
thyme
vinegar, balsamic

BEEF — STEAK TARTARE

We make **tartare** from filet mignon and hand-chop it to order, which I like so that I don't feel like I'm just eating ground beef. I season our tartare with mustard, capers, and anchovies, which I am not shy about. You want the texture of the beef to be a counterpoint.
— MICHAEL LOMONACO, PORTER HOUSE NEW YORK (NEW YORK CITY)

Skirt steak comes in a long strip and looks like a belt — it's about two feet long and a couple of inches wide. This is an incredibly flavorful cut and delicious. It is very reasonably priced as well. It is very popular in the Latin community, especially with Argentinians. You often see it flattened with a mallet to tenderize it [by breaking the meat fibers] and used in fajitas. This, along with the hanger steak, is the beefiest flavored cut of beef. We serve it in a chimichurri sauce, which is a classic Argentinian sauce made of chopped garlic, onion, and parsley, plus white [we use champagne] vinegar, red pepper flakes, and a little olive oil. It grills really well.
— MICHAEL LOMONACO, PORTER HOUSE NEW YORK (NEW YORK CITY)

Michael Lomonaco of Porter House New York on Cooking Steak

Aging: Aging is important because it tenderizes the steak. The aging process breaks down the fibers and dehydrates the steak, concentrating its flavor. A dry-aged steak has a more minerally and sharp edge to it, versus fresh meat that tastes sweeter. It is critical to the flavor and adds to the cost because it takes four weeks of aging to achieve it.

Seasoning: All our steaks are seasoned with coarse kosher salt and freshly ground black pepper just prior to cooking, which draws out the flavor while they cook. A squeeze of lemon makes a good Tuscan steak taste even better. If you are in Italy and eating "bistecca Fiorentina," what you are having is an Italian porterhouse. The steak is grilled over dried grape vines and served with a drizzle of green olive oil from the first pressing of the new harvest and lemons on the side.

Cooking: A steak should be cooked rare to medium rare. "Rare" is a little cool inside and hot on the exterior. "Medium rare" is just a shade past, and only warm in the middle. Cooking a steak beyond that point, it starts to toughen up and the fat oozes out, making it increasingly dry and tough.

Saucing: Part of looking forward is looking back. Sauces provide the connection to historical French and Italian cooking. In the gastronomic world, the saucier was the top cook in the kitchen. It is all about building layer upon layer of complexity in a sauce. It is most often sweet and sour, to cut through the richness of the fat of the steak. Red wine sauce has the acidity to cut richness, with sweetness from caramelized shallots, and it enhances the beef flavor. We also make a homemade barbecue sauce as our steak sauce, which is sweet from light brown sugar and molasses, tart from red wine vinegar, and smoky from chipotle peppers.

Hanger steak is known as an *onglet* in French and is found on bistro menus. It is also a great value, which is why you see it on menus in smaller restaurants. A hanger steak is incredibly flavorful. There is only one per carcass, and it comes from the area close to the kidneys, so it has almost an offal flavor to the beef. It has become popular because it is different and not a typical-tasting steak. I like a hanger steak grilled and served rare to medium rare. Slicing is also important, because you have to cut it on the bias so that it is tender. I like a hanger steak served with a traditional sauce, such as a caramelized shallot and red wine sauce or a bourbon peppercorn sauce. It is important to caramelize the shallots so they get sweet and offset the gaminess of the steak. I use bourbon instead of cognac because it has more punch to it, and I'll use four different peppercorns — white, black, pink, and green — with the last two modulating the flavor. Green peppercorns have the sharpness to cut through the richness.
— **MICHAEL LOMONACO**, PORTER HOUSE NEW YORK (NEW YORK CITY)

Rib steak is the most popular cut next to filet mignon. The cut comes from the rib roast, where one end meets the chuck at the fattier end and the other meets the short loin at the leaner end. The rib steak that meets the chuck end is the most popular and can even have a big knot of fat in it. This is one of my favorite steaks. A big, fatty, juicy rib steak can't be beat on the grill. I cook these bone-on because it gives more beef flavor. We do a Brandt Ranch cut that comes from California just north of Mexico. That area has lots of flavor influences, so I choose to do a chili rub on the steak. The cut is Holstein, which has a sweeter edge to its meat. We grill it so that fat melts away and bastes it as it cooks. At the end, we brush it with a blend of ancho chili, light brown sugar, toasted ground cumin seeds, chipotle chile, and a pinch of cayenne. Then we char it one more time, so that is like reseasoning the meat.
— **MICHAEL LOMONACO**, PORTER HOUSE NEW YORK (NEW YORK CITY)

The **sirloin** is a good, beefy-flavored high-quality cut. It is a cut toward the back of the animal that gets more work, so it is a little chewy, but it is a good-quality steak for barbecuing. If this cut is quickly cooked over high heat on a grill, not overcooked, and sliced correctly on the bias, you are going to get the most out of it.
— **MICHAEL LOMONACO**, PORTER HOUSE NEW YORK (NEW YORK CITY)

When you see rare roast beef, it is **top round.** It is a little tough, and that is why you see roast beef always sliced so thin. Nothing beats top round for a good old-fashioned roast beef sandwich because it doesn't have any gristle or fat — just good, beefy flavor.
— **MICHAEL LOMONACO**, PORTER HOUSE NEW YORK (NEW YORK CITY)

When I was in Ireland, I swilled Guinness [stout] and ate bangers and mash, which was essentially sausage with caramelized onions on top. It was so good that when I came back to the U.S., I started experimenting with Guinness. That's how I came up with a dish of braised short ribs that had been marinated in Guinness. The problem you often have cooking with **beer** is that sometimes the dish gets bitter. So, to counteract that naturally without using sugar, I choose to use onions. I marinate the ribs in the **beer,** then braise them, and finish the dish with a puree of roasted onions for balance.

— **ANDREW CARMELLINI,** A VOCE (NEW YORK CITY)

BEER

Taste: varies, from bitter to sweet
Weight: medium–heavy
Volume: quiet–loud

beef
cheese, cheddar
ham
marinades
meats
onions
pork
sauces
sauerkraut
sausages
shrimp
stews

BEETS

Season: year-round
Taste: sweet
Function: heating
Weight: medium
Volume: moderate
Techniques: bake, boil, carpaccio, chips, roast, soup, steam

apples
arugula
avocado
basil
beans, green
beef
beet greens
BUTTER, UNSALTED

cabbage
capers
caraway seeds
carrots
caviar
celery
CHEESE: blue, cambozola, cheddar, **GOAT, PARMESAN, ROQUEFORT, SALTY**
chervil
chicory
chiles
chives
cilantro
citrus
coriander
cream
crème fraîche
cumin
curry
dill
eggs, hard-boiled
endive
escarole
fennel
fennel seeds
fish
French cuisine
frisée
garlic
ginger
herbs
honey
herring
horseradish
leeks

LEMON: juice, zest
lemon balm
lemon thyme
lemon verbena
lime
maple syrup
milk
mint
mushrooms (e.g., shiitake)
MUSTARD, DIJON
mustard oil
nutmeg
oil: canola, peanut, vegetable, walnut
OLIVE OIL
olives, esp. niçoise
onions: red, white, yellow
ORANGE: JUICE, ZEST
parsley, flat-leaf
pasta
pears
PEPPER: BLACK, WHITE
pistachios
potatoes
radishes
rosemary
Russian cuisine
salads, esp. green
SALT: kosher, sea
scallions
SHALLOTS
sherry
soups, esp. borscht
sour cream
spinach
stocks: chicken, veal, vegetable
sugar: brown, white
TARRAGON
thyme
vinaigrette, mustard
VINEGAR: balsamic, champagne, **cider,** raspberry, red wine, sherry, tarragon, white wine
vodka
WALNUTS AND WALNUT OIL
wine, white
yogurt

Flavor Affinities

beets + chives + orange + tarragon

beets + citrus + goat cheese + olive oil + shallots

beets + crème fraîche + orange + tarragon

beets + dill + sour cream

beets + endive + goat cheese + pistachios

beets + endive + orange + walnuts

beets + goat cheese + walnuts

beets + Gorgonzola cheese + hazelnuts + vinegar

beets + honey + tarragon

beets + mint + yogurt

beets + olive oil + Parmesan cheese + balsamic vinegar

beets + orange + walnuts

beets + potatoes + balsamic vinegar

beets + shallots + vinegar + walnuts

Beets are especially delicious when accented by a salty cheese, whether queso fresco or ricotta salata.

— **SHARON HAGE,** YORK STREET (DALLAS)

People love fresh **beets.** Now I won't lay claim to inventing beet salad with Gorgonzola and hazelnuts, but how our version is different from many others is that we marinate the beets. Overnight, we'll marinate peeled beets in Barolo vinegar, shallots, olive oil, salt, and pepper. Using Russian and Polish cooking principles, marinating the beets ensures that the vinegar is able to penetrate them so that they are sure to be tangy.

— **ANDREW CARMELLINI,** A VOCE (NEW YORK CITY)

I wanted to take **beets** that are associated with winter and make them into something summery, so I used them for a ceviche. We roasted and pureed them with lime and froze them into a sorbet. We served the beet sorbet flat in a bowl so it looked like soup. From there, we layered thinly sliced raw bay scallops with segments of lime, cilantro, and red onion oil. The dish is very fresh tasting. The other key to this dish was that we had all the flavors of ceviche but did not marinate the scallops in the acid, which makes them rubbery. The scallops treated this way are more delicate, like sushi.

— **KATSUYA FUKUSHIMA,** MINIBAR (WASHINGTON, DC)

Dishes

Roasted Beet Tartare with Chianti Vinegar and Ricotta Salata
— Mario Batali, Babbo (New York City)

Roasted Beet Salad: Cabrales Blue Cheese, Endive, and Walnuts
— Daniel Boulud/Bertrand Chemel, Café Boulud
(New York City)

Roasted Beet Salad with Hazelnut, Gorgonzola, Barolo Vinegar
— Andrew Carmellini, A Voce (New York City)

Squab Borscht with Root Vegetable Pierogi
— Sandy D'Amato, Sanford (Milwaukee)

Roasted Beet Salad with a Warm Farm Egg, Caciocavallo Cheese, and Pickled Spring Onions
— Traci Des Jardins, Jardinière (San Francisco)

Roasted Beet Salad with Shaved Fennel and Chèvre
— Leslie Mackie, Macrina Bakery & Café (Seattle)

Salad of Organic Beets and Gala Apples, "Beauty Heart" Radishes and Upland Cress, Cracked Hazelnuts, Great Hill Blue Cheese, and Quince "Must" Syrup
— Carrie Nahabedian, Naha (Chicago)

Tartare of Yellow Beets with Sturgeon Caviar, and Dashi
— Kaz Okochi, Kaz Sushi Bistro (Washington, DC)

Beets, Frisée, Cambazola, Candied Walnuts, Orange Sauce
— Monica Pope, T'afia (Houston)

Beet, Apple, and Goat Cheese Tartlet with a Hazelnut-Champagne Dressing
— Thierry Rautureau, Rover's (Seattle)

We serve a salad that showcases the classic combination of **beets**, walnuts, and orange. We boil our beets, then slice them thinly on the plate. We add frisée to the salad and, since it is bitter, we mix in Cambozola cheese and candied walnuts. We dress the salad with a sherry-walnut-tarragon vinaigrette, and a mandarin orange sauce. People are surprised when they eat the dish — first, because they find out they like beets, and second, because the frisée is not bitter after being softened by the sweet touches.
— **MONICA POPE,** T'AFIA (HOUSTON)

I like to intensify the flavor of **beets** by serving them prepared in different ways on the same dish, such as accenting roasted beets with crunchy beet chips and a spiced beet coulis. And I love anything anise-flavored with beets, whether fennel or anise itself.
— **BRAD THOMPSON,** MARY ELAINE'S AT THE PHOENICIAN (SCOTTSDALE, ARIZONA)

BELGIAN CUISINE

almonds
beef
beer
Brussels sprouts
charcuterie
chocolate
endive, Belgian
game
meats
mussels, steamed
mustard
POTATOES: FRIED, mashed
shallots
soups
stews
vinegar
waffles

Flavor Affinities

beef + bay leaf + beer + thyme +
    vinegar
endive + béchamel sauce +
    nutmeg
endive + goat cheese + herbs
mussels + butter + garlic +
    parsley + shallots

BELL PEPPERS

Season: summer–autumn
Taste: bitter to sweet, from
unripe (green) to ripe (yellow to
red)
Weight: light–medium
Volume: moderate–loud
Techniques: bake, broil, grill,
roast, sauté, steam, stew, stir-fry,
stuff

anchovies
anise
arugula
bacon
BASIL
bay leaf
beef
bell peppers
butter

The sweetness of red **bell peppers** and the acidity of sherry vinegar make for a perfect combination.
— **JOSÉ ANDRÉS**, CAFÉ ATLÁNTICO (WASHINGTON, DC)

A lot of people find the skin a turnoff on green **bell peppers,** so I'll peel them and cook them, which releases their juice. They're great cooked down with chorizo, garlic, and onions, which you can serve with shrimp over rice.
— **TONY LIU**, AUGUST (NEW YORK CITY)

I'll cook red **bell peppers** with onion and garlic on the stove over a low heat for six hours or more, so that they become caramelized and intense. The bell peppers eventually turn into a concentrated red pepper paste. If you have a dish where something is missing, add a little of this and it will fix it! It is superb. I add it to all sorts of things — even pasta.
— **MICHEL RICHARD**, CITRONELLE (WASHINGTON, DC)

Green **bell peppers** are used for the equivalent of Spanish mirepoix. In Spain you don't see much celery — but you'll see green pepper, onion, garlic, and leeks.
— **ALEXANDRA RAIJ**, TÍA POL (NEW YORK CITY)

capers, esp. with roasted peppers
cardamom
carrots
cayenne
CHEESE, esp. feta, Fontina, **goat,**
    mozzarella, Parmesan
chile peppers (e.g., fresh green or
    poblano)
chives
cilantro
coriander
cream
cumin
curry
eggplant
fennel
fennel seeds
French cuisine
game
game birds
GARLIC
ginger, fresh
goulash
hazelnuts
honey

Indian cuisine
Italian cuisine
lamb
lemon, juice
lemongrass
lime, juice
lovage
marjoram
Mexican cuisine
mint
mirepoix
mushrooms (e.g., shiitake)
mustard
OIL, CANOLA
OLIVE OIL
olives (e.g., green)
ONIONS, ESP. RED OR
    YELLOW
oregano
paprika, smoked
parsley, flat-leaf
pasta
peas
pepper, black
peppers, piquillo

pine nuts
pizza
polenta
pork
potatoes (e.g., red)
quail
red pepper flakes
rice
rosemary
saffron
salads
salt: kosher, sea
sausages (e.g., chorizo, Italian)
savory
scallions
sea bass
sesame oil
shallots
squash, esp. summer
stews
stir-fried dishes
stocks: chicken, vegetable
sugar (pinch)
swordfish
Tabasco sauce
THYME
TOMATOES
tuna
VINEGAR: balsamic, champagne, cider, red wine, sherry, white wine
watercress
wine: dry white, sweet sherry
zucchini

Flavor Affinities

bell peppers + basil + currants + garlic + pine nuts + sherry vinegar

bell peppers + garlic + olive oil + onion + thyme + zucchini

Dishes

Berry Crème Fraîche Poppy Seed Cake
— Emily Luchetti, pastry chef, Farallon (San Francisco)

Fresh Fruit: Black Garnet Cherries, Strawberries, Pistachios, Marshall Farms Honey, Straus Organic Whole Milk Yogurt
— Emily Luchetti, pastry chef, Farallon (San Francisco)

Red Berry–White Chocolate Trifles
— Emily Luchetti, pastry chef, Farallon (San Francisco)

BERRIES — IN GENERAL
(See also Raspberries, Strawberries, etc.)
Season: spring–summer
Weight: light
Volume: quiet–moderate
Techniques: poach, raw

cheese, ricotta
chocolate: dark, milk, white
cream
crème de cassis
crème de menthe
crème fraîche
elderflower syrup
game
honey, wildflower
lemon: juice, zest
lime, juice
mint
pepper, black
poppy seeds
salads, fruit
sour cream
sugar: brown, white
yogurt

BITTER DISHES (e.g., greens, barbecue food)
Tips: Salt suppresses bitterness.

BITTERNESS
Taste: bitter
Function: cooling; stimulates appetite; promotes other tastes
Tips: Bitterness relieves thirst.

When a bitter component is added to a dish, it creates a sense of lightness.

The hotter the food or drink, the less the perception of bitterness.

arugula
baking powder
baking soda
beans, lima
beer, esp. hoppy (e.g., bitter ales)
bell peppers, green
bitters
broccoli rabe
Brussels sprouts
cabbage, green
caffeine (e.g., as in coffee, tea)
chard (e.g., Swiss chard)
chicory
chocolate, dark
cocoa
coffee
cranberries
eggplant
endive
escarole
fenugreek
frisée
grapefruit (bitter-sour)
greens: bitter, dark leafy (e.g., beet, dandelion, mustard, turnip)
herbs, many
horseradish
kale
lettuce, romaine

So many Western cultures don't incorporate **bitterness** into their food. In India and Asia, it is a component of a balanced dish. If you give most of America rice with lime pickle, they will not be thrilled. It will be too sour, bitter, and spicy. To introduce the bitter flavor of lime pickle, we will puree it with yogurt and use it for a marinade for whole prawns. That way, it isn't overwhelming.

— **BRAD FARMERIE**, PUBLIC (NEW YORK CITY)

I used to love dishes that were rich on rich — but the older I get, the more I look forward to that **bitterness**, the cleansing bite that makes you want to go back for your next forkful of a dish. Almost every dish in our kitchen is finished with some kind of bitter leaf to serve as a balancing component. That's why I serve cress or watercress with a steak and potato dish, and arugula with our seared bluefin tuna on braised veal cheeks, and a bed of bitter greens like watercress, frisée, arugula, and shaved endive as the base for our foie gras dish — to cut the richness.

— **SHARON HAGE**, YORK STREET (DALLAS)

liver, calf's
melon, bitter
olives (bitter-salty)
radicchio
rhubarb
spices, many
spinach
tea
tonic water
turmeric
walnuts, esp. black
watercress
wine, red, esp. tannic
zest: lemon, orange, etc.
zucchini

BLACKBERRIES

Season: summer
Taste: sour
Weight: light–medium
Volume: moderate
Techniques: cooked, raw

almonds
apples
apricots
bananas
blueberries
brandy

butter, unsalted
buttermilk
caramel
cheese, goat
chocolate: dark, white
cinnamon
cloves
cobblers
Cointreau
cornmeal
CREAM AND ICE CREAM
cream cheese
crème de cassis
crème fraîche
custard

ginger
Grand Marnier
hazelnuts
honey
Kirsch
LEMON, JUICE
lime: juice, zest
liqueurs, berry
mango
mascarpone
melons
mint
nectarines
oats
oranges
peaches
pies
pork
raspberries
salads, fruit
salt (pinch)
sour cream
strawberries
SUGAR: BROWN, WHITE
vanilla
watermelon
wine (e.g., Merlot)
yogurt

Flavor Affinities
blackberries + crème de cassis + sugar
blackberries + ginger + peaches
blackberries + honey + vanilla + yogurt

Blackberries are only okay raw, but they are really great *cooked*.
— GINA DEPALMA, BABBO (NEW YORK CITY)

Dishes

Blackberry-Almond Tart with Pineapple Carpaccio, Asian Pear, Ginger-Lime Caramel, and Beurre Noisette Ice Cream
— Michael Laiskonis, pastry chef, Le Bernardin (New York City)

Candied Ginger Shortbread Stacks with Peach-Blackberry Compote
— Emily Luchetti, pastry chef, Farallon (San Francisco)

Blackberry Sorbet–Filled Peaches
— Emily Luchetti, pastry chef, Farallon (San Francisco)

BLACK-EYED PEAS

Weight: light–medium
Volume: moderate–loud
Techniques: simmer

African cuisine
bay leaf
cardamom
carrots
cayenne
celery
chile peppers, dried red
cinnamon
cloves
coriander
cumin
garam masala
garlic
ginger, fresh
GREENS (e.g., collard)
HAM HOCKS
Indian cuisine
oil, peanut
onions: red, yellow
pepper, black
pork
red pepper flakes
rice
salt
savory
Southern cuisine (American)
tomatoes
turmeric
vinegar, white wine
yogurt

Flavor Affinities

black-eyed peas + collard greens +
    ham hocks
black-eyed peas + rice + savory

BLACK PEPPER (See Pepper, Black)

BLUEBERRIES

Season: spring–summer
Taste: sour–sweet
Botanical relatives:
huckleberries
Weight: light
Volume: quiet–moderate
Techniques: cooked, raw
Tips: Can substitute
huckleberries.

allspice
almonds
apples
apricots
bananas
blackberries
butter, unsalted
buttermilk
chocolate, white
CINNAMON
cinnamon basil
cloves
cognac
cornmeal
cream and ice cream
cream cheese
crème fraîche
custard
ginger
honey
jams
Kirsch
LEMON: juice, zest
lemon thyme
lime: juice, zest
liqueurs: berry, orange
mace
mangoes
MAPLE SYRUP
MASCARPONE
melon
mint
molasses
muffins
nectarines
nutmeg
oats and oatmeal
orange
PEACHES
pears
pecans

Cinnamon with **blueberries** really intensifies the flavor of the blueberries.
— **JERRY TRAUNFELD,** THE HERBFARM (WOODINVILLE, WASHINGTON)

If I make a blueberry cobbler, I will macerate the **blueberries** first with maple and lemon zest.
— **MICHAEL LAISKONIS,** LE BERNARDIN (NEW YORK CITY)

Blueberries and lemon go really well together. **Blueberries** are a thick fruit with a lot of pectin in them, and intensely flavored. You need some lemon to cut through that.
— **EMILY LUCHETTI,** FARALLON (SAN FRANCISCO)

Dishes

Risotto Fritters with Gingered Blueberries
— Jimmy Bradley, The Red Cat (New York City)

Warm Blueberry Crostata with Crème Fraîche and Cinnamon
— Gina DePalma, pastry chef, Babbo (New York City)

Blueberry-Apple-Lavender Faux Gelato and Anise Tuile
— Dominique and Cindy Duby, Wild Sweets (Vancouver)

pepper, black
pies
pineapple
pine nuts
port
raspberries
rhubarb
ricotta cheese
rum
salads, fruit
sour cream
strawberries
SUGAR: BROWN, WHITE
tarts
Triple Sec
vanilla
walnuts
watermelon
yogurt

Flavor Affinities

blueberries + cinnamon + cream + sugar
blueberries + cream + lemon zest + mascarpone + sugar
blueberries + honey + port + vanilla
blueberries + lemon + lemon thyme
blueberries + lemon zest + maple syrup
blueberries + mascarpone + peaches

BLUEFISH

Season: spring–early autumn
Weight: medium
Volume: loud
Techniques: bake, blacken, braise, broil, grill, pan roast, poach, sauté

chile peppers, chipotle
cilantro
lemon
lime, juice
marjoram
mustard, brown
olive oil
onions, red
rosemary

sugar
thyme
tomatoes
vinegar, cider
wine

BOK CHOY

Season: year-round
Taste: bitter
Weight: light–medium
Volume: quiet
Techniques: boil, braise, raw, stir-fry

asparagus
beef
broccoli
butter
carrots
cashews
celery
chicken
chile peppers
chili powder
cilantro
coconut milk
coriander
duck
fennel
fish
garlic
ginger
hot sauce
lemon, juice
meats
mirin
mushrooms, esp. shiitake
noodles, rice
oil: peanut, sesame, vegetable
peanuts
pork
rice
rosemary
salads
salmon
scallions
sesame: oil, seeds
shallots

shellfish
snow peas
soy sauce
tamari
tarragon
tofu
vinegar, esp. rice
water chestnuts
zucchini

BONITO FLAKES, DRIED
(See also Tuna)

Taste: salty
Weight: light–medium
Volume: moderate–loud
Tips: Use large flakes to make fish stock and small flakes to season dishes.

anchovies
capers
garlic
Japanese cuisine
oil, vegetable
scallions
stock, fish
vinegar

BOUQUET GARNI

Tips: Bundle of herbs is removed after cooking.

French cuisine
soups
stews
stocks

Flavor Affinities

bay leaf + parsley + thyme

BOURBON (See also Whiskey)

Weight: heavy
Volume: loud

apple juice
apricot brandy
barbecue
bitters

butter
butterscotch
cream
desserts
ginger
grapefruit juice
grenadine
honey
ice cream
LEMON JUICE
mint
orange juice
peaches
pecans
pineapple juice
Southern cuisine (American)
SUGAR: BROWN, WHITE
vermouth: dry, **sweet**

Flavor Affinities
bourbon + grapefruit + honey
bourbon + lemon + peaches
bourbon + lemon + sugar
bourbon + pineapple + sugar

BOYSENBERRIES
Season: summer
Taste: sour–sweet
Weight: light–medium
Volume: quiet–moderate

cream
Kirsch
lemon, juice
nectarines
peaches
sugar
vanilla
wine, esp. dry red

BRAISED DISHES
Season: winter
Tips: Check here for ideas of meats or vegetables to add to a braised dish.

artichokes
beans

beef: brisket, shanks, short ribs, shoulder
cabbage
carrots
celery
chicken: legs, thighs, wings
chili
cod
corned beef and cabbage
duck, legs
endive
fennel
ham hocks
lamb: shanks, shoulder
monkfish
octopus
onions
oxtails
pork: belly, butt, chops, loin, ribs, shank, shoulder
potatoes
pot roast
rabbit
ratatouille
short ribs
skate
stews
tripe
turkey, legs
turnips
veal: breast, rump, shank, shoulder, sirloin, sweetbreads
vegetables, root
venison, shoulder

BRAZILIAN CUISINE (See also Latin American Cuisine)
beans, black
cardamom

chile peppers
cilantro
cloves
coconut milk
garlic
ginger
greens: collard, kale
grilled dishes
meats
nutmeg
onions
orange
parsley
pepper, black
peppers
pork
pumpkin
rice
saffron
sausages
thyme

Flavor Affinities
cream + egg yolks + sugar
pork + beans + greens + onions + oranges

BRINED DISHES
Taste: salty
Tips: Brining meats (i.e., in salt water) before cooking increases their moistness, juiciness, and flavor.

chicken
game birds
pork
poultry
turkey

I don't **brine** automatically. If I have a chicken that I know will cook up on the dry side, then I will brine it first. If it is a great chicken that will cook up naturally juicy and doesn't need help, then I won't. You can make a pretty strong brine for squab or even chicken — for instance, with thyme or even chile pepper — and the meat will pick up some flavors, but it's still very subtle.
— **TRACI DES JARDINS,** JARDINIÈRE (SAN FRANCISCO)

BROCCOLI

Season: autumn–winter
Botanical relatives: Brussels sprouts, cabbage, cauliflower, collard greens, kale, kohlrabi
Function: cooling
Weight: medium
Volume: moderate
Techniques: boil, deep-fry, sauté, steam, stir-fry

almonds
anchovies
basil
bread crumbs
butter, unsalted
caraway seeds
carrots
cauliflower
CHEESE: cheddar, feta, goat, mozzarella, Parmesan, Swiss
chicken
chile peppers (esp. green)
cilantro
coriander
cream
curry and curry leaf
eggs
garlic
ginger, esp. fresh
hollandaise sauce
lemon, juice
lemon balm
mint
mustard and mustard seeds
oil: peanut, sesame
olive oil
olives
onions, esp. green
oregano
parsley
pasta
pepper, ground
red pepper flakes
rice, basmati
salt
scallions

shallots
tarragon
thyme
vinaigrette
vinegar: balsamic, red wine
wine

Flavor Affinities

broccoli + anchovies + capers + red pepper flakes + garlic + olives
broccoli + anchovies + lemon
broccoli + garlic + lemon juice + olive oil
broccoli + garlic + tarragon

BROCCOLINI

Season: year-round
Weight: light–medium
Volume: quiet–moderate
Techniques: blanch, raw, sauté, steam, stir-fry

almonds
basil
cheese: feta, Parmesan
garlic
lemon, juice
olive oil
parsley, flat-leaf
pasta
red pepper flakes
salads
sesame oil
soups
tomatoes

BROCCOLI RABE

Season: late fall–spring
Taste: bitter
Weight: medium–heavy

Our winter *pistou* features **broccoli**, and we're able to make the broccoli flavor very intense. We use not only broccoli stock, but also broccoli florets and even add broccoli puree. There's both clarity and lightness of flavor that we're able to achieve without butter or cream this way.
— DAN BARBER, BLUE HILL AT STONE BARNS (POCANTICO HILLS, NEW YORK)

Volume: moderate–loud
Techniques: boil, sauté, steam, stir-fry

almonds
anchovies
basil
beans, white
butter, unsalted
cheese, Parmesan
chicken
chickpeas
chiles
chives
cream
fish
GARLIC
Italian cuisine
lemon, juice
meats
OLIVE OIL
oregano
parsley, flat-leaf
pasta, esp. orecchiette
pepper: white, black
piquillo peppers
poultry
prosciutto
red pepper flakes
salt
sausage
stock, chicken
tomatoes
vinegar: balsamic, red wine

Dishes

Orecchiette with Rapini and Sweet Sausage
— Mario Batali, Babbo (New York City)

Broccoli Rabe with Garlic and Oregano
— Andrew Carmellini, A Voce (New York City)

Flavor Affinities

broccoli rabe + anchovies + red
    pepper flakes + garlic + olive oil
broccoli rabe + garlic + oregano
broccoli rabe + red pepper flakes
    + oregano

BRUNCH

Customers are picky at **brunch**. They have all cooked what they think they like, they think they can do it slightly better than we can, and they want it twice as fast. So, we take the classics like pancakes or French toast, use them as building blocks, and push them a little further.

We will offer seasonal pancakes. In the winter, we'll make buckwheat pancakes with cinnamon and glazed oranges. Bridging spring into summer, we'll offer corn and saffron pancakes with a spicy poached pear and fresh ricotta. Saffron and corn work really well together because of the floral nature of the saffron and sweetness of the corn. We will use poached pears on the pancakes until switching to blueberries for the summer, which give a real pop. The pears are poached in a red wine syrup with *aleppo* chile that is a sun-dried chile with a rich, round, sweet spice to it. The chile is not noticeable, but it acts like an acid by lightening, plus cutting the sugar and richness of, the pancake.

When people eat pancakes, they naturally reach for butter. I don't serve butter with my pancakes and instead serve fresh ricotta. We use ricotta from Anne Saxelby, who supplies us with a fresh, rich, velvety ricotta, and this gives a richness to the dish.
— BRAD FARMERIE, PUBLIC (NEW YORK CITY)

BRUSSELS SPROUTS

Season: autumn–winter
Taste: bitter
Botanical relatives: broccoli, cabbage, cauliflower, collard greens, kale, kohlrabi
Weight: moderate–heavy
Volume: moderate–loud
Techniques: boil, braise, sauté, simmer, steam, stew, stir-fry

almonds
apple cider
apples and apple juice or cider
artichokes, Jerusalem
BACON
basil
bay leaf
bread crumbs
BUTTER, unsalted
celery
celery root
CHEESE: blue, cheddar, goat, Parmesan, provolone, ricotta, Swiss
chestnuts
chives
coriander
cream
crème fraîche
dill
eggs, hard-boiled
fennel seeds
garlic
hazelnuts
lemon, juice
marjoram

mustard, Dijon
nutmeg
oil, mustard
olive oil
onions
pancetta
paprika
parsley, flat-leaf
pepper: black, white
potatoes, esp. mashed
salt: kosher, sea
sauces, béchamel
shallots
stock, chicken
sugar
thyme, fresh
turnips
vermouth
vinaigrette
VINEGAR: cider, white wine
water chestnuts
wine, dry white

Flavor Affinities

Brussels sprouts + bacon + garlic + cider vinegar
Brussels sprouts + bacon + onions
Brussels sprouts + cream + nutmeg
Brussels sprouts + lemon juice + thyme
Brussels sprouts + pancetta + thyme

BULGUR WHEAT

Weight: light–medium
Volume: quiet–moderate
Techniques: steam

butter
chicken
chickpeas
dill
fish (e.g., branzino, pike, striped bass)

Dishes

Brussels Sprouts, Cranberry Polenta, and Braised Fennel with a Moroccan Olive Relish
  — Thierry Rautureau, Rover's (Seattle)

I love **bulgur** [wheat] salad. In the summer, I'll serve it with greens and tomatoes, while in the fall it's paired with tangerines and pomegranates. I feel the same about it whether it is under branzino or pike or striped bass; it always makes sense.

— SHARON HAGE, YORK STREET (DALLAS)

greens
lamb
lentils
meats
Middle Eastern cuisine
oils, walnut
olive oil
orange
parsley
pilaf (key ingredient)
pine nuts
pomegranates
rice
salads
soups
tabbouleh (key ingredient)
tangerine
tarragon
tomatoes
vegetables
walnuts

BUTTER, BROWN

(aka Beurre Noisette)
bananas
fish, esp. white: halibut, skate
fruits, esp. richer ones
nuts
pears
scallops
soft-shell crabs
vinegar, esp. balsamic

Flavor Affinities
brown butter + balsamic vinegar
 + fish
brown butter + banana + nuts

BUTTERMILK

Taste: sour
Weight: medium
Volume: moderate–loud

bananas
blackberries
blueberries
cherries
cinnamon
dates
ginger
herbs
honey
lemon
lime
maple syrup
mayonnaise
mint
nectarines
nutmeg
oats
orange
peaches

plums
raisins
raspberries
rhubarb
sour cream
strawberries
sugar, brown
walnuts

BUTTERSCOTCH
almonds
chocolate
coffee
lemon
praline
rum
vanilla

Dishes
Butterscotch-Praline Ice Cream Parfait
— Rebecca Charles, Pearl Oyster Bar (New York City)

One of my favorite flavors in the world is **brown butter**. A *financier* cake made with brown butter is one of the best things ever. I have been making a brown butter vinaigrette for a jillion years! It is a super-easy pan sauce that I love as a warm sauce: I just brown my butter in a pan until it gets the *noisette* [brown] color, then add some balsamic vinegar. It doesn't even need to be expensive balsamic. You make an emulsification in the pan, and add a little salt and pepper and it's done. The flavor of brown butter, salt, and acid is one of my favorites. It works well on different fish like scallops or halibut or soft-shell crabs.

— TRACI DES JARDINS, JARDINIÈRE (SAN FRANCISCO)

Brown butter is one of my favorite flavors, and it pairs well with anything nutty, as well as richer fruits like bananas. A classic French *financier* is hands-down one of my favorite French pastries [a cookie made with brown butter, egg whites, flour, and powdered sugar].

Butter tastes great on its own, and in making brown butter you are not adding anything to it — just transforming it, so that it becomes more. The process is simple but a little tricky, as it keeps cooking even after it is off the stove. Something you can do to improve it is — halfway through the cooking process — start whisking the butter, because it intensifies the flavor if you keep the particles suspended.

— MICHAEL LAISKONIS, LE BERNARDIN (NEW YORK CITY)

CABBAGE — IN GENERAL

Season: autumn–winter
Botanical relatives: broccoli, Brussels sprouts, cauliflower, collard greens, kale, kohlrabi
Function: cooling
Weight: medium
Volume: moderate
Techniques: boil, braise, raw, sauté, steam, stir-fry

apples and apple cider
BACON
bay leaf
beef
bell peppers, red
butter, unsalted
CARAWAY SEEDS
carrots
celery: leaves, salt, seeds
Champagne
cheese: cheddar, feta, goat,
    Parmesan, Swiss, Taleggio,
    Teleme
chestnuts
chicken
chili sauce
chile peppers: dried red, fresh
    green (e.g., jalapeño)
cilantro
clove
coconut
coleslaw (key ingredient)
coriander
corned beef
cream
cumin
curry leaves
dill
duck
fat: rendered chicken, duck
fennel
fennel seeds
game birds
garlic
ginger

ham
horseradish
jicama
juniper berries
lemon, juice
lime, juice
marjoram
mayonnaise
meats
mushrooms
mustard, esp. Dijon, dry
mustard oil
mustard seeds, black
oil: peanut, sesame
olive oil
olives
ONIONS, ESP. RED
paprika
parsley
pasta
pecans
pepper: black, white
poppy seeds
pork
potatoes
poultry
prosciutto
red pepper flakes
rice

salmon
salt: kosher, sea
savory
shallots
sour cream
soy sauce
spinach
stock, chicken
sugar
tarragon
thyme
tomatoes
vinaigrettes
VINEGAR: champagne, cider, red
    wine, sherry, white wine
wine, white (e.g., Riesling)

CABBAGE, NAPA

(aka Chinese cabbage)
Season: year-round
Weight: light
Volume: quiet
Techniques: bake, braise, grill, marinate (e.g., kimchee), raw, sauté, stew, stir-fry

carrots
cashews
chicken

Cabbage often has the connotation of being heavy, but in the fall, we'll make a fine chiffonade of cabbage that's very light. I like to cut cabbage thin and roast it in a pan so that the edges just get brown because that tastes really good. We figured that out by mistake by putting cabbage into too hot a pan. After the chef raised his voice about how that is the wrong way to cook cabbage, we tasted it, and it was good! We now serve a green cabbage dish cooked this way with caraway seeds and walnuts, then deglazed with Calvados. We also add a little cider vinegar and olive oil to finish. It is a nice, easy marriage. It is not an unpredictable marriage; these things just all work together. We pair this with braised pork belly, but it would also work with a roasted breast of squab with its leg done in a confit.

— **MICHAEL ANTHONY,** GRAMERCY TAVERN (NEW YORK CITY)

I like coming up with spins using Asian ingredients — such as soaking **napa cabbage** in ice water to crisp it and serving it with a blue cheese dressing as if it were iceberg lettuce.

— **TONY LIU,** AUGUST (NEW YORK CITY)

chile peppers, jalapeño
Chinese cuisine
cilantro
coleslaw, Asian-style
cucumber
duck
fish, salmon
garlic
ginger
mint
mushrooms (e.g., shiitakes)
oil, sesame
orange, juice
pork

scallions
seafood
sesame seeds
scallops
shellfish: shrimp
soups
soy sauce
stews
stir-fries
Thai basil
tofu
vinegar, rice
wine, rice

CABBAGE, RED

Season: autumn–winter
Techniques: braise, marinate, raw

APPLES: Golden Delicious, Rome, tart
bacon
bay leaf
butter, unsalted
caraway seeds
cheese: blue, goat, Gorgonzola, ricotta salata

Dishes

Pommery Grain Mustard Ice Cream, Red Cabbage Gazpacho

— Heston Blumenthal, The Fat Duck (England)

Dishes

Sautéed Strawberries in Black Pepper–Cabernet Sauvignon Sauce
with Vanilla Bean Ice Cream and Sacristan Cookie

— Lissa Doumani and Hiro Sone, Terra (St. Helena, California)

chestnuts
cider, apple
cilantro
cream
cumin
fat: duck, goose
fruit, tart
game: rabbit, venison
game birds, pheasant
garlic
honey
lemon, juice
lime, juice
meats
mustard
nutmeg
oil, peanut
olive oil
onions: red, white
pancetta
parsley, flat-leaf
pepper, black
poultry
red pepper flakes
salt, kosher
scallions
stock, chicken
SUGAR: BROWN, WHITE
VINEGAR: balsamic, cider, red
    wine, rice wine, sherry, white
    wine
wine, dry red

Flavor Affinities

red cabbage + apples + cider vinegar
red cabbage + bacon + blue cheese + walnuts
red cabbage + balsamic vinegar + brown sugar
red cabbage + chestnuts + pork
red cabbage + duck fat + goat cheese + red wine vinegar
red cabbage + pancetta + ricotta salata cheese

CABBAGE, SAVOY

Season: autumn–winter
Techniques: boil, braise, raw, roast, steam

apples
bacon
butter, unsalted
carrots
cream
crème fraîche
garlic
leeks
lemon, juice
oil, peanut
olive oil
onions
parsley, flat-leaf
parsnips
pepper, black
potatoes
raisins, golden
salt, kosher
stock
thyme
turnips
vinegar, cider
walnuts

CABERNET SAUVIGNON

Weight: heavy red wine
Volume: loud

beef
cheese, esp. aged, blue, and/or
    stinky
game
game birds
lamb
meat, red
pepper, black
steak
strawberries

CAJUN CUISINE

cayenne
celery
chiles
crayfish
gumbo
jambalaya
onions
peppers
rice
seafood
tomatoes

CALAMARI (See Squid)

CALF'S LIVER (See Liver, Calf's)

CALVADOS

Season: winter
Weight: medium–heavy
Volume: moderate–loud
Tips: Generally an after-dinner drink.

apples
bitters, orange

French cuisine
gin
lemon, juice
orange, juice
pears
rum
sugar
vermouth, sweet

CANADIAN CUISINE

bacon, back (aka Canadian bacon)
beer
berries, esp. wild
cheese
duck
fiddlehead ferns
foie gras
game
game birds
maple syrup
meats, esp. smoked
mushrooms, wild
oysters
rabbit
salmon
seafood
wild rice
wine: ice wine, Riesling

CANTALOUPE

Season: summer
Taste: sweet
Weight: light–medium
Volume: moderate

basil
cilantro
curry powder
ginger
grapefruit
lemon, juice
lemongrass
lime, juice
melon: honeydew, watermelon

Dishes

Cantaloupe "Sashimi," Raspberry Gel, and Star Anise Dust
— Dominique and Cindy Duby, Wild Sweets (Vancouver)

mint
pepper: black, white
port
raspberries
star anise
tarragon
wine, esp. sweet
wine, Pinot Blanc (to accompany)
yogurt

CANTONESE CUISINE
(See Chinese Cuisine)

CAPERS

Taste: salty, sour, pungent
Weight: light
Volume: loud

almonds
anchovies
artichokes
arugula
basil
beans, green
butter sauces
celery
chicken
eggplant
eggs
fish
French cuisine, esp. southern
garlic
Italian cuisine, esp. southern
lamb
lemon, juice
lime
marjoram
meats, esp. richer ones, e.g.,
    rib eye steaks
Mediterranean cuisine
mustard
olives
onions
oregano

parlsey, flat-leaf
pasta
pork
potatoes
poultry
rabbit
salads
salmon
sauces, esp. Italian cuisine
shellfish, e.g., scallops, shrimp
tapenade (key ingredient)
tarragon
tomatoes
vinaigrettes
vinegar

Flavor Affinities

capers + lemon + marjoram

CARAMEL

Taste: sweet

almonds
APPLES
apricots
bananas
bourbon
cherries
chocolate
cinnamon
coffee and espresso
CREAM AND ICE CREAM
cream cheese
cumin
custard
fruits, tropical
lemon, juice
lime, juice
macadamia nuts
mangoes
nutmeg
passion fruit
peaches
peanuts
pears
pecans
plums
raisins
rhubarb

rum
sesame seeds
VANILLA

CARAWAY SEEDS

Taste: sweet, sour
Weight: light
Volume: medium–loud
Tips: Add late in the cooking process.

apples
Austrian cuisine
beef stew
BREADS, esp. pumpernickel, rye
British cuisine
cabbage
cakes
carrots
cheese (e.g., Liptauer, Muenster)
coleslaw
cookies
coriander
corned beef
cumin
desserts
duck
Eastern European cuisine
fruit
garlic
German cuisine
goose
goulash
Hungarian cuisine
juniper berries
lavender (can substitute for caraway)
marinades
meats
Moroccan cuisine
noodles
onions
parsley, flat-leaf
pork
potatoes
sauerkraut
sausages
soups
stews

thyme
tomatoes
turnips
vegetables, esp. root

CARDAMOM

Taste: sweet, pungent
Function: heating
Weight: medium
Volume: loud
Tips: Add early when cooking.

anise
apples
apricots
Asian cuisine
baked goods (e.g., breads, cakes, cookies)
bananas
beef
beverages, esp. hot
caraway
carrots
chicken, esp. stewed
chickpeas
chile peppers
chocolate
cinnamon
citrus
cloves
coffee
coriander
cream and ice cream
crème anglaise
cumin
curries
custards
dates
desserts, esp. Indian
duck, esp. roasted
fish, e.g., salmon
garam masala, Indian (key ingredient)
ginger
gingerbread
grapefruit
honey
Indian cuisine
Indonesian cuisine

lamb
legumes
lemon: juice, zest
lentils
lime
meats
North African cuisine
orange: juice, zest
paprika
parsnips
pastries
pears
peas
pepper
pistachios
pork
rice and rice dishes
saffron
salmon
Scandinavian cuisine
squash
stews
sugar
sweet potatoes
tea
vanilla
vegetables, root
walnuts
wine (e.g., mulled)
yogurt

CARIBBEAN CUISINES

allspice
bay leaf
chicken
chile peppers
cilantro
cinnamon
cloves
coconut milk
curry
dill
fish
fruits, tropical
garlic
ginger
hot sauce
jerked dishes
lime, juice

molasses
nutmeg
onions
orange
oregano
parsley
pineapple
plantains
rum, esp. dark
shellfish
sugar, brown
tamarind
thyme

Flavor Affinities

cilantro + garlic + onions (aka
    sofrito)
fish + allspice + oil + onions +
    vinegar (aka *escabèche*)

CARROTS

Season: autumn–spring
Botanical relatives: celery,
chervil, dill, fennel, parsley,
parsnips
Function: cooling
Weight: medium
Volume: quiet–moderate
Techniques: boil, braise, grill,
raw, **roast**, sauté, simmer, steam,
stir-fry

allspice
almonds
anise hyssop
apple juice
bacon
basil
bay leaf
beef
brandy
butter, brown
BUTTER, unsalted
carrot juice
celery
chervil
chicken
chile peppers: dried red, fresh
    green (e.g., jalapeño)

Thumbelina **carrots** are something I missed when I moved from working in the country [i.e., Pocantico Hills, New York, where Blue Hill at Stone Barns is located] into Manhattan. Luckily, I recently found these short, fat carrots at the green market. We sauté these carrots over an open fire so that they get a little smoky. When they are cooked, they become soft and creamy. Once cooked, we turn them into a puree with a shot of carrot juice at the last second. We pair this with farro that has been cooked like risotto, then add some pine nuts and more Thumbelina carrots that have been quartered. I don't know what is more seductive: the smooth carrot farro with its light carrot flavor or the carrots themselves that are totally creamy. The dish has no butter or cream but that is not because we are trying to be healthy. The dish just doesn't need it.
— **MICHAEL ANTHONY**, GRAMERCY TAVERN (NEW YORK CITY)

Juices are a great way to freshen up a dish. If you cook a **carrot**, you lose the "carrotiness" of it. If you make a carrot soup with cooked carrots, it doesn't become bright. So now we do a carrot base with cooked organic carrots with tops, onions, garlic, and maybe some ginger and lemongrass. With that base we make a really thick soup and then add carrot juice to it. In the end you have fresh and cooked carrots for a better flavor profile.
— **ANDREW CARMELLINI**, A VOCE (NEW YORK CITY)

I had a salad at a restaurant with grated **carrots** and tarragon leaves with pistachios — and I knew the minute I tasted it that I could adapt this salad to be my own. Instead of grating the carrots, I cut them on the bias and roasted them with a little ginger and *juca* [an African mix made of almonds, pistachios, hazelnuts, and spices]. To finish the salad, I added the whole tarragon leaves, great pistachio oil, and a raita of yogurt and golden raisins. The dish has wonderful colors and texture and those beautiful whole leaves of tarragon which I had never thought to do myself.
— **MONICA POPE**, T'AFIA (HOUSTON)

Carrots — which pair well with allspice, cinnamon, cloves, and cumin — are one of the few vegetables that shine in desserts. When I first came to the U.S. I discovered carrot cake and that you could use carrots for dessert. I have since made carrot ice cream, cookies, and fruit paste. The problem is that most people trust carrot cake but little else. When I am using carrots for dessert, I like to cook them with orange.
— **MICHEL RICHARD**, CITRONELLE (WASHINGTON, DC)

Carrots and parsnips are similar, and I like the depth of flavor that comes from combining them.
— **BRAD THOMPSON**, MARY ELAINE'S AT THE PHOENICIAN (SCOTTSDALE, ARIZONA)

Dishes

Carrot Cake with Peach-Ginger Cream and Saskatoon Berry Compote
— Dominique and Cindy Duby, Wild Sweets (Vancouver)

Carrot Cake with Vanilla Chantilly, Pecan Praline
— Emily Luchetti, pastry chef, Farallon (San Francisco)

Roasted Carrots and Minted Pea Puree, and Moscato Vinegar
— Cory Schreiber, Wildwood (Portland, Oregon)

chives
cilantro
cinnamon
cloves
cod
coriander
crayfish
cream
crème fraîche
cumin (e.g., Indian cuisine)
curry
curry leaves
dill
fennel
fennel seeds
fish
garlic
GINGER
hazelnuts
honey
lamb
leeks
LEMON, juice
lemon balm
lemon verbena
lime, juice (e.g., Indian cuisine)
lovage
mace
MAPLE SYRUP
mint: spearmint, peppermint
mirepoix (key ingredient)
mustard
mustard seeds, black
nutmeg
oil: peanut, sesame
olive oil
onions, esp. green
ORANGE, juice
PARSLEY, FLAT-LEAF
parsnips

peas
pecans
pepper: black, white
pistachios
potatoes
raisins: black, white
meats, roasted
rosemary
rum
sage
salsify
salt: *fleur de sel,* **kosher**
savory
scallops
shallots
spinach
stocks: chicken, vegetable
SUGAR: brown, white (pinch)
tamarind
tarragon
thyme
turnips
veal
vegetables, root
vinaigrette
walnuts
wine, white
yogurt

Flavor Affinities

carrots + celery + onions (aka mirepoix)
carrots + cilantro + lime
carrots + cinnamon + raisins + sugar + walnuts
carrots + cumin + orange
carrots + dill + orange
carrots + lemon juice + olive oil + parsley
carrots + maple syrup + orange
carrots + olive oil + turnips
carrots + pistachios + tarragon
carrots + raisins + yogurt

CASHEWS

Taste: sweet, rich
Function: warming
Weight: medium–heavy
Volume: loud

almonds
apricots
bananas
caramel
cheese
chicken (e.g., Indian cuisine)
chocolate, esp. white
cinnamon
coconut (e.g., Indian cuisine)
coffee / espresso
curries
dates
ginger
grapefruit
guava
honey
Indian cuisine
kiwi fruit
lemon
macadamia nuts
mango
mint
nutmeg
oil, vegetable
papaya
passion fruit
persimmon
pineapple
rice
rum
salads

salt
sauces
sugar: brown, white
vanilla
vegetables, esp. Indian

CATFISH
Weight: medium
Volume: quiet
Techniques: broil, deep-fry, grill, poach, sauté, steam, stir-fry

avocados
bacon
basil
butter, unsalted
cabbage (e.g., coleslaw)
capers
cayenne
chile peppers, chipotle
cilantro
cucumbers
garlic
greens, collard
ham
hush puppies

lemon, juice
oil: peanut, vegetable
olive oil
olives, esp. niçoise
parsley, flat-leaf
pepper: black, Szechuan
pine nuts
potatoes
salt, kosher
Southern cuisine (American)
soy sauce
stock, chicken
sugar
tomatillos
tomatoes
vinaigrette
vinegar, cider
wine, dry white

CAULIFLOWER
Season: autumn–winter
Taste: astringent
Botanical relatives: broccoli, Brussels sprouts, cabbage, collard greens, kale, kohlrabi
Function: cooling

Weight: medium
Volume: moderate
Techniques: boil, braise, deep-fry, gratin, puree, raw, roast, sauté, simmer, steam

anchovies
apples
bay leaf
bell peppers, esp. green (e.g., Indian cuisine)
bread crumbs
broccoli
brown butter
butter, unsalted
capers
cardamom
caviar
celery seeds
CHEESE: blue, cheddar, Comté, Emmental, goat, Gruyère, Parmesan, pecorino
chervil
chile peppers, dried red
chili sauce
chives

Dishes

Variation of Cauliflower with Raisins, Grenobloise Butter, and Fried Pantelleria Capers
— Daniel Boulud, Daniel (New York City)

Cauliflower Panna Cotta Topped with American Paddlefish Caviar and Cockle Emulsion
— Gabriel Kreuther, The Modern (New York City)

Cauliflower Rice Pilaf with Raita
— Vikram Vij and Meeru Dhalwala, Vij's (Vancouver)

The first time I had the combination of **cauliflower** and curry was when I worked with Daniel Boulud, and he used them together in a soup. I didn't grow up liking cauliflower, but I do now when it's well roasted or pureed. It has good water content, which makes for a very smooth puree, and it has a subtle yet distinct flavor. Apple combines well with both, as it adds acidity and crunch while cutting the stronger flavors.

— BRADFORD THOMPSON, MARY ELAINE'S AT THE PHOENICIAN (SCOTTSDALE, ARIZONA)

Our dish of spicy roasted **cauliflower** with pine nuts and lime is cauliflower with lime supremes [skinless lime sections]. I love lime because it has more character than lemon.

— HOLLY SMITH, CAFÉ JUANITA (SEATTLE)

chocolate and cocoa, when
  cauliflower is caramelized
cilantro
coriander
CREAM AND MILK
cumin
currants, dried
curry powder
dill
Eastern Mediterranean cuisine
egg, hard-boiled, esp. yolk
French cuisine
garam masala
GARLIC
ginger
greens
hollandaise sauce
Indian cuisine
leeks
lemon: juice, zest
lime
Mediterranean cuisine
mint
mussels

mustard, esp. Dijon
mustard: oil, seeds
nutmeg
OIL: canola, grapeseed, vegetable
olive oil
olives: black, green
ONIONS: green, red
orange: juice, zest
paprika
parsley, flat-leaf
pasta
PEPPER: BLACK, WHITE
pine nuts
poppy seeds
potatoes, red (e.g., Indian cuisine)
raisins
red pepper flakes
saffron
SALT: KOSHER, SEA
sauces: béchamel, brown butter,
  cheese, cream, hollandaise,
  Mornay
scallions
scallops

shallots
soups
stock, chicken
tarragon
thyme
tomatoes (e.g., Indian cuisine)
truffles, white
turmeric
vinegar: red, white wine
watercress
yogurt (e.g., Indian cuisine)

Flavor Affinities

cauliflower + anchovies + red
  pepper flakes + garlic + olive oil
cauliflower + bread crumbs +
  brown butter + parsley
cauliflower + cilantro + cloves +
  cumin + turmeric
cauliflower + cream + sorrel
cauliflower + curry + apple
cauliflower + curry + vinegar
cauliflower + garlic + mint + pasta
cauliflower + pine nuts + lime

CAVIAR

Season: winter
Taste: salty
Weight: very light
Volume: quiet–loud

blini, esp. whole wheat
bread, esp. toast points
chives
crème fraîche
eggs
French cuisine
lemon
onion, esp. raw
pepper: black, white
potatoes
Russian cuisine
salt
shallots
sour cream
vodka
white chocolate
wine, Champagne

There is an obvious reason why you could argue that white chocolate and **caviar** go together and that is because of the fact that you are pairing fat and salt. The combination, however, runs a lot deeper than that. The amine [organic chemical compounds] levels in caviar and white chocolate are such that the two ingredients almost "melt" together.

— **HESTON BLUMENTHAL,** THE FAT DUCK (ENGLAND)

Dishes

Yellowtail Tuna with Spinach Puree, Potato Salad, and Osetra Caviar and Vodka Sauce
— David Bouley, Danube (New York City)

Scrambled Egg with Lime Crème Fraîche and Sturgeon Caviar
— Thierry Rautureau, Rover's (Seattle)

Royal Ostera Caviar Served with Warm Crepes, Toast, and Crème Fraîche
— Eric Ripert, Le Bernardin (New York City)

Caviar-Pasta: Osetra on a Nest of Tagliolini, Quail Egg, and Bacon Carbonara Sauce
— Eric Ripert, Le Bernardin (New York City)

CAYENNE, GROUND

Taste: piquant
Function: warming
Weight: light
Volume: loud
Tips: Cayenne tastes hotter the more it cooks.

basil
beans
bell peppers
Cajun cuisine
cheese and cheese sauces
chili
cilantro
coriander
corn
crab
Creole cuisine
cumin
eggplant
fish
garlic
Indian cuisine
Italian cuisine
lemon
lobster
meat
Mexican cuisine
oil
onions
potatoes
rice
sardines
sauces
shellfish
soups
stews
tomatoes

AVOID
caviar
delicate flavors
truffles

Using a pinch of **cayenne** is like having a turbo versus a regular engine in your car. The cayenne goes into you so fast it is like creating an engine for your flavors. It will create a certain heat and speedy access to your flavors. I use cayenne in everything. However, it has to be done carefully. It has to be just a pinch at the last minute. If you are using basil, it will make the flavor even stronger.

— **ERIC RIPERT,** LE BERNARDIN (NEW YORK CITY)

Flavor Affinities
cayenne + coriander + cumin + garlic

CELERY

Season: year-round
Taste: astringent
Botanical relatives: carrots
Function: cooling
Weight: light
Volume: moderate–loud
Techniques: boil, braise, cream, gratiné, raw, sauté, steam, stir-fry

basil
bay leaf
beets
butter
capers
carrots
cheese, esp. **blue**, feta, goat, Gruyère, Parmesan, Roquefort
chervil
chicken and other poultry
chickpeas and hummus
chives
cream
cream cheese
curry
dill
eggs, hard-boiled
fish
garlic
legumes
lemon, juice
lovage
mirepoix (key ingredient)
mushrooms, wild
mustard, esp. Dijon

Of all vegetables, **celery** has one of the strongest flavors. To me, it is almost like a truffle. In a mirepoix, you need all the vegetables — but if I could have only one, it would be celery. I love its earthy flavor. Celery and black truffles are my favorite combination. They work in part because they come out of the ground at the same time of year. Any root vegetable also works with celery. I enjoy celery root and celery separately as well as together.

— DANIEL HUMM, ELEVEN MADISON PARK (NEW YORK CITY)

olive oil
onions, esp. red
paprika
parsley
peanuts and peanut butter
pepper, white
potatoes
rice
salads: chicken, potato, shrimp, tuna
salt
scallions
shallots
shellfish
stir-fried dishes
stocks: chicken, vegetable
stuffings
tarragon
thyme
tomatoes and tomato juice
truffles, black
turnips
vinegar: tarragon, wine

Flavor Affinities
celery + carrots + onions (aka mirepoix)
celery + tarragon + vinegar

CELERY ROOT
Season: autumn–spring
Weight: medium–heavy
Volume: moderate
Techniques: boil, deep-fry, raw, roast, steam
Tips: Always peel before using.

allspice
apples

basil
bay leaf
beef
beets
brown butter
butter
capers
carrots
celery
celery leaves
cheese: Gruyère, Parmesan, Swiss
chervil
chicken
chives
coriander
cream
crème fraîche
dill
fennel leaves
fennel seeds
garlic
leeks
LEMON, JUICE
lovage
game birds
garlic
hazelnuts
marjoram
MAYONNAISE
mushrooms
MUSTARD, DIJON
nutmeg
oil: peanut, sesame, walnut
olive oil
olives

Dishes
Celery Root Soup with Spiced Pumpernickel Bread, Confit Shallot, and Parsley Emulsion
— Charlie Trotter, Charlie Trotter's (Chicago)

onions
oregano
paprika
parsley
parsnips
pecans
pepper, black
POTATOES, ESP. MASHED
rice
rutabagas
sage
salads, esp. green, tuna
salt, kosher
seafood
soups
stews
stocks: chicken, vegetable
tarragon
thyme
truffles, esp. black
turnips
veal
vegetables, root
vinaigrette
vinegar: cider, wine
watercress
wild rice

Flavor Affinities
celery root + cream + potatoes + vinegar
celery root + lemon + mayonnaise + mustard

CELERY SALT
Bloody Marys
eggs, hard-boiled
Tabasco sauce

CELERY SEED
Taste: bitter, pungent
Function: heating
Weight: light
Volume: moderate

allspice
bay leaf
beef
breads
Cajun/Creole cuisines
cheese, e.g., blue
chervil
chicken
coriander
crab
dill
eggplant
eggs
fennel seeds
fish
German cuisine
ginger
Italian cuisine
mayonnaise
mushrooms
mustard
onions
paprika
peas
pepper
potatoes
Russian cuisine
salads and salad dressings
sauces
shellfish
soups
stews
stuffing
thyme
tomatoes
vegetables and vegetable juices
Worcestershire sauce

CHAMOMILE
Taste: sweet

Asian cuisine
chicken
chocolate, white
desserts
fish (e.g., halibut)
honey
lemon

rice
tea
veal

CHAMPAGNE
Weight: light–medium
Volume: quiet–moderate

blackberries
caviar
cherries
cranberries
lemon
lime
melon
mint
raspberries
strawberries

CHARD (aka Swiss chard)
Season: year-round
Taste: bitter
Weight: medium–heavy
Volume: moderate–loud
Techniques: boil, braise, parboil,
sauté, steam, stir-fry

anchovies
bacon
basil
bay leaf
bread crumbs
butter, unsalted
capers
cheese: Fontina, Gruyère,
   Parmesan
chickpeas
chile peppers
cilantro
cumin
cured meats
egg dishes
eggs, hard-boiled
*GARLIC
Italian cuisine, esp. pasta
lamb, esp. chops
leeks
lemon: juice, zest

mushrooms, chanterelle
oil, peanut
olive oil
olives
onions, esp. spring or yellow
orange, zest
oregano
pasta (including using to color
   green pasta)
pepper: black, white
pine nuts
polenta
potatoes
raisins
red pepper flakes
saffron
salt, kosher
shallots
spinach
stews
stocks: chicken, vegetable
thyme
tomatoes
vinegar: balsamic, red wine

Flavor Affinities
chard + bell peppers + pecorino
   cheese + eggplant
chard + red pepper flakes +
   lemon juice

CHARDONNAY
Weight: medium–heavy
Volume: quiet–loud

butter and butter sauces
chicken
crab
cream and cream sauces
fish
lobster
salmon
scallops
shellfish
veal

CHEESE — IN GENERAL

(See also specific cheeses)

Taste: sweet–sour

Function: cooling

apples
breads, esp. neutral-flavored
celery, esp. with cheese sauces
   and dishes
cherries, esp. with soft cheeses
cured meats, esp. ham
dates, esp. Medjool
dried fruits, esp. dates, figs
grapes
nuts, esp. hazelnuts, walnuts
pears

CHEESE, ASIAGO

almonds
bacon
figs

Since **cheese** is a near-perfect food, I sometimes look for the few nutrients missing in cheese that can be found in other foods. The two essential nutrients that cheese does not provide are vitamin C and fiber. This recommends fruits especially — and makes a great start to the day: cheese, some high-fiber vitamin C–rich fruit, some whole grain organic bread, and coffee. The breads I prefer with cheese are usually neutral flavored, though I fully appreciate the nutty or herbed or fruity breads as natural partners for cheeses. The main reason I prefer neutral flavors in my breads is because I don't want to meddle with the flavors in the cheeses themselves. I'm kind of a purist on that! Usually, the softer the cheese, the harder the bread — to an extent. And high-pectin, high-fiber fruits [e.g., apples, pears, apricots, plums, nectarines, peaches, figs] make natural accompaniments for many, many cheeses.

Which cheeses? My faves with my espresso to which I add a little unfiltered raw honey would be the pressed sheep milk cheeses: Ossau Iraty, Roncal, Zamorano, Berkswell, Spenwood, Trade Lake Cedar, Vermont Shepherd, manchego, or Pecorino Foglie Noce. But I'm happy with whatever is looking good, and preferably the harder aged cheeses: sheep, goat, or cow.

— **MAX McCALMAN,** ARTISANAL CHEESE CENTER (NEW YORK CITY)

With aged or strong **cheese**, you need something fruity or sweet to contrast with the strong flavor. Pecorino is very strong, so you need something sweet with it. With an aged or hard cheese, I like to serve some chestnut honey, a fruit jam, or watermelon confiture. If I have some aged goat cheese, I like a *mostarda* [Italian mustard fruit]. With sharper cheese, I also like a nice sweet wine, especially an Italian Passito. With fresh young cheese, I simply like some good bread. Chestnut honey, while good with aged cheese, does not work with a young cheese.

— **ODETTE FADA**, SAN DOMENICO (NEW YORK CITY)

Honey, jam, and *mostarda* go great with **cheese**. Most honey works best with younger cheeses and soft-ripened cheeses, especially if they have a chalky quality to them. I love mountain Gorgonzola with chestnut honey; it is crazy! In Italy, we call jam a *confitura* or *marmalata*. I like it with saltier cheeses like Parmesan, or with more assertive cheeses. *Mostarda* is made of fruits cooked in a white wine mustard syrup until they are candied. So, you have a sweet candy effect with the spicy mustard. It goes with any savory firm cheese, and particularly well with pecorino and Taleggio.

— **GINA DEPALMA**, BABBO (NEW YORK CITY)

grapes
Italian cuisine
pasta
potatoes
salads

CHEESE, AZEITAO
foie gras

CHEESE, BLUE (See also Gorgonzola, Roquefort, Stilton, etc.)
almonds
apples
beef
bread, esp. with nuts and/or raisins
celery
chestnuts, roasted
cream cheese
dill
figs, esp. with Gorgonzola
garlic
hazelnuts
HONEY, esp. chestnut or tupelo
mustard, Dijon

pasta
PEARS, esp. with Stilton
port
potatoes
salt, kosher
sour cream
steaks
vinegar, white wine
walnut bread
walnuts, esp. with Stilton
walnuts, candied
watercress

CHEESE, BRIE
almonds
apples
bread, esp. French
cherries
chicken

crudités (e.g., raw carrots, celery)
dates
fennel
figs
French cuisine
nuts
melon
onions
pears
pistachios
strawberries
white wine

CHEESE, BURRATA
beans, fava
bread
garlic
Italian cuisine
olive oil
peaches
pesto
plums
salt, esp. sea
tomatoes
vincotto (cooked wine)

CHEESE, CABRALES
figs
grapes, esp. red
ham, Serrano
honey
pears
salads
steak

CHEESE, CAMEMBERT
arugula
fruit, fresh
grapes
lettuces (e.g., baby greens)
melon

Dishes
Baked Blue Cheesecake Mousse with Rhubarb Compote and Celery Confit
— Dominique and Cindy Duby, Wild Sweets (Vancouver)

Bruschetta with Burrata Cheese, Caponata, and Fava Bean Puree
— Hiro Sone, Terra (St. Helena, California)

A wonderful combination I discovered recently that surprised me was **Azeitao cheese** with foie gras.
— MAX McCALMAN, ARTISANAL CHEESE CENTER (NEW YORK CITY)

I like **blue cheese**, either Roquefort or Stilton, served simply with a walnut bread and a glass of port.
— GABRIEL KREUTHER, THE MODERN (NEW YORK CITY)

In general, the more intense a **blue cheese** is in its own right, the lighter and more delicate the honey you'll want to pair it with. I like Colorado star thistle honey [which is creamy, with cinnamon notes].
— ADRIAN MURCIA, CHANTERELLE (NEW YORK CITY)

nuts
olive oil
pears
pecans
plums
salads
strawberries
vinegar: balsamic, sherry

CHEESE, CHEDDAR
APPLES
bacon
brandy, apple, e.g., Calvados
bread, esp. French, pumpernickel, or whole wheat
butter, unsalted
cayenne
chutney, Indian
cider
cream
dates
egg dishes
fennel
garlic
grapes
hamburgers
honey, esp. fruit (e.g., blueberry, raspberry)
mirepoix, esp. for soup

mostarda (mustard fruits)
nuts
oil, vegetable
paprika
pasta, esp. macaroni
pears and pear paste
pecans
pepper, black
potatoes
quince paste
stock, chicken
thyme
walnuts

CHEESE, COLBY
apples
bacon
beer
bread, rye
cider, apple
onions
pears
potatoes

CHEESE, COMTÉ
ham
hazelnut oil
greens, salad

Cheddar is a particularly friendly **cheese** to food pairing partners.
— ADRIAN MURCIA, CHANTERELLE (NEW YORK CITY)

CHEESE, COW'S MILK — IN GENERAL
cherries
fruits, stone (e.g., apricots, cherries, nectarines, peaches, plums, etc.)
melons

CHEESE, CREAM
(See Cream Cheese)

CHEESE, EMMENTAL
bacon
bread, rye, esp. lighter
potatoes

CHEESE, ÉPOISSES
cherries
marmalade, citrus
pears

CHEESE, EXPLORATEUR
pomegranate

CHEESE, FETA
bell peppers, red
bread: olive, pita
cheese, ricotta
chickpeas
dill
Eastern Mediterranean cuisine
eggplant
figs
garlic
grapes
Greek cuisine
honey
lamb
lemon
meats, grilled
mint
olive oil
olives: black, Greek
onions, red
pasta
pepper, black
sage

salads
sauces
shrimp
spinach
thyme
vinegar, red wine
walnuts
watermelon
zucchini

Flavor Affinities
feta cheese + chicken + mint
feta cheese + roasted red bell
   peppers + mint
feta cheese + salad greens + mint

CHEESE, FONTINA
chutney
endive
fondue
fruit, fresh
grapes
mostarda (mustard fruits)
pears
plums
salads
sandwiches
walnuts

CHEESE, FROMAGE BLANC
cranberries, sweetened
figs

CHEESE, GARROTXA
figs

CHEESE, GOAT'S MILK — IN GENERAL
almonds
honey
nuts
oil, walnut
olive oil
olives
pepper, black
pomegranate
thyme

I enjoy the combination of cherries with Lancashire [a premier English cow's milk **cheese**].
— MAX McCALMAN, ARTISANAL CHEESE CENTER (NEW YORK CITY)

Dishes
Goat Cheese Tortelloni with Dried Orange and Wild Fennel Pollen
— Mario Batali, Babbo (New York City)

Rich Goat's Milk Cheesecake with Blossom Honey Ice Cream, Fuyu Persimmons, and Huckleberries
— Elizabeth Dahl, pastry chef, Naha (Chicago)

Mixed Green Salad with Coach Farm's Triple Crème Goat Cheese, Toasted Pumpkin Seeds, and Apple Cider Vinegar
— Gabriel Kreuther, The Modern (New York City)

Goat Cheese Salad: Braised Fennel, Toasted Hazelnuts, Orange, and Extra-Virgin Olive Oil
— Alfred Portale, Gotham Bar and Grill (New York City)

CHEESE, GOAT — FRESH (e.g., chèvre)
almonds
apples, esp. green
apricots, esp. dried
basil
beets
bell peppers: green, esp. **red**
blackberries
bread, esp. French or with nuts, olives, and/or raisins, whole wheat
broccoli
butter
cauliflower
cheese: Parmesan, ricotta
cherries, sour or sweet
chervil
chives
cinnamon
cranberries, esp. dried
cream
dates
eggs
fennel
fennel seeds
figs
garlic
grapes
greens, salad, esp. arugula
herbs
honey

I enjoy pomegranate with my Ibores [a Spanish goat's milk **cheese**].
— MAX McCALMAN, ARTISANAL CHEESE CENTER (NEW YORK CITY)

Dishes
Almond-Infused Goat's Milk Cheesecake
— Carrie Nahabedian, Naha (Chicago)

Mediterranean "Greek Salad" of Mt. Vikos Feta, Kalamata Olives, Plum Tomatoes, Cucumbers, Torn Mint and Oregano, Warm Feta Cheese "Turnover"
— Carrie Nahabedian, Naha (Chicago)

I will pair thyme with **goat cheese** and cherries.

— **MICHAEL LAISKONIS,** LE BERNARDIN (NEW YORK CITY)

If you are going to make a dessert with cheese, you want it to be a softer cheese. I make a **goat cheese** cake with berries and for that I use a milder goat cheese. Goat cheese and lemon work really well together, because the acidity of the lemon juice cuts the fat of the goat cheese.

— **EMILY LUCHETTI,** FARALLON (SAN FRANCISCO)

I like strawberries with my Loire Valley **chèvres.**

— **MAX McCALMAN,** ARTISANAL CHEESE CENTER (NEW YORK CITY)

LEMON, juice
milk
mint
nutmeg
nuts
oil, sesame
olive oil
olives
onions, esp. green, Spanish, or Vidalia

orange: juice, zest
parsley, flat-leaf
pasta
pears: dried, fresh
pecans
pepper: black, white
pesto
pine nuts
pistachios
port

potatoes
raspberries
red pepper flakes
rosemary
rum, esp. light
sage
salami
salt, sea
shallots
sour cream
star anise
strawberries
sugar: brown, white
thyme
vegetables, raw
vinegar, cider
tarragon
thyme
tomatoes and tomato jam
vanilla
vinegar: balsamic, sherry
walnuts

Flavor Affinities

goat cheese + almonds + honey + pears
goat cheese + cherries + thyme
goat cheese + fennel seeds + orange zest + pasta
goat cheese + honey + persimmons
goat cheese + pancetta + shallots

Some enjoy the combination of chocolate and cheese. If the idea intrigues you, I recommend trying a good dark chocolate with an aged Alpine cheese [a style native to the French and Swiss Alps, of which **Gruyère** is one of the most famous], such as Hoch Ybrig, Appenzeller, or Prattigauer.

— **MAX McCALMAN**, ARTISANAL CHEESE CENTER (NEW YORK CITY)

Swiss mountain cheeses [e.g., Appenzeller, Comté, **Gruyère**] are a cheese snob's Holy Grail of cheeses. Their "cooked milk" character makes them great with dark, cooked fruit preserves such as fig preserves. They also go well with oloroso sherry, which has its own dark, cooked fruit flavors.

— **ADRIAN MURCIA**, CHANTERELLE (NEW YORK CITY)

CHEESE, GORGONZOLA

apples
brandy
cherries: sour, sweet
cognac
corn
cream
dulce de leche
figs
grapes
honey, esp. chestnut
Italian cuisine
mint
nuts
olive oil
pasta
PEARS
pistachios
pomegranate
prosciutto
salads (e.g., spinach)
sugar
thyme
WALNUTS
wine, sweet

Flavor Affinities

Gorgonzola + mint + walnuts

CHEESE, GOUDA

apples, esp. with aged and/or
   smoked cheese
apricots
cherries, esp. with young cheese
melon
mushrooms
peaches, esp. with young cheese
pears, esp. with aged or smoked
   cheese
spinach

CHEESE, GRUYÈRE

apples
arugula
bread
cherries
chicken
chocolate, dark, esp. with aged
   Gruyère
fondues
garlic
ham
hazelnuts
onions
soufflés
soups, esp. onion
spinach

I enjoy raspberries with my **Hoja Santa**, with a little mint thrown in.

— **MAX McCALMAN**, ARTISANAL CHEESE CENTER (NEW YORK CITY)

Swiss cuisine
thyme
walnuts

CHEESE, HOJA SANTA

mint
raspberries

CHEESE, JACK

almonds
figs
pears
pecans
prunes
quince paste
walnuts

CHEESE, MAHON

(aged Spanish cheese)
quince paste

CHEESE, MANCHEGO

ALMONDS, esp. roasted
   Spanish
anchovies
bell peppers, roasted
**bread, esp. crusty and fig or
   other fruit bread**
figs and fig cake
ham, Serrano
olive oil
olives, green or black Spanish
onions, esp. caramelized
parsley
peppers, piquillo
plum paste
***QUINCE PASTE**
salads
Spanish cuisine
tomatoes

Flavor Affinities

manchego cheese + almonds +
   quince paste

CHEESE, MASCARPONE
(See Mascarpone)

CHEESE, MONTEREY JACK
chicken
enchiladas
fresh fruit

CHEESE, MOZZARELLA
anchovies
BASIL
bell peppers, roasted
garlic
Italian cuisine
meats, cured (e.g., salami)
olive oil

olives
oregano
pancetta
pasta
pepper, black
pizza
prosciutto
radicchio
rosemary
sage
salt: kosher, sea
sopressata

spinach
*TOMATOES
tomatoes, sun-dried
truffles, black
vinegar: balsamic, red wine

Dishes

Mozzarella di Bufala, Eggplant Agrodolce, Artichoke con Pesto
— Andrew Carmellini, A Voce (New York City)

Flavor Affinities
mozzarella cheese + basil + olive
  oil + tomatoes
mozzarella cheese + olives +
  prosciutto

CHEESE, MUENSTER

apples
bread, crusty
caraway seeds
cherries
fennel
grapes

CHEESE, PARMESAN

basil
beans, fava
carpaccio
dates
fennel
figs
fruits, stone
garlic
grapes
honey, esp. chestnut
ITALIAN CUISINE
melon
mushrooms
olive oil
PASTA
pears
pizza
prosciutto
risottos
thyme
vinegar, balsamic, esp. aged
walnuts

If you open my refrigerator at home, you will always find a piece of cheese! I love many cheeses, but there will definitely be a piece of **Parmigiano-Reggiano.** It never goes bad and is so versatile. I can cut a piece off to go with a glass of Prosecco as an apéritif, serve it after dinner with red wine, slice a piece for a sandwich, or grate it over some pasta.
— **ODETTE FADA,** SAN DOMENICO (NEW YORK CITY)

I was in Parma, Italy, in a restaurant and out came my glass of Prosecco followed by the server cutting off hunks of **Parmigiano-Reggiano** to serve me. I thought it was a beautiful way to begin!
It is a way to leave your world behind, and begin your meal.
— **HOLLY SMITH,** CAFÉ JUANITA (SEATTLE)

Dishes

Parmesan Broth with Prosciutto and Peas, Scallion Parmesan Flan
— Sanford D'Amato, Sanford (Milwaukee)

CHEESE, PECORINO

bacon
bell peppers, roasted
duck confit
grapes
greens, salad
honey, chestnut
lemon, juice
mostarda (mustard fruits)
olive oil
pasta
pears
pepper, white
prosciutto
ricotta cheese
sopressata
vinegar, balsamic, esp. aged
walnuts

CHEESE, PIAVE

cured meats

CHEESE, PROVOLONE

figs
grapes
Italian cuisine

Piave cheese works with an array of different cured meats.
— **MAX McCALMAN,** ARTISANAL CHEESE CENTER (NEW YORK CITY)

lime, juice
olive oil
olives
pasta (e.g., lasagna)
pears
pizza
prosciutto

CHEESE, REBLOCHON

fennel
panforte (Italian fruit and nut cake)
pistachios

CHEESE, RICOTTA

almonds
apricots
bacon
basil
beans, fava
berries
blueberries
bread
cheese: mozzarella, Parmesan, pecorino
cheesecake
chestnuts
chives
chocolate, dark
cinnamon
coffee / espresso
cream
dates
egg dishes (e.g., frittatas, omelets)
figs, esp. dried
fruits, dried
garlic
hazelnuts
herbs
HONEY, esp. chestnut, eucalyptus, or lavender
Italian cuisine
lemon, esp. juice, zest
mace
mascarpone
nutmeg
olive oil
orange, esp. juice, zest

Gina DePalma of New York's Babbo on Babbo's Cheese Plate

At Babbo, I oversee the cheese selection, which has seven choices. The biggest challenge with Italian cheese is that there are so many "superstars" that you just can't *not* offer them. So, in the seven slots we have many standard choices but they are amazing:

- **Parmigiano-Reggiano:** This is the "undisputed king of all cheeses" according to Mario [Batali]!
- **Taleggio:** This washed-rind cheese is very wet, has the distinctive orange color, and is gooey. The interior is sweet and the rind is assertive.
- **Gorgonzola Piccante:** This is firmer, bluer, nutty, and just amazing!
- **Coach Farm Goat:** Though it is not from Italy, it is the goat cheese we choose. [Mario Batali's wife's family owns the Coach Farm Dairy.]
- **Robiola:** This is a soft-ripened cheese from Piedmont.
- **Pecorino:** This is a sheep's milk cheese that is nothing like the Pecorino-Romano that you get in your deli to grate over pasta. This is made in many areas around Italy. We may use one from the south or Tuscany or one that is rubbed with tomato or aged underground from another part of the country.
- **The Seventh Cheese:** I play around with the seventh cheese and change it often but a recent favorite is a **Piave**, which is like an English Cheddar. It is from the Veneto along the Piave River.

parsley, flat-leaf
pasta
pepper, black
pine nuts
prosciutto
Prosecco
prunes
raisins
raspberries

rum, esp. dark
salt, kosher
sorrel
spinach
strawberries
sugar
tapenade
tarragon
tomatoes
vanilla
vinegar, balsamic
walnuts, esp. candied or toasted
wine, red, sweet

Flavor Affinities

ricotta + bread + honey + Prosecco

On our brunch menu with our corn and saffron pancakes, we serve fresh **ricotta** to be used instead of butter.
— BRAD FARMERIE, PUBLIC (NEW YORK CITY)

CHEESE, ROQUEFORT

butter, unsalted
cognac
cream

figs
honey
leeks
oil, walnut
pears
pepper
potatoes, creamer
salt
vinaigrette
walnuts
wine: red, **SAUTERNES**

Flavor Affinities

Roquefort cheese + figs + pears

CHEESE, SHEEP'S MILK — IN GENERAL

almonds
apricots
bread, esp. olive
ham, esp. Serrano
honey
nuts
olive oil
olives
panforte
pepper, black
quince paste

Dishes

Bruschetta with Favas and New York State Ricotta
— Mario Batali, Babbo (New York City)

Sheep's Milk Ricotta Ravioli with Heirloom Tomato, Arugula, Vin Cotto
— Andrew Carmellini, A Voce (New York City)

Ricotta and Robiola Cheesecake with Figs and Raspberries
— Gina DePalma, pastry chef, Babbo (New York City)

Corn and Saffron Pancakes with a Spicy Poached Pear and Fresh Ricotta
— Brad Farmerie, Public (New York City)

Bellwether Farms Ricotta Fritters with Cara Cara and Blood Orange Compote, Vanilla Crème Anglaise
— Emily Luchetti, pastry chef, Farallon (San Francisco)

Ricotta Gnocchi with Fava Beans, Sage, and Lemon Oil
— Judy Rodgers, Zuni Café (San Francisco)

I'm a fan of apricot with Berkswell [an English **sheep's milk cheese**].
— **MAX McCALMAN,** ARTISANAL CHEESE CENTER (NEW YORK CITY)

CHEESE, SPANISH
(See Cheese: Cabrales, Manchego)

CHEESE, STILTON
apples
dates
honey
pears
pecans
port
salads
sauces
walnuts

CHEESE, SWISS
asparagus
bread, esp. pumpernickel
grapes
ham
pears

CHEESE, TALEGGIO
hazelnuts
mostarda (mustard fruits)
pears

CHEESE, TRIPLE CRÈME
cherries
figs
hazelnuts
herbs
honey
mostarda (mustard fruits)
nut bread
olives
pears
vegetables, roasted
walnuts

CHEESE, VACHERIN
cherries
hazelnuts

CHEESE, VALDEON
meats: cured, smoked
steak

CHEESE, VERMONT SHEPHERD
almonds
apples
fennel

CHERRIES — IN GENERAL
Season: late spring–late summer
Taste: sweet
Weight: light–medium
Volume: moderate
Techniques: flambé, poach, raw, stew

allspice
ALMONDS
amaretto
apricots
Armagnac
bourbon
brandy
butter, unsalted
buttermilk
cake
caramel
cassis
cheese: Brie, goat, ricotta
cherries, dried
CHOCOLATE, ESP. DARK, WHITE
cinnamon
cloves
coconut
coffee / espresso
cognac
coriander
CREAM AND ICE CREAM
cream cheese
crème fraîche
crust: pastry, pie

currants, red
custards (e.g., crème caramel, flan, etc.)
duck
fennel
figs
game birds
garlic
ginger
goose
Grand Marnier
hazelnuts
honey
ice cream, vanilla
***KIRSCH**
LEMON: juice, zest
lime, juice
liqueur: almond, orange
mascarpone
meats, fatty, esp. roasted
melon
meringue
nectarines
nuts
oats
orange: juice, zest
pâté
peaches
pecans
pepper: black, green
pistachios
plums
pork
port, esp. ruby
poultry, fatty, esp. roasted
quince
raspberries
rice pudding
rose hips
rum
sage, esp. with tart cherries
salads
salt
sour cream
stocks: chicken, duck, veal
SUGAR
VANILLA
vermouth, sweet

vinegar: balsamic, ice wine, red wine
vodka
walnuts
WINE: dry red (e.g., Bordeaux, Merlot), sparkling wine/Champagne
yogurt

Flavor Affinities
cherries + almonds + cream + kirsch + vanilla
cherries + chocolate + walnuts
cherries + coconut + custard
cherries + coffee + cream
cherries + goat cheese + ice wine vinegar + black pepper + thyme
cherries + honey + pistachios + yogurt
cherries + mint + vanilla
cherries + orange + sugar + dry red wine
cherries + sweet vermouth + vanilla

Cherries can stand up to a lot of flavors. They have more juice to them as well as complexity. Almonds go with cherries. Dark chocolate actually goes better with cherries than it does raspberries, and white chocolate works with cherries as well.
— **EMILY LUCHETTI,** FARALLON (SAN FRANCISCO)

If you have perfect ingredients in the summertime, you don't have to do much to them. With our perfect **cherries** [Michigan, while at Tribute restaurant], we halved them, sprinkled them with sugar, and heated them with a blowtorch so that they were just warmed through. The slightly caramelized sugar made a huge difference in the flavor. I used a goat cream cheese worked to a texture similar to mascarpone cheese, which I shaped into quenelles. Served alongside were some ice wine vinegar caramel sauce and a crispy crepe. Before serving, I added individual thyme leaves and a crack of black pepper. These are all really classic flavors, especially the cheese with black pepper and cherries.

— **MICHAEL LAISKONIS**, LE BERNARDIN (NEW YORK CITY)

I was reading an old Fannie Farmer cookbook from the late 1800s about making **cherry** jam. In the recipe, they would take the cherry pits and crush them. I thought it was crazy but tried it. When you take cherry pits and crush them, it gives you an almond flavor. I made some pickled sour cherries with the crushed pits in cheesecloth with the pickling liquid and I got this great almondy flavor that went deep inside the cherries.

— **ANDREW CARMELLINI**, A VOCE (NEW YORK CITY)

I like to let them shine on their own. But I do really like **cherries** and grappa. Mario [Batali] has a home in Michigan and he brought me back a case of cherries. They were so perfect I just macerated them in grappa and torn mint leaves. I served them in a bowl with a dollop of mascarpone. Cherries also work well with mint.

— **GINA DEPALMA**, BABBO (NEW YORK CITY)

I loved **cherries** so much growing up that I would climb up our cherry tree and eat as many as I could. Then I would realize I didn't know how to get back down and would cry until the neighbors would get me down. I still love cherries and especially in cherry pie or a *clafoutis*. Cherries work well with vanilla or poached in red wine, but I like to keep them as simple as possible.

— **GABRIEL KREUTHER**, THE MODERN (NEW YORK CITY)

Dishes

Cherry-Almond Blancmange over Frangipane and Crème Fraîche Soup
— Dominique and Cindy Duby, Wild Sweets (Vancouver)

Warm Black Garnet Cherry–Rhubarb Pie with Almond Butter Crunch Ice Cream
— Emily Luchetti, pastry chef, Farallon (San Francisco)

Black Garnet Cherries, Strawberries, Pistachios, Marshall Farms Honey, Straus Organic Whole Milk Yogurt
— Emily Luchetti, pastry chef, Farallon (San Francisco)

CHERVIL

Season: spring–autumn
Weight: delicate, soft-leaved
Volume: very quiet
Tips: Always use chervil fresh, not cooked.

asparagus
basil
beans, esp. fava, green
beets
bouquet garni (key ingredient)
carrots
cheese, ricotta
chicken
chives
crab
cream
cream cheese
dill
eggs and egg dishes
fennel
fines herbes (key ingredient, along with chives, parsley, tarragon)
fish
French cuisine
game birds
halibut
herbes de Provence (typical ingredient, along with basil, fennel, marjoram, rosemary, sage, summer savory, and thyme)
leeks
lemon, juice
lemon thyme
lettuce
lobster
marjoram
mint
mushrooms
mustard
parsley
peas
potatoes
poultry

One thing chervil has going for it is its looks. **Chervil** is so cute, it is adorable! You can very carefully make little tiny brushes of them and put them around the plate. Not only does it taste good, but it says to the people eating the dish that you are taking care of them.
— **DAVID WALTUCK,** CHANTERELLE (NEW YORK CITY)

Provençal cuisine
salads, esp. potato, and salad
   dressings
sauces, esp. creamy
scallops
shallots
shellfish
sole
soups, esp. creamy
spinach
squash
tarragon
thyme
tomatoes and tomato sauces
veal
vegetables
venison

vinaigrettes
vinegar
watercress

Flavor Affinities
chervil + chives + fish + parsley
chervil + chives + parsley +
   tarragon (fines herbes)

CHESTNUTS

Season: autumn–winter
Taste: sweet
Weight: medium–heavy
Volume: quiet–moderate
Techniques: boil, candy, grill,
puree, raw, roast

Dishes

Chestnut Spice Cake with Mascarpone Cream
— Gina DePalma, pastry chef, Babbo (New York City)

Chestnut Sugar Tart, Crème Fraîche
— Johnny Iuzzini, pastry chef, Jean Georges (New York City)

I like to take one ingredient and see how much I can do with it. I made a frozen chestnut semifreddo with bits of candied **chestnuts.** This was then set on an orange-soaked chestnut sponge cake, next to a chestnut wafer and chestnut paste. I needed a complementary flavor, and I have always liked the combination of pear and chestnut. They both have a richness but depending on how the pear is handled, it can add freshness and acidity. I roasted the pear in sugar, butter, and ice wine vinegar and finished it in the oven until soft. The pear was then diced tartare-like and had orange confit added. The juices from the pear were the only sauce.
— **MICHAEL LAISKONIS,** LE BERNARDIN (NEW YORK CITY)

Chestnuts have a bursty flavor and they work with chocolate and pears. You have to combine them with earthy flavors. If you paired chestnuts with berries, they would just get lost.
— **EMILY LUCHETTI,** FARALLON (SAN FRANCISCO)

APPLES: CIDER, FRUIT, JUICE
Armagnac
bacon
bay leaf
brandy
Brussels sprouts
butter, unsalted
caramel
cardamom
celery
celery root
celery seeds
cheese, ricotta
chicken (accompaniment)
chocolate, esp. dark or white
cinnamon
cloves
coffee
cognac
CREAM OR MILK
crème fraîche
desserts
duck
fennel
fennel seeds
figs
game (accompaniment)
ginger
ham
honey, esp. chestnut
Italian cuisine, esp. Tuscan
lemon, juice
lentils
maple syrup
mascarpone
meats
mushrooms: cepes/porcini
nutmeg
olive oil
onions
orange
pasta
pears
pepper: black, white
plums
pork (accompaniment)
poultry (e.g., chicken, turkey)
prosciutto
prunes

raisins
raspberries
risotto
rum
sage
salt, sea
sauces
sausages
shallots
sherry
stews
STOCK, CHICKEN
stuffing (e.g., for poultry)
sugar: brown, white
sweet potatoes
thyme
vanilla
wine, esp. sweet Marsala or
    sherry

AVOID
berries

Flavor Affinities
chestnuts + apples + cream
chestnuts + bacon + fennel
chestnuts + crème fraîche + sugar
chestnuts + orange + pear

CHICKEN

Function: heating
Weight: medium
Volume: quiet
Techniques: bake, braise, broil,
deep-fry, grill, poach, roast, sauté,
steam, stew, stir-fry

allspice
almonds
anise
apples
apricots, dried
artichokes
avocadoes
bacon
bananas
BASIL: regular, cinnamon

BAY LEAF
beans: red, white
beer
bell peppers: red, green, yellow
bouquet garni
brandy, esp. apple (in sauce)
bread crumbs or *panko*
BUTTER, UNSALTED
buttermilk
Calvados
capers
cardamom
CARROTS
cashews (e.g., Indian cuisine,
    etc.)
cauliflower
cayenne
celery
celery root
celery seeds
chard
cheese: Asiago, blue, Comté,
    Emmental, Fontina, Parmesan
chervil
chicken livers
chickpeas
chile peppers: dried red (e.g.,
    chipotle), fresh green (e.g.,
    jalapeño)
chives
cider
cilantro
CINNAMON
cloves
coconut milk (e.g., Indian
    cuisine, etc.)

coriander
corn
cranberries: dried
cream (e.g., French, Indian
    cuisine, etc.)
crème fraîche
cumin
currants
curry leaves (e.g., Indian cuisine)
curry powder
curry sauce
daikon
dates
dill
dumplings
endive
escarole
fenugreek
figs
fines herbes (i.e., chervil, chives,
    parsley, tarragon)
fish sauce, Thai
five-spice powder
galangal
garam masala (e.g., Indian
    cuisine)
GARLIC
GINGER: fresh, ground
Grand Marnier
grapefruit, juice
grapes and grape juice
greens
guava
ham
hazelnuts
hoisin sauce

Red beans and rice with andouille sausage is my favorite! When we opened up after the hurricane [Katrina] and were serving on paper plates, I made a roasted Tabasco **chicken** served with dirty rice, with the sausage stuffed in a bell pepper alongside red bean puree. For another dish, I was inspired by a diner down the street from us that had chicken and waffles on the menu, which is an old Southern dish. My take is to make a savory waffle and to add Boursin cheese with lots of herbs. Then I pair it with chicken thighs braised in a *coq au vin blanc* and serve it with spinach. The dish is simple, but I just love the flavors.
— **BOB IACOVONE,** CUVÉE (NEW ORLEANS)

Dishes

Taquitos de Pollo: Crispy Taquitos Filled with Chicken and Poblanos, with Homemade Sour Cream, Salsa Verde, Añejo Cheese, and Guacamole
— Rick Bayless, Frontera Grill (Chicago)

Chicken Braised in Black Pepper Gravy with Summer Root Vegetables, Hen o' Woods Mushrooms, and Rosemary Cream Biscuits
— Jeffrey Buben, Vidalia (Washington, DC)

Hoffman Ranch Breast of Chicken with Chanterelles and Thyme Jus
— Traci Des Jardins, Jardinière (San Francisco)

Chicken Tagine with Olives, Preserved Lemons, and Green Peas
— Lahsen Ksiyer, Casaville (New York City)

Half a Chicken Cut in Pieces and Braised in a Tequila–White Vinegar Sauce with Green Olives, Golden Raisins, and Almonds
— Zarela Martinez, Zarela (New York City)

"Southern Fried" Chicken Salad, Roasted Sweet Corn, Candied Pecans, Shaved Red Onions, and Buttermilk Ranch Dressing
— Carrie Nahabedian, Naha (Chicago)

Balsamic-Caramel Chicken with Broccoli and Walnuts
— Monica Pope, T'afia (Houston)

Roast Chicken Breast with Wild Mushrooms, Creamy Polenta, and White Truffle Oil
— Alfred Portale, Gotham Bar and Grill (New York City)

Boneless Chicken Breast in Peruvian Adobo Roasted in Our Wood-Burning Oven, Pumpkin and Mango Sauce, Ripe Plantain, and Eggplant Puree
— Maricel Presilla, Cucharamama (Hoboken, New Jersey)

Apricot Curry Chicken Salad with Fennel, Cilantro, and Dried Fruit
— Charlie Trotter, Trotter's to Go (Chicago)

Lemon-Ghee Marinated and Grilled Specialty Chicken Breast with Roasted Garlic and Cashews
— Vikram Vij and Meeru Dhalwala, Vij's (Vancouver)

Roasted Chicken with Green Olive, Coriander, and Ginger Sauce
— Jean-Georges Vongerichten, Jojo (New York City)

honey
kale
leeks
LEMON: juice, zest
lemongrass
lime, juice
mangoes

maple syrup
marjoram
mayonnaise
mint
mirepoix
molasses
MUSHROOMS: cultivated or wild (e.g., cepes, chanterelles, morels, portobello, shiitake, white)
mustard: Dijon, dry, yellow
mustard seeds
nutmeg
nuts: cashews, peanuts
OIL: canola, grapeseed, hazelnut, **peanut**, safflower, sesame, vegetable
OLIVE OIL
OLIVES: black, green, kalamata, niçoise
ONIONS: cipollini, pearl, red, Spanish, spring, sweet
orange: juice, zest
oregano
pancetta
paprika
PARSLEY, FLAT-LEAF (garnish)
parsnips
peaches
peanuts
pears
peas: black-eyed, green
PEPPER: BLACK, PINK, WHITE
pesto
pine nuts
polenta (accompaniment)
pomegranates and pomegranate molasses
poppy seeds
potatoes (accompaniment)
prosciutto
prunes
raisins
red pepper flakes
rice
ROSEMARY, fresh
saffron
sage
SALT: *fleur de sel,* kosher, sea
sauces, Mornay
sausages, esp. spicy (e.g., andouille)
savory

scallions
sesame seeds
shallots
sherry, dry (e.g., manzanilla)
sour cream
soy sauce
spinach
star anise
STOCKS: chicken, veal
sugar: brown, white (pinch)
sweet potatoes
Tabasco sauce
TARRAGON
THYME, FRESH
**TOMATOES AND TOMATO
  PASTE**
truffles
turmeric
turnips
vanilla
vermouth
VINEGAR: balsamic, Chinese
  black, cider, red wine, sherry,
  tarragon, white wine
waffles
whiskey
**WINE: dry to off-dry white (e.g.,
  Riesling), dry red**, rice, sweet
  wine, vermouth
yogurt

Andrew Carmellini of New York's A Voce on Cooking Chicken as a Two-Part Process — and Applying It to Chicken Cacciatore

1. *Brining:* Sometimes the older techniques inspire me for deeper flavors. Many of these techniques are overlooked. Take brining, for instance. Brining has been done forever with pork chops and chicken, and for the last five years you have heard about it with turkey. The success of brining is more about the salt and it getting in there and softening the protein strands. It is less about all the other flavoring agents.

If you want to get started in your kitchen, start with a skin- and bone-on chicken breast. Grab some kosher salt, sugar, or honey as I do, some water, and brine the breast for 30 minutes. When you pull it out of the brine, rinse it, dry it, and let it sit in the refrigerator for a couple of hours so the moisture comes out. You will notice the difference in the texture. The marinated chicken — even if you overcook it — will not be dry. It is the best.

2. *Marinating:* The chicken on my menu right now is brined and then marinated for 24 hours. It is crazy how good the chicken becomes. The marinade is made up of roasted garlic, Sicilian oregano, red pepper flakes, lots of lemon, thyme, and olive oil. We joke that it tastes like Zesty Italian Wish-Bone Dressing. It is so delicious.

The finished dish is served with poached and sautéed artichoke, roasted pepper grilled over wood, fennel, and roasted spring onions. These vegetables are all tossed with pesto, and the dish is finished with a tomato sauce made with foamy tomato water and thyme.

Chicken Cacciatore

We opened up A Voce with chicken cacciatore on our menu and when people heard the name of the dish, they'd just yawn. A lot of times, this dish is just chicken scaloppine with peppers and tomatoes. Ours is a whole different dish: the chicken is on the bone, and brined first, which makes it nice and moist. With it, we serve a homemade peperonata with roasted peppers, onions, garlic, red pepper flakes, rosemary, fresh bay leaf, fresh thyme, and *piment d'Espelette* [a pepper from France with a smoky flavor]. Here is a place where technique plays a role in the flavor: When you roast peppers, the best way to get the skin off is to put them in a bowl covered with plastic wrap and let them steam. When they are done, you are left with the pepper liquid. What we do is cook with that liquid.

To finish this dish, we put a big scoop of the pepper mixture, tomato sauce, garlic puree, onion, red wine vinegar, and fresh bay leaf on the chicken and put it in the oven to roast. The chicken cooks in its own juice then is served with roasted potatoes. It is delicious.

What we are doing is layering the flavors. You have the technique of brining the chicken, elevating the flavor profile of the peppers with the sweetness of the onions and herbs, adding a little heat from the *piment d'Espelette*, and giving body to the sauce from the pepper juice, which is distilled pepper brandy.

Flavor Affinities

chicken + andouille sausage + red beans + rice
chicken + apples + endive + walnuts
chicken + asparagus + ginger
chicken + avocado + bacon + garlic + mayonnaise + tarragon
chicken + basil + cinnamon
chicken + chanterelle mushrooms + rosemary
chicken + cloves + rosemary + yogurt
chicken + coconut + galangal + shiitake mushrooms
chicken + coriander + cumin + garlic

chicken + cream + grapefruit + pink peppercorns
chicken + cream + morels
chicken + cumin + garlic + lemon
chicken + figs + honey + thyme + dry white wine
chicken + fines herbes + mushrooms + spring onions
chicken + garlic + lemon
chicken + garlic + pancetta + sage + thyme
chicken + mustard + thyme

CHICKEN LIVERS
(See Liver, Chicken)

CHICKPEAS (aka garbanzo beans)
Season: summer
Function: cooling
Techniques: simmer

apple cider or juice
basil
bay leaf
bell peppers, esp. red
bread
butter, unsalted
cardamom
carrots
cayenne
cheese, feta
chicken
chile peppers: dried red, fresh
    green (e.g., jalapeño)
chives
cilantro
cinnamon
cloves
coriander
couscous
cumin, esp. toasted (e.g., Indian
    cuisine, etc.)
curry leaves
curry powder
fennel
fennel seeds
garam masala (e.g., Indian
    cuisine)
GARLIC
ginger
greens (e.g., chard, spinach)
ham, Serrano
hummus (key ingredient)
Indian cuisine
Italian cuisine (as garbanzo
    beans)

leeks
LEMON: juice, zest
lemon, preserved
lemon thyme
Mediterranean cuisine
Mexican cuisine
Middle Eastern cuisine
mint
OLIVE OIL
olives, black
ONIONS: RED, YELLOW
paprika, esp. smoked or sweet
parsley, flat-leaf
pasta
pepper: black, white
pork
potatoes
prosciutto
raisins
red pepper flakes
rice, esp. basmati
    (accompaniment)
rosemary
saffron
sage
salads
SALT, KOSHER
scallions
sesame seeds
shrimp
soups
spinach
squash, winter
stews
stocks: chicken, vegetable
tabbouleh (key ingredient)
tahini
tamarind
thyme
tomatoes
turmeric
vinegar, esp. balsamic, red wine,
    sherry

walnuts and walnut oil
yogurt (e.g., **Indian cuisine**)

Flavor Affinities
chickpeas + cayenne + garlic + lemon
    juice + olive oil + salt + tahini
chickpeas + cilantro + cumin
chickpeas + garlic + lemon juice +
    olive oil + thyme
chickpeas + garlic + mint
chickpeas + garlic + olive oil + parsley

CHICORY (See also Endive;
Lettuces — Bitter Greens and
Chicories; and Radicchio)
Season: autumn–spring
Weight: medium
Volume: moderate
Techniques: grill, raw

apples
bacon
capers
cheese, esp. Gruyère and/or fresh
cilantro
crème fraîche
cumin
figs
fish, smoked
garlic
ham, Serrano
lemon
lettuces
meats and poultry, richer
nuts
olive oil
paprika, smoked
parsley
prosciutto
salads
salmon, smoked
watercress

Dishes
**Preserved Lemon Hummus; Roasted Red Pepper and
Walnut Puree**
— Monica Pope, T'afia (Houston)

Dishes
**Chicory Salad with Fall Root Vegetables, Shaved Pear, and
Rapeseed-Mustard Vinaigrette**
— Daniel Boulud, Daniel (New York City)

CHILE PEPPERS — IN GENERAL

Season: summer
Taste: hot
Weight: light–medium (from fresh to dried)
Volume: moderate–very loud (from dried to fresh)
Techniques: raw, roast, sauté
Tips: Add at the end of the cooking process. The spiciness of chile peppers suggests "false heat."

Asian cuisine
avocado
bananas
basil
bay leaf
BEANS, ESP. BLACK, PINTO
Cajun cuisine
Caribbean cuisine
cayenne
cheese: Fontina, goat, mozzarella, Parmesan
Chinese cuisine
chocolate
CILANTRO, esp. in Latin American cuisine
cinnamon
coconut and coconut milk, esp. in Asian cuisine
coriander
corn
cumin
CURRIES (key ingredient)
eggplant
fennel
fish sauce, esp. in Asian cuisine
fruit, esp. citrus
GARLIC
GINGER, esp. in Asian cuisine
Indian cuisine
ketchup
Latin American cuisine
lemon, juice
lemongrass
lentils
LIME, JUICE
mangoes
marjoram
*MEXICAN CUISINE
mole sauces
mushrooms
mustard
olive oil
olives
onions
oregano
Pakistani cuisine
parsley, flat-leaf
peanuts, esp. in Asian cuisine
pineapple
rice
rosemary
saffron
salads, esp. bean
salsas and other sauces
seafood
sesame and sesame oil, esp. in Asian cuisine
shallots
Southwestern American cuisine
soy sauce
stews
sweet vegetables (e.g., beets, carrots, corn)
*THAI CUISINE
thyme
tomatoes and tomato sauces
verbena
vinegar: balsamic, red wine, sherry
yogurt

Flavor Affinities
chile peppers + cilantro + lime

CHILE PEPPERS, ANAHEIM

Taste: hot, sweet
Weight: medium
Volume: very quiet–loud

salads
salsas
stuffed peppers

CHILE PEPPERS, ANCHO

(dried poblanos)
Taste: hot, sweet
Weight: medium
Volume: quiet–loud

cashews
chili
sauces, esp. mole
soups
turkey

CHILE PEPPERS, CHIPOTLE (dried, smoked

jalapeño peppers)
Taste: very hot, smoky
Weight: medium
Volume: moderate–very loud

avocado
beans
Central American cuisine
chicken
chili
chocolate
cilantro
game
garlic
lemon, juice
lime, juice
mayonnaise
Mexican cuisine
molasses
olive oil
onions
orange, juice
paprika
pork
rice

salsas and sauces
salt, esp. kosher
soups
stews
sugar
Tex-Mex cuisine
tomatoes
vinegar, white

CHILE PEPPERS, GUAJILLO

Taste: hot
Weight: medium
Volume: moderate–loud

eggs
jicama
lime
pork
sauces
soups
stews
tomatoes

CHILE PEPPERS, HABANERO

Taste: very hot, sweet
Weight: medium
Volume: very loud+

fish (e.g., snapper)
lemon, juice
onions
pork
salsas and sauces
sugar

CHILE PEPPERS, JALAPEÑO

Taste: very hot
Weight: medium
Volume: very loud

cheese
cinnamon
lemon, juice
olive oil
onions, white
salsas and sauces
salt, sea
soups

CHILE PEPPERS, PASILLA (dried chilacas)

Taste: hot
Weight: medium
Volume: quiet–loud

mole
sauces

CHILE PEPPERS, PIMENTS D'ESPELETTE

Taste: hot
Weight: medium
Volume: quiet–moderate

cheese, French or Spanish
French Basque cuisine
olive oil
Spanish Basque cuisine

CHILE PEPPERS, POBLANO

Taste: hot
Weight: medium
Volume: quiet–moderate

chile peppers, chipotle
chiles rellenos
cilantro
corn
garlic
onions
salads

I have made a red-hot apple gelée that was a garnish to a *panna cotta*, taking apple cider and infusing it with cinnamon and **jalapeño chile** — which ended up tasting like red-hot candy. I like using fresh jalapeños in an infusion, or an *espelette* as a finishing note. I also love the idea of chipotle chile paired with chocolate ice cream.

— **MICHAEL LAISKONIS,** LE BERNARDIN (NEW YORK CITY)

salsas
tomatoes
vegetables, roasted

CHILE PEPPERS, SERRANO

Taste: very hot
Weight: medium
Volume: very loud+

Bloody Marys
chili powder
cilantro
coriander
cumin
garlic
molasses
oil, vegetable
olive oil
onions, yellow
orange, juice
salsas
stock, chicken
vinegar, white

CHILEAN CUISINE

(See also Latin American Cuisines)

chile peppers
corn
cumin
garlic
meats
olives
oregano
paprika
pepper, black
raisins

CHILI PASTE

Taste: hot
Weight: medium–heavy
Volume: loud

Asian cuisine
beef
marinades
pork
sauces

CHILI POWDER

Taste: hot
Weight: light
Volume: quiet–loud

cumin
Tabasco sauce
tequila

CHINESE CUISINE (See also Szechuan Cuisine)

Techniques: fry, stir-fry

cabbage
chicken
chile peppers
cinnamon
duck
fish
garlic
ginger

hoisin sauce
peanuts
pork
RICE
scallions
seafood
sesame: oil, seeds
shrimp: fresh, dried
snow peas
SOY SAUCE
star anise
steaming
stock, chicken
sugar
tofu
vegetables
vinegar, rice wine
wheat (e.g., noodles), esp. in
    northern China
wine, rice

In **Chinese cooking** they have a technique called "red cooking" that is a dish braised or steamed with star anise, dark soy sauce, cinnamon, and rock sugar. I cook the oxtail for my timbale of oxtail and foie gras that way, and then clarify the broth and turn it into the aspic that holds the dish together. The foie gras is cooked separately and made into a terrine. The dish is then served with gingery pickled vegetables. It is not a Chinese dish in that it is not a dish that you would find in a Chinese restaurant, but it has Chinese influences. The idea of clarifying the broth is typically French. The use of foie gras is not very Chinese. The pickled vegetables are like something you might find in Chinese cooking, but they are done in perfect dice and served as a relish.
— **DAVID WALTUCK,** CHANTERELLE (NEW YORK CITY)

Flavor Affinities

cabbage + chicken stock
garlic + ginger + pork
ginger + rice wine + soy sauce
soy sauce + sugar

CHINESE FIVE-SPICE POWDER (See Five-Spice Powder)

CHIVES

Season: spring–autumn
Botanical relatives: garlic, leeks, onions, shallots
Weight: light, soft-leaved
Volume: quiet–moderate
Tips: Always use fresh, not cooked. Use in stir-fries.

avocados
basil
beans, green
butter
CHEESE, esp. cheddar, ricotta, and cheese sauces
chervil
chicken
Chinese cuisine
cilantro
cream and cream sauces
cream cheese
crème fraîche
dill
EGGS, EGG DISHES, AND OMELETS
fennel
fines herbes (ingredient, along with chervil, parsley, tarragon)
fish

You can't cook without onions, and **chives** are a delicate way to get that flavor into a dish. They are good in a soup or a sauce. A chive oil is great drizzled around a plate for flavor as well as appearance.
— **DAVID WALTUCK**, CHANTERELLE (NEW YORK CITY)

garlic
herbs, most other
marjoram
onions, esp. green
paprika
parsley
pasta
pork
POTATOES
salads and salad dressings
sauces, esp. cheese and cream based
shellfish
smoked salmon
sole
sorrel
SOUPS, esp. cream based and cold (e.g., vichyssoise)
sour cream
tarragon
thyme
vegetables and root vegetables
vinaigrettes
zucchini

CHOCOLATE / COCOA — IN GENERAL

Taste: bitter–sweet (depending on sugar content)

achiote
allspice
ALMONDS
anise seeds
apricots
Armagnac
BANANAS
basil
beverages
boar
bourbon
brandy
brioche or challah
butter, unsalted
butterscotch
CARAMEL, esp. with dark chocolate
cardamom
cashews
cheese, ricotta

My chocolate-corn dessert [of soft chocolate ganache and sweet corn in three textures: crunchy corn and hazelnut corn sorbet, and corn tuile] was inspired by freeze-dried corn. [The kernels] are whole with a vibrant sweetness. Corn dates back to the Aztecs, who also loved **chocolate**, so it's funny when people ask, "Where'd you get the inspiration?" This starts with a layer of milk chocolate hazelnut praline paste, then the corn, and then crushed wafers that give it that Kit Kat candy bar texture; on top of that is some chocolate ganache, then a layer of chocolate. To play off those flavors I serve some *espelette* [pepper] to give a little heat and some smoked salt from Wales. This dish is about the interplay of the chocolate and the corn. The *espelette* gives a heat that reminds me of roasted corn salsa. This is an ode to the origin of the inspiration.
— **MICHAEL LAISKONIS**, LE BERNARDIN (NEW YORK CITY)

It is hard to think of a fruit or nut that is not improved by combining it with **chocolate**.
— **MICHEL RICHARD**, CITRONELLE (WASHINGTON, DC)

I love **chocolate** with fruit or nuts or both. My favorite candy bar in the world is a Cadbury Fruit and Nut bar. On my menu I have a chocolate, hazelnut, and orange dessert, which is essentially a Cadbury!
— **GINA DEPALMA**, BABBO (NEW YORK CITY)

cherries: regular, sour, dried
chicken
chile peppers
chili powder
chocolate, white
CINNAMON
cloves
cocoa powder
coconut
***COFFEE / ESPRESSO**, esp.
   with dark chocolate
cognac
Cointreau
corn syrup, light
CREAM
cream cheese
crème anglaise
crème fraîche
crust: pastry, pie
currants
custard

When it comes to **chocolate**, keep it simple. That's always good advice! For simplicity at its best, only two ingredients are necessary: heavy cream and chopped chocolate. Bring the cream to a boil, pour it over the chocolate, and it turns into ganache. Serve it warm with just a spoon. How can you do any better? In my new book, I feature a recipe called Cup O' Dark Chocolate, and essentially it is ganache poured into a cup. Then you grab a cookie, and have at it!

If you want to dip fruit into chocolate, dried fruits such as figs, pear, and pineapple all work really well. People always ask what they can serve to impress their sweetheart on Valentine's Day, and fresh strawberries are really nice in February. Just make a warm ganache, grab the strawberries, and start dipping. Fresh grapes are fantastic with chocolate. Dip them into the melted chocolate, pop them in the freezer, and when they are frozen, put them into a two-quart container. That way, you will always have a little treat in the freezer. Be careful though — they are not M&Ms, so they *will* melt in your hands!
— **MARCEL DESAULNIERS,** THE TRELLIS (WILLIAMSBURG, VIRGINIA)

dates
DESSERTS
duck

espelette
figs, dried
fruit: dried, fresh

game (e.g., rabbit, venison)
game birds
ginger
graham crackers
Grand Marnier
HAZELNUTS
honey
Kirsch
lavender
lemon
liqueurs: berry, coffee (e.g.,
    Kahlúa), nut (e.g., Frangelico),
    orange
macadamia nuts
malt (malted milk)
maple syrup
marshmallows
mascarpone
meats
Mexican cuisine (e.g., mole
    sauces)
MILK
MINT
nutmeg, esp. on hot chocolate
NUTS
oats
orange: juice, zest
orange blossom water
passion fruit
peanuts/peanut butter
pears
pecans
pepper: black, pink (pinch)
poultry
praline
prunes
raisins
RASPBERRIES, esp. with milk
    chocolate
Rice Krispies
RUM: DARK, LIGHT
salt
sauces: savory (e.g., mole), sweet
    (e.g., chocolate)
sour cream
strawberries
SUGAR: brown, confectioners',
    white

Everybody is on the **chocolate** bandwagon now, and we are not far away from the proverbial "man on the street" knowing the difference between a 72 percent and a 66 percent chocolate. The boutique chocolate makers are now coming up with estate and varietal and vintage chocolates. I love that, but honestly, once you add enough sugar and cream to chocolate, those nuances are all gone.

— **MICHAEL LAISKONIS**, LE BERNARDIN (NEW YORK CITY)

People always ask why I use bittersweet versus semisweet **chocolate**. Semisweet is chocolate that needs salt. When you add salt to it, it brings up the bitter flavor and makes it taste bittersweet. Semisweet chocolate to me tastes kind of flat. Milk chocolate can taste flat as well. Now that there is Scharffen Berger and El Rey on the market, I find both those chocolates to be really, really great, with both flavor and kick to them. But if you want a killer chocolate dessert, don't use milk chocolate.

When I write a dessert menu, there will be a couple of chocolate desserts, with one being a killer chocolate and the other a lighter option, like chocolate with bananas. If you don't have something intensely chocolate, chocolate lovers are very, very unhappy. Banana soufflé with chocolate is not considered a chocolate dessert. You have to be careful with a killer chocolate dessert — you can't just put chocolate, chocolate, and chocolate together. There has to be balance so the dessert is not too rich. To achieve balance, turn to coffee or caramel because they pair so well and help to intensify the chocolate flavor.

For some desserts, I like to combine white and dark chocolate, or milk and dark chocolate, to give balance and cut intensity. It sounds crazy, but you can use one chocolate to mellow the flavor of another.

I'm not a fan of herbs with dessert, with the possible exception of chocolate. I love the combination of chocolate with mint.

— **EMILY LUCHETTI**, FARALLON (SAN FRANCISCO)

I don't have a big sweet tooth but I do like all kinds of **chocolate**, from dark to white. Each one is completely different. I like the bitterness and clean flavor of dark chocolate. I like milk chocolate with a piece of bread like when I was a kid. You have to select your white chocolate carefully because not all of it is good. White chocolate works well in a mousse; it has a more neutral flavor and does not dictate. Dark chocolate is all about being the star, versus white, that is better to play with.

— **GABRIEL KREUTHER**, THE MODERN (NEW YORK CITY)

Dark chocolate goes really well with coffee or caramel, but if I could only pick one it would be the caramel! Caramel and chocolate play so well together despite both being strong flavors.

— **EMILY LUCHETTI**, FARALLON (SAN FRANCISCO)

tea, esp. green or Earl Grey
turkey
VANILLA

Vin Santo
walnuts

Flavor Affinities

chocolate + almonds + cinnamon + sugar
chocolate + almonds + cream
chocolate + banana + butterscotch + macadamia nuts
chocolate + banana + caramel + cream + vanilla
chocolate + butterscotch + caramel + coffee
chocolate + caramel + coffee + malt
chocolate + caramel + coffee + praline
chocolate + caramel + cream + hazelnuts + vanilla
chocolate + cherries + mint

chocolate + cinnamon + chiles + nuts + seeds
chocolate + coffee + hazelnuts
chocolate + coffee + walnuts
chocolate + cream + raspberries
chocolate + custard + pistachios
chocolate + ginger + orange
chocolate + graham crackers + marshmallows
chocolate + hazelnuts + orange
chocolate + lavender + vanilla
chocolate + rum + vanilla

Dishes

Hot Valrhona Chocolate Soufflé, Vermont Maple Ice Cream, Vanilla Ice Cream, and Chocolate Sorbet
— David Bouley, Bouley (New York City)

Austrian Chocolate-Hazelnut Soufflé with Italian Plum Ragoût and Caramel Balsamic Ice Cream
— David Bouley, Danube (New York City)

Chocolate-Hazelnut Cake with Orange Sauce and Hazelnut Gelato
— Gina DePalma, pastry chef, Babbo (New York City)

Almond and Chocolate Torte with Raspberries
— Jim Dodge, at the 2005 James Beard Awards gala reception

Crunchy Chocolate-Hazelnut Spring Roll with Mint and Mango Salad
— Dominique and Cindy Duby, Wild Sweets (Vancouver)

Milk Chocolate and Orange Parfait with Steamed Meringues and Orange and Black Truffle Brown Butter
— Dominique and Cindy Duby, Wild Sweets (Vancouver)

Chocolate-Hazelnut Mousse, Orange Sherbet, and Cardamom-Scented Oranges
— Gale Gand, pastry chef, Tru (Chicago)

Chocolate-Port Semifreddo with Chocolate-Port Bisque, Dark Chocolate Sponge Cake, and Orange-Cinnamon Truffle
— Gale Gand, pastry chef, Tru (Chicago)

Dark Chocolate, Cashew, and Caramel Tart, with Red Wine Reduction, Banana, and Malted Rum-Milk Chocolate Ice Cream
— Michael Laiskonis, pastry chef, Le Bernardin (New York City)

Flourless Chocolate Cake, Dark Chocolate Ganache, Toasted Bread, Maldon Sea Salt, Extra-Virgin Olive Oil
— Michael Laiskonis, pastry chef, Le Bernardin (New York City)

Warm El Rey Chocolate Pudding Cake with Salted Peanut Ice Cream and Peanut Brittle
— Emily Luchetti, pastry chef, Farallon (San Francisco)

Bittersweet Chocolate Pot de Crème with Coffee-Caramel Cream, Butterscotch, and Chocolate Toffee
— Emily Luchetti, pastry chef, Farallon (San Francisco)

Chocolate-Peanut Butter Crème Caramel with Strauss Family Farms Ice Milk
— Ellie Nelson, pastry chef, Jardinière (San Francisco)

Our Marjolaine Cake: A Classic Chocolate-Hazelnut Meringue Layer Cake with Raspberries
— Patrick O'Connell, The Inn at Little Washington (Washington, Virginia)

Our Perennially Popular, Molten-Centered Chocolate Cake with Roasted Banana Ice Cream
— Patrick O'Connell, The Inn at Little Washington (Washington, Virginia)

Chocolate Biscuit Soufflé with Dark Chocolate Mousse and Milk Chocolate–Ginger Parfait
— François Payard, Payard Patisserie and Bistro (New York City)

Milk Chocolate Mousse, Yuzu Citrus Cream, and Sacher Biscuit
— François Payard, Payard Patisserie and Bistro (New York City)

Trio of Desserts: Creamy Chocolate-Cheese Flan with Hibiscus Caramel, Chocolate Bread Pudding with Warm Café con Leche Sauce, Mayan Mediterranean Chocolate Rice Pudding with Cinnamon and Cacao Nib Dust
— Maricel Presilla, Zafra (Hoboken, New Jersey)

Trio of Dark, White, and Gianduja Chocolate Mousses with an Espresso Sauce
— Thierry Rautureau, Rover's (Seattle)

Dark Chocolate–Jalapeño Ice Cream Sundae
— Janos Wilder, Janos (Tucson)

I make a cake with dark **cocoa**, which makes for a bitter chocolate flavor, and then in the middle a milk chocolate cream. Many people don't realize how great the chocolate flavor of cocoa is. It adds bitterness and intensity without adding richness. That is invaluable because so many chocolate desserts are so rich. Often when I make a chocolate ice cream, I will combine melted chocolate and cocoa.

— **EMILY LUCHETTI**, FARALLON (SAN FRANCISCO)

My dessert of **milk chocolate** pot de crème, caramel foam, maple syrup, and Maldon sea salt served in an emptied-out eggshell symbolizes that a few ingredients can come together in a way that is greater than the sum of their parts. The key ingredient which ties it together is the Maldon sea salt. This combination elevates all the ingredients.

Starting with chocolate, caramel was the logical next step. At the time, I played with *fleur de sel,* red salt from Hawaii, and others, before ending up with the Maldon. I like the concept of using sugar as a seasoning, beyond its natural necessity in dessert. I also like natural sweetness from things and maple sugar brings a lot of flavor beyond sweetness. Once I hit upon this combination, I have never changed it.

— **MICHAEL LAISKONIS**, LE BERNARDIN (NEW YORK CITY)

Dishes

Creamy White Chocolate and Cranberry Risotto with Roasted Apricots
— Dominique and Cindy Duby, Wild Sweets (Vancouver)

White Chocolate and Rice Milk Flan with Pistachio Emulsion
— Dominique and Cindy Duby, Wild Sweets (Vancouver)

Valrhona and El Rey are both good. When you are looking for a **white chocolate,** you want one that has some smoothness to it. It is not going to have the acidity that dark chocolate has. When you are making a dessert with white chocolate, it is going to be a softer, smoother dessert. I don't like dark chocolate and raspberries together, but I believe I am one of the few chefs who feel this way. What I don't like is that when you take a bite of the chocolate with the berry, the acidity of the two don't blend. The acids are too similar, so it doesn't feel like a single dessert in your mouth. Instead, it is a clash with both of them bouncing into each other in your mouth. They don't bridge, and even whipped cream doesn't bring them together. But if you use white chocolate, its softness works much better with berries. The white chocolate complements the berries and brings out their flavors. Citrus, especially anything in the orange family, also works well with white chocolate. Nuts, such as almonds, work well with white chocolate. Spices also work well with white chocolate.

— **EMILY LUCHETTI**, FARALLON (SAN FRANCISCO)

CHOCOLATE, WHITE

almonds
apricots
bananas
basil
BERRIES: blackberries, blueberries, cranberries
caramel
cashews
cassis
cherries
chocolate, esp. dark
citrus
coconut
cream
dates
figs
ginger
grapes
hazelnuts
lemon: juice, zest
lime
liqueurs: berry, crème de cacao
macadamia nuts
mango
mint
orange
papaya
passion fruit
persimmons
pistachios
pomegranate
prunes
*RASPBERRIES
rum
strawberries
sugar
sweet potatoes
vanilla
yogurt

Flavor Affinities

white chocolate + basil + strawberries
white chocolate + cream + lemon + orange
white chocolate + dark chocolate + pistachios
white chocolate + ginger + pistachios + rice

CHORIZO (See also Sausages)

Taste: salty; spicy
Weight: medium–heavy
Volume: moderate–loud
Techniques: sauté, stew

apples
bay leaf
beans
bell peppers, roasted
chicken
chili
clams
garlic
hard cider
herbs
kale
monkfish
olive oil
onions
paprika
potatoes
red pepper flakes
Spanish cuisine
stews
stock, chicken
sweet potatoes
thyme
tomatoes

AVOID

delicate fish (e.g., halibut, scallops)
oily fish (e.g., sardines)

Flavor Affinities

chorizo + clam broth + herbs + monkfish

CHRISTMAS

baked goods, esp. cookies
cinnamon
cloves
eggnog
fruitcake
ginger
peppermint

CILANTRO

Season: spring–summer
Taste: sweet, sour
Weight: light, soft-leaved
Volume: loud
Tips: Always use fresh, not cooked — or, if you must, add at the very last minute.
Use cilantro to provide a cooling note to chile pepper–spiced dishes.

Asian cuisines
avocados
basil
beans
bell peppers
boar, wild
braised dishes
butter
cardamom
Caribbean cuisine
carrots
chicken
CHILE PEPPERS
chives
chutneys
coconut and coconut milk (e.g., Indian cuisine)
corn
cream and ice cream
cucumbers
cumin
curries, esp. Indian
dill
dips
figs
fish, white (e.g., cod, halibut)
garam masala (e.g., Indian cuisine)
garlic
ginger
greens
INDIAN CUISINE
lamb
Latin American cuisines
legumes
lemon, juice
lemongrass
lemon verbena
lentils
lime, juice
mayonnaise
meats, esp. white
Mediterranean cuisine
MEXICAN CUISINE
Middle Eastern cuisine
mint (e.g., Indian cuisine)
North African cuisine
onions, red

After a visit to Spain, I created a **chorizo** broth to go with monkfish. I love chorizo, with its paprika flavors and the fattiness of the pork. So I had to figure out how to make a sauce out of a dried piece of sausage. We melted the chorizo in a pan for a long time, and ended up with a flavorful grease that was not that appealing. However, we emulsified it in an herb-infused clam broth, and it became velvety. It wasn't greasy, and gave the sauce a little kick. I chose this sauce to go with monkfish because it is a meaty fish and can stand up to spice and to strong flavors really well. Chorizo would not destroy the soul of the fish.
— **ERIC RIPERT**, LE BERNARDIN (NEW YORK CITY)

Dishes

Pan-roasted Monkfish with Confit Peppers and Fiery "Patatas Bravas" with Chorizo-Albarino Emulsion
— Eric Ripert, Le Bernardin (New York City)

I like the anise-seed quality to **cilantro**, which is really good with figs.
— MICHAEL LAISKONIS, LE BERNARDIN (NEW YORK CITY)

I really like using **cilantro** for its lemony and floral qualities, even though it's very non-European. I'll put cilantro stems [not the leaves] in the cavity when I'm roasting a chicken, and I find it lifts the flavor. Cilantro stems are also wonderful in Spanish-themed stews when there's a lot of depth of flavor from ingredients like chorizo, chickpeas, oxtails, or tripe, and it needs a high note.
— TONY LIU, AUGUST (NEW YORK CITY)

Love it or hate it, **cilantro** is in a lot of my dishes! I love its citrus flavor. Cilantro has long legs; we use it to make cilantro oil as well as purees. It lends itself well to white meats but I have even put it on hanger steak and wild boar. I also like it with coconut milk.
— BRAD FARMERIE, PUBLIC (NEW YORK CITY)

orange, juice
parsley
pork
Portuguese cuisine
potatoes
rice, esp. Indian
salads, esp. Asian
SALSAS, MEXICAN
sauces
scallions
shellfish
soups
Southeast Asian cuisine
soy sauce
stews
stir-fried dishes
tamarind
Tex-Mex cuisine
Thai cuisine
tomatoes
vegetables, esp. root
Vietnamese cuisine
vinaigrettes, esp. red wine
vinegar, red wine
yogurt

AVOID
Japanese cuisine (say some)

Flavor Affinities
cilantro + chile peppers +
    coconut milk
cilantro + dill + mint
cilantro + garlic + ginger

CINNAMON

Season: autumn–winter
Taste: sweet, bitter, pungent
Function: heating
Weight: light–medium
Volume: loud
Tips: Add early in cooking.

allspice
APPLES: CIDER, FRUIT, JUICE
apricots
baked dishes and goods
bananas
beef, esp. braised, raw, stewed
bell peppers
berries
beverages, esp. hot
blueberries
breads, sweet (e.g., gingerbread)
breakfast / brunch
butter
caramel
Calvados
cardamom

cherries
chicken
chile peppers
chili powder
Chinese cuisine
CHOCOLATE / COCOA
chutneys
cloves
coffee / espresso
cloves (compatible spice)
cookies
coriander
couscous
cream and ice cream
cream cheese
cumin
curries, esp. Indian
CUSTARDS
DESSERTS
eggplant
fennel
five-spice powder (key ingredient)
French toast
fruits: fruit compotes, fruit
    desserts
game birds
garam masala, Indian (key
    ingredient)
garlic
ginger
holiday cooking
honey
Indian cuisine
Indonesian cuisine
lamb, esp. braised
lemon, juice
mace
malt
maple syrup
meats, red
Mediterreanean cuisine
Mexican cuisine
Middle Eastern cuisine
mole sauces
Moroccan cuisine
nutmeg
nuts

I use Saigon **cinnamon** that is the most amazing cinnamon you will ever try. It comes in a chip [as opposed to a stick] and is like the cinnamon used to make red-hots [candy]. I use it in a ganache.

— JOHNNY IUZZINI, JEAN GEORGES (NEW YORK CITY)

onions
orange: juice, zest
pancakes
pastries
pears
pecans
pies
plums
pork
poultry
pumpkin
quail
quatre épices (key ingredient)
raisins
ras el hanout (key ingredient)
rice
saffron
sauces (e.g., barbecue)
South American cuisine
Southeast Asian cuisine (as cassia)
Spanish cuisine
squash, esp. winter
star anise
stews
stocks and broths
sugar: brown, white
tagines
tamarind
tea
tomatoes
turmeric
vanilla
veal
vegetables, esp. sweet
waffles
walnuts
wine, red, esp. mulled
yogurt
zucchini

Flavor Affinities

cinnamon + almonds + raisins
cinnamon + cardamom + cloves + coriander + black pepper (garam masala)
cinnamon + cardamom + rice
cinnamon + cloves + mace + nutmeg

CITRUS — IN GENERAL

(See also Lemons, Limes, Oranges, etc.)
Season: winter
Taste: sour
Weight: light–medium
Volume: medium–loud

fish
Greek cuisine
lemongrass
Mediterranean cuisine
salads: green, fruit
shellfish

Dishes

Lemongrass Sorbet, Dehydrated Grapefruit, Crispy Tangerine, Lime Curd
— Johnny Iuzzini, pastry chef, Jean Georges (New York City)

CLAMS

Season: summer
Taste: salty
Weight: light
Volume: quiet–moderate
Techniques: bake, broil, deep-fry, grill, roast, sauté, steam, stew

aioli
allspice
anchovy
artichokes
asparagus
BACON
basil
bay leaf
beans, white
bell peppers, esp. red
bread, esp. French
bread crumbs
BUTTER, UNSALTED
cabbage, esp. napa
capers
carrots
cauliflower
caviar
cayenne
celery
chervil
CHILE PEPPERS, esp. dried and red (e.g., habanero, jalapeño)
chili powder
chives
chorizo
cilantro
clam juice
cocktail sauce
cod

Orange is the leading lady of **citrus** — it brings a sunny, citric flavor to dishes. Lemon and lime are the men of citrus — very strong, so use them carefully!

— MICHEL RICHARD, CITRONELLE (WASHINGTON, DC)

I love candied **citrus** for savory dishes. I love candied kumquats, orange, or lemon. They are great with sweet or savory dishes, and amazing with cheese, such as a soft, non-ashed goat cheese.

— CARRIE NAHABEDIAN, NAHA (CHICAGO)

corn
cream
cumin
fennel
fermented black beans
fish, esp. striped bass
GARLIC
ginger, fresh
gingko nuts
ham, Serrano
hominy
horseradish
Italian cuisine
Japanese cuisine
Korean cuisine
leeks
lemon, juice
lemongrass
lime, juice
marjoram
Mediterranean cuisine
milk
mint, esp. spearmint
mirepoix
mushrooms
mussels
mustard greens
New England cuisine
oil, vegetable
OLIVE OIL
onions, esp. red or Spanish
oregano
oysters
pancetta
PARSLEY, FLAT-LEAF
pasta

PEPPER: BLACK, WHITE
Pernod
pork
POTATOES, esp. Idaho, red
prosciutto
red pepper flakes
rice, esp. Arborio or bomba
romesco sauce
rosemary
saffron
sake
salt, kosher
sausage, esp. spicy (e.g., chorizo)
scallions
scallops (compatible seafood)
shallots
sherry, dry (e.g., fino)
shiso leaf
shrimp (compatible seafood)
soy sauce
spinach
squid (compatible seafood)
stocks: chicken, clam, fish
Tabasco sauce
tapenade
tarragon
Thai basil
THYME
TOMATOES, esp. plum, roasted, sauce
vermouth
WINE, DRY WHITE (e.g., Champagne, Pinot Gris, Tocai Friulano, Sauvignon Blanc)
yuzu juice

Flavor Affinities
clams + aioli + capers + tarragon
clams + bacon + lemon + scallions
clams + basil + garlic + tomatoes
clams + butter + lemon + shallots
clams + cream + curry + fennel
clams + garlic + mussels + onion + thyme + white wine
clams + oysters + potatoes + thyme

CLOVES
Taste: sweet, pungent
Function: heating
Weight: medium
Volume: loud
Techniques: Add early in cooking.

allspice
almonds
apples: cider, fruit, juice
baked goods (e.g., breads, cakes, pastries, pies)
bay leaf
beef
beets
beverages
biryani
cabbage, esp. red
cardamom
carrots
chicken
chile peppers
Chinese cuisine
chocolate
cider, hot (i.e., mulled)
cinnamon
cookies
coriander
cumin
curries (e.g., Asian, Indian)
desserts
duck
English cuisine
fennel seeds
fruits, esp. cooked
game

Dishes

Linguine with Clams, Pancetta, and Hot Chiles
— Mario Batali, Babbo (New York City)

Clam Chowder with Smoked Bacon
— Rebecca Charles, Pearl Oyster Bar (New York City)

New New England Clam Chowder Served with Cream of Bacon, Onion Jam, and Chive Oil
— Katsuya Fukushima, Café Atlántico / minibar (Washington, DC)

Braised Manila Clams, Italian Sausage, and White Beans
— Rick Tramonto, Tru (Chicago)

garam masala (key ingredient)
garlic
German cuisine
ginger
ham, baked
honey
Indian cuisine, esp. northern
ketchup
kumquats
lamb
lemon
mace
meats
Mexican cuisine
nutmeg
onions
orange
pork
pumpkin
salad dressings
sausage
spice cakes
squash
Sri Lankan cuisine
star anise
stews
stock, esp. beef
stuffing
sweet potatoes
Szechuan pepper
tamarind
tea
tomatoes
turmeric
vegetables, sweet
walnuts
wine, red, hot (i.e., mulled)
Worcestershire sauce

Flavor Affinities

cloves + cardamom + cinnamon +
  tea
cloves + cinnamon + ginger +
  nutmeg
cloves + ginger + honey

COCONUT AND COCONUT MILK

Season: autumn–spring
Taste: sweet
Function: cooling
Weight: medium–heavy
Volume: moderate–loud
Techniques: stir-fry

allspice
almonds
apricots
Asian cuisine
bananas
basil
beans, green (e.g., Indian cuisine)
beef
blackberries
Brazilian cuisine
candies
caramel
cardamom (e.g., Indian cuisine)
Caribbean cuisine
cashews (e.g., Indian cuisine)
cauliflower (e.g., Indian cuisine)

cherries, fresh or dried
chicken (e.g., Indian cuisine, etc.)
chile peppers, green or red
chili powder
chocolate, esp. dark or white
cilantro (e.g., Indian cuisine, etc.)
cinnamon
cloves
coriander
CREAM AND ICE CREAM
crème fraîche
cucumber
cumin
curries (e.g., Indian cuisine)
custard
dates
desserts
eggs
figs, dried
fish
fruit, esp. tropical
ginger
grapefruit
guava
honey

My **coconut** rice pudding strudel was the result of Takashi's influence. [Takashi Yagihashi was his chef at Detroit's Tribute restaurant.] Dessert has to make sense in the context of the rest of the meal. Being a pastry chef is exciting because you have a lot of autonomy, but you are still working within the chef's framework. Takashi's food was very Asian-influenced. This dish was meant to bring in Asian ingredients in a new way yet be something familiar.

So we have rice pudding flavored with coconut, lemongrass, ginger, and vanilla, and diced apricot for texture. At the time I was introduced to *frie de brique,* which is a Moroccan dough that is like a cross between phyllo and a wonton wrapper. I would wrap these ingredients in this dough and then sauté them in clarified butter and slice them like a spring roll. Alongside I served green tea ice cream. This covered a lot of bases for me: the warm and cold temperatures, the Asian influence, and doing something with boring old rice pudding.

The coolest compliment I ever got was from Andrew Carmellini [chef of New York's A Voce] who was sitting down with us and asked about my background. When I said I used to be a line cook, he said, "I knew it — a pastry chef would never come up with that!" It was the combination of techniques and flavors as well as sautéing something to order.

— **MICHAEL LAISKONIS,** LE BERNARDIN (NEW YORK CITY)

Dishes

Ice Wine–Lychee Gelée with Coconut Milk Sabayon and Pumpkin Seed Croquant
— Dominique and Cindy Duby, Wild Sweets (Vancouver)

Coconut Crème Brûlée with Lychee Sorbet and Sesame Tuile
— Brad Farmerie, Public (New York City)

Lemongrass and Coconut Panna Cotta
— Nora Pouillon, Asia Nora (Washington, DC)

Indian cuisine
Indonesian cuisine
kiwi
kumquats
lamb (e.g., Indian cuisine)
lemon
lemongrass
lentils (e.g., Indian cuisine)
lime, juice
lychee
macadamia nuts
Malaysian cuisine
mangoes
maple
mascarpone
milk
mint (e.g., Indian cuisine, etc.)
nutmeg
oats
orange, juice
papaya
passion fruit
peanuts
pepper, black
pineapple
pistachios
rice
rose water
rum, esp. dark
salads, fruit
salmon (e.g., Indian cuisine)
salt, kosher
sesame seeds
shellfish: shrimp, lobster
soups
sour cream
Southeast Asian cuisine
stews

SUGAR: brown, white
sweet potatoes
tea, green
Thai cuisine
tropical fruits
VANILLA
Vietnamese cuisine
vinegar, white wine

Flavor Affinities

coconut + apricot + ginger +
    green tea + lemongrass + rice +
    vanilla
coconut + honey + lime
coconut + lemongrass + vanilla
coconut + orange + vanilla
coconut milk + beef + ginger

COD

Weight: medium
Volume: quiet
Techniques: bake, boil, broil,
cakes, deep-fry, fry, grill, poach,
roast, sauté, steam

anchovies
bacon
basil
bay leaf
beans: cannellini, green, navy,
    white
bell peppers: red, green, yellow
bouquet garni
brandade
brandy
bread crumbs
BUTTER, unsalted
cabbage, savoy

capers
caraway seeds
carrots
cayenne
celery
cheese: Emmental, Gruyère,
    Swiss
chervil
chives
cilantro
coriander
cream
currants
daikon
eggplant, esp. Japanese
eggs, hard-boiled
endive
English cuisine, esp. fish and
    chips
fennel
French cuisine, esp. Provençal
garlic
ginger
ham: cured, Serrano
leeks
lemon, juice
mayonnaise
milk
miso
mushrooms, esp. cepes,
    portobello, shiitake
mustard, Dijon
New England cuisine
oils: canola, corn, grapeseed,
    peanut
olive oil
olives: black, green
onions
orange: juice, zest
paprika, sweet
PARSLEY, FLAT-LEAF
peas
pepper: black, white
pine nuts
POTATOES, esp. red, red bliss
prosciutto
radishes
risotto

Dishes

Ceviche Fronterizo: Lime-Marinated Alaskan True Cod with Vine-Ripe Tomatoes, Olives, Cilantro, and Green Chile, Served on Crispy Tostaditas
— Rick Bayless, Frontera Grill (Chicago)

Alaskan True Cod and Fresh-Shucked Oysters in Tamazula-Sparked Homemade Cocktail Sauce with Lime, Avocado, White Onion, and Cilantro
— Rick Bayless, Frontera Grill (Chicago)

Chatham Bay Codfish: Chanterelle Mushrooms, Sweet Peas, and Tarragon Sauce
— David Bouley, Upstairs (New York City)

Atlantic Cod "au Naturel" with Littleneck Clams; Roasted Artichokes, Swiss Chard, and Lemon Marmalade
— Daniel Boulud, Daniel (New York City)

Roast Cod on Edamame Risotto with Salt and Pepper Sepia and Carrot-Yuzu Sauce
— Brad Farmerie, Public (New York City)

Brioche-Crusted Cod with Baby Artichokes, Oven-Dried Tomatoes, Garlic Mashed Potatoes, and Artichoke Puree
— Bob Kinkead, Kinkead's (Washington, DC)

Cod Baked in a Salt Crust Stuffed with Baby Artichokes, Romesco, Red Wine, Olive, and Preserved Tomato Stew
— Eric Ripert, Le Bernardin (New York City)

Cod is an undervalued fish. It's light, flaky, and delicate, and I especially like it served with broths or chowders. It's also great baked for ten minutes on salt on a sheet tray. Cod pairs well with clams and shellfish, and I love the combination of fresh cod with salted cod in a dish.
— BRADFORD THOMPSON, MARY ELAINE'S AT THE PHOENICIAN (SCOTTSDALE, ARIZONA)

rosemary
saffron
sage
salt: *fleur de sel,* **kosher, sea**
sauces: hollandaise, tartar, tomato
sausage, chorizo
scallions
shallots
shellfish: clams, shrimp
stocks: chicken, fish, mussels, veal, vegetable
sugar
tarragon
thyme

tomatoes
truffles, black
VINEGAR: balsamic, champagne, red wine, sherry, tarragon, white wine
wine: dry white, red
yuzu juice

Dishes

Black Cod with Miso Sauce
— Nobu Matsuhisa, Nobu (New York City)

Broiled Sake-Marinated Alaskan Black Cod and Shrimp Dumplings in Shiso Broth
— Hiro Sone, Terra (St. Helena, California)

Flavor Affinities

cod + capers + chives + lentils + potatoes
cod + cepes (mushrooms) + garlic + lemon + potatoes

COD, BLACK

bell peppers, red
chile peppers, esp. red
chives
garlic
ginger
leeks
miso
onions
shiso
shrimp
soy sauce
sugar, brown

COD, SALT

Taste: salty
Weight: medium
Volume: moderate–loud

artichoke hearts
bay leaf
beans, white
bell peppers: green, red
bread crumbs
capers
chile peppers
cilantro
cream
French cuisine, esp. Provençal
GARLIC
greens, salad
lemon, juice
marjoram
mint

Dishes

Warm Salad of Poached Salt Cod, Porcini Mushrooms, and Yukon Golds
— David Pasternak, Esca (New York City)

Old Bay seasoning
OIL, canola
olive oil
olives, esp. black or kalamata
onions
paprika: hot, sweet
parsley, flat-leaf
pasta
pepper: black, white
potatoes
saffron
salt: kosher, sea
scallions
shallots
shrimp
sour cream
stock, fish
sugar
Tabasco sauce
thyme
tomatoes
vinegar: red wine, white wine
wine, dry
Worcestershire sauce

Flavor Affinities
salt cod + bay leaf + thyme +
    white wine vinegar

COFFEE AND ESPRESSO
Taste: bitter
Weight: medium
Volume: moderate–loud

almonds
amaretto
anise
bananas
barbecue sauce
beverages
bourbon
brandy
caramel
cardamom

cheese, ricotta
cherries
chicken
chicory
CHOCOLATE, ESP. DARK,
    white
cinnamon
cloves
COCOA
coconut
cognac
CREAM
curry
custards
dates
fennel seeds
figs
game birds
gravy
ham (e.g., with red-eye gravy)
hazelnuts
honey
ice cream, vanilla
Irish whiskey
lamb
lemon
lime
liqueurs, coffee (e.g., Kahlúa, Tía
    Maria)
macadamia nuts
maple syrup
milk, including sweetened,
    condensed
nutmeg
NUTS
oats
orange

Dishes

Espresso Cupcakes Filled with Milk Chocolate Ganache and White Chocolate Frosting
— Emily Luchetti, pastry chef, Farallon (San Francisco)

Bourbon Ice Cream on Coffee-Flavored Tapioca in a Martini Glass
— Kaz Okochi, Kaz Sushi Bistro (Washington, DC)

pears
pecans
persimmons
pork
prunes
raisins
rum
star anise
SUGAR: brown, white
VANILLA
vinegar, balsamic

AVOID
lavender

Flavor Affinities
coffee + bourbon + cream
coffee + caramel + chocolate
coffee + cinnamon + cloves +
    orange
coffee + cinnamon + cream +
    lemon + sugar
coffee + mascarpone + rum +
    sugar + vanilla

COGNAC
apples and apple cider
beef (e.g., filet mignon)
chicken
chocolate
cream
foie gras
mushrooms
mustard, esp. Dijon
pepper: black, green
pork
prunes
raisins
turkey
vanilla
vinegar, cider

In addition to seasonality, I always pay attention to temperature. I look at what I feel like eating now given that day's weather. If it is **cold** and raining, I make sure soup is on the menu.
— ANDREW CARMELLINI, A VOCE (NEW YORK CITY)

COLDNESS (of indoor
or outdoor temperature;
See also Winter)
braised dishes
butter and butter-based sauces
    and dishes
cheese and cheese dishes
cream and cream-based sauces
    and dishes
grains, heavy
hot dishes and beverages
meats, esp. red
polenta
risotto
soups, hot and hearty
spices, warming
stews and stewed dishes

COLLARD GREENS
(See Greens, Collard)

COOLING
Function: Ingredients believed to have cooling properties; useful in hot weather.

asparagus
avocados
berries
buttermilk
cucumbers
figs, fresh
fruits, esp. sweet (e.g., cherries,
    grapes)
herbs, cooling (e.g., cilantro,
    honeysuckle, lavender, lemon
    balm, mint, peppermint)
lettuce
melon
salads
spices, cooling (e.g., cardamom,
    coriander, fennel)

water
watercress
watermelon
yogurt
zucchini

Flavor Affinities
cucumbers + mint + yogurt

CORIANDER
Taste: sour, pungent, astringent
Function: cooling
Weight: light–medium
Volume: moderate–loud
Tips: Add near the end of cooking.
Toast coriander seeds to release their flavor.

allspice
anise
apples
baked goods (e.g., cakes, cookies,
    pies)
basil
beans
beef
cardamom
carrots
cayenne
chicken
chickpeas
chile peppers (e.g., fresh green)

chili
chutneys
cilantro
cinnamon
citrus and citrus zest
cloves
coconut and coconut milk
corn
crab, esp. boiled
cumin
curries (e.g., Indian cuisine)
curry powder
desserts
eggs
fennel
fennel seeds
fish
fruits, esp. autumn and dried
garam masala (key ingredient)
garlic
ginger
gingerbread
grapefruit
ham
harissa (key ingredient)
hot dogs
Indian cuisine
lamb
Latin American cuisine
lentils
mace
meats
Mediterreanean cuisine
Mexican cuisine
Middle Eastern cuisine
mint
Moroccan cuisine
mushrooms

My personal preference for the ratio of **coriander** to cumin is three-quarters of a portion of coriander to one portion of cumin.
— MEERA DHALWALA, VIJ'S (VANCOUVER)

I'll use **coriander** with peppercorns in a sachet for soups, with the pepper providing the heat and the coriander more of a fruity note.
— BRADFORD THOMPSON, MARY ELAINE'S AT THE PHOENICIAN (SCOTTSDALE, ARIZONA)

North African cuisine
North American cuisine
nutmeg
nuts
olive oil
onions
orange: juice, zest
pastries
pears
pepper, black
pickles
plums
pork
potatoes
poultry
quince
rice (e.g., as pudding)
saffron
salmon
sausages
sesame seeds
shellfish
soups, esp. cream-based
Southeast Asian cuisine
Southwestern cuisine
spinach
stews (e.g., chicken)
stocks (e.g., fish)
stuffing
sugar
tomatoes and tomato sauces
turkey
turmeric
Vietnamese cuisine

Flavor Affinities
coriander + cardamom + cinnamon + clove
coriander + cayenne + cumin + garlic
coriander + chile peppers + mustard + black pepper
coriander + cumin + curry
coriander + fish + garlic + olive oil + tomatoes

CORN
Season: summer
Taste: sweet
Function: heating
Weight: medium
Volume: moderate
Techniques: boil, grill, roast, sauté, steam

bacon
BASIL: sweet, lemon
bay leaf
beans, esp. lima
béchamel sauce
beef
BELL PEPPERS: red, green
BUTTER, UNSALTED
buttermilk
caraway seed
carrots
cayenne
celery
cheese: **cheddar**, Colby, Cotija, feta, Monterey Jack
chervil
CHILE PEPPERS: chipotle, jalapeño, serrano
chili powder
chili sauce
Chinese cuisine
chives
cilantro
clams

cornmeal
crab
CREAM, esp. heavy
crème fraîche
cumin
curry powder
dill
eggs
fava beans
fennel
fish, salmon
GARLIC
ginger, fresh
ham
leeks
lemon, juice
lemon thyme
lime, juice
lobster
lovage
maple syrup
marjoram
mascarpone
Mexican cuisine
milk
mirepoix
MUSHROOMS, esp. chanterelle, oyster, shiitake, other wild
mustard
New England cuisine
nutmeg
OIL: canola, peanut, vegetable
OLIVE OIL
ONIONS: red, Spanish, yellow
oregano
pancetta
paprika
parsley
pasta
PEPPER: BLACK, WHITE
pesto
polenta
potatoes
poultry
risottos
rosemary
saffron

sage
salads, green
salmon
salsas
SALT: kosher, sea
scallions
scallops
shallots
sherry, dry
shiso
Southern cuisine
Southwestern cuisine
squash, esp. summer
star anise
STOCKS: chicken, vegetable
sugar
tarragon
thyme
tomatoes
tortillas, corn
vermouth
vinaigrette
vinegar: cider, white wine
wine, dry white

We participate in an event called "Plate and Pitchfork" that is held on a farm with the food from the farm. The guests sit in the field among the **corn** and tomatoes, and we cook a meal for them on a couple of grills. I made a corn soup for this event. We removed the husks, then cut the kernels off the cob. Then we used the husks, which produce a juice, to make a stock for the soup. If you were to use cobs, you wouldn't get the same flavor. It is important to keep the corn flavor pure. Most cooks would throw in a bunch of vegetables in the stock, and what you'd get then is a vegetable stock with corn. I want to have a corny flavor in the end. We made a stock using the corn husks cooked with a little onion, water, and salt, and let it cook for about 45 minutes. What came out was the most amazing sweet broth. We added the corn, pureed it, and served it chilled. It was so sweet and full of corn flavor you would have sworn there were cream and sugar in it.

We now make a corn husk broth to add to a corn, chanterelle, and Dungeness crab risotto with a touch of pesto. Basil pesto and corn really speaks to me. It is a wonderful combination.
— **VITALY PALEY,** PALEY'S PLACE (PORTLAND, OREGON)

To intensify the flavor of **corn** in a dish, add [corn] juice. I'll make a corn ravioli with pureed corn and cooked corn. I add corn juice to the filling to add a fresh corn flavor to the ravioli.
— **ANDREW CARMELLINI,** A VOCE (NEW YORK CITY)

Dishes

Homemade Corn and Leek Ravioli with Maine Lobster and Silver Queen Local Corn
— Lidia Bastianich, Felidia (New York City)

Baby Corn on the Cob, Brown Butter Powder, Cilantro Emulsion
— Brad Farmerie, Public (New York City)

Arepas de Choclo: Corn Cakes Topped with Crème Fraîche and Salmon Roe
— Maricel Presilla, Zafra (Hoboken, New Jersey)

Red Bliss Potato and Corn Pizza, Parsley Pesto, and Smoked Cow's Milk Cheese
— Cory Schreiber, Wildwood (Portland, Oregon)

Flavor Affinities

corn + bell pepper + jalapeño chile + cilantro + tarragon
corn + butter + salt
corn + cayenne + lime + salt
corn + cilantro + shrimp

CORNED BEEF
(See Beef — Brisket)

CORNISH GAME HENS

cardamom
cayenne
cinnamon
cloves
cumin, esp. toasted
garam masala
garlic
ginger
lemon
oil, canola
onions
paprika
pepper, black
salt
tomatoes and tomato paste
turmeric
yogurt

COUSCOUS

Weight: light
Volume: quiet–moderate
Techniques: steep

African (North) cuisine
apricots, dried
basil
bell peppers, esp. red
butter
cabbage
carrots
cayenne
chervil
chicken
chickpeas
cilantro
cumin
fish (e.g., snapper)
ginger
lemon: juice, preserved, zest
Middle Eastern cuisine
mint
Moroccan cuisine
olive oil
olives
onions
parsley, flat-leaf
pepper, black
raisins
saffron
salt: kosher, sea
sausage, *merguez*
scallions
stocks: chicken, fish, vegetable,
tomatoes and tomato juice
turnips
zucchini

COUSCOUS, ISRAELI

Weight: medium–heavy
Volume: light–moderate

olive oil
pepper, white
pesto
shallots
stock, chicken

CRAB

Season: summer
Taste: sweet
Weight: light
Volume: quiet
Techniques: bake, boil, broil, grill, steam

aioli
apples
artichokes
asparagus
*AVOCADOS
bacon
basil
bay leaf
bell peppers, esp. green, red, yellow
bread crumbs / panko
butter, unsalted
carrots and carrot juice
cauliflower
caviar
cayenne
celery
celery root
celery salt
chervil
chile peppers: jalapeño, Scotch bonnet pepper, Thai
chili sauce
Chinese cuisine
CHIVES
cilantro
coconut and coconut milk
coriander
corn
crab roe
cream
crème fraîche
cucumber
cumin

Dishes

Jumbo Lump Crab Salad with Asparagus, Mustard Seed Dressing
— Daniel Boulud/Olivier Muller, DB Bistro (New York City)

Crab Salad with White Asparagus, Ginger, Lime, Pistachio Oil
— Daniel Boulud/Bertrand Chemel, Café Boulud (New York City)

Marinated Jumbo Lump Crabmeat with Horseradish, Coriander, Tomato, Seaweed Salad, and Ginger Vinaigrette
— Jeffrey Buben, Vidalia (Washington, DC)

Red and Yellow Tomato Gazpacho with Avocado Puree and Lump Crabmeat, with Microgreen Salad
— Bob Iacovone, Cuvée (New Orleans)

A Mélange of Jumbo Lump Crab, Mango, and Avocado in a Tropical Fruit Coulis
— Patrick O'Connell, The Inn at Little Washington (Washington, Virginia)

Signature Sushi: Blue Crab with Celery and Red Bell Pepper
— Kaz Okoshi, Kaz Sushi Bistro (Washington, DC)

Potato Gnocchi with Oregon Dungeness Crab and Preserved Lemon
— Vitaly Paley, Paley's Place (Portland, Oregon)

Spicy Crab and Peanut Soup with Okra
— Monica Pope, T'afia (Houston)

Crab Cake with Saffron-Sherry Aioli
— Monica Pope, T'afia (Houston)

Dungeness Crab and Potato Cakes, Green Beans, Cucumbers, Almonds, and Shaved Fennel
— Cory Schreiber, Wildwood (Portland, Oregon)

Michael Dean's Squash Blossom, Crabmeat, and Squash with Green Tomato Relish
— Frank Stitt, Highlands Bar and Grill (Birmingham, Alabama)

I'll never forget tasting the combination of **crab,** avocado, and almonds at chef Pascal Barbot's Paris restaurant L'Astrance.
— **MICHAEL ANTHONY,** GRAMERCY TAVERN (NEW YORK CITY)

Crab is something that you typically see steamed and served with butter. King crab is intensely flavorful, meaty, and salty. When it is caught at sea, it is cooked on the boat with heavily salted water. The first thing I did was soak the crab multiple times in ice water to draw out all the salt. I saw and created a vision of this red crabmeat within a *barigoule* with perfectly cut vegetables, artichokes, French green beans, Valencia oranges, sweet garlic, and finished with olive oil.
— **CARRIE NAHABEDIAN,** NAHA (CHICAGO)

curry
custard
dill
eggplant
eggs
endive, Belgian
fennel
fish: pike, sole
fish sauce, Thai
garlic
ginger
grapefruit
honey
LEMON: juice, zest
lemongrass
lemon thyme
lime: juice, zest
lobster
mango
mascarpone
MAYONNAISE
melon: cantaloupe, honeydew
mint
mushrooms (e.g., button, cremini, shiitakes)
mustard, Dijon
mustard powder
nutmeg
OIL: canola, grapeseed, peanut, sesame, vegetable
olive oil
Old Bay seasoning
ONIONS: green, red, spring, sweet, white
orange: juice, zest
paprika, esp. sweet
PARSLEY, FLAT-LEAF
peas, green
PEPPER: black, white
pineapple
pine nuts
ponzu sauce
potatoes
radishes
saffron
SALT: kosher, sea
scallions
sesame seeds

When making **crab** cakes, I'll use whole shrimp — the meat in the cakes, and the shrimp heads in the sauce — to intensify the shellfish flavor.

— **MICHEL RICHARD**, CITRONELLE (WASHINGTON, DC)

shallots
sherry, dry
shiso
SHRIMP
snow peas
sour cream
soy sauce
spinach
stocks: chicken, vegetable
sugar (pinch)
Tabasco sauce
tamarind
tarragon
tartar sauce
thyme
TOMATOES: fresh, sun-dried
vinaigrette, esp. citrus
vinegar: balsamic, champagne, red wine, sherry
watercress
yogurt

Flavor Affinities

crab + aioli + cilantro + jalapeño chile
crab + almonds + avocado
crab + avocado + cilantro + mango
crab + avocado + grapefruit
crab + corn + green tomatoes
crab + cucumber + lime + mint
crab + ginger + lime
crab + lime + mint
crab + mango + raspberry vinegar
crab + black pepper + snow peas
crab + saffron + shallots

CRAB, SOFT-SHELL

Season: spring–summer
Taste: sweet
Weight: light–medium
Volume: quiet–moderate
Techniques: deep-fry, grill, pan roast, sauté, tempura

almonds
arrowroot
arugula
asparagus
avocado
bacon
basil
bell peppers, red
broccoli rabe
brown butter sauce
butter: clarified, unsalted
capers
cayenne
chervil
chile peppers, jalapeño
chili powder
chives
coleslaw
couscous, Israeli
cream
crème fraîche
cucumbers
daikon
dill
fennel
garlic

ginger (e.g., pickled)
grapefruit
leeks
LEMON, JUICE
lime: juice, zest
mayonnaise
mushrooms (e.g., shiitakes)
mustard, Dijon
nori
OIL: canola, peanut, vegetable
olive oil
onions, red
orange, juice
paprika
parsley, flat-leaf
peas, sugar
PEPPER: black, white
pesto
potatoes, esp. new
rémoulade sauce
sake
SALT: kosher, sea
scallions
scallops
shallots
shiso leaf
shrimp
sorrel
soy sauce
stock, fish
Tabasco sauce

Dishes

Black and White Fettuccini with Oven-Dried Tomatoes, Almond Pesto, Calamari, and Crisp Soft-Shell Crab
— Lidia Bastianich, Felidia (New York City)

Crispy Thai-Style Soft-Shell Crab with Green Papaya Salad and Lime Dipping Sauce
— Bob Kinkead, Kinkead's (Washington, DC)

Pecan-Crusted Soft-Shell Crab Tempura with Italian Mustard Fruit
— Patrick O'Connell, The Inn at Little Washington (Washington, Virginia)

Soft-Shell Crab: Sweet Corn, Potatoes, Leeks, Spring Onions, Caper–White Wine Emulsion
— Alfred Portale, Gotham Bar and Grill (New York City)

Chesapeake Bay Soft-Shell Crabs with Young Ginger and Chinese Chive Coulis
— David Waltuck, Chanterelle (New York City)

tarragon, fresh
tartar sauce
thyme
tomatoes
vinaigrette
vinegar: balsamic, champagne, white wine
wine, dry white
zucchini

Flavor Affinities
soft-shell crab + arugula + tartar sauce
soft-shell crab + asparagus + capers + garlic + lemon + potatoes
soft-shell crab + broccoli rabe + brown butter
soft-shell crab + cabbage + mustard
soft-shell crab + lemon + parsley
soft-shell crab + orange + parsley

CRANBERRIES
Season: autumn–midwinter
Taste: sour
Weight: light–medium
Volume: loud
Techniques: boil

allspice
almonds
apples
apricots
baked goods
cheese, goat
chicken
chile peppers, jalapeño
chocolate: dark, white
cinnamon
cloves
cognac
cream
cream cheese
currants
ginger
hazelnuts
honey

LEMON: JUICE, ZEST
lime, zest
liqueur, orange (e.g., Grand Marnier)
maple syrup
nuts
oats
ORANGE: juice, zest
peaches
pears
pepper
pistachios
pork
poultry
pumpkin
raisins
quince
salt
star anise
SUGAR: brown, white
sweet potatoes
tangerines
thyme
turkey
vanilla
walnuts
wine, white

CRAYFISH (aka crawfish)
Season: spring
Weight: light–medium
Volume: moderate
Techniques: boil, broil, steam

asparagus
avocados
bacon
basil
bay leaf
butter
Cajun cuisine
carrots and carrot juice
cayenne
celery

Dishes
Crayfish, Beet, Leek, and Bacon Salad with Mustard Vinaigrette
— Daniel Boulud, at the 2003 James Beard Awards gala reception

chervil
chives
cloves
coriander
cream / milk
Creole cuisine
dill
egg yolks
endive
fennel seeds
garlic
hazelnuts
leeks
mango
mayonnaise
mirepoix
mushrooms, morels
mustard
oil, grapeseed
olive oil
onions
orange, juice
parsley, flat-leaf
pepper, black
radishes
rice
rosemary
salt
shallots
sorrel
Tabasco sauce
tarragon
thyme
tomatoes
vinegar: tarragon, white wine
wine, dry white (e.g., white Burgundy)
zucchini

Flavor Affinities
crayfish + asparagus + morel mushrooms
crayfish + carrot juice + orange juice

CREAM

When you eat a piece of pumpkin pie, the whipped **cream** is the first thing you go for! You can take this for granted in desserts, or you can dig deeper: You can think of cream as its own flavor. When I was in Japan, the cream was miles better than here in the U.S. You also need to think about your dairy choice in relation to the country. In India, everything is centered around reduced milk. The counterpart would be *dolce de leche* in Latin cuisine. I love yogurt because it is simple and complex; it can be in the forefront or in the background.

— MICHAEL LAISKONIS, LE BERNARDIN (NEW YORK CITY)

CREAM CHEESE

Taste: sour
Weight: heavy
Volume: loud

berries
blueberries
bread, esp. fruit
breakfast / brunch
cheese: fresh goat, ricotta
cherries
cloves
cream
crème fraîche
desserts
eggs
fruit, dried
ginger
graham cracker crumbs
honey
kiwi fruit
LEMON: JUICE, ZEST
liqueur, orange (e.g., Grand Marnier)
maple syrup
mascarpone
nutmeg

orange, juice
quince paste
raisins
raspberries
rum
salt (pinch)
sour cream
strawberries
sugar
vanilla
yogurt

Flavor Affinities

cream cheese + crème fraîche + orange + sugar + vanilla
cream cheese + maple syrup + mascarpone

CREAM, SOUR
(See Sour Cream)

CRÈME FRAÎCHE

Taste: sour
Weight: medium–heavy
Volume: loud

apples
caramel
French cuisine
fruit, fresh
potatoes
raspberries
sauces
strawberries
sugar, brown

CREOLE CUISINE

bouillabaisse
cayenne
crawfish
okra
onions
oysters
paprika
pepper: black, white
salt
seafood
shrimp rémoulade

CRESS (See Watercress)

CUBAN CUISINE

allspice
avocado
bay leaf
beans
beef
bell peppers
chicken
chocolate
citrus (e.g., lime, orange)
cumin
garlic
lime
olive oil
onions, esp. white
orange, juice
oregano
pineapple
plantains
pork
rice
seafood (crab, fish, lobster, shrimp)
sugar, white
watercress

Flavor Affinities

allspice + cumin + garlic + orange juice + pork
avocado + onions + pineapple + watercress
bay leaf + green bell peppers + garlic + onions + oregano (aka *safrito*)
chocolate + garlic + olive oil
citrus juice + garlic + olive oil (aka *adobo*)

Your choice of sugar suggests a country of origin. For example, **Cuban cuisine** relies on white sugar, while Mexican cuisine relies on brown sugar.

— MARICEL PRESILLA, ZAFRA (HOBOKEN, NEW JERSEY)

CUCUMBERS

Season: spring–summer
Taste: sweet, astringent
Function: cooling
Weight: light
Volume: quiet
Techniques: pickle, raw, salads, sauté, soups

allspice
bell peppers, esp. green
basil
butter
buttermilk
caraway seeds
cayenne
celery and celery seeds
cheese: blue, feta
chervil
chile peppers: fresh green, jalapeño
chives
cilantro
coconut milk
coriander
cream
cream cheese
crème fraîche
cumin
DILL
fish
fish sauce, Thai or other Asian
frisée
garam masala
GARLIC
gin
Greek cuisine
horseradish
Japanese cuisine
jicama
lemon balm
lemon, juice
lime, juice
melon, esp. honeydew
MINT (e.g., Indian cuisine)
mustard, Dijon
oil: sesame, vegetable
olive oil
ONIONS, esp. green or red
oregano
parsley, flat-leaf
peanuts
pepper: black, white
pineapple
romaine
red pepper flakes
salads
salmon
salt: kosher, sea
scallions
scallops
sesame seeds
shallots
shrimp
smoked salmon
soups, chilled (e.g., gazpacho)
sour cream
soy sauce
sprouts
sugar (pinch)
Tabasco sauce
tamari
tarragon
tea sandwiches
thyme
tomatoes
Vietnamese cuisine
vinaigrettes
VINEGAR: balsamic, champagne, cider, red wine, rice wine, sherry, tarragon, white wine
vodka
watercress
wine, white
YOGURT (e.g., Indian cuisine)

CUMIN

Taste: bitter, sweet
Function: heating
Weight: medium
Volume: moderate–loud
Tips: Add early in the cooking process.
Toast cumin seeds in a dry pan to evaporate their moisture and increase their flavor.

allspice
anise
apples
baked goods (e.g., breads)
bay leaf
beans, esp. black or kidney
beef
beets
bread (e.g., rye)
cabbage
caramel
cardamom
carrots
cayenne

Flavor Affinities
cucumber + chervil + salt + vinegar
cucumber + chile peppers + mint + yogurt
cucumber + cilantro + ginger + sugar + rice vinegar
cucumber + dill + red onion + sour cream + vinegar
cucumber + dill + salmon
cucumber + dill + yogurt
cucumber + feta cheese + garlic + mint + olive oil + oregano + red wine vinegar
cucumber + garlic + mint + yogurt
cucumber + lemon + sesame oil + vinegar
cucumber + jalapeño chile + dill + onion
cucumber + mint + yogurt

With lighter dishes like rice pilaf or lentils, I use **cumin seeds** for their gentler flavor. With heavier dishes like chickpeas, kidney beans, or red meat, I'll use the stronger-flavored **cumin powder**.

— **MEERU DHALWALA,** VIJ'S (VANCOUVER)

cheese: esp. aged, feta, Muenster
chicken
chickpeas
chile peppers
chili
chili powder
cinnamon
cloves
coriander
couscous
curries
curry leaves
eggplant
eggs
fennel
fennel seeds
fenugreek seeds
fish
fruits, dried
garam masala (key ingredient)
garlic
ginger
harissa
honey
hummus (key ingredient)
Indian cuisine
Indonesian cuisine
lamb, esp. grilled
LENTILS
mace
meats, esp. stronger-flavored, and esp. grilled
MEXICAN CUISINE
mint, dried
Moroccan cuisine
mustard and mustard seeds (e.g., Indian cuisine)
nutmeg
onions
orange
oregano
paprika
peas

pepper
pork
Portuguese cuisine
potatoes
rice
saffron
salads, esp. pasta, tomato
salmon
sauces (e.g., mole)
sauerkraut
sausages
shellfish
soups (e.g., black bean)
Spanish cuisine
squash
stews
sugar, palm
Tabasco sauce
tahini
tamarind
tequila
Tex-Mex cuisine
Thai cuisine
thyme
tomatoes
tuna
turmeric
vegetables, esp. summer
Vietnamese cuisine
yogurt

Flavor Affinities
cumin + cayenne + coriander + garlic
cumin + chickpeas + yogurt
cumin + cinnamon + saffron
cumin + palm sugar + tamarind
cumin + tomatoes + turmeric

CURRY LEAVES
Taste: sour, bitter
Weight: light
Volume: quiet–moderately loud
Tips: Add later in cooking, or to finish a dish.

allspice
Asian cuisines
bread, esp. Indian (e.g., naan)
cardamom
chile peppers
cilantro
cinnamon
cloves
coconut
coriander
cumin
curries, esp. Indian
fennel seeds
fenugreek seeds
fish
garlic
ginger
Indian cuisine
lamb
lentils
mustard seeds
paprika
peas
pepper
rice
shellfish
soups
stir-fried dishes
stocks
tamarind
turmeric
vegetables

CURRY POWDER AND SAUCES
Taste: bittersweet, pungent
Weight: medium–heavy
Volume: moderate–loud
Tips: Add early in cooking process.

beef
butter
cardamom
cashews
cayenne
cheese
chicken
chile peppers, red
cilantro
cinnamon
cloves
coconut
coriander
cream
crème fraîche
cumin
dill
eggs and egg salad
fennel
fish
garlic
ginger
Indian cuisine
lemon, zest
lemongrass
lime, juice
mace
mayonnaise
mushrooms
nutmeg
oil, vegetable
onions
paprika
pepper: black, red
potatoes
saffron
salads (e.g., chicken, egg, potato)
salt, kosher
sauces
shellfish
soups, esp. fish, pea
star anise
stews, meat
stocks: chicken, fish
tamarind
Thai cuisine
tomatoes
tuna

turmeric
vegetables
zucchini

CUSTARDS
Weight: medium–heavy
Volume: quiet

almonds
apples
apricots
bananas
berries
caramel
chai
cherries
chocolate, esp. dark or white
cinnamon
coconut
coffee
ginger
hazelnuts
lemon
liqueurs: nut, orange
mango
maple syrup
nutmeg
orange
passion fruit
pears
persimmons
pineapple
plums
prunes
pumpkin
quince
raisins

raspberries
rhubarb
strawberries
sweet potatoes
thyme
vanilla
walnuts
wine, sweet

DAIKON
Season: autumn–winter
Taste: sweet
Weight: light
Volume: quiet–moderate
Techniques: braise, marinate, raw (e.g., julienned), stew, stir-fry

basil
beef
beets
butter
cabbage
carrots
celery root
cheese, feta
chives
cream
cream cheese
cucumbers
curry powder
dill
duck
fish
ginger
honey
lemon, juice
lovage

Torrijas, which means "soaked," are a [**custardy**] dessert in the Basque country that are like French toast or *pain perdu*. We soak the bread until it is saturated in milk, then let it sit [in the refrigerator] overnight. The next morning before serving, we coat it in egg and then fry it. We serve our version of *torrijas* with poached apples and instead of serving it with maple syrup, we serve it with Pedro Ximenez [a rich, sweet, Spanish sherry] syrup that has a raisin-like quality to it. The PX is just warmed and has a little glucose added to thicken it into a syrup. I don't cook it or reduce it because I want to keep the alcohol in the syrup so it doesn't become overly cloying.

— **ALEXANDRA RAIJ,** TÍA POL (NEW YORK CITY)

Daikon is great in stews and is milder, sweeter, and more absorbent than turnips or radishes. Duck and turnips is a classic, but I like duck with daikon even better. It pairs well with other heavier flavors, such as pork or beef.

— **TONY LIU**, AUGUST (NEW YORK CITY)

marjoram
mint
miso
oil, sesame
onions, esp. green
orange, juice
oregano
parsley
pork
salmon
scallions
soups
sour cream
soy sauce
sugar
sugar snap peas
tamari
thyme
tuna
vinegar

DANDELION GREENS
(See Greens, Dandelion)

DATES
Season: autumn–winter
Taste: sweet
Function: cooling
Weight: medium–heavy
Volume: moderate

almonds
apples
apricots
Armagnac
bacon
bananas
brandy
butter, unsalted
buttermilk
cakes
caramel
CHEESE, esp. Brie, Explorateur,

Parmesan, pecorino, ricotta, Roquefort
cherries, dried
chicken
chives
chocolate, esp. dark or white
cinnamon
coconut
coffee
couscous
cranberries, dried
cream and ice cream
cream cheese
crème fraîche
currants
desserts
figs

Dishes

Chocolate and Date Pudding Cake
— Gina DePalma, pastry chef, Babbo (New York City)

Baked-to-Order Date Pudding with a Caramelized Rum Sauce and a Dollop of Freshly Whipped Cream
— Toshi Sakihara, Etats-Unis (New York City)

Medjool Dates Stuffed with Chorizo, Wrapped in Bacon
— Monica Pope, T'afia (Houston)

Medjool Dates with Maple Mascarpone, Pistachios, and Orange Blossom Water
— Monica Pope, T'afia (Houston)

ginger
hazelnuts
honey
lamb
lemon
lime
macadamia nuts
maple syrup
mascarpone
Middle Eastern cuisine
Moroccan cuisine
nuts
oats
orange blossom water
ORANGE: juice, zest
pecans
pepper, black
pistachios
prunes
quince
raisins
rosemary
rum

Someone told me about a savory **date** dish they had but could only remember that it was stuffed and wrapped in bacon. This led me into the kitchen to stuff a date with chorizo, wrap it in bacon, and then add charmoula [typically made of paprika, cayenne pepper, cumin, garlic, lemon juice, parsley, cilantro, and olive oil]. The dish just hits the mark. I also serve a sweet date dish that I stole from Judy Rodgers of Zuni Café. My version is made with Medjool dates that have maple mascarpone smeared in, pistachios crumbled on top, and orange blossom water. The orange blossom water gives people a visceral reaction because you don't see it, but you taste it. When people have the dish, they lick their fingers trying to figure it out!

— **MONICA POPE**, T'AFIA (HOUSTON)

Emily Luchetti of Farallon in San Francisco on When and How to Serve Dessert

The older I get, the more I like my dessert at 3:00 in the afternoon. I like it all by itself, it has no competition and you are usually hungry. Your taste buds are wide awake and you can appreciate what it is. Of course if we have people over for dinner I can't get away with not serving dessert!

When you serve a dessert after a meal you are already full, not in a bad way, but if you had a first course and main course your palate has gone through many flavor components. At home I always take a little break and give people a breather between dinner and dessert. I'll have my guests help with the dishes or, if it's a formal party, I'll let them talk for a half hour and finish off the red wine. It is not just for their stomachs but for the palate as well.

I hate when it comes to slicing a dessert and someone says, "No, no, that is too big!" I used to fight it and take it personally, so now I just ask in advance. The guest appreciates it, has a small piece, and then has seconds. It is recognizing that everyone has their own choice regarding how much they want to eat. If I am serving a shortcake, I will put the fruit with a little cream on the cake, then pass a bowl of whipped cream, so whether they want to pile it or keep it light, they can.

sugar: brown, white
thyme
vanilla
walnuts
wine: red, sweet

Flavor Affinities
dates + caramel + vanilla + walnuts
dates + chocolate + walnuts
dates + cream + rum
dates + maple syrup + mascarpone + pistachios
dates + orange + walnuts

DESSERTS

Tips: Sweetness satiates the appetite, so generally end a meal on a sweet note.
Even sweet desserts should be in balance (their acidity, saltiness, etc.).
Dessert wine should always be sweeter than the dessert it accompanies.

DILL

Season: spring–autumn
Taste: sour, sweet
Weight: light, soft-leaved
Volume: moderately loud
Tips: Always use dill fresh, not cooked.

asparagus
avocados
basil
beans, esp. fava or green
beef
beets
breads, esp. rye
broccoli
cabbage
capers
carrots
cauliflower
celery root
cheese: cheddar, cottage, goat, soft
chicken
chives
cilantro
coriander
corn
crayfish
cream cheese
cream sauces
crème fraîche
CUCUMBERS
eggplant
EGGS AND EGG DISHES (e.g., omelets)
European cuisines
FISH, esp. whole
garlic
German cuisine
Greek cuisine
green beans
halibut
horseradish
lemon balm
lemon thyme
lovage
meats, e.g., lamb
Mediterranean cuisine
Middle Eastern cuisine
mint
mushrooms
mustard
North American cuisine
onions
paprika
parsley
parsnips
peas
PICKLES (key ingredient)
POTATOES AND POTATO SALAD
poultry
rice, esp. pilaf
Russian cuisine
salads and salad dressings
salmon
salmon, cured (key ingredient)
salmon, smoked
sauces
scallops
Scandinavian cuisine
shellfish

Dill adds a certain freshness and cleanness to a dish. During the winter, most of my fish dishes have dill — as well as dishes like goulash with noodles, which is served with both chives and dill for their herbal freshness.
— **TONY LIU**, AUGUST (NEW YORK CITY)

shrimp
sole
soups, esp. potato
sour cream and sour cream
    sauces
spinach
squash
**TOMATOES AND TOMATO
    JUICES**
trout
Turkish cuisine
veal
vegetables
**YOGURT AND YOGURT
    SAUCES**
zucchini

Flavor Affinities
dill + cilantro + mint
dill + cucumber + salmon

DUCK

Season: autumn
Weight: heavy
Volume: moderate–loud
Techniques: braise (esp. legs),
grill (esp. breast), roast, sauté,
stir-fry

allspice
APPLES, esp. Granny Smith
apricots (sauce)
artichokes
arugula
bacon
basil
bay leaf
beans, fava
blueberries
bok choy
butter, unsalted
cabbage: green, red
caraway seeds
cardamom
carrots
celery
celery root
cheese: Asiago, Parmesan,
    pecorino, ricotta

Dishes

Duck, Butternut Squash, and Banana with Thai Flavors
— Grant Achatz, Alinea (Chicago)

Liberty Farms Duck Breast with Smoked Bacon, Savoy Spinach, and Pickled Mulberries, Ginger Consommé
— Traci Des Jardins, Jardinière (San Francisco)

Roast Duck Breast, Bok Choy, and Cassava Chips with Sesame Soy Dressing and Pickled Chiles
— Brad Farmerie, Public (New York City)

Duck with Tomato, Red Chile, and Dried Mixed Fruits
— Zarela Martinez, Zarela (New York City)

Blossom Honey "Lacquered" Aged Moulard Duck Breast, Caramelized Quince and Fennel, Broccoli Rabe, Sicilian Pistachios, and Port
— Carrie Nahabedian, Naha (Chicago)

Grilled Duck Breast with Creamy Farro, Spring Onion, and Sour Cherry Jus
— Peter Nowakoski, Rat's (Hamilton, New Jersey)

Braised Duck Legs on Wilted Watercress in an Aromatic Asian Broth
— Patrick O'Connell, The Inn at Little Washington (Washington, Virginia)

Cured Duck Meat with a Salad of Licorice-Scented Fennel Shavings and Blood Orange
— Monica Pope, T'afia (Houston)

Drake Duck "Sirloin" with Roasted Sweet Potatoes and Port Wine Sauce
— Monica Pope, T'afia (Houston)

Duck Breast with Fava Beans and Roasted Plums
— Alfred Portale, Gotham Bar and Grill (New York City)

Grilled Duck Breast over Aromatic Tamarillo Sauce, Creamy Quinoa, and Sweet Potato Puree
— Maricel Presilla, Cucharamama (Hoboken, New Jersey)

Moulard Duck Breast with Parsnips, Wild Mushrooms, and a Rosemary Sauce
— Thierry Rautureau, Rover's (Seattle)

Muscovy Duck Breast with Rainier Cherries, Pecans, and Garden Lettuces
— Judy Rodgers, Zuni Café (San Francisco)

Charcoaled Duck with Walnuts, Confit Leg, and Apricots Baked in Brown Sugar Brioche
— Lydia Shire, Locke-Ober (Boston)

Grilled Liberty Farm Duck with Duck-Liver Wontons in Wild Mushroom Sauce
— Hiro Sone, Terra (St. Helena, California)

Grilled Duck Breast in Lime Leaf Curry with Ginger, Jalapeño Basmati Rice
— Vikram Vij and Meeru Dhalwala, Vij's (Vancouver)

Spit-Roasted Duck with Quince Sauce
— Alice Waters, Chez Panisse (Berkeley, California)

CHERRIES: regular, sun-dried
chervil
chestnuts
chicory
chile peppers: ancho, jalapeño
chili paste
Chinese cuisine
chives
chocolate / cocoa
cilantro
cinnamon
citrus fruit
cloves
coconut milk
coriander
cucumbers
cumin
currants, black or red: fruit,
    preserves
curry paste, esp. Thai green, or
    curry powder, esp. Madras
dates
duck fat
farro
fennel
fennel seeds
figs
fish sauce, Thai
five-spice powder
foie gras
GARLIC
GINGER
hoisin sauce
honey, esp. lavender
horseradish
huckleberries
juniper berries
kaffir lime leaves
kumquats
lavender
leeks
LEMON, JUICE, preserved
lemongrass
lentils
lime, juice
liqueur, orange (e.g., Grand
    Marnier), peach
mangoes

Our paella made with **duck** confit, foie gras, and morels is in honor of
[the late chef] Jean-Louis Palladin. We made a paella with the fat from
the duck and morels, and to finish it we topped it with thin slices of
raw foie gras. The foie gras would get warm from the hot rice and melt
into the rice. It is an amazing paella!
— **JOSÉ ANDRÉS,** CAFÉ ATLÁNTICO (WASHINGTON, DC)

Duck is great with fruit. We serve a duck with Seville oranges that are a
little bitter. We made a puree of the pulp and a little peel that had nice
acidity and bitterness. We then added fennel that had been cooked with
butter and a little star anise.
— **DANIEL HUMM,** ELEVEN MADISON PARK (NEW YORK CITY)

For my dish of lacquered **duck** and peppercress, I make a duck cooked
with honey served with a brown butter–honey that gives the duck a
sweet, nutty flavor. To cut the sweetness, I added a reduction of
pomegranate juice and oil emulsion to give the dish a tart contrast.
— **BOB IACOVONE,** CUVÉE (NEW ORLEANS)

marjoram
Mediterranean cuisine
mint
mirepoix
morels
MUSHROOMS, ESP. WILD
    (esp. porcini or shiitake)
mustard, Dijon
nutmeg
nuts, macadamia
OIL: canola, grapeseed, peanut,
    sesame, vegetable
olive oil
olives, esp. green
ONIONS, esp. green, sweet
ORANGE: juice, zest
pancetta
parsley, flat-leaf
pasta
peaches
pears
peas
PEPPER: black, green, pink,
    white
plums: fruit, sauce
pomegranates
poppy seeds
port
potatoes

prunes
raspberries
red pepper flakes
rice, esp. basmati, wild
risotto
rosemary
sage
sake
SALT: *fleur de sel,* kosher, sea
sauerkraut
scallions
sesame seeds: black, white
shallots
sherry
SOY SAUCE
spinach
squash, butternut
star anise
STOCKS: chicken, duck, game,
    meat, turkey
stuffing
SUGAR: brown, white
sweet potatoes
Tabasco sauce
tamarind
tarragon, fresh
teriyaki sauce
Thai cuisine
thyme, fresh

tomatoes: paste, puree, raw
turmeric
TURNIPS
vegetables, root
verjus
vermouth
VINEGAR: balsamic, champagne, raspberry, red wine, rice wine, sherry, white

Flavor Affinities
duck + almonds + apricots
duck + almonds + honey
duck + apples + celery root + hazelnuts
duck + apples + parsnips (and/or other root vegetables)
duck + apricots + cherries + basmati rice
duck + arugula + lentils
duck + arugula + vinaigrette + walnuts
duck + bacon + ginger + spinach
duck + blackberries + ginger + Pinot Noir
duck + cabbage + mushrooms
duck + cherries + vinegar
duck + cinnamon + honey + orange + star anise
duck + cloves + garlic + orange + prunes + red wine
duck + dates + turnips
duck + fava beans + pecorino cheese
duck + garlic + ginger + mint
duck + ginger + honey + soy sauce
duck + ginger + kumquats + black pepper + star anise
duck + green peppercorns + sweet potatoes
duck + honey + lavender
duck + lemon + plums
duck + lentils + onions + balsamic vinegar
duck + orange + scallions
duck + parsnips + turnips

We serve a sixteen-ounce **duck** breast with a Pinot Noir, blackberry, and ginger sauce. The sauce is made from frozen Oregon blackberries, which I am not shy to admit I use, because eleven months out of the year, there is nothing better. At home, I make a version of this sauce with currant preserves: I sauté the duck, then add lots of fresh ginger and shallots, a few tablespoons of currant preserves, and some champagne vinegar to cut the sweetness.
— **MICHAEL LOMONACO,** CHEF, PORTER HOUSE NEW YORK (NEW YORK CITY)

Dishes
Duck Confit: Wild Mushrooms, Red Swiss Chard, Sweet and Sour Duck Jus
— Olivier Muller, DB Bistro Moderne (New York City)

water chestnuts
watercress
WINE, dry red (e.g., Cabernet Sauvignon, Merlot), dry white (e.g., Riesling), port, rice, sweet (Madeira, Muscat)

DUCK CONFIT
beets
cheese, Roquefort
frisée
garlic
lentils, green
mushrooms, wild
mustard, Dijon
oil: hazelnut, walnut
onions
parsley, flat-leaf
pepper, white
salt
shallots
stock, chicken
vinegar, red wine
watercress

EASTERN EUROPEAN CUISINES
allspice, esp. in desserts
bacon
beef
beets
bell peppers, green
cabbage
caraway seeds
carrots
celery
celery root
chicken
cinnamon, esp. in desserts
cloves, esp. in desserts
cream
dill
game
garlic
ginger, esp. in desserts
juniper berries
lamb
marjoram
meats
mushrooms
mustard
noodles
offal
onions
paprika

pepper, black
potatoes
rice
sour cream
sugar
tomatoes
veal
vegetables, root
vinegar

Flavor Affinities
beef + cabbage + rice
beets + dill + sour cream
cabbage + caraway + vinegar
chicken + cream + paprika
noodles + caraway seeds + sour
   cream

EGGPLANT
Season: summer
Taste: bitter
Weight: medium–heavy
Volume: moderate
Techniques: bake, boil, braise,

Dishes

Grilled Eggplant Terrine with Red Bell Pepper and Italian Parsley Sauce
— David Bouley, Bouley (New York City)

Eggplant Ravioli with Medallions of Maine Lobster and Tomato-Basil Butter
— Patrick O'Connell, The Inn at Little Washington (Washington, Virginia)

Baba Ghanoush Soup, Made with Eggplant, Tahini, Tomato Water, Garlic, and Cumin
— Michel Richard, Citronelle (Washington, DC)

Eggplant, Peas, and Paneer in Pomegranate-Cinnamon Masala with Raita and Chapati
— Vikram Vij and Meeru Dhalwala, Vij's (Vancouver)

broil, deep-fry, grill, roast, sauté,
steam, stir-fry, stuff

allspice
anchovies
artichokes
basil
bell peppers, esp. green, red
bouquet garni
bread, pita
bread crumbs

cabbage, green
capers
cashews
cayenne
CHEESE: Emmental, feta, goat,
   Gruyère, mozzarella,
   Parmesan, ricotta, ricotta
   salata, Romano, Swiss
chickpeas
chile peppers, esp. fresh green
chili powder

Chinese cuisine
chives
cilantro
cinnamon
coconut milk
coriander
cumin
curry
dips
Eastern Mediterranean cuisine
fennel
fennel seeds
French cuisine, esp. Provençal
garam masala
GARLIC
ginger
honey
Indian cuisine
Italian cuisine
Japanese cuisine
Korean cuisine
lamb
LEMON, juice
lentils
Middle Eastern cuisine
mint
miso
mushrooms, esp. button, shiitake
mustard, Dijon
oil: peanut, sesame
OLIVE OIL
olives: black, green
ONIONS, esp. red, Spanish,
    yellow
oregano
paprika (garnish)
PARSLEY, FLAT-LEAF
pasta
PEPPER: BLACK, WHITE
peppers, piquillo (e.g., Spanish
    cuisine)
pine nuts
pomegranate
prosciutto
red pepper flakes
rice
rosemary
saffron

sage
SALT: kosher, sea
sausage
savory
scallions
sesame: oil, seeds
shallots
soy sauce
squash, yellow or other
    summer
stock, chicken

sugar
tahini
tamari
thyme
TOMATOES, tomato juice,
    tomato sauce
VINEGAR: balsamic, champagne,
    red wine, rice wine, sherry
walnuts
yogurt
zucchini

Flavor Affinities

eggplant + basil + bell peppers + garlic + tomatoes
eggplant + basil + mozzarella cheese
eggplant + basil + olive oil + balsamic vinegar
eggplant + basil + ricotta salata cheese + tomatoes
eggplant + bell peppers + garlic + mustard
eggplant + garlic + lemon juice + olive oil + parsley + tahini
eggplant + garlic + onions + parsley
eggplant + lentils + yogurt

Eggplant is funny. It is a subtle vegetable that can work with strong herbs like rosemary or marjoram.
— **JERRY TRAUNFELD**, THE HERBFARM (WOODINVILLE, WASHINGTON)

Eggplant can take on an even richer, meatier flavor when it's enhanced with miso or tahini.
— **BRAD FARMERIE**, PUBLIC (NEW YORK CITY)

My **eggplant** gazpacho really tastes like a baba ghanoush soup. We start the soup by roasting eggplant and onions. Then we blend this together with tahini, tomato water, buttermilk for acidity, lemon, and garlic. The soup is garnished with three gels made of eggplant, lemon, and onion — all flavors from the soup. I love texture — people joke with me and call me "Captain Crunch" — so at the last second, we top the soup with Rice Krispies.
— **MICHEL RICHARD**, CITRONELLE (WASHINGTON, DC)

EGGS AND EGG-BASED DISHES — IN GENERAL

Taste: sweet, astringent
Function: heating
Weight: light–medium
Volume: quiet
Techniques: bake (frittata, quiche, etc.), boil (soft or hard), fry, poach, scramble

asparagus
bacon and pancetta
basil
bell peppers, esp. green
bread
butter
capers
caviar
cheeses: Comté, Emmental, **feta, Gruyère, Havarti, mozzarella, Parmesan,** Roquefort
chervil
chives
chorizo
cream
cream cheese
crème fraîche
dill
garlic
ginkgo nuts
ham: Serrano, Virginia
herbs, esp. fines herbes (i.e., chervil, chives, parsley, tarragon)
leeks
marjoram
mushrooms
olive oil
onions
parsley, flat-leaf
pepper: black, white
potatoes
salmon, smoked
salt: kosher, sea
sausage
scallions

Dishes

Frittata with Zucchini and Parmesan Cheese, with Arugula Salad
— Andrew Carmellini, A Voce (New York City)

Poached Eggs with Crispy Polenta and Tomato Hollandaise
— Andrew Carmellini, A Voce (New York City)

Warm Salad of Greens with Pancetta and Scrambled Eggs
— Cesare Casella, Maremma (New York City)

Organic Egg Frittata with Mushrooms, Zucchini, and Gruyère
— Daniel Humm, Eleven Madison Park (New York City)

Organic Farm Egg Omelet with Capriole Farms Goat Cheese, Oranges, and Citrus Hollandaise, Toasted Ciabatta, and Apple Butter
— Carrie Nahabedian, Naha (Chicago)

Organic Farm Egg and Wood-Grilled Spanish Sausage with a Salad of Italian Frisée, Smoked Red Thumb Potatoes, French Breakfast Radishes, Sweet Garlic, and Herbs
— Carrie Nahabedian, Naha (Chicago)

Organic Scrambled Egg with a Lime Crème Fraîche and White Sturgeon Caviar
— Thierry Rautureau, Rover's (Seattle)

Traditional Eggs Benedict, Shaved Canadian Bacon, Lemon-Thyme Hollandaise, and Truffle Pesto
— Nori Sugie, Asiate (New York City)

Smoked Chicken, Roasted Bell Pepper, Artichoke, and Fontina Cheese Omelet
— Nori Sugie, Asiate (New York City)

I like **frittata** as a main course at lunch or dinner. You can simply have frittata with a soup, and it's a meal. Frittata is like a risotto in its versatility; you can go crazy with it and add almost anything to them. I love my frittata with vegetables; asparagus, artichokes, mushrooms, onions, zucchini all work. With any variety of vegetables I would add some fresh herbs and cheese. Since the eggs are the protein, the only thing I don't personally care for in my frittata is meat, or maybe pickled vegetables.
— **ODETTE FADA,** SAN DOMENICO (NEW YORK CITY)

We will serve the combination of poached **egg** and spring asparagus differently at brunch versus dinner. At brunch, we will serve sliced asparagus mixed with other sliced vegetables in the bottom of a *cazuela* [clay pot] with the poached egg on top. For dinner, it will be green market asparagus topped with a poached egg and anchovy butter.
— **ALEXANDRA RAIJ,** TÍA POL (NEW YORK CITY)

shallots
sorrel
spinach
tarragon
thyme
tomatoes
truffles

AVOID
cranberries

Flavor Affinities
eggs + bacon + cheese + onions
eggs + bacon + crème fraîche + onions (Alsatian)
eggs + beets + smoked whitefish (Yiddish)
eggs + cheese + mushrooms + thyme
eggs + kale + pinkelwurst (oatmeal sausage) (Berliner)
eggs + mozzarella cheese + tomatoes (Roman)
eggs + mushrooms + red wine (Bordelaise)
eggs + potato + sausage

EGGS, FRITTATA
anchovies
artichokes
arugula
asparagus
bacon and pancetta
basil
bell peppers
cheese: feta, Gruyère, Havarti, mozzarella, Parmesan
chives
herbs
Italian cuisine
mushrooms
olives
onions
pepper, black
salt, esp. kosher
sausage
shallots
thyme
tomatoes
zucchini

EGGS, HARD-BOILED
Techniques: chop, devil, halve, sieve, slice

almonds
basil
butter, unsalted
cayenne
chile peppers, jalapeño
chives
cilantro
cream
curry
dill
garlic
ginger, pickled
leeks
mayonnaise
mint
mustard: Dijon, dry
olive oil
paprika
parsley, flat-leaf
pepper, black
salmon
salt, kosher
sauce, béchamel
scallions
shallots
sour cream
Tabasco sauce
tarragon
tomatoes

ENDIVE
Season: winter–spring
Taste: bitter, sweet
Weight: light
Volume: quiet–moderate
Techniques: braise, glaze, grill, raw, roast

almonds
anchovies
apples
arugula
avocado

Dishes

Cabbageless Sauerkraut: Pickled Onions, Fennel, Endive, and Green Apple
— Christopher Lee, Gilt (New York City)

Endive Tips with Red Pepper Puree, Maple Molasses, and Candied Walnuts
— Monica Pope, T'afia (Houston)

Endive and Grapefruit Salad with Honey Dressing and Toasted Pecans
— Monica Pope, T'afia (Houston)

Belgian Endive Salad, Shredded Carrot and Apple Salad, Concord Grapes, Sonoma Verjus Vinaigrette
— Nori Sugie, Asiate (New York City)

People shy away from **endive** because of its bitterness. But a good chef will pair it with a sweet dressing.
— **CARRIE NAHABEDIAN**, NAHA (CHICAGO)

bacon and pancetta
basil
bay leaf
beets
butter, unsalted
capers
cardamom, green
celery
CHEESE: Asiago, **blue, goat, Gorgonzola, Gruyère**, herb, **Parmesan, Roquefort**
chervil
chicken
chives
cinnamon
coriander
crab
cream
cream cheese
crème fraîche
cumin
fennel seeds
fenugreek
French cuisine
frisée
game
garlic
ginger
grapefruit
honey
horseradish

leeks
lemon, juice
mayonnaise
mushrooms
mustard: Dijon, dry, whole grain
mustard seeds
OIL: grapeseed, peanut, safflower, vegetable
OLIVE OIL
olives, black
orange: fruit, juice
parsley, flat-leaf
peanuts
pears
pecans
pepper: black, white
nuts
pistachios
pomegranate
radicchio
red pepper flakes
rosemary
salads
salt: kosher, sea
seafood
shallots
shrimp
smoked fish, esp. salmon or trout
sour cream
stocks: chicken, fish, veal
sugar: brown, white

tarragon
thyme
tomatoes
vinaigrette, mustard
VINEGAR: balsamic, raspberry, red wine, sherry
WALNUTS
watercress

Flavor Affinities
endive + argula + radicchio
endive + cheese + mushrooms

ENDIVE, CURLY (See Frisée)

ENGLISH CUISINE
cheese: Cheddar, Stilton
cream
fish (and chips)
game
jams and preserves
lamb
mutton
oats
peas
puddings (e.g., Yorkshire)
roast beef
scones
tea
tea sandwiches
Worcestershire sauce

EPAZOTE
Taste: bitter
Weight: light–medium
Volume: moderate–loud

beans, esp. black
bell peppers
Caribbean cuisine
Central American cuisine
chile peppers
chorizo
cilantro
cloves
corn
cumin
fish

I have always loved to mix meat and fish in a very delicate way. I went to Cut [Wolfgang Puck's steak restaurant] and had my first true Kobe beef steak. I begged Lee [Hefter, the chef] for his source! Surf and turf is not as much about having a piece of meat and fish on the plate as about the ideas they create for flavor combinations. The Kobe beef triggered everything. I can't serve steak at a fish restaurant, but the Kobe was so good I had to find a way to justify it on the menu. I came up with Kobe beef and **escalar,** with a brown butter that is classic with the fish. The final dish was inspired by having Korean barbecue at a friend's house, which is when I realized how to bring it together.

I wanted another element in the dish because the Kobe, escalar, and brown butter are all rich and all soft. The dish also has squash, Japanese pears, and napa cabbage marinated like Korean kimchee for just a moment. These elements add contrast, chewiness, and crunchiness.

— **ERIC RIPERT,** LE BERNARDIN (NEW YORK CITY)

garlic
goat
Latin American cuisines
legumes
lime
Mexican cuisine
mole sauces
mushrooms
onions
oregano
paprika
pepper
pork
rice
salsas
shellfish
soups
squash
tomatillos
vegetables, green

ESCALAR
brown butter
Kobe beef

Flavor Affinities
escalar + Kobe beef + brown
  butter

ESCAROLE
Season: year-round
Taste: bitter
Weight: medium

Volume: moderate–loud
Techniques: braise, grill, roast

almonds
anchovies
beans
beef
butter
cheese: Fontina, Gruyère,
  mozzarella, Parmesan,
  Roquefort
chile peppers, dried red
cream
cumin
fish
garlic
hazelnuts
lemon
olive oil
olives, black
onions
paprika, sweet
parsley
pepper: black, white
pork
poultry
red pepper flakes
salt, kosher

Escarole is a bitter but sturdy leaf, and in a salad dressed with olive oil and red wine vinegar, I like to add Cheddar for its sharpness and creaminess plus some crisp and refreshing apples.
— **TONY LIU,** AUGUST (NEW YORK CITY)

shallots
soups, esp. bean
stock, chicken
tomatoes (e.g., cherry)
vinegar, red or white wine

Flavor Affinities
escarole + apples + Cheddar
  cheese
escarole + olive oil + shallots

ETHIOPIAN CUISINE
beef, raw or stewed
injera
spices
stewed dishes
vegetables, stewed
wine, honey

EUROPEAN, EASTERN CUISINES (See Eastern European Cuisines)

FALL (See Autumn)

FENNEL
Season: year-round
Taste: sweet
Weight: light
Volume: quiet
Techniques: boil, braise, fry, grill, raw, roast, sauté, steam

almonds
anise
apples
arugula
asparagus
basil
bay leaf
beets: vegetable, juice
bell peppers
BUTTER, UNSALTED
carrots

Dishes

Wild Fennel and Ramp Soup with Broken Capellini and Alaskan King Crab
— Lidia Bastianich, Felidia (New York City)

Braised Fennel Salad with Pears and Gorgonzola
— Mario Batali, Babbo (New York City)

Puree of Fennel Soup with Apples, Almonds, and Madras Curry
— Traci Des Jardins, Jardinière (San Francisco)

CHEESE: blue, goat, Gorgonzola, Gruyère, **Parmesan**, pecorino
chicken
chives
coriander
crab
cream
crème fraîche
cucumbers
eggplant
eggs
endive
fennel pollen
fennel seeds
FISH, esp. grilled and/or whole salmon, sea bass, snapper
frisée
garlic
ginger, fresh

Italian cuisine
herbs
honey
lamb
leeks
LEMON: juice, zest
lemon balm
lettuce: Bibb, butter
lime: juice, leaf (kaffir)
lobster
lovage
meats
Mediterranean cuisine
mint
mussels
nutmeg
OIL: canola
olive oil
olives: black, green

onions, esp. red
ORANGE: JUICE, segments
pancetta
paprika
parsley, flat-leaf
pasta
pears
pecans
PEPPER: BLACK, WHITE
Pernod
pickles
pork
potatoes
prosciutto
rice
rosemary
salads (e.g., green or tuna) and salad dressings
salmon
salt: kosher, sea
sambuca
sauces
scallions
shallots
shellfish
shrimp
soups, esp. vegetable
spinach
star anise
stews, esp. fish
stocks: chicken, veal, vegetable
stuffing
sugar (pinch)
swordfish
tarragon
thyme
tomatoes and tomato sauce
tuna
veal
vegetables, esp. summer
vermouth
vinaigrettes
vinegar: champagne, cider, raspberry
walnuts
watercress
wine: dry white, vermouth
zucchini

I like **fennel** shaved raw, with just some lemon juice, olive oil, and fennel seeds. Fennel goes well with dried meats like prosciutto. It also pairs nicely with shellfish like langoustines, lobster, or crab. Fennel can work with fish as well as with meat. It goes really well with cold poached salmon or white, light meats like chicken or veal.

— **GABRIEL KREUTHER**, THE MODERN (NEW YORK CITY)

Fennel is a flavor I like so much that I have to show restraint with it. You can add anything to it because other flavors really adhere to it. You can braise it in olive oil and veal stock to get one flavor. Or you can braise it in olive oil, white wine, and water and get a whole other flavor. Or you can quarter it, caramelize it, and roast it in the oven — now you have a sugar flavor and it can become a dessert. I love fennel every way including braised, caramelized, dried, candied, and pureed. In the fall, I served raw shaved fennel with arugula, and shaved Honeycrisp apple with a dressing made of apple cider, honey, and mustard. Fennel puts the salad over the top with its crunch. In summer, we serve a fennel and fig tarte tatin with duck. You get a Fig Newton flavor from the fig and Pernod flavor from the fennel; they match really well.

— **CARRIE NAHABEDIAN**, NAHA (CHICAGO)

Flavor Affinities

fennel + almond + fennel seeds + honey + lemon
fennel + apple + pecorino cheese + watercress
fennel + asparagus + fennel seeds + garlic + olive oil
fennel + garlic + onions + tomatoes
fennel + lemon + mint + olive oil + olives + orange
fennel + lemon + olive oil + Parmesan cheese + parsley
fennel + onions + potatoes + chicken stock
fennel + orange + sambuca

FENNEL POLLEN

Taste: sweet
Weight: light
Volume: quiet
Tips: Use to finish a dish.

apricots
beef
boar
chicken
cream
fennel seeds
fish, esp. flakier white, poached
   or steamed
garlic
lamb
lemon
nuts, esp. almonds, pistachios

pasta
pork
potatoes
poultry
rabbit
rice or risotto
salads
salmon
sea trout
shellfish
vegetables
yogurt

Flavor Affinities

fennel pollen + lemon + yogurt

Fennel pollen has a light, fennel-anise flavor with a floral component. It is delicate, so you don't cook with it — you just finish a dish with it. It is great on lighter things like salads, poached or steamed flaky white fish, poultry, or pork. When a dish has fennel pollen, even before the food hits your mouth you will notice a floral smell that gets you thinking of summer, lighter foods, and freshness. I use it with my sea trout dish, which is served with a simple salad of green apple, fennel, jicama, pistachios, and dried gooseberries. The dish is topped with the pollen blended with some yogurt, lemon juice, and preserved lemon, which we drape over the fish. This dish just screams "summer." With a glass of Sauvignon Blanc on the terrace in the early evening, you're set!
— **BRAD FARMERIE,** PUBLIC (NEW YORK CITY)

I really like **fennel pollen.** The majority of the time, we use it in a marinade for meats like pork, boar, chicken, and lamb. It adds an interesting herbaceous, aromatic note and a mysterious flavor.
— **SHARON HAGE,** YORK STREET (DALLAS)

FENNEL SEEDS

Taste: sweet
Weight: light
Volume: quiet–medium
Tips: Add near end of cooking process.

apples
baked goods (e.g., breads)
basil
beans
beets
bouillabaisse
cabbage
chicken
Chinese cuisine
cinnamon
cloves
cucumber
cumin
curries
duck
fennel
figs
FISH, ESP. STEAMED
five-spice powder (key ingredient)
garam masala (key ingredient)
garlic
herbes de Provence (key ingredient)
Italian cuisine
leeks
lentils
meats, braised
Mediterranean cuisine
olives
orange
paprika
parsley
pasta
pepper, black
pickles
pork
potatoes
ras el hanout (key ingredient)
rice
saffron
salads

sauces
sauerkraut
*SAUSAGES, esp. Italian
Scandinavian cuisine
shellfish
soups, esp. fish
star anise
stews, esp. fish
stocks and broths
tarragon
tomatoes and tomato sauces
vegetables, esp. green

Flavor Affinities

fennel seeds + cinnamon + cloves + peppercorns + star anise (five-spice powder)

FENUGREEK

Season: autumn
Taste: bitter, sweet
Function: heating
Weight: light–medium
Volume: quiet–moderate

cardamom
cauliflower
cheeses, esp. creamy
chicken
cinnamon
cloves
coriander
cream, esp. sour
cumin
CURRIES AND CURRY POWDERS
Ethiopian cuisine
fennel seeds
fish
garlic
Indian cuisine
lamb

I love **fenugreek**, and its incredible aromatics. It goes well with everything from lamb to chicken to vegetables.
— VIKRAM VIJ, VIJ'S (VANCOUVER)

legumes
lentils
maple syrup, artificial (key ingredient)
mayonnaise
mint
peas
pepper
potatoes
rabbit
rice
sauces, esp. creamy
shellfish, shrimp
soups
spinach
stews, esp. tomato-based
tomatoes
turmeric
vegetables, esp. green and root
yogurt

FETA CHEESE
(See Cheese, Feta)

FIDDLEHEAD FERNS

Season: spring
Taste: bitter
Weight: medium
Volume: moderate–loud
Techniques/Tips: Always serve cooked: blanch, boil, sauté, steam.

American cuisine, esp. New England
asparagus
bacon
basil
beans, fava
beef
brown butter
butter, sweet
cayenne

Flavor Affinities

fiddlehead ferns + butter + herbs + morel mushrooms + ramps
fiddlehead ferns + garlic + morel mushrooms + salmon
fiddlehead ferns + sesame oil and/or seeds + soy sauce

Dishes

Bresaola with Fiddleheads and Pecorino
— Mario Batali, Babbo (New York City)

cheese: Comté, goat, Parmesan
chicken
fennel
fish (e.g., halibut, salmon)
garlic
hollandaise sauce
horseradish
lamb
lemon, juice
MUSHROOMS, WILD, e.g., chanterelles, morels
mustard
oil: sesame, walnut
olive oil
onions, esp. cipollini, red, spring
parsley, flat-leaf
pasta, esp. gnocchi
pepper
polenta
potatoes, esp. Yukon gold
poultry
prosciutto
ramps
salads
salt
sesame seeds
shallots
soy sauce
spinach
tarragon
thyme
veal
vinaigrettes
vinegar: balsamic, sherry
walnuts
yogurt

FIGS, DRIED
Taste: sweet
Weight: medium
Volume: moderate
Techniques: stew

almonds
anise seeds
apples
apricots, dried
bananas
bay leaf
brandy
caramel
**cheese: goat, manchego,
    Parmesan, ricotta**
cherries, dried
chestnuts
chocolate, esp. dark, white
cinnamon
cloves
coconut
coffee

cognac
cream
dates
game
ginger
HONEY
lemon: juice, zest
macadamia nuts
maple syrup
mascarpone
nutmeg
oats
ORANGE: fruit, juice
pastries
pears
pecans
pineapple
pistachios
prunes
quince
raisins, yellow
sugar, brown
sweet potatoes

vanilla
WALNUTS
WINE, RED, sweet

Flavor Affinities
dried figs + anise + oranges +
    walnuts

FIGS, FRESH
Season: summer–autumn
Taste: sweet, astringent
Function: cooling
Weight: medium
Volume: quiet–moderate
Techniques: bake, broil,
caramelize, deep-fry, grill, raw,
roast

ALMONDS
anchovies
anise, esp. green
apples
arugula

Dishes

Fresh Fig Tart with a Dollop of Mascarpone
— Gina DePalma, pastry chef, Babbo (New York City)

Fig and Ricotta Gelato
— Gina DePalma, pastry chef, Babbo (New York City)

Honey-Baked Figs Stuffed with Walnuts
— Gina DePalma, pastry chef, Babbo (New York City)

Black Mission Figs with Goat Cheese Mousse, Honey Ice Cream, and Port Sabayon
— Gary Danko, Gary Danko (San Francisco)

Rogue River Oregonzola, Black Mission Figs, Lavender Honey, Toasted Hazelnuts
— Monica Pope, T'afia (Houston)

bacon
butter, unsalted
caramel
CHEESE: blue, fromage blanc, **goat, Gorgonzola,** dry Jack, manchego, provolone, **ricotta,** Roquefort
cherries
chicken
chocolate: dark, white
cilantro
cinnamon
cloves
coffee / espresso
cognac
CREAM AND ICE CREAM
cream cheese
crème anglaise
crème fraîche
duck
fish (e.g., bass)
five-spice powder
French cuisine, esp. southern
game birds
garlic
ginger
grapes
ham, esp. Serrano
hazelnuts
HONEY
Italian cuisine, esp. southern
Kirsch
lamb

lavender
lemon: juice, zest
lime, juice
liqueurs, esp. raspberry
mango
mascarpone
meats, cured and smoked
Mediterranean cuisine
Middle Eastern cuisine
mint
Moroccan cuisine
oil, grapeseed
olive oil
onions
ORANGE: juice, zest
pancetta
pears
pecans
pepper, black
pine nuts
pistachios
pork
port
prosciutto
quail
radicchio
RASPBERRIES
rice
rosemary
rum, esp. dark
sorbets
star anise
SUGAR: brown, white

thyme
VANILLA
Vin Santo
VINEGAR: BALSAMIC, red wine, sherry
WALNUTS
wine: dry red, Marsala, port

Flavor Affinities

figs + almonds + green anise
figs + black pepper + ricotta cheese
figs + caramel + vanilla + balsamic vinegar
figs + cilantro + lime
figs + cinnamon + honey + orange
figs + cream + goat cheese + honey
figs + cream + honey + raspberries
figs + goat cheese + pine nuts
figs + honey + mascarpone
figs + lemon + rosemary
figs + olive oil + rosemary
figs + Pernod + walnuts

FILET MIGNON (See Beef — Steak: Filet Mignon)

FINES HERBES

Tips: Use late in the cooking process.

French cuisine

Flavor Affinities

chervil + chives + parsley + tarragon

FISH — IN GENERAL

(See individual fish; Seafood)

Taste: sweet
Function: heating
Weight: light–medium
Volume: quiet–moderate

anise
basil
broths
butter
cream
dill
fennel
fines herbes (i.e., chervil, chives,
    parsley, tarragon)
garlic
ginger
grapefruit
leeks
lemon: juice, zest
lemongrass
lemon verbena
lime: juice, zest
parsley
peas (accompaniment)

Think of white **fish** — dorade, Dover sole, pompano, skate, snapper — as white meat, and red fish — salmon, tuna — as red meat. Salmon is like pork, and tuna like beef, and both combine better with stronger flavors. Tuna even pairs with some of the same flavors as beef, including black pepper, red wine, and wasabi.

— **MICHEL RICHARD,** CITRONELLE (WASHINGTON, DC)

I like my **fish** simply grilled or steamed. I choose fish that have a lot of flavor so very little has to be done to them. I don't believe you need 10,000 things for a great piece of fish. Dover sole doesn't need anything. Turbot has a wonderful flavor with no help. We get our baby octopus from Sicily and they have plenty of flavor.

— **ODETTE FADA,** SAN DOMENICO (NEW YORK CITY)

Dishes

Onion-Crusted White Fish with Tomato-Water Sauce
— Michel Richard, Citronelle (Washington, DC)

peppercorns
rhubarb
salt
tomatoes
wine, esp. white

Flavor Affinities
fish + ginger + lemongrass
fish + herbs + white wine
fish + onions + tomatoes

FISH SAUCE

Taste: salty
Weight: light
Volume: loud

lime, juice
sauces, dipping
shrimp
Southeast Asian cuisines
spring rolls
sugar
Thai cuisine
Vietnamese cuisine
vegetables

FIVE-SPICE POWDER

Taste: sweet
Weight: light
Volume: quiet–moderate

beef
chicken
Chinese cuisine
duck
pork
stews
stir-fries

Flavor Affinities
cinnamon + cloves + fennel seeds
+ star anise + Szechuan
peppercorns

FLOUNDER

Season: summer
Weight: light
Volume: quiet
Techniques: bake, broil, deep-fry, fry, poach, sauté, steam, stir-fry

almonds
basil
bread crumbs or cracker crumbs
butter
capers
chili sauce
chives
coconut milk
corn
cornmeal (e.g., as a crust)
crab
curry, green
dill
lemon
lime
Mediterranean cuisine
miso
noodles
olive oil
onions, Vidalia
pasta
peas
pepper, black
ramps
salt
seaweed, esp. konbu

Dishes

Flounder Wrapped in Spring Roll Paper Served with House-Made Egg Noodles, Thai Green Curry–Coconut Milk Broth with Snow Peas, Yuzu Lime, and Honey Mushrooms
— Bob Kinkead, Colvin Run (Vienna, Virginia)

Sesame-Flavored Flounder and Wakame Seaweed Soup
— Kaz Okochi, Kaz Sushi Bistro (Washington, DC)

shiso
ume (Japanese plum)
wine, white
yuzu
zucchini

Flavor Affinities
flounder + capers + lemon
flounder + shiso + ume
flounder + konbu seaweed + shiso

FOIE GRAS

Season: autumn
Weight: heavy
Volume: moderate
Techniques: braise, sauté, terrine

allspice
APPLES
apricots
Armagnac
bacon
brandy
cabbage
cherries
chives
chocolate
cognac
endive
figs: dried, fresh
French cuisine
ginger
grapes
leeks
lemon
mangoes
miso

Dishes

Foie Gras with Roasted Plums
— Carrie Nahabedian, Naha (Chicago)

Foie Gras Sushi with Plum-Wine Jelly
— Kaz Okochi, Kaz Sushi Bistro (Washington, DC)

Seared Hudson Valley Foie Gras with Caramelized Three-Pear Salad
— Jimmy Schmidt, at the 2003 James Beard Awards gala reception

I found a recipe for olive oil cake at the same time that I was perfecting making a **foie gras** mousse that was pliable to the point that it could be made into an icing. So, I created a savory cake topped with the icing. Then one day while I was online I heard someone mention Twinkies, and the next thing I knew I was ordering real Twinkie pans online. Three days later, Twinkies stuffed with foie gras was born. I serve it with fresh strawberries and black pepper. It seems like everything has been done already, but I like to think I am the only person working with Twinkies.

— **BOB IACOVONE,** CUVÉE (NEW ORLEANS)

nutmeg
oil, grapeseed
olive oil
onions
peaches
pears
pepper, black
pistachios
plums
port
raisins
rhubarb
salt, kosher
Sauternes
shallots
stock, chicken
strawberries
sugar (dash)
tomatoes
truffles and truffle oil, esp. white
vinegar: balsamic, cider

Flavor Affinities

foie gras + cherries + balsamic
   vinegar
foie gras + cherries + pistachios
foie gras + strawberries + black
   pepper

FRENCH CUISINE — IN GENERAL

beef
cheese
CREAM
eggs
herbs
mustards
onions
parsley
pastries
pork
potatoes
poultry

roasted meats
SAUCES
sausages
sautéed dishes
seafood
shallots
spirits
STOCK
tarragon
thyme
truffles, black
veal
vinegars
wheat, esp. as flour
WINE

Flavor Affinities

butter + cheese + stock
butter + cheese + wine
butter + herbs
cream + herbs
herbs + stock
herbs + wine

FRENCH CUISINE, NORTHERN

apples: cider, fruit, juice
buckwheat (key ingredient in
   crepes)
BUTTER
cabbage
Calvados
charcuterie
cheese: Camembert
CREAM

Tarte flambée is a dish that is 200 years old and was originally made by farmers in Alsace in the village's wood-burning oven used for baking bread. The *tarte flambée* developed from what was on hand on the farm: cheese and cream from the cow, pork from the pig, and onions from the field, which they added to some dough. Since we don't have a wood-burning oven [in the middle of Manhattan], we have to tweak the recipe from the classic. We have to tweak the cream because if we don't, it breaks and just becomes grease. Instead, I use a mix of fromage blanc, cream, and sour cream so I can get the same result as cream in the original. And to compensate for not having a fire, I use an applewood-smoked bacon.

— **GABRIEL KREUTHER,** THE MODERN (NEW YORK CITY)

fish, freshwater
game
lobster
oysters
pork: bacon, ham
sausages
shellfish
veal

Flavor Affinities
bacon + cheese + cream

FRENCH CUISINE, SOUTHERN (aka Provençal Cuisine)

anchovies
anise
basil
beef, esp. stewed
bell peppers
chicken, esp. grilled
fish, esp. grilled
garlic
grilled dishes
herbes de Provence
lamb, esp. roasted
lavender
marjoram
meats
mustard
OLIVE OIL
olives
pâtés
pork
rosemary
sage
shellfish
soups
tomatoes
vegetables
wine

Flavor Affinities
basil + garlic + olive oil + Parmesan cheese
basil + olive oil + tomatoes
bell peppers + eggplant + garlic + onions + tomatoes + zucchini
chicken + garlic + olives + onions + tomatoes
garlic + egg yolk + lemon + olive oil + saffron
marjoram + rosemary + sage + thyme (aka *herbes de Provence*)
olives + basil + capers + garlic + olive oil (aka tapenade)
pork + anise + marjoram + thyme
seafood + garlic + olive oil + tomatoes

FRESHNESS

Season: spring–summer
Tips: Listed herbs are always used fresh (with little or no cooking), and add a note of freshness to a dish. Other listed flavors add a bright note to a dish. For the opposite, see listing for **Slow-Cooked.**

basil
chives
cilantro
citrus
dill
fennel pollen
mint
tarragon

FRISÉE (a fine-leaved variety of curly endive)

Season: year-round
Taste: sweet, bitter
Weight: light
Volume: quiet
Techniques: raw, wilt

almonds
anchovies
avocado
bacon / lardons
basil
bell peppers: red, yellow
beets
CHEESE: BLUE, GOAT, PARMESAN, ROQUEFORT
cherries, dried
chervil
chives
cilantro
croutons (accent)
cucumbers
eggs, esp. poached
endive
fat: bacon, duck
garlic
ginger
grapefruit
lemon, juice
lettuces: red oak leaf, red leaf
lime, juice
maple syrup
mushrooms, white
mustard, Dijon
oil: canola, grapeseed, hazelnut, walnut
olive oil
olives
onions, red
orange, juice
parsley, flat-leaf
pepper: black, white
salads, esp. warm
salt: kosher, sea
scallops
seafood
shallots
tangerines and tangerine juice
tarragon
tomatoes
vinaigrette
vinegar: sherry, white wine

Dishes

Salad "Lyonnaise": Italian Frisée, Applewood Slab Bacon, and Warm Poached Egg, Sherry Wine–Dijon Mustard Vinaigrette
— Carrie Nahabedian, Naha (Chicago)

Warm Frisée and Bacon Salad with Beet Carpaccio and Toasted Walnuts
— Lydia Shire, Locke-Ober Café (Boston)

Frisée and Spinach Salad with Dried Cherries, Blue Cheese, Walnuts, and Maple-Sherry Vinaigrette
— Charlie Trotter, Trotter's to Go (Chicago)

walnuts (accent)
watercress

Flavor Affinities

frisée + anchovies + garlic + Parmesan cheese
frisée + bacon + poached egg
frisée + bacon + Roquefort cheese + garlic + shallots + sherry vinegar

---

FRUIT, DRIED (See also Dates, Figs, Raisins, etc.)

Taste: sweet
Tips: If the fruit is hard, steam before using.

apple juice
chocolate
cinnamon
ginger
lemon
nuts
pistachios
vanilla
walnuts

FRUIT, FRESH

(See also specific fruits)
Taste: sweet
Tips: Sugar enhances the natural flavor of fruit.

almonds
ginger, fresh
lemon: juice, zest
sabayon sauce

SUGAR
vanilla

FRUIT, TROPICAL (See also specific fruits, e.g., Mangoes, Papayas, Pineapples, etc.)

Taste: sweet, sour

bananas
bourbon
caramel
chile peppers
chocolate
chocolate, white
cloves
coconut
coriander
cream and ice cream
five-spice powder
ginger
guava
honey
lemon: juice, zest
lemongrass
LIME: JUICE, ZEST
mangoes
melon, honeydew
mint
orange: juice, zest
pineapple
pomegranates
RUM
spirits, white: gin, vodka
strawberries
sugar: brown, white
vanilla
yogurt

Flavor Affinities

tropical fruit + coconut + honey + lime
tropical fruit + ginger + mint + orange + sugar

Tropical fruits are strong flavored, and stand up to chocolate better. At the same time, tropical fruits like bananas or mangoes are not overly sweet fruits, so caramel can stand up to them. With tropical fruits, I will use a little lime juice and often rum as well to help give them a little kick. With mangoes, I use a little light brown sugar — or I'll even blend light brown and white sugar together because I'll want the flavor but not want it to be too harsh.
— **EMILY LUCHETTI**, FARALLON (SAN FRANCISCO)

Dishes

Exotic Fruit Salad with Guava Sauce and Phyllo Galettes
— Dominique and Cindy Duby, Wild Sweets (Vancouver)

Chocolate Custard Cake with Exotic Fruit Gelée and Caramelized Bananas
— Dominique and Cindy Duby, Wild Sweets (Vancouver)

Tropical Fruit Salad with Rosewater and Sweet Tahini Yogurt
— Brad Farmerie, Public (New York City)

GAME — IN GENERAL

(See also Rabbit, Venison)
Season: autumn
Weight: heavy
Volume: moderate–loud
Techniques: braise, roast
Tips: The flavor of cloves adds richness to game.

allspice
cabbage, red
cayenne
cherries
chestnuts
cloves
cranberries, dried
garlic
gin
greens
Italian cuisine
juniper berries
lentils
Madeira
maple syrup
mushrooms, wild
mustard, Dijon
onions
parsley, flat-leaf
pepper, black
salt, sea
stock, beef
sugar, brown
vinegar
wine, red

GARAM MASALA

Function: warming
Tips: Add near the end of the cooking process or before serving.

Indian cuisine

Flavor Affinities

cardamom + black pepper + cinnamon + cloves + coriander + cumin + dried chiles + fennel + mace + nutmeg

GARLIC

Season: year-round
Botanical relatives: chives, leeks, onions, shallots
Function: heating
Weight: light–medium
Volume: moderate (esp. cooked)–loud (esp. raw)
Techniques: grill, raw, roast, sauté

almonds
anchovies
bacon
barbecue
basil
bay leaf
beans
beef
beets
bread
broccoli
cabbage
Cajun cuisine
caraway seeds
cayenne
cheese, Parmesan
chicken
chile peppers

Chinese cuisine
chives
cilantro
coriander
cream, half-and-half
Creole cuisine
cumin
curries
eggplant
eggs
fennel
fennel seeds
fish
French cuisine
ginger
Indian cuisine
Italian cuisine
Korean cuisine
lamb
leeks
LEMON: juice, zest
lemongrass
lentils
lime, juice
mayonnaise
meats
Mediterranean cuisine
Mexican cuisine
Middle Eastern cuisine

When **garlic** needs to be there, it needs to be there. That includes a lot of dishes, such as lamb. Garlic is also called for with all kinds of vegetables, sauces, pastas, and salads.

— **DAVID WALTUCK**, CHANTERELLE (NEW YORK CITY)

I use **garlic** primarily in two ways: infused into olive oil, or served crispy as a garnish. I'll use the garlic oil for cooking — and even if a dish will have garlic added later, I will start with this oil. For crispy brown garlic, you start by slicing it thinly like a chip. The garlic is then put into cold olive oil and cooked until it is just brown. Then, you add parsley, red pepper flakes, and an acid like lemon juice or vinegar to make a vinaigrette. You can even add some stock like a fumet, which is wonderful, too — served hot, it is great with almost any kind of fish, from something light all the way to oily blue fish.

— **ALEXANDRA RAIJ**, TÍA POL (NEW YORK CITY)

Moroccan cuisine
mushrooms
mustard
oil: canola, peanut
OLIVE OIL
onions
oregano
paprika, esp. sweet
parsley, flat-leaf
pasta and pasta sauces
pepper: black, white
pesto (key ingredient)
pork
potatoes
rice
rosemary
saffron
sage
salads (e.g., Caesar)
salt
sauces
shallots
shellfish
shrimp
soups
soy sauce
spinach
steak
stocks: chicken, vegetable
sugar
tarragon
Thai cuisine

thyme
TOMATOES AND TOMATO SAUCE
vegetables
Vietnamese cuisine
VINEGAR, esp. balsamic, red wine
wine, white
zucchini

GEORGIAN CUISINE (RUSSIAN)
fish
garlic
meats
pepper, red ground
pickles
pomegranates
vinegar
walnuts

Flavor Affinities
coriander + dill + fenugreek
    (blue) + garlic + red peppers
garlic + walnuts

GERMAN CUISINE
allspice
anise
bay leaf
beer
bread, rye

caraway seeds
chives
cinnamon
dill: seeds, weed
fish
ginger
horseradish
juniper berries
mace
meats, esp. with fruits
nutmeg
paprika, sweet
parsley
pepper, white
poppy seeds
pork
potatoes
sauerbraten
sauerkraut
sausages
sour cream
sugar
veal
vinegar

Flavor Affinities
caraway + paprika + sour cream
caraway + sauerkraut
cream + horseradish + fish or
    meat
cream + paprika + poppy seeds
dill + cucumbers
ginger + sauerbraten
juniper berries + game
mace + chicken
nutmeg + potatoes
sugar + vinegar

GIN
Weight: light–medium
Volume: quiet–loud

apple brandy
apricot brandy
basil
blackberries
celery
Champagne

Cucumber and mint is a fashionable combination in cocktails, [especially] those with Hendrick's **gin**, which has a cucumber flavor. Cucumber is a flavor that's distinct yet delicate, and very refreshing. It goes beautifully with a range of foods, from Asian cuisine to smoked salmon.

— JERRI BANKS, COCKTAIL CONSULTANT (NEW YORK CITY)

With **gin**, or even Martini & Rossi Bianco, I love the combination of blackberries and sage. Blackberries have an indescribable flavor to begin with, and the sage gives them a brooding quality.

— JERRI BANKS, COCKTAIL CONSULTANT (NEW YORK CITY)

cilantro
Cointreau
cola
cranberry juice
cucumber
Curaçao
Earl Grey tea
ginger
HERBS
honey
lemon juice
lime juice
mint
orange juice
oysters
pomegranate
pomegranate molasses
rose geranium
rosemary
sage
sugar
TONIC

Gin Flavors
Beefeater: pear
Hendrick's: cucumber, rose petals
Old Raj: saffron
Zuidam Dry: orange peel

GINGER
Season: year-round
Taste: sour, hot
Weight: light–medium
Volume: loud
Techniques: bake, stir-fry

allspice
almonds
anise
apples
apricots
Arabic cuisine
ASIAN CUISINES
bananas
basil

bay leaf
beef
bell peppers, red
beverages
butter
caramel
cardamom
carrots
cashews
celery
cheese, ricotta
chicken
chile peppers, esp. jalapeño
CHINESE CUISINE
chocolate, esp. dark, white
cilantro
cinnamon
citrus
cloves
coconut
coriander
crab
cranberries
CREAM AND ICE CREAM
cumin
CURRIES
custards
duck
eggplant
European cuisines
fennel
figs
FISH
fish sauce
five-spice powder (key ingredient)
garlic
grapefruit
guava
hazelnuts

Flavor Affinities
gin + apple brandy + lemon juice + orange juice
gin + basil + lemon
gin + blackberries + sage
gin + cilantro + lime
gin + Cointreau + lime + rosemary
gin + cucumber + mint
gin + Earl Grey tea + lemon + sugar
gin + lime + mint
gin + lime + mint + pomegranate
gin + lime + orange

Dishes
Ginger-Honey Gelato
— Gina DePalma, pastry chef, Babbo (New York City)

Ginger-Lemon Drink: Ginger, Lemon, Sugar, Salt, and Pepper
— Vikram Vij and Meeru Dhalwala, Vij's (Vancouver)

HONEY
Indian cuisine, esp. curries
Indonesian cuisine
JAPANESE CUISINE
kaffir lime leaves
Korean cuisine
kumquats
lamb
lavender
leeks
lemon
lemongrass
lemon herbs (e.g., balm, thyme, verbena)
LIME, JUICE
lobster
lychees
mangoes
maple syrup
marinades
mascarpone
meats
melon
Middle Eastern cuisine
mint
molasses
Moroccan cuisine
mushrooms
mussels
noodles and noodle dishes
North African cuisine
nutmeg
oats
oil: canola, grapeseed
olive oil
onions, esp. red
orange
papaya
passion fruit
peaches
peanuts
pears
pepper, white
persimmons
pineapple
plums
pork
prunes

pumpkin
quince
raisins
raspberries
rhubarb
rice
rum, esp. dark
saffron
salad dressings
salads, esp. Asian
salt, kosher
sauces
SCALLIONS
scallops
sesame oil
shallots
shellfish
shrimp
soups
SOY SAUCE
star anise
steak
stews
stocks: beef, chicken
strawberries
SUGAR: white, brown
sushi and sashimi
sweet potatoes
Tabasco sauce
tamarind
tarragon
tea
Thai cuisine
tomatoes
turmeric
vanilla
vegetables
verbena
Vietnamese cuisine

VINEGAR: champagne, cider, rice wine
walnuts
wasabi (e.g., with seafood)
wine, sweet
yogurt
yuzu

Flavor Affinities
ginger + carrot + celery + garlic
ginger + chile peppers + garlic
ginger + chocolate + cream + rum
ginger + cider vinegar + sugar
ginger + cilantro + garlic + scallions
ginger + cream + honey
ginger + lemon + mint
ginger + lemon + pepper + salt + sugar

GINGER, GROUND
Taste: pungent
Function: heating
Weight: light–medium
Volume: moderate–loud

Asian cuisine
baked goods (e.g., breads, cakes, cookies)
bananas
beverages
cardamom
carrots
chicken
chocolate
chutneys
cinnamon
cloves
couscous
cream and ice cream
desserts

Ginger and honey is one of my favorite flavor combinations.
— GINA DEPALMA, BABBO (NEW YORK CITY)

I'll use ginger more for its heat than its sweetness. For example, I'll juice it to add to a carrot or squash puree, which gives it heat and backbone.
— BRADFORD THOMPSON, MARY ELAINE'S AT THE PHOENICIAN (SCOTTSDALE, ARIZONA)

Dishes

Gingersnap-Lemon Ice Cream Sandwiches
— Emily Luchetti, pastry chef, Farallon (San Francisco)

Ginger is great on its own, but also works great with other flavors. It's one of those "wake up" flavors that you can hide beneath all sorts of other flavors. I think it works especially well with citrus. It works with yuzu, passion fruit, coconut, banana, and other tropical flavors.
— **MICHAEL LAISKONIS**, LE BERNARDIN (NEW YORK CITY)

My mom always had **candied ginger** in the spice cupboard when I was growing up. Today at the restaurant, we take candied ginger and combine it with whatever fruit is in season — from nectarines, to cherries, to quince — and then add Vin Santo to make a sauce for our foie gras. Vin Santo brings nuttiness and candied ginger brings spice that both cut through the fat of the foie gras. I think nectarines and candied ginger are a perfect flavor combination.
— **HOLLY SMITH**, CAFÉ JUANITA (SEATTLE)

fruits
gingerbread (key ingredient)
ham
honey
lemon
meats, esp. braised or stewed
melon
Moroccan cuisine
nutmeg
nuts
onions
oranges
paprika
peaches
pears
pepper
pineapple
pork
pumpkin
rice
saffron
squash, winter
stewed dishes
sweet potatoes
tea
tomatoes

GOAT CHEESE
(See Cheese, Goat)

GRAPEFRUIT

Season: year-round
Taste: sour
Weight: light
Volume: loud
Techniques: bake, broil, raw

arugula
asparagus
avocado
bananas
butter, unsalted
Campari
caramel
cashews
ceviche
Champagne
chicken
coconut
crab
crème fraîche
fish, esp. grilled
fromage blanc
gin

ginger, fresh
Grand Marnier
grenadine syrup
hazelnuts
honey
lemon
lime
macadamia nuts
melons
meringue
mint, fresh
miso
olive oil
onions, esp. spring
orange
papaya
pecans
pineapple
pomegranate
poppy seeds
port
raspberries
rum
salads, esp. fruit
salmon
seafood
seaweed
shrimp
sorbet
star anise
strawberries
SUGAR: brown, white
tarragon
tequila
tomatoes
vanilla
vinaigrette
vinegar, champagne
vodka
walnuts
watercress
wine, sparkling, white
yogurt

Dishes

Yuzu Cream, Caramelized Rice, Grapefruit, Green Tea Ice Cream, Crisp Meringue, Malted Rum Milk Chocolate Ice Cream

— Michael Laiskonis, pastry chef, Le Bernardin (New York City)

We serve a dish of **grapefruit**, crab salad, and mint. Grapefruit is sweet and a little bitter, which makes it fun to play with. I like mint in the dish because it refreshes and wakes your palate up. When you get a little taste of mint it brings up the other flavors of the dish.

— GABRIEL KREUTHER, THE MODERN (NEW YORK CITY)

I love tarragon with **grapefruit**. It is a classic.

— MICHAEL LAISKONIS, LE BERNARDIN (NEW YORK CITY)

I have served a **grapefruit** and seaweed crab salad with miso dressing. I also like grapefruit with asparagus.

— BRAD FARMERIE, PUBLIC (NEW YORK CITY)

Flavor Affinities

grapefruit + avocado + crème fraîche
grapefruit + caramel + meringue
grapefruit + crab + miso + seaweed
grapefruit + *fromage blanc* + pomegranate
grapefruit + mint + sugar
grapefruit + star anise + yogurt

GRAPES

Season: summer–autumn
Taste: sweet
Weight: light–medium
Volume: quiet–moderate

almonds
apples
arugula
brandy
cayenne
CHEESE, esp. blue, cow's milk, goat's milk
chicken
chocolate, white
cognac
cream
cumin
curry
curry leaf
duck
endive
fennel seeds
fish
game, esp. roasted
garlic
hazelnuts
honey
lemon
mint
mustard seeds
olive oil
paprika
pears
pecans

pistachios
pork, esp. roasted
poultry, esp. roasted
raspberries
rice
rosemary
rum
salads, esp. chicken, fruit, tuna, Waldorf
salt
sour cream
strawberries
sugar
vinegar, sherry
walnuts
wine: red, white
yogurt

GREEK CUISINE (See also Mediterranean Cuisines)

allspice
anise
basil
bay leaf
beef
bell peppers
CHEESE: FETA, goat, sheep
chicken
cinnamon
cloves
custard
dill
eggplant
eggs
fennel
figs
fish, esp. grilled
GARLIC
grape leaves
honey
kebabs

I never mess with the flavor of **Concord grapes**; I always just make them into a sorbet. I was upstate in my cabin when the first Concord grapes came into season. I wanted sorbet so badly that I cut one of my T-shirts in half to use as a strainer, and then used my broom handle with the shirt to squeeze every last bit of juice from the grapes. The sorbet was awesome!

— JOHNNY IUZZINI, JEAN GEORGES (NEW YORK CITY)

Dishes

Mediterranean "Greek Salad" of Mt. Vikos Feta, Kalamata Olives, Plum Tomatoes, Cucumbers, Torn Mint, and Oregano with Warm Feta Cheese "Turnover"
— Carrie Nahabedian, Naha (Chicago)

LAMB
LEMON
meats, esp. grilled, roasted
mint
nutmeg
nuts
octopus
OLIVE OIL
olives
onions
oregano
parsley
phyllo dough
pine nuts
pita bread
pork
raisins
rice
salads, esp. with mint
shellfish
spinach
thyme
tomatoes
yogurt
zucchini

Flavor Affinities

cucumber + dill + garlic + yogurt
dill + lemon
dill + lemon + olive oil
dill + yogurt
eggplant + custard + garlic + meat
eggplant + garlic + olive oil
eggs + lemon
lamb + garlic + lemon + oregano
lemon + olive oil
lemon + olive oil + oregano
lemon + oregano
phyllo dough + honey + nuts
rice + grape leaves
rice + nuts
spinach + feta cheese

tomatoes + cinnamon
yogurt + cinnamon

GREEN BEANS
(See Beans, Green)

GREENS — IN GENERAL
(See also specific greens)
Season: year-round
Taste: bitter
Weight: medium–heavy
Volume: moderate–loud
Techniques: blanch, raw, sauté, steam

allspice
arugula
bacon
basil
butter
caraway seeds
celery or celery seeds
CHEESE, esp. grated (e.g., Asiago, Jack, Parmesan)
chicory
chili sauce
coriander
corn
curry
dill
eggs, esp. hard-boiled
fennel
GARLIC
ginger
ham
horseradish
leeks

Dishes

A Simple Salad of Beautiful Greens, Forelli Pears, Pomegranate, and Saba Balsamic
— Carrie Nahabedian, Naha (Chicago)

legumes
lemon, juice
mushrooms
mustard, Dijon
nutmeg
nuts, toasted
oil: mustard, nut, peanut, sesame
OLIVE OIL
onions, green
oregano
paprika
parsley
pasta
peaches
pears
pomegranates
potatoes, esp. new and/or red
red pepper flakes
rice
sage
salads
salt, kosher
savory
sesame seeds
shellfish: oysters, esp. fried, shrimp
sweet potatoes
Tabasco sauce
tarragon
thyme
tomatoes
VINEGAR: balsamic, red wine

GREENS, COLLARD
Season: winter–spring
Taste: bitter
Botanical relatives: broccoli, Brussels sprouts, cabbage, cauliflower, kale, kohlrabi
Weight: medium–heavy
Volume: moderate–loud
Techniques: boil, braise, steam, stir-fry

bacon
black-eyed peas
brown butter
cheese, Parmesan
garlic
ham hocks
mustard seeds
oil: peanut, vegetable
onions, yellow
oregano
pepper, black
red pepper flakes
salt
salt pork
soul food cuisine
Southern cuisine (American)
tomatoes
vinegar, cider

GREENS, DANDELION
Season: late spring–early autumn
Taste: bitter
Weight: medium
Volume: moderate
Techniques: raw, sauté, steam

anchovies
bacon
garlic
mustard, Dijon
oil, peanut
onions
pepper, ground
salads
salt
vinegar

GREENS, KALE (See Kale)

GREENS, MUSTARD
Season: winter–spring
Taste: bitter
Weight: medium–heavy
Volume: moderate–loud
Techniques: boil, braise, grill,
stew, wilt

It's hard to even think about **bitter greens** without thinking about toasted nuts. You can get the flavor from the nuts themselves, or from toasted nut oils, which are balanced by the bright fruitiness of cider vinegar.
— **MICHAEL ANTHONY,** GRAMERCY TAVERN (NEW YORK CITY)

Asian cuisine
bacon
black-eyed peas
Chinese cuisine
ham hocks
oil, sesame
olive oil
onions
prosciutto
salads
Southern cuisine (American)
soy sauce

Flavor Affinities
mustard greens + bacon + onions
mustard greens + garlic + olive oil
    + prosciutto
mustard greens + sesame oil +
    soy sauce

GREENS, SALAD (See also
Lettuce, Sorrel, Watercress, etc.)
Season: late spring

bacon
cheese
croutons
fruit: apples, pears
garlic
olive oil
pepper, black
salt
vinegar: red wine, sherry

A salad is a tricky thing to season. If you put the salt on too early, it will wilt the **greens.** You have to be careful not to leach it of its life!
— **TRACI DES JARDINS,** JARDINIÈRE (SAN FRANCISCO)

Dishes
Wild Dandelion Greens with Anchovy Vinaigrette
— David Pasternak, Esca (New York City)

GREENS, TURNIP
Season: fall–winter
Techniques: boil, braise

bacon
black-eyed peas
eggs
ham hocks
onions

Dishes
Turnip Green and Onion Soup with Poached Egg
— Judy Rodgers, Zuni Café
(San Francisco)

GRILLED DISHES
artichokes
asparagus
bell peppers
chicken
corn, esp. on the cob
eggplant
endive
fennel
fish, whole
garlic
hamburgers
hot dogs
lamb: butterflied, chops
lobster
mushrooms

onions
pineapple
pork: chops, loin
salmon
sausages
shrimp, esp. skewered
squash, summer
steaks
swordfish
tomatoes
tuna
turkey: breasts
veal: chops, steaks
zucchini

GRITS
Techniques: simmer

cheese: cheddar, Parmesan
corn
cream
garlic
mascarpone
nutmeg
pepper, black
salt
sausage, andouille
shrimp (to accompany)
Southern cuisine (American)

GROUPER
Season: spring
Weight: medium
Volume: quiet
Techniques: bake, braise, broil, deep-fry, grill, poach, roast, sauté, steam, stir-fry

almonds
anchovies
artichokes

bacon
bay leaf
bell peppers, red
bok choy
butter
capers
carrots
cayenne
celery
cheese, Asiago
chervil
chile peppers, Anaheim
chili sauce
cucumber
endive
garlic
ginger
lemon, juice
lime, juice
Mediterranean cuisine
mushrooms, porcini
oil: corn, sesame, vegetable
olive oil
olives, picholine
onions, white
oyster sauce
parsley, flat-leaf
pepper: black, white
port
rosemary
sage
salt, sea
sesame, seeds
shallots
soy sauce
stocks: chicken, fish, pork
tarragon
thyme
tomatoes
vermouth, dry
vinegar: balsamic, sherry

wine: red, white
zucchini

GUAVAS
Season: summer–autumn
Taste: sweet
Weight: medium
Volume: moderate
Techniques: bake, juice, poach

BANANAS
cashews
cheese
chocolate, white
coconut
cream
cream cheese
curry powder
ginger
ham
honey
lemon
lime, juice
macadamia nuts
mascarpone
oil, vegetable
onions, yellow
orange
passion fruit
pineapple
pork
poultry
raisins
rum
salads, fruit
sauces
strawberries
sugar: brown, white
vanilla
vinegar, white

Dishes
Grilled American Red Grouper on Crab Hash, Pancetta–Red Onion Vinaigrette
— Sanford D'Amato, Sanford (Milwaukee)

HADDOCK (See Cod)

HALIBUT

Season: spring–summer
Weight: medium
Volume: quiet
Techniques: bake, braise, broil, grill, pan roast, poach, roast, sauté, steam

aioli (sauce)
almonds
anchovies
apples: cider, fruit, juice
artichokes
arugula
asparagus
bacon
basil
beans: black, fava, haricots verts
bell peppers: red, yellow
bok choy
butter, unsalted
capers
cardamom
carrots and carrot juice
cayenne
celery
celery root
chamomile
chard
chervil
chicory
chile peppers: dried red, fresh green
chives
cilantro
clams
coriander
cornichons
couscous
cream
cucumber
cumin
curry powder
dill
endive
fennel

fennel seeds
fenugreek seeds
frisée
garam masala
GARLIC
ginger, ground
grapefruit
hazelnuts
horseradish
kohlrabi
leeks
LEMON: juice, preserved
lemon balm
lime, juice
lovage
mint
mushrooms, esp. oyster, porcini, portobello, shiitake
mussels
mustard: Dijon, dry, grainy
OIL: canola, grapeseed
olive oil
olives: black, niçoise
onions, esp. pearl, red, spring
paprika
PARSLEY, flat-leaf
parsnips
pepper: black, white
potatoes, esp. new (e.g., fried, mashed)

pumpkin seeds
red pepper flakes
rhubarb
rosemary
saffron
salt: kosher, sea
savory
scallions
sesame seeds: black, white
SHALLOTS
sorrel
spearmint
spinach
stocks: chicken, fish
sugar (pinch)
tamarind
tapanade
tarragon
thyme
tomatoes and tomato sauce
turmeric
vinaigrette
vinegar: balsamic, sherry
walnuts
watercress
WINE: dry red, dry white (e.g., Chardonnay, Sauvignon Blanc), vermouth
yogurt
zucchini

Halibut from the East Coast is the most delicate and silky fish. It is different than Alaskan halibut, which is drier, meatier, and more robust. East Coast halibut is so delicate that anything can kill it. That is why we steam and poach so much here: Even searing it too strongly in the pan will hurt a piece of halibut.

We'll poach halibut, then serve it with a blood orange vinaigrette made with extra-virgin olive oil, which gives it a round and full flavor. The fish is then served atop a carpaccio of golden beets that have been cooked in sherry vinegar. The beets have a sweet-and-sour flavor to them. They are also very crunchy, which I like with the creamy texture of the halibut. The vinaigrette brings the right degree of acidity to the dish to make it exciting.

— **ERIC RIPERT,** LE BERNARDIN (NEW YORK CITY)

Halibut is a gentle-tasting fish, which leads to gentle herbs like cilantro, chives, or chervil.

— **JERRY TRAUNFELD,** THE HERBFARM (WOODINVILLE, WASHINGTON)

Dishes

Wellfleet Line-Caught Halibut, Sweet Corn, Shiitake Mushrooms,
and Lemon Thyme Sauce
— David Bouley, Upstairs (New York City)

Almond-Crusted Halibut with Parsnip Puree, Fava Beans, Haricots Verts,
and Wild Mushrooms
— David Bouley, Danube (New York City)

Halibut: Braised Tomato, Olives, Escarole, and Spring Salad
— Daniel Boulud/Bertrand Chemel, Café Boulud (New York City)

Olive Oil–Poached Halibut with Star Route Farm's Fava Beans, Fennel Salad, and
Niçoise Olives
— Traci Des Jardins, Jardinière (San Francisco)

Alaskan Halibut, Potato, and Black Pepper Crust
— Hubert Keller, Fleur de Lys (San Francisco)

Alaskan Halibut on a Bed of Creamy Leeks with Asparagus Puree, Fines Herbe,
Spring Ramps, Favas, and English Peas
— Bob Kinkead, Kinkead's (Washington, DC)

Chermoula Halibut with Red Quinoa, Edamame, and Shell Bean Salad with Preserved
Lemon Vinaigrette
— Monica Pope, T'afia (Houston)

Halibut with Morel Mushrooms, English Peas, and Fingerling Potatoes
— Alfred Portale, Gotham Bar and Grill (New York City)

Halibut, Kohlrabi, Celery, Verbena-Lime Emulsion
— Michel Richard, Citronelle (Washington, DC)

Halibut Poached with Sweet-and-Sour Golden and Red Beets, Citrus and Extra-Virgin
Olive Oil Emulsion
— Eric Ripert, Le Bernardin (New York City)

Alaskan Halibut Braised in the Brick Oven with Marble Potatoes, Baby Carrots,
English Peas, Butter, and Cilantro
— Judy Rodgers, Zuni Café (San Francisco)

Line-Caught Seal Rock Halibut, Leek Emulsion, Reduced Chardonnay, Bacon Vinaigrette
— Rick Tramonto, Tru (Chicago)

Flavor Affinities

halibut + anchovies + black olives
halibut + anchovies + garlic + lemon + sorrel
halibut + apples + celery root + parsnips
halibut + beets + blood orange + olive oil + sherry vinegar
halibut + bok choy + sesame seeds
halibut + chicory + grapefruit
halibut + coriander + fennel + lemon
halibut + garlic + lemon + sorrel
halibut + scallions + white wine

HAM

Taste: salty
Weight: medium
Volume: moderate–loud
(depending on smokiness)
Techniques: bake, sauté

allspice
apples and applesauce
arugula
bacon
bay leaf
breakfast / brunch
butter, unsalted
buttermilk
cayenne
CHEESE: cheddar, Emmental,
    Fontina, Gruyère, Jack,
    manchego, mozzarella,
    Parmesan, Swiss
chestnuts
chives
cinnamon
cloves
corn
cornmeal
French cuisine
eggs
garlic
greens
honey
Italian cuisine, esp. with
    prosciutto di Parma
macaroni
maple syrup
mushrooms
mustard, Dijon
nutmeg
olive oil
onions, red
orange, juice
parsley
pears
peas
pepper, black
pine nuts
potatoes
sage

Dishes

Raviolis of Virginia Country Ham and Fontina Cheese
— Patrick O'Connell, The Inn at Little Washington (Washington, Virginia)

Serrano Ham with Roasted Onions, Manchego Cheese, and Watercress
— Charlie Trotter, Trotter's to Go (Chicago)

Virtually all vegetables — from asparagus to green beans — pair well with **ham** because of its natural saltiness.
—JOSÉ ANDRÉS, CAFÉ ATLÁNTICO (WASHINGTON, DC)

One of the happiest trios in the flavor world is **Ibérico ham**, manchego cheese, and manzanilla sherry.
— ADRIAN MURCIA, CHANTERELLE (NEW YORK CITY)

If you are a first timer, the only thing you should combine with **Ibérico ham** is the warmth of your tongue. Just let it rest on your tongue and let your 37 degrees Celsius do the rest! You can use just the fat of Ibérico ham melted in a pan and make scrambled eggs or a tortilla, and it will add amazing flavor and aroma.
—JOSÉ ANDRÉS, CAFÉ ATLÁNTICO (WASHINGTON, DC)

sauce, Mornay
scallions
Southern cuisine (American)
soy sauce
spinach
stock, chicken
sugar: brown, white
sweet potatoes
tarragon
thyme
vinegar, balsamic
wine: dry sherry, Madeira red, white

Flavor Affinities
ham + cheese + mustard
ham + honey + soy sauce
ham + Jack cheese + greens + mushrooms
ham + mozzarella cheese + red onion

HAM, IBÉRICO
cheese, pressed sheep's milk (e.g., manchego)

HAM, SERRANO
asparagus
beans, green
cheese, manchego
olive oil
peppers, piquillo
Spanish cuisine
tomatoes

HAZELNUT OIL
(See Oil, Hazelnut)

HAZELNUTS
Taste: sweet, salty
Weight: medium
Volume: moderate–loud

almonds
apples
apricots
asparagus
bananas
beets
berries
butter, unsalted
buttermilk
caramel
carrots
cheese: feta, goat, Gruyère, ricotta, Taleggio
cherries
chestnuts
CHOCOLATE, esp. dark or white
cinnamon
cocoa powder
coffee / espresso
cognac
cranberries
cream and ice cream
cream cheese
custard
dates
figs
garlic
ginger
grapefruit
grapes
hazelnut oil
honey
Kirsch
kiwi
lemon
liqueur: **almond** (e.g., amaretto), hazelnut (e.g., Frangelico), orange
mango
maple syrup
mascarpone
mint
nectarines
nutmeg
oats
orange: juice, zest
pastries
peaches
pears
pecans
persimmons

plums
prunes
pumpkin
quail
raisins
raspberries
rum
sauces
soups
strawberries
sugar: brown, confectioner's,
    granulated
sweet potatoes
tea
VANILLA
vegetables
walnuts
wine: red, sweet, white

Dishes

Chocolate-Hazelnut Cake with Orange Sauce and Hazelnut Gelato
— Gina DePalma, Babbo (New York City)

Hazelnut and Chocolate Soufflé
— Odette Fada, San Domenico (New York City)

Gianduja Napoleon with Chocolate-Hazelnut Ganache, Frozen Caramel Mousse,
Crispy Hazelnut Nougatine
— Gale Gand, pastry chef, Tru (Chicago)

Hazelnuts have a complicated flavor, though not as complicated as walnuts.
— **MARCEL DESAULNIERS,** THE TRELLIS (WILLIAMSBURG, VIRGINIA)

Hazelnuts are from the north and are used in Piedmontese cooking.
Hazelnuts are very rich and round and buttery, so I will use them to
achieve a rich, fatty quality in my dessert. Hazelnuts with chocolate are a
natural. Hazelnut with grapes are great; it's like peanut butter and jelly!
— **GINA DEPALMA,** BABBO (NEW YORK CITY)

HERBES DE PROVENCE
French cuisine, southern
meats
stews, esp. vegetable
vegetables

Flavor Affinities
basil + fennel seeds + lavender + marjoram + rosemary + sage +
    summer savory + thyme

I am more of an **herb** guy than a spice guy. It comes back to a certain
conservatism I have regarding food. The French are not big on spices;
they use more herbs. I know the spices used in European cooking and
use them in moderation. I am not going to serve a dish that is wildly
nutmegged!
— **DAVID WALTUCK,** CHANTERELLE (NEW YORK CITY)

HERBS (See specific herbs)

Herbs 101
with Jerry Traunfeld of The Herbfarm, Woodinville, Washington

Working with herbs is very different from working with spices. With herbs, you can really only work with a few at a time. With spices, you can throw so many more together. An Indian dish may have more than a dozen spices in it. Here are some guidelines:

- *Know your herb.* Herbs range in intensity, so you need to know the profile of the herb you are choosing at the start. You need to be careful; for example, if you add rosemary to chervil it will over-power the chervil.
- *You want to pair delicate with delicate or strong with strong.* Chervil is possibly the most delicate herb. Lemon basil and lemon thyme would be in the middle. Lemon verbena or tarragon I would consider loud. Then you have bay leaf which is light, until you add twenty together and it becomes strong.
- *Not all herbs are created equal, and they can vary within their categories or season.* Oregano can be mild, or hot and spicy. With mint, applemint is mild while peppermint is strong. The season also has an effect on rosemary: in the winter, rosemary is mild and in the summer, it is strong.
- *Herbs have regional affinities.* Mediterranean herbs marry well together. Rosemary and marjoram or thyme and savory are naturals together. Among Asian herbs, lemongrass goes with mint and cilantro or mint and chives. In France, you have lots of combinations: chervil, tarragon, chives, and parsley. The one exception to France's herbs is tarragon, which is probably best on its own.

- *Herbs also have seasonal affinities.* Summer vegetables work with summer herbs, as do winter vegetables with winter herbs. In summer, it is basil or marjoram with tomatoes. Basil with zucchini is one of my favorite combinations. In winter, sage and rosemary work with potatoes and root vegetables. Also in winter, one of my favorite combinations is butternut squash with bay leaf and nutmeg. Pumpkin and bay leaf together make the pumpkin taste even more pumpkin-like.
- *How to use the chosen herb.* Soft-leaved herbs — such as basil, chervil, chives, cilantro, dill, lovage, and sorrel — shouldn't be cooked because they will lose their flavor. Tough-leaved herbs — such as bay leaf, savory, and rosemary — can go into dishes and stand up to heat and cooking.
- *Choose an herb that is the same intensity as your protein.* Halibut is a gentle-tasting fish, which leads to gentle herbs like cilantro, chives, or chervil. Smelt is a local fish that is oily, so here we look to stronger herbs like oregano, savory, or rosemary.
- *Herbs aren't exclusive to savory dishes.* Anise hyssop works with most stone fruits like peaches. Cinnamon basil works with blue huckleberries. Cinnamon with blueberries really intensifies the flavor of the blueberry. Lavender works with plums or peaches. Lemony herbs like basil or anise hyssop work with watermelon. Rosemary works with apples or pears. Sage works with tart cherries. Tarragon works with muskmelon.

We grow forty different tomatoes and eight different basils. Our farmer planted the tomatoes surrounded by the basil, and I thought he did it because they taste good together. It turns out that doing so attracts beneficial insects to each. Our farmer believes that tomato and basil work so well on the plate because they work so well in the field. He also explained that if you plant certain basils next to tomatoes, you can taste it in the tomato.

All our cooks take care of their own section of the **herb** garden. The garde-manger cooks [who prepare appetizers] look after the chives and chervil. The fish cooks care for the lemon herbs like lemon thyme and lemongrass, and the meat cooks for the rosemary, sage, and thyme. Our pastry cooks tend the edible flowers that can be candied, and mint and lemon verbena, which they use in sorbets.

— **DAN BARBER,** BLUE HILL AT STONE BARNS (POCANTICO HILLS, NEW YORK)

I am a big fan of roasting and resting meat on **herbs.** If you roast a rib eye, prime rib, or filet mignon, most people would put it on a sheet tray with a roasting rack. One day, I didn't have a roasting rack but I had a lot of thyme and savory and rosemary, so I threw the meat on top and roasted it. The technique did the trick by keeping the meat from the juices and it also enhanced the flavor that much more. Since then, we have stopped using roasting racks for our meats and switched to herbs. During the roasting process, I like to turn the meat so that the flavor of the herbs penetrates even more. Since you are roasting in a closed oven, the air circulates the herb flavor.

For a lamb shoulder, if you can't get hay, I would recommend using savory, thyme, sage, and rosemary. This technique is great for a whole chicken: slice some truffles to put under the chicken skin, brush it with butter, and put it on a bed of savory and thyme. It will be pretty incredible.

— **VITALY PALEY,** PALEY'S PLACE (PORTLAND, OREGON)

HONEY

Taste: sweet, astringent
Function: heating
Weight: medium–heavy
Volume: moderate–loud

almonds
apples
apricots
baked goods (e.g., biscuits, breads)
bananas
brandy
butter
buttermilk
carrots
cheese: goat, ricotta, soft
chestnuts
chicken
Chinese cuisine
chocolate: dark, white

cinnamon
coconut
coffee
cognac
CREAM AND ICE CREAM
currants, red
dates
desserts
duck
figs, esp. dried
fruit
ginger
grapefruit
grapes
Greek cuisine
guava
ham
hazelnuts
kiwi fruit
kumquats
lamb
lavender

LEMON: juice, zest
LIME, juice
liqueur, orange (e.g., Grand Marnier)
lychees
mascarpone
melon
Middle Eastern cuisines
mint
Moroccan cuisine
mustard
nutmeg
NUTS
oats
ORANGE: juice, zest
papaya
pastries
peaches
peanuts
pears
pecans
persimmons
pineapple
pine nuts
pistachios
plums
pomegranate
pork
prunes
pumpkin
quince
raisins
raspberries
red pepper flakes
rhubarb
rum
sage
sauces
Southern cuisine
soy sauce
SUGAR: brown, white
sweet potatoes
tea
tequila
thyme
Turkish cuisine
VANILLA
walnuts

I might grab **honey** when I am working with nutty flavors or to macerate some fruit. You can also scorch honey to create a whole new flavor; one of my favorite dishes is a burnt honey caramelized pistachio ice cream.

— **MICHAEL LAISKONIS,** LE BERNARDIN (NEW YORK CITY)

I use **honey** as a flavor, not as a sweetener like sugar. In my honey *panna cotta*, I add some sugar to make it sweet enough. If I used only honey as a sweetener, the flavor of honey would be too strong and the *panna cotta* would taste a little flat.

— **EMILY LUCHETTI,** FARALLON (SAN FRANCISCO)

I like the combination of fresh pineapple topped with warm **honey.** I will glaze my raspberry tart with flower honey, and my apple tart with chestnut honey. Chestnut honey gives a rustic flavor that goes well with the apple.

— **MICHEL RICHARD,** CITRONELLE (WASHINGTON, DC)

Dishes

Lavender Honey-Roasted Pig with Spiced Banana Puree
— Sandy D'Amato, Sanford (Milwaukee)

Honey Semifreddo with Tropical Consommé, Fresh Coconut, and Bloomed Basil Seeds
— Celina Tio, American Restaurant (Kansas City)

whiskey
wine: red, white

Flavor Affinities
honey + almonds + chicken + pomegranate
honey + bananas + lavender + pork
honey + cream + pistachios
honey + fruit + yogurt

HONEY, BLUEBERRY
cheese, esp. cheddar

HONEY, CHESTNUT
Taste: sweet-bitter

cheese, esp. goat, ricotta, triple crème

HONEY, RASPBERRY
cheese, esp. cheddar

HONEYDEW
Season: midsummer
Taste: sweet
Weight: light–medium
Volume: moderate

basil
blackberries
cardamom
Champagne
chiles
coconut milk
coriander
cream
cumin
figs

ginger
grapefruit
honey
lemon, juice
lemon basil
lime
melon, cantaloupe
milk
mint
nectarines
peaches
red pepper flakes
pepper: black, white
prosciutto
ricotta cheese
salt (pinch)
scallions
strawberries
sugar
tarragon
wine, sweet
yogurt

Flavor Affinities
honeydew melon + figs + mint + prosciutto

HORSERADISH
Season: spring–autumn
Taste: pungent, hot
Weight: light–medium
Volume: very loud
Tips: Use horseradish raw or add at end of cooking process. Heat diminishes the pungency of horseradish.

apples, esp. Golden Delicious
apricots

Austrian cuisine
avocados
BEEF, ESP. CORNED OR ROAST
beets
celery
chicken
chives
cinnamon
cloves
corn
CREAM
cream cheese
crème fraîche
dill
Eastern European cuisine
eggs
fennel
fish, esp. oily, smoked
garlic
German cuisine
ham
ketchup
lemon, juice
lime, juice
lobster
mascarpone
mayonnaise
meats, esp. cold
mustard
olive oil
oxtails
oysters
parsley
pears
pepper, black
pork
potatoes
Russian cuisine
salads
salmon
salmon, smoked
salt: kosher, sea
sauces
sausage
shellfish
sour cream
steak

Dishes
Honeydew-Mint Sorbet with Fresh Blackberries
— Gina DePalma, pastry chef, Babbo (New York City)

Honeydew Melon Salad with Oven-Roasted Tomatoes, Goat Cheese, and Pistachios
— Gabriel Kreuther, The Modern (New York City)

Heating grated horseradish changes the **horseradish** completely. It makes it more mellow and takes away the bite while keeping its yummy flavor. Horseradish prepared this way works well with Nantucket Bay scallops that are naturally sweet and work with the sweetness of the horseradish. We will also use it in a lemony vinaigrette and dress a smoked trout with it.

First, grate horseradish on a microplane [a fine grater]. Coat a ten-inch skillet with some Ligurian olive oil, and heat the horseradish over medium heat. Watch it very closely, because the minute it starts to turn from its blond color, it is done. From there, transfer it into cold pans to cool it quickly. When it is totally cool and has its crunch, add some lemon zest and kosher salt.

— **HOLLY SMITH**, CAFÉ JUANITA (SEATTLE)

sugar
Tabasco sauce
tomatoes and tomato paste
trout
vinegar
walnuts
Worcestershire sauce
yogurt

Flavor Affinities
horseradish + apples + pork + sour cream
horseradish + beef + beets
horseradish + beets + cream cheese
horseradish + garlic + olive oil
horseradish + salt + vinegar
horseradish + seafood + tomatoes

HOTNESS (of indoor or outdoor temperature; see also Summer)
chilled dishes and beverages
fish
grilled dishes
herbs, esp. cooling
olive oil–based dishes
raw dishes
salads, esp. fruit, vegetable

If it is **hot** outside, I make sure there are lots of salads on the menu.

— **ANDREW CARMELLINI**, A VOCE (NEW YORK CITY)

salsas, fresh
seafood
soups, cold
vegetables, esp. green leafy

HUNGARIAN CUISINE
bacon
beef
bell peppers, green
caraway seeds
chile peppers
garlic
ham
lard
mushrooms
ONIONS
PAPRIKA
pork
pork fat
potatoes
sausage
SOUR CREAM
tomatoes

wheat
wine, esp. Tokaji Aszu

Flavor Affinities
onions + paprika
onions + paprika + pork fat
onions + paprika + sour cream

HYSSOP
Taste: bitter
Weight: medium
Volume: strong

beans, green
beef
beets
cabbage
carrots
chicken
cranberries
eggs
fruits
lamb
meats
parsley
pork
rice
rosemary
salads: fruit, green
soups, esp. chicken
stews
thyme
tomatoes
turkey, esp. stuffed and roasted
vegetables
venison

In Eastern European or **Hungarian cooking**, you will see a stewed or braised dish flavored with paprika that is cut with sour cream either in it or served on top so that it mixes together as you eat it. I serve rare roasted venison in venison stock with hot and sweet paprika that is essentially a goulash. Alongside, I serve creamed sauerkraut that bleeds into the sauce and gives the same effect as a goulash. Even though the sauerkraut has an intense flavor, it is still mild because it has been cooked in cream. It is not a Hungarian dish but rather a play on a Hungarian dish, and it works in the context of the subtler intensity of flavors I like.

— **DAVID WALTUCK**, CHANTERELLE (NEW YORK CITY)

INDIAN CUISINE

allspice
almonds, esp. in desserts
anise
breads, in the north
cardamom
cauliflower
chicken
chile peppers
cilantro, esp. in the south
cinnamon
cloves
coconut, esp. in the south and/or
    in desserts
coriander
cumin, esp. in the north
CURRIES
curry leaf
eggplant
fenugreek
garlic, esp. in the north
ghee (clarified butter)
ginger, esp. in the north
herbs
lamb
lentils
mint
mustard seeds, esp. in the south
nutmeg
oil: canola, grapeseed
paprika
peas
pepper: black, white
pistachios, esp. in desserts
poppy seeds
potatoes
rice, basmati, esp. in the south
saffron
sage
SPICES
spinach
tamarind, esp. in the south
TOMATOES
turmeric
vegetables, esp. in the south
wheat, esp. in the north
yogurt

Tomatoes are as important to making **Indian cuisine** as they are to making Italian cuisine. In fact, making an Indian curry is a lot like making an Italian tomato sauce.
— MEERU DHALWALA, VIJ'S (VANCOUVER)

If my mind is in **India**, tamarind will be sneaking its way into the dish. When thinking of India, my inspirations are the flavors of clove, cardamom, and coriander seed. They are aromatic spices that really cut the fat of the dish, so it is not big, fat, and flabby on the palate.
— BRAD FARMERIE, PUBLIC (NEW YORK CITY)

I worked in an **Indian** restaurant as a waiter for four years. I love cooking with Indian ingredients. Everything I learned at the CIA was thrown out the window when I learned Indian cooking, which is where I picked up many techniques and philosophies. I now roast my own spices and create spice blends. I love creating my own flavor combinations. I came to love a garam masala made with fennel, cinnamon, clove, cumin, and coriander. Each of these five spices has a distinctive flavor, but combined they create one single flavor that is amazing. I will use my garam masala mixture in soups and sauces. When people ask about the dish, they always ask, "What was that flavor?"
— BOB IACOVONE, CUVÉE (NEW ORLEANS)

AVOID
beef, for religious reasons, say
    some
pork, for religious reasons, say
    some

Flavor Affinities
cinnamon + cloves + mace +
    nutmeg
coriander + cumin + turmeric
coriander + cumin + yogurt
cumin + garlic + ginger
cumin + garlic + yogurt
garlic + ginger
garlic + ginger + onion
potatoes + chili powder +
    turmeric
yogurt + fruit

INDONESIAN CUISINE

chicken
chile peppers
coconut
coriander
fish
garlic
grilled dishes
lemongrass
molasses
noodles
peanuts
pepper
rice
shellfish
shrimp paste
soy sauce
spices, esp. clove, nutmeg, pepper
stir-fried dishes
sugar, brown
vegetables

Flavor Affinities
chile peppers + peanuts + soy
    sauce
garlic + peanuts + soy sauce
garlic + soy sauce + brown sugar

IRANIAN CUISINE
(aka Persian Cuisine)

apricots
basil
beans
chicken
cinnamon
dates
dill
duck
fish
garlic
herbs
kebabs
lamb
lime
meats
mint
nuts
onions
parsley
plums
pomegranates
prunes
raisins
rice
saffron
stews

Flavor Affinities

cardamom + cinnamon + cloves +
    cumin + ginger + rose
duck + pomegranates + walnuts

ITALIAN CUISINE —
IN GENERAL

anchovies
artichokes
basil
beef
bell peppers
capers
**cheese: mozzarella, Parmesan,
    pecorino, ricotta**
chicken
eggplant
fennel
fish

garlic
grappa
greens
honey, esp. in desserts
lemon, esp. in desserts
Marsala
mascarpone, esp. in desserts
mushrooms
nuts
olive oil
olives
orange and orange zest, esp. in
    desserts
oregano
pancetta
parsley
pasta
pork
prosciutto
red pepper flakes
rosemary
rum, esp. in desserts
saffron
sage
sausage
shellfish
spinach
thyme
tomatoes and tomato sauces
veal
vinegar: balsamic, red wine
wine
zucchini

Flavor Affinities

anchovies + capers + lemon juice
anchovies + garlic + wine vinegar
basil + garlic + olive oil
basil + garlic + tomatoes
bell peppers + olive oil + tomatoes
capers + garlic + wine vinegar
garlic + olive oil + parsley
garlic + oregano + tomatoes
garlic + saffron + shellfish
red pepper flakes + fennel +
    sausage

ITALIAN CUISINE,
NORTHERN

asparagus
basil
beans
butter
cheeses, creamy and rich
cream and cream-based sauces
cured meats
fish
goat
hazelnuts
lemon, juice
Marsala
nuts
pasta, esp. richer egg-based
    and/or ribbon-shaped, often
    combined with other starches
    such as beans
pine nuts
polenta
potatoes
rice and risotto
truffles, white
vinegar, esp. wine
wine

ITALIAN CUISINE,
SOUTHERN

bell peppers
chile peppers
cinnamon
eggplant
fennel
garlic
marjoram
nutmeg
olive oil, heavy
oregano
**pasta, esp. tube-shaped and with
    tomato sauce**
pizza
pork
raisins
red pepper flakes
sardines
sausage
tomatoes and tomato sauces

I only half joke that if you add rum or orange zest to a dessert, it will taste **Italian.** They are very common flavors in Italy.
— **GINA DEPALMA,** BABBO (NEW YORK CITY)

There are five ingredients that any **Italian** cook must use: 1) real Italian pasta; 2) extra-virgin olive oil; 3) real balsamic vinegar; 4) Italian prosciutto; and 5) Parmigiano-Reggiano cheese.
— **MARIO BATALI,** BABBO (NEW YORK CITY)

Holly Smith of Café Juanita in Seattle on Five Flavors that Will Take You to Northern Italy

White Truffles. The perfect vehicle for white truffles is hand-cut pasta that is egg rich. Eggs that taste like real eggs make a great pasta. Our pasta is egg rich and has 35 egg yolks to a kilo (2.2 pounds) of flour. You can get them in there, it is crazy! The pasta looks like a sunset. On the pasta, I would first put butter barely scented with sage, before shaving the truffles on top.

Nebbiolo. Beef cheeks braised in Nebbiolo [wine]. To keep it simple, we serve roasted turnips and the reduced sauce with pomegranate seeds and that's it. We braise our cheeks for seven and a half hours. Most braised dishes go four hours, but not beef cheeks — anything less, and they are [still tough].

Anchovies. I love a really acidic anchovy vinaigrette for a bread salad. Anchovies with roasted garlic are like butter at this restaurant; they go in lots of dishes. We put them in lamb, we put them in between potatoes with chicken stock for a gratin. We love them. I like anchovies with sage on each side deep fried for an appetizer. We cook anchovies in olive oil with a little butter until they get toasty, throw in onions to caramelize, and serve this with fish.

Hazelnuts. Chocolate and hazelnut is the perfect combination so we make *gianduja* and put it inside crepes and warm them and put chestnut honey on top. Most of the time hazelnuts end up in salad or ground for a final dusting for a pasta. Beet pasta that looks like candy wrappers is served on top of a warm plate that has just been smeared with Gorgonzola Piccante, then topped with ground hazelnuts just before it is served. Blue cheese and hazelnuts is it for me.

Goat Meat. I just had spit-roasted goat at Da Cesare. If I knew I was going to die, I would get myself there [to the Piedmont region of Italy]. Roasted goat basted with garlic, olive oil, marjoram, mint, or rosemary is it.

JAMAICAN CUISINE

(See also Caribbean Cuisines)

jerked dishes (e.g., chicken)

JAPANESE CUISINE

bonito: dried, flakes
broiled dishes
chile peppers
daikon
dashi (kelp-based stock)
fish, cooked and raw
ginger
kelp
mirin (sweet rice wine)
noodles
pickles
poached dishes
ponzu sauce
rice
sake
scallions
sesame: oil, seeds
shellfish
*SOY SAUCE
steamed dishes
tea
vinegar, rice wine
wasabi
wine, rice
yuzu

Flavor Affinities

bonito flakes + kelp
garlic + ginger + soy sauce
ginger + scallions + soy sauce
sake + soy sauce + sugar
soy sauce + wasabi

JICAMA

Season: winter–spring
Taste: sweet
Weight: light–medium
Volume: quiet
Techniques: cooked (e.g., stir-fry), raw

avocado
cabbage, green
carrots
chicken
*CHILE PEPPERS
chili powder

Japanese cuisine is very simple. We don't mix too many ingredients together. One of the main ingredients we use in Japanese cooking is soy sauce, for both its saltiness and umami. Soy sauce is very complex: It takes months and months to make it. Same for the dried bonito used to make *dashi*, our Japanese broth. So Japanese chefs find that much of the hardest work has already been done for us!

— **KAZ OKOCHI,** KAZ SUSHI BISTRO (WASHINGTON, DC)

Dishes

Jicama Callejera: Crunchy Jicama with Oranges, Grapefruit, and Pineapple;
Orange-Lime Vinaigrette and Fresh Limes to Squeeze On
— Rick Bayless, Frontera Grill (Chicago)

Ensalada de Jicama y Aguacate: Jicama, Grapefruit, and Avocado Salad with
Pumpkin Seeds
— Traci Des Jardins, Mijita (San Francisco)

Seaweed and Jicama Salad with Ginger Dressing
— Kaz Okochi, Kaz Sushi Bistro (Washington, DC)

cilantro
cloves
cucumbers
cumin
fish
ginger
grapefruit
ketchup
lemon
*LIME, juice
Malaysian cuisine
mangoes
melon
Mexican cuisine
mustard, yellow
oil: canola, sesame
onions, red
orange
papaya
peanuts, crushed
pepper, black
pineapple
pumpkin seeds
radishes
salads (e.g., fruit)
salsa
salt, kosher
sesame oil
shrimp
soy sauce
spinach
sugar
vinegar, white

Flavor Affinities

jicama + avocado + grapefruit + pumpkin seeds
jicama + chili powder + lime juice

JUNIPER BERRIES

Season: summer–autumn
Character: refreshing
Taste: bitter
Weight: medium
Volume: moderate–loud

allspice
Alsatian cuisine
apples
bay leaf
beef
cabbage
caraway
celery
chicken
choucroute
duck
fennel
fish
GAME
game birds
garlic
German cuisine
gin
goose
ham
kidneys

lamb
liver
marinades
marjoram
Mediterranean cuisine
onions
oregano
parsley
pâtés
pepper
pork
rosemary
sage
salmon
sauces
sauerkraut
savory
Scandinavian cuisine
stuffings, esp. bread
thyme
veal
VENISON
wine, red

Flavor Affinities

juniper berries + game + garlic + rosemary

KAFFIR LIMES AND KAFFIR LIME LEAF

(See also Lemons, Limes, etc.)
Season: year-round
Taste: sour
Weight: light
Volume: moderate–loud
Techniques: stir-fry

basil, Thai
beef
cardamom
chicken
chile peppers
cilantro
coconut and coconut milk
coriander
cumin
curry pastes and curries
fish
ginger

I love the gentle, mellow tanginess **kaffir lime leaf** adds to curries.
— MEERU DHALWALA, VIJ'S (VANCOUVER)

Indian cuisine
Indonesian cuisine
lemongrass
lime, juice
marinades
mushrooms
noodles
pork
poultry
rice
salads
sesame
shellfish
soups, esp. Thai
star anise
sugar
tamarind
THAI CUISINE
turmeric
vegetables, esp. green

Flavor Affinities
kaffir lime + saffron + seafood
kaffir lime leaf + duck + ginger
kaffir lime leaf + rice + turmeric

KALE
Season: autumn–spring
Taste: bitter, sweet
Botanical relatives: broccoli, Brussels sprouts, cabbage, cauliflower, collard greens, kohlrabi
Weight: heavy
Volume: moderate
Techniques: blanch, boil, braise, sauté, steam, stir-fry

bay leaf
bell peppers, red
butter
cheese: cheddar, Parmesan
chicken, roasted
cream
GARLIC
ginger
lemon
meats, roasted

*I like **kale** blanched then sautéed with some onions, a pinch of salt, and some smoked sausage.*

— **GABRIEL KREUTHER,** THE MODERN (NEW YORK CITY)

nutmeg
OIL: grapeseed, vegetable
olive oil
onions, esp. yellow
oregano
pancetta
pasta
pepper: black, white
pork
potatoes
red pepper flakes
salt, kosher
sausage, chorizo
shallots
sour cream
soy sauce
stock, chicken
sugar
sweet potatoes
thyme
tomatoes
vinegar, red wine

Flavor Affinities
kale + garlic + olive oil + red wine vinegar
kale + onions + salt + smoked sausage

KIWI FRUIT
Season: late autumn–spring
Taste: sour
Weight: medium
Volume: quiet–moderate
Techniques: raw

bananas
berries
cherries
chocolate: dark, white
coconut
cream and ice cream
crust: pastry or pie

custard
grapefruit
hazelnuts
honey
Kirsch
lemon: juice, zest
lime
lychee
macadamia nuts
mangoes
oranges
papaya
passion fruit
pineapple
rum
salad, esp. chicken or fruit
strawberries
sugar
wine: Champagne, ice wine

KOHLRABI (See also Rutabagas, Turnips)
Season: summer–autumn
Botanical relatives: broccoli, Brussels sprouts, cabbage, cauliflower, collard greens, kale
Weight: medium (esp. when younger)–heavy (esp. when older)
Volume: moderate (esp. when younger)–loud (esp. when older)
Techniques: boil, steam, stir-fry

allspice
basil
butter, unsalted
cabbage
carrots
celery
celery leaves or seeds
celery root
cheese, esp. Parmesan, Swiss
chervil
cilantro

Kohlrabi is an underrated vegetable. I admit it has not always been one of my favorites, but it has grown on me over the years. Now, I love it. I can't precisely place its flavor, which is somewhere between a turnip, radish, and cauliflower. But it tastes great and is really versatile. You can grill it, roast it, glaze it like a carrot, or make a gratin out of it with potatoes. We have even grated it and made a rémoulade out of it like you would with a celery root. But the best way to enjoy kohlrabi is grilled, roasted, and drizzled with olive oil and sea salt. That is my favorite!

— **VITALY PALEY,** PALEY'S PLACE (PORTLAND, OREGON)

coriander
cream
dill
fennel leaves or seeds
garlic
horseradish
leeks
lemon, juice
lovage
mace
mustard (e.g., Dijon)
mustard seeds
onions
parsley, flat-leaf
pepper, black
potatoes
rosemary
salt, esp. sea
sesame oil, seeds
soups
sour cream
soy sauce
stews
tamari
turmeric
vinegar, red wine

KOREAN CUISINE

chile peppers
fish
garlic
noodles, esp. buckwheat
rice
sesame seeds
shellfish
soy sauce

sugar
vegetables, pickled (e.g., kimchi)

Flavor Affinities
chile peppers + garlic + soy sauce
chile peppers + sesame seeds + soy sauce
chile peppers + soy sauce
garlic + sesame seeds + soy sauce
garlic + soy sauce

KUMQUATS
Season: autumn–winter
Taste: sour, bitter
Weight: light–medium
Volume: moderate–loud
Techniques: raw, stew

Asian cuisines
beef
berries: **cranberries**, strawberries
brandy
caramel
cayenne
chicken
chocolate: dark, white
chutney
cinnamon
citrus
coconut
cranberries
cream
custard
dates
duck
East Asian cuisine

endive (Belgian)
fish, esp. cod, halibut, red snapper, salmon, tuna, esp. grilled
ginger
hazelnuts
honey
lemon, juice
lime
mace
mango
marinades
meats
mint
nutmeg
olive oil
onions, spring
orange
papaya
pecans
persimmons
pineapple
pistachios
pomegranates
poppy seeds
pork
pumpkin
quince
rum
SALADS: FRUIT, GREEN
salt
strawberries
sugar
vanilla
walnuts
wine, white

LAMB — IN GENERAL

Season: spring
Taste: sweet, astringent
Function: heating
Weight: heavy
Volume: moderate–loud
Techniques: braise (esp. shanks), grill (esp. leg), roast (esp. leg), stew (esp. shoulder)
Tips: Cloves add richness to the flavor of lamb.

Our signature wine-marinated **lamb** popsicles in fenugreek cream curry on spinach potatoes dish is bare rugged simplicity. You have rack of lamb that has been cooked just a few minutes. Then you have a simple sauce that is essentially just cream and garlic — and you can taste all three. We add some green fenugreek that gives an earthiness to the dish and takes it to a whole new level. It is incredibly simple. It is a dish about technique because if the garlic is cooked too long, it gets bitter. Or if you add too much fenugreek, it gets bitter and overpowers the cream. But in the right proportions, it is perfect.

— **MEERU DHALWALA,** VIJ'S (VANCOUVER)

aioli
almonds
anchovies
apples
apricots, dried
artichokes
asparagus
bacon
basil
bay leaf
beans: cranberry, **fava,**
   FLAGEOLETS, green, **WHITE**
beer
bell peppers
brandy
bread crumbs
bulgur wheat
butter: clarified, unsalted
capers
cardamom
carrots
cayenne
celery
celery root
chard
cheese: blue, feta, Parmesan,
   ricotta
chickpeas
chiles: jalapeño, red
chili powder
chives
chocolate, dark
cilantro
cinnamon
cloves
coconut
cognac
coriander
couscous
cream
cumin
curry powder
dates
dill
Eastern Mediterranean (e.g.,
   Greek, Turkish) cuisine
eggplant
endive
escarole

Dishes

Lamb, Fig, Pernod, and a Pillow of Sassafras Air
— Grant Achatz, Alinea (Chicago)

Lamb with Stew of Chickpeas, Root Vegetables, and Braised Lettuces
— Dan Barber, Blue Hill at Stone Barns (Pocantico Hills, New York)

Mint Love Letters with Spicy Lamb Sausage
— Mario Batali, Babbo (New York City)

Grilled Lamb Sirloin in a Roasted Garlic Sauce with Potato–Celery Root Gratin and Sautéed Escarole
— Ann Cashion, Cashion's Eat Place (Washington, DC)

Colorado Rack of Lamb with Roasted Fennel, Glazed Baby Carrots, Fresh Garbanzo Beans, and Cardoon Puree, Niçoise Olive–Kumquat Tapenade
— Traci Des Jardins, Jardinière (San Francisco)

Colorado Lamb Loin with Creamy Polenta, Morel Mushrooms, and Star Route Fava Beans, Perigord Truffle Jus
— Traci Des Jardins, Jardinière (San Francisco)

Roast Lamb Sirloin on Crispy Goat Cheese Polenta with Saffron-Braised Baby Vegetables and Minted Yogurt
— Brad Farmerie, Public (New York City)

"Armenian Style" Lamb Skewers, Mediterranean Chickpea Salad, "Panisses," and Minted Sheep's Milk Yogurt
— Carrie Nahabedian, Naha (Chicago)

Poached Spring Lamb with Artichoke Tart and Pine Nut–Morel Gremolata
— Bradley Ogden, at the 2003 James Beard Awards gala reception

Moroccan Spiced Rack of Lamb with Couscous Salad, Roasted Eggplant, Lemon–Black Pepper Jus
— Alfred Portale, Gotham Bar and Grill (New York City)

Pan-Roasted Lamb Rack and Eighteen-Hours-Braised Leg of Lamb; Goat Cheese Mashed Potatoes; Wild Mushroom–Red Wine Sauce
— Eric Ripert, Le Bernardin (New York City)

Lamb Black Truffle Tagliatelle with Preserved Lemon and Aged Parmesan
— Eric Ripert, Le Bernardin (New York City)

Truffle and Almond-Crusted Rack of Lamb
— Brad Thompson, Mary Elaine's at the Phoenician (Scottsdale, Arizona)

Wine-Marinated Lamb Popsicles in Fenugreek Cream Curry on Spinach Potatoes
— Vikram Vij and Meeru Dhalwala, Vij's (Vancouver)

I work with a local **lamb** farmer in the Willamette Valley who has true spring lamb in the spring. We have a spit and every Friday night we roast a whole lamb. I am a big fan of lamb shoulder. It can take a beating and in the end come out glorious tasting! There is an old French technique where they cook ham in hay. The hay is submerged in water; then they put the ham on it to cook. It is amazing. We adapted this technique to the lamb. We had our farmer collect the hay and grass in the field where the lamb grazed with the thinking that this is what the lamb actually ate. We then dry the hay by letting it sit out overnight on a tray, so it becomes really butterscotchy and barnyardy. You can use any hay for this technique but I'm just a purist.

We brine a boneless shoulder of lamb for 24 hours in a brining solution of 1 cup of salt and ¼ cup of sugar in a gallon of water, [adding] some peppercorns, bay leaf, a couple of cardamom pods, a cinnamon stick, and cumin. The brine is brought to a boil, cooled down, and the lamb goes in. After the brining we rub the lamb with garlic and summer savory and tie it up into a log and put it on the bed of hay, drizzle it with white wine, cover it, and put it in the oven. It is nature going back on itself. The lamb ate the hay, the hay makes the lamb taste better. When it's cooked, the flavors are intense but pleasant and it becomes something else. When lavender is in season, I'll throw some in the hay as well and it is delicious.

With the lamb I like to serve a stuffed tomato Provençal [typically a combination of basil, bread crumbs, garlic, olive oil]. You want to serve something simple. You could also serve a crushed potato with savory and olive oil or a medley of vegetables.

— **VITALY PALEY**, PALEY'S PLACE (PORTLAND, OREGON)

fennel
fennel seeds
fenugreek, esp. green
figs, dried black
five-spice powder
FLAGEOLETS
garam masala
*****GARLIC and garlic paste**
ginger
Greek cuisine
herbs
honey
Indian cuisine
Irish cuisine (e.g., stews)
Italian cuisine, esp. southern
lavender
leeks
LEMON: juice, zest
lemon, preserved
lentils

lime, juice
mace
marjoram
Middle Eastern cuisine
*****MINT**, esp. spearmint, mint jelly
mirepoix
Moroccan cuisine
mushrooms
MUSTARD, Dijon
nutmeg
OIL: canola, peanut, vegetable
olive oil
olives, esp. black, kalamata, niçoise
ONIONS: pearl, red, white, yellow
orange: juice, zest
oregano
paprika

PARSLEY, flat-leaf
pasta, esp. pappardelle
peas, esp. sweet
PEPPER: black, white
pesto
pine nuts
pistachios
polenta
pomegranates and pomegranate molasses
porcini mushrooms
potatoes, esp. new or red
prunes
raisins
red pepper flakes
rice: basmati, white, wild
risotto
*****ROSEMARY**
rutabaga
saffron
sage, fresh
SALT: *fleur de sel,* kosher, sea
savory
scallions
shallots
sherry, oloroso
spinach
stocks: beef, chicken, lamb, veal
sugar: brown, white
tabbouleh
tamarind
tarragon
THYME, FRESH
TOMATOES and tomato sauces
truffles, black, and truffle oil
turmeric
turnips
vanilla
vegetables, root
vermouth
vinaigrette
vinegar: balsamic, red wine, rice wine, sherry, white
watercress
WINE: dry white, red (e.g., Petite Syrah)
Worcestershire sauce
yogurt
zucchini

Flavor Affinities

lamb + broccoli rabe + Parmesan cheese
lamb + cardamom + yogurt
lamb + carrots + ginger + pistachios
lamb + carrots + lentils + parsley
lamb + chickpeas + garlic
lamb + chocolate + cinnamon + cloves
lamb + cilantro + dill + garlic + mint
lamb + cinnamon + dried apricots + preserved lemons + walnuts
lamb + cinnamon + garlic + lemon + mint + onion + oregano
lamb + cinnamon + prunes
lamb + clove + red wine
lamb + cream + fenugreek + garlic
lamb + cucumber + mint + tomatoes
lamb + escarole + lemon
lamb + fava beans + thyme
lamb + fennel + onions + turnips
lamb + flageolet beans + thyme
lamb + garlic + flageolet beans
lamb + garlic + olives
lamb + garlic + rosemary
lamb + mint + mustard
lamb + mint + olives
lamb + mint + parsley
lamb + mint + peas + risotto
lamb + mint + ricotta cheese
lamb + mint + tomatoes

LAMB, CHOPS

Techniques: broil, grill, sauté

anchovies
beans (e.g., fava)
bell peppers, red
broccoli, rabe
butter, unsalted
capers
carrots
cayenne
chard
cheese, feta
cilantro
cumin
curry
fennel
garam masala
garlic
ginger
honey
leeks
lemon
lime
mace
mint
miso
mushrooms
mustard, Dijon
nutmeg
oil: canola, peanut
olive oil
olives, black
onions, esp. pearl
oregano
paprika
parsley, flat-leaf
pepper: black, white
pomegranates
potatoes
rosemary
salad
salt: kosher, sea
savory
shallots
stock, chicken
sugar
tarragon
thyme
tomatoes
truffles
vinegar: balsamic, malt
wine, dry red
yogurt

Flavor Affinities

lamb chop + lemon + mint

LATIN AMERICAN CUISINE

beans, black
beef
café con leche
chile peppers
cilantro
cinnamon
cloves
corn
cumin
fruits
garlic
greens
lime, juice
meats

Latin American cuisine is very Mediterranean. It's based on what was brought over from Spain and Italy. You'll see the combination of garlic, onions, and peppers like you'll see in Spain and Italy, not to mention the same pantry of herbs and spices: cilantro, cinnamon, cloves, cumin, oregano, rosemary, thyme.

— MARICEL PRESILLA, ZAFRA (HOBOKEN, NEW JERSEY)

mixed grilled meats
onions
orange
oregano
peppers
pork
potatoes
rice
rosemary
sausages
seafood
tarragon
thyme
vegetables

Flavor Affinities
beef + corn + sweet potatoes
garlic + onions + peppers
meats + black beans + greens +
   orange + rice
seafood + chile peppers + cilantro
   + garlic + lime

LAVENDER
Taste: sweet, sour
Weight: light
Volume: loud
Tips: Caraway seeds can
substitute for lavender.

almonds
apples
baked goods: cakes, cookies,
   scones, shortbread
berries
blackberries

blueberries
cheese, ricotta
cherries
CHICKEN
CREAM AND ICE CREAM
crème fraîche
currants, black
custards
desserts
duck
figs
French cuisine
fruit and fruit preserves
game birds
ginger
herbes de Provence (occasional
   ingredient)
HONEY
LAMB
lemon
lemonade
marjoram
mascarpone
meats (e.g., beef, lamb, steak)
milk
mint
onions
orange
oregano
parsley
peaches
pistachios
plums
pork
potatoes
Provençal cuisine

quail
rabbit
ras el hanout (key ingredient)
raspberries
rhubarb
rice
rosemary
savory
spearmint
stews
strawberries
sugar
tea, esp. black
thyme
vanilla
vinegar, balsamic
walnuts

Flavor Affinities
lavender + cream + sugar
lavender + meat + salt

LEEKS
Season: autumn–spring
Taste: sweet
Botanical relatives: chives,
garlic, onions, shallots
Weight: light–medium
Volume: quiet
Techniques: boil, braise, fry,
grill, roast, steam
Tips: Add early in cooking
process.

anchovies
bacon
barley
bay leaf
beef
bouillabaisse
butter, unsalted
capers
caraway
carrot
cauliflower
celery
cheese: cheddar, goat, Gruyère,
   Parmesan
chervil

Lavender works with plums or peaches.
— **JERRY TRAUNFELD**, THE HERBFARM (WOODINVILLE, WASHINGTON)

Lavender and rosemary work in butter cakes, cookies, and other baked
goods.
— **JERRY TRAUNFELD**, THE HERBFARM (WOODINVILLE, WASHINGTON)

I like very little **lavender** with quail for its savory aroma, but the key
phrase is "very little" — or else it's like eating a piece of soap!
— **SHARON HAGE**, YORK STREET (DALLAS)

Dishes

Salade de Poireaux Frais: Chilled Leeks with Fingerling Potatoes and Piquillo Peppers
— Thomas Keller, Bouchon (Yountville, California)

Leek and Asparagus Pasta with Lemon, Parmesan, and Poached Egg
— Peter Nowakoski, Rat's (Hamilton, New Jersey)

chicken
chile peppers
chives
coriander
cream
crème fraîche
dill
eggs (including hard-boiled) and
    egg dishes
fennel
fish
French cuisine
garlic
Greek cuisine
lemon, juice
lovage
meats, white
mushrooms, esp. oyster
mussels
mustard
nutmeg
oil: corn, grapeseed, hazelnut,
    peanut, vegetable
olive oil
onions
oregano
paprika
parsley
pasta
pepper: black, white
potatoes
rice
sage
salads
salt, kosher
sauces, romesco
scallions
sea bass
soups
soy sauce
stews
stocks: chicken, vegetable
tamari
tarragon
thyme
tomatoes and tomato sauce
truffles, black
vinaigrette
vinegar, balsamic
wine: dry white, red

Flavor Affinities

leeks + anchovies + garlic + olive
    oil
leeks + bacon + cream
leeks + cream + thyme
leeks + mustard + vinaigrette

LEGUMES (See Beans, Lentils, Peas, etc.)

LEMONS

Season: year-round
Taste: sour
Weight: light
Volume: loud

almonds
anise

We have **lemon juice** right next to the salt when we cook. Acid is the most important aspect of how a dish tastes — whether it is there as subtle punctuation or an exclamation point!
— **SHARON HAGE**, YORK STREET (DALLAS)

Lemon zest adds a totally different dynamic than lemon juice. If you are making an apple crisp, if you added a teaspoon of zest it would taste very different than if you added lemon juice. The juice would make it taste tart, whereas the zest would actually add a lemon flavor component to it. For ice cream, custards, and tarts, use lemon juice. But if you are going to combine lemon with other flavors, that's when you use zest.
— **EMILY LUCHETTI**, FARALLON (SAN FRANCISCO)

Use **lemon juice** when you want the acid and lemony flavor of the juice. If you want the perfume of the lemon, use the zest because the skin is where you get the essential oils. I use more lemon and orange than vanilla in my cooking because they are more prevalent in Italy and in Italian cooking, and a flavor profile that people recognize as Italian.
— **GINA DEPALMA**, BABBO (NEW YORK CITY)

Lemon can be used by itself or with other ingredients because it enhances so many flavors. An orange can be a little too mellow, but lemon makes flavors much brighter. Lemon is an underlying flavor as much as the star. If there is one fruit you had to always have on hand as a basic staple, it is lemon.
— **EMILY LUCHETTI**, FARALLON (SAN FRANCISCO)

apples
apricots
artichokes
bananas
basil
bay leaf
beef
berries

beverages
blackberries
blueberries
butter, unsalted
buttermilk
capers
caramel
cardamom

cayenne
cheese: goat, ricotta
cherries
chervil
chestnuts
chicken
chives
chocolate: dark, white
cinnamon
coconut
coffee
crab
cranberries
cream / milk
cream cheese
crème fraîche
custard
dates
desserts
duck
figs: fresh, dried
FISH
GARLIC
gin
ginger
gooseberries
grapefruit
grapes
Greek cuisine
guava
hazelnuts
HONEY
kiwi fruit
lamb
lemongrass
lemon verbena
lime
liqueurs: nut, orange (e.g.,
    Cointreau, curaçao, Grand
    Marnier)
mango
maple syrup
mascarpone
Mediterranean cuisines
Middle Eastern cuisines
mint (garnish)
Moroccan cuisine
mustard, Dijon

Dishes

Ricotta-Lemon Pancakes with Blackberries and Honeycomb Butter

— Andrew Carmellini, A Voce (New York City)

nectarines
nuts, esp. hazelnuts
oats
olive oil
orange: juice, zest
oregano
oysters
papaya
parsley, flat-leaf
passion fruit
pasta and pasta sauces
peaches
pears
pecans
pepper, black
persimmons
pine nuts
pistachios
plums
poppy seeds
pork and pork chops
poultry
prunes
quince
raisins
raspberries
rhubarb
rice
rosemary
rum
sage
salads and salad dressings
salt, kosher
sauces: brown butter, parsley
sesame oil
shallots
SHELLFISH
sour cream
stock, chicken
SUGAR: brown, white
tangerine
thyme
vanilla
veal

violets
vodka
walnuts
wine: red, sweet (e.g., Muscat), white
yogurt

Flavor Affinities

lemon + berries + crème fraîche
lemon + blackberries + honey + ricotta cheese

LEMONS, MEYER

Season: autumn–spring
Taste: sour–sweet
Weight: light
Volume: moderate–loud

cream
grapefruit
honey
lemon
lime
orange
sugar
vanilla

When you are using different kinds of lemons, you need to treat them as different things. A **Meyer lemon** is different from a regular lemon. If you are using a Meyer lemon, you may want the perfume, aroma, and subtlety of it. Yet when you taste it, you may want to add a touch of regular lemon to give it a little more acidity and a little kick.
— **EMILY LUCHETTI**, FARALLON (SAN FRANCISCO)

We get a lot of **Meyer lemons** in during the season, and they have a lovely sweet-orangey lemon flavor. But there are times that they are simply too sweet and we have to either add regular lemon or some lime to balance the Meyer lemon.
— **MONICA POPE**, T'AFIA (HOUSTON)

Dishes

Meyer Lemon Cream Pie with Roasted Strawberries, Candied Coconut, Vanilla Chantilly

— Emily Luchetti, pastry chef, Farallon (San Francisco)

LEMONS, PRESERVED

Taste: sour
Weight: light–medium
Volume: moderate–loud

cinnamon
cloves
lamb
MOROCCAN CUISINE
nigella seeds
saffron

We churn through **preserved lemons**! In the middle of the summer, we buy cases so that we can age them eight months before we use them. After six months, they are great. After eight months or a year, you see God. They become incredible just by waiting those extra few months. I make preserved lemons by feel. I primarily use salt and will add some cinnamon, clove, nigella, a tiny, tiny bit of saffron, and then just tuck them away in the refrigerator. If I wasn't so greedy, I would give them away, but we are talking a year of my life here!
— **BRAD FARMERIE**, PUBLIC (NEW YORK CITY)

LEMON BALM

Season: spring–autumn
Taste: sour
Weight: light–medium
Volume: quiet–moderate

apricots
asparagus
berries
carrots
chicken
chives
dill
fennel bulb
fish
fruit
ginger
melon
mint
nectarines
parsley, flat-leaf
peaches
peas
salads, esp. fruit and green
teas

LEMON BASIL

Taste: sour
Weight: light
Volume: moderate

apricots
berries
cinnamon
desserts
fish
peaches
seafood
shellfish
soups
vegetables

LEMONGRASS

Taste: sour
Weight: light
Volume: moderate–loud

Tips: Add near end of cooking process; use in stir-fries.

basil
beef
chicken
chile peppers: red, green
chives
cilantro
cinnamon
cloves
coconut and coconut milk
coriander
crab
cream
curries
FISH
fruits
galangal
garlic
ginger
honey
Indonesian cuisine
lime, juice
lobster
Malaysian cuisine
meats
mint
noodles, rice
offal
onions
parsley
peanuts
pork
poultry
sage
salads and salad dressings
scallions
shallots
SHELLFISH
shrimp
soups, esp. chicken or turkey
Southeast Asian cuisines
spring rolls
stews
teas
THAI CUISINE
turmeric

vanilla
vegetables
Vietnamese cuisine
vinaigrettes

Flavor Affinities
lemongrass + chives + mint
lemongrass + cilantro + mint
lemongrass + cream + vanilla

LEMON THYME

Taste: sour
Weight: light
Volume: moderate–loud

asparagus
basil
bay leaf
beets
beverages (e.g., herbal teas)
bouillabaisse
carrots
chicken, esp. roasted
chives
eggs
fennel
figs
fish
fruits
ginger
halibut
lamb
marjoram
meats
mint
orange
parsley
potatoes
poultry
rabbit
rosemary
sage
salads: fruit, green
seafood
shellfish
sole
spinach
stews

Lemon verbena is amazing. I love to make a lemon verbena syrup and then poach apricots in it. It is so refreshing! We also make our own soda here, and lemon verbena is great in soda.
— JOHNNY IUZZINI, JEAN GEORGES (NEW YORK CITY)

stocks and broths: fish, seafood
stuffings
veal
vegetables, esp. spring

LEMON VERBENA
Taste: sour
Weight: light
Volume: loud

anise hyssop
apricots
baked goods (e.g., cakes, shortbread)
basil
beets
berries
beverages
blueberries
butter, unsalted
carrots
cherries
chicken
chile peppers
chives
cilantro
cinnamon
cream and ice cream
crème fraîche
currants, red
custards
desserts
fish
fruits
garlic
ginger
grapes
honey
lamb
lavender
lemon, juice
lemonade
lemongrass

lemon thyme
lime, juice
melon
milk
mint
mushrooms
nectarines
peaches
peas
plums
raspberries
rice
salads, fruit and green
salt
sour cream
strawberries
sugar
tamarind
tea, green
zucchini

Flavor Affinities
lemon verbena + apricots + sugar

LENTILS
Season: winter
Taste: sweet–stringent
Function: cooling
Weight: medium
Volume: moderate
Techniques: simmer
Tips: Green lentils are more flavorful than brown or red.

apples: cider, juice
bacon
BAY LEAF
bell peppers, esp. red
bouquet garni
bread and croutons
butter, unsalted
cardamom
CARROTS
cayenne
CELERY
celery root
cheese, goat
chervil
chile peppers: dried red, fresh green
chives (garnish)
cilantro
cinnamon
cloves
coconut

Dishes
Green Lentil Soup with Black Truffle, Smoked Quail, Crispy Shallots
— Daniel Boulud, Daniel (New York City)

Lentil Stew with Blood Sausage, Chorizo, or Ham with a Poached Egg on Top
— Alexandra Raij, Tía Pol (New York City)

A drizzle of sherry vinegar just before you serve **lentils** elevates them to another level.
— JOSÉ ANDRÉS, CAFÉ ATLÁNTICO (WASHINGTON, DC)

I like **lentils** for soup with a smoked ham hock. For seasoning the soup, I recommend thyme, bay leaf, and a pinch of cumin. You can add bacon or sausage, or serve it with potato galettes on the side.
— GABRIEL KREUTHER, THE MODERN (NEW YORK CITY)

cornichons
cream
cumin, esp. seeds
curry: leaves, powder, sauces
dill
eggplant
French cuisine
game birds, roasted (e.g., quail)
GARLIC
ginger
ham and ham hocks
honey
Indian cuisine
lamb
leeks
lemon, juice
lime, juice
meats
Mediterranean cuisine
mint, esp. spearmint
mirepoix (esp. for soups)
mustard, Dijon
mustard seeds, black
OIL: hazelnut, peanut, vegetable,
    walnut
olive oil
ONIONS, esp. red, white, yellow
oregano
PARSLEY, flat-leaf
PEPPER: black, white
pineapple
pork
poultry, roasted (e.g., chicken)
prosciutto
SALMON
SALT: kosher
sausage, esp. smoked
scallions
shallots
sorrel, esp. with green lentils
soups
soy sauce
spinach
squash, winter (e.g., butternut)
STOCKS: chicken, vegetable
thyme
tomatoes
turmeric

turnips
VINEGAR: balsamic, red wine,
    sherry
walnuts
wine, red
zucchini

Flavor Affinities
lentils + bacon + bell pepper +
    cumin + garlic
lentils + bacon + garlic + sherry
    vinegar
lentils + bay leaf + onions + thyme
lentils + cumin + turmeric
lentils + olive oil + parsley + sorrel

LETTUCES — IN GENERAL

Season: spring–autumn
Function: cooling
Weight: light–medium
Volume: quiet–loud

apples
bacon
basil
bread, breadsticks, croutons, etc.
capers
cheese (e.g., feta)
chicories, aka bitter greens
dill
eggs, esp. hard-boiled
fennel leaves
garlic
lemon, juice
mint
mushrooms
mustard, Dijon
nuts

oil: hazelnut, peanut, walnut
olive oil
olives
orange
parsley
peaches
pears
pepper, black
raisins
salt
shallots
sprouts
tarragon
vegetables, esp. raw
vinaigrette
vinegar: balsamic, cider, red wine
watercress

LETTUCE, BIBB (aka Boston or butter lettuce)

Season: spring
Taste: sweet
Weight: light–medium
Volume: quiet

arugula
avocados
basil
chervil
chives
cucumbers
fines herbes
lemon
orange
parsley
pepper, black
radishes
salt
sesame seeds

Bibb lettuce is a light, delicate, and almost creamy lettuce, so I serve it with a creamy dressing to mimic that creaminess. Because of its delicacy, to make the mayonnaise I'll use a neutral oil that's a blend of 80 percent canola and 20 percent olive. It finds a counterpoint in lemon and fines herbes, and gets a note of freshness, crunch, and spicy heat from radishes.

— **TONY LIU,** AUGUST (NEW YORK CITY)

shallots
tarragon
vinaigrette
watercress
yogurt

LETTUCES — BITTER GREENS AND CHICORIES (See Arugula, Escarole, Frisée, Radicchio)
Season: spring
Taste: bitter
Weight: light–medium
Volume: medium–loud

bacon
basil
beans, esp. "fresh shell"
butter
cheese: Asiago, Gruyère, Parmesan
cilantro
cream
eggs, hard-boiled
garlic

lemon, juice
lemon balm
nuts
olives
olive oil
onions, yellow
pancetta
parsley
pasta
red pepper flakes
rices
salt, kosher
scallions
shallots

Dishes

Hearts of Romaine and Treviso Radicchio with Spanish Serrano Ham, Manchego Cheese, White Anchovies, Fire-Roasted Peppers, and Crisp Capers
— Carrie Nahabedian, Naha (Chicago)

Caesar Salad Soup
— Nobiyuki Sugie, Asiate (New York City)

Leaves of Romaine, Creamy Garlic Dressing, Red Onions, Capers, and Parmesan
— Cory Schreiber, Wildwood (Portland, Oregon)

sugar
thyme
vinegar: balsamic, red wine, white
walnuts

LETTUCES — MESCLUN GREENS (i.e., mixed baby lettuces) (See also Lettuces — Bitter Greens and Chicories)
Season: spring
Taste: bitter
Weight: light
Volume: moderate

basil
cheese, goat
chervil
chives
confit (e.g., duck)
French cuisine
hazelnuts
lemon, juice
mushrooms, wild (e.g., morels)
olive oil
parsley, flat-leaf
pecan
pepper, black
salt
shallots
tarragon
vinaigrettes

Flavor Affinities
mesclun greens + goat cheese +
   hazelnuts

LETTUCE, ROMAINE
Season: spring–autumn
Taste: sweet, bitter
Weight: light
Volume: quiet

anchovies
avocados
bell peppers: green, red
butter
Caesar salad
capers
cayenne
CHEESE: feta, dry Jack, Monterey
   Jack, **Parmesan**, Stilton
chervil
chile peppers: jalapeño, serrano
chives
cilantro
cream
crème fraîche
croutons
cucumbers
eggs, yolk
GARLIC
grapefruit

ham
leeks
lemon, juice
lime: juice, zest
lovage
mayonnaise
mustard, Dijon
OIL: canola, vegetable
OLIVE OIL
olives, kalamata
onions, esp. red
parsley, flat-leaf
pepper: black, white
salt: kosher, sea
shallots
sour cream
stocks: chicken, vegetable
tarragon
tomatoes
vinaigrette
VINEGAR: balsamic, cider,
   raspberry, red wine, sherry,
   white wine
walnuts
Worcestershire sauce

Flavor Affinities
romaine + anchovies + Parmesan
   cheese
romaine + capers + garlic +
   Parmesan cheese + red onions

LIMES
Season: year-round
Taste: sour

Weight: light
Volume: moderate

apricots
avocados
berries: blueberries, gooseberries,
   raspberries, **strawberries**
butter
buttermilk
capers
caramel
ceviche
chicken
**chile peppers, esp. jalapeño or
   serrano**
chocolate, white
cilantro
coconut and coconut milk
cream
cream cheese
crème fraîche
dates
duck
figs, dried
fish, esp. grilled
fruits, esp. tropical
gin
ginger
gooseberries
grapefruit
green tea
guacamole
guava
hazelnuts
honey: raw, burnt

Acidity awakens flavors. I love **lime**, and just a squeeze of lime on
seafood soup or Thai soup awakens it.
— **KATSUYA FUKUSHIMA**, MINIBAR (WASHINGTON, DC)

Dishes

Key Lime Cheesecake with Macadamia Nut Crust, Lime Caramel, Key Lime Curd
— Emily Luchetti, pastry chef, Farallon (San Francisco)

**Grilled Lime Pound Cake with Crème Fraîche–Tapioca Pudding, Blueberry Gelée, and
Burnt Honey Ice Cream**
— Celina Tio, American Restaurant (Kansas City)

jicama
kiwi fruit
Latin American cuisine
lemon
lemongrass
lime: juice, zest
lobster
macadamia nuts
mangoes
maple syrup
margaritas
mascarpone
meats, esp. grilled
melon, esp. honeydew
Mexican cuisine
mint
orange, juice
papayas
passion fruit
peanuts
pecans
pie, esp. with Key limes
raspberries
rum
salt
scallops
sea bass
shellfish
shrimp
Southwestern cuisine
strawberries
sugar: brown, white
sweet potatoes
tequila
Thai cuisine
tomatoes
tuna
vanilla
Vietnamese cuisine
vodka
yogurt

Flavor Affinities

lime + blueberries + burnt honey
   + crème fraîche
lime + caramel + cream cheese +
   macadamia nuts
lime + strawberries + tequila

**LIMES AND LIME LEAF,
KAFFIR** (See Kaffir Limes and
Kaffir Lime Leaf)

LIVER, CALF'S
Taste: bitter
Weight: medium–heavy
Volume: moderate–loud
Techniques: braise, broil, grill,
sauté
Tips: Cook briefly, one minute
per side.

apples
arugula
avocado
bacon
bay leaf
bouquet garni
butter, unsalted
carrots
celery
cheese, Parmesan
chervil
chives
cream
figs
French cuisine
garlic
jasmine
lemon, juice
milk
mushrooms
mustard, Dijon
oil, canola
olive oil
olives, green
ONIONS: fried, red, Vidalia,
   white
orange, zest
pancetta
parsley, flat-leaf
pears
pepper: black, white
polenta
potatoes, mashed
prunes

rhubarb
sage
salt, kosher
sauce, brown butter
sausages
shallots
spinach
stock, chicken
sugar, brown
thyme
tomatoes
turnips
VINEGAR: balsamic, cider, red
   wine, sherry
wine: dry red or white

Flavor Affinities

calf's liver + arugula + onions +
   pancetta
calf's liver + figs + onions + red
   wine vinegar

LIVER, CHICKEN
Weight: medium
Volume: moderate–loud
Techniques: grill, sauté

anchovies
apples
bacon
bay leaf
butter, unsalted
capers
chicken fat
chives
cilantro
eggs, hard-boiled
garlic
kale
lemon, juice
lime, juice
oil, peanut
olive oil
ONIONS: fried, red, sweet (e.g.,
   Vidalia)
parsley, flat-leaf
peanuts
pepper: black, white

radishes
red pepper flakes
rosemary
sage
salt, kosher
shallots
sherry, dry (e.g., fino)
soy sauce
sugar
thyme
vinegar: balsamic, sherry
wine, dry red

Flavor Affinities
chicken livers + apples + sage
chicken livers + bacon + balsamic
   vinegar + onions + rosemary
chicken livers + kale + lemon

LIVER, DUCK OR GOOSE (See Foie Gras)

LOBSTER

Season: summer–autumn
Taste: sweet
Weight: light–medium
Volume: quiet–medium
Techniques: bake, boil, broil, grill, pan roast, poach, roast, sauté, steam

anchovies
apples
artichokes
asparagus
avocado
bacon
basil
bay leaf
beans: green, flageolets, white
beets
bell peppers, esp. red, yellow,
   and/or roasted
brandy
BUTTER, unsalted
cabbage, esp. savoy
capers
carrots

caviar
cayenne
celery
celery root
Champagne
cheese: Gruyère, Parmesan
chervil
chile peppers, jalapeño
chili paste
Chinese cuisine
chives
cilantro
cinnamon
clams
clove
coconut and coconut milk
cognac
coriander
corn
crab
cream
crème fraîche
cucumbers
cumin
curry: paste (red), powder

curry leaf
daikon
dill
eggs and egg yolks
endive
fennel
fennel seeds
fenugreek seeds
figs
fish sauce, Thai
foie gras
frisée
GARLIC
ginger, fresh
grapefruit
grapes
guacamole
haricots verts
honey
horseradish
kiwi fruit
kumquats
leeks
LEMON: juice, zest
lemon, Meyer

I love **lobster**: poached, roasted, or grilled. I like mayonnaise or a vinaigrette with my lobster much more than butter with lobster. In the summertime, I like it with small potatoes and corn. I really like it with cilantro.

   For my dish Roasted Maine Lobster in "Folly of Herbs" with Baby Fennel and Salsify, I wanted to do something different with lobster besides a lobster sauce. I make a "tea" of dried herbs: thyme, rosemary, fennel seeds, oregano, sage, mint, and tarragon. This is boiled and strained, then gets a dash of Ricard [also known as Pernod, an anise-flavored liquor]. The lobster gets finished with fresh parsley, mint, and fresh oregano. I chose these two vegetables because salsify is underused and underappreciated. I don't blanch my salsify in water because when you do, the flavor stays in the water. I roast them and caramelize them a little bit, then deglaze with just a little water with a sprig of thyme and a bay leaf. Baby fennel is good because it plays off the Ricard and fennel. I quickly blanch the fennel and then caramelize it.
— **GABRIEL KREUTHER**, THE MODERN (NEW YORK CITY)

Cooked **lobster** meat blends well with mayonnaise, but I don't think I'd use it with raw lobster — I'd use soy sauce instead.
— **KAZ OKOCHI**, KAZ SUSHI BISTRO (WASHINGTON, DC)

Dishes

Spaghettini with Spicy Budding Chives, Sweet Garlic, and a One-Pound Lobster
— Mario Batali, Babbo (New York City)

Chatham Bay Day Boat Lobster with Red Wine Sauce and Parsnip-Rosemary-Apple Puree
— David Bouley, Upstairs (New York City)

Chilled Maine Lobster: Mango, Fresh Artichoke, and Serrano Ham with a Passion Fruit and Fresh Coconut Tamarind Dressing
— David Bouley, Bouley (New York City)

Potato Gnocchi with Maine Lobster, Wild Asparagus, Meyer Lemon, and Tarragon
— Traci Des Jardins, Jardiniére (San Francisco)

Lobster and Morel Ravioli in Basil Broth, Hazelnuts, and Lobster Oil
— Sandy D'Amato, Sanford (Milwaukee)

Nova Scotia Lobster Poached with Florence Fennel and Chamomile
— Daniel Humm, Eleven Madison Park (New York City)

Warm Lobster Salad, Cauliflower and Watercress Coulis
— Jean Joho, Everest (Chicago)

Butter-Poached Lobster with Sweet Carrot Emulsion
— Thomas Keller, The French Laundry (Yountville, California)

Briny Lobster with Wasabi Mayo
— Kaz Okochi, Kaz Sushi Bistro (Washington, DC)

Maine Lobster Tails Roasted with Fingerling Potatoes, Pea Greens, Whole Garlic, and Fava Beans
— Alfred Portale, Gotham Bar and Grill (New York City)

Martini of Maine Lobster, Cucumber Salad, Belvedere Vodka, and White Sturgeon Caviar
— Thierry Rautureau, Rover's (Seattle)

Lobster Poached in a Lemon Miso Broth with Shiso and Hon Shimgeji Mushrooms
— Eric Ripert, Le Bernardin (New York City)

Baked Lobster; Braised Endives, with Enoki and Black Trumpet Mushroom with Bourbon–Black Pepper Sauce
— Eric Ripert, Le Bernardin (New York City)

lemongrass
lentils
lime: leaf (kaffir), juice
lobster roe
macaroni and cheese
mace
mâche
mangoes
mascarpone

mayonnaise
Mediterranean cuisine
mint
mirepoix
miso, white
mushrooms: button, cepes, chanterelles, cremini, porcini, shiitake, white, wild
mussels

mustard: dry, seeds
New England cuisine
nutmeg
OIL: canola, corn, grapeseed, hazelnut, peanut, sesame, vegetable, walnut
olive oil
onions, esp. pearl, red, Spanish
orange (juice, zest) and clementine
oyster sauce
papaya
paprika, sweet
parsley, flat-leaf
parsnips
pasta (e.g., macaroni)
passion fruit
peanuts
peas
peas, snow
pepper: black, white
Pernod
pineapple
port
potatoes, esp. fingerling or new
pumpkin
radicchio
red pepper flakes
rhubarb
rice, esp. sticky, and risotto
rosemary
saffron
SALT: kosher, sea, *sel gris*
sauces, béchamel
scallions
scallops
sea urchin
shallots
shrimp
snow peas
Southern cuisine
soy sauce
spinach
squid
star anise
stocks: chicken, fish, lobster, shellfish, veal, vegetable
Tabasco sauce
tamarind, puree

tarragon
thyme
TOMATOES: juice, paste, pulp
truffles: black, juice
vanilla
vermouth, dry
vinaigrette, esp. citrus
VINEGAR: red wine, rice wine,
    sherry, white wine
vodka
wasabi
water chestnuts
watermelon
whiskey
WINE: dry to off-dry white (e.g.,
    Gewürztraminer or Riesling),
    dry red (e.g., Syrah), port
Worcestershire sauce
yuzu juice

Flavor Affinities
lobster + artichokes + garlic
lobster + avocado + mayonnaise + tarragon + white wine vinegar
lobster + bacon + porcini mushrooms
lobster + basil + hazelnuts + morel mushrooms
lobster + basil + tomatoes
lobster + brandy + cream + rosemary
lobster + brown butter + orange + vanilla
lobster + butter + garlic + tarragon
lobster + celery + mayonnaise + black truffles
lobster + chanterelle mushrooms + parsley + Pernod
lobster + chanterelle mushrooms + tarragon
lobster + chive + lemon
lobster + cilantro + cumin
lobster + corn + garlic + lemon + potatoes + tarragon
lobster + fennel + lemon
lobster + mango + spinach
lobster + mayonnaise + wasabi
lobster + orange + soy sauce
lobster + pasta + peas
lobster + saffron + vanilla

LOTUS ROOT
Season: summer–winter
Taste: sweet
Weight: light–medium
Volume: quiet
Techniques: fry, raw, simmer, stir-fry

ginger
lemon
lime
oil, vegetable
salads
soups
soy sauce
stir-fried dishes
tempura
vinegar, rice
wine, rice

LOVAGE
Season: spring, autumn
Taste: sour
Weight: light–medium, soft-leaved
Volume: quiet–loud
Tips: Always use fresh, not cooked.

apples
bay leaf
beans, green
bell peppers
caraway
carrots
chard
cheese
chervil
chicken
chile peppers
chives
clams
corn
crab, Dungeness
cream cheese
dill
eggs and egg dishes
fennel
fish, e.g., halibut, skate, smoked, tuna
garlic
greens
ham
juniper berries
lamb
marjoram
mint
mushrooms
mussels
mustard
nettles, stinging
onions
oregano
parsley
pork
potatoes

Stinging nettles and **lovage** is a wonderful combination. Stinging nettles are peppery with a green flavor and lovage is celery-like. It's funny: I find nettles without lovage are kind of flat tasting. I will use this combination in a ravioli filling or with local Dungeness crab as a sauce for a soufflé.

— JERRY TRAUNFELD, THE HERBFARM (WOODINVILLE, WASHINGTON)

rabbit
rice
salads, green
sauces
shellfish
sorrel
soups, esp. fish
spinach
stews
tarragon
thyme
tomatoes and tomato juice
veal
vegetables, esp. root
zucchini

Flavor Affinities
lovage + Dungeness crab +
    stinging nettles
lovage + salmon + tomatoes

LUXURIOUS
caviar, esp. Beluga
Champagne
foie gras
Ibérico ham
Kobe beef
saffron
smoked fish
vanilla
truffles: black, white
wine

LYCHEES
Season: summer
Taste: sweet
Weight: light–medium
Volume: quiet–moderate
Techniques: raw

anise hyssop
berries
blackberries
chicken
chile peppers
cilantro
coconut and coconut milk
cream

cream cheese
curry
duck
foie gras
ginger
honey
kiwi fruit
lemon, juice
lemongrass
lime, juice
mangoes
melon, esp. honeydew
nuts
orange, tangerine
passion fruit
pears
pineapple
plums
pork
raspberries
rice
rose (French cuisine)
rum
sake
salads, fruit
shellfish: scallops, shrimp

Dishes
**Summer Raspberry-Lychee Macaroon
with Lemon Sorbet**
— Eric Bertoia, Cafe Boulud
(New York City)

strawberries
sugar, esp. palm
vodka
wine: plum, sparkling
yogurt

Flavor Affinities
lychees + ginger + lime
lychees + raspberries + rose

MACADAMIA NUT OIL
(See Oil, Macadamia Nut)

MACADAMIA NUTS
Weight: light–medium
Volume: moderate

apricots
bananas
beets
bourbon
brandy
caramel
cashews
chicken
chocolate, esp. dark or white
coconut
coffee
crab
cream
dates
desserts
figs, dried

Our **macadamia nut** tart, which we serve with banana-rum ice cream, is our take on pecan pie.
— **LISSA DOUMANI**, TERRA (ST. HELENA, CALIFORNIA)

Macadamia nuts are buttery, rich nuts. I will even pair them with sea scallops, which also have a richness to them. The macadamia nuts don't overwhelm the scallops and I put them in the dish slightly chopped — otherwise, the texture of the nut would be too chewy. We use macadamia nuts on one of the simplest yet most popular dishes on our menu — our jumbo lump crab cake with grilled asparagus and toasted macadamia nuts. Our crab cake is the only recipe we won't give out. It contains no herbs or spices. The only thing that goes in our crab cake is crab, salt, pepper, *panko* [Japanese bread crumbs], and a little mayonnaise to hold them together. You are the first people to get this recipe!
— **MARCEL DESAULNIERS**, THE TRELLIS (WILLIAMSBURG, VIRGINIA)

fish (e.g., cod, halibut, mahi
    mahi)
ginger
goat cheese
grapefruit
guava
Hawaiian cuisine
honey
kumquats
lamb
lemon
lime
mango
maple syrup
mint
orange
papaya
passion fruit
peaches
pineapple
prunes
raspberries
rum
scallops
sugar, brown
vanilla

Flavor Affinities
macadamia nuts + bananas +
    caramel + cream
macadamia nuts + beets + goat
    cheese
macadamia nuts + coconut + lime

MACE
Season: summer–autumn
Taste: pungent, sweet
Botanical relatives: nutmeg
Weight: light–medium
Volume: loud

allspice
Asian cuisine
baked goods (e.g., doughnuts)
beans
broccoli
butter
cabbage
cardamom

carrots
**cheese and cheese dishes, esp.
    creamy**
cherry pie
chicken
chocolate
chowders (e.g., fish)
cinnamon
cloves
coriander
cream / milk
cumin
curry (ingredient)
eggs
English cuisine
fish
French cuisine
garam masala (ingredient)
ginger
hazelnuts
Indian cuisine
ketchup (ingredient)
lamb
meats
New England cuisine
NUTMEG
onions
paprika
pastries
pepper
potatoes
pound cake
puddings
pumpkin
salads, fruit
sauces: béchamel, cream, onion
sausages
shellfish, shrimp
soups and consommés
spinach
stuffing
sweet potatoes
thyme
veal

vegetables
West Indian cuisine

MÂCHE
Season: autumn–spring
Weight: very light
Volume: very quiet
Techniques: raw, steam

apples
bacon
beets
butter
cheese, goat
cream
eggs, quail
endive
lemon, juice
mustard, Dijon
nuts: pistachios, **walnuts**
oil: grapeseed, nut
olive oil
orange
pomegranates
potatoes
scallops
shallots
vinegar: champagne, sherry

Flavor Affinities
mâche + apples + bacon
mâche + apples + bacon + vinegar
mâche + apples + beets + endive
    + sherry vinaigrette + walnuts
mâche + oranges + pistachios +
    pomegranates

MACKEREL
Season: summer–autumn
Weight: light
Volume: loud
Techniques: braise, broil, grill,
    marinate, poach, sauté, sear

If you go to Japan, you'll find that virtually all the sushi restaurants put
a little ginger and scallion on their **mackerel** sushi. It cuts its
"fishiness" while adding flavor.
— **KAZ OKOCHI,** KAZ SUSHI BISTRO (WASHINGTON, DC)

apples
artichokes
bay leaf
beets
bell peppers: red, yellow
butter
capers
caraway seeds
caviar
ceviche
chile peppers
chives
cilantro
cinnamon
cloves
coriander
cornichons
cream
crème fraîche
cucumber
cumin
dill
fennel
French cuisine
garlic
ginger
gooseberries
horseradish
LEMON, juice
lemon thyme
lentils
lime, juice
mint (garnish)
miso
mushrooms
mustard, Dijon
mustard seeds
OIL: canola, corn, peanut,
   sesame, vegetable
olive oil
onions
orange, juice
pancetta
parsley, flat-leaf
PEPPER: black, green, white
red pepper flakes
rosemary
saffron

sake
salmon caviar
salt, sea
scallions
sesame seeds
shallots
sorrel
soy sauce
stocks: chicken, fish
sugar
thyme
VINEGAR: champagne, red wine,
   sherry, white wine
wine, dry white

Flavor Affinities
mackerel + arugula + chickpeas +
   lemon + rosemary
mackerel + chives + Dijon
   mustard + lemon juice +
   shallots + vinegar
mackerel + ginger + scallions
mackerel + onions + thyme

MAHI MAHI
Taste: sweet
Weight: medium–heavy
Volume: quiet
Techniques: bake, broil, deep-
fry, grill, poach, sauté, steam, stir-
fry

avocado
cabbage
cilantro
coriander
dill
fruits, esp. tropical
gin
juniper berries
lemon: juice, zest
orange: juice, zest
pepper, white
salt, sea
sugar

Flavor Affinities
mahi mahi + avocado + cabbage +
   cilantro

Dishes
Taco de Pescado "Baja": Battered and
Deep-Fried Mahi Mahi in Soft Corn
Tortillas with Cabbage and Avocado-
Cilantro Cream
— Traci Des Jardins, Mijita (San
Francisco)

MALT
Taste: sweet
Weight: light
Volume: moderate

bananas
caramel
chocolate
cinnamon
coffee
cream and ice cream
nuts
sugar
vanilla

Dishes
Naha Sundae of Vanilla Malt Ice
Cream, Hickory Nut Waffle, Bananas,
and Bourbon-Pecan Syrup, Shortbread
Cookies
— Elizabeth Dahl, pastry chef,
Naha (Chicago)

Double-Malted Euphoria with Malted
Chocolate, Vanilla Mousse, and
Marcona Almond Brittle
— Celina Tio, American
Restaurant (Kansas City)

I love **malt**. It has a sweetness,
breadiness, and graininess to its
flavor. It works with the classics
like chocolate, vanilla, and caramel.
— MICHAEL LAISKONIS, LE BERNARDIN
(NEW YORK CITY)

MANGOES

Season: late spring–late summer
Taste: sweet
Weight: medium
Volume: moderate
Techniques: raw

almonds
amaretto
anise
avocados
BANANAS (compatible fruit)
basil
bell peppers, esp. red and green
beverages (e.g., cocktails,
    smoothies)
blackberries
blueberries
buttermilk
butterscotch
cabbage, green
caramel
cashews
cayenne
ceviche
Champagne
cheese, esp. mixed-milk cheeses
    (e.g., Robiola Rocchetta and
    Amarelo da Beira Baixa)
CHILE PEPPERS, esp. jalapeño,
    serrano, red, green
chocolate, white
chutneys
cilantro
cinnamon
cloves
COCONUT AND COCONUT
    MILK
coffee
cream (e.g., heavy, whipped)
crème fraîche
curry powder
custard
fish

game
garlic
ginger, fresh
grapefruit
honey
Indian cuisine
Kirsch
kiwi fruit
kumquats
lemon, juice
LIME, juice
macadamia nuts
mascarpone
Mexican cuisine
milk (e.g., evaporated)
mint
nutmeg
oil, vegetable
olive oil
ONIONS: red, sweet
ORANGE: juice, zest
orange liqueur
papaya
passion fruit
pepper, white
pineapple
pork, esp. roasted
poultry: chicken, duck
prosciutto
raspberries
rice
RUM

sake
salads, fruit
salmon
salt
Sauternes
scallions
sesame seeds
shellfish, shrimp
sorbet
squab
star anise
strawberries
SUGAR: LIGHT BROWN,
    WHITE
Tabasco sauce
Thai cuisine
tuna, esp. grilled
vanilla
vinegar: balsamic, red wine
violets
vodka
wine: Chardonnay, sweet (e.g., ice
    wine)
yogurt

AVOID
soy sauce
wasabi

Flavor Affinities
mango + almonds + lime
mango + basil + Champagne
mango + black pepper + lemon +
    mint + passion fruit
mango + coconut + rice
mango + ginger + mint + papaya
mango + salmon + sushi rice

Dishes

Mango Mousse, Pineapple Soufflé, Roasted Pineapple, Swiss Meringue
— François Payard, Payard Patisserie and Bistro (New York City)

Organic Strawberry and Grapefruit Granitas, Mango "Salad," Mascarpone
— Monica Pope, T'afia (Houston)

Mango, Pistachio, and Banana Strudel with Coconut-Curry Sauce
— Allen Susser, at the 2003 James Beard Awards gala reception

Raspberry-Mango Soufflé with Fresh Fruit and Bittersweet Chocolate Ice Cream
— Celina Tio, American Restaurant (Kansas City)

> **Mangoes** pair well with some of the mixed-milk cheeses such as Robiola Rocchetta and Amarelo da Beira Baixa.
> — MAX McCALMAN, ARTISANAL CHEESE CENTER (NEW YORK CITY)

MAPLE SYRUP

Taste: sweet, bitter
Function: cooling
Weight: medium–heavy
Volume: moderate–loud

almonds
anise
apples
apricots
bacon
baked goods, e.g., gingerbread

BANANAS
BLUEBERRIES
breakfast / brunch
butter
buttermilk
Canadian cuisine
caramel
carrots
chestnuts
chocolate, esp. dark, white
cinnamon
coffee
corn syrup
cream
cream cheese
custard
dates
desserts
duck
figs, esp. dried
foie gras
French toast
fruit
ginger
ham
hazelnuts
ice cream: coffee, vanilla
lemon, juice
lime, juice
macadamia nuts
mascarpone
nectarines
New England cuisine
nutmeg
nuts
oats
onions
orange
pancakes
peaches
PEARS
PECANS
persimmons
pineapple
plums
pork ribs
prunes
pumpkin

I typically use **maple syrup** with nuts, like in a pecan pie. I will replace the dark corn syrup in the recipe with maple syrup instead. It is always important to use a very good quality [e.g., Vermont or Canadian] maple syrup. If you are working with syrup and sugar, you need to be careful because the combination of dark brown sugar with maple syrup can become very intense.

— **EMILY LUCHETTI,** FARALLON (SAN FRANCISCO)

BLiS **maple syrup** is aged in bourbon barrels, and is good enough to drink on its own! I'll use it with everything from duck breast to foie gras.

— **BRADFORD THOMPSON,** MARY ELAINE'S AT THE PHOENICIAN (SCOTTSDALE, ARIZONA)

Dishes

Maple and Anise French Toast with Lavender Custard
— Dominique and Cindy Duby, Wild Sweets (Vancouver)

Milk Chocolate and Maple Caramel Cake
— Dominique and Cindy Duby, Wild Sweets (Vancouver)

Milk Chocolate and Maple Caramel Ice Cream, Caramelized Bananas, and Ginger Tuile
— Dominique and Cindy Duby, Wild Sweets (Vancouver)

quince
raisins
raspberries
rhubarb
rum: dark, light
star anise
strawberries
sweet potatoes
sugar: light brown, raw, white
tea
turkey
vanilla
waffles
WALNUTS
whiskey
yogurt

AVOID

sugar, dark brown, as it is too intense with maple syrup

Flavor Affinities

maple syrup + blueberries + lemon
maple syrup + butter + chocolate + cream
maple syrup + caramel + pecans
maple syrup + mascarpone + pistachios

MARJORAM

Season: summer–winter
Taste: sweet, spicy
Botanical relatives: oregano (which is stronger in flavor than marjoram)
Weight: light
Volume: quiet–moderate
Tips: Add at the end of the cooking process.

artichokes
asparagus
basil
bay leaf
beans, esp. green
beef
beets
bouquet garni (ingredient)
bread
butter
carrots
chard
cheese: fresh goat, mozzarella
chicken
chives
chowders
clams
corn
cucumber
delicate-flavored foods (e.g., those "quiet" in Volume)
duck
eggs and egg dishes (e.g., omelets)
fish
French cuisine
fines herbes (ingredient)
garlic
halibut
Italian cuisine
lamb
lemon, juice
lima beans
meats, esp. grilled
Mediterranean cuisine
Middle Eastern cuisine
mint
mushrooms, esp. wild
North African cuisine
North American cuisine
oil, peanut
olive oil
olives
onions
oregano
parsley
pasta, esp. macaroni or ravioli
peas
pizza
pork
potatoes
poultry
rabbit

risotto
rosemary
sage
**SALADS, esp. green, and salad
   dressings**
sauces
sausages
savory
shellfish
soups, esp. bean, onion
spinach
squash, summer
stews
stuffing
thyme
tomatoes and tomato sauce
tuna
veal
vegetables, esp. summer
vinaigrettes
wine, red
zucchini

Flavor Affinities

marjoram + chicken + lemon
marjoram + fresh goat cheese +
   prosciutto
marjoram + tomato sauce +
   zucchini

Mediterranean herbs marry well.
Rosemary and **marjoram,** or
thyme and savory, are naturals
together.

— **JERRY TRAUNFELD,** THE HERBFARM
(WOODINVILLE, WASHINGTON)

MASCARPONE

Taste: sweet
Weight: medium–heavy
Volume: quiet

almonds
anchovies
apricots
arugula
berries
biscotti

blackberries
blueberries
brandy
butter
caramel
cheese, ricotta
cherries
chives
chocolate, esp. dark
cinnamon
cloves
coffee/espresso
cream
cream cheese
crème fraîche
currants, red
dates
figs
fruits, tropical
ginger
guava
hazelnuts
honey
Italian cuisine
Kirsch
ladyfingers
lemon: juice, zest
lime

maple syrup
mushrooms
mustard
nectarines
nutmeg
oats
orange
pasta
peaches
pears
pepper, black
pesto
pine nuts
pistachios
prosciutto
pumpkin
quince
raisins
raspberries
rhubarb
rum
strawberries
sugar: raw, white
truffle oil
vanilla
vinegar, balsamic
walnuts
wine: red, sweet

Flavor Affinities

mascarpone + arugula + truffle oil
mascarpone + berries + figs
mascarpone + chocolate + strawberries
mascarpone + cinnamon + pumpkin
mascarpone + espresso + ladyfingers (cookies) + sugar
mascarpone + figs + prosciutto
mascarpone + maple syrup + pistachios

Dishes

Black Mission Figs with Mascarpone Foam and Prosciutto di Parma
   — Rick Tramonto, Tru (Chicago)

MEATS

Tips: Enhance the flavor of meat *before* (e.g., via brining and marinating), *during* (e.g., via selecting the best cooking technique), and *after* cooking (e.g., via condiments and sauces).

MEDITERRANEAN CUISINES (See also French [southern], Italian, Middle Eastern, Moroccan, and Spanish Cuisines)

basil
citrus
garlic
herbs
lemon, juice
marjoram
olive oil
oregano
parsley
rosemary
sage
savory
thyme
tomatoes
vinegar: balsamic, red wine

Flavor Affinities
marjoram + rosemary
savory + thyme

MELON/ MUSKMELONS — IN GENERAL (See also Cantaloupe, Honeydew, etc.)
Season: summer
Taste: sweet
Function: cooling
Weight: light–medium
Volume: moderate
Techniques: raw

almonds
anise seeds and anise hyssop

apricots
basil
beverages, esp. smoothies
blackberries
blueberries
Champagne
cherries
chile peppers, esp. serrano
chili powder
chili sauce
cilantro
cognac, esp. in cocktails
Cointreau
cream / milk
crème fraîche
cucumbers
curaçao, esp. in cocktails
cured meats (e.g., prosciutto, sopressata)
curry
fennel
ginger
Grand Marnier, esp. in cocktails
grapefruit
grapes
hazelnuts

honey
ices and ice creams
Italian cuisine
Kirsch
kiwi fruit
LEMON, juice
lemon balm
LIME, juice
lychees
macadamia nuts
Madeira
mangoes
Midori liqueur
MINT, esp. spearmint
olive oil
orange
orange-flower water
pears
pecans
pepper: black, white
port
PROSCIUTTO
raspberries
rum
sake
salads, esp. fruit

Tarragon works with **muskmelons.**

— **JERRY TRAUNFELD**, THE HERBFARM (WOODINVILLE, WASHINGTON)

salsas, fruit
salt, kosher
sambuca
soups, esp. chilled
strawberries: fruit, puree
tarragon
tequila, esp. in cocktails
vanilla

vinegar, rice
wines, sweet, esp.
  Gewürztraminer, late harvest
  wines, **Muscat Beaumes-de-**
  Venise Riesling, Sauternes
yogurt
yuzu juice

MENU

Tips: Strive for balance over an entire menu, i.e., appetizer, entrée, and dessert. Envision the course of a menu as a piece of music having a melody, rhythm, and tempo.

Three-course menu:

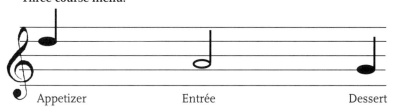

Tasting menu:

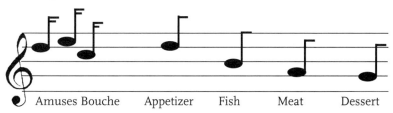

When planning a **menu,** pick the dessert or the entrée first and have the other one match it, in terms of style and preparation. If you are doing an entrée that requires last-minute time in the kitchen, don't serve a dessert that requires last-minute time as well. If you have a main course that takes last-minute work, serve a dessert that can be made a day ahead — or if your dessert is what needs last-minute attention, serve it after a stew or lasagna. When deciding what to make, remember: The heavier the main course, the lighter the dessert should be, or vice versa. I was recently going through some of my earlier books and was shocked when I looked at the recipes. One recipe for a chocolate cake that we served at Stars was served in big wedges. I was amazed we used to serve such a huge portion! People can't eat like that anymore. At the same time, the cake is so good I still want to serve it so I work backward. I will serve a chicken or something else light for the main course, not a prime rib of beef.

— **EMILY LUCHETTI,** FARALLON (SAN FRANCISCO)

MERLOT
Weight: medium
Volume: moderate

beef
cheese, esp. blue and other full-
  flavored
chicken
duck
lamb
meat, red
mushrooms
pork
steak
turkey
veal

MEXICAN CUISINE
avocados
beans
beef
chicken
*CHILE PEPPERS
chili powder
chocolate
cilantro
cinnamon
corn
cumin
epazote
fried dishes
garlic
lemon
lime, juice
nuts
onions
orange
oregano
pork
rice
saffron
salsas
scallions
seeds
squash
tomatoes
tortillas

Creating new dishes has to be more than simply intensifying flavors for dishes. In terms of visual presentation, we are shifting into a new direction where the food looks like one thing, but is really something else. That adds an extra element of challenge for us. An example of this would be a [**Mexican**-inspired] nacho dish we just created. You get something that looks like chips, sour cream, *salsa verde*, and grated cheese. The cheese is actually grated from saffron ice cream that we have thrown into liquid nitrogen, that is put into a food processor grater. The *salsa verde* is made from kiwi, mint puree, and epozote to give it a little twist. The sour cream is a yuzu crème fraîche. The chips are made from pureed corn tortilla chips that have been sweetened with powdered sugar, then pasted into triangles and deep fried. So you get something that looks like nachos, but tastes completely different. So we are taking a visual aspect of something you are comfortable with and serving it at the end of a twenty-course meal.

— **HOMARO CANTU,** MOTO (CHICAGO)

turkey
vanilla
wheat

Flavor Affinities
beans + rice
chile peppers + lime
chile peppers + tomatoes
cilantro + lime

MIDDLE EASTERN CUISINE
almonds
beans, fava
cheese, feta
chicken
chickpeas
cinnamon
cloves
coriander

cumin
dill
eggplant
fish
fruits, dried
garlic
ginger
goat
honey
lamb
lemons
lemons, preserved
lentils
meats, esp. roasted
mint
nutmeg
nuts
olive oil
olives
onions
oregano
parsley
pepper, black
pine nuts
pistachios
pomegranates
poppy seeds

raisins
ras el hanout (spice blend)
rice
roasted dishes
sesame: oil, seeds
sumac
tahini
tomatoes
walnuts
yogurt

Flavor Affinities
cilantro + cumin + ginger + red pepper
cinnamon + cloves + ginger + nutmeg
cinnamon + lemons + tomatoes
cinnamon + tomatoes
coriander + cumin + garlic
coriander + cumin + garlic + onions + parsley
coriander + cumin + garlic + pepper
eggplant + onions + tomatoes
garlic + coriander
garlic + lemon + mint
garlic + lemon + oregano
garlic + lemon + parsley
lemon + parsley
meat + cinnamon
salads + goat cheese + pomegranate seeds
yogurt + garlic + mint
yogurt + mint
yogurt + parsley

MINT — IN GENERAL
Season: spring–autumn
Taste: sweet
Function: cooling
Weight: light
Volume: quiet–moderate
Tips: Mint generally refers to spearmint.
Mint suggests "false coolness" and adds a note of freshness to dishes.

Afghan cuisine
apples
Asian cuisines
asparagus

With **mint**, applemint is mild, while peppermint is strong.
— **JERRY TRAUNFELD**, THE HERBFARM (WOODINVILLE, WASHINGTON)

I was actually brought up in the school of thought that put a sprig of **mint** on every dessert. I am not that guy anymore. I have a saying — "NFG" — which stands for two things at once: "nonfunctional garnishes" are "no fucking good." If something doesn't make sense to the dish, it won't be there. I hate ordering lamb and seeing a huge bunch of rosemary alongside it. Put it in the dish — let me taste it!
— **JOHNNY IUZZINI**, JEAN GEORGES (NEW YORK CITY)

I love **mint** flavor, but some cooks started throwing mint on desserts just because they liked the color of it. If you have a gorgeous strawberry shortcake and add some mint to it, one of two things will happen: 1) Either you don't eat it, so what's the point of putting it on the plate in the first place, or 2) If you do eat it, that one mint leaf will completely change the balance of the dessert. If you have a lemon tart that is mostly perfectly balanced lemon curd with a little whipped cream and you add a mint leaf to the dessert, the leaf will play havoc with that balance. So don't throw mint on a plate haphazardly, or you'll throw off the balance of the entire dessert.
— **EMILY LUCHETTI**, FARALLON (SAN FRANCISCO)

The first place I think of with **mint** is Morocco. From there, it is the Middle East. Mint and lamb is such a natural combination, as is mint and yogurt.
— **BRAD FARMERIE**, PUBLIC (NEW YORK CITY)

I don't use **mint** very much, but I have a serious thing for black peppermint! You will see it in one form or another on my menu. I go to the farmers' market twice a week and use it all summer. It is great with berries. It works best with something light like an infusion or granita. Last summer, we made a tangy lychee gelée that was served under oven-roasted Tristar strawberries tossed lightly with balsamic vinegar. On top of the strawberries, we scooped the black peppermint sorbet.
— **JOHNNY IUZZINI**, JEAN GEORGES (NEW YORK CITY)

basil
BEANS: black, fresh, white
beef
beets
bell peppers
berries
beverages
blackberries
bourbon
buttermilk
cardamom
carrots, esp. baby
cashews

Champagne
cheese: feta, ricotta
chicken
chile peppers (e.g., jalapeño)
chives
CHOCOLATE, ESP. DARK, white
chutneys
cilantro
cinnamon
citrus
cloves
coconut
cocktails: mint julep (ingredient),
   Pimms No. 1 Cup (ingredient)
CREAM AND ICE CREAM
crème fraîche
CUCUMBERS
cumin
curries
desserts
dill
duck
eggplant
Egyptian cuisine
endive
fenugreek
fish
FRUITS
fruits, tropical
garlic
ginger
grapefruit
grapes
Greek cuisine
halibut
honey
Indian cuisine
jellies
kumquats
***LAMB**
lavender
lemon
lemongrass
lemon verbena
lentils
lettuce
lime
mango

marinades
marjoram
meats
Mediterranean cuisine
melon
Mexican cuisine
Middle Eastern cuisine
milk
Moroccan cuisine
mushrooms
mussels
nectarines
olives, black
onions, esp. red
orange
oregano (say some)
papaya
paprika
parsley
pasta
peaches, esp. cooked
pears
peas, esp. young
pepper
pineapple
plums, esp. cooked
pork
potatoes, esp. new
poultry
pumpkin
punches, fruit
radishes
raitas
raspberries
rice and rice dishes
rosemary
sage
SALADS: bean, fruit, green,
   vegetable
salsas
sea bass
shellfish
shrimp
skate
soups, esp. bean, cold, and/or fish
soy sauce
spinach
spring rolls, esp. Vietnamese

squash, summer
stews, esp. seafood
strawberries
SUGAR
sumac
tabbouleh (key ingredient)
tea, esp. Earl Grey, green
Thai cuisine (e.g., green curries)
thyme
tomatoes
trout
tuna
Turkish cuisine
vanilla
veal
vegetables
Vietnamese cuisine
vinegar: cider, rice wine
watermelon
YOGURT
zucchini

AVOID
oregano (say some)

Flavor Affinities
mint + chocolate + cream
mint + cilantro + dill
mint + cucumber + lime
mint + cucumber + vinegar
mint + cucumber + yogurt
mint + lamb + yogurt

MINT, DRIED
Taste: sweet
Weight: medium
Volume: moderate–loud

beef
bell peppers
bold-flavored foods
cheese, feta
chicken
cucumbers
duck
Eastern Mediterranean cuisine

garlic
Greek cuisine
hummus
kebabs
lamb
leeks
lemon
lentils
meats, esp. grilled
olive oil
olives
onions, red
oregano
pasta
pork
rice
soups: chicken, vegetable
tomatoes
Turkish cuisine
yogurt
zucchini

MINT, PEPPERMINT

Taste: sweet
Weight: light–medium
Volume: very loud
Tips: Mint suggests "false coolness."

apples
berries
beverages
candies
carrots
chocolate
citrus
cream and ice cream
DESSERTS
iced desserts (e.g., granita, sorbet)
mangoes
Mediterranean cuisine
milk
strawberries
teas

AVOID
savory foods

MIREPOIX
Tips: Use as the base of stocks and soups.

French cuisine

Flavor Affinities
carrots + celery + onions

MISO AND MISO SOUP
Weight: medium–heavy
Volume: quiet–moderate (depending on light or dark miso)
Techniques: marinades, sauces, soups

beef
chicken

I like to add **miso** to purees because it adds a rich, buttery flavor and a rich texture. I will serve broiled oysters topped with a puree of miso, pineapple, and serrano chile. I am working on miso-avocado puree as well. It is delicious, but I just haven't found the right dish for it yet. I am also working with miso-huitlacoche soup with tofu, mushrooms, or corn.
— **KATSUYA FUKUSHIMA,** MINIBAR (WASHINGTON, DC)

I love **miso.** I went to a Japanese restaurant and loved the miso soup. I realized that it would give more flavor than chicken broth to my onion soup. So now I make a miso broth the night before, let it sit and separate, and use the broth for my onion soup.
— **MICHEL RICHARD,** CITRONELLE (WASHINGTON, DC)

I will use several different **misos,** depending on the purpose. I might use *saikyo*, a light, yellow, sweet miso, in marinades or with lighter fish like sweet shrimp and scallops that would be overwhelmed by dark miso. Barley miso is a distinctive strong, sweet miso that I'll use with nigiri with baby squid and shiso. I'll use wheat miso with foie gras. Sometimes I'll even mix misos.
— **KAZ OKOCHI,** KAZ SUSHI BISTRO (WASHINGTON, DC)

Dishes

Roasted Duck Breast with a Red Wine–Miso Sauce
— Gabriel Kreuther, The Modern (New York City)

Alaskan Black Cod with Chinese Broccoli, Homemade Tofu, Black Seaweed, Asian Pear, Miso Broth
— Christopher Lee, Gilt (New York City)

duck
fish: cod, salmon
garlic
ginger
honey
Japanese cuisine
legumes
lemongrass
marinades
mirin
mushrooms
mustard
oysters
pineapple
rice, brown
sake
salad dressings
sauces
sesame oil
soups
soy sauce
steak
stews
stock, chicken
sugar
tofu
vinegar, rice
walnuts

butter, unsalted
cinnamon
cream
ginger
gingerbread
Grand Marnier
lemon, juice
marinades
New England cuisine (e.g., Indian pudding)
orange
pancakes
plums
popcorn
raspberries
sugar, brown
vanilla
walnuts

MOLASSES

Taste: sweet, bitter
Weight: heavy
Volume: loud

apples
baked goods (e.g., cookies, pies)
barbecue sauce
beans, baked
bread, esp. brown

MONKFISH (See also Fish — In General)

Season: autumn–winter
Weight: medium
Volume: quiet–moderate
Techniques: braise, broil, grill, poach, roast, sauté, stew

Monkfish is great with garlic!
— ERIC RIPERT, LE BERNARDIN (NEW YORK CITY)

Dishes

Line-Caught Monkfish Loin and "Fresh Bacon" Kurobuta Pork Belly with Golden Chanterelles, Wood-Grilled Leeks, and Herb-Crusted Salsifies, Lobster Red Wine Jus
— Carrie Nahabedian, Naha (Chicago)

Sautéed Monkfish with Broccoli Rabe, Pine Nuts, and Raisins
— David Pasternak, Esca (New York City)

Roasted Monkfish with Spinach, Oyster Ravioli, Watercress Sauce
— Michel Richard, Citronelle (Washington, DC)

aioli
apples
apricots, dried
artichokes, Jerusalem
arugula
asparagus
bacon
basil
bay leaf
beans, white
beer, wheat
brandy
bread crumbs
butter: clarified, unsalted
cabbage: green, red, savoy
caperberries
capers
cardamom
carrots
cayenne
celery
chard
chervil
chile peppers
chili powder
chives
cider, hard
cilantro
cinnamon
clams
coriander
couscous
cream
cumin
curry powder

fennel
fennel seeds
GARLIC
ginger, fresh
leeks
LEMON: juice, zest
lemon, preserved
lemongrass
lemon thyme
lobster
Mediterranean cuisine
mushrooms, esp. chanterelles,
    portobello
mussels
OIL: canola, corn, peanut,
    vegetable
olive oil
olives, esp. green
onions, esp. yellow
orange, zest
oregano
pancetta
paprika, sweet
Parmesan cheese
parsley, flat-leaf
pesto
pepper: black, green, white
Pernod
pine nuts
pork: bacon, pork belly
potatoes, esp. new
red pepper flakes
romesco sauce
rosemary
saffron
sage
salmon
salmon, smoked
salt: kosher, sea
sausage
shallots
sherry, dry (e.g., fino)
soy sauce
spinach
squid
star anise

STOCKS AND BROTHS:
    chicken, clam, fish, shellfish,
    veal
striped bass
Swiss chard
tarragon
thyme
tomatoes
turmeric
vinaigrette
vinegar, white wine
walnuts
watercress
WINE: dry white (e.g.,
    Gewürztraminer), or full-
    bodied red, dry sherry

Flavor Affinities
monkfish + aioli + new potatoes
monkfish + apples + sausage
monkfish + bacon + cabbage + potatoes
monkfish + basil + Swiss chard + thyme
monkfish + curry + mussels + saffron
monkfish + leeks + mussels
monkfish + red cabbage + pancetta
monkfish + white beans + fennel + garlic + saffron + tomatoes

---

MORELS (See Mushrooms,
Morels)

MOROCCAN CUISINE
almonds
apricots
bell peppers, green
chile peppers
cilantro
cinnamon
couscous
coriander
cucumbers
cumin
dates
figs
fruits
ginger
lamb

lemon, juice
LEMONS, PRESERVED
nuts
olive oil
olives
onions
paprika
pepper
pine nuts
pistachios
raisins
ras el hanout
saffron
salads
stews, aka *tagines*

I don't know the first thing about **Moroccan cooking** other than eating Moroccan food and owning Paula Wolfert's book [*Couscous*], but I serve a lamb dish in Moroccan spices. I braise lamb shanks in cumin, saffron, and preserved lemon, with the juice being turned into a sauce. The lamb shanks are then boned and put into a cake with eggplant and molded onto a plate. This is not Moroccan cooking per se, but it suggests the flavors of Morocco.

— **DAVID WALTUCK,** CHANTERELLE (NEW YORK CITY)

sumac
tomatoes
turmeric

Flavor Affinities
chile peppers + garlic + olive oil + salt (aka harissa)
cinnamon + coriander + cumin
eggplant + cinnamon + mint
green tea + dried spearmint + sugar
lamb + cinnamon + honey + prunes
oranges + cinnamon + honey
parsley + lemon juice + olive oil
phyllo dough + almonds + cinnamon + honey
phyllo dough + honey + sesame seeds

MUSHROOMS — IN GENERAL (See also specific mushrooms)
Season: late spring–autumn
Weight: light–medium
Volume: quiet–moderate
Techniques: bake, broil, deep-fry, grill, pan roast, raw (e.g., in salads), roast, sauté, soup, steam, stew

almonds
asparagus
bacon
barley
basil
bay leaf
beans: green, lima
beef
bell peppers, esp. red
bread crumbs
BUTTER, unsalted
capers
carrots
cayenne

Dishes

Vegetarian Texas Chili: Ancho Chile Braise of Grilled Woodland Mushrooms, White Runner Beans, Green Beans, Calabacitas, Cumin, and Beer, topped with Mexican Queso Anejo and Red Onion
— Rick Bayless, Frontera Grill (Chicago)

Wild Mushroom Soup with Ramps and Croutons
— Daniel Boulud / Bertrand Chemel, Café Boulud (New York City)

Roasted Garlic Gnocchi with Wild Mushrooms, Sage, and Crispy Sweetbreads
— Gabriel Kreuther, The Modern (New York City)

Warm Mushroom Salad: Frisée, Bacon, Goat Cheese, and Sherry Vinaigrette
— Alfred Portale, Gotham Bar and Grill (New York City)

Mushroom Tart: Thin-Crust Tart Filled with Sautéed Wild Mushrooms, Celeriac Puree, and Aged Port Reduction
— Eric Ripert, Le Bernardin (New York City)

Risotto with Wild Rice, Squash, and Wild Mushrooms
— Judy Rodgers, Zuni Café (San Francisco)

Warm Wild Mushroom Spinach Salad with Chickpeas, Olives, and Preserved Lemon
— Allen Susser, Chef Allen's (Miami)

Mushroom and Asparagus Risotto with Lemon Thyme
— Jerry Traunfeld, The Herbfarm (Woodinville, Washington)

celery
cheese: Comté, Emmental, Gruyère, Parmesan, Swiss
chervil
chestnuts
chicken
chile peppers: dried red, fresh green
chives
cilantro
cloves
cognac
coriander
crab
CREAM
crème fraîche
cumin
dill
eggs
fennel
fish
French cuisine
frisée lettuce
game

garam masala
***GARLIC**
garlic chives
ginger
grappa
ham
herbs
juniper berries
leeks
lemon: juice, zest
Madeira
marjoram
meats
milk
mirepoix
mustard, Dijon
nutmeg
OIL: canola, grapeseed, peanut, vegetable
OLIVE OIL
onions: green, pearl, red, yellow

oregano
paprika, esp. sweet
Parmesan cheese
PARSLEY, flat-leaf
pasta
peas
PEPPER: black, white
pine nuts
pork
potatoes
poultry
prosciutto
radicchio
rice
risotto
rosemary
sage
sake
SALT: *fleur de sel,* kosher, sea
scallions
seafood
sesame oil
SHALLOTS
sherry, dry (e.g., manzanilla)
sour cream
soy sauce
spinach
stocks: chicken, dashi, mushroom, veal
sugar
tarragon
thyme, fresh
tomatoes
truffle oil
veal
vinegar, esp. **balsamic,** red wine, **sherry**
walnuts
WINE: dry red, white, vermouth
yogurt

Flavor Affinities

mushrooms + garlic + lemon + olive oil
mushrooms + garlic + parsley
mushrooms + garlic + shallots

Marjoram brings up the **mushroom** flavor.
— **JERRY TRAUNFELD,** THE HERBFARM (WOODINVILLE, WASHINGTON)

Dishes

Pappardelle with Chanterelles and Thyme
— Mario Batali, Babbo (New York City)

MUSHROOMS — CHANTERELLES

Season: spring–autumn
Weight: light–medium
Volume: quiet–moderate
Techniques: bake, sauté

bay leaf
butter, unsalted
chard
cheese, Parmesan
chives (garnish)
cream
eggs and egg dishes (e.g., omelets)
game
garlic
lentils
mussels
oil, peanut
olive oil
onions, esp. green
parsley
pasta
pepper: black, white
poultry
radicchio
salt, kosher
sauces
shallots
soups
STOCKS: BEEF, CHICKEN
sweet potatoes
thyme, fresh
vinegar, sherry
wine, dry white

Flavor Affinities

chanterelles + butter + cream + garlic + parsley
chanterelles + cream + garlic + thyme

MUSHROOMS — CREMINI

Season: year-round
Weight: light–medium
Volume: quiet–moderate

arugula
butter
cheese: goat, Parmesan
chives
garlic
mascarpone
olive oil
parsley, flat-leaf
pepper, white
salt
shallots
stock, chicken
thyme
truffle oil

MUSHROOMS — MATSUTAKE

Season: autumn
Weight: medium
Volume: loud
Techniques: braise, fry, grill, sauté, simmer, steam, stir-fry

butter
cabbage, savoy
chicken
cod, black
cream
custard
dashi
fish

herbs: chervil, chives, flat-leaf parsley, tarragon
Japanese cuisine
lemon, juice
mirin
mushrooms, wild
olive oil
pepper, black
rice
sake
salt
shallots
shrimp
soup
soy sauce
stock, chicken
tempura
tofu
vinegar, rice wine

MUSHROOMS — MORELS

Season: spring (May–June)
Weight: light–medium
Volume: quiet–moderate
Techniques/Tips: Always serve cooked: boil, stew

ASPARAGUS: green, white
bacon
basil
bay leaf
BUTTER, unsalted
caraway seeds
cheese: Fontina, goat, Parmesan
chervil
chicken mousse
chives
CREAM, heavy
crème fraîche
eggs, yolks
faro
fava beans

Matsutake mushrooms have a cinnamon and pine quality to them. This is a fall mushroom and works well with savoy cabbage. I like pairing luxurious ingredients with cabbage. We will roast black cod and serve it with cabbage, cream, and the matsutake.

— **JERRY TRAUNFELD,** THE HERBFARM (WOODINVILLE, WASHINGTON)

Dishes

Organic Carnaroli Risotto with Wild Spring Morels, Wood-Grilled Ramps, Confit of Green Garlic and Spinach, Parmigiano-Reggiano, and Umbrian Olive Oil
— Carrie Nahabedian, Naha (Chicago)

Our Local Morel Pizza with Fontina Cheese, Virginia Country Ham, and Frizzled Ramps. A Warm Salad of Grilled Asparagus and Freshwater Blue Prawns with Sherry Vinaigrette
— Patrick O'Connell, The Inn at Little Washington (Washington, Virginia)

Caraway seeds bring up the flavor in **morel mushrooms.**
— **JERRY TRAUNFELD**, THE HERBFARM (WOODINVILLE, WASHINGTON)

fiddlehead ferns
GARLIC: regular, spring
ham: Virginia, Serrano
herbs
lamb
leeks
lemon
Madeira
marjoram
mirepoix
oil, peanut
olive oil
onions, esp. spring
pancetta
paprika, sweet
parsley, flat-leaf
pasta
peas
PEPPER: black, white
pork
port
potatoes, esp. new
ramps
rosemary
SALT, kosher
sauces
savory
shallots
soufflés (e.g., goat cheese)
soy sauce
stocks: chicken, mushroom, vegetable
sweetbreads
tarragon

thyme
truffles, black
vinaigrette
vinegar, sherry
wine, Champagne

Flavor Affinities

morels + asparagus + ramps
morels + garlic + lemon + olive oil + parsley

MUSHROOMS — PORCINI / CEPES / KING BOLETE

Season: late spring–early autumn
Weight: light–medium
Volume: quiet–moderate
Techniques: grill, parboil, roast, sauté, stew

almonds
arugula
bacon
brandy
bread crumbs
butter, unsalted
carrots
cheese: Fontina, Garrotxa, **Parmesan**
chervil
chicken, esp. roasted
chives
coffee
cream / milk
crème fraîche
eggs
fennel
fish: grilled, white
French cuisine
garlic
hazelnuts
Italian cuisine
lemon, juice
Madeira
marjoram
mascarpone
mint
mushrooms, button or cremini
OIL, PORCINI
OLIVE OIL
onions
parsley, flat-leaf
pasta

Dishes

Raw Porcini with Arugula, Parmigiano, and Aceto Manadori
— Mario Batali, Babbo (New York City)

Salad of Porcini Mushrooms, Green Apple, and Garrotxa Cheese, with Hazelnut Vinaigrette
— Traci Des Jardins, Jardinière (San Francisco)

King Bolete — or **porcini**, as they are also known — are pretty sweet. I like them with a carrot puree in ravioli. The sauce for the dish will be the braising liquid from the ravioli as well as some carrot juice. The ravioli is then topped with fried sage and black currants.
— **JERRY TRAUNFELD**, THE HERBFARM (WOODINVILLE, WASHINGTON)

pepper, black
polenta
potatoes
prosciutto
radicchio
rice, arborio
sage
sake
salt: kosher, sea
shallots
spinach
steak
stocks: chicken, mushroom, vegetable
tamari
tarragon
thyme
tomatoes
truffles, esp. white
veal
vinegar, esp. balsamic
walnuts
wine, dry white

Flavor Affinities

porcini + almonds + balsamic vinegar
porcini + arugula + lemon + Parmesan cheese
porcini + balsamic vinegar + radicchio
porcini + carrots + sage
porcini + coffee + veal
porcini + lemon juice + olive oil
porcini + parsley + tomatoes
porcini + prosciutto + spinach

MUSHROOMS — PORTOBELLO

Season: year-round
Weight: medium–heavy
Volume: moderate
Techniques: broil, grill, roast, sauté, stuff
Tips: Gets firmer with longer cooking.

Dishes

Grilled Portobello with Manchego Cheese, Garlic, and Thyme Oil
— Ann Cashion, Cashion's Eat Place (Washington, DC)

Vegetarian Sushi: Sun-Dried Tomato and Portobello Roll
— Kaz Okochi, Kaz Sushi Bistro (Washington, DC)

Gonzales Portobello Mushroom "Steak," Texas Brown Rice and Nut Cake, Coconut-Chile Sauce
— Monica Pope, T'afia (Houston)

Pasta Salad with Sun-Dried Tomato Pesto, Portobello Mushrooms, and Grilled Squash
— Charlie Trotter, Trotter's to Go (Chicago)

Portobello Mushrooms in Porcini Cream Curry
— Vikram Vij and Meeru Dhalwala, Vij's (Vancouver)

Portobello Mushroom and Red Bell Pepper Curry on Paneer with Beet-Daikon Salad
— Vikram Vij and Meeru Dhalwala, Vij's (Vancouver)

cheese: manchego, Parmesan, ricotta
crème fraîche
garlic
lemon
mint
olive oil
pasta
polenta
spinach
thyme
tomatoes, sun-dried

Flavor Affinities

portobello mushrooms + lemon + mint + olive oil
portobello mushrooms + polenta + spinach

MUSHROOMS — SHIITAKE

Weight: medium
Volume: moderate
Techniques: grill, sauté, simmer, stir-fry

anchovies
asparagus

bacon
basil
bell peppers, roasted
brandy
butter: clarified, unsalted
cabbage, savoy
celery root
chicken
chile peppers
chives
cod
coriander
cream
cream cheese
eggplant
eggs, esp. hard-boiled
fish sauce
GARLIC
Japanese cuisine
leeks
lemon, juice
lemongrass
lime
mushrooms, oyster
OIL: canola, hazelnut, vegetable
olive oil
ONIONS, esp. red, white
parsley, flat-leaf

Vitaly Paley of Paley's Place in Portland, Oregon, on Cooking with Mushrooms

Mushrooms Year-Round

Spring. This is the start of the morel season. One of the reasons I came to work in Oregon was one day I was working in a kitchen in France and a box of morels arrived with a tag on it that said "Oregon."

Summer. The morels dwindle away, and we get a brief stint of porcini/cepes. Late summer is golden and white chanterelle season.

Fall. The porcini come back and we also get in matsutake mushrooms as well. We have [Pacific Northwest] black and white truffles here and the season starts in November. They are pretty flavorful but it is important to realize they are different from European truffles — not to mention a lot less expensive.

I'm not a big fan of cultivated mushrooms but I do like a few. King oyster or trumpet royal are the same mushroom and it is one of my favorites. Portobellos are also good, though they are a little '70s.

I am suspicious of some dried mushrooms you find in the supermarket only because you don't know how old they are and how much flavor they will have.

Buying and Cleaning Mushrooms

When it comes to mushrooms, every kind needs to be well cleaned because there is nothing worse than getting a mouthful of grit. I wash them all by soaking them in a bowl of water and pulling them out. The key to remember is that you want to use mushrooms soon after washing them. Don't wash them a day ahead.

For morel mushrooms, you need to know how to cook them, and slicing them up fresh and throwing them in a pan is not it. It is very important to clean them and I recommend blanching them. Fill a pot with cold water, toss in a handful of salt and then the mushrooms. Bring the pot to a boil, scoop out the mushrooms, spread them out, and lightly squeeze them dry. As you dry them, take a good look at them to make sure they are free of twigs and such.

Seasoning Mushrooms

When it comes to seasoning mushrooms, savory works across the board. The seasoning combination that I've used in my kitchen from day one is a raw parsley and garlic combination that in French is called *persillade*. After the mushrooms have been sautéed in butter or olive oil, at the last second you toss in this combination with a pinch of salt. That is all a mushroom needs most of the time!

If you are roasting porcini or king oyster mushrooms, roast them on a bed of savory or thyme for extra flavor.

pepper, black
pizza
polenta
pork
potatoes
rice, basmati
rosemary
sage
salt, kosher
shallots
soups

sorrel
soy sauce
spinach
stews
stock, chicken
tarragon
thyme
vinegar, balsamic
walnuts
wine, dry white

Flavor Affinities

shiitake mushrooms + basil + onions

MUSSELS

Season: autumn–winter
Weight: light
Volume: quiet–moderate
Techniques: bake, boil, grill, steam

bacon
basil
bass
bay leaf
beans: green, navy
bell peppers, esp. red and/or roasted
bread crumbs
butter, unsalted
capers
carrots
cayenne
celery
celery seeds
chanterelles
chervil
chile peppers, esp. jalapeño
Chinese cuisine
chives
cilantro
CLAMS and clam juice
cod
cognac
CREAM
curry powder
egg yolks
fennel
fennel seeds
French cuisine
GARLIC
ginger
ham
Italian cuisine
leeks
LEMON, juice
lemon thyme
lovage

Dishes

Mussel Soup with Cilantro and Serrano Chile Cream
— Robert Del Grande, Café Annie (Houston)

Mussels in a Spicy Sauce of Panca Peppers, Garlic, Cilantro, and Peruvian Dark Beer
— Maricel Presilla, Cucharamama (Hoboken, New Jersey)

Our Version of the Classic Portuguese Surf and Turf Braise: Pork Belly, Mussels, Potatoes, and Black Olives in a Savory Ají Panca and Dark Beer Sauce
— Maricel Presilla, Cucharamama (Hoboken, New Jersey)

Spaghetti with Mussels, Pine Nuts, Nutmeg, and Parsley
— Barton Seaver, Hook (Washington, DC)

Steamed Black Mussels, Coconut Broth, Red Curry Oil
— Rick Tramonto, Tru (Chicago)

marjoram
mayonnaise, garlic
Mediterranean cuisine
mint
monkfish
mushrooms
mustard, Dijon
nutmeg
OLIVE OIL
olives, black
ONIONS, esp. red, spring, white
orange: juice, zest
oregano
oysters
paella (key ingredient)
paprika: smoked, sweet
Parmesan cheese
PARSLEY: flat-leaf, curly
pasta
PEPPER: black, white
Pernod
pesto
pine nuts
potatoes
radicchio
red pepper flakes
rice and risotto
rosemary
SAFFRON
SALT: kosher, sea
scallions
SHALLOTS

shrimp
snapper
sole
squid
stews
stocks: chicken, clam, fish
tarragon
THYME
TOMATOES
vermouth
vinaigrette
vinegar: red wine, sherry
watercress
wild rice
WINE: dry white (e.g., Chardonnay, Pinot Blanc, Riesling, Sauvignon Blanc)
zucchini

Flavor Affinities

mussels + clams + garlic + onion + thyme + white wine
mussels + cream + curry + saffron
mussels + fennel + saffron + white wine
mussels + garlic + saffron + tomatoes
mussels + Dijon mustard + saffron
mussels + mustard + tarragon
mussels + olives + oranges
mussels + saffron + tarragon + tomatoes

MUSTARD

Taste: bitter
Function: heating
Weight: medium–heavy
Volume: moderate–very loud
Tips: Add at the end of the cooking process.
Use cucumbers to cut the taste of mustard.

apples: fruit, juice
avocados
bay leaf
beef, esp. corned, grilled, or roasted
beets
cabbage
capers
cheeses (e.g., blue, cheddar, Gruyère, and other hard) and cheese dishes (e.g., macaroni and cheese, soufflé)
chicken
chile peppers
cold cuts
coriander
crab
cream and sour cream
cucumbers
cumin
cured meats
curries
curry leaves

dill
egg dishes
fennel
fenugreek
fish
French cuisine, esp. southern
fruits
garlic
German cuisine
gingerbread
green beans
ham
herbs
honey
Indian cuisine, as mustard seeds
Irish cuisine
Italian cuisine, esp. southern
lamb
leeks
lemon, juice
mayonnaise
meats, cold or hot
Mediterranean cuisine
mint, esp. peppermint
mostarda (mustard fruits)
mussels
oil, canola
olive oil
onions
oregano
paprika
parsley
pastrami
pepper: black, green, white
pork
potatoes
poultry
rabbit
salads and salad dressings
salmon
salt: kosher
sauces
sauerkraut
sausages
Scandinavian cuisine
seafood
smoked fish
soy sauce

steaks
sumac
tarragon
tomatoes
turmeric
vegetable-based dishes
vinaigrettes
vinegar: balsamic, red wine, white
    wine
walnuts: nuts, oil

Good cooking transcends all cultures. You can take inspiration from all around the world and apply it to what you are cooking without making it "fusion." In some cases, you can even take a classic and make it taste better. I worked with Floyd Cardoz [chef of the Indian restaurant Tabla in New York City] and learned a lot about Indian spicing and technique from him. One technique was *turka*, which is where you fry spices in oil or ghee [Indian clarified butter] until they pop. It really opens up the flavor of the spices.

I use this cross-cultural technique when making a veal dish with a great **mustard** sauce, which is a classic French dish, and the result is not a fusion dish: Take black, yellow, and red mustard seeds and toast them in butter or olive oil until they pop; then add some shallots and vermouth and reduce it. Then, add veal stock with a splash of cream and Dijon mustard. The result is a very complex sauce with a much deeper flavor, versus simply combining some cream and mustard together in the pan.

— **ANDREW CARMELLINI,** A VOCE (NEW YORK CITY)

Flavor Affinities
mustard + curry leaves + cumin
mustard + garlic + oil + shallots +
    vinegar
mustard + garlic + oil + vinegar
mustard + oil + shallots + vinegar

MUSTARD GREENS
(See Greens, Mustard)

Tarragon leads me to **mustard** which leads me to shellfish — which leads me to mussels. The combination of the three is delicious.

— **MICHAEL ANTHONY,** GRAMERCY TAVERN (NEW YORK CITY)

NECTARINES

(See also Peaches)

Season: late spring–early autumn
Taste: sweet
Weight: light–medium
Volume: moderate
Techniques: bake, broil, grill, poach, raw, sauté

allspice
almonds, esp. toasted
apricots
beverages, esp. cocktails
blackberries
blueberries
brandy
butter, unsalted
buttermilk
caramel
Champagne
cherries
chicken
chocolate
cinnamon
cranberries
cream and ice cream
custard
desserts and dessert sauces
figs
ginger, esp. fresh
hazelnuts
honey
Kirsch
lemon: juice, zest
maple syrup
mascarpone
milk, sweetened condensed
mint (garnish)
nutmeg

oatmeal
onions
orange, juice
orange liqueur
peaches
peach liqueur (e.g., schnapps)
pecans
pepper, black
pistachios
plums (compatible fruit)
pork
raspberries
salads, fruit
salsas, fruit
soups, esp. chilled
sour cream
strawberries
SUGAR: brown, white
vanilla
vinegar, cider
WINE: red, fruity, sweet, or white: Merlot, Moscato d'Asti, Muscat, Rosé, Sauternes, Vin Santo, Zinfandel
yogurt

NORTH AFRICAN CUISINE (See also Moroccan Cuisine)

allspice
cinnamon
coriander
couscous
cumin
garlic, esp. in Egypt
ginger
lemons, preserved
meats, esp. grilled
onions

paprika
pepper, black
saffron
salads
spices, esp. in Morocco
turmeric
vegetables

NUTMEG

Season: autumn–winter
Taste: sweet
Botanical relative: mace
Weight: light–medium
Volume: loud
Tips: Use in moderation.

allspice
apples
baked dishes (e.g., biscuits, cakes, pies)
beef: braised, raw
berries
beverages (e.g., chocolate, eggnog)
broccoli
butter
cabbage
cakes
cardamom
Caribbean cuisine
carrots
cauliflower
CHEESE (ESP. RICOTTA) AND CHEESE DISHES
chicken
chickpeas
Chinese cuisine
chocolate
chowders (e.g., fish)
cinnamon
cloves
cookies
coriander
CREAM / MILK
cumin
custards
DESSERTS

Dishes

Roasted Nectarine Custard Cake with Ice Wine Sorbet and Warm Berry Compote
— Dominique and Cindy Duby, Wild Sweets (Vancouver)

New Orleans Nectar Soda "Snow Cone" with Stewed Nectarines and Fresh Raspberries — and Drizzle of Sweetened Condensed Milk
— Bob Iacovone, Cuvée (New Orleans)

EGGNOG

eggs

fish

French cuisine

fruits: dried, fresh

German cuisine

ginger

goat

Greek cuisine

green beans

hazelnuts

honey

Indian cuisine

Italian cuisine, esp. sauces

jerk pastes, e.g., Caribbean

lamb, esp. braised

Latin American cuisine

lemon, juice

MACE

meats (e.g., meatballs)

Middle Eastern cuisine

milk-based dishes

mushrooms

nuts

onions

oranges

parsnips

pasta and pasta sauces

pastries

pâtés

pears

pepper

pork

potatoes

puddings

pumpkin

quatre épices (ingredient, with cloves, ginger, and white pepper)

raisins

RICE

sauces: béchamel, white

sausages

Scandinavian cuisine

seafood

shellfish, shrimp

soufflés

soups

sour cream

Southeast Asian cuisine

SPINACH

squash, winter

stuffing

succotash

sugar, esp. brown

sweet potatoes

thyme

tomatoes and tomato sauces

vanilla

veal

wine (e.g., mulled)

yogurt

Flavor Affinities

nutmeg + allspice + cinnamon

nutmeg + cloves + cream

nutmeg + cloves + ginger + white pepper (*quatre épices*)

nutmeg + cream + spinach

NUTS — IN GENERAL

(See also Pecans, Walnuts, etc.)

Weight: heavy

Volume: moderate (varies by nut)

Tips: Always toast nuts before using to enhance flavor and texture.

I love **nuts**, and put them in everything. I find that almost all nuts pair well with a lot of different things. When I am creating a dessert, I will choose my nuts geographically. For example, if I am making a Sicilian dessert, I'll use pistachios because that is the nut they would use [in Sicily].

— **GINA DEPALMA,** BABBO (NEW YORK CITY)

The quality of chopped **nuts** can never compare with the quality of whole nuts. In 26 years, we have never bought chopped pecans because the quality is so different, despite the fact that it would be a lot less expensive.

I recommend simply chopping by hand or, in the case of something like a pecan, breaking it with your fingers. Pecans have so much moisture that if you chop them, you lose what is special about their texture. People tend to put nuts into the food processor and the next thing you know, you have powder and not pieces.

We always toast our **nuts**, 100 percent of the time. Nuts absorb a lot of moisture, so by toasting them you dry them out and heighten the flavor. You do need to be careful, because they burn so easily. Slower roasting is better. With a nut like a cashew, you want to roast them at 325 degrees to get them to be a nice, golden brown.

— **MARCEL DESAULNIERS**, THE TRELLIS (WILLIAMSBURG, VIRGINIA)

Always toast **nuts** to bring up the flavor. If you don't toast the nuts before adding them to a dish, they tend to come out soggy when the dish is done. The one exception would be if they are going on top of a tart going into the oven, because then they would be overtoasted.

Nuts work great in adding texture, especially to creamy and/or moussey desserts. The other way to balance out richness is with some phyllo dough.

— **EMILY LUCHETTI**, FARALLON (SAN FRANCISCO)

Juicing **nuts** is the new thing we are doing. We'll juice almonds, hazelnuts, and — best of all — pine nuts, which comes out like pine nut butter. Juicing pine nuts is better than grinding them, because it pulverizes their fat. We put that on some local green beans with preserved lemon zest, to serve with spring onions with lamb.

— **ANDREW CARMELLINI**, A VOCE (NEW YORK CITY)

Lavender works well with all sorts of **nuts**, including almonds, hazelnuts, pistachios, and walnuts. The one nut it doesn't work well with is chestnuts.

— **JERRY TRAUNFELD**, THE HERBFARM (WOODINVILLE, WASHINGTON)

OATMEAL / OATS

Taste: sweet
Function: heating
Weight: medium–heavy
Volume: quiet
Techniques: simmer

almonds
apples
apricots
bananas
blueberries
brandy
breakfast
butter, unsalted
buttermilk
caramel
cherries
chocolate, esp. dark, white
cider
cinnamon
coconut
coffee
cranberries
cream
currants
dates
figs, dried
ginger
hazelnuts
honey
lemon
maple syrup
mascarpone
milk
nectarines
orange
peaches
peanuts
pears
pecans
persimmons
pine nuts
plums
prunes
pumpkin
raisins
raspberries

Dishes

Cherry-Almond Granola with Greek Yogurt and Vanilla Honey
— Daniel Humm, Eleven Madison Park (New York City)

Steel-Cut Oats, Devon Cream, Cinnamon Toast, and Cider-Roasted Apples
— Daniel Humm, Eleven Madison Park (New York City)

Grown-Up Oatmeal Soufflé Served with Maple Syrup and Rum-Soaked Currants
— Patrick O'Connell, The Inn at Little Washington (Washington, Virginia)

rhubarb
rum, dark
salt (pinch)
strawberries
SUGAR: **brown**, **white**
sweet potatoes
vanilla
walnuts
yogurt

Flavor Affinities
oatmeal + currants + maple syrup
oatmeal + pears + vanilla + yogurt

OCTOPUS
Weight: medium
Volume: quiet–moderate
Techniques: grill, simmer, stew

chile peppers, jalapeño
chives
chorizo
dashi
garlic
ginger
lemon, juice
mint
olive oil
onions, red
orange, juice
pepper, black
potatoes
red pepper flakes
sake
salt, sea
soy sauce
tamarind
tangerine
tomatoes and tomato sauce

vinegar: champagne, red wine
wine, red

Flavor Affinities
octopus + chorizo + lemon
octopus + jalapeño peppers +
  mint
octopus + orange + potatoes
octopus + sake + sea salt

OIL, ALMOND
Weight: light
Volume: quiet
Techniques: bake, raw

almonds
asparagus
baked goods
chicken
Chinese cuisine
duck
fish
Indian cuisine
mustard
pasta

I like **almond oil** with asparagus salad.
— **DANIEL HUMM**, ELEVEN MADISON PARK (NEW YORK CITY)

romaine
salads
sauces
smoked salmon
vegetables
vinaigrettes
vinegar, champagne

OIL, AVOCADO
Weight: light
Volume: quiet
Techniques: emulsify, fry, grill, raw, roast, salads, sauté, stir-fry

arugula
asparagus
avocados
basil
chile peppers
corn
cucumber
emulsions
fish
garlic
grapefruit
guinea fowl
lemon, juice
lime, juice
melon
orange, juice
pasta
rabbit
salads and salad dressings
salmon
scallops

I'll poach everything from saddle of rabbit to guinea fowl to fish — from sturgeon, which holds up nicely, to New Zealand snapper to John Dory — in **avocado oil**. It gives an incredible texture and depth of flavor. I also like it with vegetarian dishes. I use it in dressings, and it seems to hold an emulsion really well. It has a nice affinity with tomato; I have made tomato water with chardonnay vinegar and avocado oil, and it makes beautiful light dressing. It also goes well with citrus like lemon, lime, or orange. Just like you like to squeeze some citrus over avocado, avocado oil works the same way in reverse.
— **BRAD FARMERIE**, PUBLIC (NEW YORK CITY)

seafood
shrimp
squid
thyme
tomatoes and tomato water
tuna
vegetables
vegetarian dishes
vinegar: balsamic, chardonnay,
    white wine
zucchini

Flavor Affinities
avocado oil + chardonnay vinegar
    + tomato water

OIL, CANOLA
Taste: neutral
Weight: light
Volume: quiet
Techniques: bake, sauté

salads and salad dressings

AVOID
deep-fry

OIL, GRAPESEED
Taste: neutral
Weight: light
Volume: quiet
Techniques: fry, raw, sauté

coconut
marinades
salads and salad dressings
sautéed dishes
vinegar

OIL, HAZELNUT
Weight: medium–heavy
Volume: moderate–loud
Techniques: raw
Tips: Avoid cooking, as it burns
easily.

apples
artichokes
broccoli

Hazelnut oil gets mixed with cider vinegar; that is a great natural marriage. This gets tossed in our baby winter spinach with mixed herbs and frisée salad. The toasted nut quality mixes well with bitter greens.
— **MICHAEL ANTHONY,** GRAMERCY TAVERN (NEW YORK CITY)

Hazelnut oil is a wonderful autumn oil. We will use it in a dark balsamic vinaigrette served with squab. It is also very good with broccoli. If you make a broccoli soup, use this along with toasted hazelnuts. It is a delicious combination.
— **DANIEL HUMM,** ELEVEN MADISON PARK (NEW YORK CITY)

cheese, fresh
desserts (e.g., candy, cookies)
figs
fish
greens, bitter
hazelnuts
lemon, juice
pastries
pears
persimmons
salads and salad dressings
sauces
spinach
squab
vinaigrettes
**vinegars, esp. balsamic, cider,
    fruity**
wild rice

OIL, MACADAMIA NUT
Weight: light–medium
Volume: moderate–loud
Techniques: bake, roast

fruit salads, esp. with tropical
    fruits
Hawaiian cuisine
macadamia nuts
rice salads
sauces

OIL, OLIVE (See Olive Oil)

OIL, PEANUT
Weight: light
Volume: quiet–moderate
Techniques: fry, raw, salads,
stir-fry

Asian cuisines
Chinese cuisine
cooking
fruits and fruit salads
garlic
ginger
lentils
meats
peanuts
salad dressings, esp. Asian, fruit
soy sauce
vinegars, esp. balsamic, malt

OIL, PECAN
Weight: medium–heavy
Volume: moderate–loud
Techniques: bake, marinade

bread
fish
meat
pasta
rice
salads and salad dressings
vegetables

OIL, PISTACHIO
Weight: medium
Volume: moderate
Techniques: bake

asparagus
avocado
beets
bread
fish
mayonnaise
meat

Pistachio oil beautifully complements tuna and asparagus in our dish Big Eye Tuna Thinly Sliced with Provence White Asparagus and Montegotterro Pistachio Oil.

— DANIEL HUMM, ELEVEN MADISON PARK (NEW YORK CITY)

pasta
salads and salad dressings
tuna

OIL, PORCINI
Weight: medium
Volume: moderate
Techniques: raw

bread
cheese
mushrooms, esp. porcini
pasta
risotto
salads and salad dressings
sauces
stews

OIL, PUMPKIN SEED
Weight: light
Volume: quiet
Tips: Use to finish a dish, not to cook.

beef, rare
citrus
corn
desserts
ice cream
maple syrup
mustard, Dijon
pastries
pumpkin seeds
rice
soups
squash, winter
vinegar: balsamic, cider, rice wine

[**Pumpkin seed oil**] is good for finishing dishes with just a little drizzle. We have even poured it over ice cream that is served with a pumpkin seed brittle.

— BRAD FARMERIE, PUBLIC
(NEW YORK CITY)

OIL, SESAME
Function: heating
Weight: light–medium
Volume: moderate–loud (light to dark versions)
Techniques: raw
Tips: Add as a flavoring to raw or cooked dishes.

Asian cuisine
beef
cabbage, napa
chicken
chili powder
Chinese cuisine
fish
fruit salads
garlic
ginger
greens, esp. Asian
honey
Japanese cuisine
Korean cuisine
lemon, juice
lemongrass
lime, juice
marinades
meats
miso soup
mustard
noodles
oil, vegetable (compatible oil)
orange
pepper, black
salads and salad dressings, esp. Asian
salt

sauces
scallions
sesame seeds
shallots
shiso
soy sauce
stir-fried dishes
tahini
tuna
vegetables
vinegar: cider, rice wine

Flavor Affinities
sesame oil + ginger + mustard +
   rice wine vinegar

OIL, TRUFFLE
Weight: light
Volume: moderate–loud
Techniques: raw

cheese
eggs
fish
mushrooms
pasta
risotto
salads and salad dressings

Dishes
Endive and Mushroom Salad, Blue Cheese, Spicy Pecans, White Balsamic–White Truffle Vinaigrette
— Monica Pope, T'afia (Houston)

OIL, WALNUT
Weight: medium
Volume: moderate
Techniques: raw
Tips: Avoid cooking as it burns easily.

Truffle oil is one of those ingredients that really gets overused, so one day I decided that I wanted to do truffle oil right. We make a dressing of truffle oil, white balsamic vinegar, and whole grain mustard. We toss it over endive, crumbled blue cheese, spicy pecans, and raw cremini mushrooms. You just can't stop eating it!

— MONICA POPE, T'AFIA (HOUSTON)

apples
baked goods
beets
bread
cheese, fresh
chicory
figs
fish, esp. grilled
frisée
greens, bitter
meats, esp. grilled
pasta
pears
persimmons
potatoes
**SALADS AND SALAD
    DRESSINGS**
sauces
steaks
vinaigrettes
vinegar: balsamic, fruit, **red
    wine**, sherry, tarragon
walnuts

OKRA

Season: summer–autumn
Function: cooling
Weight: medium–heavy
Volume: moderate
Techniques: boil, braise, deep-fry, fry, grill, sauté, steam, stew

bell peppers, esp. red
butter
cayenne
chicken
chile peppers, fresh green
cilantro
coriander
corn and cornmeal
Creole cuisine
cumin
curry powder
fennel seeds
garlic
ginger, fresh
gumbo
ham
Indian cuisine

On Selecting the Right Oil

Your choice of olive oil always depends on what you are using it for. In general, you don't want an oil that is super-assertive, green, or peppery. You want a good olive flavor. I use a 100 percent Italian blend. It is silly to cook with 100 percent extra-virgin olive oil if you are just sautéing something. If the oil is going to stay in what you are making, like a sauce, then start with extra-virgin olive oil. When I make a tomato sauce, that is what I am starting with.

If you are finishing a dish, that is also when you would use an assertive, more full-flavored **oil.** I also like to use nut oils, especially those made by Jean Leblanc. They are insane; his oils are so good that after you taste them, nothing else will do! I especially like to use nut oils in the fall. I use walnut oil dressing on salads, especially those salads that accompany meat. If you make a foie gras dish with apples and endive, an addition of walnut oil would be great.
— **ANDREW CARMELLINI**, A VOCE (NEW YORK CITY)

Olive oil comes in a wide variety of flavors and strengths even from the same region, much like wine:

• I use a heavier (e.g., Puglian, Umbrian, Sicilian) olive oil on bigger-flavored dishes. A strong olive oil goes well on bean puree or a strong vegetable like dandelion greens. In the United States, you would put a barbecue sauce on a grilled meat; in Italy, you would use a strong olive oil.

• I use a lighter (e.g., Ligurian, Tuscan) olive oil on lighter meats like veal or fish dishes and pastas. A Ligurian olive is full and bright and is great on a lighter dish.
— **ODETTE FADA**, SAN DOMENICO (NEW YORK CITY)

• I like to use single varietal **olive oil** from Australia and New Zealand. Australian olive oils can be like their wines: big, pungent, and spicy. New Zealand oils have a little more depth of flavor and green grassiness.
— **BRAD FARMERIE**, PUBLIC (NEW YORK CITY)

LEMON, juice
lime, juice
Mediterranean cuisine
Moroccan cuisine
mustard seeds
oil: peanut, vegetable
onions, esp. red
parsley, flat-leaf
peas, black-eyed
rice
salt, kosher
seafood
shrimp
soups

Southern cuisine (American)
TOMATOES
turmeric
vinegar
yogurt

OLIVE OIL

Weight: medium
Volume: quiet–loud
Techniques: cook, fry, raw, salads, sauces

almonds
anchovies

I like Greek black **olives** the best. I like them by themselves, but they also work great in a chicken, duck, or lamb dish.
— **GABRIEL KREUTHER,** THE MODERN (NEW YORK CITY)

Olives have such a strong flavor that they can overwhelm other ingredients, but salmon will stand right up to it.
— **MICHEL RICHARD,** CITRONELLE (WASHINGTON, DC)

beans, white
chickpeas
fish
French cuisine, southern
garlic
herbs
hummus
Italian cuisine
meats
Mediterranean cuisine
Middle Eastern cuisine
Moroccan cuisine
olives
Parmesan cheese
pasta
pepper, black
salads and salad dressings
salt
soups
Spanish cuisine
thyme
vegetables
vinegar

OLIVES

Taste: salty
Weight: light–medium
Volume: quiet–loud (depending on type)

almonds
anchovies
basil
bass
bay leaf
bell peppers, esp. red
brandy
bread
butter
capers

cayenne
cheese: feta, goat's milk
chicken
cognac
cream cheese
cumin
fish
French cuisine, esp. Provençal
GARLIC
Italian cuisine
lamb
LEMON: juice, zest
meats
Mediterranean cuisines
Moroccan cuisine
olive oil
onions, esp. red
orange: juice, zest
oregano
parsley, flat-leaf
pasta
pepper: black, white
peppers, piquillo
Pernod
pine nuts
red pepper flakes
rosemary
sage
salads and salad dressings
salmon
salt: kosher, sea
sambuca
scallions
scallops

Dishes

Olive and Anchovy Tapenade with Sage Crackers
— Monica Pope, T'afia (Houston)

shallots
Spanish cuisine
thyme
tomatoes: regular, sun-dried
tuna
veal
vinegar: red wine, sherry
wine, dry white

OMELETS (See Eggs and Egg-based Dishes)

ONIONS — IN GENERAL

Season: year-round
Taste: pungent (+ sweet with cooking via caramelization)
Botanical relatives: chives, garlic, leeks, shallots
Function: heating
Weight: light–medium
Volume: moderate–loud
Techniques: bake, boil, braise, deep-fry, fry, grill, roast, sauté, stir-fry
Tips: Onions increase appetite, and go with virtually all savory foods.

anchovies
apples
bacon
basil
bay leaf
beans
beef, ground, e.g., hamburgers, meat loaf
beer
beets
bell peppers
brandy
bread: croutons, crumbs
BUTTER, UNSALTED
caraway seeds
cardamom
carrots
cayenne
cheese: cheddar, Comté, Emmental, *fromage blanc,* goat, Gruyère, Parmesan, Swiss

The **onion** family is the basis for every cuisine I can think of. Of course, Asian cuisines use more green onions and garlic, while the French use more shallots and garlic, but it's the onion family providing the foundation.

— **TONY LIU**, AUGUST (NEW YORK CITY)

You can't cook without **onions.** There is not a single thing you can do without onions. There are so many things made with onions that when people come in to our restaurant and say that they are allergic to onions, I say, "No, you are not — it is impossible. You just don't like onions." People eat onions all the time and just don't know it. I remember having a conversation with [the artist] Jasper Johns, with him saying, "If truffles and onions cost the same amount of money, you would obviously choose an onion. You don't need truffles; you do need onions."

— **DAVID WALTUCK**, CHANTERELLE (NEW YORK CITY)

I roast **onions** a long, long time and use them to add a meaty flavor to soups.

— **MICHEL RICHARD**, CITRONELLE (WASHINGTON, DC)

Your cooking technique alters your flavors a great deal. If you put a lot of **onions** in your curry but don't sauté them enough first, you will get a sweet flavor. If you sauté the onions until they are almost burnt but not quite, your curry will have more of a roasted-toasted flavor.

— **VIKRAM VIJ**, VIJ'S (VANCOUVER)

chile peppers, esp. jalapeño
chili
cilantro
cinnamon
cloves
coriander
cream / milk
crème fraîche
cucumbers
cumin seeds
curry
dill
dips
eggs, e.g., omelets
garlic

greens, bitter
hamburgers
honey
lemon, juice
lime, juice
liver
mace
mangoes, esp. with red onions
marjoram
meats
milk
mint (e.g., Indian)
mirepoix (key ingredient)
mushrooms
mustard, Dijon

NUTMEG
OIL: canola, peanut, sesame, vegetable
olive oil
olives, black
orange, juice
oregano
paprika
Parmesan cheese
parsley, flat-leaf
peas
pepper: black, white
ponzu sauce
pork
potatoes
poultry
raisins, esp. golden
rice
rosemary
saffron
sage
salads
SALT: *fleur de sel*, kosher, sea
sandwiches
sauces and gravies
savory
soups
sour cream
stews
stocks: beef, chicken, veal
sugar (pinch)
Tabasco sauce
THYME, lemon
tomatoes
vegetables
vinegar: balsamic, champagne, red wine, sherry, white wine
wine: dry red, white, port

Flavor Affinities
onions + balsamic vinegar + brown sugar
onions + beer + cheese + nutmeg
onions + garlic + thyme

Dishes

Roasted Vidalia Onion Stuffed with Walnuts, Wild Rice, and Roquefort Served with Wilted Arugula, Fava Beans, and Vegetable Demi-Glace
— Peter Nowakoski, Rat's (Hamilton, New Jersey)

ONIONS, SWEET

(e.g., Vidalia)
Season: late spring–early summer
Taste: sweet
Weight: light–medium
Volume: quiet–moderate

basil
cayenne
chard
cheese: blue (e.g., Cabrales, Maytag), goat, Parmesan
chives
cilantro
ginger, fresh
herbs
lettuces
mint
nutmeg
olive oil
pine nuts
salads
salt
sandwiches
Tabasco sauce
tomatoes
vinegar: rice, sherry
yogurt

Flavor Affinities

Vidalia onions + goat cheese + tomatoes + sherry vinegar

ORANGES — IN GENERAL

Season: year-round
Taste: sour, sweet
Function: heating
Weight: medium
Volume: moderate–loud
Techniques: poach, raw
Tips: Lemon brightens the flavor of orange.

almonds
anise seeds

Dishes

Baked Chocolate Mousse with Mandarin Oranges and Anise Seed Croustillant
— Dominique and Cindy Duby, Wild Sweets (Vancouver)

Orange and Basil Soup, Alpine Strawberry Compote, and Mascarpone Mousse
— Dominique and Cindy Duby, Wild Sweets (Vancouver)

Candied Orange Sponge with Poached Rhubarb and Cream Cheese Mousse
— François Payard, Payard Patisserie and Bistro (New York City)

Orange Tart with Carrot Cake and Mandarin
— François Payard, Payard Patisserie and Bistro (New York City)

I like **orange zest** with crab and shrimp because it gives them a sunny flavor. Lemon and lime are too strong. Orange is feminine — the lady of citrus — while lemon and lime are the men!

— **MICHEL RICHARD,** CITRONELLE (WASHINGTON, DC)

I use liqueurs such as [**orange**-flavored] Grand Marnier to bring out the flavors of other ingredients. When it's done right, you don't even know it is there.

— **EMILY LUCHETTI,** FARALLON (SAN FRANCISCO)

Orange and pomegranate season overlap in the fall, making these two fruits a natural pairing.

— **JOSÉ ANDRÉS,** CAFÉ ATLÁNTICO (WASHINGTON, DC)

apples
apricots
Armagnac
arugula
avocados
bananas
basil
beets
blackberries
blueberries
brandy
buttermilk
caramel
cardamom
carrots
ceviche
cheese: goat, ricotta
cherries
chestnuts
chicken
chile peppers, esp. serrano
chives
CHOCOLATE: dark, white
cilantro
cinnamon
cloves
coconut
coffee
cognac
crabs
cranberries
cream and ice cream
crust: pastry, pie
cumin

custard
dates
desserts
fennel
figs: dried, fresh
fish
game
garlic
ginger
grapefruit
greens
grenadine syrup
guava
hazelnuts
honey
ices
juniper berries
Italian cuisine
Kirsch
kumquats
LEMON: juice, zest
lemongrass
lettuce, romaine
lime
lime leaf, kaffir
liqueurs, almond
macadamia nuts
mangoes
maple syrup
mascarpone
meats
melon
meringue
MINT

nectarines
oats
olive oil
olives, black
ONIONS, esp. green, red
orange, zest
orange liqueurs: Cointreau,
   Grand Marnier
papaya
paprika
parsley, flat-leaf
passion fruit
peaches
pears
pecans
pepper, black
persimmons
pineapple
pine nuts
pistachios
plums
pomegranates
poppy seeds
pork, roast
port
prunes
pumpkin
quince
raisins
raspberries
rhubarb
rice
rosemary
rum
saffron
salads, fruit and green
salt
sauces
scallops
shrimp
squash, winter (e.g., butternut)
star anise
strawberries
SUGAR: brown, white
sweet potatoes
tea
thyme
tomatoes

vanilla
veal
vinegar, esp. rice wine, sherry
walnuts
watercress
wine: red, sweet, white
yogurt

Flavor Affinities
orange + anise + chocolate
orange + anise + dried figs +
    walnuts
orange + basil + sugar
orange + chocolate + pistachios
orange + cinnamon + honey +
    saffron
orange + seafood + tarragon

ORANGES, BLOOD
Season: winter–late spring
Taste: sour–sweet
Weight: medium
Volume: moderate

caramel
Champagne
chocolate, white
cinnamon
cloves
cream
grapefruit
honey
kumquats
lemon
mint
pomegranates
salads
sugar, brown
tarts
vanilla

ORANGES, CLEMENTINE
(See Oranges, Mandarin)

Dishes
Blood Orange–Vanilla Creamsicle
— Emily Luchetti, pastry chef, Farallon
(San Francisco)

Dishes
Chocolate and Tangerine Semifreddo Garnished with Chopped Pistachios
— Gina DePalma, pastry chef, Babbo (New York City)

ORANGES, MANDARIN
(includes Clementines and
Tangerines)
Season: autumn–spring
Taste: sweet, sour
Weight: light–medium
Volume: moderate

almonds
apricots
bananas
Campari
caramel
chicken
Chinese cuisine (e.g., as dessert)
chives
chocolate, esp. dark
cream and ice cream
crème anglaise
cumin
custard
dates
desserts
duck
fish
garlic
ginger
grapefruit
hazelnuts and hazelnut oil
honey
kumquats
lavender
LEMON JUICE
lemongrass
lemon verbena
lettuces
lime
lime leaf, kaffir
liqueurs, orange

mascarpone
melon
mint
olive oil
onions, green
oranges and blood oranges
passion fruit
pistachios
pomegranates
raspberries
rosemary
rum, esp. dark
salads
salt
scallops
seafood
sesame oil
shellfish (e.g., crab)
shrimp
sugar
vinegar: champagne, rice, white
    wine
yogurt

OREGANO
Season: late autumn–late spring
Botanical relative: marjoram
(milder in flavor than oregano)
Weight: medium–heavy
Volume: moderate–loud
Tips: Oregano can have great
variability, i.e., from mild to hot
and spicy (e.g., Italian oregano is
"quieter" than Greek oregano).

anchovies
artichokes
arugula
basil

Avoid **oregano** with desserts. Oregano firmly belongs in savory cuisine;
one taste, and it immediately calls to mind pizza sauce!
— **GINA DEPALMA**, BABBO (NEW YORK CITY)

beans, esp. dried and/or white
beef
BELL PEPPERS
broccoli
broths
capers
cheese and cheese dishes: feta,
    mozzarella, Parmesan
chicken
chile peppers, esp. piquillo
chili con carne, esp. Mexican
    oregano
chili powder
chives
cucumbers
cumin
duck
eggs and egg dishes
eggplant
FISH, esp. oilier, and esp. baked
    or grilled
garlic
Greek cuisine
greens, bitter
grilled dishes
hamburgers
Italian cuisine
lamb
*****LEMON**
marjoram
**MEATS, esp. red and/or grilled,
    and meat-based dishes**
Mediterranean cuisine
Mexican cuisine
mint (say some)
mole sauces, esp. with Mexican
    oregano
mushrooms
olive oil
olives
onions
paprika
parsley
PASTA AND PASTA SAUCES
pepper, black
PIZZA
pork
potatoes

poultry
quail
rabbit
roasts
rosemary
sage
**salads and salad dressings, esp.
    Greek**
sauces
sausages
seafood
shellfish
shrimp
soups, esp. chicken, fish,
    vegetable
Spanish cuisine
squash, summer
squid
stews
stuffing
swordfish
Tex-Mex cuisine
thyme
*****TOMATOES AND TOMATO
    SAUCES**
veal
vegetables, esp. summer
vinaigrettes
vinegar
zucchini

AVOID
cilantro
desserts

dill
mint (say some)
tarragon

Flavor Affinities
oregano + basil + tomato
oregano + lemon juice +
    marjoram

OXTAILS (See Beef)

OYSTERS
Season: autumn–spring (aka
"months containing the letter *r*")
Taste: salty
Weight: light–heavy (e.g., light
Kumamotos to heavy Gulf Coast
oysters)
Volume: quiet–moderate
Techniques: bake, broil, deep-
fry, grill, poach, raw, roast, sauté,
steam

aioli
apples
asparagus
bacon
basil
bay leaf
beer / ale
beets
bread, esp. dark
bread crumbs, *panko*
butter, unsalted

If you come to Chanterelle during November and December, you will
see **oysters** with white truffles when they are both in season and they
are classics for this restaurant.
— **DAVID WALTUCK,** CHANTERELLE (NEW YORK CITY)

Dishes
**Oysters Served with Tomatillo-Habanero "Miñoneta," Smoky Chipotle-Garlic Salsa and
Fresh-Cut Limes**
— Rick Bayless, Frontera Grill (Chicago)

Oysters on the Half Shell with Champagne Mignonette and Fresh Horseradish
— Traci Des Jardins, Jardinière (San Francisco)

Cajun cuisine
capers
caviar
cayenne
celery
Champagne
chervil
chili sauce
chives
cilantro
clams
cocktail sauce
cornmeal (for crust)
CREAM
crème fraîche
Creole cuisine
cucumbers
daikon
fennel
flour (for dredging)
French cuisine
garlic
gazpacho
ginger
hollandaise sauce
horseradish
lavender
LEEKS
LEMON: juice, zest
lemon verbena
lime, juice
mint
mushrooms, wild
OIL: canola, peanut, vegetable
olive oil
olives
onions, Spanish
orange
oyster juice
paprika
parsley, flat-leaf
passion fruit
PEPPER: black, white
ponzu sauce
potatoes
risotto
saffron
sake

salmon, smoked
SALT: kosher, sea
sauces: cocktail, mignonette
scallions
sea urchin
seaweed
SHALLOTS
shiso leaf
shrimp
sorrel
sour cream
Southern cuisine
soy sauce
spinach
stocks: chicken, clam, fish,
   vegetable
sugar (pinch)
Tabasco sauce
tapioca
thyme
tomatoes: flesh, juice
truffles: black, white
vermouth
VINEGAR: balsamic, **champagne**,
   red wine, rice, sherry
WINE, dry white
yuzu juice

AVOID
tarragon

Flavor Affinities
oysters + caviar + leeks
oysters + caviar + tapioca
oysters + clams + potatoes + thyme
oysters + cream + horseradish +
   onions
oysters + ginger + horseradish +
   sherry vinegar
oysters + horseradish +
   champagne vinegar
oysters + Muscadet + shallots +
   vinegar
oysters + shallots + vinegar

PANCETTA
Taste: salty
Weight: medium
Volume: moderate
Techniques: fry

arugula
beans
butter
cheese: fontina, **Parmesan**
garlic
Italian cuisine
lentils
meats
olive oil
onions
parsley
parsnips
PASTA
peas
pepper, black
pistachios
poultry
SAUCES
tomatoes
vegetables

PAPAYAS
Season: summer–autumn
Taste: sweet
Weight: medium
Volume: moderate
Techniques: bake, grill, raw,
sauté

bananas
beverages (e.g., smoothies)
caramel
cashews
carrots, esp. with green
chile peppers: jalapeño, serrano
chocolate, white
cilantro
cinnamon
citrus fruits
coconut: meat, milk
cream and ice cream
curries

fish sauce
garlic, esp. with green papayas
ginger
grapefruit
honey
kiwi fruit
kumquats
lemon, juice
LIME, juice
macadamia nuts
mango
marinades
melon
mint
nectarines
orange
passion fruit
peaches
peanuts
pepper, black
pineapple
port
prosciutto
raspberries
salads, fruit
salsa
salt, esp. with green
shrimp, esp. dried with green
    papaya
sorbet
soups
sour cream
strawberries
sugar
vanilla
vinegar: rice, white wine
yogurt

PAPRIKA — IN GENERAL
Taste: sweet–hot, depending on variety (e.g., hot, sweet, smoked, etc.)
Weight: light
Volume: quiet–loud
Tips: Add at the beginning of the cooking process.

allspice
barbecue

beef
bell peppers
butter, unsalted
Cajun cuisine
caraway seeds
cardamom
cauliflower
cheese
CHICKEN, esp. baked or
    paprikash
chili
crabs
cream
crème fraîche
curries
duck
eggs, esp. hard-boiled and egg
    dishes (e.g., omelets)
European cuisines
fish, esp. baked
garlic
ginger
goulash (key ingredient)
hummus
Hungarian cuisine
Indian cuisine
lamb
legumes
lemon, juice
marjoram
meats
Middle Eastern cuisine
Moroccan cuisine
mushrooms
octopus
olive oil
onions

oregano
paprikash
parsley
pepper, white
pork
potatoes
rice
rosemary
saffron
salads: pasta, potato
salt, sea
sauces, esp. cream
sausage, esp. chorizo
seafood
shellfish
soups
sour cream
Spanish cuisine
stews, esp. fish
stock, chicken
tagines
thyme
Turkish cuisine
turmeric
veal
vegetables
yogurt

Flavor Affinities
paprika + beef + sour cream

PAPRIKA, SMOKED
Weight: medium
Volume: moderate–loud

bacon
beans, esp. white

We use lots of **smoked paprika**, but need to be careful because it can be really strong. I like to finish our fried chickpeas with this because it makes them taste like they just jumped out of the fire! We also like to mix our paprikas together, typically in equal proportions of sweet, hot, and smoked. Smoked paprika is primarily smoky and doesn't have a lot of other flavors. So if you combine it with a vibrant sweet paprika, you'll get a more rounded pepper flavor. Paprika is also very regional. In the south [of Spain] where it gets sunshine and heat, you see more smoked paprika, but in the north where it is colder and rainy, they are not into the heat.

— **ALEXANDRA RAIJ**, TÍA POL (NEW YORK CITY)

cheese
chicken
chickpeas
chorizo
clams
eggs, hard-boiled
fish (e.g., skate)
garlic
lamb
marjoram
mayonnaise
meats, esp. grilled or roasted
Mediterranean cuisine
octopus
olive oil
onions
paella
pepper, black
peppers, piquillo
pork, esp. ribs
potatoes
sage
scallions
seafood
soups
steaks
stews
tomatoes
turkey, esp. roasted
vegetables
vegetarian meals

Flavor Affinities
smoked paprika + mayonnaise +
    seafood

PARSLEY
Season: year-round
Weight: light
Volume: quiet
Tips: Use fresh. Parsley generally
refers to flat-leaf parsley. Parsley
is great for blending, as it is
compatible with virtually all other
herbs.

avocados
basil

bay leaf
beans, esp. dried
beef
bouquet garni (ingredient, along
    with bay leaf, marjoram,
    thyme)
braised dishes
bulgur wheat
butter
capers
carrots
cauliflower
cheese, esp. Parmesan, ricotta
chervil
chicken
chile peppers
chives
cinnamon
clams
cream
cream cheese
crème fraîche
dill
eggs and egg dishes
eggplant
fennel
fines herbes (ingredient)
FISH
French cuisine, esp. southern
game
GARLIC
halibut
ham
herbs (as a flavor enhancer)
Italian cuisine, esp. southern
lemon: juice, zest
lemon balm
lentils
lovage
marjoram
meats
Mediterranean cuisine
Middle Eastern cuisine
mint
Moroccan cuisine
mushrooms
mussels
oils: hazelnut, walnut

olive oil
onions
oregano
oysters
parsnips
pasta and pasta sauces
peas
pepper: black, white
pesto (ingredient)
pizza
pork
potatoes
poultry
rice
rosemary
sage
salads, esp. egg, green, pasta,
    potato, or rice
salsa verde (ingredient)
sauces
sausages
savory
scallions
seafood
shallots
shrimp
skate
snails
sorrel
SOUPS
Spanish cuisine, esp. southern
spinach
stews
stocks
stuffings
sumac
tabbouleh (key ingredient)
tarragon
thyme
tomatoes and tomato sauces
veal
vegetables
vinaigrette
vinegar, balsamic
zucchini

AVOID
desserts

The Spanish use **parsley** stems for cooking, and fresh as a garnish before serving. When you make rice or beans, you would put a stem in. To me, parsley added to fish or shellfish makes the dish tastes more "marine," as opposed to earthy. I love *salsa verde,* which is a sauce made with basically a ton of parsley, garlic, and some kind of juice like clam juice. It's wonderful served with fish.

— ALEXANDRA RAIJ, TÍA POL (NEW YORK CITY)

People do not understand **parsley;** they think it is green specks. But it is wonderful with fish. If you make a straight-up linguini with clam sauce, you want a big handful of chopped parsley in there — not for the appearance, but for the taste. It is an important component in a lot of dishes and needs to be there. It can also be used as a sauce all on its own. If you sprinkle it on a steak, it will not have the impact that it would on fish. On the other hand, if you make a Maître d'hôtel butter [butter flavored with lemon juice and parsley] and put it on the steak, the parsley has a role there. On vegetables, if you make glazed carrots or pearl onions or a stew with lots of vegetables, parsley stirred in at the last moment is good stuff. As for my choice of parsley, I always use flat Italian-style parsley.

— DAVID WALTUCK, CHANTERELLE (NEW YORK CITY)

Salsa verde is my favorite all-purpose condiment at home. I like it on fish, lamb, and steak. It is made with anchovy, garlic, shallots, olive oil, and herbs — primarily **parsley,** but also chervil, chives, tarragon, a little bit of marjoram, and sometimes a little mint if I am in the mood. I add the acid at the last moment so it won't change the color of the herbs, and will choose between Banyuls or red wine vinegar, or lemon juice. If I am serving meat, I will use vinegar; if I am serving fish, I will use lemon. Even though it changes color once the acid is added, it lasts a few days. It is really good on a piece of bread or with some fresh farmer's cheese as a snack.

— TRACI DES JARDINS, JARDINIÈRE (SAN FRANCISCO)

Flavor Affinities

parsley + bulgur wheat + garlic + lemon + mint + olive oil + scallions
parsley + butter + garlic
parsley + capers + garlic + lemon zest + olive oil
parsley + garlic
parsley + garlic + lemon zest
parsley + garlic + olive oil + Parmesan cheese + vinegar
parsley + lemon juice + olive oil + Parmesan cheese

PARSNIPS

Season: autumn–winter
Taste: sweet
Weight: medium–heavy
Volume: moderate
Techniques/Tips: Always use cooked (never raw): bake, boil, braise, deep-fry, grill, mash, puree, roast, steam

allspice
anise
apples
bacon
basil
bay leaf
beans, black, green
BUTTER, brown and/or unsalted
carrots
cheese, esp. creamy
chervil
chicken
chile peppers
chives
cinnamon
coriander
cream
cumin
curry
dill
duck
fennel: leaves, seeds
fish
game
game birds
garlic
ginger, esp. ground
greens, bitter / winter
honey
leeks
lemon, juice
lentils
lovage
mace
maple syrup
meats
mint
mirepoix
mirin

Dishes

Passion Fruit and Bonito Caramel
— Dominique and Cindy Duby, Wild Sweets (Vancouver)

Passion Fruit Flip: Passion Fruit + Honey + Lime + Raspberries + Yogurt
— Gale Gand, pastry chef, Tru (Chicago)

Passion Fruit Cream Enrobed in White Chocolate, Ginger Caramel, and Mandarin Sorbet
— Michael Laiskonis, Le Bernardin (New York City)

mushrooms, porcini
mustard
NUTMEG
oil: peanut, sesame
olive oil
onions
orange
pancetta
parsley
Parmesan cheese
pears
pepper: black, white
potatoes
rosemary
sage
salt
shallots
soups
soy sauce
stews
stocks: chicken, vegetable
sugar, brown
tarragon
thyme
vegetables, root
vinegar, balsamic
wine, dry white
yogurt

Flavor Affinities
parsnips + butter + cream + potatoes
parsnips + carrots + nutmeg + potatoes
parsnips + cream + nutmeg
parsnips + honey + mustard
parsnips + pancetta + Parmesan cheese + pasta

PASSION FRUIT

Season: year-round
Taste: sweet
Weight: medium
Volume: moderate
Techniques: puree, raw

almonds
bananas
beverages
caramel
cashews
Champagne
chicken
chives
chocolate, esp. dark, white
cilantro
citrus fruit
coconut and coconut milk
Cointreau
CREAM AND ICE CREAM
cream cheese
custard
egg whites
fish
fruits, tropical
ginger
kiwi fruit
lemon, juice
lime, juice
macadamia nuts
mangoes
orange, juice
papayas
peaches
pears
pineapples

rum, esp. dark
salads, fruit
salad dressings
soups, fruit
strawberries
SUGAR
tapioca
tequila
vanilla
wine, ice
yogurt

Flavor Affinities
passion fruit + banana + orange
passion fruit + caramel + coconut
passion fruit + caramel + ginger + white chocolate
passion fruit + cream + ice wine
passion fruit + dark chocolate + ginger + raspberries

PASTA

Weight: medium–heavy (depending on the cut)
Volume: quiet

anchovies
artichokes
asparagus
bacon
basil
beans, e.g., fava, white
beef
bottarga (tuna roe)
bread crumbs
broccoli
broths, esp. chicken, esp. with small pasta
butter
capers
cauliflower
CHEESE: cheddar, Comté, Emmental, Fontina, goat, Gorgonzola, Gouda, Gruyère, **mozzarella, PARMESAN, pecorino, ricotta,** ricotta salata
chicken
chickpeas

Dishes

Goat Cheese Tortelloni with Dried Orange and Fennel Pollen
— Mario Batali, Babbo (New York City)

Mint Tagliatelle with Lamb and Olives
— Mario Batali, Babbo (New York City)

Spaghettini with Spicy Artichokes, Sweet Garlic, and Lobster
— Mario Batali, Babbo (New York City)

Spaghetti Primavera with Prosciutto, Spring Garlic, Sugar Snap Peas, and Parmigiano
— Andrew Carmellini, A Voce (New York City)

Homemade Pappardelle with Lamb Bolognese and Sheep's Milk Ricotta
— Andrew Carmellini, A Voce (New York City)

Homemade Soft Egg Yolk–Filled Raviolo with Truffled Butter
— Odette Fada, San Domenico (New York City)

Homemade Straccetti with Pesto and Clams
— Odette Fada, San Domenico (New York City)

Linguini with Clams, Pancetta, and Spicy Fresno Chile Pesto
— Matt Molina, Osteria Mozza (Los Angeles)

Farfalle with Stridoli, Walnuts, and Chanterelles
— Matt Molina, Osteria Mozza (Los Angeles)

Tagliatelle with Chanterelles and Parmigiano Reggiano
— Holly Smith, Café Juanita (Seattle)

Butternut Squash Ravioli with Oxtail Ragôut and Sage Cream
— David Waltuck, Chanterelle (New York City)

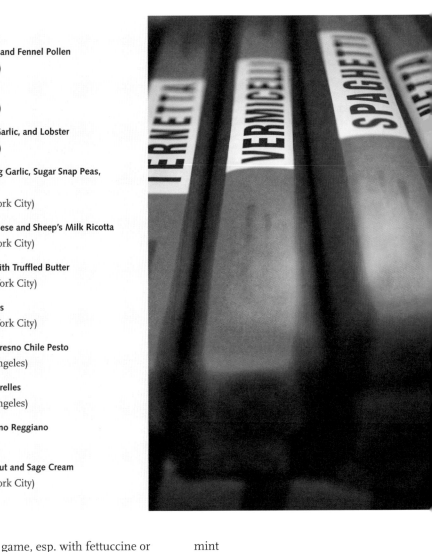

chile peppers
chives
clams
cream, esp. with fettuccine, festonate, gnocchi, or pappardelle
cured meats: bacon, ham, pancetta, prosciutto
duck confit
eggplant
eggs
fennel
figs
fish (e.g., cod, salmon, swordfish, tuna)

game, esp. with fettuccine or pappardelle
garlic
greens (e.g., arugula, radicchio, stridoli)
ITALIAN CUISINE
lamb
leeks
lemon, juice
lobster
mascarpone
meat, esp. beef, lamb, oxtail, pork, venison
meat, ground, esp. with penne and rigatoni

mint
mushrooms, esp. wild
mussels
mustard, Dijon
nutmeg
octopus
OLIVE OIL, esp. with linguini and spaghetti
olives
onions
pancetta
parsley, flat-leaf
parsnips
peas, esp. with penne and rigatoni
pecans

Pairing Pastas with Sauces

Which sauces pair best with which pastas? We asked chef Odette Fada of New York City's San Domenico restaurant.

- **Angel hair:** In Italy, angel hair pasta is served to old people who can't chew. It's for grandparents, or for others to eat when they are sick. The problem with angel hair pasta is it's so thin it's hard to cook al dente, and I like my pasta a little chewy.
- **Bow tie:** Fresh bow tie is great when made by hand, because it stays folded and doesn't open into a square. I like to serve it with vegetables and tomato-based sauces.
- **Fettuccine:** This is a flavorful pasta and is good with a Bolognese sauce.
- **Fusilli:** I like their [corkscrew] shape, but they tend to break easily so they are not that attractive when you cook them in a restaurant setting. I like them at home in a salad or with some pesto because the pesto sticks to it.
- **Hollow pasta** [e.g., macaroni, penne, rigatoni]: Good with sauces that have big chunks in them so that the sauce pieces go inside whole. I like to do penne with fresh peas because the peas will slip inside, so you'll sometimes get a little surprise when you're chewing.

- **Pappardelle:** This is a strong, rustic pasta. I like it with rabbit sauce, a ragoût, or a fish sauce that has some character.
- **Small pasta** [e.g., rice-, shell-, or star-shaped]: These are good for soups and brothy dishes. For example, you would use them with a brothy fish dish.
- **Spaghetti:** Everything goes with spaghetti! It is a pasta that sauce sticks to. Everything from tomato sauce to pesto to pecorino with black pepper is great with spaghetti.

Or, if you're starting with the sauce:

- **Carbonara:** Spaghetti or bucatini, you want a pasta that the sauce will stick to.
- **Cream:** Fettuccine, pappardelle, or gnocchi, since cream is so rich you want a strong-flavored pasta or, in the last case, gnocchi — one that is made with some egg in it.
- **Game:** Pappardelle or fettuccine; you want an egg-rich pasta with some flavor.
- **Olive oil and garlic:** Spaghetti.
- **Pesto:** Fusilli.
- **Tomato:** This works with almost all pasta shapes, from small to large.

I have played with lots of flavored pasta doughs. One of my favorites is olive because it holds its flavor. Other flavors that hold up well are squid ink and saffron. I have also made a pappardelle with cocoa powder that I paired with game sauce that worked great. If you wanted to achieve a particular color, you could create red pasta with beets, green pasta with spinach, and black pasta with squid ink.

pepper: black, white
pine nuts
pork
potatoes
prosciutto
pumpkin
rabbit, braised, esp. with
   pappardelle
raisins
red pepper flakes

rosemary
saffron
sage
salt, esp. kosher
sardines
SAUCES: Bolognese (esp. with fettuccine), carbonara (esp. with bucatini or spaghetti), Mornay (esp. with macaroni), pesto (esp. with fusilli), rabbit (esp.

with pappardelle), sardines (esp. with bucatini), tomato
sausage
scallops
seafood: clams, crab, lobster, mussels, octopus, scallops, shrimp, squid
shallots
shrimp
spinach

squash: summer, winter
squid
sweet potato
thyme
tomatoes
tomatoes, sun-dried
truffles: black, white
veal
vegetables
venison
vinegar, esp. balsamic
walnuts
zucchini

Flavor Affinities

pasta + anchovies + bread crumbs + capers + red pepper flakes + garlic
    + olives
pasta + anchovies + mozzarella cheese
pasta + artichokes + garlic + lobster
pasta + bacon + black pepper + eggs + olive oil + pecorino cheese
pasta + basil + garlic + tomato
pasta + basil + peas + shrimp
pasta + basil + scallops + tomato
pasta + bread crumbs + greens + shrimp + white beans
pasta + bread crumbs + raisins + sardines
pasta + chickpeas + garlic + sage
pasta + chile peppers + lobster + mint
pasta + clams + pancetta
pasta + cream + peas + prosciutto
pasta + duck confit + wild mushrooms
pasta + fennel + sausage + tomato + white beans
pasta + figs + pancetta
pasta + Gorgonzola cheese + spinach + walnuts
pasta + Gruyère cheese + nutmeg + ricotta cheese
pasta + lamb + lemon + rosemary
pasta + lamb + mint + olives
pasta + lobster + peas
pasta + mushrooms + pumpkin + sage
pasta + pancetta + stridoli
pasta + Parmesan cheese + sage + tomato
pasta + pesto + white beans
pasta + pumpkin + pecans + ricotta cheese + sage
pasta + red pepper flakes + fennel + sardines + tomatoes
pasta + red pepper flakes + garlic + olive oil
pasta + ricotta cheese + veal shanks
pasta + rosemary + venison
pasta + spinach + ricotta cheese
pasta + tomatoes + ricotta cheese

Chef Odette Fada of New York's San Domenico on Making Ravioli

I love ravioli! Anything and everything goes in my ravioli — I have used everything from chestnuts to cheese to fish, meat, and vegetables. You can vary the ravioli dough as well as the stuffing. For example, I serve ravioli stuffed with sea urchin and the dough is light and made with just flour and water. For a stronger filling like lamb, I will use some egg in the dough which makes it bigger flavored. One of my favorite ravioli stuffings is black truffle and pancetta. The truffle provides a crunchiness when you bite into it.

One of the greatest ravioli we do dates back to the chef for the last king of Italy at the beginning of the twentieth century. It is stuffed with spinach, truffle, Parmesan cheese, and an egg yolk, and served with butter, truffle, and Parmesan cheese. When the ravioli is cooked, it is served with the yolk warm but not cooked. It is truly an amazing dish.

In Italy during the winter, you would typically have some slices of sausage on top of a plate of lentils. I decided to combine the two into a ravioli dish. Now, one of my other favorite dishes is our ravioli stuffed with *cotechino* [sausage] and lentils. The lentils are cooked with rosemary, garlic, extra-virgin olive oil, and prosciutto skin, and go into the ravioli with the sausage, parsley, and Parmesan cheese. The dish is finished with some strong extra-virgin olive oil, parsley, and a crack of pepper.

PEACHES

Season: late spring–early autumn
Taste: sweet
Function: heating
Weight: medium
Volume: moderate
Techniques: bake, broil, grill, poach, raw, roast, sauté

allspice
ALMONDS, esp. toasted
anise hyssop
apples
apricots, puree
arugula
basil
bay leaf
beverages, esp. cocktails
blackberries
BLUEBERRIES
bourbon
brandy
butter, unsalted
buttermilk
Calvados
caramel
Champagne
cherries
chile peppers, green (e.g., jalapeño)
chocolate: dark, white
CINNAMON
cloves
coconut
cognac
Cointreau
*CREAM AND ICE CREAM
crème fraîche
currants, red: fruit, jelly
custards
desserts and dessert sauces
figs
fruit crisp
ginger
Grand Marnier
grenadine
hazelnuts
honey
ice, esp. pistachio
ice cream, esp. vanilla
Kirsch
lavender
LEMON: juice, zest
lemon thyme
lemon verbena
lime, juice
liqueurs: nut, orange, peach (e.g., schnapps)
mace
Madeira
maple syrup
Marsala
mascarpone
mint
molasses
nectarines
nutmeg
oatmeal

Dishes

Jim Core's Peaches Upside-Down Cake with Blueberry Sorbet
— John Besh, August (New Orleans)

Saffron Panna Cotta with Peaches, Peach Sorbetto, and Lemon Balm
— Gina DePalma, Babbo (New York City)

White Peach Melba with Raspberry Granita
— Emily Luchetti, pastry chef, Farallon (San Francisco)

Warm Ginger Cake Sabayon with Spiced Peaches
— Chuck Subra, La Côte Brasserie (New Orleans)

When I think of the essence of **peaches,** it's their smell — so I think of echoing that with the floralness of Moscato d'Asti. I'll add acidity, sweetness, and a little fat, such as through crème fraîche.
— TONY LIU, AUGUST (NEW YORK CITY)

I try not to cook **peaches,** or if I do, only for a short amount of time. A peach pie never tastes as good to me as a blueberry pie, because it tastes too cooked by the time you get it thick enough. So if I get peaches, I'll chop them up and put them on a tart shell that is already cooked instead.
— EMILY LUCHETTI, FARALLON (SAN FRANCISCO)

I like **peaches** with rich, round flavors like vanilla and honey.
— GINA DEPALMA, BABBO (NEW YORK CITY)

Japanese baby **peaches** are tiny peaches about the size of olives. We wanted to showcase the peaches and thought, What do peaches go with? Cream. We took that one step further and used yogurt instead. So we chose Greek yogurt, paired it with the peaches, then garnished the dish with Hawaiian pink sea salt, Greek olive oil, reduced balsamic vinegar, and micro mint. We turned the water strained from the yogurt into "air" [foam]. This is a dish that we serve as a pre-dessert and it works well because it is sweet and savory.
— KATSUYA FUKUSHIMA, MINIBAR (WASHINGTON, DC)

oil, vegetable
olive oil
onions, yellow
ORANGE: juice, zest
papaya
passion fruit
pecans
pepper: black, white
pineapple
PISTACHIOS

plums
port
raisins
RASPBERRIES: fruit, puree
rum
saffron
salads, fruit
salsas, fruit
salt
soups, esp. cold

sour cream
star anise
STRAWBERRIES (e.g., fruit, puree)
SUGAR: BROWN, confectioners', white
tarragon
tea
thyme
VANILLA
vinegar: balsamic, champagne, cider, red wine, rice, white
Vin Santo
violets, esp. candied
walnuts
watercress
whiskey
WINE: dry or fruity red or white or sweet (e.g., Asti, **Burgundy,** Merlot, sweet Muscat, Riesling, Rosé, Zinfandel)
yogurt
zabaglione

Flavor Affinities

peaches + apples + vanilla
peaches + blueberries + mascarpone
peaches + cream + honey + vanilla
peaches + figs + maple syrup
peaches + ginger + sugar
peaches + orange liqueur + vanilla
peaches + sugar + yogurt

PEANUT OIL (See Oil, Peanut)

PEANUTS AND PEANUT BUTTER (See also Nuts — In General)

Taste: sweet, astringent
Function: heating
Weight: medium–heavy
Volume: moderate–loud

African cuisine
apples
BANANAS
basil

beef
bell peppers
Burmese cuisine
butter
caramel
cayenne
chicken
chile peppers (e.g., jalapeño)
Chinese cuisine
CHOCOLATE, ESP. DARK,
 MILK
cilantro
coconut and coconut milk
coffee
curries
curry paste, Thai red
curry powder
desserts
fish sauce, Thai
garlic
grape jelly
honey
Indonesian cuisine
lemon, juice
lime, juice
mole sauces
noodles
oatmeal
oil: peanut, vegetable
olive oil
onions
parsley
pears
pork
raisins
raspberries
Rice Krispies
salads
salt
sauces
shrimp
Southern cuisine (American)
soy sauce
stir-fried dishes
strawberries
sugar: brown, white
tarragon
Thai cuisine

Anything we put **peanuts** on sells! Peanuts are associated with the South, so there is a regional appeal. We had a chicken breast with sugar snap peas, white radishes, toasted peanuts, basmati rice, and spicy peanut sauce.

— **MARCEL DESAULNIERS**, THE TRELLIS (WILLIAMSBURG, VIRGINIA)

Peanuts are not as versatile as other nuts. They have a great flavor and are pretty generic so you can use them on a lot of things and they pair well. Milk chocolate and peanuts work really well together. Peanuts pair great with bananas, especially if you cover the banana in chocolate and then roll it in peanuts and freeze it.

— **EMILY LUCHETTI**, FARALLON (SAN FRANCISCO)

tomatoes
turmeric
vanilla
Vietnamese cuisine
vinegar, red wine

PEARS

Season: autumn–winter
Taste: sweet
Weight: medium
Volume: quiet–moderate
Techniques: bake, deep-fry (e.g., as chips), grill, poach, raw, roast, sauté, stew

allspice
ALMONDS and almond paste
anise
apples: fruit, juice
apricots, esp. dried or pureed
arugula
bacon
basil
beets
blackberries
blueberries
borage
bourbon
brandy, esp. pear
butter, brown
BUTTER, unsalted
butterscotch
Calvados
CARAMEL
cardamom

cassis
celery
Champagne
CHEESE: BLUE, Brie, Cabrales,
 Cambozola, Camembert,
 Cantal, cheddar, feta, **goat,**
 Gorgonzola, Monterey Jack,
 Parmesan, pecorino, ricotta,
 Romano, **ROQUEFORT,**
 Stilton
cherries: dried, fresh
chestnuts
Chinese cuisine, esp. featuring
 Asian pears
CHOCOLATE, esp. dark, white
cider
CINNAMON
CLOVES
cranberries
cream and ice cream
cream cheese
crème anglaise
crème fraîche
custards
dates
dill
duck and duck confit
endive
fennel
figs
French cuisine
game
ginger
Grand Marnier
hazelnuts

HONEY
ice cream, vanilla
Italian cuisine
Kirsch
LEMON: JUICE, ZEST
liqueurs: almond, hazelnut,
    orange
macadamia nuts
mace
maple syrup
Marsala
MASCARPONE
meats, esp. fatty, grilled, and/or
    roasted
Mediterranean cuisine
mint (garnish)
mustard
nutmeg
nuts
oats
oil, canola
olive oil
onions, green
ORANGE: fruit, juice, zest
parsley, flat-leaf
passion fruit
peanuts
pear brandy
pear cider
pecans
pepper: black, white
pine nuts
pistachios
Poire William
pork
port: red, white
poultry
praline
prosciutto
prunes
quinces
radicchio
raisins
raspberries: fruit, puree
rhubarb
rice (e.g., pudding)
rosemary
rum

This salad has roasted **pear**, Roquefort cheese, lemon, and olive oil and is garnished with borage flowers. The sauce is burnt caramel with pepper deglazed with Coteaux du Layon, which is sweet but higher in acid than Sauternes. The caramel sauce keeps you awake!

Cheese and fruit: Blue cheese is sharp and hits your palate, then the pear calms it down.

Salad greens: We use herbs in our salad and this one has fennel, thyme, tarragon, parsley, and anise hyssop.

Borage flowers: Eating a borage flower is like eating an oyster! It is briny. In the summer when they are in season, if you taste a couple it is reminiscent of a mild oyster.

— **GABRIEL KREUTHER,** THE MODERN (NEW YORK CITY)

Apples are more popular than **pears** because when you go to the store, pears are all hard. You buy them, bring them home, and wait forever for them to ripen. You have to have a premeditated use for pears.

— **EMILY LUCHETTI,** FARALLON (SAN FRANCISCO)

I like **pears** poached because I'm not fond of their texture. I also make a pear tart with pears poached in lemon zest and vanilla, and then combined with custard, honey, lemon, and vanilla. It is paired with a honey grappa zabaglione and topped with grated Pecorino Toscano cheese grated over it as if it were pasta. The dish sounds a little crazy but all these flavors are classic combinations found in Italy. Pears are often infused with grappa in the north of Italy. Pears, honey, and pecorino is a classic combination in Tuscany. Pecorino goes with every flavor. Honey carries all the flavors forward.

— **GINA DEPALMA,** BABBO (NEW YORK CITY)

sabayon
salads: fruit, green
salt (pinch)
sour cream
squab
squash: butternut, winter
star anise
strawberries, esp. sauce
SUGAR: brown, white
sweet potatoes
toffee
VANILLA
VINEGAR: balsamic, champagne, sherry, white, white wine
WALNUTS
watercress
whiskey
WINE: red (e.g., Burgundy), strong red (e.g., Cabernet Sauvignon, Zinfandel), dry white (e.g., Riesling), sparkling (e.g., Champagne), sweet (e.g., ice wine)

Flavor Affinities

pears + amaretto + hazelnuts
pears + arugula + Parmesan cheese + vinaigrette + walnuts
pears + bacon + bitter greens + goat cheese
pears + blue cheese + olive oil + red wine vinegar + watercress
pears + caramel + balsamic vinegar
pears + caramel + chestnuts + crème fraîche
pears + caramel + chocolate
pears + cinnamon + ginger + honey
pears + fennel + Parmesan cheese + balsamic vinegar + walnuts
pears + ginger + honey + vanilla
pears + Gorgonzola cheese + vinaigrette + walnuts
pears + honey + lime + vanilla
pears + honey + rosemary
pears + maple syrup + walnuts
pears + mascarpone + pistachios + red wine
pears + pecorino cheese + balsamic vinegar
pears + Roquefort cheese + sugar + vanilla + red wine
pears + Roquefort cheese + walnuts
pears + Stilton cheese + hazelnuts + balsamic vinegar

Dishes

Pear and Fresh Pecorino–Filled Ravioli with Aged Pecorino and Crushed Black Pepper
— Lidia Bastianich, Felidia (New York City)

Grilled Pear and Roquefort Tart with Caramelized Onions and Walnuts
— Sandy D'Amato, Sanford (Milwaukee)

Grilled Pear Steak with Polenta Frites and Orange-Tarragon Sauce
— Dominique and Cindy Duby, Wild Edibles (Vancouver)

Salad of Spicy Poached Pear, Fresh Ricotta, Smoked Almonds, and Edamame with Verjus Dressing
— Brad Farmerie, Monday Room (New York City)

Sticky Toffee Pudding with Cinnamon-Sautéed Pears
— Gale Gand, at the 2005 James Beard Awards gala reception

Warm Semolina Pancake, Poached Pears, Cumin
— Johnny Iuzzini, pastry chef, Jean Georges (New York City)

Honey-Roasted Pear Napoleon
— Kate Zuckerman, pastry chef, Chanterelle (New York City)

PEAS — IN GENERAL

(See also Snap Peas)
Season: late spring–summer
Taste: sweet
Weight: light–medium
Volume: quiet–moderate
Techniques: boil, braise, sauté, steam

arugula
asparagus
bacon
BASIL
bay leaf
bouquet garni
BUTTER, unsalted
cardamom
CARROTS and carrot juice
cayenne
celery
cheese, esp. Parmesan, ricotta
chervil

chicken
chile peppers: dried red, fresh
  green
chives
cilantro, (e.g., as Indian cuisine)
cinnamon
cloves
coriander
crab
CREAM, HEAVY
crème fraîche
cumin
curry powder
dill
fava beans
fish
French cuisine
garam masala
garlic
ginger
ham and ham hocks
honey
Italian cuisine
leeks
lemon, juice
lettuce, Boston
lime, juice
lobster
marjoram
mascarpone
MINT
mushrooms, esp. morels
oil, peanut
olive oil
onions: pearl, red, spring, white
pancetta
parsley, flat-leaf
pasta
pepper: black, white
pork
potatoes
poultry
prosciutto
risotto
rosemary
sage
salt: kosher, sea

savory, winter
scallions
scallops
shallots
shrimp
snap peas
sorrel
Spanish cuisine, esp. southern
spinach
stocks: chicken, vegetable

sugar
tarragon
thyme
tomatoes
turmeric
vinaigrette
vinegar, champagne
watercress
wine, dry white
yogurt

Flavor Affinities

peas + bacon + cream + shallots

peas + basil + potatoes

peas + celery + olive oil + onions + chicken stock + sugar

peas + custard + Parmesan cheese

peas + lobster + pasta

peas + marjoram + mascarpone + Parmesan cheese

peas + mint + morel mushrooms

peas + mushrooms + ricotta cheese

peas + onions + pancetta + sage

Bronze fennel grows all over Seattle. One day I walked outside eating **peas** while going out to get mint for my pea salad. I ate a bite of fennel and thought, "By Jove, I've got a dish!" Bronze fennel is a non-bulb fennel that has an amazing fennel and earthy flavor.

— HOLLY SMITH, CAFÉ JUANITA (SEATTLE)

Dishes

Spring Pea Fricassée with Morels and Butter Lettuce

— Daniel Boulud, at the 2003 James Beard Awards gala reception

Chilled Sweet Pea Soup "à la Française" Thumbelina Carrot Salad with Cilantro and Lobster

— Daniel Boulud, Daniel (New York City)

Pea Velouté with Apple-Smoked Bacon, Louisiana Crayfish, Savory Cream

— Daniel Boulud, Daniel (New York City)

Garden Pea Soup with Morel Cream

— Daniel Humm, Eleven Madison Park (New York City)

Sweet Pea Soup with Caramelized Vidalia Onion, Apple-Smoked Bacon, and Mint

— Alfred Portale, Gotham Bar and Grill (New York City)

Sweet Pea Sorbet with Preserved Green Almond and Marcona Almond Milk, Fuji Apple with Butterscotch, Rye, and Thyme

— Charlie Trotter, Charlie Trotter's (Chicago)

Fresh Pea Ravioli with Sweet Onions Sauce and Smoked Pork Reduction

— David Waltuck, Chanterelle (New York City)

PECAN OIL (See Oil, Pecan)

PECANS (See also Nuts — In General)

Season: autumn
Taste: bitter–sweet
Weight: medium–heavy
Volume: quiet–moderate

almonds
apples
apricots
baked goods (e.g., breads, cookies, pies)
bananas
blackberries
blueberries
bourbon
brandy
breakfast (e.g., pancakes, waffles)
butter, unsalted
butterscotch
CARAMEL
cheese, goat
cherries
chicken
chocolate: dark, white
cinnamon
coffee
cognac
corn syrup: light, dark
cranberries
cream
dates
ginger
grapefruit
grapes
hazelnuts
honey
ice cream
kumquats
lemon, juice
liqueurs, orange
MAPLE SYRUP
mascarpone
Mexican sauces
nectarines
nutmeg
oats and oatmeal
orange
peaches
pears
persimmons
plums
pork
prunes
pumpkin
quince
raisins
raspberries
rice, wild
rum
salads
salt
sour cream
Southern cuisine (American)
squash, butternut
stir-fried dishes

Dishes

Pecan Praline Cheesecake
— Terrance Brennan, Artisanal (New York City)

Pecan Praline Pancakes with Brown Butter Bananas and Rum Raisins
— Daniel Humm, Eleven Madison Park (New York City)

Southern Butter Pecan Ice Cream with Hot Caramel Sauce
— Patrick O'Connell, The Inn at Little Washington (Washington, Virginia)

Phyllo Spirals with Garden Herbs, Rio Grande Organic Pecans, and Pure Luck Feta
— Monica Pope, T'afia (Houston)

We are using **pecans** on a savory dish of scallops and shrimp, ham, shiitake mushrooms, shallots, and pecan-studded basmati rice.
— MARCEL DESAULNIERS, THE TRELLIS (WILLIAMSBURG, VIRGINIA)

strawberries
stuffing
SUGAR: BROWN, white
sweet potatoes
tea
vanilla
walnuts
whiskey
wine: red, sweet

PEPPER, BLACK

Taste: pungent, hot
Function: warming
Weight: light–medium
Volume: moderate–loud
Tips: Pepper suggests "false heat" and also stimulates the appetite. Add at the end of the cooking process.

apricots
basil
BEEF, esp. roasted
berries
cardamom
cheese
cherries
cinnamon
cloves
coconut milk
coriander
cumin
eggs

fruit, fresh
game
garlic
ginger
Indian cuisine
lamb
lemon, juice
lentils
lime, juice
meats, red
nutmeg
nuts
olive oil
olives
parsley
pineapple
pork
poultry
pumpkin (e.g., pie)
rosemary
salads
SALT
sauces
sausages
seafood, heartier
soups
spice cake
STEAKS, esp. grilled
strawberries
thyme
tomatoes
turmeric
veal

PEPPER, GREEN (as peppercorns)

Taste: hot
Weight: light–medium
Volume: moderate
Tips: Add at the end of the cooking process.
The flavor is less sharp than black pepper.

avocados
bay leaf
beef
brandy
butter
chicken
cream
curries
duck
game
garlic
ham
meats, esp. grilled and/or red
mustard
parsley
pâtés
pork
sage
salads and salad dressings
salmon
sauces: creamy, white
seafood
shrimp
stock, veal
turkey
veal
vegetables
venison
wine, white

PEPPER, PINK

Taste: hot
Weight: light–medium
Volume: moderate–loud
Tips: Add at the end of the cooking process.

butter
chervil

chicken
chocolate
desserts
duck
eggs
fennel
fruit
game
lemongrass
lime leaves, kaffir
lobster
meats, esp. richer and/or
    stronger
mint
olive oil
parsley
pâtés
pears
pepper: black, green
pineapple
pork
poultry
salad dressings
sauces: fruit, white
scallops
seafood
shrimp
steak
veal
vinegar, esp. balsamic
Worcestershire sauce

PEPPER, RED
(See also Cayenne, Ground)
Taste: hot
Weight: light
Volume: loud
Tips: Add at the end of the
cooking process.

Caribbean cuisine
chili powder (ingredient)
Indian cuisine
Italian cuisine
jerk seasoning (ingredient)
meats
Mexican cuisine
mole negro (ingredient)
seafood

I like **white pepper** with most white fish, and **black pepper** with tuna and red meat. White pepper works with halibut because it does not overwhelm the fish. Black pepper has a complex flavor and is spicy, which can be distracting. The problem with many peppers like cayenne or chipotle is that they are so strong they can burn. That is not a problem for me, but it is for our clientele. We use *piment d'Espelette,* which is spicy but sweet.

— **ERIC RIPERT,** LE BERNARDIN (NEW YORK CITY)

You have to be careful with **black pepper** because it can be a vehicle to add flavor — but if misused, it will mask flavor. I might add the tiniest little pinch before a dessert gets served to punch it up. I use black pepper with fresh fruit, especially cherries.

— **MICHAEL LAISKONIS,** LE BERNARDIN (NEW YORK CITY)

To me, tuna doesn't even taste like tuna anymore unless it's seared with my **pepper** mix of toasted and ground black and pink peppercorns, coriander, and star anise. The same mix is also great on beef, buffalo, and venison.

— **SHARON HAGE,** YORK STREET (DALLAS)

We don't have sixteen types of **pepper** here; we use a basic black Tellicherry peppercorn and a little bit of red pepper flakes. I will occasionally go to an Asian market to get a pepper that has a sweet element to it, as these also tend to have a fruitiness to them that works well in braised dishes.

— **SHARON HAGE,** YORK STREET (DALLAS)

PEPPER, WHITE
Taste: hot
Weight: light–medium
Volume: moderate (Note: White pepper is "quieter," i.e., milder, than black pepper.)
Tips: Add at the end of the cooking process.

Asian cuisines
charcuterie
cloves
European cuisines
fish, esp. white
ginger
halibut
Japanese cuisine
lemongrass
nutmeg
potatoes
quatre épices (key ingredient)
sauces, esp. light-colored or white
soups, esp. light-colored or white
Thai cuisine
**white and other light-colored
    foods**

PEPPERS, BELL
(See Bell Peppers)

PEPPERS, CHILE (See Chile Peppers)

PEPPERS, PEPPADEW
Peppadew peppers, which are from South Africa, started coming to the U.S. just a few years ago. I stuff them with goat cheese and wrap them in Serrano

ham before frying them. You get sweetness and spice from the peppers, saltiness from the ham, creaminess from the cheese, and crunchiness from the frying. Doing so gives them so much flavor, I don't need to add anything else.

— **BOB IACOVONE,** CUVÉE (NEW ORLEANS)

PEPPERS, PIQUILLO

(Spanish peppers)

Taste: hot
Weight: medium
Volume: moderate–loud
Techniques: roast

aioli
almonds
anchovies
artichokes
asparagus
beef
bread
calamari
CHEESE: goat, **manchego**
chicken
chickpeas
chocolate, bitter
chorizo
clams
crab
eggs
fish, esp. cod, redfish, white
garlic
lamb
lemon
meat
mushrooms

Dishes

Green Olives Stuffed with Piquillo Peppers and Anchovies
— José Andrés, Café Atlántico (Washington, DC)

Piquillo Peppers Filled with Manchego Cheese, Avocado Leaf — and Hoja Santa — Seasoned Refried Beans and Vanilla — Bitter Chocolate Sauce
— Maricel Presilla, Zafra (Hoboken, New Jersey)

OLIVE OIL

olives
onions
orange
paprika, smoked
pork
potatoes
salads
salmon
salt
seafood
shrimp
soups
Spanish cuisine
stews
sugar
tomatoes
tuna

PEPPERS, SPANISH

Guindilla peppers are used to give heat in Spanish cooking. If you were cooking beans, you would add your parsley sprig, half an onion, garlic, carrot, and one guindilla pepper. **Nora peppers** are smoked, bell-shaped peppers from Catalonia used for romesco sauce. They are similar to Mexican guajillo peppers. **Chorizero peppers** are bittersweet. Their pulp is used in *salsa vizcaina,* which is a red sauce made with a lot of onions cooked down sweet, the chorizero pepper pulp, and either fish or bean stock. It's great served on fish or tripe.

— **ALEXANDRA RAIJ,** TÍA POL (NEW YORK CITY)

PERSIMMONS

Season: autumn–winter
Taste: sweet–sour
Weight: medium–heavy
Volume: moderate–loud
Techniques: bake, broil, raw

almonds
apples
avocados
bourbon
brandy
caramel
cashews
cheese, esp. creamy, goat
chile peppers, serrano
chocolate, white
cinnamon
cloves
coffee
cognac
cream and ice cream
custard
endive
frisée
ginger
grapes, esp. red
hazelnuts
honey
Kirsch
kiwi
kumquats
lemon: juice, zest
liqueurs, esp. orange
mace
maple syrup
nutmeg
oatmeal
oil, hazelnut
olive oil
orange
pears
pecans
pepper, black
pomegranates
pork
poultry
prosciutto

Because of the texture and unique flavor of a **persimmon**, no matter what you do it will always taste like persimmon pudding. I decided two years ago to stop trying to do anything else with persimmons. Why try and reinvent the wheel? To work with persimmons, you first put them in the freezer overnight to ripen, then peel and puree them. Persimmons are pretty astringent, so you need to add a lot of spices and sugar to them. The combination of allspice, cinnamon, and ginger that you see in traditional recipes is nice with persimmons, and adds an interesting complexity to the flavor.

— EMILY LUCHETTI, FARALLON (SAN FRANCISCO)

puddings
radicchio
raisins
rum, esp. dark
salads: fruit, green
salt
seafood
sorbet
sugar: brown, white
sweet potatoes
vanilla
vinegar: champagne, red wine, sherry, white wine
walnuts
watercress
wine, sweet (e.g., Sauternes)
yogurt

Flavor Affinities
persimmons + allspice + cinnamon + ginger

PHEASANT

Season: autumn
Weight: medium
Volume: moderate
Techniques: grill, roast
Tips: Wrap with bacon to keep from drying out when roasting.

apples
bacon
basil
bay leaf
butter
buttermilk
cabbage, esp. savoy
Calvados
chestnuts
cider
cinnamon
cream: heavy, sour
foie gras
French cuisine, esp. southern
GARLIC
Italian cuisine, esp. southern
lemon, juice
mushrooms, esp. wild
nutmeg
olive oil
onions
orange
parsley, flat-leaf
port
POTATOES
raisins
sage
sauerkraut
shallots
Spanish cuisine, esp. southern

Dishes

Pheasant: Cider, Shallot, and Burning Leaves
— Grant Achatz, Alinea (Chicago)

Cinnamon-Roasted Pheasant with Applewood-Smoked Bacon and Red Chile Pecan Sauce
— Robert Del Grande, Café Annie (Houston)

squash, winter
tarragon
THYME
truffles
wild rice
wine

Flavor Affinities
pheasant + apples + potatoes

PICKLES

I lived in Japan for two years where I fell in love with **pickles** and pickling. For pickling, I use the proportions that are common for seasoning Japanese sushi rice, though I'll admit that there might be a sushi chef out there who might disagree with me: 9 parts vinegar to 5 parts sugar, 1 part salt, and 1 part water. Pickles are one of those things I love to have in my pantry because they are so fun to use and make so many things yummy. It is definitely one of my tricks that I keep stashed away. I like to pickle Swiss chard stems with raw beets and star anise. They are great together and work as a garnish on our Nantucket Bay scallop dish.

— MICHAEL ANTHONY, GRAMERCY TAVERN (NEW YORK CITY)

PIMENTON (See also Paprika)

I don't even like to use the word "paprika" when referring to *pimenton.* It is not the same as Hungarian paprika, which is just dried pepper and doesn't taste like anything else. The Spanish were the first to plant peppers. Our *pimenton* has the right touch of sweetness, bitterness, and smoke. Used in a dish it makes the dish a whole new thing. Sprinkled on octopus, it is astonishing.

— JOSÉ ANDRÉS, CAFÉ ATLÁNTICO (WASHINGTON, DC)

Dishes

Pineapple-Vanilla Vacherin with Coconut Gelée
— Daniel Boulud, Restaurant Daniel, New York City

Warm Pineapple Cake "Sottosopra" with Rum Zabaione
— Gina DePalma, pastry chef, Babbo (New York City)

Exotic Fruit and Mint Salad, Star Anise Tuile
— Dominique and Cindy Duby, Wild Sweets (Vancouver)

Pineapple Rum Soup with Passion Fruit and Mango Gelée, Coconut Tapioca, Pink Peppercorn–Pineapple Sorbet
— Gale Gand, pastry chef, Tru (Chicago)

Pineapple Sorbet, Candied Pine Nut Tart, and Pineapple Chip
— Thomas Keller, The French Laundry (Yountville, California)

Fermented Pineapple Peel Drink
— Maricel Presilla, Zafra (Hoboken, New Jersey)

Grilled Pineapple, Avocado, and Watercress
— Maricel Presilla, Zafra (Hoboken, New Jersey)

Roasted Pineapple with Pistachio Ice Cream
— Eric Ripert, Le Bernardin (New York City)

PINEAPPLES
Season: winter–summer
Taste: sweet
Weight: medium
Volume: moderate
Techniques: bake, broil, grill, poach, raw, roast, sauté

allspice
apricots
avocado
baked goods
BANANAS
basil
brandy
butter, unsalted
caramel
cardamom
cashews
cayenne
cheese: blue (some)
chicken

Pineapple is 80 to 90 percent water. We'll freeze the pineapple, then pull it out and put it in a colander, and let the juice run out of it — which has all the flavor of the pineapple. After pressing out all the juice, we'll throw out the now-flavorless pulp, and use just the juice. You can do the same with strawberries or other fruits to obtain a clear juice, which you can use in drinks or, frozen and scraped, as fruit crystals to serve with a dessert.

— DOMINIQUE AND CINDY DUBY, WILD SWEETS (VANCOUVER)

I like the combination of rosemary with **pineapple**.

— MICHAEL LAISKONIS, LE BERNARDIN (NEW YORK CITY)

Pineapple benefits from a touch of vanilla.

— GINA DEPALMA, BABBO (NEW YORK CITY)

chile peppers: fresh, dried, red, green (e.g., jalapeño)
chocolate
cilantro
cinnamon
cloves
COCONUT: meat, milk
cognac
Cointreau
cream and ice cream
cream, Bavarian style
curry
fennel seeds
fruits, tropical
ginger
Grand Marnier
grapefruit
ham
honey
Kirsch
kiwi fruit
kumquats
lemon: juice, zest
lemongrass
LIME: juice, zest
macadamia nuts
MANGOES
maple syrup
marinades
meat
mint
olive oil
onion, red

oranges: fruit, marmalade
papaya
passion fruit
pepper, black
pistachios
pomegranate
poultry
raspberries
rice/rice pudding
rosemary
RUM
saffron
salads, fruit
salt, esp. *fleur de sel,* kosher
seafood (e.g., shrimp)
shallots

spinach
star anise
strawberries
SUGAR: brown, white
sweet potatoes
Szechuan pepper
tamarind
tapioca
VANILLA
vinegar, rice
walnuts
watercress
wine, sweet (e.g., Vin Santo)
yogurt

Flavor Affinities
pineapple + avocado + watercress
pineapple + banana + ginger + rum + sugar + vanilla
pineapple + berries + citrus + mangoes + star anise
pineapple + coconut + honey + oranges
pineapple + ice cream + brown sugar + vanilla
pineapple + lime + sugar
pineapple + Madeira + brown sugar + vanilla
pineapple + rum + sugar
pineapple + rum + vanilla + walnuts

You have to be careful with **pine nuts** because they are so strong that they will dominate a dessert. If I use even a small amount in an apple dessert, it turns it into a pine nut dessert.

— **EMILY LUCHETTI**, FARALLON (SAN FRANCISCO)

Pine nuts are really fatty and luxurious, so I like to use salt with them for balance. Even in a pesto, you notice the flavor of pine nuts versus using walnuts or no nuts.

— **GINA DEPALMA**, BABBO (NEW YORK CITY)

PINE NUTS
Weight: light
Volume: moderate
Techniques: toast

apples
apricots
basil
bell peppers
Central American cuisine
cheese: feta, goat, Parmesan, ricotta
cookies
Eastern Mediterranean cuisine
French cuisine, esp. southern
garlic
honey
Italian cuisine, esp. southern
lemon
liqueurs, orange
mascarpone
Mexican sauces
Middle Eastern cuisine
Moroccan cuisine
olive oil
onions
orange
pears
PESTO (key ingredient)
prunes
raisins
raspberries
rice
rum
sauces
Spanish cuisine, esp. southern
sugar
vanilla
vegetables, esp. roasted
walnuts
wine: red, sweet

Flavor Affinities
pine nuts + apples + apricots + rosemary
pine nuts + basil + garlic + olive oil + Parmesan cheese (pesto)

PINOT NOIR
Weight: light–medium
Volume: quiet–moderate

beef
chicken
duck
lamb
mushrooms
pork
salmon
tuna
veal

PIQUANCY
Taste: hot
Volume: loud
Function: warming
Tips: Stimulates appetite; enhances other flavors (e.g., salty, sour).

Heat [aka **piquancy**] can come from a grind of black pepper when you are cooking, or at the last second on top of a salad before it goes out. Heat can also come from some jalapeño in steamed cockles with ginger and lemongrass. In either case, heat adds a brightness to the dish.

— **SHARON HAGE**, YORK STREET (DALLAS)

cayenne
chile peppers
garlic
ginger
horseradish
mustard, hot
onions, esp. raw
pepper, black
red pepper flakes
spices, many
wasabi

PISTACHIO OIL (See Oil, Pistachio)

PISTACHIOS (See also Nuts — In General)
Season: year-round
Weight: medium
Volume: moderate
Techniques: raw, roast, salt

anchovies
apples
apricots
artichokes
arugula
asparagus
bananas
basil
beets
cardamom
cauliflower
cheese: goat, Parmesan, ricotta, Taleggio
cherries
chicken
chocolate: dark, white
coconut
cranberries
cream and ice cream

Dishes

Pistachio and Chocolate Semifreddo
— Gina DePalma, pastry chef, Babbo (New York City)

A Checkerboard Terrine of Pistachio and White Chocolate Ice Cream with Blackberry Sauce
— Patrick O'Connell, The Inn at Little Washington (Washington, Virginia)

Pistachios are a distinctively flavored nut. You need to be sure that what you pair with them will stand up. They go well with raspberries but not strawberries because the latter are softer in flavor.
— **EMILY LUCHETTI**, FARALLON (SAN FRANCISCO)

Pistachios look great with other nuts because you get green and brown alongside each other. They can be pretty mild so they are less about flavor and more about color and texture. Since pistachios are so mild I like to feature them solo or in a large quantity so they don't get lost. I make a chocolate semifreddo and there is pistachio in the semifreddo, there is pistachio paste, they are on the plate, and they are in the sauce. They are front and center.
— **GINA DEPALMA**, BABBO (NEW YORK CITY)

dates
duck
Eastern Mediterranean cuisine
endive
figs: dried, fresh
foie gras
ginger
gooseberries
honey
Italian cuisine
kumquats
lavender
leeks
lemon
mangoes
mascarpone
Moroccan cuisine
nectarines
orange
parsley
pasta and pasta sauces
pastries
pâtés
PEACHES
poultry
prunes
quince

raisins, esp. golden
raspberries
rice
rosemary
rose water
sausages
sugar
vanilla
watermelon
yogurt

AVOID
strawberries, which pistachios
   can easily overpower

PLANTAINS, GREEN

Botanical relatives: bananas
Weight: medium
Volume: quiet–moderate
Techniques: bake, boil, deep-fry, mash, sauté
Tips: Look for green plantains without any yellow.

African cuisine
bacon
butter

cardamom
Central American cuisine
chicken
chile peppers
cilantro
cinnamon
cloves
coriander
cumin
curry
fruits, tropical
garam masala
garlic
ginger
lime, juice
Mexican cuisine
molasses
oil: canola, vegetable
onions, esp. red
pepper, esp. black
pork
rice
salsa
salt, esp. kosher
soups
stews
yogurt

PLANTAINS, SWEET

Taste: sweet
Botanical relatives: bananas
Weight: medium
Volume: moderate
Techniques: bake, boil, deep-fry, sauté
Tip: Look for yellow to black plantains that ripen to black.

African cuisine
allspice
butter
Central American cuisine
chicken
chocolate
cinnamon
cloves
coconut
cranberries
cream and ice cream

fruits, tropical
ginger
honey
lemon, juice
lime, juice
Mexican cuisine
molasses
oil: canola, vegetable
orange: fruit, juice, zest
pepper, black
rice
rum, esp. dark
salt
star anise
sugar, esp. brown
toffee

PLUMS

Season: late spring–early autumn
Taste: sweet, astringent
Weight: light
Volume: moderate
Techniques: bake, poach, raw, stew

allspice
almonds
anise
anise hyssop
apricots, pureed
arugula
bay leaf
brandy, esp. plum
butter, unsalted
buttermilk
caramel
cardamom
cherries
cider
CINNAMON
cloves
coriander
cornmeal
cream and ice cream
crème fraîche
custard
French cuisine
gin
ginger

hazelnuts
honey
juniper berries
Kirsch
lavender
LEMON: juice, zest
liqueurs: almond, orange, plum
mace
maple syrup
mint
nectarines
nutmeg
oatmeal
olive oil
onions, red
ORANGE: juice, zest
peaches
pecans
pepper, black
pies
prosciutto
raisins
raspberries
rum, dark
sage
salads
sour cream
strawberries
SUGAR: brown, confectioners', white
thyme
VANILLA
vinegar: balsamic, cider
walnuts
whiskey
wine, dry red or white or dessert
wine: port or sweet (e.g., plum)
yogurt

Dishes

Plum and Bay Leaf Soup with Vanilla Yogurt Sorbetto
— Gina DePalma, pastry chef, Babbo (New York City)

Plum Cornmeal Cake with Plum Sorbet
— Emily Luchetti, pastry chef, Farallon (San Francisco)

Flavor Affinities

plums + arugula + prosciutto
plums + bay leaf + vanilla
plums + cinnamon + cloves + red wine + sugar
plums + cinnamon + orange
plums + cream + sugar + vanilla
plums + ginger + raspberries
plums + ginger + yogurt

PLUMS, DRIED (aka prunes)

Season: year-round
Taste: sweet
Weight: medium–heavy
Volume: moderate
Techniques: raw, stew

allspice
almonds
anise
apples
apricots, dried
*ARMAGNAC
bacon
baked goods
bay leaf
brandy, esp. apple, pear
caramel
cheese, esp. blue, goat, ricotta
chestnuts
chocolate: dark, white
cinnamon
cloves
coffee
cognac
cream and ice cream
crème fraîche

I like **plums** with anise hyssop. That is a classic flavor combination and I serve it every year. They also work well with sage, and I have made sage ice cream to serve with plums.
— **GINA DEPALMA**, BABBO (NEW YORK CITY)

cumin
currants
custard
dates
figs, esp. dried
French cuisine
game
game birds
ginger
hazelnuts
honey, wildflower
lemon, zest
liqueurs: almond, other nut
macadamia nuts
maple syrup
Moroccan cuisine
oatmeal
orange, zest
pâté
pears
pecans
pepper, black
pine nuts
pistachios
pork
port, esp. tawny
quince
rabbit
raisins
rice pudding
rum
Southern Comfort
star anise
stews
sugar: brown, white
teas, esp. black or Earl Grey
thyme
turkey
vanilla
vinegar: champagne, white wine
WALNUTS
whiskey
WINE: dry red (e.g., Bordeaux,
    Cabernet Sauvignon),
    Sauternes, sweet white
    (e.g., Muscat)

Flavor Affinities

prunes + allspice + bay leaf + cinnamon + black pepper
prunes + apples + brandy + vanilla + yogurt
prunes + Armagnac + chocolate
prunes + Armagnac + crème fraîche
prunes + brandy + cream + vanilla
prunes + cheese + cumin + walnuts
prunes + cognac + honey + Sauternes

POLENTA

Weight: medium
Volume: quiet
Techniques: simmer
Tips: Grill or sauté cooked
polenta.

bay leaf
beef
bell peppers, esp. red
butter, unsalted
CHEESE: Fontina, Gorgonzola,
    Gruyère, mozzarella,
    Parmesan, Taleggio
chervil
chicken
chives
cream / milk
egg, yolks
game birds
garlic
herbs
honey
Italian cuisine, esp. northern
marjoram
mascarpone
mushrooms, esp. chanterelles,
    porcini, shiitakes
oil: truffle, walnut
olive oil
parsley, flat-leaf
pepper: black, white

pork
red pepper flakes
rosemary
salt: kosher, sea
sausages
scallions
stocks: chicken, vegetable
thyme
tomatoes and tomato sauce
truffles, white
walnuts

Flavor Affinities

polenta + chanterelle
    mushrooms + white truffle oil
polenta + Gorgonzola cheese +
    mascarpone + walnuts
polenta + Parmesan cheese +
    rosemary

POMEGRANATES

Season: autumn
Taste: sour, sweet
Function: cooling
Weight: light–medium
Volume: moderate
Techniques: raw, ice/sorbet

allspice
almonds
arugula
avocados

Dishes

Cornish Game Hens with Pomegranate Sauce and Toasted Almonds
— Rafih Benjelloun, Imperial Fez (Atlanta)

Pomegranate Glazed Specialty Chicken Breast with Coconut-Onion Curry
— Vikram Vij and Meeru Dhalwala, Vij's (Vancouver)

bananas
beets
cardamom
chicken
chile peppers
chocolate, white
cinnamon
cloves
coconut
coriander
couscous
cream
cucumbers
cumin
curry
desserts
fish
garlic
ginger, esp. fresh
grapefruit
hazelnuts
honey
hummus
kumquat
lamb
legumes
lemon, juice
lime, juice
meats, roasted
Middle Eastern cuisine
nutmeg
olive oil
onions
orange, juice
parsley
pine nuts
pomegranate molasses (key
    ingredient)
pork
poultry (e.g., turkey)
SALADS, esp. cucumber, fruit,
    green
sesame seeds
sorbets
stewed dishes
sugar
tequila
turmeric

What is nice about **pomegranates** is that they are very flavorful but don't have a lot of sugar in them. They also have a unique flavor that is not like anything else. It is one of the few flavors that have come around in popularity because they have made it easier to use [via pomegranate juice, molasses, etc.]. Cleaning them to use just the seeds can be a pain in the neck. However, I use the juice because it makes a great sorbet.

— **EMILY LUCHETTI,** FARALLON (SAN FRANCISCO)

vinegar: balsamic, red wine
walnuts
wine: port, red, white

Flavor Affinities
pomegranates + almonds +
    cinnamon + cloves + garlic +
    ginger + honey
pomegranates + chicken +
    coconut + curry + onions
pomegranates + lemon + sugar

POMEGRANATE MOLASSES
Taste: sweet, sour
Weight: medium–heavy
Volume: moderate–loud

allspice
beef
chicken
chile peppers
cinnamon
cloves
duck
game
game birds
ginger
lamb
marinades
meats
Middle Eastern cuisine

Pomelo is good in salads. During the summer, we will mix it with pickled ginger and a couple of other ingredients and serve it on chicken or fish.

— **BRAD FARMERIE,** PUBLIC
(NEW YORK CITY)

mustard
mustard seeds
olive oil
pepper
pork
poultry
salad dressings
vinegar, balsamic
walnuts

POMELOS (See also Grapefruit)
Taste: sour, sweet
Weight: light
Volume: loud
Techniques: broil, raw

avocado
chicken
chili powder
coconut
crab
fish
fish sauce
ginger, pickled
lemongrass
maple
onions
peanuts
pomegranate
salads
salt
scallops
shrimp
spinach

Flavor Affinities
pomelo + pickled ginger + fish
pomelo + salt + chili powder

PONZU SAUCE

Taste: sour
Weight: light–medium
Volume: moderate–loud

beef
dashi
fish, esp. grilled or raw
Japanese cuisine
meat, esp. grilled
sashimi
shellfish
soy sauce
ume (Japanese plum)

POPPY SEEDS

Taste: sweet
Weight: light
Volume: quiet

apples
Asian cuisine
BAKED GOODS (e.g., breads, cakes, cookies, pastries)
beans, green
butter, unsalted
buttermilk
cabbage
carrots
cauliflower
cheese, ricotta
cinnamon
cloves
cream
curry powder
desserts
eggplant
eggs and egg dishes
fish
fruits
ginger
honey
Indian cuisine
lemon
Mediterranean cuisine
noodles
nutmeg
onions, esp. sweet

pasta
pastries
potatoes
rice
salads and salad dressings, esp. creamy
sauces, esp. creamy
sesame seeds
sour cream
spinach
strawberries
sugar
Turkish cuisine
vanilla
vegetables
walnuts
zucchini

PORK — IN GENERAL

Season: autumn
Taste: sweet–astringent
Function: heating
Techniques: Use dry-heat cooking (e.g., broil, grill, roast) for tender cuts of pork, and moist-heat cooking (e.g., braise, stew) for tougher cuts of pork.

aioli
almonds
anchovies
anise
APPLES: cider, fruit, juice
apricots
asparagus
bacon
barbecue dishes
basil
bay leaf
beans: green, navy, white
beer
bell peppers: green, red
bourbon
brandy
bread crumbs
butter, unsalted
cabbage: green, red
Calvados

capers
caraway seeds
cardamom
carrots
cayenne
celery
cheese: Gruyère, Jack
chile peppers, esp. anchos, dried red, jalapeño
chili powder
Chinese cuisine
chives
cider
cilantro
cinnamon
cloves
coconut milk
coriander
cornichons
corn
cranberries
cream
cumin
curry powder
fennel
fennel seeds
figs
fish sauce, Thai
French cuisine, esp. southern
fruit: dried, fresh
GARLIC
ginger: fresh, ground dried
ham, Serrano
honey
horseradish
Italian cuisine, esp. southern
ketchup
Korean cuisine, esp. northern
LEMON: juice, zest
lemongrass
lemon verbena
lentils
lime, juice
mace
mangoes: green, ripe
marjoram
Mexican cuisine
mint, esp. spearmint

Dishes

Rack of Pork, Marinated in Oranges, Thyme, and Garlic, Served with Fennel and Black Olive Ouzo and Orange Sauce
— Ann Cashion, Cashion's Eat Place (Washington, DC)

Suckling Pig with Quince Paste and Romesco Sauce
— Suzanne Goin, at the 2003 James Beard Awards gala reception

Roasted Rack of Pork with Apple Butter Glaze, Country Ham Spoon Bread, Roasted Apples, Mustard Greens, and Bourbon Glaze
— Bob Kinkead, Colvin Run (Vienna, Virginia)

Beer-Braised Pork Belly with Sauerkraut and Ginger Jus
— Gabriel Kreuther, The Modern (New York City)

Organic Berkshire Pork Tenderloin Marinated in Wheat Beer with Barley Risotto, Turnips, and Chicory Emulsion
— Gabriel Kreuther, The Modern (New York City)

Pork with Fig Maple Jus and Dutch Cabbage
— Monica Pope, T'afia (Houston)

Cuban Roast Pork Marinated in an Allspice-Cumin Adobo with Ripe Plantains, Rich Oaxacan Six-Chile Mole Sauce, and "Moors and Christians" Rice
— Maricel Presilla, Zafra (Hoboken, New Jersey)

Trio of Pan-Seared Pork Tenderloin with House-Made Sausage and Potato Pierogis
— Celina Tio, American Restaurant (Kansas City)

Marinated Pork Medallions with Garlic-Yogurt Curry and Naan Bread
— Vikram Vij and Meeru Dhalwala, Vij's (Vancouver)

You'll often see what is essentially clam chowder [without the clams] used as a sauce: the combination of **pork** — whether it's bacon, chorizo, or whatever — and thyme, served with potatoes and cream. It could be served with something poached or sautéed. It is a cute reworking of something that is classic.
— **DAVID WALTUCK**, CHANTERELLE (NEW YORK CITY)

I like the combination of **pork** with fruit. With a pork chop, fresh and dried figs or strawberries would all work.
— **MARCEL DESAULNIERS**, THE TRELLIS (WILLIAMSBURG, VIRGINIA)

Sauces often don't do justice to the meat they're saucing. For that reason, we don't use veal stock with **pork**, which hides the flavor of the meat. Instead, we want to do everything we can to emphasize the flavor of the pork itself. So, we'll roast the pork scraps and bones and make a pork stock instead. In the summertime, to keep it light, we won't even add wine.
— **DAN BARBER**, BLUE HILL AT STONE BARNS (POCANTICO HILLS, NEW YORK)

mirepoix
molasses
mushrooms, esp. shiitake
mustard, Dijon
mustard seeds
noodles/pasta
nutmeg
OIL: canola, grapeseed, sesame, vegetable
olive oil
olives
ONIONS, esp. green, pearl, red, sweet, white, yellow
ORANGE: juice, zest
oregano
paprika: smoked, sweet
parsley, flat-leaf
peanuts and peanut sauce
pears
peas, black-eyed
pecans
*****PEPPER: black,** white
pineapple
pine nuts
piquillo peppers
plums
port
potatoes, mashed or roasted
prosciutto
prunes
quince
radicchio
red pepper flakes
rice or risotto
ROSEMARY
saffron
sage
salt: kosher, sea
sauerkraut
shallots
sherry, cream
sour cream
soy sauce
spaetzle
Spanish cuisine, esp. southern
squash: acorn, butternut
star anise
stock, chicken

Pork can handle all the sweet spices, including allspice, cinnamon, and clove.

— **BRADFORD THOMPSON,** MARY ELAINE'S AT THE PHOENICIAN (SCOTTSDALE, ARIZONA)

sugar (pinch)
sweet potatoes
Tabasco sauce
tangerine, juice
tea, black (e.g., Lapsang Souchong)
THYME
tomatoes and tomato paste
turmeric
turnips
vanilla
verjus
vermouth, dry
Vietnamese cuisine
VINEGAR: balsamic, red wine, rice wine, sherry, white wine
walnuts
watercress
wine: dry red, white
Worcestershire sauce
yogurt

Flavor Affinities
pork + allspice + mace
pork + apples + mustard
pork + bacon + mustard + sauerkraut
pork + chile peppers + cilantro + garlic + lime + peanuts
pork + cinnamon + star anise
pork + coriander + honey + soy sauce
pork + clove + garlic + orange
pork + cream + potatoes + thyme
pork + curry + garlic + yogurt
pork + fennel + garlic
pork + garlic + ginger + molasses
pork + ginger + honey + soy sauce
pork + mustard + sauerkraut
pork + port + rosemary

PORK — BACON
(See Bacon)

PORK — BELLY
Techniques: braise, double-cook, pan-fry

apples
bacon
bay leaf
beets
caraway
carrots
celery
cilantro
cinnamon
citrus
cumin
eggs
fennel
garlic
leeks

mushrooms
oil, peanut
olive oil
onions
paprika
parsley, flat-leaf
parsnips
pepper, black
potatoes
rosemary
sake
salt: kosher, sea
shallots
soy sauce
star anise
stocks: chicken, veal
thyme
vegetables, root
vinegar, champagne
zucchini

PORK — CHOPS
Techniques: dry-heat cooking (e.g., broil, grill, roast, sauté)

APPLES: cider, fruit, sauce
arugula
beans
bread crumbs
broccoli rabe
butter
cabbage, red
coriander
corn
fennel
fennel pollen

I'm sometimes inspired by looking back to my childhood and the combinations of flavors I liked. I was a pretty picky eater growing up, but I loved my macaroni and cheese, and bacon and eggs. I came up with a take on bacon and eggs substituting **pork belly** for the bacon. I love pork belly — it is a poor man's foie gras, the way it just melts in your mouth. I make the eggs in a double boiler that gives them a creamy texture, and finish them with fresh herbs. For the belly, we grill it and then braise it in citrus, champagne vinegar, and veal stock for six hours. Then at serving, we grill it again and top it with a "sweet heat" sauce which is like a barbecue sauce with layers and layers of flavor.

— **BOB IACOVONE,** CUVÉE (NEW ORLEANS)

Dishes

Grilled Pork Chop with Artichokes, Cipollini, and Aceto Manodori
— Mario Batali, Babbo (New York City)

Pork Chop, Creamed Sweet Corn, Pan-Fried Summer Squash, and Crushed Blackberries
— Cory Schreiber, Wildwood (Portland, Oregon)

garlic
ginger
greens
honey
lemon, juice
lentils
molasses
mustard (esp. Dijon) and
   mustard seeds
olive oil
onions
peaches
pepper, black
polenta
potatoes: mashed, steamed
prosciutto
rosemary
SAGE
sauerkraut
spinach
stock, chicken
sugar: brown, white
tomatoes
vanilla
vinegar: balsamic, cider

Flavor Affinities
pork chop + apples + ginger +
   sage
pork chop + arugula + tomatoes
pork chop + greens + sweet
   potatoes
pork chop + peaches + balsamic
   vinegar

PORK — HAM (See Ham)

PORK — LOIN
Techniques: dry-heat cooking
(e.g., bake, braise, grill, roast,
sauté)

bay leaf
brandy
cabbage, red
chile peppers, ancho
cilantro
cinnamon
figs
garlic
ginger
lemongrass
lime, juice
maple syrup
mustard
mustard seeds
onions
oregano
port
potatoes
rosemary
sage
sake
soy sauce
stock, chicken
thyme
vinegar, white
wine, white

Flavor Affinities
pork loin + figs + onions
pork loin + red cabbage + port
   wine

PORK — RIBS
Techniques: bake, barbecue,
braise, broil, grill, roast, sauté

allspice
bay leaf
beer
bourbon
butter

cabbage
chile peppers, guajillo
chili powder
cider
coffee
coriander
cumin
garlic
ginger
hoisin sauce
honey
hot sauce
ketchup
lemongrass
liquid smoke
mirepoix
molasses
mustard, Dijon
olive oil
onions, esp. white
oregano
paprika: hot, smoked
parsley, flat-leaf
pepper, black
potatoes
salt: kosher, sea
sesame oil
soy sauce
sugar, brown
Tabasco sauce
thyme
tomatoes and tomato puree
vinegar: apple cider, balsamic,
   red wine, sherry, white wine
Worcestershire sauce

PORK — SAUSAGE
(See Sausages)

PORK — SHOULDER
Techniques: moist-heat
cooking (e.g., barbecue, braise,
stew)

achiote
allspice
andouille sausage (key
   ingredient)

apples
barbecue sauce
bay leaf
cayenne
chile peppers
cinnamon
coriander
cornmeal (e.g., grits, polenta)
couscous
cumin
five-spice powder
GARLIC
ginger
honey
lemon
lime
maple syrup
milk
mushrooms
orange
oregano
paprika
port
quince
rice
rum
sage
soy sauce
sugar, brown
thyme
tomatoes
vinegar
wine, red

Flavor Affinities
pork shoulder + bay leaves + wild mushrooms
pork shoulder + chipotle peppers + cumin + tomatoes
pork shoulder + plantains + rice + rum

PORK — TENDERLOIN
Techniques: dry-heat cooking (e.g., broil, grill, roast, sauté)

artichokes, Jerusalem
bacon

beans, green
cardamom
cilantro
cinnamon
corn
fennel
ginger
lime
maple syrup
marjoram
mushrooms, porcini, dried
mustard
olive oil
onions: cipollini, yellow
orange
oregano
pancetta
parsley
pepper, black
polenta
potatoes
red pepper flakes
rosemary
rum, esp. dark
sage
savory
sherry
sour cream
sugar, brown
tarragon
turmeric
vinegar, balsamic
yogurt

PORTUGUESE CUISINE
anise
bread
chile peppers, piri piri
cilantro
cinnamon
clams
cod
custards
eggs
fish
garlic
kale
olive oil

onions
paprika
parsley
pork, esp. cured
port
potatoes
rice
saffron
shellfish
tomatoes
turkey
vanilla

Flavor Affinities
clams + garlic + paprika + pork
cod + eggs + onions + potatoes
garlic + kale + onions + potatoes
piri piri peppers + garlic + lemon juice + olive oil + salt

POTATOES
Season: year-round
Function: cooling
Weight: medium–heavy
Volume: quiet
Techniques: bake, boil, deep-fry, gratin, grill, mash (use older, starchier potatoes), puree, roast, sauté, steam

arugula
bacon
basil
BAY LEAF
BEEF
bell peppers, green, esp. roasted
BUTTER, unsalted
buttermilk
caraway seeds
cardamom
carrots
cauliflower (e.g., Indian cuisine)
caviar
cayenne
celery
celery root
CHEESE: Brin d'Amour, Cantal, cheddar, Comté, Dry Jack,

Emmental, Fontina, goat,
Gouda, Gruyère, manchego,
Parmesan, pecorino, raclette,
Roquefort, Torta del Casar
chervil
chicken
chickpeas (e.g., Indian cuisine)
chicory
chile peppers (e.g., Indian, Thai
cuisine)
chili oil
CHIVES
cilantro
cinnamon
cloves
coriander
CREAM / MILK
crème fraîche
cumin
curry
dill
eggs
French cuisine
garam masala
GARLIC
ginger
greens, winter
herbs
kale

> We make a **potato** stew with bacon, olives, mushrooms, and onions, which is perfect for cold winter Sunday suppers. We add two strong flavors — bacon and olives — to the potato. Onions and porcini mushrooms add another layer of flavor.
>
> — **MICHEL RICHARD,** CITRONELLE (WASHINGTON, DC)

lamb
lavender
LEEKS
lemon, juice
lovage
marjoram
mayonnaise
morels
mushrooms, esp. wild
mussels
mustard: Dijon, dry
nutmeg
OIL: canola, peanut, vegetable
olive oil
olives, e.g., black
ONIONS: green, red, Spanish,
Vidalia
oysters
paprika
parsley, flat-leaf
parsnips
peas
PEPPER: black, white

pork and pork belly
ramps
ROSEMARY
rutabagas
saffron
sage
salads
SALT: kosher, sea
salt cod
sausages: chorizo, Italian
savory
scallions
shallots
sorrel
sour cream
spinach (e.g., Indian cuisine)
squash, winter (e.g., butternut)
STEAK
STOCKS: chicken, vegetable
sweet potatoes
THYME
tomatoes
truffles, black

turmeric
turnips
vegetables, root
vinaigrettes
vinegar: champagne, sherry, white wine
wine, dry white
yogurt

Flavor Affinities
potatoes + bacon + cheese + onions
potatoes + chives + sour cream
potatoes + cream + garlic + Parmesan cheese + rosemary
potatoes + cream + leeks + oysters
potatoes + Gruyère cheese + winter squash
potatoes + leeks + nutmeg

POTATOES, NEW

Season: spring–summer
Weight: medium
Volume: quiet
Techniques: boil, roast, steam
Tips: New potatoes are best not baked or fried.

chives
cream
garlic
mint
olive oil
paprika
parsley
pepper, black
rosemary
salt
savory
shallots
tarragon
thyme
vinegar

Flavor Affinities
new potatoes + garlic + shallots + tarragon + vinegar

POULTRY (See Chicken, Turkey, etc.)

PROSCIUTTO

Taste: salty
Weight: light–medium (depending on thinness of slicing)
Volume: moderate

almonds
apples
arugula
asparagus
basil
cheese: Fontina, Gruyère, Parmesan, provolone
chestnuts
chicken
chicory
cilantro
fennel
FIGS
grapes
hazelnuts
honey
Italian cuisine
lemon, juice
lime, juice
*__MELON__, esp. cantaloupe, honeydew
mushrooms
mustard, esp. Dijon
mustard seeds
nectarines
olive oil
pasta
pears
pepper: black, white
pine nuts

Dishes

Prosciutto San Daniele with Black Pepper Fettunta and Figs
— Mario Batali, Babbo (New York City)

Fig and Prosciutto Pizza
— Todd English, Figs (Charlestown, Massachusetts)

pomegranate molasses
sage
spinach
tomatoes
walnuts

PRUNES (See Plums, Dried)

PUMPKIN (See also Squashes, Winter)

Season: autumn
Taste: sweet
Weight: medium–heavy
Volume: moderate
Techniques: bake, braise, grill, puree, roast

allspice
amaretti cookie crumbs
apples
bay leaf
brandy, esp. apple
BUTTER, unsalted
caramel
carrots
cayenne
CHEESE: feta, Gruyère, Parmesan
chile peppers
chocolate, white
cilantro
CINNAMON
CLOVES
coconut
cognac
cranberries
CREAM
cream cheese
crème anglaise
crème fraîche

Dishes

Pumpkin, Brown Sugar, and Tempura with Cinnamon Fragrance
— Grant Achatz, Alinea (Chicago)

Pumpkin "Lune" with Butter, Sage, and Amaretti
— Mario Batali, Babbo (New York City)

Creamy Pumpkin and Cream Cheese Custard with Orange-Rum Raisins
— Gina DePalma, pastry chef, Babbo (New York City)

Grilled Pineapple and Caribbean Pumpkin Salad with Pumpkin Seeds and Cacao Nib Vinaigrette
— Maricel Presilla, Zafra (Hoboken, New Jersey)

cumin
curry
custard
duck
garlic
GINGER: fresh, ground
hazelnuts
honey
Italian cuisine
kumquats
lemon, juice

lime, juice
lobster
mace
maple syrup
marjoram
molasses
mushrooms
NUTMEG
nuts
oatmeal
oil: sesame, vegetable

olive oil
onions: red, white
orange: juice, zest
orange liqueur (e.g., Grand Marnier)
oysters
pasta (e.g., ravioli, tortelli)
pecans
pepper: black, white
pine nuts
pork
potatoes
pumpkin: oil, seeds
radicchio
raisins
risotto
rosemary
rum, esp. dark
SAGE
salt, kosher
scallops
shrimp
soups
sour cream

With **pumpkin** or even sweet potatoes, the combination of allspice, cinnamon, ginger, and clove works great. If you buy canned pumpkin that has spices already added, it tastes a little off and artificial. Depending on how you like your spices, you typically add equal amounts of ginger and cinnamon and less allspice and clove because the last two are very strong.
— **EMILY LUCHETTI,** FARALLON (SAN FRANCISCO)

Pumpkin and butternut squash juices are great in dishes featuring [each respective vegetable]. What the juice does is intensify their flavor, making the dishes taste more natural.
— **ANDREW CARMELLINI,** A VOCE (NEW YORK CITY)

I had to come up with a recipe for a vegan cookbook, and ended up making a **pumpkin** and coconut milk custard thickened with agar-agar that was so delicious, I put it on the menu!
— **BRADFORD THOMPSON,** MARY ELAINE'S AT THE PHOENICIAN (SCOTTSDALE, ARIZONA)

Pumpkin and bay leaf together make the pumpkin taste even more pumpkin-like.
— **JERRY TRAUNFELD,** THE HERBFARM (WOODINVILLE, WASHINGTON)

My **pumpkin** pie soup dish was inspired by walking through Whole Foods and seeing pumpkins. I thought, How do I like my pumpkin? I like pumpkin pie, and thought it would actually make an interesting soup. I made a pumpkin soup and found the soup to be very savory with its spicing, and added smoked duck to it. I wanted a contrasting flavor, so I added some sweet meringue as a garnish. Then I needed a contrast to the creaminess, so I put in a piece of pie crust a second before serving as well as toasted pecans for even more crunch.
— **BOB IACOVONE,** CUVÉE (NEW ORLEANS)

stews
stock, chicken
SUGAR: brown, white
sweet potatoes
Thanksgiving
thyme
turnips
vanilla
vinegar, balsamic
walnuts
wine, dry white
wine, sweet
yogurt

PUMPKIN SEED OIL
(See Oil, Pumpkin Seed)

PUMPKIN SEEDS
Season: autumn
Weight: light
Volume: quiet
Techniques: bake, roast

caramel
chile peppers, jalapeño
cilantro
coriander
cumin
Mexican cuisine
salt

PURSLANE
Season: summer
Taste: sour
Weight: light
Volume: moderate
Techniques: raw, sauté

beans, green
cucumber
garlic

Flavor Affinities
pumpkin + allspice + bay leaf + cinnamon + salt
pumpkin + allspice + cinnamon + ginger
pumpkin + amaretti cookie crumbs + butter + pasta + sage
pumpkin + apples + curry
pumpkin + brown sugar + pine nuts
pumpkin + butter + garlic + chicken stock + thyme
pumpkin + chile peppers + garlic
pumpkin + cream cheese + orange + rum
pumpkin + cream cheese + pumpkin seeds + sugar
pumpkin + custard + garlic
pumpkin + honey + balsamic vinegar
pumpkin + olive oil + rosemary

Dishes

Pepitas: Toasted Pumpkin Seeds Seasoned with Cumin, Coriander, and Jalapeño
— Traci Des Jardins, Mijita (San Francisco)

Cilantro and Pumpkin Seed Pesto
— Jerry Traunfeld, The Herbfarm (Woodinville, Washington)

herbs: chervil, cilantro, mint
olive oil
smoked trout
tomatoes
vinegar, white wine
yogurt

QUAIL
Season: late spring–autumn
Weight: light–medium
Volume: quiet–moderate
Techniques: braise, broil, grill, pan roast, roast, sauté

almonds
anchovies
anisette
apples
arugula
bacon

bay leaf
bell peppers, esp. red
bourbon
brandy
butter, unsalted
capers
cardamom
carrots
chard
chestnuts
chicken livers
chile peppers, esp. green
chili powder
cinnamon
cloves
coconut
cognac
coriander
cream
cumin
currants
curries
dandelion greens
fennel
figs
foie gras

Wild **purslane** has a lemony flavor and waxy leaves. It makes me think of a salad of very young green beans that are three inches long and tossed with the purslane and a splash of white wine vinegar and Ligurian olive oil.

— **MICHAEL ANTHONY**, GRAMERCY TAVERN (NEW YORK CITY)

frisée
garlic
ginger, fresh or ground
grapes, esp. seedless
ham
honey
Italian cuisine
leeks
lemon, juice
lentils
maple syrup
marjoram
mint
molasses
mushrooms, wild
mustard, Dijon
OIL: canola, peanut, sesame,
   vegetable
olive oil
onions, spring

orange: juice, zest
oysters
pancetta
parsley, flat-leaf
pears
peas
pepper, black, pink
pine nuts
pistachios
polenta
pomegranates and pomegranate
   molasses
potatoes, esp. creamer
prosciutto
rosemary
saffron
sage
salsify
salt
sausage

scallions
shallots
sherry
soy sauce
stocks: chicken, vegetable
stuffing
sugar, brown
sumac
Tabasco sauce
tamarind
tarragon
THYME
tomato paste
truffles, white
vinaigrette
VINEGAR: balsamic, red wine,
   sherry
walnuts
wine: red, white

Quail is too delicate for rosemary, so I like it with a little lavender, pink
peppercorns, and *fleur de sel*.
— **SHARON HAGE,** YORK STREET (DALLAS)

Dishes

**Quail Corn Bread and Pecan Stuffed Breast, Leg Confit, Sweet Corn Pudding, and
Chanterelle Mushrooms**
— Jeffrey Buben, Vidalia (Washington, DC)

Glazed Quail with Caramelized Fennel Bulb and Tangerine Marmalade
— Thomas Keller, The French Laundry (Yountville, California)

**Walnut-Glazed Quail with a Ragout of Organic Shell Beans, Shiitake Mushrooms, and
Applewood-Smoked Bacon**
— Gabriel Kreuther, The Modern (New York City)

**Roast "Brace" of Quail and La Quercia "Americano" Prosciutto with a "Fondant"
of Austrian Crescent Potatoes, Roasted Acorn Squash, Red Pearl Onions, Swiss Chard,
and Tarragon**
— Carrie Nahabedian, Naha (Chicago)

Two Texas Cross Quail and Braised Cabbage with Apple and Hazelnuts
— Monica Pope, T'afia (Houston)

Roasted Quail with Smoked Bacon, Brussels Sprouts, and a Quail Jus
— Thierry Rautureau, Rover's (Seattle)

Pan-Fried Coriander Quail Cakes with Coconut Curried Vegetables
— Vikram Vij and Meeru Dhalwala, Vij's (Vancouver)

Flavor Affinities

quail + arugula + pomegranate
quail + bacon + Brussels sprouts
quail + bacon + garlic + lemon
quail + bourbon + molasses +
   pears
quail + chanterelle mushrooms +
   tarragon + tomato
quail + cinnamon + sumac
quail + figs + vinaigrette
quail + marjoram + olive oil +
   rosemary + sage + thyme

QUATRE ÉPICES

beef, esp. braised
charcuterie
duck
foie gras
French cuisine
game
pâté
sausages
soups
stews
vegetables
venison, esp. braised

Flavor Affinities

cloves (allspice or cinnamon) +
    ginger + nutmeg + black
    and/or white pepper

QUINCE

Season: autumn
Taste: sour
Weight: medium
Volume: moderate
Techniques: bake, poach, stew

almonds
*APPLES: fruit, juice
Armagnac
bay leaf
beef
brandy
butter, unsalted
Calvados
caramel
cardamom
CHEESE, ESP. GOAT,
    MANCHEGO, RICOTTA, and
    esp. with quince paste
cherries
chicken
cinnamon
cloves
cranberries
cream and ice cream
custards
dates
figs, esp. dried
fruits, dried, esp. apricots,
    cherries, plums
ginger
hazelnuts
honey
jams and jellies
kumquats
lamb
lemon, juice
liqueurs, nut
maple syrup
mascarpone
meats
nutmeg

Dishes

Roasted Quince, Foie Gras, and Candied Fennel with Sweet Spices
— Grant Achatz, Alinea (Chicago)

Quince and Marcona Almond "Crisp," Mascarpone Sorbet, and Pedro Ximenez Sherry Caramel
— Elizabeth Dahl, pastry chef, Naha (Chicago)

Quince-Filled Maple-Whiskey Cake with Goat Cheese Ice Cream
— Dominique and Cindy Duby, Wild Sweets (Vancouver)

Granny Smith Apple Sorbet, Quince, Quinoa, Pecans
— Johnny Iuzzini, pastry chef, Jean Georges (New York City)

Quince is something that will never be mainstream because of its unique flavor and the fact that you just can't peel it and eat it. But if you peel quince and cook it forever and show it some love, it is so much better than an apple or a pear.
— **EMILY LUCHETTI**, FARALLON (SAN FRANCISCO)

orange
*PEARS
pecans
pepper, black
pies (e.g., apple)
pistachios
poultry
raisins
raspberries
Spanish cuisine (quince paste)
star anise
sugar: brown, white
vanilla
walnuts
whiskey
wine: red, sweet
wine, white, e.g., Riesling
yogurt

RABBIT (See also Game — In General)

Season: autumn–winter
Taste: sweet–astringent
Function: heating
Weight: medium
Volume: quiet–moderate
Techniques: barbecue, braise (esp. legs, thighs), broil, grill, roast, sauté, stew

almonds
apples
artichokes
arugula
asparagus, white
BACON, esp. smoked
barbecue sauce
basil
bay leaf
beans: fava, green, white
beer
bell peppers
brandy
bread crumbs
butter, unsalted
cabbage, esp. red
carrots
cayenne
celery root
cherries
chervil
chiles, esp. Thai
chives
chocolate, esp. dark
cider
cilantro
cinnamon
cloves
coconut milk

Dishes

Rabbit Enchiladas with Red Chile Mole and Pumpkin Seeds
— Robert Del Grande, at the 2003 James Beard Awards gala reception

Braised Rabbit with Winter Vegetables, Abita Beer Bread, Truffled Parsnips
— Bob Iacovone, Cuvée (New Orleans)

Roast Loin of Rabbit with a "Ragoût" of Braised Rabbit, Confit Garlic Crushed Potatoes, Applewood Slab Bacon, "Hen of the Woods" Mushrooms, Glazed Young Carrots, and Turnips
— Carrie Nahabedian, Naha (Chicago)

Roasted Rabbit Saddle with Root Vegetables, Green Lentils, and a Game Jus
— Thierry Rautureau, Rover's (Seattle)

Rabbit Braised in Arneis with Chickpea Crepe and Pancetta
— Holly Smith, Café Juanita (Seattle)

Rabbit Consommé, Morels, Pea, and Lavender Emulsion
— Rick Tramonto, Tru (Chicago)

coriander
corn
cream
cumin
currants (e.g., currant jelly)
curry paste, Thai yellow
fennel leaves
fennel seeds
fish sauce, Thai
French cuisine
GARLIC
ginger
hazelnuts
Italian cuisine
leeks
lemon: juice, zest
lemongrass
lime: juice, leaves
Marsala
Mediterranean cuisine
mint
mirepoix
mushrooms
MUSTARD: Dijon, dry
OIL: canola, grapeseed, hazelnut, peanut, vegetable, walnut
olive oil
olives, esp. green, black, kalamata

ONIONS, esp. pearl, Spanish, yellow
orange, zest
oregano
pancetta
paprika: smoked, sweet
parsley, flat-leaf
pasta/noodles, egg
PEPPER: black, pink, white
pine nuts
plums
port
potatoes

prunes
rice and risotto
rosemary
saffron
sage
salt: kosher, sea
sesame seeds
shallots
soy sauce
spinach
star anise
STOCKS: chicken, rabbit, veal
sugar (pinch)
Tabasco sauce
tarragon
THYME
tomatoes and tomato paste
vegetable puree
VINEGAR: balsamic, cider, red wine, sherry, white wine
WINE: dry red, dry white (e.g., Riesling), Champagne

Flavor Affinities

rabbit + bacon + rosemary
rabbit + garlic + potatoes + rosemary + shallots
rabbit + mushrooms + noodles
rabbit + mushrooms + tarragon
rabbit + mustard + red wine
rabbit + vinegar + red wine
rabbit + rosemary + tomato
rabbit + shallots + white beans

A dish I am really proud of is our saddle of **rabbit** served with green olives, shallots, marjoram, and fennel jam. This is a light and beautifully balanced dish that reminds me of Liguria [in Italy]. The olives are salty, the marjoram is strong, and the fennel is sweet. This has been on our menu for over a year but it took me a few tries to get right. I tried black olives, but they were too strong. I tried rosemary, but it was too earthy. I tried Brussels sprouts, but they were a little too bitter and didn't complement the same way sweet fennel did. So though the combination didn't work for the saddle, the black olives and rosemary led me to add some rabbit liver and stuff a whole boned rabbit. That dish did work. The two dishes were different in the sense that the saddle with the green olives was a little more sophisticated while the whole rabbit was more of a peasant dish. Customers like both!

— **ODETTE FADA,** SAN DOMENICO (NEW YORK CITY)

RADICCHIO

Season: year-round
Taste: bitter
Weight: medium–heavy
Volume: moderate–loud
Techniques: braise, grill, roast, sear

anchovies
apples
arugula
bacon
beans, esp. shell, white
beef
butter
capers
CHEESE, esp. pungent and/or Asiago, blue, dry Jack, feta, **Gorgonzola**, Gruyère, **PARMESAN**
chicken, esp. roasted
chives
duck
eggs, esp. hard-boiled
endive
fennel
figs
fish
garlic
horseradish
ITALIAN CUISINE
lamb
lemon: juice, zest
lime, juice
lobster
mushrooms, wild
mustard, Dijon
oil, corn
OLIVE OIL
onions, red
orange: juice, zest
pancetta
parsley, flat-leaf
pasta
pears
pecans
pepper: black, white

pine nuts
pizza
pork
poultry
prosciutto
pumpkin and pumpkin oil
red pepper flakes
risotto
rosemary
salads and salad dressings
salami
SALT
seafood, esp. grilled or roasted
shallots
shrimp
squab
VINEGAR: BALSAMIC, red wine, sherry
walnuts
wine, dry white

Flavor Affinities

radicchio + arugula + endive
radicchio + Asiago cheese + olive oil + balsamic vinegar
radicchio + duck + risotto + reduced balsamic vinegar
radicchio + fennel + prosciutto
radicchio + Gorgonzola cheese + pears
radicchio + hard-boiled eggs + olive oil + prosciutto + sherry vinegar + walnuts
radicchio + mushrooms + risotto + balsamic vinegar

It's vital that you taste your ingredients to determine the best way to serve them. We got a new **radicchio** in that is so bitter it just won't work as a salad. Instead, we will turn it into a pesto or a tiny garnish.
— MONICA POPE, T'AFIA (HOUSTON)

Dishes

Grilled Radicchio Trevisano with Asiago and Horseradish
— Mario Batali, Babbo (New York City)

Radicchio Salad with Parmesan Balsamic Vinaigrette
— Hiro Sone and Lissa Doumani, Terra (St. Helena, California)

RADISHES

Season: spring–autumn
Taste: pungent
Function: heating
Weight: light
Volume: moderate–loud
Techniques: braise, raw

anchovies
avocados
basil
bread: French, rye
BUTTER, esp. sweet
celery
cheese, esp. blue, feta
chervil
chives
cilantro
crab
cream

There is a time of year when all there seems to be in the green market is **radishes.** You get sick of seeing them and they are there for months. I needed to create something new and all there was were radishes. So, I came up with a radish salad served with lobster. We blanch turnip rounds and fold in a little baby ginger to get this wonderfully peppery salad. The sauce with the lobster is a pistachio vinaigrette that is bound by onion puree and brightened by the juice that pickled the ginger. We finish the dish with toasted pistachios and add a pistachio oil. The pistachio nut and oil add an earthy quality and depth of flavor to the dish.

— MICHAEL ANTHONY, GRAMERCY TAVERN (NEW YORK CITY)

cream cheese
cucumbers
curry powder
dill
fennel
fish, esp. white
lemon, juice
lettuces
lobster
lovage
marjoram
mint
olive oil
onions
orange: fruit, juice
oregano
parsley, flat-leaf
pears
pecans
pepper
rosemary
salads
SALT, esp. SEA
scallions
sesame oil
shallots
shrimp
soy sauce
tamari
thyme
vinaigrettes
VINEGAR: cider, white wine

Flavor Affinities
radishes + bread + butter + salt

RAISINS

Taste: sweet
Weight: medium
Volume: moderate
Techniques: bake, raw, stew

allspice
almonds
anise
apples
apricots, dried
baked goods (e.g., cookies)
bananas
brandy
breakfast (e.g., cereals, oatmeal)
butter, unsalted
buttermilk
caramel
carrots
cheese: goat, ricotta

chestnuts
chocolate: dark, white
cinnamon
cloves
cognac
crème fraîche
currants
custard
dates
desserts
figs, dried
ginger
hazelnuts
honey
ice cream
Indian cuisine
Italian cuisine, esp. Venetian
lemon: juice, zest
liqueurs, nut
maple syrup
mascarpone
mole sauces
Moroccan cuisine
nutmeg
nuts
oatmeal
orange: juice, zest
peanuts
pears
pecans
pine nuts
pistachios

prunes
pumpkin
quince
raisins
rice (e.g., pudding)
RUM
salads
sour cream
Southern Comfort
stuffings
sugar: brown, white
sweet potatoes
vanilla
walnuts
whiskey
wine: red, sweet, white
yogurt

Flavor Affinities
raisins + orange + rum

RAMPS (aka wild leeks; see also Leeks, Onions, and Scallions)
Season: spring–summer
Weight: light
Volume: quiet–moderate
Techniques: cook, raw

asparagus
bacon
butter
carrots
cheese, Parmesan
chicken
chives
cream
cured meats (e.g., speck)
fish (e.g., halibut, salmon, trout)
ham
lentils, green
mushrooms, wild (e.g., morels)

Dishes

Spaghetti with Local Ramps, American Speck, and Parmesan
— Andrew Carmellini, A Voce (New York City)

Roasted Pork Chop with Spiced Pulled Pork, Green Lentils, and Ramps
— Gray Kunz, Café Gray (New York City)

olive oil
onions
pasta
pepper, black
pork
potatoes, esp. new
prosciutto
risotto
shallots
stock, chicken
wine, white

Flavor Affinities
ramps + asparagus + morels
ramps + lentils + pork
ramps + Parmesan cheese + risotto
ramps + pasta + speck

RASPBERRIES
Season: summer
Taste: sweet
Weight: light
Volume: quiet–moderate

almonds
apricots
beverages
blackberries
blueberries
brandy, esp. berry-flavored
buttermilk
caramel
Champagne
cheese: goat, ricotta
CHOCOLATE, ESP. DARK (say some)
***CHOCOLATE, WHITE**
cinnamon
cloves
cognac

Cointreau
corn syrup, light
CREAM
crème anglaise
crème fraîche
currants, esp. red
custard
desserts
figs, esp. fresh
Framboise
ginger
graham crackers
Grand Marnier
grapefruit
grapes
hazelnuts
honey
ICE CREAM, vanilla
jams
Kirsch
LEMON: juice, zest
lemon verbena
lime: juice, zest
liqueurs, esp. berry, nut
macadamia nuts
mangoes
maple syrup
mascarpone
melon
meringue
milk, sweetened condensed
mint (garnish)
nectarines
oatmeal
orange: juice, zest
peaches
peanuts
pears
pecans
pineapple
pine nuts
pistachios
plums
quince
raspberry preserves
rhubarb
rum, dark
salads: fruit, green

Dishes

Flambéed Peaches with Crepes and Raspberry-Lemon Ice Cream
— Gary Danko, Gary Danko (San Francisco)

Raspberry Mousse and Star Anise Tuile
— Dominique and Cindy Duby, Wild Sweets (Vancouver)

Almond Tart Shell Filled with Rose Cream and Raspberries with Lychee Granité, and Pistachio Crème Anglaise
— Michael Laiskonis, pastry chef, Le Bernardin (New York City)

When working with **raspberries**, I will try not to cook them too much. The problem is that often fresh raspberries are not that great. If I am making a sauce, even in the middle of summer I will use frozen raspberries. You can use frozen fruit as long as it doesn't have sugar or anything else added. The fruit is picked in the field when it is ripe and frozen right away. So, the frozen raspberries will have better flavor than those that have been put in a little carton and shipped across the country. Of course, local farmers' market raspberries are a different story. If I am making a sauce in the summer, the frozen raspberries will taste great. On the other hand, you would not use frozen raspberries on top of a tart.

— **EMILY LUCHETTI**, FARALLON (SAN FRANCISCO)

salt, sea
sauces
sour cream
star anise
strawberries
SUGAR: brown, white
tequila
wine: red, sweet (e.g., Riesling)
VANILLA
yogurt

AVOID
chocolate, dark (say some)

Flavor Affinities
raspberries + almonds + lemon
raspberries + almonds + vanilla
raspberries + cream + star anise
raspberries + crème fraîche + lemon
raspberries + custard + mint
raspberries + lemon + peaches
raspberries + sugar + vanilla + white chocolate

RED SNAPPER (See Snapper)

RHUBARB
Season: late spring–summer
Taste: sour
Weight: medium
Volume: loud
Techniques: bake, puree, sauté, stew

almonds
ANGELICA
apples
bay leaf
berries
blood orange
brandy
butter, unsalted
buttermilk
caramel
cardamom
cheese: blue, Stilton
chives
chocolate, white

cinnamon
citrus fruits
cloves
CREAM AND ICE CREAM
cream cheese
crème fraîche
crust: pastry, pie
custard
duck
eggs
fennel
fish, mild
foie gras
fruit
game birds
garlic
GINGER: fresh, crystallized, powdered
Grand Marnier
grapefruit
grenadine
hazelnuts
honey
Kirsch
lemon: juice, zest
lime: juice, zest
liver
maple syrup
mascarpone
mint, esp. spearmint
nutmeg
oatmeal
oil, peanut
onions
orange, juice
pecans
pepper, black
pies
plums
pork
port
raspberries
salt: kosher, sea
sour cream
***STRAWBERRIES**
SUGAR: BROWN, CONFECTIONERS', WHITE
trout

Dishes

Cool Rhubarb Soup with Orange and Mint Fior Di Latte
— Gina DePalma, pastry chef, Babbo (New York City)

Ricotta Cheesecake with Rhubarb and Sweet Vanilla Cream
— Gina DePalma, pastry chef, Babbo (New York City)

Rhubarb Stilton and Port Wine Reduction Chocolate
— Dominique and Cindy Duby, Wild Sweets (Vancouver)

Rhubarb Consommé, Vanilla-Poached Rhubarb, Strawberry Crisp
— Gale Gand, pastry chef, Tru (Chicago)

Vanilla Yogurt Mousse, Rhubarb-Citrus Compote, Blood Orange Sorbet, and Coulis
— Michael Laiskonis, pastry chef, Le Bernardin (New York City)

Warm Apple and Rhubarb Turnovers with Rhubarb-Gewürztraminer Jam and Candied Ginger–Crème Fraîche Ice Cream
— Emily Luchetti, pastry chef, Farallon (San Francisco)

Rhubarb Napoleon with Mascarpone Cream and Fennel Compote
— Ellie Nelson, pastry chef, Jardinière (San Francisco)

Old-Fashioned Rhubarb Crisp with Cinnamon-Walnut Ice Cream
— Michael Romano, Union Square Café (New York City)

Rhubarb and Angelica Pie
— Jerry Traunfeld, The Herbfarm (Woodinville, Washington)

Rhubarb-Mint Cobbler
— Jerry Traunfeld, The Herbfarm (Woodinville, Washington)

I like to pair **rhubarb**, caramelized sugar, and blood orange juice — which has more character than orange juice — because their seasons barely overlap. I am not a fan of rhubarb desserts because they always tend to be one note — either very tart, or very sweet to make up for the tartness. Caramel works well with rhubarb because it makes the rhubarb not too sweet.
— **MICHAEL LAISKONIS**, LE BERNARDIN (NEW YORK CITY)

There is not a lot of fruit available in the spring, so that pretty much leaves you with **rhubarb**. The good news is that rhubarb works well in custards and ice creams.
— **JERRY TRAUNFELD**, THE HERBFARM (WOODINVILLE, WASHINGTON)

VANILLA
verbena
vinaigrette
vinegar: cider, raspberry

wild rice
wine, sweet white (e.g., Riesling)
yogurt

Flavor Affinities

rhubarb + blood orange + caramelized sugar
rhubarb + caramel + orange
rhubarb + cardamom + orange
rhubarb + cardamom + sugar + vanilla
rhubarb + cinnamon + cream + walnuts
rhubarb + cream cheese + lime + vanilla
rhubarb + fennel + mascarpone
rhubarb + honey + lemon + vanilla
rhubarb + lemon + yogurt
rhubarb + mint + orange
rhubarb + mint + sugar + vanilla
rhubarb + Stilton cheese + port wine
rhubarb + strawberry + vanilla

RICE, WHITE — IN GENERAL

Function: cooling
Weight: light–medium
Volume: quiet
Techniques: boil, steam

anise
bacon
beans
butter, unsalted
chicken
cinnamon
coconut and coconut milk
cream / milk
curry powder
fish
fish sauce, Thai
garlic
ginger, fresh
lemon, zest
meats
nuts: almonds, pecans, pistachios, walnuts
onions
peas
raisins
rhubarb
SAFFRON
salt
shellfish

shrimp
stocks: chicken, vegetable
sugar
tomatoes
vegetables

RICE, ARBORIO OR CARNAROLI (aka risotto)

Weight: medium–heavy
Volume: quiet
Techniques: sauté, then simmer

arugula
asparagus
bacon
basil
butter, unsalted
celery

cheese, Parmesan
chicken
chile peppers, red
chives
crab
fennel
garlic
Italian cuisine
lemon
lemon thyme
lime, zest
mushrooms (e.g., chanterelles, morels, shiitake)
mussels
mustard seeds
onions
parsley, flat-leaf
peas

pepper, black
prosciutto
saffron
scallions
shallots
shellfish
shrimp
sorrel
squid
stocks: chicken, fish, vegetable
tarragon
thyme
tomatoes
truffles
veal
vermouth
wine: dry red or white
zucchini blossoms

Flavor Affinities

risotto + artichokes + lemon + prosciutto
risotto + asparagus + chervil + morel mushrooms
risotto + asparagus + saffron + scallops
risotto + bacon + butternut squash + maple syrup + sage
risotto + chanterelle mushrooms + zucchini blossoms
risotto + chorizo + clams + saffron
risotto + corn + Parmesan cheese + scallions
risotto + corn + Parmesan cheese + shrimp
risotto + mussels + parsley + peas
risotto + pancetta + Parmesan cheese + pumpkin
risotto + peas + prosciutto
risotto + sweet onions + Parmesan cheese
risotto + veal + black truffles

RICE, BASMATI

Function: cooling
Weight: light
Volume: quiet–moderate
Techniques: boil, simmer

almonds
basil
bay leaves
bell peppers
butter
buttermilk
cardamom
chicken
chile peppers, esp. dried red
cinnamon
coconut
coriander
cream / milk
cumin
currants
curry leaves
fennel seeds
garam masala
garlic
ginger
Indian cuisine
lamb
lemon
lime, juice
milk
mint
nuts

oil: canola, macadamia
onions, esp. green, red
orange
peas
pepper: black, white
pistachios
potatoes
raisins, yellow
saffron
salt, kosher
spinach
sugar
thyme
tomatoes and tomato paste

RICE, CARNAROLI
(See Rice, Arborio)

RICE, JASMINE
(See Thai Cuisine)

RICE, WILD

Weight: medium
Volume: moderate
Techniques: simmer

butter, unsalted
celery
game
game birds
lemon, zest
Midwestern American cuisine
oil: hazelnut, vegetable, walnut

olive oil
onions
pepper, ground
pine nuts
salt
sausage, smoked
scallions
stock, chicken
tarragon
walnuts
wine, dry white

RIESLING
Weight: light
Volume: quiet–moderate

apples
cheese, esp. blue, soft, triple crème
chicken
curries, esp. milder
duck
fish
fruit, esp. summer
ham, esp. baked
pork
salads
salmon
salmon, smoked
scallops
seafood
shellfish
trout, esp. sautéed

Dishes

Rose and Almond Panna Cotta
— Gina DePalma, pastry chef, Babbo (New York City)

Tropical Fruit Salad with Rosewater and Sweet Tahini Yogurt
— Brad Farmerie, Public (New York City)

Floral flavors, when done well, can be really amazing. This is also special because it is something that I never grew up with. Someone from India may not find it a big deal.

I tend to think in threes. I'll pair two classic ingredients, and add a third to elevate the combination. I make my own **rose**-flavored dessert that was inspired by [French pastry chef] Pierre Hermé and his rose macaroon with raspberry and lychee, which is one of the greatest things I have tasted in my life. I coat a standard tart shell with a layer of liquid raspberry; on top of that I place a rose parfait, which I pair with lemon and pistachio. To make the rose flavor not so overbearing, I use it in three different forms. I infuse rosebuds [used to make rosewater] in the milk for the parfait, and I also use rose syrup, which adds color and sweetness, and finally rosewater as well. You have to be careful with rose because it can be like eating perfume. That is why I take a lot of care using three layers to make it one flavor.

— **MICHAEL LAISKONIS,** LE BERNARDIN (NEW YORK CITY)

ROASTED DISHES
artichokes, Jerusalem
beef
beets
carrots
celery root
chicken
fennel
ham
lamb
onions
parsnips
pork
potatoes
rutabagas
shallots
squash, winter (e.g., butternut)
turkey
turnips
veal: loin, rib
vegetables, root
venison
yams

ROMAINE
(See Lettuce, Romaine)

ROSE (Hips, Petals, Water)
Taste: sweet
Weight: light
Volume: moderate–loud

almonds
baked goods (e.g., cakes)
cream / milk
desserts
fruit
honey
ice cream
Indian cuisine desserts
lemon
lychee
pistachios
raspberries
rice and rice pudding
vanilla
yogurt

Flavor Affinities

rose + almonds + cream/milk
rose + honey + yogurt
rose + lemon + pistachios
rose + lychee + raspberries

ROSEMARY

Season: year-round
Taste: pungent
Weight: heavy, tough-leaved
Volume: loud
Tips: Add early in the cooking process.
In winter, rosemary is milder; in summer, it is stronger.

anchovies
apples
apricots
asparagus
bacon
baked goods (e.g., breads, cakes, cookies)
bay leaf
BEANS, esp. dried, fava, white, green
beef
bell peppers
bouquet garni (key ingredient)
braised dishes
breads
Brussels sprouts
butter
cabbage
carrots
cauliflower
celery
chicken, esp. grilled
chives
cream
cream cheese
duck
eggs and egg dishes
eggplant
fennel
figs
FISH, esp. grilled
focaccia

French cuisine, esp. Provençal
fruit
game: rabbit, venison
***GARLIC**
gin
grains
grapefruit: juice, zest
grapes
grilled dishes, esp. meats, vegetables
herbes de Provence (key ingredient)
honey
Italian cuisine
***LAMB**
lavender
lemon: juice, zest
lemon verbena
lentils
lime: juice, zest
liver
lovage
mackerel
marinades
marjoram
MEATS, esp. grilled, roasted
Mediterranean cuisine
milk
mint

mushrooms
mussels
octopus
OLIVE OIL
ONIONS
orange: juice
oregano
parsley
parsnips
pasta
pears
peas
pepper, black
pizza
polenta
PORK
POTATOES
poultry
radicchio
rice
risotto
roasted meats
sage
salmon
sardines
sauces
savory
scallops, esp. grilled

Rosemary has a strong flavor, so it's always going to be the star. It works with strong, assertive fish like swordfish or tuna — and, of course, it is a classic with lamb.
— **DAVID WALTUCK**, CHANTERELLE (NEW YORK CITY)

Rosemary works with apples or pears.
— **JERRY TRAUNFELD**, THE HERBFARM (WOODINVILLE, WASHINGTON)

When I think of **rosemary**, I think of octopus. It works so well in a ceviche with octopus, black olives, and potato.
— **KATSUYA FUKUSHIMA**, MINIBAR (WASHINGTON, DC)

Rosemary can be strong with seafood unless it is a full-flavored seafood. We will skewer mussels with rosemary and panfry them because they work with the piney flavor of the mussels.
— **JERRY TRAUNFELD**, THE HERBFARM (WOODINVILLE, WASHINGTON)

Rosemary works well with citrus and honey.
— **GINA DEPALMA**, BABBO (NEW YORK CITY)

shellfish
sherry
shrimp
soups
spinach
squash: summer, **winter**
steaks
stews
strawberries
strongly flavored foods
sweet potatoes
swordfish
thyme
TOMATOES, tomato juice, tomato sauce
tuna
veal
vegetables, esp. grilled, roasted
vinegar, balsamic
wine
zucchini (say some)

AVOID
corn
Middle Eastern cuisine
salads
zucchini (say some)

Flavor Affinities
rosemary + anchovies + garlic
rosemary + butter + lemon
rosemary + garlic + lamb
rosemary + garlic + lemon
rosemary + garlic + wine
rosemary + onions + potatoes
rosemary + Parmesan cheese + polenta
rosemary + pork + sherry

RUM
Weight: light–heavy (light to dark rum)
Volume: moderate–loud

apples: fruit, juice
bananas: fruit, liqueur
butter
butterscotch

The Martinique **rums** tend to be drier, while Haitian rums tend to be spicier. I use more spices with rum in general, and herbs with spirits such as gin.
— **JERRI BANKS,** COCKTAIL CONSULTANT (NEW YORK CITY)

I love the combination of **rum** with carrots. Carrot juice provides a bright color that sends a message, especially to women. It has its own natural sweetness, and a little goes a long way. Carrots go beautifully with lemon thyme and orange, but I especially love the combination of carrots and ginger. In the autumn months, I'll combine gold rum with carrot and apple juices and autumn spices. I'll infuse allspice, cinnamon, and nutmeg into a tea or tisane, and add that to the cocktail.
— **JERRI BANKS,** COCKTAIL CONSULTANT (NEW YORK CITY)

Caribbean cuisine
carrot: juice
chestnuts
chocolate
cinnamon
Coca-Cola
coconut: fruit, milk, water
cream and ice cream
fruit juice
ginger
grapefruit
grenadine
LEMON: JUICE
LIME: JUICE
maple syrup
maraschino liqueur
mint
nutmeg
nuts
ORANGE: JUICE
passion fruit
pineapple
pumpkin
punch (key ingredient)
raisins
SPICES: allspice, cinnamon, nutmeg, star anise
SUGAR, ESP. BROWN
tropical fruits
vanilla
vermouth: dry, sweet

Flavor Affinities
rum + apples + butter + nuts + vanilla
rum + apples + carrot juice + spices
rum + apples + cinnamon + pumpkin
rum + coconut water + tropical fruits
rum + lime + banana + sugar
rum + lime + mint + sugar
rum + lime + pineapple + sugar

RUSSIAN CUISINE
beets
cabbage
caraway seeds
caviar
cilantro
cinnamon
cloves
cumin
dill
fish: pickled, smoked
fruits and fruit sauces
garlic
ginger
herring
lamb, grilled
meats, skewered and grilled
mint
mushrooms
nutmeg
onions
paprika

parsley
pepper, black
poppy seeds
potatoes
saffron
sausages
sour cream
tarragon
vinegar
vodka
yogurt

Flavor Affinities
mushrooms + cloves + pepper +
vinegar

RUTABAGAS
Season: autumn–spring
Taste: sweet
Weight: medium–heavy
Volume: moderate–loud
Techniques: boil, braise, deep-
fry, puree, roast, steam

allspice
apples
basil
bay leaf
beets
broccoli
butter, clarified
caraway seeds
cardamom
carrots
cayenne
celery
celery root
cheese: blue, **Gruyère**, Parmesan
chives
cinnamon
cream
cream cheese

Dishes
Apple-Rutabaga Soup
— Patrick O'Connell, The Inn at Little Washington (Washington, Virginia)

cumin
dill
duck
garlic, esp. roasted
ginger
greens, bitter
honey
lamb
leeks
lemon, juice
mace
maple syrup
marjoram
mustard
nutmeg
olive oil
onions
orange, zest
oregano
parsley
parsnips
pears
pepper: black, white
pork
potatoes
rabbit
raisins
rosemary
saffron
sage
salt
savory
scallions
soups
squash, butternut
star anise
stock, chicken
sweet potatoes
tarragon
thyme
tomatoes
tuna

turnips
vanilla
vinaigrette / vinegar
watercress

Flavor Affinities
rutabagas + apples + maple
    syrup
rutabagas + cheese + potatoes
rutabagas + potatoes +
    rosemary

SAFFRON
Taste: sour–sweet–bitter
Function: cooling
Weight: very light
Volume: very loud
Tips: Add later in the cooking
process; saffron is activated by
the heat of cooking.
This bright yellow/orange-hued
spice is used for its color as well
as its flavor.
A little saffron goes a very long
way — never add more than
necessary.

anise
artichokes
asparagus
basil
beef
BOUILLABAISSE
breads
cardamom
carrots
cheese
chicken
cinnamon
citrus
cloves
coriander
corn
couscous
cream and ice cream
cumin
curries
custards

Dishes

Saffron Panna Cotta with "Agrumi Misti" and Blood Orange Sorbetto
— Gina DePalma, pastry chef, Babbo (New York City)

I would definitely have **saffron** on hand for Spanish cooking. It lends itself to rice, seafood, meat, and poultry. You can combine saffron and salt together for a saffron salt that is incredibly aromatic. Saffron also works very well on a salad. People forget that saffron is a flower and, sprinkled on a salad, it aromatizes the greens.
— **JOSÉ ANDRÉS,** CAFÉ ATLÁNTICO (WASHINGTON, DC)

Saffron has a sweet power. It is a classic flavor to add to shellfish, but the minute you taste the saffron in a dish, there is too much.
— **MICHEL RICHARD,** CITRONELLE (WASHINGTON, DC)

I wanted to come up with a *panna cotta* that was unlike anyone else's. I was walking down the street thinking of Italian dishes and risotto Milanese [which is made with **saffron**] came to mind. This led me to think about saffron, and the idea of adding saffron to my *panna cotta*. After Ruth Reichl mentioned it in the *New York Times* review of Babbo, Mario [Batali] told me I could never take it off the menu!

Saffron has a bright metallic flavor, and with quince — which is floral, delicate, and perfumed — it is wonderful. Over the years, I have found that saffron unexpectedly changes its flavor depending on what fruit is paired with it. Each fruit I work with either turns up its floral component or its metallic flavor. Saffron is great with stone fruits like apples, peaches, pears, plums, and figs. It also works with citrus like blood oranges, kumquats, and grapefruit. On the other hand, it doesn't work with many berries. It makes strawberries a little flat, and is downright awful with cranberries.
— **GINA DEPALMA,** BABBO (NEW YORK CITY)

eggplant
eggs
fennel
FISH
fruit
game birds
garlic
ginger
halibut
ice cream
Indian cuisine
Italian cuisine
lamb
leeks
mayonnaise

meats
Mediterranean cuisine
Middle Eastern cuisine
Moroccan cuisine
mushrooms
mussels
North African cuisine
nutmeg
onions, esp. Spanish, Vidalia
orange
paella
paprika
pepper
potatoes
rabbit

ras el hanout (ingredient)
*RICE
*RISOTTO
sauces
scallops
SHELLFISH
shrimp
soups, esp. chicken, fish
Spanish cuisine
spinach
squash, winter
stews, esp. fish
tomatoes
turbot
vanilla
veal
vegetables
yogurt

Flavor Affinities
saffron + fish + rice
saffron + ginger + vanilla
saffron + monkfish + rice

SAGE

Season: late spring–early summer
Taste: sweet, bitter, sour
Weight: moderate–heavy
Volume: loud
Tips: Always use cooked (never raw); add near the end of the cooking process.

apples
asparagus
bay leaf
BEANS, esp. dried, green
beef
blueberries
bread
butter
cabbage
caraway
carrots
CHEESE, esp. Brie, feta, Fontina, Gruyère, Parmesan, ricotta
cherries, esp. tart

Sage has a much better flavor when it is cooked first. We will cook it in butter, olive oil, or bacon fat.

— JERRY TRAUNFELD, THE HERBFARM (WOODINVILLE, WASHINGTON)

CHICKEN, esp. roasted
chickpeas
citrus
corn
cream
cream cheese
duck
eggplant
eggs
European cuisine
fattier foods, esp. meats
fennel
fish, esp. oilier
French cuisine
game
game birds
garlic
ginger, dried
goose
Greek cuisine
honey
Italian cuisine
lamb
lemon
lemon herbs (balm, thyme, verbena)
liver
lovage
marjoram
meats, fattier, richer, and/or roasted
Mediterranean cuisine
mint
mushrooms
offal
olive oil
ONIONS
orange
oregano
oysters (e.g., stuffing)
pancetta
paprika
parsley, flat-leaf

PASTA, esp. gnocchi, ravioli
pears
peas
pepper, black
***PORK**
potatoes
poultry
prosciutto
pumpkin
rice
rich dishes
rosemary
salads: pasta, potato
sausages
savory
shellfish
shrimp
skate
slow-cooked dishes
soups, esp. legumes
Spanish cuisine
squash, winter
steak
stews
stocks
STUFFING
swordfish
thyme
tomatoes
tuna

turkey
veal
vegetables, esp. root
walnuts
wine, esp. white

Flavor Affinities
sage + marjoram + thyme
sage + parsley + rosemary + thyme
sage + pasta + walnuts
sage + stuffing + turkey + walnuts

SAKE
Weight: light
Volume: quiet

cucumber
fish
gin
JAPANESE CUISINE
lemon juice
lime juice
salads
sashimi and sushi
shellfish
sugar (simple syrup)
vodka

Flavor Affinities
sake + cucumber + lime

SALADS (See also Lettuces and other vegetables)

Every **salad** should have elements of bitter, salt, heat, and texture. For us, the bitter component is often the greens. We use a lot of frisée, radicchio, and endive. But there always needs to be some crunch in a salad. Even if it is a delicate salad, you need to find a way to get a crunch in there. For a delicate salad, you can get crunch using fried shallot rings or crispy sage leaves. We often use nuts for crunch. Our leaf salad has a cashew brittle, which is made by caramelizing sugar then seasoning it with salt, black pepper, a hint of madras curry, a pinch of our Moroccan spice blend (eighteen ingredients), and a pinch of pepper mix (four ingredients) before tossing the nuts in. The other components of the salad are pomegranate seeds, bacon, and a South American blue cheese.

— SHARON HAGE, YORK STREET (DALLAS)

When you are eating a **salad**, the greens are the main ingredient, so whatever you add has to elevate them. Lettuce is boring by itself, so you elevate it with the vinaigrette. We will use herbs in our salads, but they must not overpower the greens; they have to be very subtle and used in small amounts. We will use chives or fresh parsley leaves or a combination of the two. We may also add some mint to the mix because it pushes the flavors of the greens.

— **ERIC RIPERT,** LE BERNARDIN (NEW YORK CITY)

SALMON (See also Fish — In General)

Season: spring–early autumn
Weight: medium
Volume: moderate
Techniques: bake, braise, broil, grill, marinate, panfry, poach, raw (e.g., sashimi, tartare), roast, sauté, sear, steam

anchovies
apples, esp. Golden Delicious or Granny Smith, and apple cider
artichoke hearts
arugula
asparagus (accompaniment)
bacon
barbecue sauce
basil: leaf, oil
bass
bay leaf
beans: fava, flageolets, white
beets
beurre blanc
bread crumbs: regular, *panko*
Brussels sprouts
BUTTER, unsalted
cabbage, esp. green, savoy
capers
cardamom
carrots
caviar
cayenne
celery
Champagne
chervil
chile peppers: dried, fresh, green, jalapeño, red, Thai

**King White Salmon by Gabriel Kreuther
of New York City's The Modern**

The **salmon** is roasted, and served with warm, slightly charred cucumbers, which I like because they are rarely used cooked. We use market vegetables that right now are bok choy and peas. I have added some trout caviar for a briny flavor because salmon is on the sweet side. The dish is then finished with a hickory broth.

For the hickory broth, we smoke some hickory chips, wrap them in cheesecloth with juniper berries and peppercorns, and then submerge them in water to make a broth. This creates a smoked sauce that is light and tasty. What we have here is a "wood stock" that makes perfect sense with the salmon because so often salmon is smoked. After the wood comes out, you taste the broth to adjust it. It may need some more water to cut the wood and smoke flavor, or it might need to be reduced to intensify it. We finish the sauce with a little half-and-half, and foam it with a handheld mixer.

CHIVES (garnish)
cilantro
cinnamon
citrus
cloves
coconut: shredded, milk
cognac
coriander
corn
cornichons
crab
CREAM, HEAVY
cream cheese
crème fraîche
cucumbers
cumin
curry: leaves, powder, sauce
   (esp. red)
daikon
dill
eggs: hard-boiled, scrambled
fennel
fennel seeds
fenugreek seeds
GARLIC
ginger: fresh
grapefruit: juice, zest
greens, bitter
horseradish
juniper berries
kelp
leeks
LEMON: juice, zest
lemon, preserved
lemongrass
LENTILS
lettuces (e.g., frisée)
licorice
LIME: juice, leaves, zest
lovage
Madeira
mangoes
marjoram
mayonnaise
mint, esp. spearmint
mirepoix
mirin
miso, white

Salmon has been my favorite fish since I learned to cook it correctly. It is so versatile: you can smoke it, marinate it, or even serve it raw. Because it is rich and fatty, it pairs well with everything from a red wine sauce to a simple vinaigrette.
— **MICHEL RICHARD**, CITRONELLE (WASHINGTON, DC)

Tomato and pineapple with **salmon:** This dish goes back to 1975 when someone gave me a salad of tomato and pineapple. I didn't know what to do with it, so I stored the idea away. Today, I will cook the tomato, pineapple, a dash of white wine for acid, miso, and the salmon head, which bridges and brings the flavors together. Tomato gets fruitier when cooked with pineapple. The end result doesn't taste like either tomato or pineapple; it is a new flavor. This sauce is perfect with salmon.
— **MICHEL RICHARD**, CITRONELLE (WASHINGTON, DC)

Dishes

Salmon Gravlax with Chickpea Pancake, Caviar, and Mustard
— Tom Valenti, Ouest (New York City)

Dishes

Seared Salmon with Potatoes, Leeks, and Mustard-Chive Sauce
— Lidia Bastianich, Felidia (New York City)

Pistachio-Crusted Salmon Medallions with Garlic Mashed Potatoes, Crispy Fennel, Arugula, Olives, Roasted Peppers, and Savory Tomato Butter
— Bob Kinkead, Kinkead's (Washington, DC)

Wild Salmon with Horseradish Crust, Cabbage, and Riesling
— Gabriel Kreuther, The Modern (New York City)

House-Made Graviax with Scrambled Eggs, Pumpernickel, Herb Crème Fraîche, and Red Onions
— Tony Liu, August (New York City)

Salmon Rubbed with Ground Red Chile and Lime and Pan Seared. Served with a Tangy, Spicy Tomatillo, Jalapeño, and Lime Juice Sauce
— Zarela Martinez, Zarela (New York City)

Wild Alaskan Troll Red King Salmon, Yukon Potato Gnocchi, Braised Artichokes and Leeks, Enriched Chicken Jus with Chives and Chervil
— Carrie Nahabedian, Naha (Chicago)

Signature Sushi: Salmon with Mango Puree; Seared Salmon Belly with Lemon Soy
— Kaz Okochi, Kaz Sushi Bistro (Washington, DC)

Pistachio-Crusted Salmon with Curried Spinach Salad, Mandarin Orange Vinaigrette
— Monica Pope, T'afia (Houston)

Salmon with Grilled Vegetables, Baby Artichokes, Israeli Couscous, Warm Vegetable Vinaigrette
— Alfred Portale, Gotham Bar and Grill (New York City)

Wild Salmon: Barely Cooked Wild Alaskan Salmon; Morels and Spring Vegetables in a Wild Mushroom Pot au Feu
— Eric Ripert, Le Bernardin (New York City)

Slow-Roasted Scottish Salmon, Caramelized Fennel, Red Wine–Fennel Emulsion
— Rick Tramonto, Tru (Chicago)

Darjeeling Tea–Cured Salmon with English Cucumber and Crème Fraîche
— Charlie Trotter, Trotter's to Go (Chicago)

Roasted Salmon with Sweet Corn Flan, Chanterelles, Prosciutto, Zucchini, Corn-Chive Butter, and Shrimp Oil
— Tom Valenti, Ouest (New York City)

---

mushrooms, esp. black trumpet, button, chanterelles, cremini, morels, oysters
mussels
MUSTARD: Dijon, whole grain
mustard seeds
nutmeg

OIL: canola, corn, grapeseed, peanut (for cooking), sesame, vegetable (for cooking)
OLIVE OIL
olives, esp. black, niçoise, picholine, Provençal

ONIONS, esp. pearl, red, Vidalia, white
orange: juice, zest
oysters
pancetta
paprika
PARSLEY, flat-leaf
peas
PEPPER: black, green, pink, red, white
Pernod
pike
pineapple and pineapple juice
pistachios
polenta
ponzu sauce
port
POTATOES
radishes
ramps
rice (e.g., basmati, sushi)
roe: flying fish, **salmon**
rosemary
saffron
sake
SALT: kosher, sea
sauces: béarnaise, beurre blanc, brown butter hollandaise
scallions
scallops
sesame seeds
SHALLOTS
shiso leaves
smoked salmon
sole
sorrel
sour cream
soy sauce
spinach
STOCKS: chicken, fish, mussels, veal, vegetable
sugar: brown, white
Tabasco sauce
tamarind
tarragon
THYME
tilefish
TOMATOES

tomatoes, sun-dried
truffles: oil, shaved, white
turmeric
vanilla
vermouth
vinaigrette
VINEGAR, e.g., balsamic,
champagne, cider, red wine,
rice, sherry, white wine
watercress
WINE: dry white or red
(Cabernet Sauvignon, Pinot
Noir)
zucchini

Flavor Affinities

salmon + apple + horseradish + rosemary
salmon + avocado + chile peppers + grapefruit
salmon + bacon + cabbage + chestnuts
salmon + bacon + lentils + sherry vinegar
salmon + basil + white beans
salmon + beets + crème fraîche + cucumber + horseradish
salmon + caviar + vermouth
salmon + chervil + chives + leeks + lemon + morels + peas + potatoes
salmon + cucumber + balsamic vinegar
salmon + cucumber + dill
salmon + cucumber + dill + horseradish
salmon + cucumber + tomato
salmon + lemon juice + Dijon mustard
salmon + marjoram + peas
salmon + miso + pineapple + tomato + white wine
salmon + mustard + scallions
salmon + orange + tomato
salmon + peas + potatoes
salmon + pineapple + tomatoes
salmon + potato + watercress

SALMON, CURED

Taste: salty
Weight: medium
Volume: moderate–loud

aquavit
avocados
basil
beans, white
bell peppers, red
bread: pumpernickel, rye
caviar
cayenne
Champagne
chives
cream
cream cheese
crème fraîche
dill
honey
horseradish
lemon: juice, zest
lentils, green
lime: juice, zest
mustard: Dijon, dry
olive oil
orange, zest
pepper: black, white
potatoes
salt: kosher, sea
shallots
sour cream
sugar
tarragon
tomatoes

SALMON, SMOKED

Taste: salty
Weight: medium
Volume: moderate–loud

artichokes
avocados
bell peppers, roasted
blini
bread: bagels, pumpernickel, rye,
white

My signature sushi roll pairs **salmon** with mango puree and sushi rice. However, I wouldn't serve salmon with mango puree as sashimi. The balance would be lost. Also, mango doesn't pair well with either soy sauce or wasabi.

— **KAZ OKOCHI,** KAZ SUSHI BISTRO (WASHINGTON, DC)

We roast **salmon** wrapped in squash blossom and it imparts a slight zucchini flavor to the salmon. The blossom is mild and makes a perfect package for the salmon by steaming it as it cooks. With the salmon we serve a [zucchini] squash cut into spaghetti seasoned with lemon thyme and basil. The herbs work with both the zucchini and the salmon.

— **JERRY TRAUNFELD,** THE HERBFARM (WOODINVILLE, WASHINGTON)

I love combining fruit and proteins. I am one-half Hawaiian, and in Hawaiian cooking a classic dish is Spam cooked with fresh pineapple. I grew up with my father making it for us, and it is delicious. You'll also see a lot of sushi chefs combine kiwi and scallops, as fruit adds a nice cleansing note to the protein you are working with. Our take on this combination is pineapple **salmon** with avocado and quinoa. We cut pineapple very thin, then wrap it around salmon belly, which is very rich. When we cook it, the pineapple gets caramelized and helps cut the fat of the salmon. On the dish is a sweet-hot sauce of avocado, honey, scallions, and serrano chiles. To garnish the dish and add some crunch we add quinoa that is cooked then dried for three days before cooking it in olive oil, which makes it puff like Rice Krispies.

— **KATSUYA FUKUSHIMA,** MINIBAR (WASHINGTON, DC)

breakfast / brunch
butter: clarified, unsalted
capers
caviar
celery
celery root
Champagne
chervil
chicory
CHIVES
cilantro

cream
CREAM CHEESE
crème fraîche
cucumbers
cumin
daikon
DILL
eggs, esp. hard-boiled, and egg
    salad
frisée
garlic

ginger, fresh
horseradish
juniper
leeks
LEMON: juice, zest
lime: juice, zest
mascarpone
monkfish
mussels, smoked
mustard, Dijon
oil, canola
olive oil
onions, esp. red, sweet
orange
oysters
parsley
pasta
PEPPER: black, white
Pernod
potatoes and potato salad
radishes
salmon
salmon roe
salt: kosher, sea
scallions
scallops
shallots
shiso leaf
sorrel
sour cream
soy sauce
spinach
stocks: clam, fish
Tabasco sauce
tarragon
tea sandwiches
tomatoes
vinaigrette
vinegar: red wine, rice wine,
    sherry, white wine
Worcestershire sauce
yogurt (say some)

AVOID
mayonnaise
yogurt (say some)

Dishes

Smoked Salmon with Crispy Potatoes and Horseradish Cream
— Jean Joho, Brasserie Jo (Chicago)

Rosti Potato Cake with Herb Mascarpone and Fresh-Smoked Salmon
— Monica Pope, T'afia (Houston)

Leek Tart with Smoked Salmon and Crème Fraîche
— Michel Richard, Citronelle (Washington, DC)

Flavor Affinities

smoked salmon + chives + crème fraîche + dill + pumpernickel-rye blini
smoked salmon + chives + dill + scrambled eggs + potatoes
smoked salmon + cream cheese + lemon juice + shallots + sour cream
smoked salmon + cucumber + horseradish + mint
smoked salmon + dill + horseradish + lemon juice + sour cream

SALSIFY

Season: autumn–winter
Taste: sweet
Weight: medium
Volume: moderate
Techniques: bake, braise, pan roast, stew

anchovies
butter
cheese, Parmesan
chives
cream
duck prosciutto
fish (e.g., halibut)
hollandaise sauce
LEMON, JUICE
maple syrup
mascarpone
mayonnaise
mushrooms
nutmeg
oil, peanut
onions
orange
parsley
pepper, black
polenta
prosciutto
rice
sage
salmon, smoked
salt, kosher
scallions
shallots
sorrel

soups
stock, chicken
thyme, fresh
truffles, black
vinaigrettes

Flavor Affinities

salsify + Parmesan cheese + prosciutto

SALT — IN GENERAL

Taste: salty
Function: warming

SALT, FLEUR DE SEL

chicken
cold dishes
meats
radishes
salads
steak

SALT, HAWAIIAN

ceviche
chicken
lamb
meat, esp. barbecued
pork
seafood
steak
vegetables, esp. tomatoes

I like to use **Hawaiian salt** on a dish where I want a little crunch. This holds up better than other salts that will dissolve more

We use *fleur de sel* on cold dishes, such as salads. We also use it on meats like beef, buffalo rib eye, or roast chicken after they are sliced and a moment before serving.
— **SHARON HAGE,** YORK STREET (DALLAS)

quickly. I will use it on ceviche, which has a little broth.
— **DANIEL HUMM,** ELEVEN MADISON PARK (NEW YORK CITY)

SALT, JAPANESE

fish
foie gras
salmon
sashimi
squid

Japanese salt has ground seaweed in it and works on sashimi. I use this in Japanese dishes.
— **DANIEL HUMM,** ELEVEN MADISON PARK (NEW YORK CITY)

SALT, KOSHER

breads
brines
charcuterie
cocktails, esp. rims
cooking
cures
meats
potatoes
pretzels
toasts
water for blanching or for pasta

We use **kosher salt** primarily for meats.
— **SHARON HAGE,** YORK STREET (DALLAS)

SALT, MALDON

fish, esp. raw
finishing dishes
lobster

[Maldon] is the finest of all **salts** in regard to both flavor and texture. I appreciate its delicacy on fish, especially lobster.
— **DANIEL HUMM,** ELEVEN MADISON PARK (NEW YORK CITY)

SALT, SEA — COARSE

meats
seafood
seasoning
vegetables, hearty

SALT, SEA — FINE

baking
fish
seasoning
vegetables, delicate

For delicate foods like vegetables or fish, we use ground **sea salt** right before it goes into the pan.

— **SHARON HAGE,** YORK STREET (DALLAS)

SALT, SMOKED

brines, esp. for pork
chicken
fish, esp. raw
meats: barbecued, red
pork
potatoes, baked
seafood
salmon
sardines
steak
tuna
vegetarian dishes

The **Danish smoked salt** we use is smoked over Chardonnay vines. For us, using smoked salt provides the flavor of cooking over grape vines as they do in Spain. Smoked salt is also great if you don't have a grill, because even a gas grill can't provide a smoky flavor. I like smoked salt sprinkled on sardines, which in Spain will be cooked over a fire on the beach where they get really smoky. I can give that sense of place by using this salt on my sardines.

— **ALEXANDRA RAIJ,** TÍA POL (NEW YORK CITY)

SALT, TRUFFLE

egg dishes
pastas
popcorn
potatoes
risotto
salads and salad dressing

SALT, VANILLA

chicken
chocolate, esp. dark
lamb
meats

mussels
nuts
pork
pumpkin
shellfish, esp. lobster or scallops
squash, winter
sweet potatoes

SALTINESS

Taste: salty
Function: heating; stimulates salivation; enhances the flavors of ingredients
Tips: Adding salt to a dish diminishes the effects of bitter, sour, and sweet.

anchovies
bacon
capers
caperberries
caviar and other fish roe
cheeses, salty (e.g., feta, manchego, Parmesan, pecorino)
clams and clam juice
cured meats
dashi (e.g., Japanese stock)
finnan haddie
fish sauce, Asian
gravlax
ham
ingredients with added salt (e.g., chips, nuts)
kelp
lemons, preserved
lox
nuts, salted
olives
oysters
oyster sauce
pancetta
pickles (salty-sour)
prosciutto
salmon, smoked
salt
salt cod
salt pork

sardines
sausages, salty (e.g., chorizo)
sea urchin
sea vegetables
seaweed

If you have a piece of Ibérico or Serrano ham in your refrigerator, you'll eventually end up with this little end of dried-out salt-cured meat. While some might just throw it away, we know there's a lot of flavor left — so we grind it up in a coffee grinder and use it as meat-flavored salt. We call this "**ham salt**," and will use this on a salad to emphasize the aroma and flavor of pork. . . . In Spain we have *mojama*, which is tuna loin cured like ham. We'll grind it up in a coffee grinder and it becomes tuna salt. When I sear tuna, I will sprinkle this on and emphasize the tuna with its own tuna flavor. It is simple and dramatic. I even showed this technique to the owner of the best tuna restaurant in the world — called El Campero in Barbate, Spain — where he serves tuna a hundred ways. He loved it!

— **JOSÉ ANDRÉS,** CAFÉ ATLÁNTICO (WASHINGTON, DC)

We use three different kinds of salt — but we also use **capers, anchovies, olives, preserved lemons,** and even **prosciutto** for adding another dimension of saltiness. Even when using these other salty components, 99 percent of the time we'll use them in addition to salt, not instead of it.

— **SHARON HAGE,** YORK STREET (DALLAS)

Chefs on Selecting and Using Salt

*Kosher salt has larger, harder crystals and won't break down too fast. I use this for pasta water, brining, curing meat, and charcuterie. I use **French sea salt** (esp. Baleine) for general seasoning. I like Maldon salt a lot. This is what I use for finishing dishes. It has a really fine crystal and the flavor is great. It even gives some crunch and melts like snowflakes. It is great sprinkled on raw fish.*
— **ANDREW CARMELLINI,** A VOCE (NEW YORK CITY)

Salt is now used very often in desserts and unfortunately it doesn't always make sense. I was served a green apple sorbet with salt and it didn't work. Salt does work on sweet oranges, though. If you cut a Cara Cara orange into wedges and sprinkle sea salt on them, they are delicious. Salt also makes sense with caramel and butterscotch. The salt is a contrast to the super sweet, which is why we like PayDay candy bars.
— **GINA DEPALMA,** BABBO (NEW YORK CITY)

*I use **Maldon salt** flakes as a salt for finishing dishes, and kosher salt for blanching water or when I roast on salt. I'll sometimes use **smoked salt** with raw fish or in a brine for pork, but it's really strong so you have to be careful with it.*
— **BRADFORD THOMPSON,** MARY ELAINE'S AT THE PHOENICIAN (SCOTTSDALE, ARIZONA)

*There is salt in almost all of my desserts. However, you would not know it was there until I took it out — which is how it should be. You don't need to taste the salt, but it helps open the palate and stimulates your taste buds. With something fatty like chocolate, you need some salt to brighten it up. I use all sorts of salts with my desserts. We are making a peanut butter and jelly bonbon that I pair with **smoked Brittany sea salt.** Maldon salt is shaved and more about texture, because it is not as strong; I would use it on a pancake or something creamy. Fleur de sel is a salt with texture and ocean floral notes, and would go well on our panini which have cheese, arugula, and vinaigrette.*
— **JOHNNY IUZZINI,** JEAN GEORGES (NEW YORK CITY)

*Salt goes into almost every dough we make and is something that makes flavors pop. Some chefs can go a little overboard, but desserts should still be sweet. Salt works well with caramel and chocolate, obviously. I also use a **vanilla salt** with a classic sweet potato tart that is cut into four slices with a few grains on each slice. The salt reinforces the savoriness of the sweet potato and plays off the brightness of the preserved lemon on the plate.*
— **MICHAEL LAISKONIS,** LE BERNARDIN (NEW YORK CITY)

*To counteract **oversalting** a dish, you need to increase the volume of whatever you are making. That can be tricky, because you don't want to end up with something too watery. Whenever there is a puree involved, whether it is mashed potatoes or butternut squash soup, I encourage my cooks to make it thick. You can always add, but not take away.*
— **ANDREW CARMELLINI,** A VOCE (NEW YORK CITY)

seeds, salted
shrimp paste
smoked foods, esp. fish, meats
smoked salmon and trout
soy sauce
tamari
Worcestershire sauce

SARDINES
Season: spring–summer
Taste: salty
Weight: light
Volume: loud
Techniques: braise, broil, fry, grill, marinate, poach, sauté

anchovies
basil
bay leaf
bell peppers, red
bread crumbs
capers
carrots
cayenne
chives
coriander seeds
currants
eggplant
fennel
fennel pollen
fennel seeds
French cuisine
garlic
ham
Italian cuisine, esp. southern
lemon: juice, zest
mirin
oil, peanut
OLIVE OIL
onions: red, white

orange: juice, zest
parsley, flat-leaf
pasta
pepper: black, white
peppers, piquillo
pine nuts
raisins, esp. yellow
red pepper flakes
rosemary
saffron
sage
sake
salt, sea
sour cream
soy sauce
thyme
tomatoes and tomato sauce
verjus
vinaigrette
vinegar, e.g., balsamic, red wine, sherry, white wine
walnuts
wine, dry white (e.g., Chenin Blanc, Grenache, Viognier)
zucchini

SAUERKRAUT
Taste: sour
Weight: medium
Volume: loud
Tips: Sauerkraut is shredded cabbage that is fermented in salt and spices.

apples
bacon
bay leaf
beans, esp. kidney and/or red
caraway seeds
carrots

cider
cloves
duck
Eastern European cuisine
fat: duck, goose
French cuisine, esp. Alsatian
garlic
German cuisine
gin
ham: hocks, meat
JUNIPER BERRIES
Kirsch
olive oil
onions
pepper, black
pork, esp. loin
potatoes
rhubarb
salt, kosher
SAUSAGES, esp. blood, bratwurst, frankfurter, kielbasa
stock, chicken
vinegar: champagne, white wine
wine: dry to off-dry white (e.g., Alsatian, Riesling)

SAUSAGES (See also Chorizo)
Weight: light–heavy
Volume: quiet–loud
Techniques: bake, grill, poach, sauté, stew

apples
basil
bay leaf
beans, white
beer
bell peppers: green, red
breakfast
broccoli rabe
butter, unsalted
carrots
celery root
celery seeds
fennel
garlic
leeks
lemon, juice

Dishes

Marinated Fresh Sardines with Caramelized Fennel and Lobster Oil
— Mario Batali, Babbo (New York City)

Whole Wheat Spaghetti with Fresh Sardines and Walnuts
— David Pasternak, Esca (New York City)

Dishes

Homemade Alsatian Country Sausage with Turnip Choucroute and Whole Grain Mustard Sauce

— Gabriel Kreuther, The Modern (New York City)

lentils
Mediterranean cuisine
mustard, Dijon
oil, canola
olive oil
ONIONS: white, yellow
oregano
parsley, flat-leaf
pasta
pepper, black
potatoes, esp. boiled, mashed,
    pureed
radicchio
rosemary
salt, kosher
sauerkraut
scallops
shallots
thyme
tomatoes
vinegar, balsamic
wine, dry white

Flavor Affinities

sausages + mustard + sauerkraut
sausages + onions + potatoes +
    tomatoes
sausages + radicchio + white
    beans

SAUVIGNON BLANC

Weight: medium
Volume: moderate

asparagus
chicken
cilantro
fish
garlic
herbs
oysters, esp. raw
peppers
pork

salads
shellfish
tomatoes
turkey
vegetables

SAVORY

Weight: medium, tough-leaved
Volume: moderate–loud
(Summer savory is quieter, winter
savory is louder.)
Tips: Can stand up to cooking.
Use summer savory with
summer vegetables, and winter
savory with winter vegetables.

basil
bay leaf
***BEANS, esp. dried, summer**
    (e.g., fava, green, lima)
beef
beets
bell peppers
bouquet garni
braised dishes
Brussels sprouts
cabbage
cheese (e.g., goat) and cheese
    dishes

chicken
chicken livers
chives
cumin
eggs and egg dishes
fennel
fines herbes (ingredient)
fish, esp. baked or grilled
garlic
herbes de Provence (ingredient)
herbs, other (as a blending herb)
kale
lamb
lavender
legumes
lentils
mackerel
marjoram
meats, esp. grilled, roasted,
    stewed
Mediterranean cuisine
mint
mushrooms
nutmeg
olives
onions
oregano
paprika
parsley
peas
polenta
pork
potatoes
poultry, esp. grilled

Savory in any form — whether summer or winter savory — is my
favorite herb. It is not as woody as thyme, not as piney as rosemary, and
not as pungent as sage. It also has the ability to stay flavorful throughout
the cooking process. I like it with potatoes, with polenta, and with
mushrooms. Savory and mushrooms are great. I especially like grilled
porcini mushrooms with savory. I'll grill the mushrooms then put them
on a bed of savory to finish roasting them. Savory also works in a sherry
or red wine vinaigrette with shallots, and is great on salads.
— **VITALY PALEY,** PALEY'S PLACE (PORTLAND, OREGON)

Savory is an herb that is very compatible in the same way fresh thyme is.
You could use savory in dishes that call for thyme.
— **MARCEL DESAULNIERS,** THE TRELLIS (WILLIAMSBURG, VIRGINIA)

rabbit
rice
rosemary
sage
salads and salad dressings
sauces and gravies
soups, esp. tomato-based
squash, summer
stews, esp. meat
stuffings (e.g., poultry)
tarragon
thyme
tomatoes and tomato sauces
veal
vegetables, esp. root
vinegar
wine, red
zucchini

Flavor Affinities

savory + garlic + tomatoes

SCALLIONS

Season: summer
Weight: light
Volume: moderate
Techniques: braise, grill, raw, sauté, stir-fry

anise
basil
bay leaf
bell peppers
butter, unsalted
carrots
cheese: goat, Parmesan
chile peppers
cilantro
cinnamon
cloves
cream
cream cheese
curry
dill
egg dishes
garlic
greens, bitter
honey

Japanese cuisine
Korean cuisine
lemon, juice
mushrooms
mustard, Dijon
nutmeg
olive oil
oregano
paprika
parsley
pepper, white
potatoes
rice
rosemary
sage
salt, kosher

sesame oil
sugar
Thai cuisine
thyme
tomatoes
vinegar

SCALLOPS

Season: summer–autumn
Taste: sweet, esp. bay scallops
Weight: light–medium
Volume: quiet
Techniques: broil, deep-fry, gratin, grill, marinate, pan sear, poach, raw, roast, sauté, sear, steam, stir-fry, tartare

Dishes

Callos de Hacha en Adobo: Chipotle-Glazed, Grilled "Dry Pack" New England Sea Scallops in Classic Adobo Sauce (Anchos, Garlic, Orange) with Plantain-Studded Black Bean Rice, Wood-Grilled Green Beans, and Crispy Onions
— Rick Bayless, Frontera Grill (Chicago)

Fresh-Grilled Sea Scallops Baked Over Rosemary Salt, with Creamy Polenta and Tomato-Citrus Vinaigrette
— Daniel Boulud, Daniel (New York City)

Diver Sea Scallops: Fennel Ravioli, Fricassee of Chanterelles, Artichoke, and Arugula
— Daniel Boulud/Olivier Muller, DB Bistro Moderne (New York City)

Maine Diver Scallops with English Peas, Smoked Bacon, Pickled Ramps, and Perigord Truffle Nage
— Traci Des Jardins, Jardinière (San Francisco)

Maine Diver Scallops Grilled with Ruby Grapefruit, Spring Potatoes, and Basil
— Daniel Humm, Eleven Madison Park (New York City)

Sea of Cortez "Mano de Leon" Scallops Scented with Citrus, Spices, and Vanilla Bean, Caramelized Belgian Endive, Ruby Red Grapefruit, Mâche, and Mint
— Carrie Nahabedian, Naha (Chicago)

Bay Scallops with Mushrooms, Peppers, and Grilled Italian Sausage
— Patrick O'Connell, The Inn at Little Washington (Washington, Virginia)

Delicate Sake-Poached Sea Scallops with Lemon and Cilantro
— Kaz Okochi, Kaz Sushi Bistro (Washington, DC)

Linguine with Taylor Bay Scallops, Maine Mussels, Hot Red Pepper, and Pancetta
— David Pasternak, Esca (New York City)

Scallops with Roasted Brussels Sprouts and Pancetta
— David Pasternak, Esca (New York City)

almonds
apples, esp. Granny Smith
artichokes
arugula
asparagus
avocado
bacon and other cured meats
   (e.g., Serrano ham)
basil
bay leaf
beans: cannelini, fava, green,
   haricots verts, lima
bell peppers: red, green, yellow
bread crumbs
Brussels sprouts
BUTTER: brown, clarified,
   unsalted
capers
carrots and carrot juice
cauliflower, esp. pureed
caviar
cayenne
celery
Champagne
cheese: Asiago, Parmesan
chervil
chile peppers: jalapeño, poblano
Chinese cuisine
chives (garnish)
cilantro
citron
citrus
clams
cloves
coconut and coconut milk
corn
coriander
crab
cream
cream cheese
crème fraîche
cucumbers
curry powder
dashi
dill
duck fat
edamame
eggs, hard-boiled
fennel

We have served cinnamon-dusted sea **scallops**, and they were very tasty.
— **MARCEL DESAULNIERS**, THE TRELLIS (WILLIAMSBURG, VIRGINIA)

You'll find sushi chefs combining **scallops** with kiwi.
— **KATSUYA FUKUSHIMA**, MINIBAR (WASHINGTON, DC)

We offer Gulf of Maine sea **scallops** scented with citrus, spices, and vanilla bean, caramelized Belgian endive, ruby red grapefruit, mâche, and mint. The dish came about because I love vanilla and grapefruit. I came up with the idea that I would use dry citrus to powder my scallops. Then I realized that was just one note, so I added some spice which led to star anise, fennel, and anise seed. I sauce the dish with a beurre blanc and grapefruit syrup made of fresh grapefruit, candied peel, and fresh vanilla bean. Since the sauce has butter and cream, I had to be careful not to turn this into vanilla crème brûlée! I love caramelized endive because you have a bitter vegetable that you make sweet. We cook it in whole butter and just as it starts to brown we sprinkle in sugar. This balances the tart and sweet of the grapefruit and the sweetness of the scallops.
— **CARRIE NAHABEDIAN**, NAHA (CHICAGO)

Sear **scallops** on one side only, or else they'll be overcooked. Accent them with coconut milk, garlic, ginger, or lemongrass. Or, puree sea scallops with cream and cook them slowly in a double boiler, which gives them the appearance of white scrambled eggs. This pairs beautifully with caviar, chopped raw onion, or truffles.
— **MICHEL RICHARD**, CITRONELLE (WASHINGTON, DC)

Scallops with chanterelles and green parsley sauce is as beautiful on the plate as it is on the palate.
— **HIRO SONE**, TERRA (ST. HELENA, CALIFORNIA)

Nantucket bay **scallops** are magically delicious, and pairing them with duck fat is an unusual combination that works. It is essentially scallops Provençal, but instead of using olive oil you use duck fat that gives you a silky quality. It is an enormously fun dish to cook and you use your eyes and nose to cook it. You heat up duck fat, getting it really hot, then sauté the scallops really fast. After taking them out, add chopped garlic and tomato *concasse*. It moves along quickly; hit it with chicken stock, adjust it with some lemon juice, and let it reduce and emulsify. You add your scallops back in with some chiffonade of basil and it's done.

   The dish smells so good while you're cooking it, between the garlic, the scallops, and the duck fat. The whole thing is done in one shot. No resting, no slicing, no elaborate plating. It's fun, and it's delicious.
— **DAVID WALTUCK**, CHANTERELLE (NEW YORK CITY)

fennel seeds
fish sauce, Thai
French cuisine
GARLIC
ginger
grapefruit: juice, zest
gremolata
ham
haricots verts
honey
horseradish
kaffir lime
kiwi fruit
leeks
LEMON: juice, zest
lemongrass
lemon thyme
lentils
LIME: juice, zest
lobster
mango
marjoram
mascarpone
mint
morels
mushrooms: button, chanterelle, cremini, Japanese, porcini, portobello, shiitake
mussels
mustard, Dijon
OIL: canola, corn, grapeseed, peanut, vegetable
oil: almond, hazelnut
olive oil
onions, esp. red, white, yellow
orange: juice, zest
pancetta
PARSLEY, flat-leaf
passion fruit
pasta
peas
PEPPER: black, white
Pernod
pineapple
pomegranates and pomegranate juice
potatoes, esp. mashed
red pepper flakes
rice

rosemary
saffron
sake
salmon roe
salsify
SALT: kosher, sea
sauce, béchamel
sausages, chorizo
scallions
sea urchin
sesame: seeds, oil
SHALLOTS
shrimp
sole
soy sauce
spinach
squash, butternut
squid
stocks: chicken, clam, fish, shrimp, veal, vegetable

Flavor Affinities

scallops + almonds + cauliflower
scallops + apples + bacon + watercress
scallops + apples + tarragon
scallops + asparagus + butter + lemongrass
scallops + avocado + lemon + lobster
scallops + bacon + chives
scallops + bacon + garlic + chanterelle mushrooms
scallops + bacon + leeks
scallops + basil + caviar + chives + tomatoes
scallops + basil + chicken stock + duck fat + garlic + lemon juice + tomatoes
scallops + basil + grapefruit
scallops + bay leaf + vanilla
scallops + Brussels sprouts + pancetta
scallops + carrot juice + pomegranate juice
scallops + cauliflower + cream
scallops + cilantro + lemon + sake
scallops + coriander + crab + lemon + thyme
scallops + dashi + Japanese mushrooms
scallops + edamame + mint
scallops + fennel + lemon + parsley
scallops + fennel + orange + rosemary
scallops + garlic + mushrooms
scallops + ginger + mint
scallops + ginger + scallions
scallops + ham + pineapple
scallops + kaffir lime + lemongrass + peanuts
scallops + parsley + salmon roe

sugar
Tabasco sauce
tarragon, fresh
THYME, FRESH
tomatoes: canned, fresh, paste
truffles, esp. black, white
tuna
turnips
vanilla
vermouth
vinaigrette
VINEGAR: balsamic, champagne, cider, red wine, rice wine, sherry, tarragon, white wine
watercress
WINE, DRY WHITE (e.g., Chablis, Chardonnay, Meursault, Riesling, Sauvignon Blanc)
Vermouth
yuzu juice
zucchini

SCANDINAVIAN CUISINE

aquavit
cardamom, esp. in baked goods
cinnamon
cucumbers
dill
fruits, esp. stewed
ginger
herring, pickled
juniper berries
nutmeg
onions
salmon, cured (aka gravlax)
soups, fruit
sour cream

Flavor Affinities
apples + cinnamon + sugar
cardamom + ginger + cinnamon
   + nutmeg + cloves
cucumbers + dill + onions + sugar
   + vinegar

SEAFOOD — IN GENERAL (See also specific fish and Shellfish)

Tips: Tap these ideas when cooking a medley of assorted seafood.

apples, esp. green
avocados
brandy, dry
capers
citrus
fennel
fruit
garlic
ginger
LEMON JUICE
mint
Old Bay seasoning
olive oil

SCOTCH

Weight: medium–heavy
Volume: moderate–loud

bitters
Earl Grey tea
gin
ginger
lemon, juice
lime, juice
orange, juice
soda
tamarind syrup
vermouth

Flavor Affinities
scotch + Earl Grey tea + tamarind
   syrup
scotch + ginger + lemon juice

During the winter months, I'll turn to bourbon and brown spirits to make cocktails. But non–scotch drinkers might turn their noses up at a cocktail with **scotch** in the name, so I created the Scotty and Tammy — an Earl Grey tea–based scotch drink made with tamarind syrup that goes especially well with Indian food.
— **JERRI BANKS,** COCKTAIL CONSULTANT (NEW YORK CITY)

The combination of ginger and **scotch** is explosive! I think the combination of ginger and lemon is such a welcoming flavor and can take on almost any spirit. Ginger itself is one of the most compelling scents and flavors in the world. Nothing else comes close.
— **JERRI BANKS,** COCKTAIL CONSULTANT (NEW YORK CITY)

I love citrus and fruit in general with savory food because they add acidity. Fruit works really well with **seafood** because seafood is also sweet. During the winter, we served a seafood consommé with green apple and ginger. We added a little green apple juice in the end for the acid balance.
— **DANIEL HUMM,** ELEVEN MADISON PARK (NEW YORK CITY)

We use the **Seafood** Watch guide from the Monterey Bay Aquarium to help select the fish we serve.
— **MONICA POPE,** T'AFIA (HOUSTON)

Our Seafood Watch regional guides contain the latest information on sustainable **seafood** choices available in different regions of the United States. Our Best Choices are abundant, well managed, and fished or farmed in environmentally friendly ways. **Seafood** to avoid are overfished and/or fished or farmed in ways that harm other marine life or the environment. You can view the guides online or download a pocket-size version.
— **MONTEREY BAY AQUARIUM SEAFOOD WATCH**

We work to inspire a closer relationship with the sea through science, art, and literature [including its Guide to Ocean Friendly Seafood].
— **BLUE OCEAN INSTITUTE**

olives
onions
parsley, flat-leaf
pepper: white, black
red pepper flakes
rosemary
saffron
salt
shallots
sherry
vinaigrettes
vinegars
wine: dry white (e.g., Sancerre, Soave)

Flavor Affinities
seafood + brandy + sherry
seafood + fennel + lemon + mint
seafood + green apple + ginger

Dishes

Spicy Gazpacho with Chilled Seafood Salad and Sweet Herbs
— Vitaly Paley, Paley's Place (Portland, Oregon)

Seafood Salad: Scallops, Squid, Japanese Octopus, Lobster, Avocado, Lemon Vinaigrette
— Alfred Portale, Gotham Bar and Grill (New York City)

The Cure Crudo: Tuna Bresaola, Citrus Sardine, and Smoked Scallop with Blood Orange
— Barton Seaver, Hook (Washington, DC)

Seafood Salad with Chickpeas, Celery, and Black Olives
— Hiro Sone, Terra (St. Helena, California)

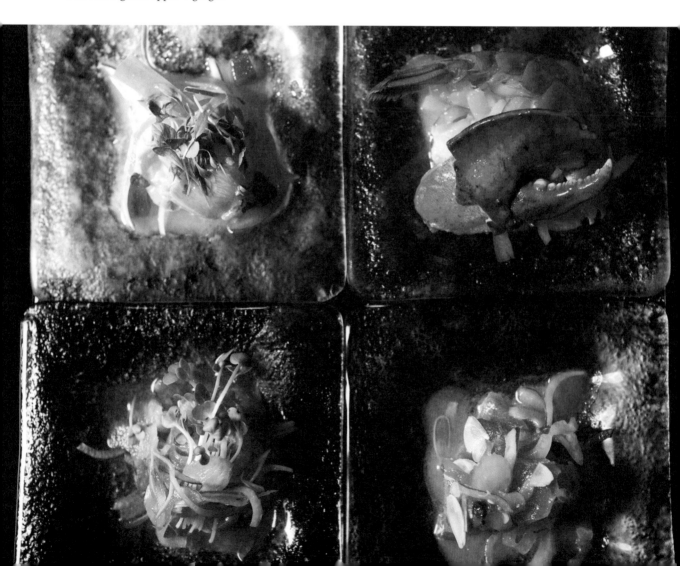

SESAME OIL
(See Oil, Sesame)

SESAME SEEDS, BLACK
Taste: bitter
Weight: light
Volume: quiet
Tips: Use whole seeds.

apples
Asian cuisine
bananas
Chinese cuisine
fish
Japanese cuisine
lemon, juice
meats
mirin
rice
salt
seafood
sesame seeds, white
soy sauce
vegetables
vinegar, rice wine

SESAME SEEDS, WHITE
Taste: sweet
Function: heating
Weight: light
Volume: quiet
Tips: Toast before using; use ground or whole.

allspice
apples
Asian cuisines
baked goods (e.g., bagels, breads, cakes, cookies)
bananas
beef
beets
breads and breadsticks
cardamom
chicken
chickpeas
chile peppers
Chinese cuisine (e.g., dim sum)
cilantro

cinnamon
cloves
coriander
duck
eggplant
fish
garlic
ginger
honey
hummus
ice cream
Indian cuisine
Japanese cuisine
lamb
Lebanese cuisine
legumes
lemon
meats
mole sauces
Middle Eastern cuisine
noodles
nutmeg
orange
oregano
paprika
pepper
rice
SALADS (green, pasta) and salad dressings
scallions
scallops
sesame oil
shellfish
shrimp
soy sauce
spinach
stir-fried dishes
sugar
sumac
tahini paste (key ingredient)
thyme
Turkish cuisine
vanilla
vegetables, esp. cold, green
zucchini

Flavor Affinities
sesame seeds + honey + tahini paste + vanilla

sesame seeds + garlic + soy sauce + spinach

SHALLOTS
Season: summer
Taste: sweet
Botanical relatives: chives, garlic, leeks, onions
Weight: light–medium
Volume: moderate
Techniques: blanch, braise, deep-fry, fry, roast, sauté, stir-fry
Tips: Shallots are milder than garlic or onions.

beef
butter
capers
chicken
chives
cod
cognac
cream
fish, esp. baked, grilled
French cuisine, esp. sauces
garlic
halibut
lemon, juice
meats, esp. grilled, roasted
mustard, Dijon
nutmeg
olive oil
oysters
parsley, flat-leaf
pasta
pepper, white
port
salads and salad dressings
salt
sauces (e.g., béarnaise, bordelaise, red wine)
sherry
squash, butternut
steak
stock, chicken
sugar (pinch)
tarragon
thyme
tomatoes

veal
vinaigrettes
vinegar: balsamic, champagne, cider, red wine, sherry, white wine
wine

SHELLFISH (See also Crab, Lobster, Scallops, Shrimp, etc.)
Season: summer

almonds
bacon
basil
celery
chives
cilantro
coconut
cream
curry
fennel
fines herbes (i.e., chervil, chives, parsley, tarragon)
fruit
garlic
ginger
grapefruit
hoisin sauce
LEMON
lemongrass
Old Bay seasoning
orange
saffron
tarragon
tomatoes
vanilla
vinegar
watermelon
wines, dry white (e.g., Sauvighon Blanc)

Flavor Affinities
shellfish + almonds + vanilla
shellfish + curry + lemongrass
shellfish + saffron + cream

SHIITAKE MUSHROOMS
(See Mushrooms — Shiitakes)

Fruit works easily with **shellfish**. You need to be careful, though, and counteract some of the sweetness of the fruit with vinegar or a citrus juice like lemon. Watermelon works well with shellfish, and I particularly like it with lobster, shrimp, and crab.
— **GABRIEL KREUTHER,** THE MODERN (NEW YORK CITY)

I love Provençal-style **shellfish** cooked with saffron and cream.
— **HIRO SONE,** TERRA (ST. HELENA, CALIFORNIA)

I love vanilla with **shellfish** because it brings out the sweetness. It works with scallops, lobster, or shrimp. I make a lobster-vanilla bisque that is one of my favorite soups. I also serve a scallop dish with vanilla, almonds, and orange. The vanilla brings up the sweet, the almonds add crispness to the creamy rich scallops, and the orange adds some acid. The dish also works really well with grapefruit instead of orange and gives it a tart flavor as well.
— **BOB IACOVONE,** CUVÉE (NEW ORLEANS)

SHISO LEAF
Weight: light
Volume: moderate–loud
Techniques: raw

apples
avocados
basil
beef
cabbage
chicken
chives
clams
crab
cucumbers
fish, esp. fried or oily
fried foods
ginger
Japanese cuisine
Korean cuisine
lemon
lemongrass
lime
meat
melon
mint
miso
noodles
onions
orange
parsley
pears
pickles
prawns
radishes
rice
salads: green, fruit
sea urchin

Visually you can't beat **shiso**; it is a big, beautiful leaf. It is great with fried foods, oily fish, and sea urchin, and pairs with big, robust flavors. Instead of grabbing lemon or soy sauce, you can use shiso to liven up a dish.
— **BRAD FARMERIE,** PUBLIC (NEW YORK CITY)

Shiso is a very versatile herb and works with a lot of things. It can work with pears as well as apples, not to mention a variety of seafood like Dungeness crab and spot prawns.
— **JERRY TRAUNFELD,** THE HERBFARM (WOODINVILLE, WASHINGTON)

seafood
shrimp
soups
soy sauce
sushi and sashimi
tempura
turnips
vinegar
wasabi
yellowtail

Flavor Affinities
shiso leaf + avocado + crab
shiso leaf + clams + onions

SHORT RIBS (See Beef — Short Ribs)

SHRIMP (See also Shellfish)
Season: year–round
Weight: light–medium (depending on size)
Volume: quiet
Techniques: bake, barbecue, boil, broil, deep-fry, grill, poach, roast, sauté, steam, stir-fry

allspice
almonds
apples and apple cider
artichokes
arugula
asparagus
avocado
bacon
basil
bay leaf
beans: black, cranberry, fava, green, white
beer
bell peppers, red
bonito flakes (e.g., Japanese)
brandy
bread crumbs, *panko*
brown butter sauce
butter, unsalted
cabbage: green, red
Cajun cuisine

capers
carrots and carrot juice
caviar
cayenne
celery
celery root
chervil
chicory
CHILE PEPPERS, e.g., ancho, chipotle, dried red, jalapeño, serrano
chili oil
chili paste
chili powder
chili sauce
Chinese cuisine
chives
cilantro (garnish)
cinnamon
clams
cloves
coconut: milk, shredded
cognac
coriander
corn
CRAB
cream
Creole cuisine
cucumbers
cumin
curry leaf
curry powder or sauce
dill
eggs
endive
fennel
fennel seeds
fish, white
fish sauce, Thai
*GARLIC
ginger
greens, esp. beet, dandelion, collard, mustard, turnip
grits
hazelnut oil
honey
horseradish
Japanese cuisine

kaffir lime leaf
ketchup
Korean cuisine
leeks
LEMON: juice, zest
lemongrass
lettuce
lime: leaves, juice, whole, zest
lobster
mango
marjoram
mayonnaise
Mediterranean cuisine
melon, cantaloupe
Mexican cuisine
mint
mirin
monkfish
mushrooms, (e.g., chanterelles, shiitakes)
mussels
mustard: country, Dijon, dry (sauce)
mustard seeds
nutmeg
OIL: canola, corn, grapeseed, peanut, vegetable
oil: peanut, sesame (for drizzling)
Old Bay seasoning
olive oil
olives, black
ONIONS, esp. red, Spanish, white
orange: juice, zest
oregano
oysters
paprika
parsley, flat-leaf
pasta
peanuts
PEPPER: black, white
pesto
pike
pineapple and pineapple juice
pine nuts
pistachios
pumpkin

Dishes

Black Spaghetti with Rock Shrimp, Spicy Salami Calabrese, and Green Chiles
— Mario Batali, Babbo (New York City)

Ceviche Yucateco: Steamed Organic Shrimp and Calamari Tossed with Lime, Orange, Habanero, Avocado, and Cilantro
— Rick Bayless, Frontera Grill (Chicago)

Phyllo-Crusted Shrimp with Crabmeat in an Ocean Herbal Broth
— David Bouley, Bouley (New York City)

Shrimp Sautéed in a Spicy Sauce with Jalapeño, Mint, and Garlic, Topped with Shredded Fresh Coconut
— Zarela Martinez, Zarela (New York City)

Chipotle Shrimp Corn Cakes
— Mark Miller, Coyote Café (Santa Fe)

Shrimp with White Bean Salad and Italian Sausage
— Patrick O'Connell, The Inn at Little Washington (Washington, Virginia)

Sweet Shrimp Risotto: Roma Tomatoes, Wilted Arugula, and Crisp Bacon
— Alfred Portale, Gotham Bar and Grill (New York City)

Shrimp in Light Three-Pepper Red Mole Sauce (Coloradito) over Cuban-Style Fresh Corn Polenta and Sautéed Kale
— Maricel Presilla, Zafra (Hoboken, New Jersey)

Fricassee of Rock Shrimp, Mango, Leeks, and Coconut Rum
— Allen Susser, Chef Allen's (Aventura, Florida)

Shrimp and Avocado Ceviche, Kaffir Lime, Coconut Milk, Scallions, and Pappadam
— Allen Susser, Chef Allen's (Aventura, Florida)

Shrimp shells are a base for a great sauce. They are really sweet, and you want to be sure to brown all the shrimp shell surfaces to get the maximum sweetness. This sauce came about by smelling the shells while they were cooking, and working with the flavors that came to mind. I added vanilla and whiskey, and something magical happened.
— **CARRIE NAHABEDIAN,** NAHA (CHICAGO)

radishes
red pepper flakes
rice (e.g., Arborio, bomba)
risotto
rosemary
rum, dark
saffron
sage
sake

salsa
SALT: kosher, sea
sauce, romesco
sausages (e.g., andouille)
scallions
scallops
sesame: oil, seeds
shallots
shiso leaf

snow peas
sour cream
Southern cuisine
soy sauce
spinach
squid
squid ink
star anise
stocks: chicken, clam, fish, shrimp
sugar: brown, white
sweet potatoes
Tabasco sauce
tarragon
tea sandwiches
tempura
Thai cuisine
thyme, lemon
TOMATOES and tomato paste, sun-dried
turmeric
vanilla
vermouth
Vietnamese cuisine
vinaigrette
vinegar: balsamic, rice wine, sherry, tarragon, wine
wasabi
watercress
WINE: dry white, rice, Sauternes
Worcestershire sauce
yogurt
yuzu juice
zucchini

Flavor Affinities

shrimp + bacon + chives
shrimp + basil + garlic + jalapeño chile
shrimp + black beans + coriander
shrimp + cayenne + cinnamon + orange
shrimp + cepes mushrooms + curry powder + Dijon mustard
shrimp + chiles + lime juice + brown sugar
shrimp + coriander + tarragon
shrimp + crab + Old Bay seasoning
shrimp + crab + pistachio nuts + watercress
shrimp + garlic + grits + mascarpone + tomato
shrimp + garlic + lime
shrimp + garlic + mustard + tarragon
shrimp + ginger + green apple + saffron
shrimp + horseradish + ketchup + lemon
shrimp + white beans + bell pepper + orange + sausage

SKATE

Season: summer
Weight: medium–heavy
Volume: quiet–moderate
Techniques: broil, grill, poach, roast, sauté, steam

almonds
anchovies
arugula
bay leaf
butter and butter sauces (e.g., brown butter)
CAPERS
carrots
cayenne
celery and celery leaves
chives
cilantro
clams
cloves
dill
eggplant
fennel
garlic
leeks
LEMON, juice
lemon balm
lovage
mustard, Dijon
OIL: canola, peanut, sesame, vegetable
OLIVE OIL
onions
orange, juice
parsley, flat-leaf
parsnips
pasta
pepper: black, green, white
pistachios
polenta
ponzu sauce
potatoes
pumpkin seeds
rosemary
saffron
sage

Dishes

Skate with Hen-of-the-Woods (Mushrooms) and Butternut Squash
— Mario Batali, Babbo (New York City)

Chanterelle-Stuffed Skate, Creamy Spinach, "Carotte Fondante," and Bordelaise Sauce
— Daniel Boulud, Daniel (New York City)

Sautéed Skate Wing with Caper Brown Butter
— Jean Joho, Brasserie Jo (Chicago)

Skate Wing and a Cannelloni of "Sunchoke" with Butter-Poached Chesapeake Bay Lump Crab, Jerusalem Artichokes, and Oyster Mushrooms
— Carrie Nahabedian, Naha (Chicago)

Sage goes really well with **skate** — it gives the skate a masculine touch.
— **ERIC RIPERT**, LE BERNARDIN (NEW YORK CITY)

I make a sautéed **skate** dish that is basically a version of linguini with white clam sauce. The sauce with the skate is made from the juice from the clams, garlic, anchovy, and olive oil and it is finished with a parsley puree. With the fish I also serve angel hair pasta. All these flavors are what you will find in white clam sauce, but are just served in a different form.
— **DAVID WALTUCK**, CHANTERELLE (NEW YORK CITY)

We still have the same philosophy as when we opened: The fish is still the star of the plate. We have not budged from there, but every dish has a sauce that completes the dish, and brings together all the elements on the plate and creates harmony. We pay homage to seafood and are dedicated to it, but use a wide palette from rich sauces to broths and a variety of spices and emulsions.

What makes a dish work is the way we make and treat our sauce. We don't make a sauce in the morning and use it for the day. Can you imagine if you made coffee in the morning and came back at noon to taste it? It would be disgusting. The same for tea: if you left a tea bag in your tea all day, at night it would be awful.

We used to make a garlic sage broth and I found it to be very volatile. I realized that the sauce is really only good for three minutes. After that, the sage kills the garlic or vice versa and the sauce loses its balance. What we ended up doing is making a base with chicken stock, then using a tea bag with ingredients in it to infuse the sauce, and we serve it right away. This sauce is paired with **skate** roasted in goose fat with green peppercorns. On the side we serve artichokes with pistachios and Parmesan cheese.
— **ERIC RIPERT**, LE BERNARDIN (NEW YORK CITY)

sake
salt: kosher, sea
shallots
shrimp
spinach
squid
star anise
tapenade
tarragon
thyme
tomatoes and tomato paste
vinaigrette
VINEGAR: balsamic, red wine,
   rice wine, sherry
walnuts
wine: dry white, red

Flavor Affinities
skate + butter + pistachios
skate + capers + garlic + lemon
   juice
skate + capers + sherry vinegar
skate + fennel + onions
skate + garlic + sage

SLOW-COOKED
Season: autumn–winter
Tips: These herbs and flavorings
taste better with longer cooking.
For the opposite of slow-cooked,
see **Freshness.**

cumin
garlic
ginger
horseradish
onions
oregano
rosemary
shallots
thyme

SMOKED SALMON
(See Salmon, Smoked)

SMOKINESS
Tips: Add a smoky component to
provide a "meaty" flavor to a dish

or to counteract the richness of
certain meats and seafoods.

bacon
barbecued foods
beer, smoked
cheese, smoked
chile peppers, chipotle
duck, smoked
fish, smoked (e.g., salmon, trout)
grilled foods
ham, smoked
liquid smoke
paprika, smoked
salmon, smoked
salt, smoked
sausage, smoked
tea, Lapsang Souchong
whiskey, scotch

SNAP PEAS
(aka sugar snap peas)
Season: spring
Taste: sweet
Weight: light
Volume: quiet
Techniques: blanch, raw, steam,
stir-fry

almonds
basil
brown butter sauce
butter
carrots
celery
chervil
chives
cilantro
cream
curry
dill
garlic
ginger
halibut
leeks
lemon, juice
marjoram
mint

Dishes
Alaskan King Salmon with Sugar Snap Peas
  — David Pasternak, Esca
(New York City)

mushrooms
nutmeg
olive oil
onions
oregano
parsley
pepper, white
potatoes
rice
rosemary
saffron
sage
salmon
scallions
sesame oil
sesame seeds
shrimp
stock, vegetable
tarragon
thyme
yogurt

Flavor Affinities
snap peas + brown butter + sage

SNAPPER (aka red snapper)
Season: late spring–early
autumn
Weight: medium
Volume: moderate
Techniques: bake, braise, broil,
deep-fry, grill, poach, roast, sauté,
steam, stir-fry

almonds
apricots, esp. dried
artichokes
basil (garnish)
bay leaf
bell peppers: green, red, yellow
butter, unsalted
cabbage

capers
carrots
cayenne
celery and celery leaves
chile peppers: chipotle, jalapeño
chives
cilantro
clams
coconut
coriander
couscous
crab
cream
cumin
dill
fennel
fennel seeds
five-spice powder
GARLIC
ginger
grapefruit
hazelnuts
leeks

LEMON: fruit, juice, zest
lemon thyme
lime, juice
mint
miso: dried, white
mushrooms: cepes, chanterelles
mustard, Dijon
OIL: canola, corn, grapeseed,
    vegetable
OLIVE OIL
olives: black, kalamata
onions: red, white
orange: juice, zest
papaya
paprika
parsley, flat-leaf
peas, sugar snap
pepper: black, white
pesto
pistachios, esp. as crust
port
potatoes
red pepper flakes

Dishes

Marinated Thai Snapper with Wasabi Cream;
Shaved Radishes and Poppy Seed Tuile
— Daniel Boulud, Daniel (New York City)

rice
rosemary
saffron
SALT: kosher, sea
sauces: brown butter,
    hollandaise, romesco
sausage, esp. spicy
scallions
seaweed (for presentation)
sesame
shallots
shrimp
spinach
star anise
stocks: chicken, fish
sugar
sweet potatoes

tarragon
thyme
TOMATOES: canned, fresh, paste
turnips
vinegar: red wine, sherry, white
wine, dry white

Flavor Affinities
snapper + clams + romesco sauce + sausage
snapper + fennel + olives + orange + saffron
snapper + coconut + crab + papaya
snapper + garlic + potatoes + rosemary
snapper + lemon + thyme + tomatoes

SOLE
Weight: light
Volume: quiet
Techniques: pan sear, poach, sauté, steam

artichokes
asparagus
basil: sweet, lemon
bass
bay leaf
beans, fava
bread crumbs
BUTTER, unsalted
buttermilk
capers
carrots
cayenne
celery and celery leaves
chervil
CHIVES
coriander
cornmeal
couscous
cream
dill
endive
French cuisine
garlic
ginger
greens, collard
LEMON: juice, slices

lobster
mayonnaise
Mediterranean cuisine
milk
mint, esp. spearmint
mushrooms: button, morels
mussels
noodles
oil: canola, corn, grapeseed, olive, peanut, vegetable
olive oil
onions, esp. white
oysters
paprika
PARSLEY, flat-leaf
peas
PEPPER: black, pink, white
potatoes
quince
ramps
salmon
SALT: kosher, sea
sauces: brown butter, hollandaise
SHALLOTS
shrimp
spinach
star anise
stock, fish
TARRAGON
thyme
tomatoes
truffles
vinegar, balsamic

watercress
WINE, DRY WHITE
  (e.g., Chablis)

Flavor Affinities
sole + butter + lemon + parsley
sole + paprika + potatoes

SORREL
Season: spring–autumn
Taste: sour
Weight: medium, soft-leaved
Volume: moderate–loud
Tips: Always use fresh; as a soft-leaved herb, it will lose flavor in sauces, soups.

almonds
apples
avocados
bacon
basil
BUTTER, UNSALTED
carrots
caviar
chard
CHEESE: Emmental, goat, **Gruyère, Parmesan,** pecorino, **ricotta,** Swiss
chervil
chicken
chives
cilantro
collard greens
CREAM
crème fraîche
cucumbers
dandelion greens
dill
EGGS: egg-based dishes, omelets
escarole
FISH
French cuisine
garlic
grapes
greens
leeks
lemon, juice

Dishes

Puree of Sorrel Soup with Toasted Marcona Almonds and Poached Sultanas
— Thomas Keller, The French Laundry (Yountville, California)

Sorrel has a green vegetal quality and is tangy. It is a little like tasting fish sauce: on its own it is nasty, but with food it is great! Sorrel also works with eggs as well as seafood. One of the seafood dishes we make is roasted oysters with bacon and sorrel sauce.
— **JERRY TRAUNFELD**, THE HERBFARM (WOODINVILLE, WASHINGTON)

lemon verbena
lentils, esp. green
lettuce
lovage
marinades
meats
mint
mushrooms
mussels
mustard
nutmeg
olive oil
onions
paprika
parsley, flat-leaf
parsnip
pepper: black, white
pork
potatoes, esp. new, russet
poultry
rice
salads (say some)
salmon
salmon, smoked
salt
sauces, cream
seafood
shad
shallots
shellfish
SOUPS, esp. creamy vegetable
sour cream
SPINACH
STOCKS: chicken, veal, vegetable
stuffings
tarragon
tea sandwiches

thyme, lemon
tomatoes
trout
veal
vegetarian dishes
vinegar, red wine
watercress
wine, dry white

AVOID
salads (say some)

Flavor Affinities
sorrel + butter + chicken stock
sorrel + garlic + spinach
sorrel + leeks + potatoes
sorrel + nutmeg + ricotta cheese

SOUR CREAM
Taste: sour
Weight: medium–heavy
Volume: moderate–loud
Tips: Use fresh, or cook at low temperatures only.

baked goods (e.g., cakes, cookies)
borscht
caviar
desserts
dill
dips

I like galangal, lemongrass, and ginger. They all have natural **acidity** and zingy spice that will perk anything up. Even if you are not adding [a liquid] acid to coconut milk but add aromatics instead, your dish won't taste heavy.
— **BRAD FARMERIE**, PUBLIC (NEW YORK CITY)

European cuisine, esp. eastern and northern
fruit
horseradish
Hungarian cuisine
lemon, juice
mustard
paprika
pepper
potatoes, esp. baked
Russian cuisine
salads and salad dressings
sauces
Scandinavian cuisine
soups

SOURNESS
Taste: sour
Function: heating; stimulates appetite; increases thirst
Tips: Sourness tends to sharpen other flavors.
In small doses, sour notes enhance bitterness, while in large doses, they suppress bitterness.

apples, tart (e.g., Granny Smith, Winesap)
blackberries
buttermilk
caraway seeds
cheese, sour (e.g., chèvre, other goat cheese)
cherries, sour
citrus
cloves
coriander
cornichons
cranberries
cream cheese
cream of tartar
crème fraîche

A defining factor for American cooks is hitting high notes with **acidic** tones. Using acidity to create brightness in dishes stands out from the cooking I did in France. French cooking is all about harmony, while American cooking is about hitting the high notes. In American fine dining, you have to have some boundaries with your acidity because you are working with wine. It is important to hit the high notes but you have to do it without destroying the wine pairing.

— **MICHAEL ANTHONY,** GRAMERCY TAVERN (NEW YORK CITY)

Almost every dish has to have some sort of **acid**, or else it will taste flat. It is a question of taste — some chefs like sour, some like sweet — and there is no right or wrong. Lemon juice is used in small amounts to bring out other flavors. I use all kinds of vinegars — banyuls, red wine, rice wine, and sherry, just to name a few.

— **DAVID WALTUCK,** CHANTERELLE (NEW YORK CITY)

I have a cupboard full of acids! Every culture is doing the same thing when it comes to using **acid** in its food: it is all about enhancing flavor without adding salt. We use a lot of citrus, whether it is lemon, lime, or something else. When I lived in England, they joked with me because I would add orange juice to almost everything, especially vinaigrettes. I really like its acidity and the light, fruity flavor it adds. On a totally different end of the spectrum is tamarind. We always have tamarind water in our refrigerator and use it to finish sauces. Depending on the country of inspiration, I will use a different acid: for India, tamarind; Japan, ponzu, yuzu; Middle East, sumac, preserved lemon, and yogurt; and for Southeast Asia, lemon, lime, and tamarind.

— **BRAD FARMERIE,** PUBLIC (NEW YORK CITY)

I select my **acids** as carefully as I select my sweeteners. I could use lemon juice for everything, but in some cases, *verjus* will add a brightness that balsamic or sherry vinegar won't. I love *verjus* and have served it alone as a sorbet. I have also served it with apple and pears. I like ice wine vinegar with roasting fruits. Aged balsamic vinegar isn't shocking anymore — it is great straight over fruit or added to an ice cream.

— **MICHAEL LAISKONIS,** LE BERNARDIN (NEW YORK CITY)

When you add **acid** to a sauce, it lifts everything up. Lemon is my favorite; I use lemon and orange the way a chef uses salt and pepper. Whether I add the juice, zest, or confit depends on the cooking application:

- **Juice:** If a recipe calls for water, why use that? Why not add flavor and use orange juice?
- **Zest:** If I make *panna cotta*, it will have orange zest in it but it will not taste orangey. If I make a cake, I also use zest.
- **Confit:** I use this most often as a garnish.

— **MICHAEL LAISKONIS,** LE BERNARDIN (NEW YORK CITY)

currants
fermented foods
fruits: sour, unripened
galangal
ginger
grapefruit
grapes, green
kaffir lime
kiwi fruit
kumquats
lemon: juice, zest
lemon, preserved
lemongrass
lime: juice, zest
milk, goat's
miso
mushrooms, enoki
orange: juice, zest
pickled foods
plums, esp. unripe
ponzu
quince
rhubarb
rose hips
sauces, reduced-wine
sauerkraut
sorrel
sour cream
soy sauce
sumac
tamarind
tomatoes, esp. green
verjus
vinegars
whey
wine, dry
yogurt
yuzu

SOUS-VIDE COOKING

What *sous-vide* ["under vacuum"] cooking does is give you a long, very controlled cooking time. I like to use it on vegetables because no air hits the vegetable. All the white vegetables come out really white. It also keeps the whiteness in fruits like apples and pears.

— **DANIEL HUMM**, ELEVEN MADISON PARK (NEW YORK CITY)

Instead of *sous-vide,* with poultry I'll use a poaching technique I learned from my grandmother: I'll cover a whole chicken or turkey or pheasant with cold liquid, mirepoix, garlic, and herbs; cover the pot with a tight-fitting lid; bring it to a boil; drop it to a simmer; and then turn it off. This technique creates a vacuum seal that transfers all the flavor into the chicken. It's ten times better than straight poaching, because you don't lose any moisture. I'll serve the chicken cold with a hot ginger sauce that's two parts fresh ginger to one part each garlic, scallions, and cilantro. I heat oil to smoking, pour it over the herbs, and serve the hot ginger-herb sauce over the cold poached chicken. It's delicious.

— **TONY LIU**, AUGUST (NEW YORK CITY)

SOUTHEAST ASIAN CUISINES

Tips: Balance hot + sour + salty + sweet tastes.

chile peppers
coconut milk
curries
fish sauce
galangal
ginger
lemongrass
lime
mint
soy sauce
sugar
tamarind
vegetables: fresh, fermented

Flavor Affinities

chile peppers + fish sauce + lime + sugar
fish sauce + lime + tamarind

SOUTHERN CUISINE (AMERICAN)

baked goods, e.g., biscuits
barbecue
black-eyed peas
chicken, esp. fried
gravy
greens, esp. collard
grits
ham
pies
pork
potatoes
rice
sweet potatoes
tea: iced, sweet

SOUTHWESTERN CUISINE (AMERICAN)

avocados
beans
beef
cheese
chicken
chiles
chocolate
cilantro
cinnamon
corn
limes
nuts
onions
pork
rice
squash
tomatoes
tortillas

SOY SAUCE

Taste: salty
Weight: light
Volume: moderate–loud
Tips: Add at the end of the cooking process, or to finish a dish. Use in stir-fries.

basil
beef
broccoli
chicken
Chinese cuisine
coriander
fish: cooked, raw
garlic
ginger
honey
Japanese cuisine
Korean cuisine
lime juice
lobster, raw
marinades
meats
mirin
molasses

I add **soy sauce** to my onion soup because it gives it a meaty flavor. I use so much soy sauce at home my kid is starting to look Asian!
— **MICHEL RICHARD,** CITRONELLE (WASHINGTON, DC)

White soy sauce is something I fell in love with while cooking in Japan for two years. It is like liquid smoke. It is not really soy sauce, but more of a brewed wheat product. It has a smoky quality, too, but it is still so light you can use it on hamachi with sesame seeds and olive oil.
— **MICHAEL ANTHONY,** GRAMERCY TAVERN (NEW YORK CITY)

White soy sauce is lighter on the palate and has a cleaner, more direct flavor than regular soy sauce. Regular soy sauce has a touch of caramel for color, flavor, and body, which makes it more a part of the dish rather than simply enhancing the ingredient. White soy sauce will let the ingredient sing. It is very pale, and if you make a ponzu sauce with mirin and rice wine vinegar, you'll get something almost clear.
— **BRAD FARMERIE,** PUBLIC (NEW YORK CITY)

orange zest
peanuts
red pepper flakes
salt
scallions
seafood
sesame oil
sugar
wasabi

Flavor Affinities
soy sauce + coriander + honey
soy sauce + garlic + ginger
soy sauce + molasses + sugar

SPANISH CUISINE
almonds
anchovies
bay leaf
bread
chorizo
custards
eggs
fish
fruits
garlic
ham, Serrano
hazelnuts
lemon
meats, esp. roasted

olive oil
olives
onion
orange
paprika, sweet
parsley
peppers, esp. guindilla or
    piquillo, esp. roasted
pine nuts
pomegranates
pork
rice
roasts
saffron
shellfish
sherry
soups
stews
thyme

tomatoes
vanilla
vegetables
vinegar, sherry
walnuts

Flavor Affinities
almonds + garlic + olive oil
almonds + olive oil
garlic + olive oil
garlic + onions + paprika + rice +
    saffron
garlic + onions + parsley
red peppers + onions + tomatoes
tomatoes + almonds + olive oil +
    roasted red peppers

Dishes

Hearts of Romaine and Treviso Radicchio with Spanish Serrano Ham, Manchego Cheese, and White Anchovies, Fire-Roasted Peppers, and Crisp Capers
— Carrie Nahabedian, Naha (Chicago)

Petite Red Oak Lettuce Salad with Manchego Cheese, Cinnamon Almonds, and Aged Sherry Vinaigrette
— Celina Tio, American Restaurant (Kansas City)

Spain in the New World:
How American Chefs Are Influenced by Spain

Sweet Potato, Feta, and Smoked Paprika Tortilla with Minted Lemon Raita: We looked at Spain and the tortilla as the starting point for this dish. A traditional tortilla is made all together in one pan, but we played with that a little. We roast our sweet potatoes first with spicy-smoky paprika that tempers the sweetness with the heat and aromatic smokiness. We add feta cheese for the salt factor and caramelized onion for another layer of flavor. We then mix up a bunch of eggs, combine everything together, and cook it tortilla-style in a hot pan with a lot of olive oil on the stove and then in the oven to finish cooking. When we serve it, we cut it tortilla-style in a wedge and serve it at room temperature. The idea of eggs and potatoes always feels a bit heavy, which is why there is a zesty yogurt on the plate along with a crunchy watercress salad.

— **BRAD FARMERIE,** PUBLIC (NEW YORK CITY)

Hearts of Romaine and Treviso Radicchio with Spanish Serrano Ham, Manchego Cheese and White Anchovies, Fire-Roasted Peppers and Crisp Capers: This dish is an homage to Guillermo, who supplies our Spanish products. His anchovies are so good that if someone asks for them on the side, the waiter just replies, "Trust me. . . ." The reason there is radicchio on the salad is because I like to change people's opinions of ingredients that have been wronged. When it is added to this salad, it is so good you can't believe it. It adds a wonderful crunch and balances the romaine and other flavors. I add the fried capers to add some acidity and crunch.

— **CARRIE NAHABEDIAN,** NAHA (CHICAGO)

In Spain, eggs aren't eaten for breakfast; they are more for dinner. The Spanish also don't eat brunch, but at Tía Pol, brunch is a way to celebrate the Spanish egg cookery that is a huge part of their diet. The Spanish cook eggs beautifully and in a huge variety. In the Basque country, they really value a soft scrambled egg with a great ingredient in it — whether tiny mushrooms, asparagus, or baby pink shrimp. The Spanish also cook eggs in olive oil. When we serve a fried egg, we cook it in so much oil it is almost deep-fried; instead of using a spatula, we use a spider [a weblike wire mesh strainer] to remove the egg from the pan.

— **ALEXANDRA RAIJ,** TÍA POL (NEW YORK CITY)

We use olive oil as a condiment. In Spain it is not uncommon to see something swimming in olive oil. Anchovies will be covered in oil, and after you eat the anchovies you just dip your bread in the oil. Even a dish that is cooked in olive oil will get a drizzle of raw oil on top for finishing. In Spanish cooking it is hard for me to name a dish that doesn't get olive oil. We will cook mushrooms in olive oil and serve them with oil on top.

Sautéed vegetables in Spain may get cooked in a little pork fat and then served with diced ham on top. The Spanish also like to braise vegetables, and will add a ham end similar to a trotter [pig's foot] during the cooking. Any pot of stew or beans, such as garbanzos, will get ham added to it as well. What the ham end adds to what is being cooked is a little funky flavor but in a good way — like the flavor mold adds to a cheese.

— **ALEXANDRA RAIJ,** TÍA POL (NEW YORK CITY)

SPICES (See also individual spices)

Just a pinch of **spices** such as fennel, coriander, cumin, and cayenne is great for finishing a sauce. Cayenne is great if you want to raise the heat level. You want to use only a pinch so that you don't even know it is there. If you are making a French lemon sauce with beurre blanc, lemon puree, and diced lemon zest, adding a pinch of cayenne will bring up the flavor without making it spicy.

— ANDREW CARMELLINI, A VOCE (NEW YORK CITY)

I am sure every kitchen has its own **pepper mix** that is not just pepper. We have a mix that is specific for meat and occasionally for pork or tuna. It is a combination of black peppercorns, pink peppercorns, coriander seeds, and toasted ground star anise. The other thing I always have next to me is a tray we call "the four seasons": *fleur de sel;* red pepper flakes — the ultimate marriage of heat and fruit; dry mustard, which I use all the time; and sumac, for an acidic component.

— SHARON HAGE, YORK STREET (DALLAS)

To counteract **overspicing**, you need to increase the quantity of whatever you are making. This is a case where you might want to add a puree of something, or add some sweetness because sweetness balances spice. With an Indian curry that is too powerful, you could puree some dried apricot into it. The apricot puree adds sweetness, binds the sauce, and increases the overall quantity.

— ANDREW CARMELLINI, A VOCE (NEW YORK CITY)

SPINACH (See also Greens — In General)

Season: year-round
Taste: bitter
Function: cooling
Weight: medium
Volume: moderate
Techniques: boil, raw, sauté, steam, stir-fry, wilt

almonds
anchovies
apples
bacon
basil
*BUTTER, unsalted
cayenne
chard
CHEESE: aged, Comté,
Emmental, feta, goat,
Parmesan, ricotta
chicken, esp. grilled
chickpeas
chives
crab
CREAM / MILK
cream cheese
crème fraîche
cumin
curry
dill
eggs, esp. hard-boiled
fennel
fish (e.g., striped bass)
French cuisine
GARLIC
ginger
greens, collard

Indian cuisine
Italian cuisine
Japanese cuisine
lamb, esp. grilled
lemon, juice
lentils
lovage
marjoram
mascarpone
mint, esp. spearmint
mushrooms, esp. shiitake
mustard, Dijon
mustard seeds
NUTMEG
OIL: canola, peanut, sesame, vegetable, **walnut**
olive oil
onions, esp. sweet
pancetta
paprika, sweet
parsley
pasta
pecans
PEPPER: black, white
pesto
pine nuts
potatoes
prosciutto
quince
raisins
red pepper flakes
saffron
SALT: kosher, sea
salt cod
sauces: béchamel, Mornay
scallions
SESAME SEEDS
shallots
shrimp
smoked salmon
sorrel
sour cream
soy sauce
stocks: chicken, vegetable
sugar (pinch)
Tabasco sauce
thyme, fresh
tomatoes

Dishes

Warm Mushroom and Baby Spinach Salad with Black Bean Sauce
— Kaz Okochi, Kaz Sushi Bistro (Washington, DC)

Spinach and Walnut Cannelloni in the Style of the River Plate Region, Creamy Manchego and Parmigiano-Reggiano White Sauce, and Tomato Sauce
— Maricel Presilla, Cucharamama (Hoboken, New Jersey)

I love **spinach.** It is best sautéed in a little oil, because if you blanch it, it tends to lose its flavor [to the blanching water]. I like to add some garlic to it, and from there you can go almost anywhere. Sautéed spinach is delicious with a poached egg.
— **GABRIEL KREUTHER,** THE MODERN (NEW YORK CITY)

Spinach and bacon is simply a great combination. The key to our creamed spinach is that we steam our fresh-leaf spinach just until it wilts, then drain it and chop it slightly. [In a pan,] we start with a little butter and flour to thicken, then add cream, nutmeg, and an *onion piqué* [an onion spiked with cloves], and reduce the cream by half. Then we add the barely cooked spinach to the cream and heat them together briefly so just a little juice infiltrates the cream. You end up with velvety spinach, which we top with [chunks of] Nueske's bacon, which is an applewood-smoked bacon from the Midwest.
— **MICHAEL LOMONACO,** PORTER HOUSE NEW YORK (NEW YORK CITY)

Our warm mushroom and baby **spinach** salad with black bean sauce works so well because of the garlic, which is the last thing added to the dish. Too often, garlic is overpowering. You want to add just enough.
— **KAZ OKOCHI,** KAZ SUSHI BISTRO (WASHINGTON, DC)

tuna
vinaigrette, esp. sherry
VINEGAR: balsamic, cider, red
   wine, rice wine, sherry
walnuts
yogurt

Flavor Affinities

spinach + bacon + garlic + onions + cider vinegar
spinach + bacon + walnuts
spinach + chives + goat cheese + mascarpone
spinach + cumin + garlic + lemon + yogurt
spinach + fennel + Parmesan cheese + portobello mushrooms +
   balsamic vinegar
spinach + feta cheese + lemon juice + oregano
spinach + garlic + mushrooms
spinach + garlic + sorrel

SPRING
Weather: typically warm
Techniques: pan roast and other stove-top methods

artichokes (peak: March–April)
asparagus: green, purple, white
   (peak: April)
beans, fava (peak: April–June)
cauliflower (peak: March)
crayfish
dandelion greens (peak:
   May–June)
fiddlehead ferns
garlic, green (peak: March)
greens: salad, spring
lamb, spring
leeks
lemons, Meyer
lettuces
lighter dishes
limes, key
loquats
mushrooms, morel (peak: April)
onions: spring, Vidalia (peak:
   May)
oranges, navel (peak: March)
peas (peak: May)
ramps (peak: May)
rhubarb (peak: April)
soft-shell crabs
sorrel (peak: May)
soufflés
spices, cooling (e.g., white
   peppercorns)
strawberries
tomatoes, heirloom
watercress
zucchini blossoms

Spring is when people are looking for all the young salads that they have been missing all winter. I really look forward to asparagus that I will serve simply with mayonnaise or a mousseline.
— **GABRIEL KREUTHER,** THE MODERN (NEW YORK CITY)

Spring is when everyone's moods start to lighten. It may be cold, but people are looking for lighter things. This is rhubarb and strawberry season. Citrus plays a bigger role; in the winter, it is an alternative to chocolate, but in the spring, it is the lighter and more aromatic option.

— **EMILY LUCHETTI**, FARALLON (SAN FRANCISCO)

Spring lamb is one of the quintessential dishes of **spring**.

— **MICHEL RICHARD**, CITRONELLE (WASHINGTON, DC)

Dishes

Squab, Watermelon, Foie Gras, and Black Licorice
— Grant Achatz, Alinea (Chicago)

Barbecued Squab with Roasted Beet "Farrotto" and Porcini Mustard
— Mario Batali, Babbo (New York City)

You may be thinking about licorice but don't want a licorice sauce. So you may simply just grate some fennel over **squab** and you get this great aroma and when you take a bite you'll taste this root beer–Pernod flavor that is not overbearing that will still work with squab, foie gras, medjool dates, and green peppercorns. Some flavors are meant to be just a soft accent on a dish. I like to think of them as "eye shadow"!

— **CARRIE NAHABEDIAN**, NAHA (CHICAGO)

SPROUTS
Season: year-round
Function: cooling
Weight: light
Volume: quiet
Techniques: sauté, steam, stir-fry
Tips: Cook for less than 30 seconds, or they'll wilt.

cucumbers
egg salad
salads, esp. more delicate sprouts
sandwiches
stir-fried dishes, esp. heartier sprouts

SQUAB
Weight: medium
Volume: moderate
Techniques: braise, broil, grill, roast, sauté

bacon
beans, fava
beets
cabbage
cherries
fennel

figs
foie gras
garlic
juniper berries
lentils
mushrooms, wild, esp. porcini
mustard
olive oil
olives
onions
pancetta
pears
peas
pepper, black
prunes
rice and risotto
rosemary
sage
salt
vinegar, balsamic
wine, esp. red

SQUASH, ACORN (See also Pumpkin; Squash, Butternut; and Squash, Winter)
Season: autumn–winter
Taste: sweet
Weight: medium–heavy
Volume: moderate
Techniques: bake, mash

allspice
bay leaf
butter, esp. brown
cheese, Parmesan
cinnamon
cream
eggs, custard
garlic
ginger, fresh
maple syrup
mascarpone
mushrooms, esp. shiitake
nutmeg
nuts
olive oil
onions, esp. cipollini
parsley
pork
SAGE
salt, kosher
sugar, brown
thyme
vanilla
vinegar, sherry

Flavor Affinities
acorn squash + custard + sage
acorn squash + ginger + maple syrup

Dishes

Heirloom Autumn Squash Salad with Local Pears, Currants, Roasted Chestnuts, Sankow Farm Feta Cheese, and Brown Butter Dressing
— Michael Nischan, Dressing Room (Westport, Connecticut)

Butternut Squash Soup with Honey-Glazed Parsnips, Spaghetti Squash, and Smoked Duck, Maple Syrup, Styrian Pumpkin Seed Oil, and Crisp Garnett Yams
— Carrie Nahabedian, Naha (Chicago)

I find **butternut** to be the best **squash**. It is nutty, sweet, and has a balanced flavor to it.
— **DANIEL HUMM**, ELEVEN MADISON PARK (NEW YORK CITY)

In winter, one of my favorite combinations is **butternut squash** with bay leaf and nutmeg.
— **JERRY TRAUNFELD**, THE HERBFARM (WOODINVILLE, WASHINGTON)

SQUASH, BUTTERNUT

(See also Pumpkin; Squash, Acorn; and Squash, Winter)
Season: early autumn
Taste: sweet
Weight: medium–heavy
Volume: moderate
Techniques: bake, braise, mash, roast, steam, tempura-fry

allspice
anchovies
apples, esp. green
artichokes, Jerusalem
bacon
basil
bay leaf
bourbon
bread crumbs
brown butter
BUTTER, UNSALTED
carrots
cayenne
celery
celery root
CHEESE: Fontina, **goat**, Gruyère, **PARMESAN**, pecorino, **ricotta**, ricotta salata

chervil
chestnuts
chickpeas
chile peppers, esp. fresh green, jalapeño
chili sauce
chives
cilantro
cinnamon
cloves
coconut milk
coriander
couscous
cream
crème fraîche
cumin
curry: paste (yellow), powder
duck
fenugreek
fish sauce, Thai
garlic
ginger: fresh, ground
honey
Japanese cuisine (e.g., tempura)
leeks
lemon, juice
lemongrass
lime, juice

maple syrup
marjoram
mascarpone
mint
Moroccan cuisine
mushrooms, esp. porcini
nutmeg
nuts
OIL: canola, grapeseed, peanut, **pumpkin seed**, vegetable
olive oil
ONIONS, esp. red
orange, juice
pancetta
parsley, flat-leaf
parsnips
pears
PEPPER: black, white
pork
potatoes
pumpkin seeds
red pepper flakes
risotto
rosemary
SAGE
salsify
SALT: kosher, sea
shallots
shrimp
soups
sour cream
spinach
STOCKS: chicken, vegetable
sugar: brown, white
tarragon
thyme
truffle oil
vanilla
vinegar: balsamic, champagne, sherry
walnuts
watercress
wine: dry white, Vin Santo
yams
yogurt

Flavor Affinities

butternut squash + anchovies + bread crumbs + onions + pasta
butternut squash + bacon + maple syrup + sage
butternut squash + bay leaf + nutmeg
butternut squash + cilantro + coconut + ginger
butternut squash + crème fraîche + nutmeg + sage
butternut squash + ricotta cheese + rosemary
butternut squash + risotto + sage

SQUASH, KABOCHA
(See also Squash, Winter)

Flavor Affinities
kabocha squash + coconut + sweet curry
— **DOMINIQUE AND CINDY DUBY,** WILD SWEETS (VANCOUVER)

SQUASH, SPAGHETTI
(See also Squash, Winter)
Season: early autumn–winter
Weight: medium
Volume: moderate
Techniques: bake, boil, or steam; then sauté

bacon
basil
bell peppers
cheese: feta, Gorgonzola, Parmesan
chicken
chives
duck
garlic
ginger
honey, chestnut
olive oil
olives, black
oregano
parsley, flat-leaf
pasta
pepper, ground
salt
seafood: fish, scallops
tomatoes
vinaigrette

SQUASH, SUMMER
(See also Zucchini)
Season: summer
Weight: light–medium
Volume: quiet–moderate
Techniques: bake, blanch, boil, braise, deep-fry, grill, sauté, steam, stir-fry

basil
bell peppers
butter
cheese: goat, Gruyère, mozzarella, Parmesan
chile peppers: dried red, fresh green
chives
cinnamon
coconut
coriander
corn
cream
cumin
curry leaves
dill
eggplant
garlic
lemon, juice
marjoram
mint
mustard seeds, black

olive oil
onions
oregano
parsley, flat-leaf
pecans
pepper, black
rosemary
sage
salt
sausage, Italian
thyme
tomatoes
turmeric
walnuts
yogurt

SQUASH, WINTER
(See also Pumpkin; Squash, Acorn; and Squash, Butternut)
Season: autumn–winter
Weight: medium–heavy
Volume: moderate
Techniques: bake, braise, grill, mash, puree, roast, sauté, steam

allspice
APPLES: cider, fruit, juice
bacon
BUTTER
caraway seeds
cayenne
celery, leaves
cheese: Fontina, Gruyère, Parmesan, pecorino, Romano
chili powder
cinnamon
cloves
coconut milk
coriander
cream
cumin

Dishes
Red Curry Squash Flan, Orange Jelly, Coconut Emulsion, Sweet Gnocchi, and Curry Gel
— Dominique and Cindy Duby, Wild Sweets (Vancouver)

Roasted Squash Ice Cream, Crispy Pumpkin Seeds, Sage
— Johnny Iuzzini, pastry chef, Jean Georges (New York City)

When **winter squash** is at its peak, it is already sweet, and yet the tendency is to want to reach for the cinnamon or maple syrup to season it. To keep it a savory dish, I'll reach for fresh ginger, which adds a sweet heat.

— BRADFORD THOMPSON, MARY ELAINE'S AT THE PHOENICIAN (SCOTTSDALE, ARIZONA)

curry
GARLIC
ginger
honey
lamb
leeks
lemongrass
lime, juice
maple syrup
marjoram
mushrooms
mustard
NUTMEG
nuts
olive oil
ONIONS
orange: juice, zest
oregano
paprika, sweet
parsley, flat-leaf
pasta, esp. ravioli
pears
pecans
pork
pumpkin
pumpkin seeds
quince
radicchio
red pepper flakes
risotto
rosemary
SAGE
savory
soups
stocks: chicken, vegetable
SUGAR, BROWN
THYME
truffles, white
vinegar, sherry
walnuts
wild rice

Flavor Affinities
winter squash + butter + garlic + sage
winter squash + garlic + olive oil + parsley
winter squash + onions + Parmesan cheese + chicken stock

SQUASH BLOSSOMS
(See Zucchini Blossoms)

SQUID (aka calamari)
Weight: light–medium
Volume: quiet
Techniques: deep-fry, grill, marinate, roast, salad, sauté, stew

aioli
almonds
anchovies
arugula
basil
bay leaf
beans, white
bell peppers: green, red, yellow
butter, unsalted
cabbage: green, red
caperberries
capers
carrots
cayenne
celery
chard
chile peppers, esp. piquillo
chives

Dishes
Grilled Squid with Tapioca and Meyer Lemon
— Charlie Trotter, Charlie Trotter's (Chicago)

chorizo
cilantro
cloves
cornichons
cornmeal (for breading)
couscous, esp. Israeli
currants
GARLIC
ginger
hoisin sauce
honey
ketchup
Italian cuisine
leeks
LEMON, JUICE
lime, juice
lobster
marjoram
mayonnaise
Mediterranean cuisine
melon, esp. cantaloupe, watermelon
oil: grapeseed, peanut (for frying), walnut
OLIVE OIL
olives, esp. black, kalamata
onions, esp. sweet, white
orange, zest
oregano
PARSLEY, FLAT-LEAF
pasta
PEPPER: black, white
pine nuts
polenta
potatoes, new
red pepper flakes
rice: Arborio, bomba
risotto
saffron
salads
SALT: kosher, sea
scallions
scallops

sesame seeds

shallots

shiso

shrimp

soy sauce

squid ink

stock, fish

sugar

Tabasco sauce

tarragon

thyme

tomatoes

VINEGAR: balsamic, red wine, rice wine, sherry, white wine

walnuts

wine, dry white

yuzu juice

zucchini

Flavor Affinities

squid + aioli + anchovies

squid + basil + bell peppers + chiles + garlic + orange + tomatoes + red wine

squid + garlic + lemon + parsley

STAR ANISE (See Anise, Star)

STEAK (See Beef)

STRAWBERRIES

Season: late spring–summer

Taste: sweet–sour

Weight: light

Volume: moderate

Techniques: raw, sauté

Tips: Adding sugar enhances strawberry flavor, as does adding an acid such as citrus juice or vinegar.

almonds

amaretto

apricots, pureed

bananas

berries

biscuit

blackberries

Dishes

Strawberries in Chianti with Black Pepper Ricotta Cream
— Gina DePalma, pastry chef, Babbo (New York City)

Fresh Strawberry Tart with Orange Curd and Moscato Gelée
— Lissa Doumani, Terra (St. Helena, California)

Citrus-Strawberry Salad, Honey Parfait, and Charentais Melon Puree
— Michael Laiskonis, Le Bernardin (New York City)

Strawberry, Mango, and Basil "Ice Cream Sandwich" and Organic Strawberry Juice
— Michael Laiskonis, Le Bernardin (New York City)

Strawberry-Rhubarb Shortcake with Crème Fraîche Ice Cream
— Patrick O'Connell, The Inn at Little Washington (Washington, Virginia)

blueberries

boysenberries

brandy

buttermilk

caramel

cardamom

Champagne

Chartreuse

cheese: Queso de los Beyos, ricotta

chocolate: dark, white

cinnamon

I remember asking myself, How can I make a salad into a dessert? The result of my experimentation bore no resemblance to a salad: I used olive oil to make an almond *financier*; because a *financier* is not a *financier* without the brown butter, I substituted olive oil for half the brown butter. I served this with a balsamic vinegar ice cream, and a basil-infused **strawberry** consommé.

A note about the strawberries is that I cooked them on very low heat. It comes from the idea of gentleness, slowness, care, respect for the ingredients, and, in the end, a better-tasting fresh ingredient. I could have extracted more juice from the strawberries by bringing them up to a boil with a bunch of sugar, but that results in cooked strawberries and not the fresh strawberry flavor you're after.
— **MICHAEL LAISKONIS**, LE BERNARDIN (NEW YORK CITY)

A tiny bit of vanilla makes **strawberries** yummy! It has to be just a little because you don't want a vanilla-strawberry dessert; you want a strawberry dessert that has a little vanilla on the palate that people have to search for.
— **GINA DePALMA**, BABBO (NEW YORK CITY)

You still can't go wrong with a classic. For years I tried to come up with the end-all be-all **strawberry** dessert. Four years ago, I said forget it — the strawberries I get from my purveyor in the farmers' market are perfect. Now, I serve strawberry gelato with lots of strawberries and 25-year-old balsamic vinegar. It became an injustice to try to do anything else with the perfect strawberries I was getting.
— **GINA DePALMA**, BABBO (NEW YORK CITY)

Strawberries pair beautifully with Cabernet Sauvignon, and black pepper takes the combination even further.
— LISSA DOUMANI, TERRA (ST. HELENA, CALIFORNIA)

When I taste **strawberries** at the store I close my eyes and ask, Is this a [perfect] strawberry or does this need a little help? If they are a little dry, to help them, you cook them on top of the stove a little and that will release their perfume and juice. You can add Grand Marnier or Kirsch, which will help their flavor as well. If you follow these steps, though, this will lead you to wanting to serve them warm. If you chill them down, they will not look great. So I would serve a warm berry compote over vanilla ice cream. If you have some berries that aren't perfect, with a little love and attention they'll adapt. In spring, when the strawberries are early and not that good, I'll roast them in the oven with red wine, balsamic vinegar, sugar, corn syrup, and water, and they turn wonderfully jammy.
— EMILY LUCHETTI, FARALLON (SAN FRANCISCO)

I love fresh **strawberries** with dense and dry cow's milk cheeses, such as Queso de los Beyos from Spain. It hits your tongue like dry plaster, then melts, releasing its slightly sour fresh milk flavor. Both also go very well with rosé Champagne.
— ADRIAN MURCIA, CHANTERELLE (NEW YORK CITY)

Strawberries have a rose note to them so I find rose geraniums bring that out. The two have similar flavors.
— JERRY TRAUNFELD, THE HERBFARM (WOODINVILLE, WASHINGTON)

cloves
cognac
coriander
***CREAM AND ICE CREAM**
cream cheese
crème de cassis
crème fraîche
crust: pastry, pie
custard
elderflower syrup
gelatin (for texture)
ginger
gooseberries
grapefruit
grapes
grappa
guava
hazelnuts
honey
KIRSCH
kumquats
LEMON: juice, zest
lemon verbena
lime: juice, zest
liqueurs, berry or orange (e.g., Cointreau, **curaçao**, Framboise, **GRAND MARNIER**
loquats
mangoes
maple syrup
mascarpone
melon
mint (for garnish)
nutmeg
oatmeal
ORANGE: juice, zest
papaya
passion fruit
peaches
peanuts
pecans
pepper, black
pies
pineapple
pine nuts
pistachios
plums
pomegranates

port
RASPBERRIES
*RHUBARB
rum
sake
sherry
shortcake
SOUR CREAM
*SUGAR: brown, white
tarts
VANILLA
*VINEGAR, BALSAMIC, ESP.
    AGED
walnuts
WINE: RED OR ROSÉ (e.g.,
    Beaujolais, Cabernet
    Sauvignon), sweet white (e.g.,
    Moscato d'Asti, Muscat,
    Riesling, Sauternes, Vin Santo)
yogurt
zabaglione

AVOID
salt

Flavor Affinities
strawberries + almonds + cream
strawberries + almonds + olive oil + balsamic vinegar
strawberries + almonds + rhubarb
strawberries + balsamic vinegar + black pepper
strawberries + black pepper + ricotta cheese + red wine
strawberries + Champagne +
    Grand Marnier
strawberries + rhubarb + sugar

STRIPED BASS
(See Bass, Striped)

STUFFING
Season: autumn–winter
Weight: medium–heavy
Volume: quiet–moderate

apples
bread crumbs
butter, unsalted
celery
chestnuts

chicken fat
chicken livers
corn bread
garlic
mushrooms (e.g., shiitakes)
olive oil
onions
parsley, flat-leaf
pecans
pepper: black, white
prosciutto
rosemary
sage
salt, kosher
sausage, esp. chicken, pork
stocks: chicken, turkey
thyme
walnuts

SUGAR
Taste: sweet
Function: cooling
Tips: Balance sweetness with acid (e.g., vinegar) and salt. Avoid dark brown sugar with maple syrup, as the combination is too intense.

SUGAR, PALM
Taste: sweet
Tips: Avoid with lighter dishes, which would be overwhelmed.

coconut
curries
custards
desserts
Indian cuisine
tamarind
Thai cuisine

SUGAR SNAP PEAS
(See Snap Peas)

SUMAC
Taste: sour
Weight: light–medium
Volume: moderate

allspice
avocados
beets
cheese, feta
CHICKEN, ESP. ROASTED

We rely a lot on **sumac,** which I love because it is a good way to add another layer of tartness and acidity to a dish without having to add liquid. I could not imagine our beet salad without it. Sumac works well with chicken, vegetables, and salads, as well as in a vinaigrette or with cheeses you might marinate like feta. I avoid it with red meat or steak; I think it is the wrong kind of tartness for them.
— **SHARON HAGE,** YORK STREET (DALLAS)

Sumac's distinctly sour flavor and reddish-purple color can both lift a dish.
— **LISSA DOUMANI,** TERRA (ST. HELENA, CALIFORNIA)

If my mind is in the Middle East, I will be reaching for **sumac** or preserved lemon or yogurt. I use sumac at the very end of the cooking process to enhance the acid already being used in the dish.
— **BRAD FARMERIE,** PUBLIC (NEW YORK CITY)

chickpeas
chile peppers
chili powder
coriander
cucumbers
cumin
eggplant
fennel
FISH, ESP. GRILLED
garlic
ginger
kebabs
lamb
Lebanese cuisine
lemon, juice
lentils
lime
meats, esp. grilled
Middle Eastern cuisine
mint
Moroccan cuisine
onions
orange
oregano
paprika
parsley
pepper, black
pine nuts
pomegrantes
rosemary
salads and salad dressings
salt
seafood
sesame seeds
shellfish
stewed dishes
thyme
tomatoes
Turkish cuisine
vegetables
walnuts
yogurt

Flavor Affinities
sumac + lamb + black pepper
sumac + salt + sesame seeds + thyme
    (aka Middle Eastern *za'atar*)

My favorite fruit to work with is a toss-up between all of the stone fruits [i.e., cherries, plums, apricots, nectarines, and peaches]. Late July, August, and September is my favorite time of year!
— **GINA DEPALMA**, BABBO (NEW YORK CITY)

When I compose a dish, I work with the season — but like to play with that as well. People will ask how we can have braised short ribs on the menu in **summer.** I can, because I play with the other elements of the dish. For example, I pair seared watermelon with my short ribs for a refreshing note. From this base, I add other elements to lighten the dish further. The dish also has watermelon radishes that are bright green on the outside and red on the inside so you get another take on "watermelon on watermelon." The radish also adds a little heat and freshness to cut the richness of the short ribs. The last note in the dish is feta cheese, which adds overall creaminess and goes back to the combination of watermelon and feta that you see in Greek restaurants.
— **KATSUYA FUKUSHIMA**, MINIBAR (WASHINGTON, DC)

What I like about working with the seasons is that everything that is in season at the same time works together. During the **summer** when you have tomatoes, melon, and basil, you can make a dish with them and it will work. [His menu includes a salad of grilled watermelon with tomatoes, basil, and aged balsamic.] I don't try to create new combinations of ingredients. I saw the combination of tomatoes and basil everywhere I ever worked. Should I do something different with tomatoes? No — why? The reason everyone serves this combination is because it is amazing! My approach is to find a new way to serve the tomatoes or the basil. I may make a tomato gazpacho and serve it with basil sorbet, or I could serve different preparations of tomatoes on the plate — fresh, a confit, a juice — and then do the same with the basil, serving it as an oil or a puree.
— **DANIEL HUMM**, ELEVEN MADISON PARK (NEW YORK CITY)

Look at the weather and the occasion. You want your dessert to match the style and appropriateness of the meal. If it is a barbecue in the **summer,** I would serve a fruit crisp or pie, summer pudding, or ice cream, and that is pretty much it. People always talk about using fresh and local ingredients, which is very important. But, if you are using chocolate, which is available year-round, and if it is 85 degrees out with 85 percent humidity, the last thing you want is a hot chocolate soufflé. You want chocolate ice cream instead.
— **EMILY LUCHETTI**, FARALLON (SAN FRANCISCO)

Summer vegetables work with summer herbs. In the Northwest, you will see the same set of ingredients in season in the same week every year. So, you just put them together. For example, sockeye salmon comes into season [during the summer] when squash does, and so do the herbs used in a fines herbes mixture. There's your dish!
— **JERRY TRAUNFELD**, THE HERBFARM (WOODINVILLE, WASHINGTON)

SUMMER

Weather: typically hot
Techniques: barbecue, grill, marinate, panfry, pan roast, raw

apricots (peak: June)
basil
beans, fava
beans, green (peak: August)
blackberries (peak: June)
blueberries (peak: July)
boysenberries (peak: June)
cherries
chilled dishes and beverages
corn (peak: July/August)
cucumbers (peak: August)
eggplant
figs (peak: August)
fish

flowers, edible
garlic (peak: August)
grapes
grilled dishes
herbs, cooling (e.g., basil, cilantro, dill, fennel, licorice, marjoram, mint)
ice cream
ices
limes (peak: June)
mangoes
melons (peak: August)
nectarines (peak: July)
okra (peak: August)
onions (peak: August)
onions, red (peak: July)
peaches (peak: July/August)
pears, Bartlett (peak: August)
peppers

picnics
plums (peak: August)
puddings, summer
raspberries (peak: June, August)
raw foods (e.g., salads)
salads: fruit, green, pasta
salsas, fresh
shellfish
sorbets
soups, cold
spices, cooling (e.g., peppercorns, white; turmeric, etc.)
squash, summer
steaming
strawberries
tomatillos (peak: August)
tomatoes
vegetables, green leafy
Vidalia onions (peak: June)

watermelon
zucchini (peak: July)

SUNCHOKES (See Artichokes, Jerusalem)

SWEDISH CUISINE

allspice
bay leaf
cardamom
cinnamon
cloves
DILL
fish
ginger
herring, pickled
meatballs
mushrooms
mustard
nutmeg
onions
peas
pepper
pickled dishes (e.g., fish, meat, vegetables)
potatoes
shellfish
soups, esp. fruit
sugar

AVOID

garlic
piquancy

Flavor Affinities

beef + bay leaf + dill + nutmeg + onions
herring + sour cream + vinegar
red wine + allspice + cinnamon + cloves + raisins + sugar
veal + allspice + onions

SWEETBREADS

Weight: medium
Volume: moderate
Techniques: braise, deep-fry, grill, pan roast, sauté

In the fall, I use walnut vinegar which is red wine vinegar with macerated walnuts in it. It is great on a **sweetbread** and hazelnut dish.
— **ANDREW CARMELLINI,** A VOCE (NEW YORK CITY)

Dishes

Sweetbreads, Cauliflower, Burnt Bread, and Toasted Hay
— Grant Achatz, Alinea (Chicago)

artichokes, Jerusalem
asparagus
BACON
butter, unsalted
cabbage
capers
celery
celery root
cream
fennel
fennel seeds
flour (for dredging)
French cuisine
garlic
greens
ham
hazelnuts
honey
Italian cuisine
lemon, juice
liver, esp. duck
Madeira
mushrooms, esp. wild (e.g., chanterelles, morels)
mustard
oil, peanut
olive oil
onions: red, white
parsley, flat-leaf
peas
pecans
PEPPER: black, white
port
raisins
salt: kosher, sea
scallions
shallots
soy sauce

spinach
stock, chicken
sugar
thyme, fresh
truffles, black
vermouth
VINEGAR: balsamic, red, rice, sherry, white
wine, white

Flavor Affinities

sweetbreads + asparagus + morels
sweetbreads + bacon + capers
sweetbreads + bacon + garlic
sweetbreads + bacon + onions + sherry vinegar
sweetbreads + capers + lemon
sweetbreads + celery + truffles, black
sweetbreads + hazelnuts + red wine vinegar + walnuts
sweetbreads + Madeira
sweetbreads + mustard + raisins

SWEETNESS

Taste: sweet
Function: cooling; sweetness satiates the appetite
Tips: The colder the food or drink, the less the perception of sweetness. Sweetness tends to round out flavors, while acidity sharpens them.

apple: cider, fruit, juice
apricots
bananas
barley
basil, sweet
beans
beets
bell peppers: red, yellow
brandies, fruit (e.g., Calvados)
butter

At dessert time, you don't have the same philosophy as you do at the beginning of the meal. You don't want people coming back for more — you want to finish them off! Dessert is the easy course, because **sweetness** is easy and obvious. I don't want big structure; the work is done. As long as the apple tastes like apple, you are there! A dessert is about manipulating the sugar in some way to bring out the best of the apple, chocolate, lemon, pecans, or whatever you are working with. From there, you want to balance the sugar with the fat to bring out the best of the star ingredient. I am not a pastry chef, so I try to stick to simple things, like chocolate *pot de crème* and lemon pudding. The key is that, though they may be simple, I always use very good ingredients.
— **SHARON HAGE**, YORK STREET (DALLAS)

I'm not such a fan of white sugar because it only adds **sweetness** and little sophistication. Maple, honey, or brown sugar add so much more. When making a baba in France, you use only sugar and water. I use molasses because it gives texture and sweetness. In France you use a lot of simple syrup. I like to use orange juice instead of water, and instead of using white sugar, I'll use brown.
— **MICHEL RICHARD**, CITRONELLE (WASHINGTON, DC)

I love jaggery [the unrefined sugar used in India, also known as palm sugar] because it has a fermented flavor and provides more complexity. Dates can be a primary source of **sweetness** in a dessert instead of sugar, as can vegetables such as beets, carrots, parsnips, and corn, which all have an earthy sweetness. However, I don't want to pound people over the head with a beet sorbet.
— **MICHAEL LAISKONIS**, LE BERNARDIN (NEW YORK CITY)

caramel
carrots
cherries, sweet
chestnuts
chocolate: dark, milk, white
clementines
cloves
cocoa, sweetened
coconut and coconut milk
corn
corn syrup
crab
cream
currants
daikon
dates
figs
fruits: dried, ripe
fruit juices

garlic, roasted
ginger, candied
grapes
guava
hoisin sauce
honey
jicama
ketchup
lentils
licorice
liqueurs, sweet
lobster
lotus root
lychee nuts
Madeira
mangoes
maple syrup

melons (e.g., cantaloupe, honeydew)
milk
mirin (Japanese sweetener)
molasses
nectarines
onions: cooked, sweet (e.g., Vidalia)
oranges, sweet (e.g., navel)
papaya
parsnips
passion fruits
peaches
pears
peas and sugar snap peas
persimmons
pimentos
pineapple
plantains, esp. ripe
plums, sweet
plum sauce
pomegranates
potatoes
prunes
pumpkin
raisins
raspberries
rice
roasted foods
sake
scallops, esp. bay
sherry, sweet (e.g., cream, oloroso)
shrimp
squash, winter (e.g., acorn, butternut)
strawberries
sugar: brown, palm, white
sweet potatoes
tangerines
tomatoes
vermouth, sweet
vinegar, balsamic
watermelon
wheat
wines, sweet

Dishes

Sweet Potato, Feta, and Smoked Paprika Tortilla with Minted Lemon Raita
— Brad Farmerie, Public (New York City)

Warm Sweet Potato Cake with Cranberries and Dates
— Johnny Iuzzini, pastry chef, Jean Georges (New York City)

Szechuan Peppercorn and Salt-Roasted Sweet Potato Skewers with Sweet-Hot Mustard Sauce
— Monica Pope, T'afia (Houston)

SWEET POTATOES

Season: autumn–winter
Taste: sweet
Weight: medium–heavy
Volume: moderate–loud
Techniques: bake, boil, deep-fry, fry, grill, mash, roast, sauté, steam

allspice
anise
apples and apple juice
bacon
bananas
basil
bay leaf
beans
bell peppers: green, red
bourbon
brandy
BUTTER, unsalted
caramel
cheeses
chestnuts
chile peppers
chives
chocolate, white
cilantro
CINNAMON
cloves
coconut
coriander
cranberries
cream
crème fraîche
cumin

curry powder
custards
dates
dill
duck
figs, dried
fruits and fruit juices
garlic
ginger
greens, bitter
ham
hazelnuts
honey
kale
ketchup
leeks
lemon: juice, zest
lime, juice
liqueurs: nut, orange
maple syrup
meats, esp. roasted
molasses
mushrooms, chanterelle
mustard, esp. Dijon
NUTMEG
oatmeal
oil: nut, peanut, sesame
olive oil
onions, esp. red
ORANGE: juice, zest
paprika, smoked
parsley, flat-leaf
peanuts
pears
pecans
pepper: black, white

persimmons
pineapple
pork
potatoes: new, red
poultry, esp. roasted
prosciutto
pumpkin
pumpkin seeds
raisins
red pepper flakes
rosemary
rum
sage
salt, kosher
sausage: andouille, chorizo
sesame seeds
sour cream
stock, chicken
SUGAR, BROWN
tarragon
thyme
tomatoes
vanilla
vinegar: balsamic, cider
walnuts
whiskey
wine, sweet
Worcestershire sauce
yogurt

Flavor Affinities
sweet potatoes + allspice + cinnamon + ginger
sweet potatoes + apples + sage
sweet potatoes + bacon + onions + rosemary
sweet potatoes + chile peppers + lemon zest
sweet potatoes + chorizo sausage + orange
sweet potatoes + cilantro + lime juice
sweet potatoes + kale + prosciutto
sweet potatoes + maple syrup + pecans

SWISS CHARD (See Chard)

SWORDFISH
Season: early summer–early autumn
Weight: heavy
Volume: quiet–moderate
Techniques: braise, broil, grill, poach, sauté, sear, steam, stir-fry

apples, esp. Granny Smith
bacon
basil
bay leaf
beans, white
bread crumbs
butter
capers
caponata
carrots
cayenne
celery
chili powder
cilantro
coconut milk
coriander
cream
cumin
currants
curry
fennel
garlic
lemon: juice, zest
lemon, preserved
lemongrass
lime: juice, leaf (kaffir), zest
mint
OIL, corn
olive oil
olives, esp. black
onions, esp. pearl

orange, juice
oregano
parsley, flat-leaf
pepper: black, red
pineapple
pine nuts
pistou
potatoes
red pepper flakes
rosemary
saffron
salt: kosher, sea
scallions
shallots
star anise
stocks: chicken, fish, shrimp
Tabasco sauce
tomatoes and tomato sauce
vinegar, balsamic
wine, dry white

SZECHUAN CUISINE
(See also Chinese Cuisine)
Volume: loud
Techniques: braise, pickle, roast, simmer, steam, stir-fry

bamboo shoots
beef
cabbage, Chinese
chicken
chile peppers
chili paste
duck
garlic
ginger
meats, smoked
peanuts
PORK
soy sauce
***SZECHUAN PEPPER**

tangerine peel, dried
wine, rice

SZECHUAN PEPPER
Taste: sour, hot, pungent
Weight: light–medium
Volume: loud
Tips: Add at the end of the cooking process.

Asian cuisines
beans, black
chicken
chile peppers
Chinese cuisine
curry powder
duck
five-spice powder (key ingredient)
fried dishes
fruits, citrus
game
game birds
garlic
ginger
grilled dishes
honey
lemon
lime
meats, esp. fattier
mushrooms
onions
orange
peppercorns: black, green, white
pork
quail
salt
scallions
sesame: oil, seeds
soy sauce
squid
star anise
stir-fried dishes
Tibetan cuisine

Flavor Affinities
Szechuan pepper + ginger + star anise

Dishes

Seared Swordfish with Lemon and Caper Shallot Dressing
— David Bouley, Bouley (New York City)

Swordfish with Eggplant Caviar and Teardrop Tomato Salad
— Gabriel Kreuther, The Modern (New York City)

TAMARIND

Season: spring–early summer
Taste: sour
Weight: medium
Volume: moderate–loud
Tips: Add at the beginning of the cooking process.

African cuisine
allspice
almonds
Asian cuisines
bananas
beans
beverages, esp. fruit
cabbage
cardamom
Central American cuisine
chicken
chickpeas
chile peppers, esp. Thai
chili powder
Chinese cuisine
chutneys
cilantro
cinnamon
cloves
coconut and coconut milk
coriander
cumin
curries, curry paste, curry powder
dates
duck
fennel seeds
fenugreek
fish
fish sauce
fruits
game
garlic
ginger
greens
honey
INDIAN CUISINE
Indonesian cuisine
Jamaican cuisine
lamb
Latin American cuisine
lentils
lime, juice
mangoes
marinades
meats
Middle Eastern cuisine
mint
mushrooms
mustard
oil, grapeseed
onions, red
orange
paprika
peaches
peanuts
pears
pepper, black
pineapple
pork
potatoes
poultry
rice
sauces
scallops
sea bass
shellfish
shrimp
soups
Southeast Asian cuisine
soy sauce
star anise
stews
sugar: brown, palm, white
Thai basil
Thai cuisine
turmeric
vegetables
vinaigrette
Worcestershire sauce (key ingredient)
yogurt

Flavor Affinities
tamarind + chicken + yogurt

TANGERINES (see Oranges, Mandarin)

TARRAGON

Season: late spring–summer
Taste: sweet
Weight: light
Volume: loud
Tips: Add at the end of the cooking process.

acidic foods and flavors
(e.g., citrus)
anise
apples
apricots
artichokes
asparagus
basil (say some)
bass
bay leaf
beans, green
beef
beets
broccoli
capers
carrots
cauliflower
celery seeds
cheese, esp. goat, ricotta
chervil
***CHICKEN**
chives
chocolate
corn
crab and crab cakes
cream
crème fraîche
dill
EGGS AND EGG DISHES
(e.g., omelets), egg salad
fennel bulb
fennel seeds
fines herbes (key ingredient)
FISH
French cuisine
game
game birds
garlic
grapefruit
greens, bitter

The flavor of **tarragon** is fabulous. You get the flavor of Provence and of fennel . . . it is wonderful. I use it a lot, but you have to be careful. Most people chop tarragon too thin and it oxidizes before it goes into the dish. You want to just cut it into three pieces, and that's it. Chop, chop, chop — that's it. Otherwise, between the knife and the cutting board, it will oxidize and give the herb a bad taste.

— MICHEL RICHARD, CITRONELLE (WASHINGTON, DC)

I like **tarragon** when it is used in moderation. It is a fairly particular and strong herb, and for that reason it doesn't have the same applications as other herbs. It is good in a lot of things, such as with fish and chicken — and you can't make béarnaise without it!

— DAVID WALTUCK, CHANTERELLE (NEW YORK CITY)

Tarragon is my all-time favorite herb. I like the licorice flavor and the light perfume of the herb. This is an herb that marries well with other flavors. We serve a dish right now of flounder, white corn, and sugar snap peas with tarragon butter that is delicious.

— MARCEL DESAULNIERS, THE TRELLIS (WILLIAMSBURG, VIRGINIA)

Tarragon is best on its own [as opposed to combined with other herbs], . . . Tarragon works with muskmelon.

— JERRY TRAUNFELD, THE HERBFARM (WOODINVILLE, WASHINGTON)

halibut
leeks
LEMON, JUICE
lemon herbs (balm, thyme, verbena)
lentils
lettuces (e.g., frisée)
lime
lobster
lovage
marjoram
mayonnaise
meats, white
melon
mint
mushrooms
mussels
mustard: Dijon, Chinese (ingredient and complement)
olive oil
onions
orange, juice
oysters
paprika

PARSLEY
pasta
peaches
peas
pepper, black
Pernod
pork
potatoes
poultry
rabbit
radishes
rice
salads (e.g., fruit, green) and salad dressings
salmon
salsify
sauces, e.g., **BÉARNAISE** (key ingredient), creamy, hollandaise, tartar

savory
scallops
shallots
SHELLFISH
shrimp
sole
soups
sorrel
soy sauce
spinach
squash, summer
steaks
stock, vegetable
stuffings
TOMATOES
veal
vegetables
vinaigrette
VINEGAR, esp. champagne, sherry, white wine
wine, red
zucchini

AVOID
basil (say some)
desserts
oregano
rosemary
sage
savory
sweet dishes

Flavor Affinities
tarragon + anise + celery seeds
tarragon + chicken + lemon
tarragon + orange + seafood

TECHNIQUES

We believe that food preparation is 60 percent ingredients and 40 percent **technique**.

— DOMINIQUE AND CINDY DUBY, WILD SWEETS (VANCOUVER)

I find it a bit of a nightmare to find quality fruit and vegetables in this country. I think that for this reason **technique** began to be the primary driving force for a new dish.

— HESTON BLUMENTHAL, THE FAT DUCK (ENGLAND)

TEQUILA
Weight: medium
Volume: moderate

chile peppers
cilantro
Cointreau
fruit juice
ginger
grenadine
lemon, juice
LIME, JUICE
MEXICAN CUISINE
orange, juice
pomegranate, juice
sage
salt
sugar
vermouth: dry, sweet

Flavor Affinities
tequila + cilantro + lime
tequila + Cointreau + lime juice +
    pomegranate juice
tequila + Cointreau + lime juice +
    sage
tequila + lime juice + salt

TEX-MEX CUISINE
(See Mexican Cuisine,
Southwestern Cuisine)

THAI CUISINE
Tips: Authentic Thai cuisine
strives for a balance of hot + sour
+ salty + sweet.

basil, Thai
bell peppers
CHILE PEPPERS
cilantro
coconut
coriander
cumin
curries
fish
fish sauce
garlic

ginger
herbs, fresh
lemongrass
lime
mint
noodles, as in Pad Thai
peanuts
rice
shrimp paste
sugar
turmeric
vegetables

Flavor Affinities
chile peppers + cilantro + coconut
    milk
chile peppers + curry
chile peppers + curry + fish sauce
chile peppers + curry + peanuts
chile peppers + fish sauce
chile peppers + garlic
chile peppers + peanuts

THYME
Season: early summer
Weight: medium
Volume: moderate–loud
Tips: Add at the beginning of the
cooking process; use dried or
fresh.

allspice
apples
bacon
basil
BAY LEAF
beans, esp. dried, green
beef
beer
bell peppers
bouquet garni (key ingredient,
    along with bay leaf, marjoram,
    parsley)
braised dishes
bread and other baked goods
broccoli
Brussels sprouts
cabbage
caramel
carrots
casseroles
celery
CHEESE: FRESH, GOAT
CHICKEN, esp. roasted
chile peppers
chives
chowders, clam
cloves
cod
coriander

Thyme works well with so many things, especially soups and stews. I can't think of anything that it wouldn't work with if used properly. It is often a supporting-role herb and not the star; it is not an herb that bangs you over the head.
— DAVID WALTUCK, CHANTERELLE (NEW YORK CITY)

This is one of those cases where I remember the first time I ever tasted **thyme**. I'd ordered a cup of real clam chowder in Newport, Rhode Island, and found out that fresh thyme was the secret to it being the best I had tasted at the time. I still use thyme in my chowder to this day, though now I use dried thyme. You would have to use a considerable amount of fresh thyme to get the flavor of the dried.
— MARCEL DESAULNIERS, THE TRELLIS (WILLIAMSBURG, VIRGINIA)

Thyme works well with citrus and honey.
— GINA DEPALMA, BABBO (NEW YORK CITY)

In Spanish cooking, **thyme** is used very lightly. You will just toss a sprig in something. You don't want it to be strong; it is just a note. I use it when making *escabeche* [marinated poached or fried fish] or when cooking beans.
— ALEXANDRA RAIJ, TÍA POL (NEW YORK CITY)

corn
cranberries
curries
dates
dill
eggplant
eggs and egg dishes
fennel
figs
FISH
French cuisine
fruits, dried
game
garlic
Greek cuisine
gumbos
herbes de Provence (ingredient)
honey
Italian cuisine
Jamaican cuisine
jerk seasoning
lamb, esp. grilled, roasted
lavender
leeks
legumes

lemon
lemon verbena
lentils
lovage
marinades
marjoram
MEATS and meat loaf
Mediterranean cuisine
Middle Eastern cuisine
mint
mole sauce
MUSHROOMS
mustard
nutmeg
olive oil
ONIONS
orange
oregano
oysters, esp. stewed
paprika
parsley
parsnips
pasta and pasta sauces
pâtés
pears

peas
pepper
pork, esp. roasted
POTATOES
poultry
rabbit
rice
roasts
ROSEMARY
sage
salads and salad dressings
sauces, esp. rich and/or tomato
    sauces, red wine
sausages
SAVORY
seafood
SOUPS, esp. vegetable
Spanish cusine
spinach
STEWS
stocks
stuffings
tarragon
TOMATOES
vegetables, esp. winter
venison
vinaigrettes
wine, red, and red wine sauces
zucchini

Flavor Affinities
thyme + goat cheese + olive oil
thyme + savory

THYME, LEMON
(See Lemon Thyme)

TOFU
Weight: light
Volume: quiet
Techniques: grill, sauté, stir-fry, tempura-fry

asparagus
cabbage, esp. napa
garlic
ginger
Japanese cuisine

miso
mushrooms
noodles, esp. soba, udon
rice, esp. fried
salads and salad dressings
scallions
sesame: oil, seeds
soups
soy sauce
tamari
teriyaki

TOMATILLOS

Season: year-round
Taste: sour
Weight: light–medium
Volume: moderate

avocado
chicken
chile peppers, fresh
   (e.g., jalapeño, serrano)
cilantro
cucumber
fish
garlic
grilled dishes
guacamole
lime
Mexican cuisine
onions
pork
salsas, esp. green
salt: kosher, sea
scallions
shellfish
shrimp
sour cream
stews
tequila
tomatoes

TOMATOES

Season: summer–early autumn
Taste: sour, sweet
Function: heating
Weight: medium
Volume: moderate

Dishes

Warm Goat Cheese Salad: Vine-Ripe Tomatoes, Frisée, Watercress, and Almond Dressing
— David Bouley, Upstairs (New York City)

Heirloom Tomato Salad, Warm Brin d'Amore (Corsican Sheep's Milk Cheese), Teammate Coulis, Raspberry Vinegar, Globe Basil
— David Bouley, Upstairs (New York City)

Cherry Tomatoes with Milk-Poached Buffalo Mozzarella, Country Ham, Jalapeño, Purple Basil, and Tomato Water
— Jeffrey Buben, Vidalia (Washington, DC)

Chilled Gazpacho with Cucumber Relish and Parsley Cream
— Sanford D'Amato, Sanford (Milwaukee)

Chilled Tomato Soup with Watermelon, Ginger Oil, Coconut Cream, and Basil
— Katsuya Fukushima, minibar (Washington, DC)

Summer Vegetable Bread Pudding with Warm Tomato Vinaigrette and Tomato-Basil Salad
— Vitaly Paley, Paley's Place (Portland, Oregon)

Heirloom Tomato Salad with Crème Fraîche and Herbs
— Alice Waters, Chez Panisse (Berkeley, California)

Tomatoes with watermelon is a simple, refreshing, and perfectly balanced combination. The acidity of the tomatoes is a counterpoint to the sweetness of the watermelon.

— JOSÉ ANDRÉS, CAFÉ ATLÁNTICO (WASHINGTON, DC)

A romesco sauce combines some of Spain's best-loved ingredients: tomatoes, peppers, onions, bread, and almonds.

— JOSÉ ANDRÉS, CAFÉ ATLÁNTICO (WASHINGTON, DC)

Strattu is a Sicilian tomato paste that I'm finishing many dishes with now. It is delicious and very sweet. It looks like red Silly Putty and comes in jars, and doesn't taste anything like canned tomato paste. I recently used it in a garlic aioli that we served with calamari. It gave the mayonnaise a wonderful color, sweetness, and depth of flavor.

— ANDREW CARMELLINI, A VOCE (NEW YORK CITY)

Gazpacho is awesome. As a restaurant chef, I can't just make gazpacho. I have to do something that you can't do at home, but that is interesting — and not in a weird way. We use the ingredients that you would find in gazpacho but instead of using only tomatoes, we will use 80 percent strawberries and 20 percent tomatoes. My gazpacho is made up of toasted country bread, cucumber, bell pepper, a little garlic, strawberries, tomatoes, olive oil, and white balsamic vinegar. The dish is then garnished with Hawaiian blue prawns, diced strawberries, and slices of *guanciale* (cured pork jowl), olive oil, basil, and black pepper.

— DANIEL HUMM, ELEVEN MADISON PARK (NEW YORK CITY)

My parents had a large garden with almost 120 tomato plants. I would go out in the garden and pick a tomato and eat it like an apple. I love heirloom tomato season. I like to serve them with a little salt and pepper, a drizzle of lemon juice or cider vinegar, and a piece of mozzarella cheese. You need to taste your tomatoes before you season them. Yellow tomatoes are pretty sweet, which is why I like to add a little vinegar.

— GABRIEL KREUTHER, THE MODERN (NEW YORK CITY)

Techniques: bake, broil, confit, fry, grill, raw, roast, sauté, stew

aioli
allspice
almonds
anchovies
arugula
avocados
*BASIL: lemon, purple
bay leaf
beans: fava, green

beets
BELL PEPPERS: red, green, yellow
bread, bread crumbs
broccoli
butter, unsalted
capers
carrots
cauliflower
cayenne
celery and celery salt
CHEESE: blue, Cabrales, cheddar,

feta, **goat, Gorgonzola, mozzarella, Parmesan, pecorino,** ricotta, ricotta salata, sheep's milk
chervil
chicken
chickpeas
chile peppers: chipotle, habanero, jalapeño, serrano, and/or dried sweet
chili
chili sauce
chives
cilantro
cinnamon
coconut milk
coriander
corn
crab
cream
cream cheese
cucumbers
cumin
curry
dill
eggplant
eggs
fennel
fennel seeds
fish, esp. poached, grilled
French cuisine
GARLIC
garlic chives
ginger
ham
hazelnuts
honey
horseradish
Italian cuisine
lamb
lavender
leeks
legumes
LEMON: juice, zest
lemon balm
lime, juice
lovage
Madeira

mango
marjoram
mayonnaise
meats
Mediterranean cuisine
melon, esp. cantaloupe,
    honeydew
Mexican cuisine
mint, esp. spearmint
mushrooms
mustard, esp. whole grain
oil: grapeseed, vegetable
okra
OLIVE OIL
olives: black, niçoise
ONIONS, esp. pearl, red,
    Spanish, sweet, Vidalia, white,
    yellow
orange, juice
oregano
paprika, esp. sweet
parsley, flat-leaf
pasta and pasta sauces
peas
PEPPER: black, white
pineapple
pizza
port
raspberries
red pepper flakes
rice
rosemary
saffron
sage
salads, green
SALT: *fleur de sel,* **kosher, sea**
sandwiches
sauces
shallots
shellfish
soups
Spanish cuisine
squash
stews
stocks / broths: beef, chicken,
    vegetable
strawberries
sugar (pinch)

Tabasco sauce
tarragon
THYME
tomato paste
veal
vinaigrettes
VINEGAR: balsamic, raspberry,
    red wine, rice, sherry, tarragon,
    white, wine
watermelon
wine: red, rosé, vermouth, white
yogurt
zucchini

Flavor Affinities

tomatoes + avocado + basil + crab
tomatoes + avocado + lemon
tomatoes + basil + chervil + garlic + tarragon
tomatoes + basil + goat cheese
tomatoes + basil + mozzarella cheese + garlic + olive oil + balsamic
    vinegar
tomatoes + basil + olive oil + orange juice + prosciutto + watermelon
tomatoes + basil + oregano + thyme
tomatoes + basil + ricotta cheese
tomatoes + chile peppers + garlic + onions
tomatoes + fennel + Gorgonzola cheese
tomatoes + garlic chives + lemon basil
tomatoes + horseradish + lemon
tomatoes + olive oil + balsamic vinegar

TROUT

Season: midsummer
Weight: medium
Volume: moderate–loud
Techniques: bake, broil, grill,
panfry, pan roast, poach, roast,
sauté, steam

almonds
anchovies
apples: cider, fruit
bacon
bay leaf

beans, green
bell peppers, esp. red
bread crumbs
brown butter sauce
butter, unsalted
capers
carrots
cayenne
celery
cheese: manchego, Parmesan
chili powder
corn
crayfish
cream
escarole
fines herbes
garlic
ham, esp. Serrano
leeks
lemon, juice
lentils
mint
mushrooms
oil: canola, peanut
olive oil
onions
oregano
parsley
pine nuts
parsley, flat-leaf
pepper: black, white
potatoes
sage
salt, kosher
sauces, béarnaise
shallots
stock, mushroom
thyme
tomatoes
vinegar, esp. sherry, wine
wine: dry red, white

Flavor Affinities
trout + bacon + lentils + sherry
  vinegar
trout + capers + lemon

Dishes

Pan-Roasted Trout with Almonds, Brown Butter, and Haricots Verts
— Thomas Keller, Bouchon (Yountville, California)

Smoked Trout with Purslane Salad
— Mario Batali, Babbo (New York City)

TROUT, SMOKED
Taste: salty
Weight: medium
Volume: loud

apples
beans, green
bell pepper, roasted **red**
cayenne
chives
corn
cream
crème fraîche
dill
greens, baby
horseradish
lemon, juice
marjoram
nutmeg
olive oil
pepper: black, white
purslane
radishes
salt, sea
sour cream
walnut oil
wine, white (e.g., Riesling)

Flavor Affinities
smoked trout + apples +
  horseradish
smoked trout + crème fraîche +
  dill
smoked trout + horseradish +
  lemon juice + olive oil +
  purslane

TRUFFLES, BLACK
Season: winter
Weight: light
Volume: loud (in a subtle way!)
Techniques: shave

bacon
beef
cauliflower
chicken
cod
eggs: chicken, quail
foie gras
French cuisine
langoustines
lemon, juice
mushrooms (e.g., cepes, morels)
olive oil
pears
potatoes
rabbit
scallops
shellfish
stock, chicken
tarragon
vinegar, balsamic

TRUFFLES, PACIFIC NORTHWEST
Season: autumn
Weight: light
Volume: moderate–loud (in a subtle way!)

beef, esp. with black truffles
butter
celery root
crab, esp. with white truffles
eggs
game birds, esp. with black
  truffles

Jerry Traunfeld of Woodinville, Washington's The Herbfarm on Pacific Northwest Truffles

Northwest truffles are very good for what they are. What they are *not* is French or Italian truffles, which are stronger. Northwest truffles pair really well with celery root puree. We serve a ravioli filled with celery root and an egg yolk. The egg yolk is raw when the ravioli is cooked; when it is served, the dish is topped with butter and shaved truffle.

The white truffles are milder than the black. I especially like the white truffles with seafood such as shellfish, especially crab. They also work with root vegetables and potatoes.

The black truffles are a little funkier, and work with red meats and game birds.

We like to prepare melted leeks, which are leeks cooked in water until they are incredibly soft, which then get a shaving of black truffle and are served with wagu beef.

leeks, melted, esp. with black truffles

meats, red, esp. with black truffles

pasta, esp. with white truffles

potatoes, esp. with white truffles

salads, esp. with white truffles

seafood, esp. with white truffles

shellfish, esp. with white truffles

vegetables, root, esp. with white truffles

TRUFFLES, WHITE

(and White Truffle Oil) (See also Oil, Truffle)

Season: autumn
Weight: light
Volume: loud (in a subtle way!)
Techniques: shave
Tips: Shave over dishes at the last minute.

Dishes

Pappardelle with Butter, Parmesan, and White Truffles
— Mario Batali, Babbo (New York City)

Homemade Yolk-Filled Ravioli in Truffle Butter
— Odette Fada, San Domenico (New York City)

artichokes, Jerusalem
butter
cheese, Parmesan
cream / milk
eggs
Italian cuisine
onions
pasta
pears
pepper
potatoes
prosciutto
risotto
salt
thyme

Flavor Affinities

truffles + eggs + pasta

TUNA

Season: summer–autumn
Weight: heavy
Volume: moderate
Techniques: braise, broil, grill, poach, raw (e.g., sushi, tartare), sauté, sear, steam, stir-fry

aioli
anchovies
arugula
asparagus
avocado
bacon
basil
bass, black
bay leaf
beans: black, fava, green, white
beets
bell peppers, esp. green, red, yellow
butter, unsalted
cabbage, green
capers
caponata
carrots
caviar
cayenne
celery
chervil
CHILE PEPPERS: dried or fresh, esp. green (e.g., jalapeño, Thai)
chili oil
chili sauce
CHIVES

I really look forward to **truffle** season. I love a poached egg with truffle, or a truffle salad. A truffle needs to be the central component and the dish needs to be simple. One of my favorite dishes is Jerusalem artichokes with a poached egg and shaved white truffle. We serve this in a [mason] jar that clamps on the side, and when you pop it open you get a burst of truffle aroma.
— **GABRIEL KREUTHER,** THE MODERN (NEW YORK CITY)

When you have a nice ripe **truffle**, it will have a sweet, fruity pear smell to it. I mix pear and truffle together to make a little salad. I make a sauce with chicken stock, olive oil, and add little bits of tarragon, then serve it with langoustine, which is a very sweet shellfish.
— **GABRIEL KREUTHER,** THE MODERN (NEW YORK CITY)

CILANTRO
coconut milk
cognac
coriander
corn
cornichons
cucumbers
cumin
curry
daikon
dashi
dill
eggs (e.g., hard-boiled)
fennel
fennel pollen
fennel seeds
fish sauce, Thai
frisée
GARLIC
GINGER: pickled, fresh, juice
honey
jicama
leeks
LEMON: juice, zest
lettuce, red oak
LIME, juice
mayonnaise
mint, esp. spearmint
mirepoix
mirin
miso, sweet
mizuna
mushrooms: cultivated, shiitakes
mustard: Dijon, seeds
nectarines
noodles: angel hair, vermicelli,
   rice
nori
OIL: canola, grapeseed, peanut,
   sesame, vegetable
olive oil
olives, esp. black, kalamata,
   niçoise
ONIONS: green, pearl, red,
   Spanish, spring

Dishes

Marinated Yellowfin Tuna with Anchovy Dressing: Quail Egg, Haricots, and Fried Panelleria Capers
— Daniel Boulud, Daniel (New York City)

Spicy Tuna Tartare with Cured Lemon, Harissa, Cucumber Yogurt
— Daniel Boulud/Bertrand Chemel, Café Boulud (New York City)

Tuna Marinato with Zucchini, Gaeta Olives, and Orange
— Andrew Carmellini, A Voce (New York City)

Grilled Rare Marinated Tuna with Cumin Wafers and Cilantro Dressing
— Sanford D'Amato, Sanford (Milwaukee)

Signature Sushi: Tuna with Roasted Almond, Kalamata Olive, Foie Gras, or Italian Black Truffle
— Kaz Okochi, Kaz Sushi Bistro (Washington, DC)

Grilled Tuna with Wasabi and Pickled Ginger
— Chris Schlesinger, East Coast Grill (Cambridge, Massachusetts)

Toasted Cumin and Tangerine Seared Rare Tuna: Wasabi Mash Potato, Green Papaya Slaw, Pineapple-Ginger Nage
— Allen Susser, Chef Allen's (Aventura, Florida)

Japanese Hamachi with Roasted Bell Pepper, Kalamata Olive Sorbet, Spanish Paprika, and Basil Oil
— Charlie Trotter, Charlie Trotter's (Chicago)

Bluefin Tuna with Spicy Miso
— Charlie Trotter, Charlie Trotter's (Chicago)

One dish that we always make the same is **bluefin tuna** over braised veal cheeks. It is our take on *vitello tunato*. This dish has to be made with bluefin because it is meatlike and gets seasoned like meat. The fish is cooked rare and served with a little *tunato* sauce and arugula.

— **SHARON HAGE,** YORK STREET (DALLAS)

orange, blood or regular, juice
pancetta
paprika
PARSLEY, flat-leaf
passion fruit
pasta
PEPPER: black, green, white
pine nuts
potatoes
prosciutto
radicchio
radishes
rice
rosemary
sage
sake
SALT: kosher, sea
SCALLIONS
scallops
SESAME: oil, seeds
shallots
shiso
SOY SAUCE
spinach
stock, chicken
sugar
sweet potatoes
Tabasco sauce
tahini
tarragon
THYME
TOMATOES, tomato juice, tomato paste
veal and veal cheeks
vinaigrette
VINEGAR: balsamic, champagne, red wine, rice wine, sherry, white wine
vodka
wasabi
watercress

wine: dry red (Grenache, Pinot Noir, Syrah), rosé
yuzu: juice, rind

Flavor Affinities

tuna + aioli + capers + tomatoes
tuna + anchovies + green beans + olives + potatoes
tuna + arugula + bacon
tuna + avocado + ginger + radish
tuna + avocado + lemon + soy sauce
tuna + beets + lemon
tuna + black pepper + cilantro + cucumber + soy sauce
tuna + cilantro + cumin
tuna + cilantro + dill + garlic + mint
tuna + cilantro + dill + mint
tuna + cucumber + ginger + miso + shiso
tuna + fennel + fennel pollen
tuna + ginger + mustard
tuna + ginger + vinaigrette
tuna + jalapeño chile + cilantro + ginger + sesame oil + shallots + soy sauce
tuna + lemon + olive oil + tomatoes + watercress
tuna + sesame + wasabi

TURBOT

Weight: medium
Volume: quiet–moderate
Techniques: bake, broil, grill, poach, roast, sauté, steam

asparagus
butter, unsalted
Champagne
chervil
chives
crème fraîche
fennel
garlic
ginger
hollandaise sauce
leeks
lemon: juice, zest
marjoram
miso
mushrooms
olive oil
parsley, flat-leaf
pepper: black, white
potatoes, esp. red, white
rosemary
saffron
sage
salt, sea
shallots
spinach
stocks: fish, mussel

When I create a dish, I start with the fish and ask, What is the inspiration of the moment? I will choose a culture and start there. For a recent dish, I was in a Japanese mood and wanted something light and refined. I used a piece of **turbot** and paired it with miso and mushroom broth. The mushrooms don't relate so much to the culture but the miso definitely does. I created a lemon miso paste with white miso and lemon confit. The fish would sit on the paste and at the last second the waiter would add the mushroom broth. If you add the broth too soon, the miso kills the mushroom flavors.

— ERIC RIPERT, LE BERNARDIN (NEW YORK CITY)

Turbot is a beautiful, delicate fish that calls to mind special occasions and celebrations. It poaches well, and takes on richer garnishes such as caviar or truffles.

— BRADFORD THOMPSON, MARY ELAINE'S AT THE PHOENICIAN
(SCOTTSDALE, ARIZONA)

When you get in fresh **turbot**, you automatically think of pairing it with delicate flavors. It is like looking at the Queen of England: You look at it with unbelievable respect, and there is no way you are going to overload this delicate piece of fish. I like turbot with a nage with periwinkles, chervil, and parsley puree. Or I'll make it with tiny pearl onions with a drizzle of red wine reduction made from the bones of the turbot.

— CARRIE NAHABEDIAN, NAHA (CHICAGO)

Dishes
Steamed Turbot with Osetra Caviar in Champagne Sauce
— David Bouley, Danube (New York City)

tarragon
tomatoes
vanilla
wine: Champagne, white

Flavor Affinities
turbot + butter + lemon +
   marjoram
turbot + caviar + Champagne
turbot + lemon + miso +
   mushrooms

TURKEY
Season: summer–autumn
Weight: medium
Volume: quiet
Techniques: braise, grill, poach, roast, sauté, stir-fry

allspice
apples
bacon
bay leaf
bread crumbs
butter, unsalted
cardamom
carrots
celery
cheese: white sheep or goat's milk
   (similar to feta)

chestnuts
chile peppers: dried red (esp.
   sweet); fresh green
cinnamon
cloves
corn bread
cranberries
cumin
fenugreek leaves
figs, dried
garam masala
garlic
ginger
grapes, white
innards: turkey heart, liver
juniper berries
leeks
lemon, juice
lime, juice
mushrooms, esp. wild (e.g.,
   chanterelles)
oil: canola, grapeseed, peanut,
   vegetable
olive oil
onions, esp. sweet, white
orange, juice
paprika
parsnips
parsley, flat-leaf
pepper: black, white
phyllo dough
pine nuts
potatoes
raisins, esp. yellow
rosemary
sage
salt, kosher
sausage, esp. Italian
shallots
soy sauce
spinach
stocks: chicken, turkey
stuffing
sugar
tarragon
thyme
tomatoes
vermouth, dry

walnuts
wine, dry white, rosé
yogurt

TURKISH CUISINE

beef
chicken
cinnamon, esp. in desserts
cloves, esp. in desserts
cumin
dill
eggplant
fish
garlic
goat / sheep cheese
honey, esp. in desserts
kebabs, meat, esp. lamb
lamb, esp. grilled
lemon
mint: dried, fresh
nutmeg, esp. in desserts
olive oil
onions
paprika
parsley
pepper, black
phyllo dough
rice
sesame seeds
spinach
tomatoes
walnuts
yogurt

Flavor Affinities

chicken + garlic + paprika +
   parsley
cumin + lemon + parsley
eggplant + garlic + meat + onions
   + tomatoes
fish + dill + lemon + black pepper
lamb + cumin + dill + mint

TURMERIC

Season: year-round
Taste: bittersweet; pungent
Function: heating
Weight: light–medium
Volume: medium

Fresh **turmeric** gives you fruitiness and upfront flavor, plus a touch of acid that perks up a dish. If you add fresh turmeric to your curry, you will make a world of difference. When you smell the powdered stuff, it smells like nothing. Dried turmeric hurts me. It hurts the soul. It is really not what turmeric is. Unfortunately, frozen turmeric isn't a good substitute, either. You have to use it fresh.

— **BRAD FARMERIE**, PUBLIC (NEW YORK CITY)

Turmeric is always the first spice I add to a curry, like the primer on a canvas. The amount of turmeric controls the entire path that curry will take. I cook in layers of flavor, so only when I am happy with the aroma of one layer will I then add ingredients to create the next layer. If I am making curry, the pan will have onions, garlic, and tomatoes, and then the very first thing to go in is the turmeric. If I use a lot of turmeric, it's destined to be a richer-spiced curry, as I'll also have to put in more of all the other spices to balance the flavors.

— **MEERU DHALWALA**, VIJ'S (VANCOUVER)

Asian cuisine
beans
beef
butter
Caribbean cuisine
cheese
chicken
chile peppers
chutneys
cilantro
cloves
coconut milk
coriander
cumin
***CURRY LEAVES, POWDER**
eggplant
eggs
fennel
fish
garlic
ginger
Indian cuisine
Indonesian cuisine
kaffir lime, leaves
lamb
lemongrass
lentils
meats, esp. white
Middle Eastern cuisine
Moroccan cuisine

mustard
mustard seeds
North African cuisine
paella
paprika
parsley
pepper
pickles
pork
potatoes
poultry
ras el hanout (key ingredient)
rice
sauces, esp. creamy
sausage
seafood
shallots
shellfish
shrimp
soups
Southeast Asian cuisine
spinach
stewed dishes
tamarind
Thai cuisine
vegetables, esp. root
yogurt

Flavor Affinities

turmeric + cilantro + cumin + garlic + onion + paprika + parsley + pepper (Moroccan chermoula)

turmeric + coriander + cumin (Indian cuisine)

TURNIP GREENS
(See Greens, Turnip)

TURNIPS
Season: year-round
Taste: sweet
Weight: medium–heavy
Volume: moderate–loud
Techniques: boil, braise, deep-fry, roast, simmer, steam

bacon
bay leaf
butter, unsalted
carrots
celery root
cheese, Parmesan
cream
curry
dill
duck, esp. roasted
garlic
honey
juniper berries
lamb
leeks
lemon, juice
marjoram
nutmeg
onions, esp. green, yellow
parsley
pepper: black, white
poppy seeds
pork, esp. roasted
potatoes
prosciutto
salt: kosher, rock, sea
shiso
stock, chicken
sugar (pinch)
sweet potatoes
thyme
vinegar

UMAMI
Taste: savory or savory + salty

aged foods (e.g., cheese)
anchovies
beef, esp. aged
bonito flakes
broccoli
carrots
cheese, aged (e.g., blue, Gruyère, Parmesan, Roquefort)
chicken
clams
cured foods
fermented foods
fish sauce, Asian
grapefruit
grapes
ketchup
lobster
mackerel
meats
miso
mushrooms, esp. shiitake
oysters
pork
potatoes
ripe ingredients
sardines
sauces, meat-based
scallops
seafood
seaweed, dried
soy beans
soy sauce
squid
steaks, esp. dry-aged, grilled
stocks, meat-based
sweet potatoes
tea, green
tomatoes and tomato sauce
truffles

tuna
vinegar, balsamic
walnuts

VANILLA
Taste: sweet
Weight: medium
Volume: quiet

allspice
almonds
apples
apricots
BAKED GOODS, e.g., cakes, cookies
bay leaf
beans, black
beef
berries
beverages (e.g., eggnog, soft drinks)
brown butter
butter
butterscotch
cakes
candies
caramel
cardamom
cheese, ricotta
chicken
chiles
CHOCOLATE
cilantro
cinnamon
cloves
coconut
COFFEE
cookies
CREAM AND ICE CREAM
cream cheese
custards
DESSERTS
eggs
figs
fish
fruits, esp. poached
ginger
honey

Dishes

Vanilla Bean Bavarese with Brown Butter and Laurel
— Gina DePalma, pastry chef, Babbo (New York City)

Vanilla Bean Pain Perdu with Mascarpone Custard, Tondo Balsamic Syrup, Strawberries
— Emily Luchetti, pastry chef, Farallon (San Francisco)

I always overlooked **vanilla** when I was growing up. After I made my first vanilla ice cream, however, it was no longer just "the white one"! I like the nuances that different kinds of vanilla offer. Working at Le Bernardin where quality is paramount, for our ice cream it has to be Tahitian. When vanilla is the star, this is the bean you choose. It has an interesting woody, cherrylike flavor to it that I just love. Bourbon vanilla is a great workhorse bean that does well in a supporting role.

— MICHAEL LAISKONIS, LE BERNARDIN (NEW YORK CITY)

If I poach a pear, I will always add **vanilla**. Vanilla also pairs really well with sweet herbs, especially tarragon and bay leaf.

— GINA DEPALMA, BABBO (NEW YORK CITY)

So many dessert recipes call for **vanilla** that it is like salt for dessert. But sometimes it doesn't have a place and can muck up things. Vanilla should be the star of the show. I love vanilla in dairy desserts. I do a vanilla bean Bavarese (an Italian Bavarian cream) that I serve with brown butter and bay leaf. Vanilla and fresh bay leaf bring each other alive, it is a fantastic combination. Bay leaf is very sweet; it is like a truffle in that it is more about the aroma than the flavor.

— GINA DEPALMA, BABBO (NEW YORK CITY)

*ICE CREAM
lamb
lavender
lemon: juice, zest
lemongrass
lobster
mascarpone
meats
melon
Mexican cuisine
milk
mint
mussels
nutmeg
nuts
orange
peaches
pears
plums

pork
puddings
rhubarb
rice
rosemary
saffron
salads, fruit
scallops
seafood
seeds: poppy, sesame
shellfish
soups
stocks
strawberries
SUGAR
tamarind
tea
tomatoes
vegetables (e.g., root)

vinegar, balsamic
whiskey
wine, Champagne
yogurt

Flavor Affinities
vanilla + almonds + cream + whiskey
vanilla + bay leaf + brown butter
vanilla + chicken + cream

VEAL — IN GENERAL

Season: spring
Weight: light–medium
Volume: quiet
Techniques: braise (shanks), pan roast (chops), roast, stew (breast, shoulder)

almonds
anchovies
apples
asparagus
basil
bay leaf
beans, esp. flageolets, haricots verts
beef, short ribs
beets
bell peppers: green, red, yellow
brandy
bread and bread crumbs
butter, unsalted
capers
caraway seeds
carrots
celery
celery root
cheese: Emmental, Gruyère, Parmesan, Swiss
chervil
chile peppers
chives
cider
coconut milk
cream
crème fraîche
cucumbers, sautéed

dill
eggs, esp. hard-boiled
French cuisine
GARLIC
gremolata
ham: smoked, hock
hazelnuts
Italian cuisine
leeks
LEMON: juice, zest
lemon verbena
lime: juice, leaves
Madeira
marjoram
milk
MUSHROOMS: button,
    chanterelle, morels, oyster,
    porcini, shiitake, white, wild
mustard, Dijon
nutmeg
OIL: canola, corn, peanut,
    vegetable
olive oil
olives, black
ONIONS, esp. pearl, sweet, white
orange: juice, zest
parsley, flat-leaf
parsnips
pasta, esp. fettuccine
peas, spring
PEPPER: black, white
polenta
potatoes
prosciutto
rice
rosemary
sage
SALT: kosher, sea
shallots
spaetzle
spinach
STOCKS: beef, chicken, veal,
    vegetable
tarragon
thyme
TOMATOES: canned, paste,
    plum, sauce
truffles

tuna
turnips
vanilla
vinegar: balsamic, chamapagne
watercrêss
WINE, DRY WHITE
zucchini

Flavor Affinities
veal + asparagus + morels
veal + basil + lemon
veal + capers + lemon
veal + cream + mushrooms
veal + cucumber + mustard
veal + garlic + Parmesan cheese +
    tomatoes
veal + gremolata + orange
veal + Marsala wine +
    mushrooms
veal + orange + polenta
veal + prosciutto + sage

VEAL — BREAST
Techniques: braise, grill, roast

beans, white
cheese, Fontina
garlic
olive oil
onions, esp. Spanish
pancetta
parsley, flat-leaf
rosemary
stock, chicken
thyme
wine, white

VEAL — CHEEKS
When we make **veal cheek** osso
buco on polenta, each dish gets a
squeeze of orange and orange
zest on it.
— **ANDREW CARMELLINI,** A VOCE (NEW
YORK CITY)

VEAL — CHOP
Techniques: braise, grill, pan
roast, sauté, stuff

artichokes
basil
beans, esp. fava
broccoli rabe
butter
Campari
capers
chives
cilantro
coriander
garlic
ginger
gnocchi
leeks
lemon, juice
Madeira
marjoram
mint
mirin
miso
mushrooms (e.g., black trumpet)
mushrooms, wild, esp.
    chanterelle, porcini
mustard, Dijon
olive oil
olives: black, kalamata
onions
parsley, flat-leaf
peas
pepper, white
pine nuts
polenta
potatoes
prosciutto
radishes
red pepper flakes
salt
sesame: oil, seeds
shallots
soy sauce
stock, chicken
sugar, brown
thyme
tomatoes, sun-dried
watercress
wine, dry white

Dishes

"San Angelo" Veal Rib Chop with "Texas Grits" and Saffron Aioli
— Monica Pope, T'afia (Houston)

Fricassee de Veau Printanière: Savory Veal Stew with English Peas, Asparagus, Morels, and Spring Vegetables
— Michael Romano, at the 2005 James Beard Awards gala reception

Sautéed Wisconsin Veal Chop, White Polenta, Wild Mushrooms
— Jean Joho, Everest (Chicago)

Veal Chop with Truffled Leek Pierogies, Roasted Spring Onion, Creamed Spinach, and Chive Crème Fraîche
— Peter Nowakoski, Rat's (Hamilton, New Jersey)

Organic Veal Chop with Madeira Sauce and Truffled "Macaroni and Cheese"
— David Waltuck, Chanterelle (New York City)

Flavor Affinities

veal chop + artichokes + basil
veal chop + celery root + cream + Dijon mustard
veal chop + garlic + chanterelle mushrooms
veal chop + leeks + peas
veal chop + leeks + polenta
veal chop + mushrooms + watercress

VEAL — LOIN

Techniques: braise, grill, pan roast, roast, sauté

arugula
basil
cheese, Fontina
chestnuts
cider, apple
citrus
cranberries
garlic
mushrooms, wild (e.g., chanterelles, morels)
nuts (e.g., almonds, hazelnuts, pine nuts, pistachios)
onions
oregano
pasta
pumpkin
risotto
rosemary
sage
stock, veal
tarragon
thyme
tomatoes
wine, red

VEAL — SHANKS

Techniques: braise

bay leaf
carrots

Dishes

Grilled Veal Loin Medallions on Pumpkin Fettuccine
— Marcel Desaulniers, The Trellis (Williamsburg, Virginia)

Pan-Seared Tenderloin of Veal with Wild Morel Mushrooms, Local Asparagus, and Raviolis of Virginia Country Ham and Fontina Cheese
— Patrick O'Connell, The Inn at Little Washington (Washington, Virginia)

Roasted Veal Loin with Caramelized Onions, Almonds, Pine Nuts, and Pistachios
— Charlie Trotter, Charlie Trotter's (Chicago)

celery
cilantro
cinnamon
cumin
garlic
gremolata
horseradish
lemon: juice, **zest**
marjoram
mushrooms, porcini
olive oil
olives
onions, esp. red, white
oranges
osso buco (ingredient)
parsley
pepper
pine nuts
raisins, yellow
risotto
rosemary
salt
stocks: chicken, veal
thyme
tomatoes: paste, sauce
truffles, white
WINE, WHITE

Flavor Affinities

veal shanks + capers + gremolata + olives
veal shanks + lemon + olives
veal shanks + onions + tomatoes
veal shanks + tomatoes + thyme

VEAL — TENDERLOIN

Techniques: braise, grill, sauté, sear

asparagus
bacon
basil
capers
cheese, Fontina
cream
ham
mushrooms, morel
mustard, Dijon
onions, red
sage
tarragon
thyme
truffle oil
wine, white

Flavor Affinities

veal tenderloin + asparagus + morel mushrooms

veal tenderloin + cream + morel mushrooms

veal tenderloin + garlic + pancetta

VEGETABLES

(See specific vegetables)
Tips: Onion enhances the flavor of vegetables, and brings out their sweetness.

VEGETABLES, ROOT

(See specific root vegetables, e.g., Carrots)
Techniques: roast

VEGETARIAN DISHES

Tips: To add a deep, meaty flavor to vegetarian dishes — without adding meat — try:

chile peppers, chipotle — use adobo sauce from canned chiles
liquid smoke
miso
mushrooms
onions, roasted
paprika, smoked
shallots, roasted
soy sauce

All year long, I make a *pistou* [a **vegetable** soup seasoned with basil, garlic, and olive oil]. However, it changes not only by the season, but by the week. In the spring, I'll add peas. In the summer, it will have zucchini and basil. In the fall, I'll add salsify, scallions, and leeks, and in the winter, broccoli and even soybeans along with parsley.
— **DAN BARBER**, BLUE HILL AT STONE BARNS (POCANTICO HILLS, NEW YORK)

Root vegetables are so sweet and full of sugar in the fall. Fall and winter vegetables thrive on cold and frost. The plant's water converts to sugar and when it is picked you have a really sweet vegetable. A root vegetable, like a sweet carrot or parsnip, is similar in sweetness to fruit, so you can put the two in a salad and they will go well together.
— **DAN BARBER**, BLUE HILL AT STONE BARNS (POCANTICO HILLS, NEW YORK)

Because **venison** doesn't have much fat, you need to be careful how you cut its richness. I will use chutney that has nice fruit acids with the addition of a little vinegar.
— **BRAD FARMERIE**, PUBLIC (NEW YORK CITY)

We offer **venison** medallions with huckleberry sauce and glazed pears. Venison is a pretty sweet meat. Huckleberries are found in the woods and pears are autumnal. The pears are poached with star anise and cinnamon, and then they are roasted to caramelize them a little, which adds extra depth to them and to the dish.
— **GABRIEL KREUTHER**, THE MODERN (NEW YORK CITY)

One of my favorite dishes is medallions of ranch **venison**, huckleberries, roasted chestnuts and Brussels sprouts, celery root, and Honeycrisp applesauce. I love a sweet flavor with venison. A traditional marinade is with vinegar, red wine, herbs, and juniper berries. A natural pairing would be roasted pears or apples.
— **CARRIE NAHABEDIAN**, NAHA (CHICAGO)

VENISON (See also Game — In General)
Season: autumn
Weight: heavy
Volume: moderate–loud
Techniques: braise, broil, grill, roast, sauté

Dishes

New Zealand Venison Crusted in Pink Peppercorns: Jerusalem Artichoke and Young Garlic Confit, Roasted Brussels Sprout Leaves
— David Bouley, Bouley (New York City)

Shiitake-Crusted New Zealand Venison Loin, Peppered Spinach, Sweet Potato Dauphinoise, and Sour Cherry Compote
— Brad Farmerie, Public (New York City)

Smoked New Zealand Venison Carpaccio with Licorice Pickled Onions
— Brad Farmerie, Monday Room (New York City)

Medallions of Ranch Venison with Huckleberries, Roasted Chestnuts and Brussels Sprouts, Celery Root, and Honeycrisp Applesauce
— Carrie Nahabedian, Naha (Chicago)

Venison Medallions, Grilled Grits, and Green Peach Relish with Okra and Tomato
— Frank Stitt, Highlands Bar and Grill (Birmingham, Alabama)

Millbrook Farm Venison Loin with Kohlrabi, White Runner Beans, Pickled Garlic, and Spiced Dates
— Charlie Trotter, Charlie Trotter's (Chicago)

American cuisine
apples
artichoke, Jerusalem
bacon
bay leaf
beets
bourbon
brandy
Brussels sprouts
butter, unsalted
cabbage, red
cardamom
carrots
celery
cheese, Asiago
cherries, dried or fresh, esp. black
chervil
chestnuts
chiles
chives
cinnamon
cloves
cognac
coriander
corn
cranberries
cream
currants, dried or fresh, esp. red
curries and curry powder
fennel
garlic
gin
ginger: grated, ground, minced
greens: arugula, chicory, dandelion, mâche, radicchio, spinach
honey
horseradish
huckleberries
JUNIPER BERRIES
lemon, juice
lemongrass
lime, juice
Marsala
mirepoix
mushrooms: button, porcini, shiitake, **wild**
mustard
nectarines
nutmeg
nuts: almonds, cashews
oil: canola, grapeseed, peanut, walnut
olive oil
ONIONS
orange: juice, zest

pancetta
parsley, flat-leaf
parsnips
peaches
PEARS
PEPPER: black, green, pink,
   Szechuan, white
pineapple
pomegranate
port
potatoes
pumpkin
raisins
rosemary
sage
salt, kosher
savory
shallots
soy sauce
spinach
squash: acorn, butternut
star anise
STOCKS: beef, chicken, venison
sweet potatoes
thyme
tomatoes and tomato paste
turnips, esp. yellow
vinegar: balsamic, red wine, rice,
   sherry
watercress
WINE: red (e.g., Cabernet
   Sauvignon), dry white

Flavor Affinities
venison + curry + pomegranate
   seeds
venison + garlic + juniper berries
   + rosemary
venison + garlic + peppercorns
venison + garlic + rosemary +
   tomatoes + red wine
venison + parsnips + pepper
venison + pears + rosemary

VERJUS

Taste: sour–sweet
Tips: Use instead of vinegar or
lemon juice, or as a seasoning.
Verjus is often more wine friendly
than vinegar.

apples
apricots
asparagus
berries
cheese, goat
chicken
cranberries
cucumbers
fennel
fish (e.g., halibut, salmon, tuna)
foie gras
FRUIT
garlic
ginger
herbs (e.g., dill, mint, thyme)
lamb
lettuces
marinades
meat
melon
mustard, Dijon
olive oil
onions
pears
pomegranate
pork
poultry
quail
quince
rabbit
SALADS: FRUIT, GREEN
sauces
shellfish (e.g., crab, scallops,
   shrimp)
soups
soy sauce
spinach
strawberries
sugar: brown, white
tuna
vegetables
vinegar, rice wine

VIETNAMESE CUISINE

basil, Thai
bean sprouts
beef, in soup (*pho*)
chicken
chile peppers
cilantro
cucumbers
fish
fish sauce
garlic
ginger
lemon
lemongrass
lettuce
lime
milk, sweetened condensed
   (e.g., in coffee)
mint
noodles
pork
raw foods
rice
scallions
shallots
shellfish
shrimp
star anise
sugar

Flavor Affinities
chile peppers + fish sauce +
   lemon
fish sauce + herbs
fish sauce + lemon

VINEGAR — IN GENERAL

I use a variety of **vinegars** and right now I am using cider vinegar, balsamic, and white balsamic. What vinegar you grab really depends on how far you can push the product. When we make a walnut sauce, it can handle a good-sized dash of cider vinegar. In a fluke tartare, we'll only use a drop of vinegar.

— **MICHAEL ANTHONY**, GRAMERCY TAVERN (NEW YORK CITY)

VINEGAR, BALSAMIC

Taste: sour, sweet
Weight: medium–heavy (depending on age)
Volume: moderate–loud
Tips: Use when you want a sweet, low-acid vinegar.

Add at end of cooking (and never boil!) or use to finish a dish.

apricots
arugula
basil
beans, green
bell peppers: green, red
berries, esp. strawberries
brown butter
cabbage
cheese, Parmesan
cherries
chicken
chicory
eggplant
endive

fish, esp. white
fruit
greens, salad
grilled dishes
hazelnut oil
honey
Italian cuisine
marinades
meats
mustard, esp. Dijon
mustard: dry, seeds
oil
onions
pepper, black
radicchio
raspberries

High-quality **vinegars** such as Gegenbauer vinegars [from Vienna, Austria], have a place in my kitchen. I'll use a few drops of cucumber vinegar with cucumbers, a raspberry vinegar with raspberries, and a tomato vinegar with tomatoes to intensify the flavor of the ingredient.

— **SHARON HAGE**, YORK STREET (DALLAS)

Balsamic vinegar is wonderful with fruit. I love the Italian dish of strawberries with balsamic vinegar.

— **GABRIEL KREUTHER**, THE MODERN (NEW YORK CITY)

I like **white balsamic vinegar** because it has fruitiness and a hint of sweetness to it, but not aggressive acidity.

— **DANIEL HUMM**, ELEVEN MADISON PARK (NEW YORK CITY)

SALADS AND SALAD DRESSINGS
sesame oil
steak
*STRAWBERRIES
*TOMATOES
vegetables
vinaigrette
vinegar: red wine, sherry (blending vinegars)
walnut oil
watercress
white truffle oil

Flavor Affinities
balsamic vinegar + brown butter + fish
white balsamic vinegar + white truffle oil + whole grain mustard

VINEGAR, BANYULS
Taste: sour–sweet
Weight: light
Volume: quiet–moderate
Tips: Can substitute for red wine vinegar. Use to deglaze a pan.

beets
cheese: blue, Parmesan

I'll use **Banyuls vinegar** as our everyday vinegar for finishing dishes. A crispy fish like ivory salmon served on the rare side will get a drop of Banyuls vinegar right before it goes out to the table. I'll also use it as a delicate finish for birds like quail.

— **SHARON HAGE**, YORK STREET (DALLAS)

cream
duck
fish
foie gras
honey
lettuces
marinades
meats
mushrooms
nuts
oil: hazelnut, walnut
olive oil
pears
pepper, black
quail
salads and salad dressings
salmon, ivory
salt
sauces
scallops
shellfish
tomatoes
vegetables
walnuts

Flavor Affinities
Banyuls vinegar + blue cheese + lettuce + pears + walnuts

VINEGAR, CABERNET SAUVIGNON
We finish most of our *jus* for meat dishes with **cabernet vinegar**. If you use it at the beginning of the cooking process, it cooks out because it is so light.

— **BRAD FARMERIE**, PUBLIC (NEW YORK CITY)

VINEGAR, CHAMPAGNE
Taste: sour
Weight: light
Volume: quiet–moderate
Tips: Champagne vinegar is the most delicate vinegar.

artichokes
avocados
delicate dishes
fennel
fish
greens, delicate salad (e.g., baby greens, butter lettuce)
leeks
oils: nut, truffle
olive oil

Sorbet is about pure flavor and should be a very intense experience of the fruit's flavor. You can jack up the flavor of your sorbet by choosing the correct acid to balance it. For example, lemon juice is really strong. If you have sweet sorbet, you can add a ton of lemon juice that will balance the sweetness but give you a lemon dessert. For some sorbets, I prefer to use **champagne vinegar**. It is light and easy to use. Vinegar is a more potent fruity acid, so you can use less and bring up the fruit of your dessert. I use champagne vinegar for mango or raspberry sorbet. It is made from grapes, which are berries, and is a natural for berry desserts — berries with berries.

— **GINA DEPALMA**, BABBO (NEW YORK CITY)

Most of our ingredients are pickled with **cider vinegar** and a touch of sugar. I like its fresh green appley flavor and the way it makes things pop.

— **BRAD FARMERIE**, PUBLIC (NEW YORK CITY)

potatoes
raspberries
salads
shellfish
strawberries
vegetables

VINEGAR, CHARDONNAY

Chardonnay vinegar is a sweet acid, so you don't have to add additional sugar to your pickling mixture.

— **BRAD FARMERIE,** PUBLIC (NEW YORK CITY)

VINEGAR, CIDER

Taste: sour
Weight: light
Volume: quiet–moderate

American cuisine
apples
coleslaw
fruits, esp. in salads
ginger
grains
herbs
oil
pears
peas
pork
salads and salad dressings
sauces
smoked fish
smoked meats
sugar

Flavor Affinities
cider vinegar + ginger + sugar

VINEGAR, FRUIT

Taste: sour, sweet
Weight: light
Volume: quiet–moderate

avocados
chicken

Inniskillin **ice wine vinegar** is really delicious, but expensive. It is delicious with foie gras. It is a fairly reduced sweet and sour vinegar and works as just a drizzle on a plate. It is also good dressed on a salad that you would serve alongside a foie gras terrine.

— **TRACI DES JARDINS,** JARDINIÈRE (SAN FRANCISCO)

Minus 8 is an **ice wine vinegar,** so named because the grapes are frozen to minus 8 degrees and then squeezed to make the vinegar. It still has acid to it, but it is more viscous, sweet, and tart. It is great with foie gras.

— **SHARON HAGE,** YORK STREET (DALLAS)

fruit salads
hazelnut oil
meats, white
oils, esp. nut
peanut oil
pears
salads and salad dressings
turkey
walnut oil

AVOID
cheese
eggs

VINEGAR, ICE WINE

Taste: sour, sweet
Weight: light
Volume: quiet–moderate, with 5 percent acidity

berries
FOIE GRAS, ESP. TERRINE
fruit
lobster
oil: grapeseed
onions
oysters
peaches
salads
sauces
scallops
seafood
sorbets

strawberries
vegetables

VINEGAR, MALT

Taste: sour
Weight: light
Volume: loud, with moderate acidity
Tips: Sprinkle on foods judiciously.

dressings
fish, fried
oil: hazelnut, peanut
olive oil
pickles

AVOID
sauces

VINEGAR, RED WINE

Taste: sour
Weight: light–medium
Volume: loud, with high acidity
Tips: Red wine vinegar can stand up to spices and stronger herbs.

beans, green
chard
cherries
chicken
cinnamon
cold dishes

Red wine vinegar is my workhorse vinegar for cold dishes. I use it in dressings and marinades.

— **SHARON HAGE,** YORK STREET (DALLAS)

dandelion greens
greens: salad, stronger
grilled dishes
heartier dishes
kale
marinades
meat, red
mushrooms
mustard
oils, nut
olive oil
salads and salad dressings
sauces
spinach
tomatoes
vinaigrettes

VINEGAR, RICE WINE

Taste: sour, sweet
Weight: light
Volume: quiet, with lower acidity

Asian cuisine
cilantro
coriander
cucumbers
fruit, esp. salads
ginger
honey
Japanese cuisine
lemon
mirin
noodles
oils: peanut, sesame
pepper: black, pink
rice (e.g., for sushi)
salads
salmon
scallions
sesame seeds
soups, esp. creamy, potato
soy sauce
star anise
wasabi

The minute **sherry vinegar** is added to a dish, the music gets turned up. It's not just its flavor, but its aroma as well. It makes things sizzle. It is not just when it is used in salads, but it is also the spark that makes gazpacho the unique soup it is. It is the spark that makes a humble lentil stew made with carrots, garlic, onion, and water a new thing. At the end, you add just a touch of vinegar and you have this wonderful flavor that sparkles. . . . We have made sorbet out of sherry vinegar and what you get is something that makes "the king of refreshing" even *more* refreshing! You can go either savory or sweet with this sorbet: You could serve orange segments with the sherry sorbet on top, a touch of olive oil, an anchovy, a couple of black olives, and you have a salad. Or you could take the same oranges, add a touch of honey on top, manchego cheese, the sherry vinegar sorbet, and have a sweet dessert.
— JOSÉ ANDRÉS, CAFÉ ATLÁNTICO (WASHINGTON, DC)

For our meat dishes, we deglaze with vinegar or *verjus* — and most often it will be **sherry vinegar.** That's my workhorse vinegar for hot dishes.
— SHARON HAGE, YORK STREET (DALLAS)

There is a range of **sherry vinegar** from light to heavy, and I use them all. I love sherry vinegar on almost all vegetables, but especially asparagus and cucumbers.
— KATSUYA FUKUSHIMA, MINIBAR (WASHINGTON, DC)

VINEGAR, SHERRY

Taste: sour, sweet
Weight: light
Volume: moderate

apples
asparagus
beans
chicken
cucumbers
duck
figs
fish
gazpacho
greens, esp. bitter
meat dishes
mustard, grainy
nuts
oils: nut, walnut
onions
orange
pancetta
pears
radicchio
rich dishes
salad dressings
salads, esp. with apples, nuts, pears
sauces
Spanish cuisine
tomatoes
tortilla, Spanish
vegetables

VINEGAR, TARRAGON
(herb-flavored vinegar)
Taste: sour
Weight: light
Volume: moderate–loud

endive
lettuces, esp. Bibb, iceberg, romaine
oil, mild (e.g., peanut)
olive oil

Vincotto is a byproduct of balsamic vinegar, and is sweet and sour. It is very syrupy and good drizzled over fruit or cheese.

— SHARON HAGE, YORK STREET (DALLAS)

VINEGAR, VINCOTTO
(Cooked Wine)

Taste: sour–sweet
Weight: medium–heavy
Volume: moderate–loud

almonds
bacon
cheese, burrata
desserts
fennel
figs
fruit
Italian cuisine
peaches
pears
plums
meats, esp. grilled, roasted
salads and salad dressings
yogurt

VINEGAR, WHITE WINE

Taste: sour
Weight: light
Volume: quiet–moderate
Tips: Can substitute champagne vinegar if needed.

artichokes
avocados
delicate dishes
fennel
fish
leeks
oils: safflower, sunflower
olive oil (extra virgin)
potatoes
shellfish

VODKA

Weight: light–medium
Volume: quiet

amaretto
apples and apple juice
beef consommé
beet juice
berries
blackberries
caraway
carrots, juice
caviar
celery and leaves
celery root
cilantro
cinnamon
cloves
coffee
coconut
cranberry juice
cream
cucumber
currants, black
ginger
grapefruit juice
honey
horseradish
kaffir lime leaf

Kahlúa
LEMON, JUICE
lemongrass
lemon thyme
lemon verbena
licorice
lime, juice
mangoes
maraschino liqueur
melon
oats
olives, green
orange, juice
pepper, black
pineapple juice
Polish cuisine
pomegranate juice
raspberries
rose
RUSSIAN CUISINE
smoked fish
star anise
sugar (simple syrup)
tomato juice
triple sec
vanilla

Using **vodka** as a base spirit in a cocktail makes it drier, while propelling flavors and knitting them together. . . . I love the combination of Chopin vodka, carrot juice, lemon thyme. If I have it, I'll use Farigoule — a liqueur from Provence made with wild thyme — and lime.

— JERRI BANKS, COCKTAIL CONSULTANT (NEW YORK CITY)

I love to draw on the roots of a spirit, and to link a cocktail back to the foods of the table of their country of origin. I'll pair [Eastern European] **vodkas** with the flavors of the *zakuski* table [which historically features several small dishes of beets, cabbage, eggplant, and mushrooms], such as beets, caraway, and horseradish.

— JERRI BANKS, COCKTAIL CONSULTANT (NEW YORK CITY)

Flavor Affinities

vodka + amaretto + cream + Kahlúa
vodka + apple + beet + caraway + horseradish
vodka + apple + cinnamon + cloves + cranberry
vodka + beef consommé + celery leaf + horseradish
vodka + blackberries + black pepper + rose
vodka + carrot juice + lemon thyme + lime
vodka + celery + lime juice
vodka + cilantro + coconut + lime + sugar
vodka + cilantro + lime
vodka + coffee + cream
vodka + cranberry + orange
vodka + cranberry + star anise
vodka + grapefruit + maraschino liqueur
vodka + honey + oats
vodka + lemon + lemon verbena
vodka + lime + pineapple

Walnuts are my favorite nut. I like their bitter quality. They pair well with honey, apples, and pears.

— **GINA DEPALMA**, BABBO (NEW YORK CITY)

Walnuts are not as versatile as other nuts. If you look at its flavor, it is the opposite end of the spectrum from a macadamia nut because it has a more complicated flavor. You are not getting something that is buttery that coats your palate; you are getting more nut flavor. I can't think of many times when you wouldn't use it, but you might use a smaller amount.

— **MARCEL DESAULNIERS**, THE TRELLIS (WILLIAMSBURG, VIRGINIA)

Walnuts are an oilier nut but still not as strong or dominating as a pecan. I like to combine walnuts with maple in desserts. They work with apples as well as pears or quince.

— **EMILY LUCHETTI**, FARALLON (SAN FRANCISCO)

WALNUT OIL
(See Oil, Walnut)

WALNUTS (See also Nuts — In General)
Season: autumn
Taste: bitter, sweet
Function: heating
Weight: medium–heavy
Volume: quiet–moderate

almonds
anise
APPLES
apricots
Armagnac
bananas
bourbon
brandy
breakfast (e.g., pancakes, waffles)
butter, unsalted
buttermilk
caramel
carrots
cheese: blue, Cheddar, goat, Parmesan, ricotta, Roquefort, Stilton
cherries
chestnuts
chicken

chocolate: dark, milk, white
cinnamon
coffee
cognac
cookies
corn syrup: light, dark
cranberries
cream
cream cheese
crème fraîche
cumin
dates
ENDIVE
figs, esp. dried
garlic
ginger
grapefruit
grapes
hazelnuts
HONEY
ice cream
Italian sauces
kumquats
lemon: juice, zest
liqueurs, orange
maple syrup
mascarpone

Mediterranean cuisine
Mexican sauces
molasses
nectarines
oatmeal
olive oil
orange: juice, zest
peaches
PEARS
pecans
pepper, esp. white
persimmons
pine nuts
plums
pomegranates
port
praline
PRUNES
pumpkin
quince
raisins
raspberries
rum
salads
salt
sauces
stuffings

Dishes

Warm Apple and Walnut Budino with Cinnamon Gelato
— Gina DePalma, pastry chef, Babbo (New York City)

Walnut-Prune Tart with Thyme Sherbet and Caramel Gastrique, Served with a 30-Year-Old Tawny Port
— Ellie Nelson, pastry chef, Jardinière (San Francisco)

SUGAR: brown, confectioners', white
sweet potatoes
tea
vanilla
walnut oil
whiskey
wine: dry, sweet
yogurt

Flavor Affinities

walnuts + anise + dried figs + orange
walnuts + apples + honey
walnuts + caramel + prunes
walnuts + coffee + cream
walnuts + cumin + prunes

WARMING

Function: Ingredients believed to have warming properties; useful in cold weather.

alcohol
barley
chile peppers
coffee
cranberries
fruits, dried (e.g., dates)
garlic
grains (e.g., polenta, quinoa)
honey
hot beverages
meat, red
mustard
nuts
oils: almond, mustard
olive oil
onions

spices, warming (e.g., black pepper, cayenne, cinnamon, cloves, ginger, nutmeg, turmeric)
vegetables, root (e.g., carrots, potatoes)
vinegar
walnuts

WASABI

Taste: hot
Weight: medium
Volume: very loud

avocados
beef
crab
cream
fish
ginger (e.g., with seafood)
JAPANESE CUISINE
mirin
miso
olive oil
onions, green
rice
salmon
sauces
seafood
sesame: oil, seeds
shrimp

Dishes

Insalata "A Voce" with Green Apple, Marcona Almonds, Watercress, Pecorino
— Andrew Carmellini, A Voce (New York City)

Watercress and Endive Salad with Mediterranean Cucumber, Marinated Beets, and Mascarpone Croutons
— Judy Rodgers, Zuni Café (San Francisco)

soy sauce
sushi and sashimi
tofu
tuna
vinegar, rice wine

WATER CHESTNUTS

Season: summer–fall
Taste: sweet
Weight: light–medium
Volume: quiet
Techniques: raw, stir-fry

bacon
chicken
Chinese cuisine
garlic
ginger
scallions
sesame: oil, seeds
soy sauce
sugar
vinegar, rice wine

WATERCRESS

Season: spring, autumn
Taste: bitter, sweet
Weight: light
Volume: moderate
Techniques: raw

almonds
apples
asparagus, esp. white
bacon
bean sprouts
beef, esp. roasted
beets
bell peppers, esp. red

butter, unsalted
buttermilk
cheese: blue, goat, pecorino
chervil
chicken, esp. roasted
Chinese cuisine
chives
cilantro
cream
crème fraîche
cucumbers
duck
eggs
endive
fennel
fish
fish sauce, Asian
French cuisine
garlic
ginger
Italian cuisine
lamb
leeks
lemon, juice
lime, juice
mascarpone
meats, roasted
mint
mushrooms
mustard
OIL: grapeseed, sesame, vegetable, walnut
OLIVE OIL
onions: red, white, yellow
orange
oysters
parsley, flat-leaf
pears
peas
pepper: black, white
potatoes
radicchio
rice
salads
salmon
salt: kosher, sea
scallions

scallops
seafood
sesame seeds, black
sesame oil
shallots
shrimp
smoked salmon
sorrel
soups, esp. Asian, vegetable
soy sauce
STOCKS: chicken, fish, seafood, vegetable
sugar (pinch)
tarragon
tea sandwiches
tomatoes
veal
vinaigrette
vinegar: champagne, red wine, rice, sherry
walnuts
wine: rice, white
yogurt

Flavor Affinities

watercress + almonds + green apple + pecorino cheese

watercress + bacon + cream

watercress + endive + Roquefort cheese + walnuts

watercress + ginger + lemon + shrimp

WATERMELON

Season: summer
Taste: sweet
Weight: light
Volume: quiet–moderate
Techniques: raw

anise hyssop
basil
beverages
blackberries
blueberries
CHEESE: FETA, goat
chili powder
cilantro
cinnamon
cream
cucumber
fennel
honey
jicama
kaffir lime
lemon: juice, zest
lime, juice
melon, esp. cantaloupe
mint
olive oil
orange
parsley, flat-leaf
pepper: black, white
pistachios
pomegranate
raspberries
salads, fruit
salt: kosher, sea
sorbet
soups, esp. chilled
sugar: brown, white
tequila

I thought the combination of **watermelon** and feta cheese sounded horrible when I first heard it. Then I tasted it, and it works.
— **MICHAEL LAISKONIS,** LE BERNARDIN (NEW YORK CITY)

Lemony herbs like basil or anise hyssop work with **watermelon**.
— **JERRY TRAUNFELD,** THE HERBFARM (WOODINVILLE, WASHINGTON)

tomatoes
vanilla
vinegar: balsamic, rice, sherry

Flavor Affinities

watermelon + cilantro + cream + tequila
watermelon + fennel + lemon juice + parsley + salt
watermelon + feta cheese + red onions
watermelon + kaffir lime + vanilla

I started working on my **watermelon** salad years ago at Jean Georges restaurant. It started out as a watermelon and goat cheese salad for summertime. The dish was a very refreshing summer dish with the rich goat cheese and the fresh sweet watermelon. You felt like you were eating in a garden! It then went on to become watermelon with fresh tomatoes, but I still wasn't happy with it. The texture of the tomato didn't work with the texture of the watermelon. I then turned the tomatoes into a confit, cooking them in the oven over two hours with olive oil to concentrate their flavor. The dish is now watermelon, with a layer of tomato confit, topped with pistachios that just get browned in the oven, then a drizzle of olive oil and salt and pepper. The whole thing is then flashed in the oven for just a minute or two to warm it. Just before serving it gets a drizzle of balsamic vinegar. It is not only a beautiful play of flavors, but of colors as well.

— **GABRIEL KREUTHER,** THE MODERN (NEW YORK CITY)

WHISKEY (See also Bourbon)
Weight: heavy
Volume: loud

allspice
chocolate
cinnamon
cream and ice cream
dried fruits
figs
ginger or ginger ale
honey
lemon juice
orange curaçao
pears
spices: cinnamon, star anise
sugar: brown, white
sweet potatoes
vanilla

Flavor Affinities

whiskey + cinnamon + dried
    fruits + ginger + lemon + star
    anise
whiskey + lemon + orange
    curaçao

WILD RICE (See Rice, Wild)

WINE (See individual varietals)

WINTER
Weather: typically cold
Techniques: bake, braise, glaze,
roast, simmer, slow-cook

bananas
beans
beef
braised dishes
broccoli (peak: February)
Brussels sprouts (peak:
    December)
cabbage
caramel
chocolate
citrus fruit

dates (peak: December)
game
grains, heavy
grapefruit (peak: February)
greens, winter
lemons (peak: January)
lentils
limes
lobster
maple syrup
mushrooms, wild (peak:
    December)
mussels
orange, mandarin (peak: January)
passion fruit
pears (peak: December)
plantains
pork
potatoes
roasted dishes
root vegetables
rosemary
sage
soups

spices, warming
squashes, winter
squid
stewed dishes
sunchoke
sweet potatoes (peak: December)
tangerines (peak: January)
turnips (peak: December)
venison
water chestnuts (peak: February)
yams (peak: December)

YAMS (See Sweet Potatoes)

YOGURT
Taste: sour
Function: heating
Weight: medium–heavy
Volume: moderate–loud

almonds
apricots
bananas

Winter vegetables work with winter herbs. Sage and rosemary work with potatoes and root vegetables.
— **JERRY TRAUNFELD,** THE HERBFARM (WOODINVILLE, WASHINGTON)

I think of beef and pork as **winter** meats.
— **MICHEL RICHARD,** CITRONELLE (WASHINGTON, DC)

With my desserts, I focus on chocolate all year round, but use it even more in **winter**. In California, the fruit is so wonderful in the summer that that is the place to focus. In summer, I can write my whole menu and forget chocolate — that is how good the fruit is here! In winter, it is the opposite. There are not eight unique things to focus on. So chocolate comes into play because it is a real comfort food and warming, too. Winter with its cool nights becomes soufflé season. Winter is when all the special citrus fruits are available. Thank God for that, because you can work with Cara Cara oranges, lemon, and tropical fruits like passion fruit. Mangoes are available year-round, but winter is when I use them because there's no competition from berries and other summer fruits. What is great about the tropical fruits in winter is that they also bring color to the menu. Pies and tarts work year-round because you can put anything in them, from chocolate to fruit.

— **EMILY LUCHETTI,** FARALLON (SAN FRANCISCO)

Dishes

Yogurt with Caramel, Aged Balsamic, and Pine Nut Brittle
— Gina DePalma, pastry chef, Babbo (New York City)

One of my favorite desserts is Greek **yogurt**, warm caramel sauce, and aged, 25-year-old balsamic vinegar. The yogurt is really rich and not too acidic. On the yogurt, I put a salty pine nut brittle, and then the drizzle of vinegar. It works because of the beautiful balance of salt, sweet, and acid.

— GINA DEPALMA, BABBO (NEW YORK CITY)

beef
beets
blackberries
blueberries
breakfast
cardamom
cayenne
chicken
chickpeas
cilantro
cinnamon
coconut
coriander
CUCUMBER
cumin
curry
desserts
dill
Eastern Mediterranean cuisine
eggplant
fruit
garlic
grapes
Greek cuisine
honey
Indian cuisine
lamb
LEMON: JUICE, ZEST
lemon, preserved
lime
mangoes
maple syrup
meats
Middle Eastern cuisine
mint

nectarines
nutmeg
nuts
oatmeal
okra (e.g., Indian cuisine)
onions
orange: juice, zest
parsley
pasta
peaches
pecans
pepper, white
pineapple
pistachios
potatoes
radishes
raisins
raspberries

rhubarb
saffron
salt, kosher
scallions
squash
strawberries
sugar: brown, white
tamarind
Turkish cuisine
vanilla
veal
vegetables
walnuts
zucchini

Flavor Affinities

yogurt + apricots + pistachios
yogurt + caramel + pine nuts + balsamic vinegar
yogurt + cilantro + garlic
yogurt + garlic + lemon + salt

YUZU FRUIT

Season: winter–spring
Taste: sour
Weight: light–medium
Volume: loud

apricots
beef
beverages

Fresh **yuzu** is expensive, so I use yuzu juice to add acid to a dish. It is great on seafood. It is not as pungent as lime, and has a little sweetness to it. When you put it on something hot like fish, it also brings out its floral notes.

— KATSUYA FUKUSHIMA, MINIBAR (WASHINGTON, DC)

I had just come back from Japan and was inspired, so I made a **yuzu** curd served with green tea ice cream. The dish has some small bit players like segments of grapefruit which I have always liked with green tea. When you have a perfect grapefruit, it is a little bitter and sweet, just like green tea. Grapefruit reinforces the yuzu because though it is citrus it is a very different flavored citrus. I'll be honest — it looks cool as well, with the pink and green being served together. For texture I add caramelized Rice Krispies. This makes it a homage to Japan: You have rice, green tea, yuzu, and a little ginger caramel.

— MICHAEL LAISKONIS, LE BERNARDIN (NEW YORK CITY)

Just like the lemon that is often served on the side with grilled fish, just a splash of **yuzu juice** makes a lot of things delightful. I love both its aroma and flavor with lighter fish, such as flounder, fluke, and scallops. I recently went to a restaurant where a young chef was trying to be creative, and he paired sweet shrimp with scallion oil, which hid the flavors of the shrimp. I tried to politely suggest that he try yuzu juice instead, which would bring out the sweetness of the sweet shrimp.

— **KAZ OKOCHI**, KAZ SUSHI BISTRO (WASHINGTON, DC)

Dishes

Yuzu Green Tea Tart with Lychee and Green Tea Marshmallows
— François Payard, Payard Patisserie and Bistro (New York City)

caramel
carrots
ceviche
chicken
Chinese cuisine
fish, esp. sweeter, either cooked or raw (e.g., ceviche, sashimi)
flounder
fluke
garlic
gin
ginger
grapefruit
greens
hamachi
hoisin sauce
Japanese cuisine
lemon
mangoes
mirin
miso and miso soup
mushrooms, Japanese
OIL: canola, **GRAPESEED**, vegetable
olive oil
onions, esp. green
orange, juice
pepper, black
poultry
rice
salmon
scallops
seafood
sesame seeds

shellfish
shrimp
soy sauce: regular, white
sugar
tea, green
teriyaki
Thai basil
tofu
tuna
vinegar, rice wine
vodka

Flavor Affinities

yuzu + caramel + grapefruit + green tea

ZUCCHINI (See also Summer Squash)
Season: spring–summer
Taste: sweet, astringent
Function: cooling
Weight: light–medium
Volume: quiet–moderate
Techniques: fry, grill, pan roast, roast, sauté

BASIL
bell peppers: green, red, yellow
bread crumbs
butter
CHEESE: cheddar, **dry feta, goat**, Gruyère, mozzarella, **PARMESAN, pecorino**, queso fresco, **RICOTTA**

chile peppers: dried red (e.g., chipotle), fresh green (e.g., jalapeño)
chives
cilantro
cinnamon
coriander
corn
cream
curry leaf
dill
EGGPLANT
fish
French cuisine, esp. Provençal
GARLIC
Italian cuisine
lemon: juice, zest
lemon balm
lemon thyme
marjoram
meats
mint
mustard seeds, esp. black
OIL: pecan, vegetable, walnut
OLIVE OIL
olives, esp. black, niçoise
ONIONS, esp. Spanish, white
oregano
PARSLEY, FLAT-LEAF
pasta
pecans
PEPPER: BLACK, WHITE
Pernod
pesto
pine nuts
red pepper flakes
rice or risotto
rosemary
saffron
sage
salmon
SALT: KOSHER, SEA
sausage, esp. chorizo
scallions
scallops
sesame seeds
shallots
shrimp

ZUCCHINI BLOSSOMS
(See also Zucchini)

Season: early summer
Weight: light
Volume: quiet
Techniques: fry, steam

basil
**cheese: goat, mozzarella,
    Parmesan, ricotta**
corn
eggs
flour
Italian cuisine
lobster
marjoram
Mexican cuisine
olive oil
onions
parsley, flat-leaf
pepper, black
pesto
risotto
sage
salads
salt, kosher
savory
shrimp
soup
stock, chicken
tomatoes and tomato sauce

My wife was the inspiration for my **zucchini** dish. She makes a fantastic zucchini soup. She peels the zucchini and boils them in water, then purees them with a little of the water and adds a white cheese like goat or Philadelphia [cream cheese], then some olive oil and salt. It is amazing! It is creamy, velvety, and refined. We cook the zucchini and use the cooking water to make a gelatin. Then we take the white zucchini meat and make a mousse with olive oil. So the bottom of the dish is the mousse, then a layer of seeds — cleaned one by one, which is very labor intensive — then a layer of gelatin that is topped with Spanish caviar. The dish is sweet and savory, and we are proud of its simplicity [of taste].

— **JOSÉ ANDRÉS,** CAFÉ ATLÁNTICO (WASHINGTON, DC)

Dishes

Zucchini–Olive Oil Cake with Lemon Crunch Glaze
— Gina DePalma, pastry chef, Babbo (New York City)

sour cream
squash, yellow
stocks: chicken, veal, vegetable
tarragon
THYME
TOMATOES
vinegar: balsamic, champagne,
    red wine, sherry, white
walnuts
wine, dry white
yogurt
zucchini blossoms

Flavor Affinities

zucchini + basil + garlic
zucchini + cream + Parmesan cheese
zucchini + eggplant + garlic + onions + tomatoes
zucchini + pecorino cheese + pecan oil + pecans
zucchini + Pernod + walnut oil

ACKNOWLEDGMENTS

"We don't accomplish anything in this world alone . . . and whatever happens is the result of the whole tapestry of one's life and all the weavings of individual threads from one to another that creates something."
— **SANDRA DAY O'CONNOR**

We'd like to thank some of the many people whose invaluable threads helped to create the tapestry that is *The Flavor Bible*.

First and foremost are all the experts who took the time to speak with us at length about the way they approach flavor development and innovation — and whose insights in this book will surely inspire the next generation to new heights of creativity in the kitchen.

At Little, Brown, thanks to our editor, Michael L. Sand, whose advice and counsel we are both lucky and grateful to have had leading this team. He was not only a trusted sounding board for editorial issues, but his great taste extends from his keen eye overseeing this book's gorgeous design to our delectable lunches at restaurants including Alto and Park Avenue Winter.

We'd also like to thank the other fabulous folks at Little, Brown, including Sophie Cottrell, vice president and Hachette communications director; Michael Pietsch, publisher; Carolyn O'Keefe and Luisa Frontino, publicists; Peggy Freudenthal, Jayne Yaffe Kemp, and Julie Stillman, copy editors; Jean Wilcox, designer; and Zinzi Clemmons, editorial assistant. Thanks, too, to Karen Murgolo and Jill Cohen, our acquiring editor and publisher, for kicking things off.

Many thanks to our inimitable literary agent Janis Donnaud of Janis A. Donnaud and Associates, for sharing her wisdom and her own delicious taste in everything from publisher matchmaking to Moroccan tagines to barbecued spareribs.

Photography: Our heartfelt thanks to our photographer and very dear friend, the multitalented Barry Salzman, who created the extraordinary photography for this book. Barry traveled all over to get the right shot and even supplied his own home as a studio. We join Barry in extending thanks to all of the restaurants (and professionals, plus their staffs) who were enormously helpful to us in setting up the photo shoots. They include: August (Tony Liu), A Voce (Dante Camara), Babbo (Gina DePalma), Bette (Amy Sacco), Casaville (Lahcen Ksiyer), Chikalicious (Chika and Don Tillman), Chinatown Brasserie, Darna (Mourad El-Hebil), Despaña, DiPalo, Essex Street Market, Fairway Market, Formaggio Essex, Gilt (Tobie Cancino), Inside (Charleen Badman and Anne Rosenzweig), Kalustyan's (Aziz Osmani), La Esquina, Maremma (Cesare Casella), Saxelby Cheesemongers (Anne Saxelby), Solera (Ron Miller), and the Modern (Gabriel Kreuther).

Friends and Family: Thanks to all of those without whose love and support our lives wouldn't be a fraction as delicious: Susan Bulkeley Butler; Rikki Klieman and Bill Bratton; Laura Day, Samson Day, and Adam Robinson; Cynthia and Jeff Penney; Gael Greene and Steven Richter; Susan Davis and Walter Moora; Julia Davis; Blake Davis;

Susan Dey and Bernard Sofronski; Valerie Vigoda and Brendan Milburn; Michael Gelb and Deborah Domanski; Ashley Garrett and Alan Jones; Jimmy Carbone and Pixie Yates; Heidi Olson; Deborah Pines and Tony Schwartz; Steve Beckta and Maureen Cunningham; Jody Oberfelder and Juergen Riehm; Julia D'Amico and Stuart Rockefeller; Rosanne Schaffer-Shaw; Katherine Sieh Takata; Steve Wilson; Trey Wilson; Stephanie Winston; and everyone else we inadvertently missed.

Our DC Outpost: Thanks to our editor, Joe Yonan, and his talented Food section staff at the *Washington Post,* with which we've been proud to be affiliated since March 2007.

Rave: Thanks to all of our friends and family who were among the first online buyers of *What to Drink with What You Eat:* Craig Atlas, Gerry Beck, Ken Beck, Gregory Bess, Susan Bishop, Bill Bratton, Stacey Breivogel, Susan Bulkeley Butler, Jimmy Carbone, Chris Crosthwaite, Laura Day, Carla Dearing, Mark Dornenburg, Meredith Dornenburg, Amy Drown, Robyn Foster, Ashley Garrett, Steven Greenberger, James Incognito, Alan K. Jones, Rikki Klieman, Laura Lau, Dave Mabe, Susan Mabe, Brendan Milburn, Elizabeth Morrill, Marilynn Scott Murphy, Jody Oberfelder, Kelley Olson, Scott Olson, Juergen Riehm, Ann Rogers, Josh Silverman, Gina Silvestri, Renie Steves, Sandra Suria, Valerie Urban, Valerie Vigoda, Janet McCabe White, and Pixie Yates.

Virtual Book Tour: We wouldn't have had as much fun introducing our last book, *What to Drink with What You Eat,* to the world if it hadn't been for the overwhelmingly warm support of the Web sites and blogs who agreed to host a stop on our Virtual Book Tour in October 2006. We gratefully thank them for their participation: Sally Bernstein of Sallys-Place.com; Betsy Block of MamaCooks.com; Enoch Choi of EnochChoi.com; Paul Clarke of CocktailChronicles.com; Hillel and Debbie Cooperman of TastingMenu.com; Joe Dressner of JoeDressner.com; Chef James T. Ehler of FoodReference.com; Jeremy Emmerson of GlobalChefs.com; Jack Everitt and Joanne White of ForkandBottle.com; John Foley of AllBusiness.com; Ayun Halliday of DirtySugarCookies.blogspot.com; Robert Hess of DrinkBoy.com and TheSpiritWorld.net; Ron Hogan of Beatrice.com; Meg Hourihan of MegNut.com; IACP Blog Team of international-iacp.blogspot.com (including Ruth Alegria, Scott Givot, Elena Hernández, Kate McGhie, and Yukari Pratt); David Lebovitz of DavidLebovitz.com; David Leite of LeitesCulinaria.com; Chris McBride and Jennifer McBride of SavoryTidbits.com; Paul McCann of KIPlog.com; Amy McDaniel of MexicanFood.BellaOnline.com; Dave McIntyre of dmwineline.com; Brett Moore of GourmetFood.About.com; David Nelson of Chef2Chef.net; Adam Roberts of AmateurGourmet.com; Derrick Schneider of ObsessionWithFood.com; Amy Sherman of CookingWithAmy.blogspot.com; Cheri Sicard of FabulousFoods.com; Charlie Suisman of ManhattanUsersGuide.com; Lenn Thompson of LennThompson.typepad.com; and Molly Wizenberg of Orangette.blogspot.com.

Others Who Got the Word Out: We're grateful to the award-winning host Leonard Lopate of WNYC Radio for being the first journalist to put *What to Drink with What You Eat* on the map in a big way, and to Executive Producer Jessica Stedman Guff, who turned it into a series for ABC's *Good Morning America Now.*

Where Better Books Are Sold: We'd like to give a special thank-you to Brad Parsons, Lee Stern, and Scott Ferguson, without whom you'd never be able to find our books in the nation's leading bookstores. And a special thank-you to Barbara-jo McIntosh of Barbara-Jo's Books to Cooks in Vancouver, Ellen Rose of the Cook's Library in Los Angeles, and Nach Waxman of Kitchen Arts & Letters in New York City, whose stores are specialty treasures.

. . . And the Rest: We can't imagine working or living without the seasoned professionals supporting these restaurants, an invaluable source of help and even inspiration to us: Tobie Cancino, Christopher Day, Jason Ferris, and Christopher Lee (Gilt); Heather Freeman (Café Atlántico); Heather Gurfein and Ryan Ibsen (August); Ron Miller (Solera); Rubén Sanz Ramiro (The Monday Room); Rachel Hayden (The Inn at Little Washington); Michael Poli (Wild Edibles); Heather Ronan and Scott and Heather Fratangelo (Spigolo).

Thornton Wilder wrote, "We can only be said to be alive in those moments when our hearts are conscious of our treasures." As we think of those who have been there for us with such generosity, we feel very much alive indeed.

— **ANDREW DORNENBURG AND KAREN PAGE**
April 2008

P.S. from Andrew Dornenburg: *The Flavor Bible* is our first book with Karen's name listed first on the cover, even though she has always been the prime conceptualizer and writer of all of them. Karen generously suggested before our first book came out in 1995 that we list our names alphabetically — a tradition that continued more out of publishing convenience (having all our books alphabetized together on bookstore shelves, for example) than anything else. However, she is long overdue to be properly credited as the primary force behind our work together. I couldn't be happier about the change!

ABOUT THE EXPERTS

The expert contributors listed here invite you to learn more about their work at the Web sites they have provided at the end of their biographical notes.

José Andrés is the chef-owner of Café Atlántico, Jaleo, minibar, and Zaytinya in Washington, DC, and the author of *Tapas: A Taste of Spain in America*. In 2003 he received the James Beard Foundation Award as Best Chef: Mid-Atlantic and in 2008 he was nominated as Outstanding Chef. www.joseandres.com

Michael Anthony is the executive chef of the Gramercy Tavern, and in 2008 he was nominated as Best Chef: New York City. He was formerly a chef at Blue Hill in Manhattan and at Blue Hill at Stone Barns in Pocantico Hills, New York. He is an alumnus of Daniel and March. www.gramercytavern.com

Jerri Banks is a beverage consultant based in New York City. She is known for her innovative use of exotic flavorings, fresh herbs and flowers, and teas. Her employers and clients have included Gotham Bar and Grill, Cellar in the Sky, Moët Hennessy USA, Diageo, and Bacardi.

Dan Barber is the chef-owner of Blue Hill at Stone Barns in Pocantico Hills, New York, and of Blue Hill in Manhattan. He has written op-eds on food for the *New York Times*. In 2006 he received the James Beard Foundation Award as Best Chef: New York City, and in 2008 he was nominated as Outstanding Chef. www.bluehillstonebarns.com

Homaro Cantu is the chef-owner of Moto and Otom in Chicago. He has appeared on the cover of *Gourmet* magazine, and his avant-garde cuisine has been featured widely in the media, from *Fast Company* to the *New York Times* "Technology" section. www.motorestaurant.com

Andrew Carmellini is the chef-owner of A Voce and was previously the chef at Café Boulud in New York City. He is the author of *Urban Italian* (2008). In 2005 he received the James Beard Foundation Award as Best Chef: New York City. www.avocerestaurant.com

Gina DePalma was the pastry chef at Babbo in New York City. She is the author of *Dolce Italiano* and is writing another book. From 2002 to 2006 and again in 2008 she was nominated for the James Beard Foundation Award as Outstanding Pastry Chef. www.babbonyc.com

Marcel Desaulniers is the chef-owner of the Trellis in Williamsburg, Virginia, and is the author of several cookbooks, including *I'm Dreaming of a Chocolate Christmas*. In 1999 he received the James Beard Foundation Award as Outstanding Pastry Chef, and in 1993 he won as Best Chef: Mid-Atlantic. www.thetrellis.com

Traci Des Jardins is the chef or chef-owner of Jardinière, Acme Chophouse, and Mijita Cocina Mexicana in San Francisco. In 2007 she received the James Beard Foundation Award as Best Chef: Pacific, and in 1995 she was named Rising Star Chef. www.tracidesjardins.com

Meeru Dhalwala is the chef and co-owner of Vij's in Vancouver. A native of India, she is coauthor, with Vikram Vij, of the award-winning cookbook *Vij's: Elegant and Inspired Indian Cuisine*. www.vijs.ca

Dominique Duby and **Cindy Duby** are the pastry chefs and co-owners of Wild Sweets, near Vancouver, and coauthors of *Wild Sweets* and *Wild Sweets Chocolate*. They trained under master pastry chefs at Lenôtre in Paris and Wittamer in Brussels. www.dcduby.com

Odette Fada has been the chef at San Domenico in New York City for more than a decade. A native of Brescia, Italy, she is an alumna of Rex in Los Angeles. In 2003 she was nominated for the James Beard Foundation Award as Best Chef: New York. www.sandomeniconewyork.com

Brad Farmerie is the chef at Public and the Monday Room in New York City. He earned a Grand Diplôme at Le Cordon Bleu and is an alumnus of Chez Nico, Le Manoir aux Quat' Saisons, and the Providores and Tapa Room. www.public-nyc.com

Katsuya Fukushima is a chef at minibar and Café Atlántico in Washington, DC. He is an alumnus of Verbena in New York City and El Bulli in Spain and he has spoken at the Cooper Hewitt in New York City. www.cafeatlantico.com

Sharon Hage is the chef-owner of York Street in Dallas. She is an alumna of Neiman Marcus. From 2004 to 2008 she was nominated annually for the James Beard Foundation Award as Best Chef: Southwest. www.yorkstreetdallas.com

Daniel Humm is the chef at Eleven Madison Park in New York City. Since 2003 he has been nominated three times by the James Beard Foundation for its Rising Star Chef Award. www.elevenmadisonpark.com

Bob Iacavone is the executive chef at Cuvée in New Orleans. An alumnus of the Culinary Institute of America and holder of a sommelier certificate, he has won acclaim for his inventive cuisine. www.restaurantcuvee.com

Johnny Iuzzini is the executive pastry chef at Jean Georges, Nougatine, and Perry St. in New York City. He is the author of *Dessert 4 Play* (2008). In 2006 he received the James Beard Foundation Award as Outstanding Pastry Chef. www.johnnyiuzzini.com

Gabriel Kreuther is the chef at the Modern, which in 2006 won the James Beard Foundation Award as Best New Restaurant. In 2008 he was nominated as Best Chef: New York City. He was previously the chef at Atelier and Jean Georges in New York. www.themodernnyc.com

Michael Laiskonis is the pastry chef of Le Bernardin in New York City. He was previously the pastry chef at Tribute in Detroit. In 2007 he received the James Beard Foundation Award as Outstanding Pastry Chef. www.le-bernardin.com

Tony Liu is the chef at August in New York City. A native of Hawaii, he is an alumnus of the Culinary Institute of America, as well as of the kitchens at Babbo, Daniel, and Lespinasse. www.augustny.com

Michael Lomonaco is the chef-owner of Porter House New York in New York City and the author of *Nightly Specials* and *The "21" Cookbook*. He was previously executive chef at Windows on the World and "21." www.porterhousenewyork.com

Emily Luchetti is the executive pastry chef at Farallon in San Francisco and the author of several cookbooks, including *Classic Stars Desserts*. In 2004 she received the James Beard Foundation Award as Outstanding Pastry Chef. www.farallonrestaurant.com

Max McCalman is the dean of curriculum at chef Terrance Brennan's Artisanal Cheese Center in New York City and has overseen the cheese programs at Picholine and Artisanal restaurants. He is the author of *Cheese: A Connoisseur's Guide to the World's Best* and *The Cheese Plate*. www.artisanalcheese.com

Adrian Murcia is the fromager and assistant sommelier at Chanterelle in New York City. He worked for three years under Max McCalman at Picholine. www.chanterellenyc.com

Carrie Nahabedian is the chef-owner of Naha in Chicago. From 2006 to 2008 she was nominated for the James Beard Foundation Award for Best Chef: Great Lakes. www.naha-chicago.com

Kaz Okochi is the chef-owner of Kaz Sushi Bistro in Washington, DC. A native of Japan, he is an alumnus of the Tsuji Culinary Institute in Osaka. www.kazsushibistro.com

Vitaly Paley is the chef-owner of Paley's Place in Portland, Oregon, and an alumnus of Chanterelle, Remi, and Union Square Café in New York City. In 2005 he received the James Beard Foundation Award as Best Chef: Northwest. www.paleysplace.net

Monica Pope is the chef-owner of T'afia and a founder of the Midtown Farmers Market in Houston. In 2007 she was nominated for the James Beard Foundation Award as Best Chef: Southwest. www.tafia.com

Maricel Presilla is the chef-owner of Cucharamama and Zafra in Hoboken, New Jersey, and the author of several books, including *The New Taste of Chocolate*. In 2007 and 2008 Dr. Presilla was nominated for the James Beard Foundation Award as Best Chef: Mid-Atlantic. www.maricelpresilla.com

Alexandra Raij is the chef at Tía Pol and El Quinto Pino in New York City. She is an alumna of the Culinary Institute of America, as well as of Meigas, Prune, and the Tasting Room in New York City. www.tiapol.com

Michel Richard is the chef-owner of Citronelle and Central in Washington, DC, of Citronelle by Michel Richard at the Carmel Valley Ranch resort, and of Citrus at Social in Los Angeles. He is also the author of *Happy in the Kitchen* and *Michel Richard's Home Cooking with a French Accent*. In 2007 he received the James Beard Foundation Award as Outstanding Chef. www.citronelledc.com

Eric Ripert is the chef-partner of Le Bernardin in New York City and Westend Bistro in Washington, DC. He is also the author of *The Le Bernardin Cookbook* and *A Return to Cooking*. In 2003 he received the James Beard Foundation Award as Outstanding Chef. www.le-bernardin.com

Holly Smith is the chef-owner of Café Juanita in Seattle. She is an alumna of Brasa and Dahlia Lounge in Seattle. From 2006 to 2008 she was nominated for the James Beard Foundation Award as Best Chef: Northwest. www.cafejuanita.com

Bradford Thompson was the chef at Mary Elaine's at the Phoenician in Scottsdale, Arizona, from 2003 to 2007, and he previously cooked under Daniel Boulud in New York City. In 2006 he received the James Beard Foundation Award as Best Chef: Southwest.

Jerry Traunfeld was the chef at the Herbfarm in Woodinville, Washington, and is the author of *The Herbal Kitchen* and *The Herbfarm Cookbook*. In 2000 he received the James Beard Foundation Award as Best Chef: Northwest. www.theherbfarm.com

Vikram Vij is the chef and co-owner of Vij's in Vancouver. A trained sommelier, he is the coauthor, with Meeru Dhalwala, of the award-winning cookbook *Vij's: Elegant and Inspired Indian Cuisine*. www.vijs.ca

David Waltuck is the chef-owner of Chanterelle in New York City, which in 2004 was named Outstanding Restaurant by the James Beard Foundation. He is also the author of *Staff Meals from Chanterelle*. In 2007 he received the James Beard Foundation Award as Best Chef: New York City. www.chanterellenyc.com

ABOUT THE AUTHORS

Karen Page and **Andrew Dornenburg** are the award-winning team behind some of today's most groundbreaking books on gastronomy, including their most recent, *What to Drink with What You Eat,* the first book in history to win both the International Association of Culinary Professionals Cookbook of the Year Award and the Georges Dubeouf Wine Book of the Year Award. Their previous books *Becoming a Chef, Dining Out,* and *The New American Chef* were all winners of or finalists for Gourmand World Cookbook, IACP, and/or James Beard book awards. The couple, frequent guests on radio (National Public Radio) and television (*Good Morning America* and *Today*), were cited as two of a dozen "international culinary luminaries" in the Winter 2007 issue of the Relais & Châteaux magazine *L'Ame & L'Esprit,* along with Gael Greene, Patrick O'Connell, Alice Waters, and Tim and Nina Zagat. Since March 2007, they have penned a weekly column for the *Washington Post,* in which capacity they served as judges of the Oyster Riot wine pairing competition. A native of Detroit, Karen Page holds degrees from Northwestern and the Harvard Business School. San Fancisco native Andrew Dornenburg is a former restaurant chef who studied with the legendary Madeleine Kamman at the School for American Chefs and was cited by Regis Philbin on *Regis and Kelly* as one of the most famous former employees of McDonald's, along with Jeff Bezos, Jay Leno, and Sharon Stone. Paired personally as well as professionally, the couple have been married since 1990, when they ran the Montreal International Marathon together on their honeymoon. They reside in New York City. Their Web site is www.becomingachef.com.

ABOUT THE PHOTOGRAPHER

After a twenty-year corporate career, **Barry Salzman**, a Harvard MBA who ran a large global media organization employing thousands of people, embarked on a career transition to pursue his passion on a full-time basis. He is a professional photographer focused primarily on lifestyle, food, and travel. Salzman is a winner of the international Golden Light award, which is judged by Jeff Rosenheim, associate photography curator of the Metropolitan Museum of Art, and Susan White, photography director for *Vanity Fair.* Salzman's work has appeared in such publications as *Vanity Fair, Vogue Entertaining + Travel, Harper's Bazaar, AdNews, Australian Geographic,* and *OutTraveler.* His work can be seen at www.barrysalzman.net.